BOSTON ACCESS®

P9-EDY-396

Orientation

The charm of the *Walker's City* begins with its quirky, appealingly inefficient streets, imprinted by old Indian trails, colonial cowpaths, earlier shorelines, pedestrian shortcuts twixt house and fields, markets, wharves. Even their names offer snippets of history. This seaside city is a patchwork of distinctive neighborhoods that create their own lasting impressions: the Old-World **North End** where Boston began, now an Italian enclave; red-brick **Beacon Hill** with its pretty English propriety; sophisticated, urbane **Back Bay**; multicultural, neighborly **South End**; bustling **Financial District/Downtown** with its flourishing skyscraper crop; tiny, colorful **Chinatown** and revitalizing **Theater District**; the waterfront recalling Boston's maritime glories; the *New Boston* of

Government Center and inspired commercial recycling of historic **Faneuil Hall Marketplace**; and **Kenmore Square/Fenway**'s odd mix of museums, baseball, and students. (Actually, perhaps not so odd—culture, sports, and academics are all major Boston preoccupations, joined by politics and religion.)

Boston enshrines its history in architecture, museums, annual events, historic reenactments, memorials, plaques, place names. Thus, modern developments with meaningless monikers like **One Financial Center**, at home in **New York** or **Dallas**, stand out like gauche social climbers here, lacking the good breeding of Boston's well-preserved old buildings. This most American and most European of US cities has the 7th-largest population in the country, yet it's a compact, manageable, liveable town. This Grande Dame of American cities is becoming livelier and more cosmopolitan every year (although most nightlife still winds down by 1-2AM). When Boston seems too big, quiet escapes are close by; when Boston seems too small, New York City is within easy reach. Expect unpredictable weather that tries even Bostonians' patience—harsh winters and too-short springs are common complaints. And forget about driving—already impossible for novices to navigate with ease, Boston faces the spectre of the *Big Dig*. Unless current plans go awry, the car-clogged skyway known as the **Central Artery** is to be replaced shortly by an 8-10 lane underground highway with a third auto harbor tunnel built as well; driving will likely be nightmarish for the 4-8 years the 7-mile-long construction project is underway. Remember, Boston has been a pedestrian city throughout most of its history, and the oldest subway system in the country will transport you quite pleasantly if you weary of walking. Carry a street map and wear comfortable shoes.

Transportation In and Out

Airport
Logan International Airport *BOS*
Airport Information ...:	561.1804
Airport Security	561.1700
Customs & Immigration	565.4658
Ground Transportation Hotline	800/235.6426
Medical Emergencies	569.1900
Parking Information	561.1672
Travelers Aid	542.7286

Lost or damaged baggage: See airline representative in baggage claim area.
Lost and Found	567.1714
ATMs:	Cirrus, NYCE, Yankee 24

In Boston, a *regular* means coffee with cream, and some coffeeshops automatically add sugar unless you ask them not to.

Rental Cars
Shuttle from baggage claim to rental car counters. 24 hours.
American	569.3550
Avis	561.3500
Budget	787.8200
Hertz	569.7272
National	800/227.7368
Thrifty	569.6500

Serving domestic and international flights, Logan is 3 miles from downtown Boston and is accessible by the **Fitzgerald Expressway**, commonly called the **Central Artery**, with a tunnel in either direction—**Callahan** out to Logan from Boston; **Sumner** in to Boston from Logan. (Poor timing will find you inching along in either tunnel.) To get to Logan by public transportation, take the MBTA **Blue Line** to the **Airport** stop, where Massport shuttle buses transport travelers free (every 12 minutes) to the airport terminals and back to the Airport stop. From

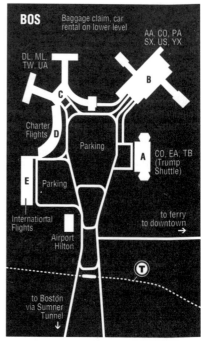

the Airport stop it's a 15- to 20-minute ride to the **Aquarium** or **Government Center** stops in downtown Boston. The **Airport Water Shuttle** also takes travelers to and from Logan: a free shuttle bus takes you from your airline terminal to the **Logan Boat Dock**, and from there it's a 7-minute ferry ride (fare charged) across **Boston Harbor** to **Rowes Wharf** (Atlantic Ave) on the edge of downtown Boston. Taxi stands are located at all airport terminals; the common practice is to share a ride with others heading your way. Although it's a mere 2¹/₂ miles from Logan to downtown Boston, legendary traffic snarls can lengthen the trip to 30-45 minutes or more, and run up a hefty taxi fare. You can also take limousines or minibuses: **Airway Transportation** (267.2981) runs daily between Logan and mainly Back Bay hotels. **Hudson Limousine** (395.8080) runs between Logan and outlying areas of Greater Boston and beyond, including southern New Hampshire. To sum up, the MBTA Blue Line is the cheapest way to Logan and often takes no more time; the Airport Water Shuttle charges a moderate fare, takes a scenic route, and avoids traffic entirely; and limos and taxis are most expensive, with taxi fares fluctuating greatly during peak travel times. Plan your itinerary so you'll never arrive at or leave from Logan between 4-6PM on a weekday—especially a Friday. Parking is available at the airport and nearby.

Distances and Times to major American cities

City	Miles	Drive Time	Flight Time
Atlanta	1037	22 hrs	3.5 hrs
Chicago	963	17.5 hrs	2 hrs
Dallas	1748	39.5 hrs	4.5 hrs
Denver	1949	37.5 hrs	6 hrs
Detroit	695	14 hrs	3 hrs
Los Angeles	2979	64 hrs	7 hrs
Miami	1504	29 hrs	3.5 hrs
New Orleans	1507	34 hrs	4 hrs
New York	206	4 hrs	1 hr
Philadelphia	296	6 hrs	1 hr
Salt Lake City	2343	49.5 hrs	5 hrs
San Francisco	3095	63 hrs	6 hrs
Seattle	2976	63.5 hrs	7 hrs
Washington DC	429	9 hrs	1 hr

Long Distance and Commuter Buses
There are 2 bus terminals in Boston, about 10 blocks apart. The **Greyhound/Trailways Terminal** is at 10 St. James Ave, Back Bay. The **Peter Pan Terminal** is near South Station at 555 Atlantic Ave, Waterfront. Several lines use each terminal and some lines use both, depending on destination. Assume nothing. Call. They're very helpful.
Bonanza .... 423.5810 (Northeast US)
Concord Trailways .... 426.7838 (New Hampshire)
Greyhound .... 423.5810 (Nationwide)
Peter Pan ...... 426.7838 (Central Mass. and to NY City)
Plymouth & Brockton .... 773.9400 (the Cape)
Trailways .... 292.4702 (Nationwide)

Bostonians *never* call Boston *Beantown*, a nickname that lingers nonetheless.

An 1833 law prohibits the unseemly practice of public cow-washing: *No person shall, in any street, wash or clean any animal....*

Trains
North Station: 150 Causeway St, information 227.5070, 800/392.6099. MBTA commuter trains (the **Purple Lines**) for destinations north and west of the city leave from this station. Here's where Bostonians in droves catch trains to the **North Shore** and its beaches. The **Rockport Line Commuter Rail**, nicknamed the *beach train*, fills up fast on hot summer days. The MBTA **Green** and **Orange Lines** stop at North Station.

South Station: Atlantic Ave at Summer St, information 482.3660, 800/872.7245; MBTA commuter rail 800/

392.6099. **Amtrak** trains depart from South Station, also stopping at **Back Bay Station**, 145 Dartmouth St, and 15 minutes west of Boston at **Route 128 Station**, Westwood. MBTA commuter trains (the **Purple Lines**) leave from South Station for points south of the city. The MBTA **Red Line** stops at South Station and the **Orange Line** stops at **Back Bay/South End** station (which also serves as Amtrak's Back Bay Station).

Local Transportation
Buses
Crosstown and local service is offered throughout Greater Boston and Cambridge. Token, exact fare, or MBTA pass required. For information, call the MBTA at 722.3200 or 800/392.6100.

Driving and Parking
If there's a choice, don't do it. This is a pedestrian city, with confusing street patterns in many neighborhoods. Even if you've the derring-do to drive among Boston's notoriously brazen drivers, be forewarned that signage is generally poor and there are lots of one-way streets. Have a city street map. Street parking is limited and highly regulated, so read signs carefully. Many neighborhoods, such as **Beacon Hill**, have almost no parking for nonresidents. It's very common to be ticketed, or towed away to Boston's hinterlands; if your car is towed, retrieving it will be costly and time-consuming. On highways, the speed limit is 55 miles per hour. Right turn on red is permitted in Massachusetts except where prohibited by posted signs. Tolls are charged for using the **Mass Pike** (I-90), tunnels, and various bridges.

There are numerous **Parking Garages** in town, and various open lots. Some are listed below. Prices vary widely for hourly and day rates, with the most expensive in the **Downtown/Financial District** area.

Auditorium Garage ♦ 50 Dalton St (near Hynes Convention Center). 247.8006

Boston Common Garage ♦ 0 Charles St (beneath Boston Common). 954.2096

Boston Harbor Garage ♦ 70 East India Row. 723.1731

Charles Square Garage ♦ 5 Bennett St, Harvard Sq, Cambridge. 491.6779

Copley Place Parking ♦ One Copley Pl. 375.4488

Government Center Garage ♦ 50 New Sudbury St. 227.0385

Harvard Square Parking Garage ♦ 65 JFK St, Cambridge. 354.4168

John Hancock Garage ♦ 100 Clarendon St. 421.5050

Prudential Center Garage ♦ 5 Huntington Ave. 267.2965

Subway

The **Massachusetts Bay Transportation Authority** (MBTA) operates subways, streetcar lines, buses, commuter trains, commuter boats, and vans for riders with special needs. For information, call 722.3200 or 800/392.6100, TDD 722.5146. For daily recorded service conditions, call 722.5050. (Unfortunately, when calling the first number there's inevitably a wait.) The rapid transit system, the **T**, is the nation's oldest subway system. Four lines—**Red, Blue, Orange, Green**—radiate from downtown, where they intersect below-

Orientation

ground; some operate aboveground beyond. Both the Red and Green lines have branches off them, so check destinations carefully. The Red Line splits to run from **Alewife** to **Braintree** or **Ashmont**. The Green Line branches into the **B, C, D** and **E** lines. (There used to be an A line; it's defunct now.) The symbol indicates stops. *Inbound* refers to trains going in to central downtown stations: **Park Street, Downtown Crossing, State**, and **Government Center**. Outbound heads away from these stations. Tokens, exact fare, or passes must be used; purchase tokens at stations.

The T has minor eccentricities, best learned from experience. On the Green Line many street-level stations do not have ticket booths and you must have exact change ready. Tokens are also accepted, supplemented by change. Drivers do not make change, although helpful passengers will. *Note*: Going inbound, certain lines charge higher fares from outlying stations; ask. And going outbound on the Green Line, no fare is charged if you board at an aboveground station. Smoking is not allowed in stations or on trains. MBTA lines operate M-Sa 5AM-12:45AM, Su and holidays 6AM-12:45AM. Special discount passes for elders available at **Downtown Crossing Concourse**, student passes available at schools, children 5-11 pay half fare, children under 5 ride free. For information on access services (called **The RIDE**) for those with special traveling needs, call 722.5123, 800/533.6282, TDD 722.5415. The **Boston Passport**, a special visitor pass good for 3 or 7 days, is sold at the **Information Booth** on **Boston Common**, daily 9AM-5PM, or at the **Airport** T station, daily 9AM-4:30PM. Monthly passes are available at various rates, with the option to combine subway and bus travel. Call 722.5219 for pass information and locations where sold.

Taxis

There are usually enough of them around town, except 3-7PM (especially Friday) and in the worst weather. They're easiest to find near major hotels, **Newbury St, Downtown Crossing, Faneuil Hall Marketplace**. Available cruising taxis have a lighted sign on the roof. The standard tip is 15%. Boston taxi companies include Checker 536.7000, I.T.O.A. 426.8700, Red Cab 734.5000, Town Taxi 536.5000, Red and White 742.9090. Cambridge taxi companies include Ambassador Brattle 492.1100, Cambridge Yellow Cab 876.5000, 547.3000, and Checker Cab of Cambridge 497.1500.

In Boston, the first black representatives to sit in any state legislature did so in 1866.

The first American labor organization was founded 18 October 1648 by Boston shoemakers.

FYI

Information Centers

Boston Common Visitor's Information Booth ♦ Daily 9AM-5PM. Boston Common at Tremont St. 426.3115

Cambridge Discovery Information Kiosk ♦ M-Sa 9AM-6PM, Su 1-6PM June-Labor Day; M-Sa 9AM-5PM, Su 1-5PM Labor Day-late June. ♦ Harvard Sq. 497.1630

Charlestown Navy Yard National Park Service ♦ Daily 9AM-5PM. 242.5601

Greater Boston Convention & Visitors Bureau ♦ M-F 9AM-5PM. Prudential Plaza, Back Bay. 536.4100

Massachusetts Tourism Office ♦ M-F 9AM-5PM. 100 Cambridge St, Government Center. 727.3201, 800/727.3221

National Park Service Visitor Center ♦ Daily 9AM-5PM. 15 State St, Financial District. 242.5642

Tours

By Trolley, Bus, or Car
Beantown Trolley ♦ 287.1900
Boston Trolley Tours (The Blue Trolley) ♦ 427.TOUR, TRO.LLEY
Brush Hill Transportation ♦ 287.1900
Commonwealth Limousine Service ♦ 787.5575
The Gray Line ♦ 426.8805
New England Sights ♦ 492.6689
Old Town Trolley Tour of Boston ♦ 269.7010
Uncommon Boston ♦ 731.5854

On Foot
Boston by Foot/Boston by Little Feet ♦ 367.2345
Historic Neighborhoods Foundation ♦ 426.1885
National Park Service Visitor Center ♦ 242.5642
Uncommon Boston ♦ 731.5854

Other
Boston by Sail ♦ 742.3313
Boston Helicopter Tours ♦ 357.6868
(Other boat tours listed in Waterfront chapter)

Bed-and-Breakfasts

Hotels are listed in the neighborhood where they're located. Many B&B organizations serve a number of neighborhoods and towns.

AAA Land & Sea Accommodations ♦ 491.6107, 800/232.9989

Bed & Breakfast Associates, Bay Colony ♦ 449.5302

Bed and Breakfast of Cambridge and Greater Boston ♦ 576.1492

A Cambridge House ♦ 491.6300, 800/232.9989

Host Homes of Boston ♦ 244.1308

New England Bed & Breakfast, Inc. ♦ 244.2112

Tickets

Here are a number of ticket sources for Boston-area events. Per-ticket service charges vary by outlet.

Bostix Half-price tickets for same-day events: sports, cultural, music, theater, dance, special. Bostix sells full-price tickets too, and is a Ticketron outlet. ♦ Faneuil Hall Marketplace. No credit cards. 723.5181

Charg-Tix Comedy clubs and other shows (credit card only). ♦ 542.8511

Concertcharge Sports, theater, concerts, special events (credit card only). ♦ 497.1118, 800/442.1854

Concertix Tickets for the Regattabar jazz performances and other events. ♦ 876.7777

Hub Ticket Agency Sports and theater. ♦ 240 Tremont St, Theater District. 426.8340

Out-of-Town Ticket Agency Sports, theater, concerts, special events (no credit cards). ♦ Harvard Square MBTA station, O Harvard Sq, Cambridge. 492.1900

Ticketmaster Cabarets, concerts, circuses, sports. A computerized ticket service (credit card only); ask for cash-only outlet locations. ♦ 931.2000

Ticketron Sports, theater, dance, music, others (credit card only). Also a computerized ticket service; ask for cash-only outlet locations. ♦ 720.3400, 800/302.8080

Hints
Flat shoes Comfortable shoes with good soles are a must for cobblestones, bumpy brick sidewalks (especially in Cambridge), subway stairs.

Hotels Always ask about special rates, since many Boston hotels offer weekend or holiday packages, and discounts for children, elders, the military, students. In many hotels, children under certain ages stay in parents' room free.

Safety Watch traffic, since Boston drivers are aggressive and run red lights. Use common sense; be careful if you venture off well-worn paths in the city. The subways are safe within Boston and Cambridge and mostly without; keep your wits about you. After dark, avoid the parks, Boston Common, the Combat Zone, alleys, and side streets. Be cautious using multilevel parking garages at night. Keep a grip on purses, briefcases, hand luggage—it isn't enough to simply keep belongings in sight, since some thieves distract expertly.

Recreation
A sporting town like Boston naturally has plenty of municipal sports facilities. The **Parks and Recreation Department** and the **Metropolitan District Commission** (MDC) are responsible for maintaining different facilities, with some overlapping. Most are available on a first-come first-served basis; some require reservations or permits. Call the Parks and Recreation Department at 725.4006 if you're interested in baseball and Little League diamonds; softball fields, basketball, tennis, and street hockey courts; ice-skating rinks (free public skating is also permitted on the **Public Garden** lagoon in winter, with skates rented on the spot by a local shop). Call the MDC at 727.9547 or 727.5215 (recorded information) for information on baseball diamonds, football fields, tennis courts, swimming pools, public beaches, public freshwater fishing areas, skiing, skating rinks. (One of the most popular MDC skating rinks is the **Steriti Rink** on Commercial St in the **North End**, where you can skate with a fine view of Old Ironsides and the **Bunker Hill Monument** in **Charlestown** across the way.)

If you want to play golf, try the **Franklin Park Golf Course**, 436.7586, a newly refurbished public 18-hole course designed by Donald Ross, a renowned golf-course architect. The par-70 course is the country's second-oldest municipal golf course. For **camping** and **hiking** information, call or drop in at the **Appalachian Mountain Club, 5 Joy St,** 523.0636 (they can tell you about skiing too); the **Sierra Club**, 3 Joy St, 227.5339; or the **National Park Service Visitor Center**, 15 State St, 242.5642.

Ranking high among cushy jobs is the position of fence viewer, established by a 1693 state law still on the books. A similarly unboastworthy position—measurer of leather—was created by an 1841 measure that hasn't been repealed.

There are numerous **public beaches** around Boston (including on some **Boston Harbor Islands**) under the supervision of MDC. For information, call 727.7090. But many MDC beaches—although not all—are on dirty **Boston Harbor**, which awaits a long-overdue cleanup, so better to drive or take a beach train (Rockport Line Commuter Rail) from **North Station**, 227.5070, to one of the popular North Shore swimming spots such as **Singing Beach** in **Manchester-by-the-Sea**. Other favorite area beaches include the **Crane Memorial Reservation** in **Ipswich**; the **Parker River National Wildlife Refuge** on **Plum Island** near **New-**

buryport; **Wingaersheek** and **Good Harbor Beaches** in **Gloucester**; **Nantasket Beach** in **Hull** (MDC-run); **Duxbury Beach** in **Duxbury**.

Weather
Since you're likely to be on foot, be prepared. Depending on the season, have warm, waterproof boots, an umbrella, light colored clothing, an extra sweater. Weather can be wildly variable in all seasons: summer can be very hot and humid but is often cooled by the sea; winter can be cold and damp with snow and ice or brisk and sunny. The easiest times are spring and fall, but each season has its charms.

Month	Average Temp. °F	No. Rain Days
Dec-Feb	30	11
Mar-May	46	11
June- Aug	69	10
Sep-Nov	53	9

Smoking and Drinking
You must be 21 to purchase liquor; Blue Laws vary slightly in Cambridge and Boston, also depending on the establishment's license. In general, no liquor is sold in bars before noon on Sunday and only until 1AM. In stores, no liquor is sold after 11PM Monday-Saturday, and none on Sunday except near the New Hampshire border. There's strong anti-smoking sentiment in Boston and Cambridge, especially Cambridge, with occasional restaurants banning it entirely. Most public places forbid smoking; most restaurants have smoking and nonsmoking sections.

Money
Foreign Currency and Traveler's Checks Boston banks do not commonly exchange for foreign currency, so bring US dollars or exchange at **Logan International Airport** at Bay Bank Foreign Money Exchange, Terminal E, 567.2313. You can buy foreign currency at **Thomas Cook Foreign Exchange**, 426.0016; **Shawmut Bank of Boston**, 292.2000; **Bank of Boston**, 434.2200. Banks, many stores, and restaurants accept traveler's checks, generally requiring a photo ID. Purchase them at **American Express**, 723.8400; **Barclay's Bank**, 800/825.5210; **Thomas Cook**, 720.2285, 800/223.4030.

Sales Tax In Massachusetts, a 5% tax is charged on all purchases except services, food bought in stores (not restaurants), and clothing under $175. A 9.7% hotel tax is also assessed. New higher taxes on some goods and services will likely be in effect soon.

Tipping Tip 15-20% in restaurants and for personal services.

Newspapers and Periodicals

Local publications useful for news and events information include *The Boston Globe* (daily); *Boston Herald* (daily); *Christian Science Monitor* (M-F); *The Boston Phoenix* (weekly); *Boston Magazine* (monthly); *New England Monthly* (monthly); *The Tab* (neighborhood weekly, with different editions for different neighborhoods). Especially helpful for events information are the *Globe's Calendar*, published Thursday; the *Herald's Scene*, published Friday, and the *Phoenix*, published Friday.

Orientation

Phone Book

Unless otherwise stated, the area code is 617 (outlying areas use 508; area code for western MA is 413; ask the information operator or check telephone book). As of press time, New England Telephone (NET) and AT&T pay telephones still cost 10¢ for a local call, with no charge for information (dial 411 for local information). However, a number of other companies have installed pay telephones that cost 25¢. Have plenty of change; these amounts are for limited minutes and calls are disconnected without further payment.

Emergencies

Coast Guard	565.9200
Dental	956.6828
FBI	742.5533
Medical	726.2000, 956.5566
Poison Control	232.2120
Police/Fire/Ambulance	911
Police (nonemergency)	247.4200
Rape Hotline	492.7273
Suicide Samaritan	247.0220
24-hr drugstores (Boston)	523.1028/4372
(Cambridge)	876.5519

Important Numbers

American Youth Hostels (AYH)	731.5430
Back Bay Station	482.3660
Bay State Line (ferry service)	723.7800
Boston Parking Violations	725.4410
Boston Public Library	536.5400
Cambridge Parking Violations	498.9036
Greater Boston Convention & Visitors Bureau	536.4100
Greyhound Bus	423.5810
Handicapped Visitor Information	727.5540, 800/462.5015
Local directory assistance	411
Logan International Airport	561.1806, 800/23LOGAN
Long distance information	1/area code/555.1212
Mass Bay Line (ferry service)	542.8000
Massport Ground Transportation	800/23LOGAN
MBTA	722.3200, 800/392.6100
North Station (MBTA commuter rail)	227.5070, 800/392.6099
Operator assistance	0
Peter Pan (bus service)	426.7838
South Station/Amtrak	482.3660, 800/872.7245
TDD (Boston Public Library AccessCenter)	536.5400 ext 295
Traveler's Aid	542.7286/9875
24-hr convenience stores	227.9534, 424.6888
US Customs	565.6155
US Immigration and Naturalization	656.3879
US Passport Office	565.6998
Zip Code	654.5767, 800/872.7245

Recorded Information

Boston Parks and Recreation	725.4006
Children's Museum	426.8855
MBTA service (daily conditions)	722.5050
Marine Weather Forecast	569.3700
Museum of Fine Arts	267.9377
Museum of Science	723.2500
Time	637.1234, NER.VOUS
US Postal Service	451.9922
Weather	936.1234/1212

Sports and Recreation

Appalachian Mountain Club	523.0603
Bicycling	491.RIDE
Boston Bruins (hockey)	227.3200
Boston Celtics (basketball)	523.3030
Boston Parks and Recreation	725.4006 (recorded) 725.4505
Boston Red Sox (baseball)	267.8661
Canoeing	527.2799
Ice skating	725.4006, 727.5215
Mayor's office for events	725.4500
National Park Service	242.5642
New England Patriots (football)	800/543.1776
Sierra Club	227.5339
Skiing conditions	828.5070 (MA) 800/258.3608 (NH), 802/229.0531 (VT)
State Fisheries and Wildlife	727.3151
State Forests and Parks	727.3180

Services

Hair, nail, and skin care (Bon Visage)	536.0800
Massage (Repose)	267.9115
Same-day glasses (Eye World)	437.1070
Shoeshine and repair (La Rossa's)	227.8499, 345.0656

Boston Reading

The Proper Bostonians Cleveland Amory

Uncommon Boston Susan Berk with Jill Bloom

in and out of Boston with (or without) children Bernice Chesler

Historic Walks in Boston John Harris

Historic Walks in Cambridge John Harris

Lost Boston Jane Holtz Kay

Flashmaps Instant Guide to Boston Toy Lasker

The Boston Globe Restaurant Book Robert Levey

Common Ground J. Anthony Lukas

The City Observed: Boston Donlyn Lyndon

Make Way for Ducklings Robert McCloskey

About Boston: Sight, Sound, Flavor and Inflection David McCord

Car-Free in Boston Association for Public Transportation

Boston's Best Restaurants Steven Raichlen

New England Off the Beaten Path: A Guide to Unusual Places Corinne Madden Ross and Ralph Woodward

A.I.A. Guide to Boston Susan and Michael Southworth

Boston: A Topographical History Walter Muir Whitehill

Zagat Boston Restaurant Survey

Frederick Law Olmsted and the Boston Park System Cynthia Zaitzevsky

In *Boston Streets*, published by the **Boston Department of Public Works**, 19 pages list squares named in honor of veterans.

Annual Events

A plethora of offices, organizations, community groups, institutions, and individuals are involved in Boston's myriad events. Locations and telephone numbers change frequently, so it's easiest to track down whatever happenings interest you by calling the Greater Boston Convention & Visitors Bureau, 536.4100. They'll tell you what you need to know or help direct you to the right source.

January
First Night, 31 Dec-1 Jan
Chinese New Year (or February)
Japanese New Year Festival, Children's Museum

February
Black History Month
Thaddeus Kosciuszko Day
Massachusetts Camelia Show
Frederick Douglass Day, Roxbury
Uncommon Boston Valentine Chocolate Tour
   (731.5854—private company)
Annual Valentine's Festival
Kid's Computer Fair at the Computer Museum
Beanpot Tournament at Boston Garden
New England Boat Show

March
Crispus Attucks/Boston Massacre Ceremony
New England Spring Flower Show, Bayside Exposition Center
St. Patrick's Day Parade, South Boston
Evacuation Day (17th), when the British fled in 1776
Easter Parade (or April)
Great Boston Egg Race, Science Museum (or April)
Great Chefs Fair (326.7225, National Kidney Foundation)

April
Artists' Ball, Cyclorama in South End
Boston Marathon (3rd Monday)
Patriots Day (3rd Monday), Reenactment of the Battle of Lexington, Paul Revere's and William Dawes' rides, and other events
Opening Day at Fenway Park (baseball season)
Swan Boats return to Public Garden Lagoon
Duckling Day, Public Garden
Mass Special Olympics
Wake up the Earth Day in Jamaica Plain (or May)
Boston Kite Festival, Franklin Park

May
Boston Pops season begins, Symphony Hall
Art Newbury Street
Art South Street
Lilac Sunday at Arnold Arboretum
Magnolias bloom on Comm Ave, Back Bay
Beacon Hill Hidden Garden Tour
The Big Apple Circus
Memorial Day Parade, Copley Sq
Brimfield Outdoor Antique Show
Walk for Hunger

Writing on Boston's notoriously changeable weather, **David McCord** observed: *Old Bostonians never mention it; but not so the stranger. He speaks of it in comparative terms. It is wetter than Kansas, drier than Washington, colder than Virginia, hotter than Minnesota, clearer than the Labrador, foggier than New Mexico, and stranger than all get out.*

America's first postal route was established between Boston and **New York City** on 22 January 1673.

June
Dorchester Day Parade
The Ancient and Honorable Artillery Company Parade
Victorian Promenade (alternate years)
Boston Globe Jazz Festival
Gay Pride March
Dairy Festival, Boston Common
Bunker Hill Day in Charlestown (17th)
Tanglewood Music Festival begins in the Berkshires
Cambridge River Festival
Dragon Boat Festival, Esplanade
Blessing of the Fleet, Provincetown and Gloucester

July
North End Italian *Festas*
Boston Pops Esplanade Orchestra Concerts, Esplanade
Boston Harborfest
Boston Pops Annual 4th of July Concert, Hatch Memorial Shell, Esplanade
Independence Day Oration and Parade, Old State House 725.3911
USS *Constitution* Turnaround (4th)
Chowderfest
US Pro Tennis Championships at Longwood
National Folk Festival, Lowell
Bastille Day, Marlborough St, Back Bay

August
North End Italian *Festas*
August Moon Festival in Chinatown (or September)
Tugboat Parade and Muster
Caribbean Carnival Festival, Franklin Park
Newport (RI) Jazz Festival

September
Boston Film Festival
South End Open Studios
Art Newbury St
Charles Street Fair
Balloon Festival in Cummington

October
Topsfield Fair
Boston Globe Book Festival
Columbus Day Parade, East Boston-North End
Head of the Charles Regatta
Halloween Costume Ball, Hammond Castle Museum, Gloucester
Monster Dash in costume

November
Boston International Antiquarian Book Fair
Veteran's Day Parade, Comm Ave in Back Bay
Jordan Marsh Thanksgiving Road Race (*Turkey Trot*)

December
Crafts at the Castle
Reenactment of the Boston Tea Party
Bill Rogers Jingle Bell Run
Christmas Tree Lighting, Prudential Center
Tree-lighting on Boston Common
Boston Ballet's *Nutcracker*
The Revels, Sanders Theatre, Cambridge
Handel & Haydn Society's *Messiah*, Symphony Hall
Uncommon Boston Victorian Christmas Tour
   (731.5854—private company)
First Night, 31 Dec-1 Jan

Ray Bolger, the **Scarecrow** from the Hollywood blockbuster *The Wizard of Oz*, came from Boston.

Beacon Hill

Stroll across **Boston Common**, an enormous grassy blanket that Bostonians have put to fascinating use since the city's birth. Then be ready—with comfortable shoes—to double-back, dead-end, poke about, and peer into the nooks and crannies of historic **Beacon Hill**. You'll quickly find Boston, this neighborhood especially, a walker's dream and a driver's nightmare. Beacon Hill is a red-brick quarter of handsome houses crowding along close crazy-quilt streets lit by flickering gaslights. Boston is one of America's most European cities, with Beacon Hill looking ever-so-English. It's easiest to navigate its slopes in good weather, but well worth slipping and sliding a bit to enjoy Beacon Hill's serene winter stillness.

A fashionable enclave today, *the Hill* in Colonial times was infant Boston's undesirable outskirts—crisscrossed with cowpaths, covered with brambles, berries, and scrub. The **Puritans** called it **Trimountain** for its 3-peaked silhouette resembling a man's head and shoulders. Whittled away by early developers to create new lots and landfill, today only Beacon Hill remains. The completion of the majestic **State House** in 1798, designed by **Charles Bulfinch**, spotlighted the Hill's potential and drew affluent **Brahmins** who settled here. Beacon Hill blossomed in the first half of the 19th century as the city's intellectual and artistic Renaissance unfolded; cultural luminaries gathered here.

Beacon Hill itself is divided roughly into 3 districts. The **flats** is the newer, more orderly section running down to the **Charles River** from Charles St. Up from Charles St is the Hill's sunny **south slope**, reaching from Beacon St to Pinckney St, and the

shady **north slope**, descending from Pinckney to Cambridge St. While the south slope's mansions and row houses exude Brahmin privilege, the north slope's smaller houses and former tenement walk-ups relay a different, often-overlooked history: one of ethnic diversity and the struggle of many groups—especially blacks—to make their way on the Hill. Coursing through the Hill, infusing it with vitality, is **Charles Street**, an eclectic, surprisingly friendly commercial way. Most of Beacon Hill's shops, services, and businesses are located here.

In older cities, the chicken-or-the-egg question is: which came first, the streets or the dwellings? As you meander about the hodgepodge Hill, it's clear that houses came first and streets have simply made do. Wend your way over bumpy brick sidewalks, observing that Beacon Hill wouldn't be so appealing if it were level—gone would be the interesting inclines, the jigs-and-jogs of the streets, the surprise of **Louisburg Square**, the glimpses of the glistening river below. The Hill is an intimate people-scaled place where idiosyncratic touches reveal the layers of lives that have enriched this large

heap of brick and granite. Iron handrails fastened to buildings help on steep ways; gardens and gatherings enliven rooflines; ornate doorknockers, bootscrapers, and wrought-iron embellishments dress up some of the most modest facades; tunnels lead to concealed courtyards and hidden houses.

Most Beacon Hill homes are Greek Revival or Federal in style, but refreshing upstarts have sneaked in here and there. Master carpenters, satisfyingly called *housewrights*, built most structures since the trained American architect was a brand-new breed. Notice the many graceful **bowfronts**, a Beacon Hill innovation. In 1955 the Hill was declared a **historic district**, and plaques are everywhere. Today the **Beacon Hill Civic Association** watchdogs its precious repository of buildings, even dictating exterior color choices. Come back in 10, 20, 30 years, and it will all look the same. True, as buildings change hands there's less single ownership, more condos and luxury apartments belonging to young professionals instead of *Proper Bostonians*. Yet Beacon Hill lore lingers. Holding sway here for generations, Boston's famous *First Families*—the **Cabots**, the **Lodges**, the **Codmans**, the **Lowells**, to name a few—have passed their stories on, facts fuzzied by time and telling. Yes, the Hill clings to its elitist past, but Jewish and Italian immigrants, Depression-era bohemians, artists, and students have also made their homes here, and today there's a large gay population.

If the Hill's tranquil charm and careful-when-you-touch air begin to be tiresome, remember there's a startling or delightful nuance to discover just ahead. Watch the world go by over a *caffè* at **Il Dolce Momento**; find that slip of a street called **Acorn**; then come down from the heights and take an afternoon promenade in the **Public Garden**.

1 **Boston Common** (1634) Fifty sprawling acres, the pentagonal Boston Common is the oldest public park in the country. The city and the Common grew up together. Now the city's heart, the Common was once its hinterland. It was part of the farm belonging to **Reverend William Blaxton**, the first English squatter on the Shawmut Peninsula, where Boston sprouted by the sea. A reclusive bachelor in the style of **Henry David Thoreau**, Blaxton shattered his own blissful solitude: he generously invited the city's Puritan founders to settle on his peninsula and share its fresh water. His neighbors then too close for comfort, Blaxton sold them the Common in 1634 and retreated to the heights of Beacon Hill. There the city's first—but not last!—eccentric tended to his beloved books, garden, and orchard, reputedly

riding about on his Brahma bull for recreation. But when the busybody Puritans then tried to convince Blaxton to join their church, he fled south to Rhode Island.

The Common has belonged to Bostonians ever since, and they've found every imaginable use for it. Cattle grazed its grass until outlawed in 1830. Justice—of a sort—was meted out with whipping posts, stocks, and pillories. Indians, pirates, and persecuted Quakers were hanged here; so was **Rachell Whall** in the late 1700s for the crime of highway robbery: she stole a 75-cent bonnet. Until 6 July 1836, blacks couldn't pass freely on the Common. Here Redcoats camped during the Revolution, and Civil War troops mustered. In 1789, newly elected **President Washington** dropped by to revisit the site of his greatest military victory. **General Lafayette** returned to the US in 1824 and shot off a ceremonial cannon here, and the **Prince of Wales**, future **King Edward VII**, reviewed the troops here in 1860.

The 4 subway stops most convenient to Boston Common, Beacon Hill, and the Public Garden are **Park Street** (**Red** and **Green Lines**), **Boylston, Charles** (**Red Line**), and **Arlington** (**Green Line**). The entire neighborhood can be easily walked starting from any of these stations.

Great public outdoor theater—sermons, duels, puppet shows, balloon ascensions, promenades, hopscotch championships, fire engines and flying-machine demonstrations, horse racing, antislavery meetings, fireworks, hoop rolling, and ox roasting—the Common is still one of Boston's best people-watching places. Arrive before 9 on a sunny morning and relish your leisure while working folk push on to their jobs, leaving you to saunter along the Common's intersecting walkways among the magicians, musicians, mounted police, artists, baby strollers, religious proselytizers, skateboarders, soapbox orators, pigeons, and pushcart vendors. Return some summer evening to watch a

Beacon Hill

softball game in one corner of the Common, while in another corner an unofficial dog-walking group meets after work to chat while 57 varieties of their quadripedal pals romp. Here a delightful bull terrier named Willie won hearts and launched a modeling career that culminated with her appearance on a poster advertising beer on view at Jacob Wirth in the Theater District. One cautionary word: as is true of most urban parks, the Common isn't a safe place to be after dark.

1 Park Street Station (1897, **Wheelwright and Haven**) The first subway system in the US opened here to incredible fanfare on 1 September 1897. *First Car Off the Earth!* trumpeted *The Boston Globe.* (The subway line originally ran only as far as today's Boylston station, just one stop across the Common at Tremont and Boylston streets.) Before you hurry aboveground to leave the dankness, popcorn and donut smells, and throngs on the subway platforms, look for the mosaic mural immediately inside the turnstiles. It depicts the first streetcar entering the subway, with a woman rider holding aloft that day's *Globe.* Aboveground, Park St Station's 2 copper-roofed, granite-faced kiosks are National Historic Landmarks, although truthfully they look more like overgrown Parisian restrooms.

Head a short distance down the Common along Tremont St to the blue-trimmed **Visitor's Information Booth**, where you can find out about all the local doings—from museum exhibitions to helicopter rides to whale watches. On the way is *Brewer Fountain* (1868), a bronze replica of the lauded fountain of the 1855 Paris Exposition and a popular rendezvous.

2 The Freedom Trail At the Information Booth begins the famous self-guided, 3-mile tourist pilgrimage on which you track an elusive red line connecting 16 historical sites from Colonial and Revolutionary times. You'll end up in Charlestown, which means a trek or ride back, and you really could invent a more entertaining odyssey of your own. But if you're in the mood to follow in the footsteps of countless others, the tour takes about 3 hours.

The wonderful wrought-iron of the balconies of Beacon Hill, much of it Colonial or Spanish in origin, is sometimes called *Boston black lace.*

The Freedom Trail

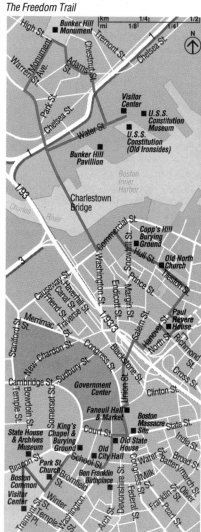

2 Parkman Plaza Left of the Information Booth, facing the Common, the plaza's bronze figures solemnly enshrine Puritan values. Take the path just left of *Industry*—called **Railroad Mall** because it led to the terminal of one of Boston's first railroads in 1835—for a brief, lovely stroll to the Neoclassical **Parkman Bandstand.** Mount this sadly neglected but still-handsome structure, where you can ignore the graffiti and watch the squirrels skitter while you imagine long-silent strains of music. In the fall, surrounded by rustling leaves and frequented by Boston homeless people, this is one of the city's most mournful but evocative settings.

3 Central Burying Ground (1756) Once you're in a thoroughly contemplative mood, follow Railroad Mall to find history written on tombstones. Legend claims that here lie American soldiers who died at the **Battle of Bunker Hill** and British soldiers who succumbed to illness during the **Siege of Boston.** At least a dozen **Boston Tea Party** guests are here, as is portraitist **Gilbert Stuart,** who painted **Martha** and

George Washington. Stuart died in poverty, humiliated to be eclipsed by less talented but more socially skilled painters. The inscriptions that mention *strangers* refer to Irish Catholic immigrants buried here. In early Colonial graveyards like this one, headstones often faced east—from where would come the Day of Judgment trumpet call—and were paired with footstones, creating a cozy bed for the occupant's eternal rest.

3 Boston Common Ranger Station Stop here on the Tremont St side of the Common for information on the walks led by **Park Rangers**, including historic tours of the Common and **Granary Burying Ground**, and a *What's in Bloom?* walk or *Family Stroll* in the **Public Garden**. For kids, there's the *Make Way for Ducklings* tour, which includes reading the famous storybook and meets at the Public Garden's bronze ducklings; and the *Horse of Course* program about a day in the life of a Park Ranger horse.

4 Flagstaff Hill Climb the Common's highest point, atop which the *Soldiers and Sailors Monument* commemorates Civil War combatants. Gunpowder was stored here long ago. In October 1979, **Pope John Paul II** held an outdoor Mass on the northwest slope.

4 Frog Pond True, it's a frogless, sometimes-water-filled concrete hollow instead of the marshy amphibian abode it once was (**Edgar Allan Poe** derisively called Bostonians *Frogpondians*), but in steamy weather the pond is filled with children cavorting under its fountain. (Even the cynical Poe called the Common *no common thing*.)

5 Beacon Street Mall In the shadow of the State House, this wide, dappled promenade along the Common's north side is where **Ralph Waldo Emerson** and **Walt Whitman** paced back and forth, arguing about taking the sex out of Whitman's *Leaves of Grass*. Emerson was utterly convincing, Whitman concluded: *I could never hear the points better put—and then I felt down in my soul the clear and unmistakable conviction to disobey all, and pursue my own way.* Despite their disagreement, the friends went off together to partake of *a bully dinner*.

6 Headquarters House (1808, **Asher Benjamin**; National Historic Landmark) This graceful pair of brick bowfronts, now joined, is adorned with many of the delicate Greek architectural details Benjamin favored. The lefthand house, now headquarters for the **National Society of Colonial Dames**, inspired the setting for *The Virginians* by British author **William Makepeace Thackery**, a houseguest of a former owner. On Wednesday, you can peruse the Colonial and Victorian artifacts collected and preserved by the Dames, but only if you take the tour. ♦ Admission. W 10AM-3PM. 54-55 Beacon St (Spruce St) 742.3190

Restaurants/Clubs: Red   Hotels: Blue
Shops/Parks: Green   **Sights/Culture:** Black

7 45 Beacon Street (1805–1808, **Charles Bulfinch**) The last and largest of the 3 imposing residences designed by Bulfinch for the larger-than-life grandee **Harrison Gray Otis**, one of Boston's first big-time developers, a Boston mayor, a US senator, and a man who believed in living the good life. He added a fourth repast to his regular meals, breakfasted daily on pâté de foie gras, and—surprise, surprise—was a gout victim for 40 years. Each afternoon the politicians and society guests gathered in Otis' drawing room consumed 10 gallons of spiked punch from a waiting punchbowl perched on the landing. Otis feted all of fashionable Boston in his magnificent rooms. Yet, as no tour guide

will omit telling you, even Harry's house didn't have plumbing. (Bathwater was considered a health menace because it supposedly attracted cockroaches, so tubs weren't allowed until the 1840s.) **The Society for the Preservation of New England Antiquities** (SPNEA, see page 38) has opened 2 floors of the house as a museum that brings to life the Federalist era, during which Otis led Bostonians in lavish spending, extravagant hospitality, and shrewd politicking. Imagine horsehooves clattering along the cobblestone courtyard leading to a carriage house behind. The **American Meteorological Society** is now the fortunate resident. ♦ Spruce-Walnut Sts

7 Somerset Club (1819, **Alexander Parris**; National Register of Historic Places) Painter **John Singleton Copley** lived in a house that once stood on this site, until he went to England in 1744 and never returned. Now an ultraexclusive private club, the Greek Revival granite bowfront that replaced Copley's house aggressively protrudes beyond its neighbors' facades. **Colonel David Sears** erected the first (righthand) half in 1819, adding the left half in 1832—doubling Parris' original design and spoiling it in the process. Look for the baronial iron-studded portal with its lions' head knockers—a very showy, un-Beacon Hill touch. ♦ 42 Beacon St (Spruce-Walnut Sts)

8 Appleton-Parker Houses (1818, **Alexander Parris**; addition 1888, **Hartwell and Richardson**; National Historic Landmark) This pair of Greek Revival bowfronts were, respectively, the abodes of Boston's merchant prince **Nathan Appleton** of the textile manufacturing family and his former partner, **Daniel Parker** of the **Parker House**, Boston's oldest remaining hotel. **Henry Wadsworth Longfellow** courted and married **Fanny Appleton** in her family's front parlor in 1843. And sardonic **Edgar Allan Poe**, characteristically misbehaving before the ladies at an Appleton soiree, was given the heave-ho. No. 40 is now headquarters for the **Women's City Club of Boston**, best known for its well-attended *Literary Hour* series that lures famous authors to the city. Before you go in, look up at the elaborate fanlights over the entrances. ♦ 39-40 Beacon St (Walnut St)

8 Purple Window Panes The famed *purple panes* of Beacon Hill are the lavender-hued windowpanes that are the proud possession of a handful of houses on the Hill. Actually, the treasured tint was a fluke—in shipments of glass sent from Hamburg to Boston between 1818-1824, manganese oxide reacted with the sun to create the color. Although numerous copies exist, very few authentic panes have survived. You can look for the originals at **Nos. 39-40** and **63 Beacon St**, and **29A Chestnut St**, among others.

Beacon Hill

9 Little, Brown and Company (1825) Imagine **Louisa May Alcott** dropping by to look over the galley proofs for *Little Women*. Established in 1837, this venerable Boston publishing house also has on its backlist **John Bartlett** (of that household tome *Bartlett's Familiar Quotations*), **J.D. Salinger, Evelyn Waugh, Fanny Farmer** of cookbook fame, **Margaret Atwood**, and **Berke Breathed**, creator of the recently retired *Bloom County* cartoon strip. The firm moved its headquarters here in 1909. ◆ 34 Beacon St (Joy St)

9 George Parkman House (1825, **Cornelius Coolidge**, builder) In one of the most sensational murders of the century, **George Francis Parkman**'s father, **Dr. George Parkman**, was murdered in 1849 allegedly by Harvard college professor **John Webster**, a fellow Boston socialite who had borrowed money from the doctor. Webster finally was hanged for the crime; it so happened the judge handling the case, **Lemuel Shaw**, was related to the victim. After the furor, Parkman's son retreated with his mother and sister from public scrutiny, remaining a recluse in this house until his death in 1908. The house overlooks the Common, and Parkman must have found solace in this unchanging landscape because he left $5\frac{1}{2}$ million dollars in his will for its maintenance. For generations, Boston mayors lived in this house, which belongs to the city but is now used only for civic functions. ◆ 33 Beacon St

Known as *The Way to the Poorhouse* in the 17th century, because of the almshouse located at the corner of Park St, **Beacon St** began as an undeveloped area on Boston's edge. Here the free-spirited **Reverend Blaxton** cultivated the first named variety of American apple—*Blaxton's Yellow Sweeting*—in his beloved orchard near today's Charles St. Formally laid out in 1708, Beacon St began to acquire its present sedate and stately character when its brick row houses, most in early Federal style, were built in the first half of the 19th century, following the State House's lead. This bright thoroughfare bordering the Common became known as *the sunny street that holds the sifted few.*

10 The State House (1795–1798, **Charles Bulfinch**; restored, 1896–1898; rear annex 1889–1895, **Charles E. Brigham**; wings 1914–1917, **Chapman, Sturgis and Andrews**; National Historic Landmark) The gilded dome of the Massachusetts State House glitters above the soft, dull hues of Beacon Hill, luring the eye. In fact, the capitol building (always, always called the *State House*, never the *Capitol*) itself was the lure that first drew wealthy Bostonians away from the crowded waterfront to settle on the more salubrious Hill, still considered *country* at the start of the 18th century.

Charles Bulfinch spun out his remarkable designs at a breathtaking rate, leaps and bounds ahead of city officials in his brilliant urban planning maneuvers. The State House is his finest surviving gift to the city. When construction began, **Governor Samuel Adams**, the popular Revolutionary War patriot, laid the cornerstone with **Paul Revere**'s help. Looking up from Beacon St, imagine away the 2 marble wings, added more than a century later. Facing the Common, Bulfinch's imposing south facade is dominated by a commanding portico with 12 Corinthian columns, surmounting an arcade of brick arches. Topping the lantern above the dome is a gilded pinecone, a symbol of the vast timberlands of northern Massachusetts, which became the state of Maine in 1820.

This striking Neoclassical edifice cut a much less flashy figure in Bulfinch's time: the dome was originally whitewashed wood shingles, replaced in 1802 with gray-painted copper sheet-

Boston's nickname, *the Hub*, comes from an article published by **Oliver Wendell Holmes**—doctor, author, and father of the famous jurist—in *The Atlantic Monthly* in 1858. Holmes grandiosely wrote: *Boston State House is the hub of the solar system.* Not a bad image, so Bostonians have since stretched it to include the entire city.

Charles Bulfinch (1763–1844) For his enduring stamp on Boston buildings and topography, this architectural genie deserved to have many more places in the city named after him; after all, painter **John Singleton Copley**'s name appears all over, and that Anglophile left America for good on the eve of the Revolution. No matter, Bulfinch didn't hanker after fame and fortune. The first Bostonian to take up architecture as a profession, he was a creative dynamo who began life in a notable Boston family, then skirted poverty throughout his adulthood because he was a poor businessman and gave too much free architectural advice. A patriot through-and-through, Bulfinch nonetheless emulated English architecture, infusing his concern for harmony, hierarchy, public order, propriety—he was Boston's police chief, after all, and head selectman for many years. Bulfinch didn't stop at buildings, either; he had grand visions for entire city segments. A pioneer urban designer, he was one of the **Mount Vernon Proprietors** engineering the shaping of **Brahmin** Beacon Hill. With entire streets and scores of houses, public buildings, churches, banks, hospitals, offices, and schools to his credit, it was Bulfinch who turned an 18th-century town into a 19th-century city. A happier chapter of Bulfinch's life was spent in Washington DC, where he felt much more appreciated—well-paid at last—and contributed to the design of the **US Capitol**.

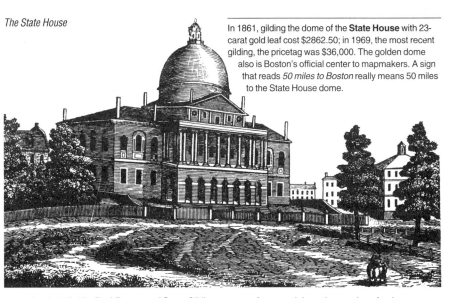

The State House

ing, installed by **Paul Revere and Sons**. Gilding wasn't applied until 1861; the dome was briefly blackened during World War II to hide from moonlight during blackouts, so it wouldn't offer a target to the Axis bombers who never came. In 1825, the red-brick walls were painted white (a common practice when granite or marble was too costly); in 1845 repainted yellow; then white again in 1917 to match the new marble wings. Not until 1928 was the red brick exposed once more. Around the back is the monstrous yellow-brick heap of an extension, 6 times the size of the original building.

Beneath the central colonnade stand statues of the spellbinding orator and US senator **Daniel Webster**, educator **Horace Mann**, and Civil War general **Thomas Hooker** on his charger. On the lawns below the 2 wings are pensive images of **Anne Hutchinson** (left), who was banished from Boston in 1645 by the Puritan community for her free-thinking religious views (not until 1945 did the **Great and General Court of Massachusetts** revoke the edict of banishment), and Quaker **Mary Dyer** (right), who was hanged on the Common for protesting Anne's banishment. A new statue of a young, serious, striding **John F. Kennedy** was recently added. Climb the steps and enter Bulfinch's **Doric Hall** on the 1st floor under the dome, named for its 10 colossal columns. The hall's main doors only open when a US president visits or a Massachusetts governor leaves the State House for the last time.

On the 2nd floor is the resplendent **House of Representatives** gallery. Here hangs the *Sacred Cod* carved in pine, presented to the legislature in 1783 by Boston merchant **Jonathan Rowe** as a reminder of the fishing industry's importance to the state economy. This wooden fish effigy was given such ridiculous reverence that in 1895 it was wrapped in an American flag and carried to the new State House by 4 messengers, escorted by a committee of 15 House members. And on 26 April 1933, when the fish was codnapped by the **Harvard Lampoon** as a prank, all business in the House was suspended

for several days, the members fuming over their missing fish. The thieves relented, and phoned to tell the House that their mascot was concealed in a closet beneath their chamber. In the barrel-vaulted **Senate Reception Room**, the original Senate Chamber, each of 4 original Ionic columns by Bulfinch was carved from a single pine tree. Directly beneath the gold dome is the sunburst-ceilinged **Senate Chamber**, where **Angelina Grimke** was the first woman to address a US legislative body when she gave an antislavery speech in 1838. ♦ Building: M-F 9AM-5PM. Information and tours: M-F 10AM-4PM, Doric Hall. Closed state holidays ⑤ Enter from Bowdoin St

11 Robert Gould Shaw Memorial (1897)
Across from the main entrance to the State House, sculptor **Augustus Saint-Gauden**'s monument honors the **54th Massachusetts Regiment** volunteers of African descent, and the nation's first black regiment, which enlisted in Boston. The troops fought in the Civil War under the command of 26-year-old Shaw, son of a venerable Boston family. For 2 years, until a shamefaced Congress relented, members of the 54th refused their pay because they received only $10/month instead of the $13 paid to whites. Shaw and half his men died in a valiant assault on Fort Wagner SC, in 1863. It took Saint-Gaudens 13 years to complete this beautifully wrought bas-relief, which Shaw's abolitionist family insisted must honor the black infantrymen as well as their son. The monument today seems somewhat patronizing for its portrayal of the white Shaw as a heroic figure on horseback towering above the black troops, but it was, in fact, remarkably democratic in its day. Draw near and study the portraitlike, ennobling, expressive treatment of the men's faces. The angel of death hovers above. A Hollywood movie about Shaw and his brave regiment, called *Glory*, was released in 1989. Charles McKim, of the prestigious architectural firm **McKim, Mead, & White**, designed the memorial's classical frame. It sits on a petite plaza whose granite balustrade overlooks the Common.

12 Park Street Called Sentry Lane in the 17th century, this was the pathway the sentry took to the top of Beacon Hill, where a bucket of tar mounted on a post in 1634 was ever-ready for emergency lighting until it blew down in 1789. An almshouse, house of correction, insane asylum, and *bridewell*—a lovely name for a jail —populated this street when it was part of Boston's outskirts; now Park St is home to a number of decidedly reputable institutions. In 1804, architect **Charles Bulfinch** straightened out the lane and designed 9 residences facing the Common that became known as **Bulfinch Row**. Only the **Amory-Ticknor House** at the corner of Beacon St survives—disastrously altered.

Beacon Hill

12 The Union Club The flag bearing the Union Club's logo forever waves over No. 8, now the street's only handsome structure, and formerly separate 19th-century mansions (the right-hand one was demolished in 1896 and replaced) owned by 2 of Boston's most illustrious families. If you're in a perverse mood, sample one of the chilliest receptions you'll ever encounter by walking into the genteel lobby of this private club. As the receptionist will frostily inform you, Boston's First Family members use the Club's *Social Register* as their telephone book and chat about strictly nonbusiness topics over lunch. Members coming and going will give you a not-so-subtle once-over. ♦ 8 Park St

12 Houghton Mifflin Company (1877, **Snell and Gregerson**, extensively altered) No. 2 isn't much to look at, but it has been the home of Houghton Mifflin Company's editorial offices since 1880. Many beloved and respected books have been launched here, including works by Willa Cather, Henry James, Kate Douglas (*Rebecca of Sunnybrook Farm*), **G.A. Rey**'s *Curious George* series, and **Roger Tory Peterson**'s famous bird guides. ♦ 2 Park St

13 Park Street Church (1810, Peter Banner) When heading northeast on the Common, all eyes irresistibly rise to this majestic church looming at Park and Tremont streets, opposite the subway station. **Henry James** heaped praise on this elegant late-Georgian edifice, pronouncing it *perfectly felicitous* and *the most interesting mass of brick and mortar in America*. Influenced by his much more illustrious English compatriot **Christopher Wren**, Banner capped the crowning glory of his career with a stalwart 217-foot telescoping steeple that points to the sky like an orator's emphatic forefinger. Locals have always relied on its easy-to-read clock for time and rendezvous. Here the anthem *America* was first sung on 4 July 1831; 24-year-old **Samuel Francis Smith** reputedly dashed off its lyrics a half-hour before school children sang it on the church steps. And the illustrious **Handel & Haydn Society** formed here in 1815, drawing many of its voices from the church choir. The church once stood next to a workhouse, the Puritan answer to homelessness and poverty. ♦ Daily 10AM-4PM, July-Aug; by appointment only, Sep-June. 1 Park St (Tremont St) 523.3383

13 Brimstone Corner Where Tremont and Park streets meet supposedly was dubbed for the fire-and-brimstone oratory of the Park Street Church's Congregational preachers—including abolitionist **William Lloyd Garrison**, who gave his first antislavery address here in 1829. But a more banal explanation is that brimstone, used to make gunpowder, was stored in the church crypt during the War of 1812.

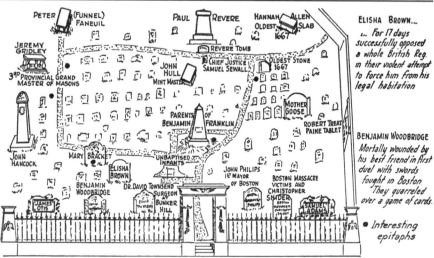

13 Granary Burying Ground (1660; gateway 1830, **Solomon Willard**) Nestled to the right of the Park Street Church, this graveyard was named for the 1738 granary that the church replaced. It is the third oldest graveyard in the city. In this shady haven lie many Revolutionary heroes—**Samuel Adams, John Hancock, James Otis, Robert Treat Paine**, and **Paul Revere**—although headstones have been moved so often that one can't be sure who's where. The 5 victims of the **Boston Massacre**, philanthropist **Peter Faneuil** (for whom

Faneuil Hall is named), **Benjamin Franklin's parents** (he's in Philadelphia), and **Mary Mother Goose** are also here. **Judge Samuel Sewell**, too, rests easy, having cleared his conscience as the only judge to ever admit publicly that he was wrong to condemn the **Salem Witches**. But the best reason to visit this free museum *en plein air* is to examine the tombstones' extraordinary carvings—remember, rubbings are forbidden here—of astonishing posing skeletons, urns and willow fronds, hopeful flowers, somber winged skulls, and contemplative angels. In this haunting place, one is transported back to the 17th-century, from which the earliest tombstones date. The winged hourglasses carved into the Egyptian-style granite gateway were added in the 19th century. ◆ Daily 8AM-4PM

14 **The Boston Athenaeum** (1840, **Edward Clarke Cabot**; enlarged and rebuilt 1913–1914, **Henry Forbes Bigelow**; National Historic Landmark) Although the architect modeled the building after **Palladio**'s *Palazzo da Porta Festa* in Vicenza, Italy, the Athenaeum is a Boston institution to its bones. Only 1049 ownership shares exist to this private library, founded in 1907, and all can be traced to their original Brahmin owners. But even those who aren't to the Athenaeum born can tour and look at—but not touch—books on the 1st and 2nd floors. Two groups frowned upon in most public places—dogs and smokers—are welcome. Take a tour and visit Boston's most pleasant place for musing, the high-ceilinged, airy **Reading Room** on the 5th floor, with its sunny alcoves. As **David McCord** wrote, the room *combines the best elements of the Bodleian, Monticello, the frigate Constitution, a greenhouse and an old New England sitting room.* Make sure you step out onto the 5th-floor terrace, with its gorgeous plantings and view of the **Granary Burying Ground**.

The Athenaeum's superb collections include **George Washington**'s private library and Confederate imprints, as well as history, biography, English, American, and Gypsy literature. There's a notable mystery collection too. An early Athenaeum librarian set up the classification system that baffles users to this day. Members and visitors who've connived special dispensation can actually touch many of the books, but may receive a lesson in the proper way to remove a volume from its shelf (work your fingers *around* its sides, *don't* pull it out from the top!). Take a ride in the charmingly hand painted elevator, a former employee's handiwork, with its framed bookplate display. Part of the library's appeal is the way Oriental carpets and art treasures are casually strewn about. Keep an eye out for the wonderful statue of *Little Nell* on the 1st floor by the stairs. Tours are offered Tuesday and Thursday, reservations required. You'll leave full of envy for the fortunate 1049. ◆ M-F 9AM-5:30PM; Sa 9AM-4PM. Closed August. 10¹/₂ Beacon St. 227.0270

15

always be right on Beacon Hill, George T. Goodspeed, son of the founder, has promised. ◆ M-F 9AM-5PM; Sa 10AM-3PM. Closed mid June-2nd week September. 7 Beacon St (Somerset St) 523.5970. Also at: 310 Washington St (Old South Meeting House). 523.5970

Beacon Hill

16 **Black Goose** ★$$ Crowds are just catching on to this newcomer's Coliseum-size Caesar salads and luxuriant pesto served in the midst of majestic Corinthian columns. In good weather, find a sun-warmed table out front for lunch, and watch scholars and book-browsers coming and going beneath the **Boston Athenaeum**'s dignified sandstone facade across the way. ◆ Italian ◆ M-W 11:30AM-10PM; Th-F 11:30AM-11PM; Sa 5-11PM. 21 Beacon St. Reservations recommended. 720.4500 &

17 **The Golden Dome** ★$ Just *The Dome* will do. The Hill's legislators hold court daily in this clubby little pub, which has been called *the State House Annex*, and it's a show worth catching. When there's a roll call at the State House, someone phones over and a waitress yells to the house; watch how no one moves. Those fingers just keep hoisting their precious cargo, such as the Dome's delectable turkey clubs—the turkey's roasted on the premises—and toothsome fried-potato wedges. Daily specials keep the pols happy. ◆ American ◆ M-F 11AM-11PM (kitchen 11:30AM-3PM) 150 Bowdoin St. No credit cards. 227.7100

17 **The Fill-A-Buster** $ When this little eatery lost its lease on Park St and nearly closed several years ago, the weekday breakfast and lunch crowd went into early mourning. But eureka, another spot opened just 2 blocks away! Gracious **Vaios Grigas**' friendly crew are still serving up their hearty fare with Greek highlights—egg-lemon soup, falafel, spinach-cheese pie, and kabobs—for the same old clientele of pols and media types. The breakfast specials are just as bountiful, plus you can smell Grigas' famous homemade muffins a block away. Once you're a regular here, they'll have your coffee poured and waiting before you've crossed the threshold. Ah, the working life. ◆ Greek/American/takeout ◆ M-F 7AM-4PM. 142 Bowdoin St. 523.8164

18 Tangiers ★$ This tiny stepdown grotto moves at its own langorous tempo, a world apart from the hubbub of the nearby hospital, student, and government beehives. It serves up Lebanese dishes that are so good and cheap, you'll suspect the restaurant of altruistic motives. (The owner's been known to concoct a special tea to soothe a customer's sore throat.) *Lamajune, munazali, kubbeh, mujadarra*—it's a heady selection, so come with friends who like to share. If you're in a talkative mood, linger over an exotic coffee or *mentha*, a cool concoction of soda water, milk, and mint extract. The hours can be erratic, since the owner will often stay up with his last customers, then open late

Beacon Hill

the next day. He deserves his rest. Call ahead to check. ♦ Middle Eastern/takeout ♦ M-Th, Su 11AM-10PM; F-Sa 11AM-11PM. 37 Bowdoin St. 367.0273

19 Lyman Paine House This understated house's distinctive character comes from its intriguing asymmetrical windows and refined Greek Revival ornamentation. ♦ 6 Joy St (Mt Vernon St)

20 Appalachian Mountain Club Founded in Boston in 1876, the AMC can give you plenty of information on outdoor recreation around Boston and New England. ♦ M-F 8:30AM-5:30PM. 5 Joy St. 523.0636

21 32 Mount Vernon Street Julia Ward Howe and **Dr. Samuel Gridley Howe** took up housekeeping here in the 1870s. Anthem-author Julia's husband is best known for founding the **Perkins Institute for the Blind**. But he also organized the **Committee of Vigilance** to protect runaway slaves, which helped at least 300 fugitives and pulled off an occasional daring rescue when word arrived that slaves were aboard ships in **Boston Harbor**. **General Ulysses S. Grant** and writer **Bret Harte** were among the Howes' notable houseguests. ♦ Joy-Walnut Sts

---

Mount Vernon Street, said **Henry James**, is like *some good flushed lady of more than middle age*. This most proper and elegant of American addresses today, the Mt Vernon peak of what the Puritans called **Trimountain** was sniggeringly called *Mount Whoredom* late into the 18th century. Wrote a visiting English lieutenant in 1775: [Bostonians] *were too puritanical a set to admit of such lewd Diversions, tho' ther's perhaps no town of its size cou'd turn out more whores than this cou'd*. But Mt Whoredom was due for a complete *Pygmalion* turnabout. Sharpwitted **Harrison Gray Otis'** syndicate of wealthy investors, the **Mount Vernon Proprietors**, finagled the purchase of Boston painter **John Singleton Copley**'s hilltop acreage while he was in England. The enraged painter failed to stop the sale when he learned his land had become a gold mine after the State House was built. The Proprietors then lopped 60 feet off Mt Vernon to create Walnut, Chestnut, Pinckney, and Mt Vernon streets. One of America's earliest railroads, operating by gravity and horsepower, carried the soil and gravel away in carts, dumping the loads to create **Charles St**. By 1848, majestic mansions had shooed all the bawdy houses over to the Hill's north slope.

22 Nichols House Museum (1804, **Charles Bulfinch**) Remarkable **Miss Rose Standish Nichols**, niece of sculptor **Augustus Saint-Gaudens**, spent most of her genteel life here. A gardening author, world traveler, peace advocate, and pioneer woman landscape architect who earned her own living, Miss Rose also founded the **International Society of Pen Pals** in her front parlor. Stop in to see the furnishings, memorabilia, and ancestors' portraits—collected by Miss Rose and her family over centuries—which she bequeathed to the public along with her home as a museum. The curator will take you on a witty tour. Call for hours. ♦ Admission. 55 Mt Vernon St. 227.6993

Within Nichols House Museum:

The Beacon Hill Garden Club Their annual spring **Hidden Gardens Tour** is your one chance to roam through greenery that otherwise can only be glimpsed tantalizingly beyond brick walls. ♦ Tour info: 227.4392

23 John Callender's House (1802) One of the first houses on the street, Callender's *small house finished for little money* cost $2155 for the lot and $5000–$7000 for construction. A lavish garden blooms behind this bargain-basement structure. ♦ 14 Walnut St (Mt Vernon St)

24 13, 15, and 17 Chestnut Street (1804–1805, **Charles Bulfinch**; No. 13, National Historic Landmark) Bulfinch kept busy building for patrons' daughters, and in fact this most famous trio of row houses were dubbed the *Daughter Houses*. While her husband, **Colonel James Swan**, cooled his heels in a French debtors' prison, Boston heiress **Hepzibah Swan** built these houses for her 3 daughters as wedding gifts. ♦ Walnut St

25 29A Chestnut Street (1799–1800, **Charles Bulfinch**; remodeled, c. 1818) In 1865 tragedian **Edwin Booth** was enjoying a succcessful run in *The Iron Chest*, a drama about a murderer haunted by his crime, and was staying here at the home of the theater manager. But on the eve of Edwin's last performance, brother **John Wilkes Booth** murdered **President Abraham Lincoln**. Edwin's last performance was canceled, he left secretly for New York, and didn't appear before an audience again for nearly a year.

26 Acorn Street Stand at the crown of this, one of Boston's skinniest streets, and watch cars shimmy and shake as they torturously climb its cobbled length. On one side, look up at the trees waving from the hidden gardens backing Mt Vernon St; on the other side are the diminutive houses that belonged to coachmen serving families in mansions on Chestnut and Mt

---

If you pass by the **State House Library** on the 3rd floor, stop in and ask the librarians to show you the fascinating binders in which popular Q&As and trivia about anything Massachusettsian have been entered for decades, such as the argument carried out in local newspapers about the actual thickness of the dome's gilding.

Restaurants/Clubs: Red
Shops/Parks: Green
Hotels: Blue
Sights/Culture: Black

Vernon streets. The opposite of ostentatious, these simple abodes have been spruced up with window boxes and plantings. Study the entrances to **Nos. 1, 3**, and **5** and notice the ornamental acorns that correspond in number with each address. The original, humble home-owners would be pleased to know their houses now hobnob with the best on the real-estate market.

27 Second Harrison Gray Otis House (1800–1802, **Charles Bulfinch**; National Register of Historic Places) Ever an onward-and-upward kind of fellow, Otis abandoned a spanking-new manse on **Cambridge St**, also by Bulfinch, to take up residence in this fashionable neighbor-hood of his own making. One of the only houses on the Hill with ample elbow room, towering No. 85 was intended to set a Joneses standard of freestanding mansions on gener-ous landscaped grounds, but Boston's popula-tion boom soon made this impossible. ◆ 85 Mt Vernon St

28 Louisburg Square (plan, 1826, **S.P. Fuller**, construction 1834–1848) Suddenly, the po-litely jostling houses of the Hill open wide, and you're swung in a new direction, at the edge of one of Boston's most serenely patrician places: Louisburg—pronounce that *s*; you'll horrify locals if you say *Louie-burg!*—Square. If Bul-finch would have had his way, the square would be 3 times larger and 3 decades older, but the **Mount Vernon Proprietors** didn't act on his plan. The red-brick row houses and the oval park they overlook aren't extraordinary in themselves; it's the square's timeless aura that has always appealed to Bostonians. Only home-owners' keys unlock the tall iron fence flanking the park, in which famously bad, deteriorating statues of **Aristides the Just** and **Columbus** coolly survey all comers.

Finally a literary success, **Louisa May Alcott** brought her perenially penniless family to **No. 10**, where mercury poisoning—she got it while a Civil War nurse—slowly crippled her. **No. 20** is a happier address: here **Jenny Lind** (*The Swedish Nightingale*) skyrocketed to fame by **P.T. Barnum**—was married in 1852 to her ac-companist. **Samuel Gray Ward**, a representa-tive of Lind's London bankers, also lived here; among his banking coups was arranging America's purchase of Alaska from Russia for $7,500,000. ◆ Pinckney-Mt Vernon Sts

29 Pinckney Street Begin at its base, and with luck you'll time your arrival at the summit as the late-afternoon sunlight turns molten, and the trees become sparkling lanterns stretching down toward the Charles River. Called by one author the Cinderella street of Beacon Hill, Pinckney was once the dividing line between those who were and those who were not. Pinckney's buildings—many handsome, many humble—are idiosyncratic and utterly delight-ful. It's the Hill's most wonderful street.

29 62 Pinckney Street (1846) Owned by **George S. Hilliard**, this residence was a stop on the underground railroad that began its run through Boston in the 1850s. Whether Hilliard

knew fugitives were harbored in his home is debatable, but his staunchly abolitionist wife certainly did. Workmen discovered the secret attic chamber in the 1920s. ◆ Anderson St

30 Boston English High School The first inter-racial public school in Boston, accepting boys only, opened in this austere cruciform edifice —now condos—in 1844; the city's explosive battle over court-ordered school integration was a tragedy belonging to the century to come. ◆ 65 Anderson St (Pinckney St)

31 Pie-Shaped House The interior reveals what the exterior conceals: squeezed between its neighbors, this house comes to a point like a

piece of pie. Look at the roofline for a clue. ◆ 56 Pinckney St

32 House of Odd Windows (renovation 1884, **William Ralph Emerson**) When **Ralph Waldo Emerson**'s nephew renovated this former car-riage house, he turned the facade into a mon-tage of windows—each singular and superbly positioned—in an inexplicable burst of artistry. Notice the quirked eyebrow dormer at the top. ◆ 24 Pinckney St

32 20 Pinckney Street **Bronson Alcott**, mystic, educator, *other-worldly philosopher*, and noto-riously bad provider, brought his wife and 4 daughters to live here from 1852–1855. The close-knit family and their struggle with poverty inspired daughter Louisa's heartstring-tugger *Little Women*.

33 9¹/₂ Pinckney Street The Hill's hodgepodge evolution created labyrinthine patterns of streets and housing that led to hidden gardens, even hidden houses (**No. 74¹/₂** is the famous **Hidden House**, left to your imagination). The iron gate here at No. 9¹/₂ opens onto a tunnel, or *sally port*, which passes through the house and into a courtyard skirted by 3 hidden houses. Crouch down for a glimpse.

33 Middleton-Glapion House (1795) **George Middleton**, a black jockey, horsebreaker, and Revolutionary War veteran, and **Louis Glapion**, a hairdresser and barber, collaborated on this minute clapboard house, so untouched by time that the pair might have strolled out the front door this morning. ◆ 5 Pinckney St

---

Boston was the center for the abolitionist movement in the 19th century and many illustrious locals played a part. **Charles Sumner** was the most vigorous opponent to slavery in the US Senate; **Harriet Beecher Stowe** wrote *Uncle Tom's Cabin*, which made many Ameri-cans aware for the first time of slavery's human cost; and reformer and lecturer **Wendell Phillips** became known as the *Orator of the Antislavery Cause*. Shame-fully overlooked by history is the part black Bostonians played in helping fugitive slaves and organizing early civil rights campaigns. Not all Bostonians were recep-tive to the antislavery cause, however; a hostile crowd tarred and feathered **William Lloyd Garrison** on one occasion, and the well-born Phillips wasn't allowed to enter many a front door.

34 Myrtle Street When Brahmin restrained elegance begins to stultify, seek out this narrow street's down-to-earth personality. North- and south-slope architecture—tenements and Greek Revival row houses—commune along Myrtle's length, along with the laundries, markets, shoe-repair shops, playground, pizza parlor, and other unfashionable establishments that make this the most for-real neighborhood on the Hill. Look at the rooflines and spot the funky gardens that aren't found on any *Hidden Gardens of Beacon Hill* tour. Perched here in the Hill's heights, you can see the lazy **Charles River** and techy **Massachusetts Institute of Technology**.

Beacon Hill

35 African Meeting House (1806; National Historic Landmark) Free black artisans built this meeting house, the oldest black church still standing in the US, and **Asher Benjamin**'s architecture influenced its townhouse style. Nicknamed *Black Faneuil Hall* during the abolitionist era, here is where **William Lloyd Garrison** founded the **New England Anti-Slavery Society** in the midst of a fierce winter storm on 6 January 1832. Late last century, blacks began migrating to the South End and Roxbury; by the '20s, Irish and Jewish immigrants moved in. The Meeting House was sold to an Orthodox Jewish congregation and remained a synagogue until purchased by the **Museum of Afro American History** in the '70s. ♦ 8 Smith Ct

35 Abiel Smith School The first grammar-and-primary school for black children in Boston opened in 1834, replacing the school that had met in the Meeting House basement; it was named for the businessman who bequeathed the funds for its construction. The school closed 20 years later when the state upheld the black community's demand for integrated schools, ending the practice of taxing blacks to support the schools excluding their children. The **Museum of Afro American History** now inhabits the former school building, where you can explore African-American history in New England. ♦ Free. Tu-Su 10AM-4PM. 46 Joy St (Smith Ct) 742.1854

The American Revolution was a turning point for **African-Americans** in Massachusetts; at its end there were more free blacks than slaves. Early in the 19th century, blacks left the North End for the Hill's better living quarters, settling in **Smith Court**. Antislavery activity and reform movements percolated in this tiny pocket. The **Black Heritage Trail**, a guided walking tour that retraces the history of Boston's 19th-century black community, begins at the **Robert Gould Shaw Memorial** (see page 13). Call the **Boston African American National Historic Site**, 742.5415.

The firebrand **Reverend Cotton Mather** had harsh words for the city in the 17th century: *Boston is almost a hell upon earth, a city full of Lies and Murders and Blasphemies; a dismal Picture and an emblem of Hell.*

35 William C. Nell House (1799; National Historic Landmark) America's first published black historian and a member of **William Lloyd Garrison**'s circle, Nell boarded in this wooden farmhouse from 1851–1856. He led the crusade for integrated public schools in the city, and his **Equal School Association** organized the boycott of neighbor **Abiel Smith School** until the state legislature finally abolished restrictions on black children's access to public schools. Black clothing-dealer **James Scott** purchased it and ran it as a rooming house starting in 1865; he sheltered fugitive slaves here. ♦ 3 Smith Ct

36 Venice Ristorante ★$ This is the kind of place you can walk by a hundred times without noticing, but stop in once and try the food—poof!—you're a regular. Crisp-crusted pizzas topped with ultrafresh ingredients even come in a *personal* size for one. Or choose from an enormous selection of salads, pastas, subs, and daily specials. Free delivery. ♦ Pizza/takeout ♦ M-Th 11AM-1AM; F-Sa 11AM-2AM; Su noon-1AM. 204 Cambridge St (S. Russell St) No credit cards. 227.2094 ♿

37 Rollins Place (1843) Countless passersby have glanced down Rollins Place and been charmed by the little white house tucked snugly at its end. But this inviting Southern-style facade is really a false front—an intriguing anomaly in a neighborhood touting unimpeachable authenticity. The architectural trompe l'oeil masks an old cliff running between Revere and lower Phillips streets. Continue down the same side of the street and slip into **Goodwin Place** (No. 73), **Sentry Hill Place**, and **Bellingham Court**, all charming cul-de-sacs along Revere that also disguise the cliff, but without such fanciful deceit. ♦ 27 Revere St

38 Lewis Hayden House (1814) A fugitive slave himself, Hayden became one of the most famous abolitionists, and his home a station on the underground railroad. **William** and **Ellen Craft**, a famous couple who escaped by masquerading as master and slave, stayed here. And in 1853, **Harriet Beecher Stowe**, who had already published *Uncle Tom's Cabin*, visited Hayden and met 13 newly escaped slaves—the first she'd ever met. The Haydens reputedly kept 2 kegs of gunpowder in the basement, threatening to blow up the house if anyone tried to search it. No one did. ♦ 66 Phillips St

39 Phillips Drug Don't bother to go in now, but if your head starts pounding after the bars close or you wake up in the night with a killer cough, remember Phillips—it's open 24 hrs/day in a city where so much closes so early. Prices can be steep, though. Don't forget the pay phones inside; they're few and far between around the Hill. You can also depend on getting a cab out front. ♦ 24 hrs. 155 Charles St. 523.1028

40 The King & I For the past 5 years, Boston's passionate, some say obsessive, affair with Thai cuisine has created so many offspring that it's often hard to tell them apart. This bright, courteous restaurant has always stood out, however, for its entrancing, delicate versions of dishes like paradise beef, which carries on its own little flirtation with coriander seed. For an after-dinner treat of a different sort, cross Charles St and enter the passage to the left of the **Charles Street Animal Clinic**. You'll see an arch framing trees, the river, passing cars. Enter here and admire the curved charm of **West Hill Place**. ♦ Thai/takeout ♦ M-Th 11:30AM-2:30PM, 5-9:45PM; F 11:30AM-2:30PM, 5-10:45PM; Sa 5-10:45PM; Su 5-9:45PM. 145 Charles St. Reservations recommended for dinner. 227.3320. Also at: 259 Newbury St. 437.9611

41 Period Furniture Hardware Company The 50-year-old shop is aglow with gleaming surfaces to stroke. Many antiquers have abandoned their wearisome Holy-Grail quest for such-and-such genuine wall sconce from such-and-such period for the somewhat-as-satisfying pleasures of these reproductions of hardware from the 18th century onward. If only the price tags weren't the real thing. ♦ M-F 8:30AM-5PM; Sa 10AM-2PM. 123 Charles St. 227.0758

41 C.A. Ruppert Antiques It's like entering someone's home when you visit this intimate parlor-level shop, located in one of Charles St's oldest residences. Although owner **Craig Ruppert** deals mainly with the trade, his shop is open to browsers, too. A comparative newcomer to the street, Ruppert fits right in among the venerables with his stately stock of 18th-, 19th-, and early 20th-century Continental and English furniture and decorative this-and-thats. Look for the shop's original warming oven and brick hearth. ♦ Tu-Sa 10AM-5PM. 121 Charles St. 523.5033

41 Boston Antique Coop I & II These 2 cooperatives in one building set out a tempting smorgasbord of American, Asian, and European antiques. The place has all the ambiance of a garage sale, but it's great fun and local antique dealers snoop about here too. Downstairs at Coop I, 4 dealers display sterling, porcelains, paintings, jewelry, bottles, vintage photography, bric-a-brac, and more. Upstairs at Coop II, 8 dealers specialize in decorative items, vintage clothing, and textiles. Items change constantly, so check back from time to time. ♦ Coop I: M-Th, Sa 11AM-7PM; F 10AM-6PM; Su 1-6PM. Coop II: M-Sa 10AM-6PM; Su noon-6PM. 119 Charles St. Coop I 227.9810, Coop II 227.9811

Don't waste time trying to park on Beacon Hill because most of the district is strictly zoned for residential use. To squeeze into impossibly small spaces, experienced Boston drivers perform *muscle parking*, also called *bumper-car parking*, which involves boldly nudging the bumpers of the cars ahead and behind to create more room. And as parking becomes more scarce, another urban pitfall has opened up: a band of city employees regularly ride the streets checking license numbers, on the lookout for cars that have racked up numerous unpaid tickets. Your prize, should you reach the current magic number, is the *Denver Boot,* a yellow-steel wheel attachment that immoblizes the car.

42 Danish Country Furniture Brightly colored, appealing objects—rugs, tableware, crafts, folk art—can be found in, on, and among the handsome blond furniture dating from the mid-18th century onward. So often antique furniture cringes from returning to active service, but owner **John Kilroy**'s Danish desks, armoires, tables, chests, and chairs sturdily welcome the prospect. His shop is cheery after the dark-and-dour environment of many other Hill establishments. ♦ M-W 10AM-6PM; Th 10AM-7PM; Sa 10AM-5PM; Su 1-5PM. 138 Charles St. 227.1804

42 Marika's You'll need to navigate carefully through this crowded collection of glassware,

furniture, paintings, tapestries, and treasures from all around the world. Owner **Matthew Raisz**'s grandmother Marika emigrated from Budapest and founded this shop, which is particularly prestigious for its extraordinary jewelry. Everybody on the antique circuit knows Marika's. ♦ Tu-Sa 10AM-5PM. 130 Charles St. 523.4520

43 George Gravert Antiques The pleasant proprietor of this shop has been in the antiques business for 30 years, specializing in European furniture and accessories that are clearly chosen by an expert eye. There's something timeless and trustworthy about the place that makes you want to linger even after you've ogled everything twice. Although he caters mainly to wholesalers, Gravert won't mind at all if you come in and browse, but you'll have to strike it lucky because he's only open to the public *by chance.* ♦ 122 Charles St. 227.1593

43 Helen's Leather Shop Care to prance about in python or buckle on some buffalo? You can even opt for ostrich in this leather emporium, which boasts an exotic collection of handmade boots. The mammoth wooden boot out front tells you you've arrived at New England's biggest Western boot dealer, and Helen's also sells shoes, clothing, briefcases, backpacks, and other leather what-have-yous in many popular brands. ♦ M-Sa 10AM-6PM; Su noon-6PM. 110 Charles St. 742.2077

44 Kiku Sui Gallery The name means *floating chrysanthemum.* The largest of its kind in New England, this gallery is one of Charles St's more exotic residents, with an unusual inventory of reasonably priced Japanese prints from the last 3 centuries, ceramics, books, cards, kimonos, flower-arranging materials, and other gifts. You can also get Japanese translated here. The carefully composed window displays reflect owner **David Welker**'s fascination with Japanese art forms. A particularly appealing one showcased hundreds of miniature cats ensconced on pillows. According to a Japanese legend, these tiny figures are talismans; their upraised paws beckon good luck. ♦ M, W-Su 11AM-6PM. 101 Charles St. 227.4288

Restaurants/Clubs: Red   Hotels: Blue
Shops/Parks: Green   **Sights/Culture:** Black

44 The Coffee Connection ★$ The coffee is unsurpassable; walk in and let the potent, sultry aroma of romancing beans engulf you. Sit at one of the tiny windowside tables and nurse your brew or, better still, carry it over to the Public Garden. ◆ Café/takeout ◆ M-F 7AM-6PM; Sa 8AM-6PM; Su 9AM-5PM. 97 Charles St (Pinckney St) 227.3812. Also at: 2 Faneuil Hall Marketplace. 227.3821; Copley Pl. 353.1963; 36 JFK St, Harvard Sq, Cambridge. 492.4881

45 Romano's Bakery & Coffee Shop ★★$ It's short on decor but long on great cheap food, so people keep wending their way back to this cozy downstairs eatery. The clutter of newspapers tells you to sit, relax, take your time. The fresh-

Beacon Hill

baked goods, quiches, salads, sandwiches, and soups always hit the spot at lunchtime, and leave you with plenty of money to splurge on dinner. If you're in a dangerous mood, there's always a lethal pastry or chocolate something to rev you up for the afternoon. ◆ Café/takeout ◆ Daily 7:30AM-8PM. 89 Charles St. No credit cards. 523.8704

45 The Sevens ★★$ This is the neighborhood's favorite pub. Often crowded, with free-for-all conversations bouncing between the bar and the booths, the gregarious Sevens is a good place to sit back and sip a draft when the world seems a little lonely. You can find the funniest bartender in Boston, **Mark Linehan**, here on Tuesday-Friday nights. Try the pub lunch—a generous, satisfying sandwich and bargain-priced mug of draft beer. Good chili, soups, salads, too. They don't take credit cards, *just pictures of dead presidents*. ◆ Bar food ◆ Daily noon-midnight. 77 Charles St. 523.9074

45 The Hungry i ★★$$ If you're claustrophobic, think twice before stepping down into this extremely intimate restaurant. Yet for many, this is one of the city's most romantic choices. You can also dine alfresco in a diminutive courtyard. The salads arrive in enormous wooden bowls, and fish and game star in the brief but inventive menu. ◆ New American ◆ M-Sa 6-9:30PM; Su 11AM-2PM, 6-9:30PM. 71½ Charles St. Reservations recommended. 227.3524

46 The Grand Trousseau The ornamental screen in the window is dripping with strings of beads and awash with luxuriant velvets, embroidered brocades, shimmering silk, and fabrics one never sees swirling along the street any more. While classical music and jazz entwine you, explore this treasure chamber bursting with romantic vintage clothing and accessories—mostly women's—from the Victorian and Edwardian eras and the '20s and '30s. Owner **Candace Savage** and manager **Twyla Reardon** emphasize that everything sold here is meant to be functional, and they enjoy helping customers feel comfortable with this striking finery. Alterations available, too. ◆ M-Sa 11AM-7PM; Su noon-5PM. 88 Charles St. 367.3163

46 Samuel L. Lowe, Jr. Antiques On a decidedly seaward tack, this shop holds a bounty of marine art, scrimshaw, navigational instruments, model and bottled ships, whaling gear, and a stash of nautical books that will make you long *heigh-ho, for the life of a sailor!* You can add folk art and Chinese porcelain to your booty as well. ◆ M-F 10:30AM-4:30PM; Sa 10:30AM-4PM. 80 Charles St. 742.0845

46 Eugene Galleries It's easy to lose all track of time in this enthralling emporium of old prints, maps, postcards, photographs, and oddments of every sort—a Victorian dustpan, sheet music, paperweights, fire-and-brimstone sermons, and a *History of the Great Fire of Boston* to name a few. Specializing in Boston views and maps, Eugene's is the ideal place after touring the city to see how your favorite sights have been commemorated through the centuries. Two hundred fifty other categories are available too: botanical, medical, legal, women, transportation, and on and on. ◆ M-Sa 10:30AM-5:30PM. 76 Charles St. 227.3062

Courtesy John Sharratt Associates

47 Charles Street Meeting House (1804, **Asher Benjamin**; renovation 1982, **John Sharratt Associates**; National Register of Historic Places) It's a shame they stuck a food shop in the front of this forthright structure; come Sunday morning when it's closed. An octagonal belfry crowns the rectangular central tower, a handsome ensemble by the architect who designed **Faneuil Hall** and inherited Bulfinch's unofficial role of architect laureate of Boston. The meeting house's first congregation, the **Baptist Society**, found the nearby Charles River convenient for baptisms. Although abolitionists often orated from the pulpit—including **William Lloyd Garrison, Frederick Douglass, Harriet Tubman, Sojourner Truth**—church seating was segregated. **Timothy Gilbert**, a member of the congregation, challenged the tradition and was expelled for inviting several black friends to sit in a white pew. (Gilbert then founded the **Tremont Temple** in 1842, Boston's first integrated place of worship.) The **African Methodist Episcopal Church** met here from 1867 until the '30s, with the Unitarian Universalists moving in after the Depression. Later, when the **Afro-American Culture Center** was located here, poet **Langston Hughes** gave readings. Shops and private offices have since replaced community activities. ◆ 121 Mt Vernon St (Charles St)

God made Boston on a wet Sunday.

Raymond Chandle

48 Church of the Advent (1875–1888, **Sturgis and Brigham**) The story goes that flamboyant parishioner **Isabella Stewart Gardner**, who founded her signature museum in the Fenway, scrubbed the church steps during Lent as penance. The story also goes that Proper Bostonians sniffed and wondered why Isabella wasn't required to scour the entire edifice. This Gothic Revival distributes its great girth on an awkward site through a chain of conical-roofed chapels, amiably accommodating nearby domestic architecture as a good Hill neighbor should. The interiors are also ingeniously arranged, splendidly embellished. The church boasts one of the finest sets of carillon bells in the United States and a restful garden. ♦ Mt Vernon St at Brimmer St

49 Sunflower Castle (1840; remodeled 1878, **Clarence Luce**) This amusing Queen Anne cottage began life as a plain-Jane anonymous little building; now it takes its name from the enormous, gaudy sunflower ornament pressed on its brow. Maybe boredom with Beacon Hill's *de rigueur* palette and mincing details inspired Luce to paint the stuccoed 1st floor brilliant yellow and sheath the 2nd story in China-red tile. Whimsy now unleashed, he added exuberantly carved brackets and posts, and a griffin. ♦ 130 Mt Vernon St (River St)

50 Another Season ★★★$$$
London-born owner **Odette Bery** proves that the English can cook. Her monthly menus are eclectic and international; her food modern, understated, often mercifully free of butter and cream, and served in petite portions. The well-heeled clientele includes many Hill regulars, who don't mind if their knees bump in the cramped dining alcoves because they're fond of the Gay Nineties bistro murals; pleasured by the inventive turns beef medallions take here; enamored of the expressive chocolate or fruit-based desserts. Insist on the front room. You may not become a passionate habitué, but stroll up to Mt Vernon's summit afterward, and pronounce the evening perfect. ♦ New American ♦ M, Sa 6-10PM; Tu-F noon-2PM, 6-10PM. Reservations recommended; required for dinner F-Sa. 97 Mt Vernon St. 367.0880

51 Charles Street Supply A really good hardware store is an alluring place. Even if you've never gone to war with weeds or handled a 2x4, you'll itch to tackle some project, *any* project, at the sight of all the handy wares spilling onto this overstuffed store's sidewalks. Sure, prices are high, but then gregarious owner **Richard Gurnon**'s operation dispenses a lot more than tools and how-tos. *We're the friendly store*, he says, and it's true. The staff often steers disoriented people in the right direction, and in the neighborhood they're famous for doing *a lot of*

those little things that smooth the bumpy course of urban life. If you need a converter, by the way, stop in. ♦ M-Sa 8AM-6PM. 54-56 Charles St. 367.9046

51 The Lyric Stage The oldest resident professional theater company in Boston will likely re-

locate to larger quarters on **Clarendon St** after approximately 1 September 1991. Its season generally running from late September-early June, the Lyric Stage performs neglected classics such as **George Bernard Shaw**'s works. Led by artistic director **Ron Ritchell**, the company emphasizes intimate theater experiences. ♦ Seats 103. 54 Charles St. 742.1790

51 Blackstone's of Beacon Hill Owner **Bob Smith** stocks reproductions for historical societies all across the US, so this is the place to come for trivets, candlesnuffers, doorknockers, and such in brass and mahogany. Blackstone's has handmade stained-glass frames and porcelain and enamel renditions of the Public Garden's famous **Swan Boats** designed for the shop by **Limoges** and **Crummles**. ♦ M-F 10AM-6:30PM; Sa 9AM-6PM; Su noon-6PM. 46 Charles St. 227.4646

51 Paramount Restaurant $ This is a Greek diner squeezed into a Charles St shoebox. A gathering spot for locals, it offers typical greasy-spoon breakfasts that one is expected to consume with dispatch during busy hours. You'll know if you're too slow. Yet *so* many are dedicated to the place, there must be some larger appeal a sensitive soul will perceive. Nothing's small here—try the Greek salad, moussakka, or souvlaki. Self-serve and very cheap. ♦ Greek/American/takeout ♦ M-Sa 7AM-10PM; Su 8AM-9PM. 44 Charles St. 523.8832

Boston Brahmins Boston aristocracy does not, as many believe, hark back to the early Puritan settlers or the *Mayflower* set; instead, Boston's elite descended from 19th-century merchant princes, some of whom had made money in rather unsavory ways. Many of these early, privileged Bostonians justified their worldly gains by founding and funding cultural and charitable organizations. Brahmins came to epitomize high standards of thrifty, moral, and simple living. **Oliver Wendell Holmes** coined this upperclass set's famous label—*Brahmins*—after the ascetic Hindu caste that performed sacred rituals and set moral standards. **Cabot, Coolidge, Forbes, Lawrence, Lodge, Lowell, Saltonstall**—their names have been recycled and intermingled through the years, but still convey the best and worst of their all-powerful ancestors who once ruled the city.

51 Bel Canto ★$ This local chain cooks up tasty *tortas*—thick-crusted (wheat or white) pizzas—perfect for 2, so come with an even-numbered party or include a renegade who'll happily tackle a calzone instead. Mix and match toppings to your heart's content, but if you order fresh garlic, advise the waiter that you have no fear of vampires and don't need an entire head thrown on. ◆ Pizza/takeout ◆ M-Th, Su 11AM-10PM; F-Sa 11AM-11PM. 42 Charles St. 523.5575 ♿

51 Eric's of Boston Eric's inventory is a Christmas list run amuck; stuffing a stocking with these pricey treasures and toys could easily run into the thousands. Most famous for annual

arrays of spectacular tree ornaments you'll be afraid to breathe on, the shop is decked out for lots of other occasions. The splendid selection of international cards and wrapping papers, and the jewelry, porcelains, and miniatures just waiting to become keepsakes, will satisfy many a whim. But spend too much time in the midst of this preciosity, and you'll need a good dose of down-home yard-sale shopping. ◆ M-Sa 9:30AM-6PM. 38 Charles St. 227.6567

51 James Billings Antiques & Interiors Handling the antiques side of things is **James Billings**, who concentrates on 18th-century English and Continental furniture. **Lise Davis**, his wife and partner, is an interior decorator who specializes in the ever-more-popular English country-house look. Both belong to the British Antique Dealers Association and have been in business in Essex, England, for 30 years, and in Boston for 8. Their talents blend beautifully in this spacious opulently-appointed shop. It's impossible to pass by without peering within, even if the owners' particular interests aren't your cup of tea. As one glance will inform you, everything comes dear here. ◆ M-Sa 10AM-6PM. 34 Charles St (Chestnut St) 367.9533

52 Victorian Bouquet One of Boston's most inspired florists, **Susan Bates** uses locally-grown flowers and Holland imports, and dried and silk varieties too. Her bouquets are simply great. Unfortunately, there's no access for the handicapped, but the attentive staff willingly provides streetside service. ◆ M-Sa 9AM-6PM. 53A Charles St. 367.6648

52 Ristorante Toscano ★★★$$$ Conscientiously patrolled by its 3 owners, this brisk, friendly Florentine trattoria offers a diverting lineup of daily specials, headlining such luscious stars as rack of lamb, smoked-salmon pasta, and *carpaccio*. This is one of the only places you're likely to encounter *bolito misto* (Italian boiled dinner). Start out rifling the bread basket for *focaccia* and *schiacciata*, and end in dignified rapture over *tiramisú* and espresso.

Having conquered its growing pains, this restaurant is now one of Boston's favorites. ◆ Italian ◆ M-Th 11:30AM-2:30PM, 5:30-10PM; F-Sa 11:30AM-2:30PM, 5:30-10:30PM; Su 5:30-10PM. 41 Charles St. Valet parking evenings. Reservations recommended. 723.4090

53 Cedar Lane Way When evening has nearly crept over the Hill, enter this skinny lane from Chestnut St. Say hello to the cats in the windows of the tiny dwellings, and use sonar to sidestep residents' trash and potted plants while you look up and admire their gardens spilling over brick retaining walls. The lane turns to cobblestones after crossing Pinckney St and ends beneath a gas lantern's intimate glow.

54 The Book Store Just a few strides away from the commotion of Charles St, this little shop seems to shrink back into the safe embrace of its residential surroundings. A familiar presence on the Hill, as the unassuming name implies, The Book Store has catered to residents for 35 years. Soft-spoken owners **Susan Timken** and **Linda Cox** stock many books no one else seems to have, with wonderful choices in art, children's, and local books. They'll special-order anything for you. ◆ M-F 10AM-6PM, Sa 10AM-5PM. 76 Chestnut St. 742.4531

55 Il Dolce Momento ★$ We'll tell you up front that the service is inexplicably harried and hare-brained, and the pastries and cappuccino only so-so in this red-and-brick storefront café. But take a look around, and you'll know right away why you came. Long after the last drop of espresso is a memory, people linger here gazing out at the Charles St parade. Every table is near a plate-glass window and it's a good place to write a long letter on a winter afternoon. Plus the *biscotti di Prato*—say almond cookies, or get a blank look—are great dunkers and the gelati *perfetto*, from amaretto to zuppa inglese. Okay sandwiches too. ◆ Caffè ◆ Daily 10AM-11:30PM. 30 Charles St (Chestnut St) No credit cards. 720.0477 ♿

55 Lauriat's Housed in a handsome former hotel, Lauriat's offers the Hill's biggest book selection. They sell a little bit of everything, with strong sections in cookbooks, gardening, and books on the Boston area. ◆ M-Sa 10AM-10PM; Su noon-6PM. 20 Charles St. 523.0188. Also at: 45 Franklin St. 482.2850; Copley Pl. 262.8857 ♿

Massachusetts became a *Commonwealth* in 1780, when it adopted its constitution, which became a model for the Constitution of the United States. Although it's been amended more than 100 times, the state document is the oldest written constitution in effect in the world today. Only 3 other states are Commonwealths: Kentucky, Pennsylvania, and Virginia.

The handsome Federalist row houses along quiet, tranquil **Chestnut St** don't aspire to the grandeur showcased on Mt Vernon St, which runs parallel, but rather offer a compendium of delicately improvised architectural details—with a few more of those amethyst panes—against a backdrop of red brick. Once you've arrived at the base of the street, look back and see how the State House appears ready to take off from its peak on a space voyage.

56 O'Tansey's Have you ever seen a barber shop like this one? As one Hill resident put it, *you're absolutely convinced you can get as good a haircut elsewhere for half the price, but there's just something about the atmosphere at Rick's.* The brick-and-wood surroundings, comfy leather furniture, and grandfather's clock ticking away in the corner will make you feel right at home in this cozy 2-chair shop. Ever-cheerful **Rick O' Tansey** cuts the men, his associate cuts the women. Rick maintains sunrise to sunset hours, and is so busy he never bothers to advertise. ◆ M-Sa 7:30AM-6:30PM. 21 River St. 227.2335

57 Rebecca's ★★$$ Yes, it's trendy, and you won't want your heart to suspect how much butter the succulent monkfish is swimming in. But silence those qualms and enjoy owner **Rebecca Caras'** consistently good formula of seasonal bounty, which made this cheerful bistro such a success that she's launched little takeout satellites all over the city. In the open kitchen watch the chefs assemble excellent omelets, salads, and pasta concoctions, or ogle the chorus line of desserts, which always includes pies with sky-high crusts. To avoid the crush, come early for dinner while the loyal clientele are still at their health clubs, or try brunch some Sunday when you wake up ravenous. While waiting for a table on a late summer's evening, walk down Chestnut St toward the river and look for No. 101 on your right. Surrounding a charming interior court, these condos look like English mews. And on your way back, watch for No. 90, an architectural oddity on the opposite side. Handicapped access for takeout only. ◆ New American ◆ M 7-10:30AM, 11:30AM-4PM, 5-10PM; Tu-Th 7-10:30AM, 11:30AM-4PM, 5-midnight; F 7-10:30AM, 11:30AM-4PM, 5:30-midnight; Sa 8-10:30AM, 11:30AM-4PM, 5:30-midnight; Su 11AM-4PM, 5:30-10PM. Valet parking evenings. Reservations recommended. 21 Charles St. 742.9747

58 Beacon Hill Thrift Shop Don't be hoity-toity about stopping in here; Boston's resourceful Brahmins would surely look askance at anyone silly enough to snub a bargain. One of Boston's oldest thrift shops, it's pleasingly cramped and cluttered with knickknacks and doodads, plus some truly fabulous finds. Manager **Leonard Peterson** is always ready to make a deal, ably assisted by a loyal corps of women volunteers from the Hill. **Winnie Cunningham**, now retired, worked here for 30 years until she was 95, and **Frannie Keene**, the ribbon-cutter at the shop's 1957 opening, is still at her post behind the front counter. All proceeds benefit the New England Baptist Hospital League Nursing Scholar-

Beacon Hill

ships. ◆ M-Th, Sa 11AM-4PM, during daylight-saving time; M-Th, Sa 10:30AM-3:30PM, rest of the year. 15 Charles St. 523.4343

58 DeLuca's Market This market has all sorts of gourmet fixings for a sumptuous picnic on the Esplanade or supper by a fire. (If it's Oreos you're looking for, you can find them, too.) Expect lines and tight squeezes because the whole Hill shops here. Of course, such quality commands a high price. There's a little bit of everything here, but if you can't find your favorite treat, they'll order it. In business for 70 years, DeLuca's wangled a wine-and-liquor license (a *major* feat on Beacon Hill) some years back and purveys an extensive selection. ◆ Daily 7AM-10:30PM. Closed Christmas Day. 11 Charles St. 523.4343. Also at: 239 Newbury St. 262.5990

Courtesy
The Bostonian Society

One of America's early industries, ropemaking, began in Boston in the 1630s. By the 19th century, *ropewalks* were commonplace fixtures on the town's outskirts. These buildings extended up to 1000 feet to house the cumbersome hemp-winding process. Inside, the rope-maker walked backward as the hemp fiber unwound from the skein encircling his waist, and was simulta-

neously twisted into yarn. Ropewalks once crisscrossed the Public Garden and the north slope of Beacon Hill, for example, presenting physical barriers that even influenced how neighborhoods developed. Since a coating of hot pitch was often applied to the rope as a preservative, ropewalks were smelly, hazardous firetraps avoided by townspeople out walking.

59 Hampshire House (1909, **Ogden Codman**) This townhouse, borrowing from Greek and Georgian Revival and Federal styles, was built for Brahmins by a Brahmin, and the silver-spoon spirit still thrives. Try Sunday brunch at the **Oak Room Bar and Cafe** (★★★$$) on the 1st floor. The polished paneling, leather chairs, and mooseheads create a men's-club milieu, which becomes more and more pleasant, just fine, really, when the splendid eggs Benedict and crisp corned-beef hash arrive. Then it's time for a second impeccable Bloody Mary, while the piano playing gently eases the morning along. And some evening soon, return with a serious new flame to gaze at the Public Garden. The Oak

Beacon Hill

Room offers a café menu at dinner, or you can dine more formally in the adjacent **Georgian Room** (★$$$). Either one is perfect for a taste of the *original* Beacon Hill. Several of the fabulous chandeliers are house originals. ♦ American ♦ M-F 11:45AM-2:30PM, 6-10PM; Sa 6-10PM; Su 10:30AM-2PM, 6-10PM. Oak Room daily 5-10PM. 84 Beacon St. Free parking 5-10PM. Reservations recommended for dinner. 227.9600

Within Hampshire House:

Bull & Finch ★$ The bar in the TV sitcom *Cheers* was modeled after this pub, and all the brouhaha has eclipsed a lot of its authentic charm. Still, if you time it right you can sidestep the boisterous throngs of tourists and college students by slipping in at a quiet hour for a beer and one of the great burgers or other pub-style fare. One of Boston's nicest bartenders, **Eddie Doyle**, works here days. Doyle has raised hundreds of thousands of dollars over the years for all kinds of causes. Look for the paper placemats—Doyle's design. ♦ Bar food ♦ Daily 11AM-closing. Dancing Th-Sa 10PM-closing. 84 Beacon St. 227.9605

Two places whose names befuddle even Bostonians are the **Boston Public Garden** and the **Boston Garden**. The first refers to the city's lovely botanic oasis across from **Boston Common**, while the second is the sports arena at North Station where the **Celtics** and **Bruins** star. Although some of us like to pretend the Public Garden is our own backyard and call it simply *the garden*, most Bostonians hearing that nickname would envision the architectural monument to Boston's beloved pastime, spectator sports. The key word is *Public*—make certain you say that if you ask for directions, and you'll find yourself surrounded by trees instead of bleachers.

Restaurants/Clubs: Red   **Hotels:** Blue

Shops/Parks: Green   **Sights/Culture:** Black

60 Public Garden (1859; landscape design, **George Meacham**) The Boston Common belongs to the people and is bedraggled from their freewheeling use, but the Public Garden belongs to the city and has a much more manicured look. Though you can't lounge as freely on the grass here, the garden is an idyllic, lush retreat that always seems larger than it truly is. Artists love to paint here, and the advertising and film communities stage photo shoots all over. Several out-of-the-way bowers offer haven from urban tumult. And there's no better place for a springtime romance to bloom than this splendid spot.

One of the oldest botanical gardens in America, the garden began as desolate, soggy saltmarsh flats located along a great bay of the Charles River estuary. Ropewalks spanned the area and Bostonians clammed and fished when the tides allowed. In April 1775, the **British soldiers** embarked by boat, near the garden's Charles St Gate, for **Lexington** and **Concord**—the American Revolution's debut, which catapulted **Paul Revere** and **William Dawes** on their historic horseback dashes to warn the populace and alert the **Minutemen**. There's also a remarkable history of outspoken citizen involvement enshrined in the Public Garden. Throughout the early 1800s, real-estate developers hankered after its 24 acres, only to be thwarted again and again by vigilant citizens dreaming of a magnificent botanical park. Bostonians finally ratified a bill in 1859 that made the garden forever public. That same year, Meacham, a novice local architect, won $100 for his English-inspired vision of a Public Garden dominated by a sinuous pond and ribboned with paths. His grandiloquent scheme was toned down in the final form. Today the garden is watched over and beautified by *garden* angels: **The Friends of the Public Garden**, formed in the '70s.

Within the Public Garden:

Footbridge (1867, **William G. Preston**) Enter by the ceremonial **Haffenreffer Walk** off Charles St and step onto the spunky, whimsical footbridge, an appealing exaggeration of the engineering marvel of its day—the suspension bridge. Repaired and reinforced, the bridge's spiderweb cables are only decorative now. Lean back against the baby bridge and gaze across the garden toward **Beacon St**, ignoring the ugly downtown stretch in the distance along **Tremont St**. From bridgeside, watch Boston's entire socioeconomic spectrum pass by on the walkway traversing garden and Common, linking the city's residential and commercial districts.

 Swan Boats and Lagoon One of Boston's most famous sights, the Swan Boats cruise serenely on the 4-foot-deep, 4-acre lagoon, among flotillions of chatty ducks waiting for handouts. A pair of swans, ceremoniously escorted to the lagoon every spring, sail snootily about. Rowboats, canoes, and a little sidewheeler named the *Dolly Varden* once plied these waters, but the Swan Boats have reigned alone now for more than a century. Their creator, **Robert Paget**, an English immigrant and

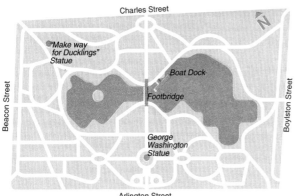

Charles Street

"Make way for Ducklings" Statue

Beacon Street

Boat Dock

Footbridge

Boylston Street

George Washington Statue

Arlington Street

Statues Sure, some of the garden's sculpture is mediocre, but all in all it's an oddly appealing lot. The most striking statue is Charlestown native **Thomas Ball**'s gallant *George Washington* on horseback (1869), facing Commonwealth Avenue (near the Arlington St Gate). Anecdotes tell how Ball was obsessed with accurately depicting the triumphant patriot's steed; he frequented local stables and employed a famous local charger, Black Prince, as his model. To George's right (facing Commonwealth Ave) is the granite-and-red-and-white marble *Ether Fountain,* the garden's oldest monument, which was donated in 1866 to honor the first use of anesthesia, 20 years before, at Massachusetts General Hospital in Boston.

Some others to seek out: Tucked away is a Beaux-Art monument and fountain honoring *George Robert White,* a benevolent Bostonian (1924, statue, **Daniel Chester French**; base, **Henry Bacon**). Facing Boylston St are abolitionist senator *Charles Sumner* **(Thomas Ball)**; anti-slavery spokesman *Wendell Phillips* (1914, statue, Daniel Chester French; base, Henry Bacon); Polish independence leader *Tadeusz Kosciuszko* (1927, **Theo Alice Ruggles Kitson**). By the Charles St Gate is philanthropist *Edward Everett Hale* (1913, **Bela Lyon Pratt**), patriot **Nathan Hale**'s nephew. Flamboyant Unitarian preacher and transcendentalist *William Ellery Channing* (1903, **Herbert Adams**) faces Arlington St. Channing's writing influenced many young authors of his day, including **Ralph Waldo Emerson.** Four fountain statues, all by women, portray images of childhood. Near Arlington St: *Boy and Bird* (1914, **Bashka Paeff**) and *Small Child* (1929, **Mary E. Moore**). Near Charles St: *Triton Babies* (**Anna Coleman Ladd**) and *Bagheera* (1986) by **Lilian Swann Saarinen**, wife of architect **Eero Saarinen**, which illustrates the scene from **Rudyard Kipling**'s *Jungle Book* in which the black panther Bagheera tries to trap an owl.

Ducklings (1987, **Nancy Schön**) The newest and already best-beloved garden statues are Boston artist Schön's larger-than-life bronzes of **Mrs. Mallard and her eight ducklings**, the heroes of **Robert McCloskey**'s children's tale *Make Way for Ducklings* (1941). As the story tells, after stopping all the traffic on **Beacon St**, the canard clan marches off to rendezvous at the lagoon with Mr. Mallard. It's easy to spot the ducks along the path between the lagoon and the gateway at Charles and Beacon streets; you'll always see children sitting on them, embracing and patting them or waddling nearby— quacking. In 1989, news that one of the ducklings had been stolen even made *The New York Times.* A pair of Boston bartenders—**Eddie Doyle** of the nearby **Bull & Finch**, aka *Cheers* bar and **Tommy Leonard** of the Back Bay **Eliot Lounge** together started the *Bring Back Mack* fundraising campaign; now **Mack** is back with his pack.

Meanwhile Mrs. Mallard had reached the Corner Book Shop and turned into Charles Street, with Jack, Kack, Lack, Mack, Nack, Ouack, Pack and Quack all marching in line behind her. Everyone stared. An old lady from Beacon Hill said: "Isn't it amazing!" and the man who swept the streets said: "Well, now, ain't that nice!" and when Mrs. Mallard heard them, she was so proud that she tipped her nose into the air and walked along with an extra swing in her waddle.

Robert McCloskey, *Make Way for Ducklings*

Boston's land mass today is more than 4 times the area of the original **Shawmut Peninsula**. The city's original 785 acres or so have grown to more than 4000 acres, owing to landfill projects that began in 1803 and continue today.

Government Center/ Faneuil Hall

This part of town is not really a neighborhood. It's more a collection of interesting and worthwhile things to see sprinkled among impersonal office towers and heavily trafficked, characterless streets, more or less fitting within **Cambridge St** to the west, the tangle of highways intersecting at the edge of the **Charles River** to the north, **Court** and **State** streets to the south, and the **Central Artery** to the east. The main attractions are **Faneuil Hall Marketplace**, with its irresistible blend of history and contemporary consumer delights; the **Blackstone Block**, a tiny remnant of *Old Boston*; and **Boston Garden** sports arena, home of the **Celtics** basketball team, the **Bruins** ice hockey team, and their devoted fans.

Established communities did exist here once. They were swept away in the '60s, when the stagnating city tried to rejuvenate itself through drastic and painful urban renewal, forcing thousands of city residents to move elsewhere. **I.M. Pei**'s 1960 master urban-design plan imposed monumental order on 56 acres: 22 streets were replaced with 6; slots for big, bold new buildings carefully plotted; and a vast plaza created and crowned with an iconoclastic city hall symbolizing *New Boston*.

The name **West End**, nearly forgotten now, at one time referred to 48 acres stretching from the base of **Beacon Hill** to **North Station**. The West End's fashionable days had ended in the 19th century, and by the 20th many considered the area a slum. Yet more than 10,000 people of 23 nationalities—Russians, Greeks, Albanians, Irish, Italians, Poles, Jews, Lithuanians—inhabited 3- and 4-story brick row houses on lively, intimate streets. Older Bostonians recall when **Government Center** was the raucous and irrepressible **Scollay Square**, where Boston's racier nightlife caroused in saloons, burlesque shows, shooting galleries, adult theaters, pawnshops, tattoo parlors, cheap hotels. Indulging in some romantic afterthought, many still regret that this historic free-wheeling square was obliterated to make way for business, federal, state, and city offices—somewhat more reputable but much less colorful.

Incredibly altered and dislocated from its past, this area seems oddly situated abutting the history-drenched waterfront, North End, and Beacon Hill. Government Center is more a passageway to other destinations than a place to linger. Only vestiges of the old remain, like **Old West Church**, **Harrison Gray Otis House**, **Bulfinch Pavilion** and **Ether Dome** at **Massachusetts General Hospital** (MGH), **Sears Crescent** and the famous **Steaming Kettle** landmark. Most of the contemporary architecture has a '60s look, often alienating and aloof. The newest buildings still can't decide what they're doing here, such as **Graham Gund**'s theatrical **One Bowdoin Square** office building, a controversial addition to the skyline. The old authentic languages, layers, color, complexity are gone; some say the West End's demise was necessary to let a new city image live. While it's true that much of what's gone doesn't merit mourning, most of the new is nothing to brag about either.

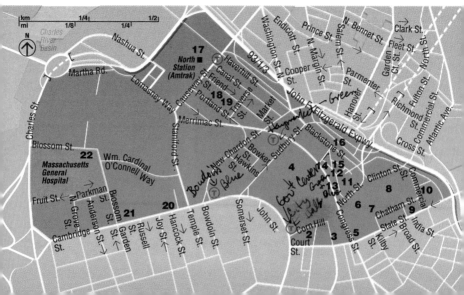

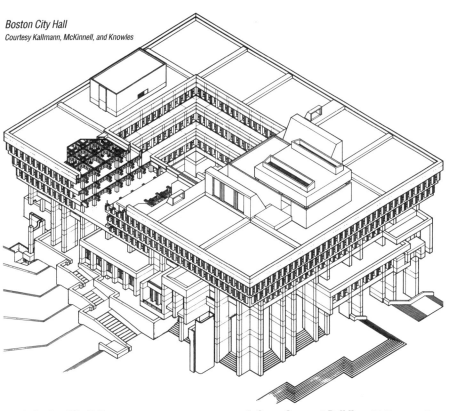

Boston City Hall
Courtesy Kallmann, McKinnell, and Knowles

1 Boston City Hall (1968, **Kallmann, McKinnell, and Knowles**) This dramatic building towering over a windswept brick plain looks precisely like what it is—a factory where Boston governmental operations crank along. **Gerhard Kallmann** and **Michael McKinnell**, also architects for the **Hynes Auditorium** in Back Bay and the **Boston Five Cents Savings Bank** on School St, won a national competition for this project, the eye-catching centerpiece of New Boston. Like Boston's old warehouses, the building's exterior frankly communicates the functions and hierarchies of what's happening inside: its sprawling open lower levels house departments that directly serve the public, while more aloof bureaucracy is relegated to the upper floors, with the publicly accountable mayor's and city council's offices suspended between. Civic activities such as summertime concerts and year-round political events spill onto **City Hall Plaza**. Although its interior is dim and neglected-looking, City Hall is an edifice of heroic intentions, its massing and shadows always eloquent. ♦ City Hall Plaza. 725.4000 ᵯ

The best starting point for this neighborhood is the **Government Center** (**Green** and **Blue Lines**) T stop at **City Hall Plaza**, but the **Haymarket** (**Green** and **Orange Lines**) and **Bowdoin** (**Blue Line**) subway stops are also convenient. **North Station** (**Green** and **Orange Lines**) is the stop for **Boston Garden**; **Charles St** (**Red Line**) stop takes you nearest to **Massachusetts General Hospital** and **Massachusetts Eye and Ear**. (Note: the Haymarket bus and subway stop is behind the **Government Center Garage**, about a block's distance down **New Congress St** from the outdoor Haymarket.)

2 Sears Crescent Building (1816; renovation 1969, **Don Stull Associates**) A holdover from old **Scollay Sq**, this gracefully curving building moderates **City Hall**'s aggressive stance and softens 9-acre **City Hall Plaza**'s impersonality. The crescent recalls the days when Boston streets sprouted every which way and the city didn't care that the shortest distance between 2 points is a line. Built by **David Sears**, whose Beacon Hill mansion is now the **Somerset Club**, this block was once Boston's publishing center, where **Emerson, Hawthorne**, and other literary types gathered. Cozying up to the crescent is the little **Sears Block** building (1848), where Boston's homey landmark, the gilded **Steaming Kettle**, puffs around the clock. The city's oldest animated trade sign, the kettle was cast in 1873 by coppersmiths **Hicks and Badger**, commissioned by the **Oriental Tea Co.** at 57 Court St. Fed steam by a pipe from the company's boiler room, the kettle was an instant curiosity. Its big day came when Oriental held a contest to guess its mascot's capacity. Weeks of fervent speculation ended on 1 January 1875, when more than 10,000 people gathered to watch **Mr. William F. Reed**, City Sealer of Weights and Measures, decree the official measure of 227 gallons, 2 quarts, 1 pint, and 3 gills—now engraved on the kettle's side. Eight winners shared the prize: a chest of premium tea. Reporting on the event, the *Boston Sunday Times* referred to the famous **Boston Tea Party** and bragged, *The tea-kettle excitement has run nearly as high as the tea excitement of old, and is almost a historical incident in the career of our noble city.*

We have long had the biggest organ, the biggest monument, the biggest bass drum, and now we have got the biggest tea kettle in the country; and permit us to doubt if any other city could have produced 8 men to guess within 3 gills of its capacity. Once Scollay Sq was razed, the kettle was relocated in 1967 to the Sears Block. There it graced the popular unassuming Steaming Kettle Coffee Shop, recently defunct. ♦ One City Hall Plaza

Within Sears Crescent Building:

Warburton's $ Liberally dotting the town, this chain bakes respectable morning muffins, also savories, scones, Danish, brownies, soups, and sandwiches. City government folk come here often, just as state employees frequent the Warburton's by the State House. ♦ Takeout ♦ M-F 7AM-5PM. No credit cards. 523.7338. Also at: 22A Beacon St. 720.1094; 1 Federal St. 451.0825; 27 Brattle St, Harvard Sq, Cambridge. 876.1609

3 Ames Building (1889, **Shepley, Rutan & Coolidge**; National Register of Historic Places) Fourteen-stories high, the proud and distinctive Ames was once the tallest office building on the Eastern seaboard. Abounding with arches, modulating from the weighty ones at the base to the delicate chain under the cornice, the vigorous building was designed by **H.H. Richardson**'s successor firm. Although the great architect had died a few years earlier, his influence clearly was not forgotten, especially in the Romanesque architectural details and lacy carvings. One of Boston's first skycrapers, the sturdy Ames is supported by 9-foot-thick masonry walls—the 2nd-tallest such structure in the world—not the light-steel frame that became popular soon afterward. The building only briefly dominated the city's skyline. No matter that it's been dwarfed by 20th-century behemoths—the Ames exerts enduring presence. ♦ 1 Court St (Cambridge-Congress Sts)

Within the Ames Building:

Ames Coffee Shop $ Entering the building from **Court St**, notice the vaulted lobby's handsome mosaics, then turn left to find this little luncheonette, which looks as if it hasn't changed in decades. Sit at the old-fashioned counter and enjoy a dose of nostalgia along with all-homemade soups, salads, hash-and-eggs, pancakes, sandwiches. Corn chowder on Wednesday. As they say, *You name it, we've got it.* ♦ American/takeout ♦ M-F 7AM-3:30PM; Sa 7AM-noon. No credit cards. 523.8903

4 John F. Kennedy Federal Office Building (1967, **The Architects Collaborative** and **Samuel Glaser Associates**) Indifferent and impersonal in appearance, this one-million-square-foot building designed by **Walter Gropius**' firm is a perfectly appropriate home for the **Internal Revenue Service, Federal Bureau of Investigation**, and other federal agencies one doesn't want to tangle with. A **Robert Motherwell** mural marks the spot where the 26-story tower unites with its long low-rise mate. ♦ City Hall Plaza (Cambridge-Sudbury Sts)

5 Bay Tower Room ★★$$$ Boston's best space-station experience. It's a private club by day, but come evening this restaurant offers its stunning views, festive atmosphere, and costly but good food to all. Try to arrive before sunset. Located on the 33rd floor, the dramatic dining room is an assemblage of alcoves and tiers where every table claims a view: closeups of Faneuil Hall Marketplace crowds and the Custom House Tower, vistas with boats crossing Boston Harbor, and planes circling Logan Airport. The cuisine is sometimes uneven and sometimes just fine, with successes including lobster ravioli, oysters, country-style pâté, châteaubriand, seafood mixed grill, rack of lamb, roasted venison tenderloin, an extraordinary fruit shortcake. After dinner, ascend to the postage stamp-size lounge and dance to music by a small combo. If you're driving, there's free validated parking under the building; enter from **Merchant's Row**. ♦ New American ♦ M-Th 5:30-10PM; F-Sa 5:30-11PM. 60 State St (Congress St) Jacket required in dining room. Reservations recommended. 723.1666 ♿

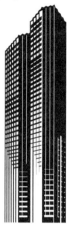

5 Houlihan's $$ Mostly, people come here for the people. One in a national chain of 56, this watering hole has predictable passable food—stick to appetizers and simpler fare—and is usually crowded, especially with the big business-lunch crowd and major after-work singles scene. The decor is a clutter of English and Irish memorabilia, and there's a sports bar. A DJ entertains nightly, Monday-Friday 5PM-2AM and Saturday-Sunday 7PM-2AM, attracting people in their late 20s and 30s. (A reservation does not reserve your party a particular table; it puts your name at the top of the waiting list when you arrive.) ♦ American ♦ M-Sa 11:30AM-2AM; Su 11AM-2AM. 60 State St (Congress St) No jeans or sneakers in lounge after 7PM. Reservations recommended. 367.6377 ♿

5 Walking Distance Locator A marvelous machine that's perfect for Boston, the walker's city, this computerized information terminal prints out free maps of *nearby* places. Pick the category of information you're interested in, such as General Retail, Food & Beverage, Transportation & Lodging, Cultural & Entertainment; then push a button to select the subcategory to be included in your map printout, such as department stores, cafés, movie theaters, gas stations. Out comes an easy-to-read map with numbers corresponding to a list of establishments below. It couldn't be simpler. Special features include *What's on Sale Today*, and *City Happenings*. Other locators, with many more to come: **Boylston St** in front of the **Prudential Tower**, next to **Hynes Auditorium** in Back Bay; on **Boston Five Cents Savings Plaza**, **School** and **Washington** streets; at the **Bank of Boston, Congress** and **Franklin** streets. ♦ 60 State St (Congress St)

5 Dock Square The open area between **Congress St** and **Faneuil Hall** earned its name in Colonial times when it was young Boston's landing-place. The **Town Dock** was eventually built out into **Town Cove**. Later filled in to create more land, this was an important threshold to the New World, with newcomers, visitors, and goods passing constantly across the square to and from the boats docked near its edge. On the way to Faneuil Hall, look for **Anne Whitney**'s 1880 bronze of **Samuel Adams**.

6 Faneuil Hall (1742, **John Smibert**; renovation 1806, **Charles Bulfinch**) From the heights of the steps behind **City Hall**, look for the most familiar and beloved of Boston's many curious objects of affection: spinning in harbor-sent breezes and glinting in the

sun atop Faneuil Hall is master tinsmith **Deacon Shem Drowne**'s gold-plated grasshopper (1742), a weathervane that was modeled after a similar one topping the **London's Royal Exchange**. Grasshoppers symbolize good luck; in a city where many a fine old building has been lost to fire or progress, this critter certainly has done right by Faneuil Hall. When wealthy French Huguenot and Bostonian merchant **Peter Faneuil** offered in 1740 to erect a market building for the town at his own-expense, citizens voted on his proposal. It barely passed, 367-360, a lukewarm welcome for the landmark named for its donor that has been a historic center of Boston life ever since.

Painter John Smibert designed the original structure housing open market stalls, a meeting hall, and offices; gutted by fire in 1761, an

identical building was soon rebuilt. Peddlers and politicians have always peacefully coexisted here, inspiring local poet **Francis W. Hatch** to write: *Here orators in ages past have mounted their attack/Undaunted by proximity of sausage on the rack*. As the Revolution approached, the impassioned oratory of patriots such as **Samuel Adams** and **James Otis** fired up the populace, drawing huge crowds and earning Faneuil Hall the nickname *Cradle of Liberty*. At a 1772 town meeting here, Adams proposed that Boston establish the **Committee of Correspondence** and invite the other colonies to join, thus establishing the clandestine information network that promoted united action against the British repressions. The hall's claim to its nickname was further cemented when Boston's famous antislavery orator **Wendell Phillips** presented his first address here in 1837; **William Lloyd Garrison** and Massachusetts senator **Charles Sumner** joined the battle for the abolitionist cause from the same rostrum.

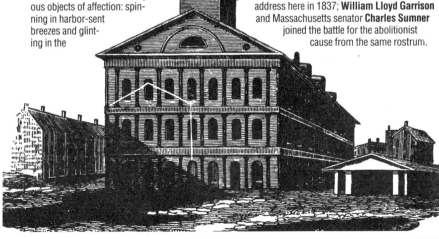

There's one and only one **Faneuil Hall**—the littlest building with the grasshopper on top—but the entire marketplace is usually collectively called *Faneuil Hall*, and sometimes *Quincy Market*. Officially, **Faneuil Hall Marketplace** includes Faneuil Hall, **Quincy Market** (with its **Rotunda, Colonnade, North** and **South Canopies**), and the **North Market** and **South Market** buildings.

Pronunciations of *Faneuil* abound and there's little agreement about which is correct: Funnel, Fan'l, Fannel, Fan-you-ill, Fan-yul, Fan-ee-yul, to name some. The first is closest, but the last 2 are most common.

Restaurants/Clubs: Red   **Hotels**: Blue
Shops/Parks: Green   **Sights/Culture**: Black

29

When the crowds just couldn't squeeze in anymore, Charles Bulfinch handsomely remodeled and enlarged the cramped hall, preserving its stalwart simplicity but doubling its width, adding a floor and creating a marvelous 2nd-floor galleried assembly room that citizens groups constantly use to this day. Among the room's dozens of portraits of famous Americans, look for **George P.A. Healy**'s *Liberty and Union, Now and Forever* depicting Massachusetts **Senator Daniel Webster** on the floor of the US Senate defending the Union in 1830 against a southern senator's contention that states could veto federal laws; and **Gilbert Stuart**'s well-known portrait of **George Washington** taking Dorchester Heights from the Redcoats. On the 3rd floor reside the headquarters and museum of the **Ancient and Honorable Artillery**

Government Center/Faneuil Hall

Company of Massachusetts, a ceremonial organization with a proud past as the oldest military organization in the western hemisphere, chartered in 1638 by Massachusetts' first governor, **John Winthrop**. The company displays its collection of arms, uniforms, documents, and memorabilia.

Back at ground level, get a foretaste of **Quincy Market** across the way by making a quick tour of the souvenir shops and food counters that have replaced the more down-to-earth provender purveyed in Faneuil Hall of old. Times have changed, but the adaptable hall thrives on. Its political pulse also beats strong; during presidential election years, contenders in the state's primary debate here. A major renovation is underway, with completion scheduled for late 1992. ♦ M-Sa 10AM-9PM; Su noon-7PM. 523.3886

Supposedly the oldest chartered military organization in the world, the **Ancient and Honorable Artillery Company of Massachusetts** was formed in 1638 by **Governor John Winthrop** to defend the **Massachusetts Bay Colony** in case of riots or Indian attacks, although the name wasn't official until 1738. Somehow it appears there really wasn't all that much for the *Ancient and Honorables* to do. Even when that little matter of the Revolutionary War came to pass, the group didn't play an important role and hasn't served as a body in any war since. The 700-or-so members have met since 1748 on the top floor of **Faneuil Hall**, and duties gradually evolved: to dress up in full regalia, put on parades, attend the annual spring commission ceremony with the governor, and go on a fall tour of duty to a foreign land. Every important Massachusetts public ceremony now includes the Ancient and Honorables, whom the infamous Boston mayor **James Michael Curley** once declared *Invincible in peace. Invisible in war.* It must be said that numerous members have distinguished themselves individually, some even awarded the Congressional Medal of Honor. Four Ancient and I Ionorables have served as US President: **James Monroe, Chester Alan Arthur, Calvin Coolidge,** and **John F. Kennedy.**

Within Faneuil Hall (south side):

United States Post Office Except for the Logan International Airport branch, this is the only post office in Boston that takes mail on Sunday. Currently closed during renovations.

6 Bostix Stop by this outdoor kiosk to purchase half-price tickets on the day of performance, or advance full-price tickets, to many of Boston's arts and entertainment events. This is an in-person, cash-only service selling tickets for 52 local theater companies, Broadway shows, 19 local dance companies, 47 local music organizations, plus comedy clubs, sports events, jazz concerts, campgrounds, rock/pop clubs and events, dinner theaters, tourist attractions, and summer festivals and theaters. ♦ Tu-Sa 11AM-6PM; Su 11AM-4PM. Faneuil Hall Marketplace (So side of Faneuil Hall) Recorded info 723.5181 ♿

7 The Limited and Express Representative of New Boston's sometimes cavalier attitude toward the city's history, this new building by **Graham Gund Associates** strives to relate to the other marketplace structures. But as hard as it tries, it's a new kid on the block with too much style and not enough substance. For a quick shopping foray that's sure to overwhelm, step inside and explore The Limited's superstore: floor upon floor of moderately priced fashions and accessories primarily for women —but some for men and children too—including Express' international assortment of pricier *Euro*-looks. There's a whole floor of lingerie. Teenagers and college students adore this place. ♦ M-Sa 10AM-9PM; Su noon-6PM. One Faneuil Hall Sq. 742.6837 ♿

7 Bertucci's $ Another spacious outpost of the popular local pizza-and-pasta chain, this Bertucci's is hopping in tune with nearby Faneuil Hall Marketplace. Count on tasty fresh pizzas, calzones, salads. Look for the fun mural, depicting pizza-making, located above the bar. ♦ Pizza/takeout ♦ M-Th 11AM-11PM; F-Sa 11AM-midnight; Su noon-11PM. 22 Merchant's Row. 227.7889. Also at: 43 Stanhope St. 247.6161 ♿

7 Clarke's $$ On one side, there's a big neighborly saloon where crowds flock to watch sports events on TV, eye prospective dates, or wind down after work; on the other, a comfortable no-frills restaurant and bar where you can order straightforward New England dishes like scrod. Try the big sandwiches and burgers with a side of great fries. There's a shuttle from here to **Boston Garden** events. Co-owner **Dave DeBusschere**, formerly of the **New York Knicks**, sometimes drops by to watch the **Celtics** play. ♦ American ♦ M-F 11:30AM-2AM; Sa-Su noon-2AM. 21 Merchant's Row (State St) Reservations recommended for large parties. 227.7800 ♿

On the **South Market** side of Faneuil Hall Marketplace, look for the bronze statue of longtime **Boston Celtics** coach and manager **Red Auerbach**. The team's famous leader is seated on a bench, ready to light the customary cigar that signals a victory at hand.

Restaurants/Clubs: Red   Hotels: Blue
Shops/Parks: Green   **Sights/Culture**: Black

Drawing Courtesy Benjamin Thompson & Assoc/Carlos Diniz

8 Faneuil Hall Marketplace (1826, **Alexander Parris**; reuse 1978, **Benjamin Thompson & Associates**) Beyond **Faneuil Hall** stands a long, low trio of buildings bursting with international and specialty food stalls, restaurants, cafés, boutiques, bars, and an army of pushcarts peddling wares to tempt the impulse buyer. The extravaganza ranges from junk food to gourmet, kitsch to haute couture. The whole ensemble attracts 14 million visitors a year, inviting comparisons to Disney World. But touristy and slick as it is, the marketplace possesses the authentic patina of history. It has lived a long useful life. Many people are turned off by the throngs and buy-buy-buy mood of this shop-and-snack mecca, but it definitely deserves a visit—if only to glance over the worthy old buildings and enjoy the outdoor spectacle of pedestrians and street performers. (An information desk is located under the South Canopy. It isn't easy to spot among the pushcarts, and the staff is often indifferent, but pick up the extremely helpful printed directory.)

The marketplace's 535-foot-long granite centerpiece, a National Historic Landmark, **Quincy Market** is named for **Josiah Quincy**, the Boston mayor who revitalized the decrepit waterfront by ordering major landfills, 6 new streets, and the construction of a market house to supplement overcrowded Faneuil Hall. Architect Alexander Parris crowned the Greek Revival central building with a copper dome and planted majestic Doric colonnades at either end. The building projected a noble face seaward, for it was right at the harbor's edge in those days. Two granite-faced brick warehouses, today called **North** and **South Markets**, later rose on either side according to Parris' plans. For a century and a half, the ensemble was the dignified venue for meat and produce distribution and storage. By the 1970s, however, the marketplace was decaying, in danger of demolition. **Ben and Jane Thompson** of Benjamin Thompson & Associates convinced the city and developers (Rouse) that the complex could become Boston's gathering place again, if recycled to suit contemporary urban life. Thompson's firm restored as much of the complex as possible, adding innovations such as the glass canopies flanking the central building and festive signage. On the South Market side, the cobbled pedestrian way is more

31

spacious, with plenty of benches. Even in chilly weather, you'll see plenty of people enjoying the show while savoring baklava, barbecue, chowder, fudge, gourmet brownies, pizzas, salads, sausage-on-a-stick, raw oysters, Indian pudding, French fries, ice cream—the whole gastronomic gamut. Under the canopy on the north side of Quincy Market, a popular piano bar draws a big after-work crowd from the Financial District and nearby offices, inspiring many an impromptu sing-a-long. When Boston winter finally gives up, outdoor cafés dot the pedestrian streets. An outdoor flower market near the north side of Faneuil Hall blankets the cobblestones with greenery, bringing colors and smells of each season to this corner of the city: autumn pumpkins, Christmas trees and poinsettias, harbingers of spring, summer bouquets.

Government Center/Faneuil Hall

All in all, breathing life back into the old buildings was gently done, and the scheme has proven a fantastic success, a model for renewal projects across the United States. Boston lost its waterside meat-and-potatoes-style market, but colorful abundance of another sort has moved in. Come early in the morning and enjoy a quiet pickup breakfast in Quincy Market's central rotunda, or brave Saturday afternoon crowds when the place is really hopping, full of competing aromas and voices. You'll notice crowds are often ringing the cobbled square between Faneuil Hall and Quincy Market's West Portico, the prime spot for musicians, dancers, magicians, jugglers, and other entertainers. Don't try to wear high heels! ♦ General marketplace shop hrs M-Sa 10AM-9PM; Su noon-6PM. Info 523.3886

Within Quincy Market:

Boston & Maine Fish Company Live lobster up to a whopping 25 lbs and other super-fresh seafood are packed for travel or shipped anywhere in the US from this retail market. Prices are high, but sometimes worth it to satisfy a hankering for fruits of the Atlantic. You can even get all the fixings for an authentic New England clambake, minus the seaside pit: lobsters, steamer clams, chowder, and utensils. Or, if you just want some steamers to take home for supper, they'll steam them for you here if you ask. ♦ M-Sa 8AM-9PM; Su 8AM-6PM. Colonnade. 800/6-BOSTON; 723.3474 (that's 723.FISH!) &

Restaurants/Clubs: Red | Hotels: Blue
Shops/Parks: Green | **Sights/Culture: Black**

The Salty Dog Seafood Bar and Grille $$ Get some of the best oysters in town, good chowder and fried clams, and other fresh and basic undisguised seafood in this noisy little seafood hut of a place. No pastry cart *here*, and no reservations. There's outdoor seating April-1 November. A lot of regulars stay away during the summer to avoid the throngs. ♦ Seafood/American ♦ M-Sa 11AM-1AM; Su 10AM-1AM. Lower level. 742.2094

Boston Chipyard They only sell that classic milk-and-cookies combo, and they're the best chocolate chippers in town—award-winning mouthfuls that are always fresh, whether the plain traditional favorite or mixed with other ingredients like peanut butter, extra chocolate, nuts, oatmeal and raisins. A California parent came more than 14 years ago and opened the shop with her own recipe, loved by her son and his friends. Come for a late-night fix. Mail order too. ♦ Daily 10AM-midnight. North Canopy. 742.9537 &

La Rossa's Instant Shoe Repair Seventy years in the business, this shop promises while-you-wait service Monday-Saturday 9AM-6PM that's both swift and good. La Rossa's also fixes luggage, handbags, and other leather goods, and does leather dyeing. ♦ M-F 9AM-9PM; Sa 10AM-9PM; Su noon-6PM. South Canopy. No credit cards. 227.8499. Also at: South Station. 345.0656; Filene's Basement, Washington St. 338.8656; 290 Main St, Kendall Sq, Cambridge. 864.1801

Within North Market:

Marketplace Café ★$$ A light, bright, and casual bistro where you can dine outdoors in the summer and in a greenhouse setting in the winter, on a variety of appetizers, salads, sandwiches, and simple entree offerings. The café is especially festive and welcoming on warm evenings. ♦ American ♦ M-Th 11AM-11:30PM; F 11AM-1AM; Sa 10AM-1AM; Su 10AM-11:30PM. 227.9660 &

The Boston Beach Club Attracting a younger crowd, BBC books live bands and plays up its seaside theme with surfboard tables, a fish tank, tropical drinks, Hawaiian leis, assorted games and toys. T-shirts, hats, records, trips, and other freebies are handed out on special promotion nights. Drinks only. ♦ Daily 6PM-2AM. 227.9660 &

Brasserie les Halles ★$$ Located above the **Marketplace Café**, this quiet, pleasant French bistro is a welcome change from Faneuil Hall's frenetic hubbub. While imbibing French wine by the glass, from big windows you can watch the throngs you've escaped. The restaurant features a wine-and-cheese bar (open past dining hours) and serves hearty and traditional country French fare in generous portions. Ask about validated parking. ♦ French ♦ M-F 11:30AM-3:30PM, 5:30-11PM; Sa 5:30-11PM. Reservations recommended. 227.1272 &

Durgin Park ★★$ For true Yankee cooking and a taste of Boston's bygone days, you must come here. Don't listen to detractors who say Durgin Park is overrated; give it a try and enjoy a fast-paced, filling meal. Founded in 1827, this cranky-creaky but well-loved institution dates from the marketplace's old days, when produce held the fort instead of today's gourmet melée. Notice the ancient plank floors and tin ceilings. Waitresses legendary for their brisk gotta-job-to-do manner—some have 47+ years of experience—serve up raw clams and oysters, phone book-size prime rib, starchless fish chowder, Boston scrod and Boston baked beans *of course*, chops, steaks, fresh seafood, chicken potpie, cornbread, and more solid old favorites. Save room for Durgin's scrumptious fresh strawberry shortcake made on the premises, and rich Indian pudding. Everybody dines family-style at tables set for 16 and decked out in red-checkered cloths. Visitors from around the country and the world follow the well-worn path here, where 500,000 people are served annually. Durgin Park stuck it out during the market's '70s transformation; now the venerable restaurant is one of the most genuine features of the place. Ask about validated parking. ♦ Yankee ♦ M-Sa 11:30AM-10PM; Su 11AM-9PM. Street level. No credit cards (some traveler's checks accepted) 227.2038

Downstairs at Durgin Park:

The Oyster Bar at Durgin Park ★★$ Serving appetizers and sandwiches only, this is a great alternative to the big noisy place upstairs if you want a light repast and a little calm. Try the soothing clam chowder and briny steamers. No tables; just the bar and bar-style counters. Though dessert's not on the menu, just ask and someone will transport it from upstairs. ♦ 227.2038

Tales with Tails See the kids squeezing and hugging fuzzywuzzies of all kinds. Family-owned and operated, this shop specializes in a menagerie of stuffed animals and toys that debuted in books, such as **Paddington**, **Babar**, **Celeste**, **and Arthur**, **Curious George**, **Raggedy Ann** and **Andy**, **Beatrix Potter** and **Sesame Street** characters, and more. You can get the storybooks, too. Makers include Gund, Dakin, Applause. ♦ M-Sa 10AM-9PM; Su noon-6PM. 2nd level 227.8772

Within South Market:

Serendipity 3 $ Tourists, families, and a younger crowd flock here. This good-humored food boutique makes no bones about its eccentricities, from the whimsical décor to an enormous illustrated menu—you'll want to color it with crayons. It will take forever to decide what to order, but everything's pretty good. Be basic with a burger or omelet, or venture into

blue-corn nachos with goat cheese, scrod Rockefeller, Ftatateeta's Toast, an Eiffel Tower sandwich, the famous frozen hot chocolate. Monday-Friday, complimentary hors d'oeuvres are served during the 4-8PM *Attitude Adjustment* hours, and live jazz plays Wednesday and Thursday nights. In warmer weather, tables migrate outdoors. Desserts are still available a half-hour after dining times. By the way, if you see something you like here, be it a T-shirt, statuette, or lighting fixture, it's likely for sale. ♦ American ♦ M-Th 11:30AM-11:30PM; F 11:30AM-12:30AM; Sa 10:30AM-midnight; Su 10:30AM-11PM. Street level. Reservations recommended F-Sa nights, Su brunch. 523.2339 ㋴

Siam Malee Come here for a feast of fabrics —iridescent, shimmering, gorgeously colored silks, cottons, and linens, all imported from

Government Center/Faneuil Hall

Thailand—metamorphosed into butterflylike day and evening fashions. Almost all are for women, although there's a vivid array of men's ties. Styling is simple but clever, with unusual detailing. Glittery and festive jewelry, beaded bags, jackets, and belts too. ♦ M-Sa 10AM-9PM; Su noon-6PM. Street level. 227.7027 ㋴

Alan Lawrence The 2 friendly young owners put their first names as well as their heads together to create this chic and cozy high-end men's boutique with its emphasis on customer service and *Euro-classic* looks in exceptional textures, colors, fabrics. Men of all ages come in for custom-made suits and shirting, casual wear, and accessories, some designed by the owners and produced internationally. There's a tailor on the premises. Custom consultations offered by appointment. ♦ M-Sa 10AM-9PM; Su noon-6PM. Street level. 227.1144

Le Baggerie This snug shop features unusual individually selected bags of every sort: briefcases, duffels, purses, portfolios, totes, hand-beaded evening bags. Things to put in the bags are sold, too, like calendars, wallets, coin purses. A specialty is the Laurel Burch line of bags, jewelry, T-shirts, mugs, handpainted and silkscreened sweatshirts. ♦ M-Sa 10AM-9PM; Su noon-6PM. Street level. 367.0578

The pushcart parades under and just beyond **Quincy Market**'s canopies are known collectively as the **Bull Market**, named for the bull weathervane above the gold dome.

Quincy Market was the first large-scale use of granite and glass in post-and-beam construction. Another innovation is the cast-iron columns marching the length of the markethouse.

For former **West Enders**, the famous line *You can't go home again* has had tragic aptness. Forced out of their neighborhood after the city declared it a slum and replaced affordable housing with luxury apartments and offices, their plight became a casebook example of the terrible consequences of '60s-style urban renewal. **Herbert Gans**' famous 1962 study, *The Urban Villagers*, spotlights the West End's fate.

Folklorica One of the renovated market's older tenants, this shop has established its fine reputation on its captivating mix of antique and contemporary designer jewelry from Victorian to New York funk. For a wide range of prices, you can pick up a lovely necklace of Murano Venetian glass beads, a marcasite brooch, a Bakelite bracelet, gold estate pieces. The owner/buyer will search for special requests. Pearl

Government Center/Faneuil Hall

stringing and custom design offered. ♦ M-Sa 10AM-9PM; Su noon-6PM. 2nd level. 367.1201 ♿

9 The Black Rose ★$ Its name is translated from *Roisin Dubh*, a Gaelic allegorical name for Ireland that symbolizes Irish Catholic repression by the British. Famous Irish faces and mementos line the walls and Irish music accompanies bargain-priced meals like meatloaf, lamb stew, fish-and-chips, Yankee pot roast, boiled lobster. Don't look for gourmet here. This big hospitable bar offers numerous Irish beers and stout on tap and live Irish music every day; ask for times. It's a great place to meet after work, sing along with folk music, watch the **Celtics** game on the big-screen TV, slowly sip Irish coffee. ♦ American/Irish ♦ M-Sa 11:30AM-1:45AM; Su noon-1:45AM. 160 State St. 742.2286

10 Marketplace Center (1985, **WZMH Group**) This gauche gate-crashing building tries to look like it belongs on this important historic site, even mimicking its venerable neighbors somewhat in materials and style. While it could have been worse, the building is awkward, especially its graceless atrium gateway with makeup-mirror-style fixtures. Although the opening preserves the pedestrian walk-to-the-sea leading to **Boston Harbor** at **Christopher Columbus Park**, the too-tall, too-wide building is a barrier where none existed before. It adds to the marketplace's stockpile of shops, including many chain stores like Brookstone, Banana Republic, Mrs. Fields, Williams-Sonoma, Carroll Reed, Sharper Image, The Gap, and more. ♦ 200 State St

Within Marketplace Center:

Pavo Real Discover beautifully hued and patterned sweaters here that can't be found elsewhere. The shop imports most of its luxurious alpaca wool and pima cotton. Custom-designed handknit sweaters for men and women from Peru and Bolivia with hefty mark-ups. Delightful jewelry, hats, gloves, scarfs, wallets, pocketbooks too, some quite whimsical in design. ♦ M-Sa 10AM-7PM, Su noon-6PM, Jan-Mar; M-Sa 10AM-9PM, Su noon-6PM, Apr-Dec. Street level. 439.0013

Doubleday Book Shop Spacious and bright, with a friendly staff, this link in the Doubleday chain carries books for the general public, with strong sections in fiction, cooking, local information. It's convenient too, since bookstores in this neighborhood are scarce. Pick up some reading to accompany a pickup lunch from Quincy Market. ♦ M-Sa 10AM-9PM; Su noon-6PM. Street level. 439.0196. Also at: 99 Park Plaza. 482.8453 ♿

Peacock Papers Almost always crowded and busy, this gift and novelty shop carries the full Peacock Papers line, plus a trendy, amusing, and irreverent selection of cards, wrapping papers, office items, T-shirts, ornamented pencils stamped with mottos, and just-for-fun gismos and games. ♦ M-Sa 10AM-7PM, Su noon-6PM, Jan-Mar; M-Sa 10AM-9PM; Su noon-6PM, Apr-Dec. Street level. 439.4818 ♿

Chocolate Dipper Through the window, watch thick streams of fragrant, gooey chocolate blending away while the staff readies luscious fresh fruit and truffles for dipping. Try strawberries, raspberries in season, banana, pineapple, cherries, grapes, orange slices and orange rinds enrobed in dark, milk, or white chocolate. The extra-rich truffles come in 7 or 8 flavors, and a big variety of other chocolates are also made on the premises. Chocolate lovers can't stay away. ♦ M-Sa 10AM-7PM, Su noon-6PM, Jan-May; M-Sa 10AM-9PM, Su noon-6PM, Apr-Dec. Street level. 439.0190 ♿

On the site of **No. 16 North St** resided **William Dawes**, who rode to **Lexington** on the evening of 18 April 1775 to warn **John Hancock** and **Samuel Adams** that the British were coming. Meanwhile, **Paul Revere** was en route to **Charlestown** to warn patriots there, after watching for the signal at the **Old North Church** in the **North End**.

The historic **Green Dragon Tavern** once stood on **Union St**, the popular patriots' meeting place that **Daniel Webster** called *the Headquarters of the Revolution*. The Boston Tea Party was planned here.

Restaurants/Clubs: Red   Hotels: Blue
Shops/Parks: Green   **Sights/Culture**: Black

11 The Bostonian Hotel $$$$ Intimate and gracious, the Bostonian has been one of the most pleasant places to stay in Boston since opening in 1982. Much of the hotel's charm comes from its residential scale and the way it blends with the historic **Blackstone Block**: incorporated into the new hotel complex are an 1890 warehouse built by **Peabody** and **Stearns** (architects for the **Custom House Tower**) and an 1824 building. Many of the Bostonian's 152 rooms have French doors opening onto private balconies that overlook Faneuil Hall Marketplace; request rooms that have an imprint of history in the 19th-century Harkness wing. Ten honeymoon suites have Jacuzzis and working fireplaces, 2 rooms have canopy beds. The lobby is appealingly low-key, with historic displays on permanent loan from the **Bostonian Society**. The airy **Atrium** cocktail lounge is a comfortable place to relax, snack on appetizers, and listen to nightly live jazz (no jeans or sneakers). Amenities include babysitting, complimentary overnight shoeshining. Valet and paid parking. Request nonsmokers' or handicapped-accessible accommodations. Rooms equipped for the deaf are also available. No pets allowed. ◆ Deluxe ◆ Faneuil Hall Marketplace. 523.3600, 800/343.0922; fax 523.2454 ₺

Within the Bostonian Hotel:

Seasons ★★★★$$$$ The swank, glass-enclosed dining room atop the Bostonian offers generous cityscapes and marvelous views of Quincy Market's gold dome, the famous Faneuil Hall grasshopper weathervane, and the Custom House Tower's fabulous glowing clock. This is a lovely place to introduce someone to Boston. The enticing menu changes with the seasons, featuring flawless New England and international treats like duckling with ginger and scallions, lemon mousseline, charred rack of lamb and pumpkin couscous, swordfish with grilled fennel and clam hash, chanterelle mushroom and cheddar-cheese pancakes. Even the humble clam fritter becomes special here. Service is gracious. The award-winning, all-American wine list is impressive, and the staff ably recommends. The billowy ceiling balloon shades add a romantic touch, and piano music filters up from the **Atrium** lounge. Politicos and businesspeople come for power breakfasts. Private club at lunchtime. ◆ New American ◆ M-F 7-10:30AM, 11:30AM-2PM, 6-10PM; Sa, Su 7-10:30AM, 6-10PM. Valet parking. No jeans or sneakers at dinner. Reservations recommended. 523.4119

12 Union Oyster House (c. 1713-1717; newer half, 1724) ★★$$$ Dine in one of the few spots in Boston where time simply refuses to move forward. Boston's oldest restaurant and the oldest in continuous operation in the United States, Union Oyster House has been serving its specialty here since 1826. Look in the window and watch oyster-shucking at the bar. This is truly a one-of-a-kind place, best on a cold winter's day when you can follow chilly oysters with steaming chowder or oyster stew and fresh seafood entrees of every kind. The 1st-floor booths are the original ones, with a plaque adorning the booth where **JFK** liked to dine. No reservations taken, so come in the mood for a predinner amble. If there's enough time, have an aperitif at the nearby Bostonian hotel's Atrium lounge.

The block's oldest and best-known building is actually a compatible pair of plain brick row houses. In 1742, **Hopestill Capen** ran a fancy dry-goods business and lived with his family here. Before landfill pushed **Boston Harbor** far

Government Center/Faneuil Hall

away, ships used to dock directly out back to deliver goods. From 1771-1775, printer **Isaiah Thomas** published the outspoken *The Massachusetts Spy* on the 2nd floor, a newspaper so openly supportive of American independence that Thomas was forced to flee to Worcester MA, where he resumed publication. The exiled **Duc de Chartres**, France's future **King Louis Philippe**, lived on the 2nd floor in 1797, paying his way by teaching French to Bostonians until family funds arrived. When **Atwood** and **Bacon** opened their oyster and clam bar, they installed the current half-circle mahogany bar that supposedly became **Daniel Webster**'s favorite haunt. Webster reputedly downed each half-dozen oysters with a tumbler of brandy and water, and he rarely consumed fewer than 6 platefuls. ◆ Seafood/American ◆ M-Th, Su 11AM-9:30PM; F-Sa 11AM-10PM. 41 Union St. 227.2750 ₺ (1st flr only)

13 Statues of Mayor Curley (1980, Lloyd Lillie) Follow North St to the amiable little park tucked between Union and Congress streets. Here 2 statues of Boston's controversial but beloved **Mayor James Michael Curley** (1874-1958) share the active street scene. In one, Curley is seated on a bench in a very approachable pose; many a photo has been taken of Curley seemingly chatting with whomever plops down next to him. The other statue portrays an upright Curley as the man-of-action and orator. Four times mayor, four times congressman, former Massachusetts governor too, Curley was born in Boston's South End. Truly a self-made man, his flamboyant political career gave Bostonians plenty to admire, gossip about, and remember him by. Curley smoothly ran Boston's infamous and powerful Irish political machine, inspiring poet **Francis W. Hatch** to quip, *Vote often and early for Curley*. **Edwin O'Connor** had Curley in mind when he wrote *The Last Hurrah*. But Curley was also known as the *Mayor of the Poor*, and his civic contributions included establishing **Boston City Hospital**.

The toothpick was first used in the United States at the **Union Oyster House**

13 Marshall House ★★$$ When the **Union Oyster House** is too crowded or too much for your wallet—often the case—come here. You may have a wait, but it won't be as long. This place is less than a decade old, yet manages to look as if it's been here 100 years, with plenty of brass and wood. Eat informally at the bar or bar tables, or in the snug rear dining room. Start off with the raw bar—oysters, steamers, cherrystones, littlenecks, etc—and proceed with fresh seafood entrees prepared in the open kitchen in the middle of the restaurant. There are 2 lobster specials every day and a wide choice of beers. Big burgers and sandwiches, too. You can't make a reservation, so leave your name and take a stroll around **Faneuil Hall Marketplace**; you won't be bored. Until recently the city's oldest hardware store

Government Center/Faneuil Hall

stood next door, but times sadly change and now a **McDonald's** franchise is moving in, hungry for tourist trade. ♦ Seafood/American ♦ Daily 11:30AM-11PM. 15 Union St. 523.9396 &

14 Bell in Hand Tavern Operating since 1795, though not always at this site, this is the oldest tavern in the US. On a cold afternoon, duck in here for a giant draft beer and an appetizer, burger, or sandwich; kitchen hours vary, so food isn't always available. With its moniker illustrated by the curious old sign on its plain facade, the Bell in Hand is very like an English pub. It was named by original proprietor **Jim Wilson**, Boston's town crier until 1794, who rang a bell as he progressed though town announcing the news. **Benjamin Franklin**'s childhood home once stood on this site. ♦ M-F 11:30AM-closing; Sa-Su noon-closing. 45 Union St. 227.2098

15 Ebenezer Hancock House (c. 1760) The **Blackstone Block**'s second oldest building, this 3-story red-brick house was probably built by **John Hancock**'s uncle **Thomas**, from whom John later inherited it. Here John's younger brother **Ebenezer** lived and maintained his office as deputy paymaster of the Continental Army. His biggest duty came in 1778 when **Admiral D'Estaing**'s fleet conducted 2 million silver coins from **King Louis XVI** of France to pay local troops, salvaging their morale. Restored, the house is now lawyers' offices and not open to the public. ♦ 10 Marshall St

15 Blackstone Block A charming snippet of old Boston, this tiny block is laced with winding lanes and alleys, whose names, such as **Salt Lane, Marsh Lane**, and **Creek Square**, echo an era when water still flowed here. The neighborhood's history dates to Colonial times; its architecture spans the 18th, 19th, and 20th centuries. People, chickens, geese, hogs, garbage, and carts laden with goods from nearby ships once commingled on the block's dirt streets. This area was on the narrow neck—frequently under water—that led from the **Shawmut Peninsula** to the **North End**. Meat

markets flourished here throughout the city's history, and still do along **Blackstone St**, named for Boston's first settler **William Blaxton** (his name was spelled both ways). **Benjamin Franklin** lived in this neighborhood as a boy, the youngest of the 10 children who survived out of 17, on the 2nd floor of his father **Joseph**'s chandlery and soap-boiling shop at the corner of **Union** and **Hanover** streets. Walking along diminutive **Marshall St**, look for the historic **Boston Stone** embedded in the base of an 1835 building's rear wall across from the **Ebenezer Hancock Building**. In 1701, a nearby merchant named **Thomas Child**, who specialized in painting shopsigns, used this stone to grind and mix pigment. Decades after Child's death, legend claims this fragment of the original stone was recovered from his backyard and inscribed with the date 1737. The stone was eventually set into this wall and long served as a marker for measuring distances from Boston.

16 The Haymarket On Friday and Saturday, a fleet of pushcart vendors selling fruits, vegetables, and fish sets up for open-air business along **Blackstone St**, in front of old establishments like the **Puritan Beef Co.** and **Pilgrim Market**, which purvey meats and cheeses supplementing Haymarket offerings. There's a great greasy stand-and-eat pizza place. The narrow sidewalk is clogged with veteran shoppers making their rounds, and bewildered novices trying to learn the ropes. Saturdays are busiest. Come for bargains, especially at the end of the day, but be forewarned that the vendors, many of them North Enders, will treat you brusquely if you pick over their merchandise selectively. *They* fill the bags; you just pay, European style. So what if a tomato or 2 is worse for wear; it's satisfying to have avoided the supermarkets' boring sterility. Boston's last great outdoor market has been squeezed by urban development. A *mysterious* fire destroyed the Blackstone St shops nearest the Bostonian hotel, leaving an ominous hole that really should be recycled for market uses. When the Haymarket finally winds down for the day, squashed produce and scattered cartons make passage here challenging, but the place is soon restored for the next day's deluge. This debris has been honored in **Mags Harries**' bronze reliefs of everyday garbage, embedded in asphalt at the intersection of Blackstone and Hanover streets, where a crossing leads to the passageway bringing visitors under the expressway to the North End. ♦ F-Sa dawn-dusk. Blackstone St (North-Hanover Sts)

17 Boston Garden Visit this hulking old barn while you still can, since it's due for demolition in the next few years to make way for a slick new garden. That's been the off-again, on-again plan for quite a while, but it looks like it will finally happen—sometime. Many will miss its funky Art Deco facade, interestingly juxtaposed with elevated rails that will also come down. Home of the **Celtics** basketball team and the **Bruins** ice hockey team, Boston's beloved sports arena also hosts family events and concerts year-round. Not to be confused with the

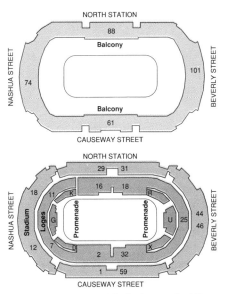

NORTH STATION

NASHUA STREET

BEVERLY STREET

88

Balcony

101

74

Balcony

61

CAUSEWAY STREET

NORTH STATION

29 31

16 18

18 11 K R

Stadium Loges G Promenade Promenade U 25

12 7 D X

2 32

1 59

CAUSEWAY STREET

verdant **Boston Public Garden** near Back Bay, this outdated dilapidated 1928 structure is much too old for its heavy workload, but still manages somehow. On game nights, the place pulses with energy, festooned with championship banners and retired numbers of star players. Notice the famous parquet floor, built during WWII when only short wood was available. If you attend a basketball game, stay past the final score: when the buzzer sounds, even before the last player has left the basketball court, garden staff whip in and start unscrewing the bolts holding down 264 five-foot-square panels, storing them within a mere 30 minutes and replacing them with a sea of hockey glass. Then head over to the **Scotch 'n Sirloin** warehouse restaurant at 77 North Washington, a popular after-game spot for steaks, seafood, and chicken, nice harbor views, and dancing Wednesday-Saturday; or the **Commonwealth Brewing Company** at 138 Portland St; or just follow diehard fans to nearby bars. ♦ 150 Causeway St. Recorded info 227.3200

Behind Boston Garden:

North Station Just like the comfortable current arrangement, the Garden of the Future will combine with North Station to make it easy for fans coming in by train from north of the city. Trains operating from here also transport daily flocks of commuters from the North Shore. In the summertime, the station rings with voices as cheerful crowds await the beach train—the route stopping at **Beverly, Manchester, Gloucester, Rockport**, and other towns up the line blessed (or cursed, their residents might say) with spacious public beaches. Located across the street from North Station's main entrance, the MBTA's Green Line carries riders in and out of central Boston.

No. 1 has never been worn by a **Boston Celtic** because it was retired in honor of **Walter Brown**, the team's founder.

Restaurants/Clubs: Red   **Hotels:** Blue
Shops/Parks: Green   **Sights/Culture:** Black

18 Hilton's Tent City The name is no empty boast. What began as a modest Army surplus store in 1947 has ballooned into the biggest and best source of tents, with 5 floors holding the largest set-up tent display in the country and complete accessories for family camping and backpacking. Hilton's also sells men's and women's clothing for all seasons, for skiing, mountaineering, and backpacking. They don't stock running shoes or sneakers, but carry hiking, work, and sporty boots and shoes. Remember the old hardware store in your hometown? This is that kind of funky dusty place packed with indispensable bargains. And Hilton's guarantees the lowest prices around on all its stock. When the mountains and hills of New England beckon, prepare for your adventure here. ♦ M-F 9AM-9PM; Sa 9AM-6PM; Su

Government Center/Faneuil Hall

noon-6PM. 272 Friend St (Causeway St) 227.9242 ♿

19 Commonwealth Brewing Company ★$$
Let no man thirst for the lack of real ale is the motto here. This working brewery and restaurant produces 10 or so kinds of English ale on the premises, including the acclaimed Boston's Best Burton Bitter, all dispensed on tap at the appropriate 52 degrees. For those who insist, 4 of the beers are served bottled and chilled. The cavernous main level glows with copper tables—polished nightly—fixtures, pipes, and huge tanks of beer. In the downstairs tap room, redolent with fermenting yeast, watch the brewing process through glass walls. Light meals and snacks available, but the main attraction is definitely the ale. A lot of people come here before and after **Boston Garden** games, and needless to say it gets pretty noisy. Live bands play Saturday night. Free brewery tours—but no samples—are offered Saturday and Sunday at 3:30PM (not handicapped-accessible). ♦ American ♦ M-Th 11:30AM-midnight; F-Sa 11:30AM-1AM; Su 11:30AM-11PM. 138 Portland St (Valenti Wy) 523.8383 ♿

20 Old West Church (1806, Asher Benjamin; National Historic Landmark) A 1737 wood-framed church stood on this site until the British razed it in 1775, suspicious that Revolutionary sympathizers were using the steeple to signal the Continental troops in Cambridge. The decorous red-brick Federal replacement is kin to **Charles Bulfinch's Massachusetts State House** and **St. Stephen's Church**, and Benjamin's **Charles Street Meeting House**—all flat-surfaced and delicately ornamented with Classical motifs. The church—formerly Unitarian and now Methodist—exerts quiet composure along Cambridge St's physical and architectural chaos. Inquire about concerts featuring the fine **Charles Fisk** pipe organ. ♦ 131 Cambridge St (Staniford St) 227.5088

In 1960, Congressman **John F. Kennedy** walked from his **Bowdoin St** apartment on **Beacon Hill** to vote at the **Old West Church** polling place during his presidential campaign.

20 Harrison Gray Otis House (First) (1796, **Charles Bulfinch**) This house was a trial run for Otis and his architect-of-choice, the first in a series of 3 increasingly lavish residences that Bulfinch designed for his friend, who had a taste for flamboyant living and fine architecture. Otis lived here for just 4 years before moving his family to grander quarters on Mount Vernon St, followed by another move to Beacon St. When he lived at House No. 1, Harry Otis was a prestigious lawyer and freshman member of Congress; he ultimately became Boston's third mayor and a major land speculator who transformed rustic Beacon Hill into a wealthy enclave, again with Bulfinch's help. Set in what was briefly fashionable Bowdoin Sq, this Federalist mansion is austerely handsome, much more opulent inside than out. By the end

Government Center/Faneuil Hall

of the 19th century, Bowdoin Sq's elegance had frayed away, and Otis' former home endured a spotty career as a women's Turkish bath, then a patent medicine shop, and finally a boarding house defaced with storefronts. In 1916, the **Society for the Preservation of New England Antiquities (SPNEA)** acquired the house—now one of 34 New England properties which they run—and meticulously restored its former splendor. SPNEA is headquartered here, including its fabulous architectural and photographic archives, and offers tours of the interior. The house's decor dates from 1790-1820 and includes some Otis family belongings. With its next-door neighbor, the **Old West Church**, the Otis house steps back into the early years of the Republic. The two lonely survivors refuse to be overwhelmed by their overdeveloped high-rise surroundings. ♦ Admission. Tu-F noon-5PM; Sa 10AM-5PM. Guided 40-min tours on the hr, last tour 4PM; groups limited to 15, by reservation only. 141 Cambridge St (Lynde St) 227.3956

21 Holiday Inn-Government Center $$$ Adjacent to **Massachusetts General Hospital**, this 15-story hotel has 300 rooms, with the nicest on the Executive level. There's a seasonal outdoor pool, rooftop lounge with DJ and dancing, rooftop dining room for breakfast and dinners only, and **Blossoms Food and Spirits** offering a light menu for lunch and dinner. Nonsmokers' and handicapped-equipped rooms available. You can easily walk from here to **Government Center** and **Faneuil Hall Marketplace**, or cross **Cambridge St** and meander over **Beacon Hill**. Discounted parking available. ♦ 5 Blossom St (Cambridge St) 742.7630, 800/465.4329 (request fax at this number also)

America's first medical instruction was a medical chemistry course offered at **Harvard Medical School** (then part of Massachusetts General Hospital) in 1871. The nation's first coeducational medical school was **Boston University School of Medicine**, organized in 1874.

Restaurants/Clubs: Red
Shops/Parks: Green
Hotels: Blue
Sights/Culture: Black

38

22 Bulfinch Pavilion and Ether Dome at Massachusetts General Hospital (MGH) (1816-1821, **Charles Bulfinch**; National Historic Landmark) Although a hospital is rarely a voluntary destination, make a trip to MGH to visit the remarkable seed from which sprouted this preeminent institution, consistently named as the nation's best general hospital. To locate the Bulfinch Pavilion in the MGH maze, enter from **North Grove St** off **Cambridge St**, or ask directions at the **George R. White Memorial Building** on **Fruit St**, the main hospital building. (Built in 1939 by **Coolidge, Shepley, Bulfinch**, and **Abbott**, this late Art Deco city landmark is also worth a look.)

In 1817, Boston's trailblazing architect Charles Bulfinch won the commission to create this edifice of Chelmsford granite, quarried by inmates of the Charlestown state prison. Questions persist about Bulfinch's actual role in the pavilion commission, since it was his last project before he was called to Washington by the president to design the **United States Capitol** rotunda. His assistant **Alexander Parris**—who later gained fame in his own right, particularly for designing **Quincy Market**—prepared the working drawings and supervised construction, probably influencing the pavilion's final form much more than its name suggests. Delayed by the War of 1812, the cornerstone was laid in 1818 and the first patient was admitted in 1821. Today the building is still used for patient care, offices, and research.

Progressive for its day and gracefully proportioned, the Greek Revival building is special in itself. But its enduring fame derives from the historic medical achievements that took place in the amphitheater beneath the skylit dome. It was in this theater, MGH's operating room from 1821-1867, now called the Ether Dome, that the first public demonstration of the use of ether in a surgical procedure took place. On 16 October 1846, **Dr. John C. Warren**, cofounder of MGH and its first surgeon, operated on a patient suffering from a tumor in his jaw. A dentist named **Thomas Green Morton** administered the ether with his own apparatus, after supposedly almost missing the operation because he stayed up late the night before perfecting the inhaler device. When the procedure was finished, the patient awoke and said he felt no pain. Dr. Warren announced to his colleagues, *Gentlemen, this is no humbug.* Within a year, ether was in use worldwide to prevent surgical pain. In 1869, another medical milestone: **Dr. Joseph Lister** of Scotland introduced antiseptic surgery in the amphitheater. And in 1886, **Dr. Reginald Fitz** of MGH identified appendicitis; subsequently, MGH surgical staff performed the first appendectomies, the first procedures to entail opening the abdominal cavity.

Not only does the amphitheater house memories of medical successes, it's home to **Padihershef**, a mummy from Thebes, Egypt, who was brought here in 1823. The hospital's largest fund-raiser, Padihershef is also the only remaining witness to the Ether Dome's finest moments. To visit the Ether Dome, call ahead to be sure it's not in use. There's no charge. ♦ 55 Fruit St. 726.2000

Michael and Susan Southworth

Urban Designers, Planners, and Authors of *A.I.A. Guide to Boston*.

Going for long walks through the streets, boulevards, lanes, and alleys almost anywhere in the city—Boston is the most walkable and explorable city in the country!

Italian gelati and cappuccino at a North End *caffé*.

Friday afternoon at the Symphony—**Symphony Hall** is the Stradavarius of concert halls and on Friday afternoon you can observe Boston Yankees in droves.

Exploring the **Underground Railroad** and the many other significant black history sites in Boston.

Candlelight concerts by talented young musicians at Mrs. Jack Gardner's Venetian Palace, now the **Gardner Museum**.

German sausage, sauerkraut, and beer at **Jake Wirth's**, a restaurant that is almost unchanged since it was founded in 1868.

The luscious *tarte tatin* at **Maison Robert**.

Chile *relleños* at **Casa Romero**, an intimate Mexican restaurant that transcends tacos and smashed beans.

The **Ritz-Carlton** dining room, the essence of Brahmin elegance.

The first day the Swan Boats paddle the pond in the **Public Garden** each spring—winter cannot return!

The *Shaw Memorial*, by Augustus Saint-Gaudens, honoring the first regiment of freed blacks to serve in the Civil War.

The Boston **Early Music Festival** and its cacophony of virginals, clavichords, and sackbuts—often imitated but never equaled.

The Italian Renaissance Revival interiors of McKim, Mead & White's **Boston Public Library**.

The **Nichols House** (Beacon Hill) and **Gibson House** (Back Bay) museums that transport us to domestic life in 19th-century Boston.

The **Essex Institute** in Salem, with its collection of important museum houses, furniture, and artifacts of the China Trade.

Saturday morning shopping at the Italian street markets in the **North End**.

A Sunday afternoon walk through the **Back Bay Fens** with its tall rushes, winding waterway, and stone bridge (by H.H. Richardson), followed by visits to the **Museum of Fine Arts** and the **Gardner Museum**.

Celebrating St. Patrick's Day in any South Boston tavern.

Evacuation Day, because it's the holiday no other city celebrates.

Robert Campbell

Architect and Architecture Critic

Lots of cities surpass Boston's food or its architecture or its shopping. But none can top its streets and neighborhoods. The characteristic joy in Boston is a walk down **Beacon Hill**, along **Mount Vernon Street** to **Louisburg Square**, perhaps on Christmas Eve when the candles are in the windows and the carolers move from house to house. Or through the **Public Garden** or out **Commonwealth Avenue** or along the **Charles River Esplanade** or past the little shops of **Charles Street**.

Other streets where the city's karma seems to collect: **Union Park Square** in the South End, with sunlight falling through the trees on the bowfronts. **Marlborough Street**, the best proportioned and preserved of the streets of the Back Bay—easily the most successful *planned* residential neighborhood in American history. **Paul Revere Mall** behind Old North Church in the North End, Boston's only European-style *outdoor room*. **Harvard Yard** in November, the essence of austere, Puritan New England—so poignantly contrasted with Harvard Square next door, an explosion of punks and consumers. **Newbury Street** in the Back Bay, a humanly scaled shopping street, its stores tucked into 3 levels of what once were houses.

Two classic examples of an especially American kind of streetscape, shaped by a canopy of trees and a row of congenial mansions: **Brattle Street** in Cambridge and **Chestnut Street** in Salem.

Art:

The Fitzhugh Lane seascapes at the **Cape Ann Historical Society** in Gloucester—America's greatest painter?—and his *View of Penobscot Bay* in the **Museum of Fine Arts**; the **Robert Gould Shaw Memorial** by Saint-Gaudens in Boston Common; the **Richard Haas mural** on the Boston Architectural Center; **Mount Auburn Cemetery** in Watertown, in May, when the landscape is in bloom.

Food:

The special pizza at **Bertucci's**; the brownies at **Rosie's** in Inman Square; **Locke-Ober**, an Edwardian survival; the tables outdoors at the **Harvest** in Harvard Square. And a frank on a summer evening at **Fenway Park**, one of the last of the intimate ballparks that isn't an impersonal stadium, the home of a team that we know in our Puritan hearts will never win a world championship because of our guilt.

Buildings:

McKim's **Boston Public Library**, especially the old grand stair; the **Isabella Stewart Gardner Museum** (maybe at Sunday concert time); the **Peabody Museum** in Salem, especially the **South Seas** and **China Trade exhibitions**; the **Harvard Lampoon** on Mount Auburn Street, a rare example of a funny building; **Rowes Wharf**, approached from across the harbor on the airport shuttle.

The lovely New England villages:

Stockbridge and **Edgartown** and **Nantucket** and so many more; or the exquisite mill village of **Harrisville** up in New Hampshire; or the colony of miniature, brightly painted cottages—originally a religious encampment—at **Oak Bluffs** on **Martha's Vineyard**. Or a tour of the mills of **Lowell**.

And lastly, of course, the annual influx of college students, tens upon tens of thousands of them, as central to a Boston autumn as new grass is to spring, keeping an old city fue!ed up and alive.

North End

Old men convene on corners and lounge in door ways, gossiping, while women hurry past on their way to noisy markets. Children switch between English and Italian with ease, depending on their company: school friends or family. Tangled streets squeeze between rows of red-brick facades, monotonous except at street level, where gala window displays tempt and entertain. Alluring aromas escape from *pasticcerie*, *trattorie*, *ristoranti*, *mercati*, and *caffè* and wind around each other. And through this insular, fiercely proud Italian enclave winds the red ribbon of the **Freedom Trail**, directing tourists to **Paul Revere's house**, the **Old North Church, Copp's Hill Burying Ground**, and other vestiges of Colonial Boston.

This is the spirited, colorful, bursting-at-the-seams North End. Don't come here by car; it's best reached on foot by an ignominious route: from the **Government Center T stop**, head behind **City Hall**, then cross **Blackstone St** at the **Haymarket**, with its pushcart vendors, to a short pedestrian tunnel that sneaks under the elevated **Fitzgerald Expressway**, commonly called the **Central Artery**. Your path is messy and smelly, but cheered with outdoor artist **Mags Harries'** bronze reliefs of everyday garbage embedded in the pavement below, North End children's mosaics in the tunnel walls, and local artists' outdoor murals that greet you at **Cross Street**, once you've reached the North End side of the expressway.

The North End is exceedingly *Old World*, and one of the oldest parts of the *New World*. The heart of this vivacious, voluble district is Mediterranean today, but Italians have held sway only since 1920 or so. This is Boston's original neighborhood, where the city's early Puritan residents settled during the 17th century, their eyes on the sea. As piers, wharves, and markets

Boston's subway service doesn't bring you into the North End, but rather deposits you near its edge. Although making your way into this out-of-the-way neighborhood can be confusing, there are always crowds of tourists heading in that direction. In addition to the **Government Center** T stop (**Green** and **Blue Lines**), the **Haymarket** (**Green** and **Orange Lines**) and **Aquarium** (**Blue Line**) stops are the most convenient to the North End.

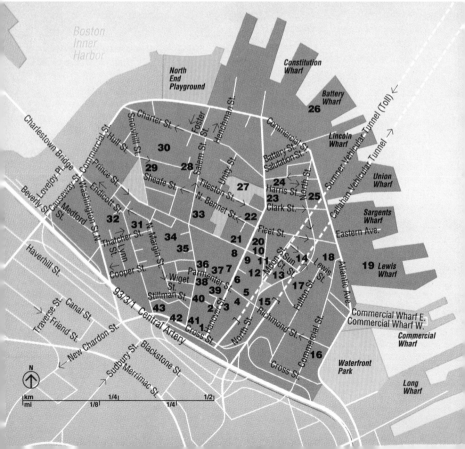

sprang up along the waterfront, the North End was known as *the wealthiest, most populous, and in every way the most important part of town*. It has undergone many a sea-change since then. Those glory days ended following the Revolution, when the North End's aristocratic Tory population fled to England and elite Bostonians moved elsewhere in the city, to **Beacon Hill** and **Bay Village**. The black community gradually migrated to the Hill also. In the 19th century, waves of immigrants—first Irish, then eastern European Jews, then Portuguese, then Italians—poured into the North End, which had deteriorated into a slum. Over some 60 years, Italian-Americans have industriously restored the neighborhood. Their traditions have become the North End's bulwark, with social life focusing on the family, the church, social clubs, caffès, rituals, and festivals.

North End Beach and bridge to Copp's Hill Terraces

North End

Buildings date from the late 19th and 20th centuries, with a few venerable ones tucked in. Most streets follow their jumbled 17th-century pattern, giving you the flavor of Colonial history seasoned with Italian culture. When infant Boston still fit onto the **Shawmut Peninsula**, the North End was a second peninsula—almost an island—divided from the first by **Mill Creek**. Today, following the old creek's track, the Central Artery's green mass cleaves the North End from downtown. The current plan is to dismantle and depress the elevated highway. Hated at first, the highway has proven to be a blessing in disguise by protecting the North End from gentrification's full force. Without this barrier, North Enders fear for their neighborhood's future; a new boundary will be exposed to assault.

Perhaps North Enders' fears won't be realized. But irreversible change is afoot, so spend time here while the fascinating layers remain in place. The people you pass on the streets are still the children and grandchildren of *paesani* from villages in **Sicily**, **Abruzzi**, **Calabria**. On **Hanover Street**, the North End's main commercial street, the caffè jukeboxes play Italian pop music. Parallel and to the left is **Salem Street**, where meat and provisions shops do brisk business; a block to the right brings you to quaint **North Square** and **North Street**, the district's third major thoroughfare that originally followed the shoreline until landfill pushed it blocks away. As you walk, notice the loaded laundry lines—you won't see *those* on Beacon Hill—little building ornament except a bit of wrought iron here and there, and aside from some well-used parks and rooftop gardens, no room for greenery. Glance up; more than one elderly North Ender is leaning out, checking on who's coming, who's going, who's doing what they shouldn't be doing. This is a close-knit place, after all, where people watch out for each other and strangers get the onceover more than once. Return before noon on a Sunday, when only the restaurants and caffès are open, filled with families in their Sunday best. In the summertime, join the throngs for one of the weekend *feste* in July and August, when North Enders commandeer the streets for morning-till-night processions, dancing, eating, praying—each weekend dedicated to a different patron saint.

1 Hanover Street The labyrinthine North End's straightest, widest route—which isn't saying much—Hanover St runs through the heart of the district and boasts the greatest concentration of restaurants, bakeries, caffès, banks, services, and shops selling everything from saints' figures to Italian leathergoods. Two famous department stores began here: At **No. 168 Eben Jordan** started a drygoods store that eventually became the **Jordan Marsh Company**; and **Rowland H. Macy** opened a similar operation nearby that grew into the **R.H. Macy Company** of New York City. Block after block, 4- and 5-story buildings crowd in so closely that the waterfront's nearness stays a secret until you reach the bend by **Charles Bulfinch's St. Stephen's Church**. Tourists stream along the narrow sidewalks as they follow the **Freedom Trail** to the **Old North Church**, or seek out popular dining spots such as **The European** or **The Daily Catch**. But most of the street scene belongs to the people who live here. Even on a sleepy Sunday afternoon, Hanover St pulses with the vigor of Italian-American culture.

1 Theatre Lobby and Natalie's Restaurant
A newcomer to Hanover St, this terrific little combination theater/cabaret/restaurant fills a giant gap in Boston's nightlife with aplomb. Nowhere else in the city can one enjoy an evening of entertainment with such leisurely European style. Owners **Anthony** and **Sally Capodilupo** have created a graceful, satisfying setting for performers and audiences. Natalie's offers new Italian fare. The wraparound square theater and the mauve-and-cream cabaret/caffè, which also

serves as the theater's lobby, are intimate and comfortable; sound and lighting are superb; the cabaret's handsome antique Steinway is beautifully reconditioned. Because the theater is young, the program and showtimes tend to change. Call for showtimes, and information. Discounts are usually available on combination tickets. ◆ Italian ◆ Seats 175 (theater). Admission. Restaurant, daily 5-10PM. 216 Hanover St. 227.9872

1 The European ★$ The North End's *old reliable* since 1917, The European isn't much to look at inside, but its famous clock and neon sign outside are familiar features in a landscape threatened with change. Your finickiest friend will be satisfied with the mammoth menu, and service is usually brisk and friendly. Huge, gloppy portions of Italo-American fare are reasonably priced—no exciting finds, but the extra-large pizza is surely Boston's biggest. Although lines are long, the elephantine dining rooms mean the wait is generally endurable. The mood here is often boisterous; practically every visit some table of 20 bursts into *Happy Birthday*. Still, once in a while this just seems like the right place to be. A good place to bring kids—they can bounce off the walls and no one will notice. After your meal, cross over Hanover St to **Mechanic St**, which ends in a funky cul de sac. Through the wire fence is a great view of the stalwart **Customs Tower** downtown and its beautiful clock. To the left is the **Sumner Tunnel** (1934) entranceway, with its wonderful pair of Art Deco reliefs: one angel in flight escorts a vintage truck, the other a car. ◆ Italian ◆ M-Th, Su 11AM-12:30AM; F-Sa 11AM-12:45AM. 218 Hanover St (Cross-Parmenter Sts) Reservations recommended for large parties, M-F only. 523.5694 ♿

Earlier in this century, a popular schoolchildren's song went:

> *My name is Solomon Levi*
> *At my store on Salem Street*
> *That's where you'll find your coats and hats*
> *And everything that's neat.*

1 Trio's Using recipes from Abruzzi and Sicily, some of which go back 300 years, the Trio family—**Tony, Genevieve**, their son **Louis**—whips up an awesome array of handmade pastas and companion sauces. To name just a few, you can take home gnocchi, tortellini, tortelloni, agnolotti, cavatelli, ravioli, red-pepper linguine, lemon fettuccini—and top them off any which way with ginger-vermouth, gorgonzola, anchovy-nut, white-clam, piquant marinara, or pesto sauces. Everything's made fresh on site; look into the kitchen where the pasta machines are churning out that day's supply. The Trios prepare lasagnas and other entrees for takeout; there are a handful of tables if you can't wait to dig in. ◆ Takeout ◆ M-Sa 9AM-6PM; Su 9AM-1PM. 222 Hanover St. No credit cards. 523.9636

2 A&J Distributors Here's where budding vintners or brewers come for supplies. A&J's also stocks Italian kitchenware from the practical (6 kinds of meat grinders) to the frivolous (the gleaming row of Italian cookie presses). There are plenty of heavy-duty pasta and espresso machines to choose from, plus all those little gismos for specialized tasks that become so mysteriously indispensible. ◆ M, W 9:30AM-5:30PM; Tu, Th-F 9:30AM-7PM; Sa 9:30AM-8PM; Su by chance. 236 Hanover St. 523.8490

3 Caffè Paradiso Espresso Bar ★$ Stop by on the night of a *festa* or other celebration when the whole neighborhood seems to be here having a great time. The mainstay of Paradiso's decor is mirrors—they're everywhere, magnifying the caffè's hectic atmosphere. A sunnier setting is much nicer during the day, but this place is—for Boston—a night-owl spot, with the only 2AM liquor license on the street. The lively crowd keeps the jukebox cranking. The *gelati*, *sorbetti*, and spumoni are homemade. There's a full line of Italian bitter aperitifs, plus an enormous array of designer desserts you won't see in the local bakeries. ◆ Caffè ◆ Daily 7AM-2AM. 255 Hanover St. 742.1768. Also at: One Eliot Pl, Harvard Sq, Cambridge. 868.3240; 3 Water St. 742.8689

Upstairs at the Caffè Paradiso:

Il Sole $$ Run by Paradiso's owners. A lot of younger locals name this as one of their North End favorites. There are interesting offerings, such as a spicy seafood stew, as well as the usual fish, veal, chicken, and pasta selections. ◆ Italian ◆ M-Sa 11:30AM-11:30PM. 255 Hanover St. Reservations recommended. 742.1768

18 January 1950, **Tony Pino** and 10 partners in crime pulled off their famous heist of more than $1.75 million in cash from the **Brinks Garage**, located at the intersection of Prince and Commercial streets.

3 Modern Pastry Giovanni Picariellos junior and senior are renowned for their diabolically delicious homemade *torrone*, a nougat-and-almond confection drenched in chocolate. This ever-popular 60-year-old *pasticceria* offers great *sfogliatelli*, *pizzelles*, and cannoli too. ♦ Bakery ♦ Daily 7AM-9PM. 257 Hanover St. No credit cards. 523.3783

4 Villa Francesca $$ Not to be outdone by their high-profile neighbor (Felicia's) across the way, this restaurant's owners claim their share of star diners too, including a slew of **Red Sox** baseball players. The food is nothing special—big portions spruced up with lots of lemon and white wine—but there's an Italian singer Monday-Friday who draws a big following and provides the finishing touch to Francesca's overblown, old-world ambiance. When you want a little schmaltz with your romance, try this place. Bring a date who has a sense of humor. ♦ Italian ♦ M-Th 5-10:30PM; F-Sa 5-11PM; Su 4-10PM. 150 Richmond St. 367.2948

5 Salumeria Italiana This grocery store's name means *Italian market*, which tells you that you won't be rubbing elbows with many North Enders here. But most of the neighborhood stores rely heavily on the tourist trade, as proprietor **Erminio Martignetti** will candidly confirm. It's definitely worth a stop to pick up some *prosciutto di Parma*, an import that wasn't available for years. The store also sells a good variety of cheeses, breads, salamis, olive oils, and espresso coffees. Come at lunchtime and Martignetti will make you what chef **Jasper White** calls *probably the greatest cold-cut sandwich in the world*. ♦ M-Th, Sa 8AM-6PM; F 8AM-7PM. 151 Richmond St. 523.8743

5 Felicia's ★$$ Owner and chef **Felicia Solimine**'s place banks on past prestige; it's undeniably a North End institution. For proof, look at the de rigueur gallery of celebrities' photos on your way upstairs to the dining room. See **Bob**

Hope? See **Tom Selleck**? This is an overpriced classic red-sauce-and-chianti-bottle-lamp kind of spot; still, most North End *ristoranti* overcharge for spiffed-up spaghetti, and Felicia's can be campy and fun if you come with a large group. The chicken *verdiccio* (made with mushrooms, artichokes, acidic white wine) is worth a try. ♦ Italian ♦ M-Sa 4-10PM; Su 2-9PM. 145A Richmond St. 523.9885 ♿

Touring **Beacon Hill** by car is a bad idea; attempting the same in the still-more-crowded **North End** is lunatic. First of all, there's practically no place to leave the car. Second, there are out-of-the-way streets and sights you'd never come upon in a car. And since local residents are made truly miserable by the noisy, slow-moving strings of vehicles that practically park on their doorsteps, why not be kind to them: take public transportation and then walk.

6 Galleria Umberto ★★$ Come from the far reaches if necessary; don't miss out on the best pizza and calzones the North End has to offer, not to mention Italian finger foods like *panzarotti* (Italian dumplings) and *arrincini* (deep-fried balls of meat filled with rice). They serve only lunch, there's no table service, lines are long, and when the food's gone it's gone. When a new pan of pizza is delivered from the oven, watch the server attack it with his pizza wheel, ferociously *wap-wapping* it into steaming squares overflowing with fragrant cheese and oil. Join the steady stream of North Enders, including gaggles of school kids in uniform, and rejoice at how inexpensive absolute gluttony can be. ♦ Pizza/takeout ♦ M-Sa 11AM-2 or 3PM. 289 Hanover St. No credit cards. 227.5709 ♿

6 Caffè dello Sport ★$ The sunniest caffè on the street. No question about which sport its name refers to: fluttering everywhere are pennants for Italian soccer teams. Take a window-

side seat and sip one of the excellent frothy espressos while you join in the North End's favorite pastime: people-watching. It gets ever more lively as the day progresses. ♦ Caffè ♦ Daily 6AM-midnight. 307 Hanover St. 523.5063

7 Ristorante Saraceno ★$$ Another family-owned and operated restaurant, this one concentrating on Neopolitan recipes. In addition to the usual antipasti and entree lineup, Saraceno's features good veal saltimbocca, shrimp and lobster *fra diavolo*, linguine with seafood. The scrolled menus add a note of pretension to an otherwise straightforward, pleasant place recommended by many North Enders. Dine in the small upstairs room; downstairs is rather confining with gaudy murals of Capri, the Bay of Naples, Amalfi. ♦ Italian ♦ M-Sa noon-10:30PM; Su noon-9:30PM. 286 Hanover St. Reservations recommended. 227.5888 ♿

8 Caffè Vittoria ★$ This place is almost too much, with its *faux* marble tables and ornament, *il cortile* that isn't *really* a courtyard, *il grotto* that isn't *really* a grotto, and more-lurid-than-life murals of Venice and the Bay of Sorrento at the back. But a little *braggadocio* isn't all bad, and this 60-year-old caffè—Boston's first—exerts a full-bodied charm all its own. The antique coffee grinders are absolutely real, so are the black-and-white photos of North Enders on the walls and the operatic espresso makers by the windows. Venture beyond cappuccino; try an *anisetta*, *grappa*, or Italian soda, maybe a gelato, too. Come during the day when your caffè companions are older men lingering over newpapers, chatting in Italian, and you'll get a sense of how deeply rooted Italian culture is in this neighborhood. At night it's a totally different place—festive and boisterous. ♦ Caffè ♦ Daily 8AM-midnight. 296 Hanover St. No credit cards. 227.7606

Restaurants/Clubs: Red   Hotels: Blue
Shops/Parks: Green   **Sights/Culture: Black**

43

MIKE'S PASTRY

8 Mike's Pastry Mike's is always hopping because it sells every type of caloric Italian treat one could possibly crave—cream cakes, candy, cookies, breads, cannoli, even that most un-Italian of baked goods, the oat-bran muffin. Since Mike's tries to cover all the bases, quality varies and you should scout out the smaller *pasticcerias* for your favorite sweets. But the *biscotti di Prato* are very good and cinnamony here, or go whole hog and try a *lobster tail*, a particularly diet-devastating concoction of pastry with cheese, custard, *and* whipped cream. There are some tables and you can get coffee here. A popular stopover for Freedom Trail pilgrims. ♦ Bakery ♦ M-Th, Su 8AM-9PM; F-Sa 8AM-10PM. 300 Hanover St. 742.3050

North End

9 Daily Catch ★★$$ That's the tiny restaurant's official moniker, but the name *Calamari Cafe* and portrait of a squid lovingly handpainted on the front window tell the real story. Owners **Paul** and **Maria Freddura** have dedicated their culinary careers to promoting this cephalopod, even mounting a traveling squid-tasting show in the '70s when their favorite's popularity sunk to its lowest. A happy ending—calamari has become a big star and can be devoured here in many delicious ways. Since the Fredduras understand that squid is not for everyone, the menu's supporting cast includes Sicilian-style seafood options. Linguine with white- or red-clam sauce is another hit. The half-dozen-or-so tables flank the open kitchen, so enjoy the show as the young chefs deftly, flamboyantly toss your meal together. Then be prepared, because once the sizzling skillets are casually plunked down before you, you'll nearly reel from the intense garlic that sneaks into practically every dish. As long as you stay among good friends all evening, it's worth it. The drawbacks: there's no bathroom, but it doesn't take much resourcefulness to find neighboring facilities. And there's always a line, so come in good weather when you feel gregarious, or eat early. This original Daily Catch has spawned offspring, including 261 Northern Avenue, Waterfront. 338.3093. ♦ Italian ♦ Daily 11AM-10:30PM. 323 Hanover St. No credit cards. 523.8567

The **Prince Spaghetti Company** used to be located at 45-69 Atlantic Avenue. For years, it ran a television ad campaign with the famous line: *In the Italian North End of Boston, Wednesday is Prince Spaghetti Day.* Many Americans can still picture the commercial's star, a boy named Anthony, rushing home through the streets of the North End as his mother calls him to a steaming plate of spaghetti at the crowded family table.

As you walk along, notice the pillows (often custom-made) resting on apartment windowsills; they're there to make people-watching a more comfortable pastime.

10 Ristorante Carlo Marino ★★$$ The gay green awning announces **Anna Marino**'s place, named for her late father. When you've had your fill of silk flowers, travel posters of *Italia*, and the reds and golds splashed about too many North End dining rooms, Anna's crisp forest-green-and-white-enamel decor is downright refreshing. And her flowers are real. Seating's snug but doesn't detract from the pleasant spirit. The affable owner is committed to tasty classical renditions of enduring Northern Italian peasant dishes, such as *fritto di ricotta, minestra di spinachi, penne all'Amatriciana.* ♦ Italian ♦ Tu-Sa 5-10:30PM; Su 4-9PM. 8 Prince St (Hanover St-North Sq) 523.9109

11 North Square Idiosyncratic interpretations of the civic *square* abound in Boston; this one is, in fact, a cobbled triangle. Nearly overwhelmed by the massive chain along its perimeter—a heavyhanded, almost ludicrous nod to a nautical past—the square is still winsome, made more so by its circular garden. The first part of the North End to be settled, a stone's throw from the waterfront, the square soon boasted a diverse community of artisans, merchants, seafarers, and tradesmen. The **Second Church of Boston**, nicknamed *Old North*, the seat of the powerful preaching **Mathers**, was located where **Moon Street** enters the square until torn down by the British in 1776. By late Colonial times this had become a prestigious neighborhood. Boston's 2 most lavish mansions overlooked the square, called **Clark Square** then. Today, 17th-, 18th-, 19th-, and 20th-century structures commune here. Just off the square is Boston's most charmingly named intersection: the celestial meeting of Sun Court and Moon streets. Just around the corner is **4 Garden Court Street**, home for 8 years to **John F. *Honey Fitz* Fitzgerald**, ward boss, congressman, Boston mayor, and one of the city's most famous citizens. His daughter **Rose, President John F. Kennedy**'s mother, was born here in 1890, in what she described as *a modest flat in an 8-family dwelling.* While in residence at No. 4, Honey Fitz began his political ascent with his election to Congress in 1894, soon acquiring the nickname the *Napoleon of the North End.* After leaving Garden Court, Honey Fitz took his family elsewhere in the North End to No. 8 Unity St. Throughout his career, Honey Fitz spoke so often of the *dear old North End* that North Enders were dubbed the *Dearos*, a name that was adopted by the Irish political and social organization he led.

Honey Fitz was born nearby on Ferry St in 1863. (Both the Fitzgeralds and the Kennedys emigrated to Boston in the mid 1800s to escape the Irish potato famine. Honey Fitz's father became a grocer on North St and on Hanover St. The North End was always beloved by both families.) US **Senator Ted Kennedy** has reminisced about how he and brothers **John** and **Robert** used to play a game to see who could cross **Hanover St** first *in a hop, a skip, and a jump.*

At 409 Commercial St, the U.S.S. *Constitution* was built at **Constitution Wharf**. The ship's keel was laid in 1794 and it was launched in 1797.

12 Moses Pierce-Hichborn House (1710; restored 1950) This stalwart structure to the left of **Paul Revere**'s house was home to Paul's cousin **Nathaniel Hichborn**, a boatbuilder. Another prized Colonial urban relic, it was built by a glazier named Moses Pierce. Overstimulated modern eyes might not notice the fact, but this English Renaissance brick structure stylistically leaps far ahead of the Revere's Tudor in a very brief timespan. Even the central stair is innovative—simple and straight instead of windy and cramped like that of the Revere house. The pleasing 3-story residence reflects a pioneering effort to apply formal English architectural principles to early Boston's unruly family. When the house left Hichborn's family in 1864, it, too, fell on hard times, becoming a tenement until restored in 1950. It is now undergoing further refurbishing as a museum-in-progress. Four rooms are open to the public for guided tours given twice daily, the only times to see the interior. Enter at the Revere house gate. ♦ Admission. Daily 9:30AM-5:15PM, 15 Apr-Oct; daily 9:30AM-4:15PM, Nov-14 Apr. Tours 12:30, 2:30PM. Closed Monday in Jan-Mar; major holidays. 19 North Sq. 523.1676

Around the corner:

Bakers Alley Ends in a pretty residential piazza ingeniously tucked in among the backsides of apartment buildings. Lucky residents—they have a number of handsome specimens of that scarce North End commodity: trees.

12 Mariner's House (1838) Dedicated to the service of seamen, this very respectable Federalist edifice is a remnant of Boston's great seafaring days, now long gone, which fueled the city's rapid growth and residents' fabulous fortunes. From the cupola atop its roof, mariner residents reputedly kept watch on the sea, much nearer then than today. Peer in the windows at the exceedingly nautical decor. Bonafide seamen still board here. ♦ 11 North Sq

12 The Paul Revere House (c. 1677; rebuilt mid-18th century; restored 1908, **Joseph Chandler**; National Historic Landmark) Here is where America's most famous messenger hung his hat. A descendant of Huguenots named Revoire, **Paul Revere** was an exceptionally versatile gold- and silversmith as well as copper engraver and a maker of cannons, church bells, and false teeth—reputedly including a pair for **George Washington**.

Busloads upon busloads of tourists stream in nonstop, but it doesn't take long to see the humble rooms open to the public in Revere's tiny, 2-story wooden clapboard abode. It's worth inching along because this house and the **Moses Pierce-Hichborn** residence next door are remarkable, rare survivors of Colonial Boston. Built nearly 100 years before the *Son of Liberty*'s midnight ride, the house has been restored—over-restored, really—to what it looked like originally, before Paul added an extra story to accommodate his big family. Revere and his second wife, **Rachel** (who gave birth to 8 of his 16 children), owned the house from 1770–1800 and lived here for a decade until the war-ruined economy forced them to move in

with relatives. From here Revere hurried off to his patriotic exploits, including participating in the **Boston Tea Party**. By the mid-19th century, the North End was an impoverished, blighted neighborhood, abandoned to poor immigrants by middle-class and wealthy Bostonians. The Revere house slipped into decrepitude and became a sordid tenement with shabby storefronts. The wrecking ball loomed at the start of this century, but a great-grandson of Revere's formed a preservation group that rescued the house.

From across **North Sq**, look toward the medieval overhanging upper floor and leaded casements. These throwbacks to late 16th-century Elizabethan urban architecture are reminders that architectural styles were exported to the Colonies from England and adapted with Yankee ingenuity long after they were out of fashion in Europe. Built after the devastating Boston fire of 1676, the fashionable townhouse violated the building

code because it was made of wood, not brick. Today, 90 percent of its frame and one door are genuine, its skin and insides reproductions. See how artfully the house tucks into its tiny site—every inch of space was built in the Colonial North End, with rabbitwarren clusters of small houses linked by a maze of alleyways. The low-ceilinged, heavy-beamed dark rooms with their oversize fireplaces bear few traces of the Revere family, but recall Colonial domestic arrangements. The pretty period gardens in back are equally interesting when you study them with the help of the posted illustrated key and an informative pamphlet sold at the ticket kiosk. The multipurpose plantings—with old-time names like Johnny jump-up, Bee balm, Dutchman's pipe, Lady's mantle—remind visitors that gardens were once commonplace sources in city life for ornament, pharmaceuticals, food, and domestic aids. ♦ Admission. Daily 9:30AM-5:15PM, 15 Apr-Oct; daily 9:30AM-4:15PM, Nov-14 Apr. Closed Monday in Jan-Mar, major holidays. 19 North Sq. 523.1676

Across the street:

Rachel Revere Park Named for Paul's wife and dedicated by the **Massachusetts Charitable Mechanics Association**, a philanthropic group that was founded in 1795 with Revere as its first president.

13 Sacred Heart Church (1833) **Walt Whitman** described this former bethel (a place of worship for seamen) as *a quaint ship-cabin-looking church*. The church opened in 1833, and for 38 years seamen flocked to hear the legendary Methodist preacher **Father Edward Taylor**, once a sailor himself. *I set my bethel in North Square*, said Taylor, *because I learned to set my net where the fish ran*. Whitman came to services, calling Father Taylor the only *essentially perfect orator*. **Ralph Waldo Emerson** anointed Taylor *the Shakespeare of the sailor and the poor* and often spoke from his close friend's pulpit. On one of his Boston visits, **Charles Dickens** made a special trip to hear the preacher, accompanied by **Longfellow** and **Charles Sumner**, abolitionist and US senator. In 1871, the bethel was sold and enlarged as a Catholic church. ♦ Daily 7AM-7PM, 1st 2 levels only. Upper level open only on Su and special occasions. 12 North Sq. 523.1225/5638

Ottavio's

14 Ottavio's ★★$$$ Owner and chef **Sammy DiPasquale** freely acknowledges that his clientele doesn't include a lot of North Enders because *who cooks better than their own mother —and my mother cooks here.* His mamma's specials include soups, the usual array of pasta dishes, rich ricotta pies. He also serves rabbit and baby lamb dishes, authentic North End fare you can't get in *ristoranti* catering to tourists' notions of Italian cuisine. A number of dishes are prepared tableside. It's no accident that the

North End

plates and glasses are 8-sided; Ottavio's is named for Sammy's grandfather, who was the eighth child in his family. This is not a hustle-and-bustle place, so relax and linger over your cappuccino and homemade cannoli. ♦ Italian ♦ M-W, Su 4-10PM; Th-Sa 4-11PM. 257 North St. Reservations required F-Su. 723.6060 &

From early June until the end of August, a different *festa* takes over the North End's streets every weekend. Each celebration is organized by one of the neighborhood's religious societies, most of which honor the patron saint of a village in Italy or Sicily whence their original members came. Most start off with a parade on Friday, when the saint's statue is transported to a temporary chapel along a traditional route winding through the North End. All weekend long there's music, dancing, and lots of eating—with vendors selling *quahogs*, calzones, sausage, pizza, fried dough, fried calamari, *zeppoli*, and every other wonderful greasy food you can think of. The weekend's finale is the extravagant procession on Sunday, which brings the saint home to the meeting place of the host society. Shouldered by men who may plod along under its weight for 8 hours or so, the saint is paraded in a cloud of confetti throughout the gaily decorated neighborhood. Elderly women clutch rosaries, their eyes on the passing saint. Religious offerings are made by pinning money to long ribbons fastened to the figure; the men will raise the statue so that people reaching from apartment windows can pin on their bills. The most popular festas are the largest, nicknamed the *Big St. Anthony,* and the most colorful, the **Feast of the Madonna del Soccorso,** nicknamed the *Fisherman's Feast.* This feast's most famous feature is the *flight of the angel,* in which a young girl *flies* from a window over North St down to the Madonna to offer a bouquet. The festas have become commercial over time, and many North Enders avoid them now because they draw hordes of outsiders and turn their neighborhood into a circus. Still, these exuberant celebrations are the fullest expression of North End culture you'll encounter.

Restaurants/Clubs: Red	Hotels: Blue
Shops/Parks: Green	Sights/Culture: Black

46

15 V. Cirace & Sons Jeff and Lisa Cirace are the third generation and the second *brother-sister act* to run this 83-year-old Italian wine establishment. Cirace's was recently voted the best shop of its kind in the US by Italy's Wine and Food Institute. About half of the store's 1500+ wines are Italian, and there's an extensive collection of cognacs, cordials, and venerable vintages. The Ciraces also carry cheeses, pâtés, and other gourmet items. This is not a self-service place; the staff is friendly and helpful, and will assemble quite gorgeous gift baskets if you desire. The *V* in the name, by the way, is for *Vincenza,* the owners' grandmother. ♦ M-Th 9AM-7:30PM; F-Sa 9AM-10PM. 173 North St. 227.3193

16 Bibelots Housed in the **Mercantile Wharf** building (1857, **Gridley Bryant**; renovated 1976, **John Sharratt Associates**), a renovated, enormous granite warehouse, **Renée Koller** and **David Bastian**'s international folk art and gift store is great fun because practically every item is one-of-a-kind and at least slightly eccentric. Most are handmade, imported from Mexico, Guatemala, Africa, England, all over. There are amusing interpretations of teapots, napkin rings, salt-and-pepper shakers; jewelry shaped like flora, fauna, and other creatures that can't be categorized; fanciful figurines and ornaments just waiting to become someone's unlikely treasure—plus more practical items such as dinnerware that resembles a stylish version of Fiestaware. A small gallery downstairs exhibits local artists' work. ♦ Tu-W, F 11AM-7PM; Th noon-8PM; Sa-Su noon-6PM. 75 Commercial St. 523.7336

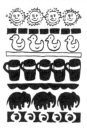

17 McLaughlin Building (c. 1850; renovated 1979, **Moritz Bergmeyer**; National Register of Historic Places) It's worth going out of your way to see New England's first cast-iron building, its soft brownish-mauve facade adorned with lacy rows of arched windows crowned by fanlights. The most delicate of colonettes divide the windows, seeming to melt into the wall of glittering glass. The **McLaughlin Elevator Company** once resided here, now condos do. ♦ 120 Fulton St (Richmond-Lewis Sts)

18 Michael's Waterfront and Wine Library $$ Its interior crowded with wine bottles and books, this restaurant announces up front the 2 features that keep it from being just another fern-filled bar. The books, some of which are quite old and quite odd, are donated by libraries and individuals, and patrons may borrow them. With one of Boston's largest wine lists, Michael's offers a big selection of international wines by the glass. The sports-oriented bar is frequented by a nonbookish crowd that occasionally includes rock musicians, entertainers, TV people. As for the food, it's basic New England cuisine and seafood, featuring a great rack of lamb. Shuttle service is available to Boston Garden events, the theater district, local hotels. ♦ American ♦ M, Sa 5:30-10:30PM; T-F 11:30AM-2:30PM, 5:30-10:30PM; Su 11:30AM-3PM, 5:30-10PM. 85 Atlantic Ave. Valet parking available 4:30PM-closing. Reservations recommended. 367.6425

18 Jasper's ★★★★$$$$ Tell a Bostonian that you'd like to take him or her out for an extravagant, sumptuous dinner—no matter the expense—and this will be one of your friend's first choices. Owner and chef **Jasper White** is lauded nationally for his culinary wizardry, which Pygmalianlike, transforms even the heartiest ethnic food into an elegant, refined dish. Not *too* refined, however—White clearly thinks food is just wonderful and that it should always taste that way. No Yankee stick-in-the-mode, his nouvelle New England cuisine globetrots. Some of White's inventions are his famous grilled lobster sausage; garlicky pork and clams, Portuguese *Alentejo* style; Maine rock crabcakes; grilled duck salad with papaya and spiced pecans. Consider trying the seafood tasting menu. Soups and desserts are special here. The dining rooms are spacious, muted, unremarkable—a perfect unobtrusive setting for any evening drama you'd like to supply. Service is highly professional. Some critics say Jasper's has off nights, especially when he's not around, and that would certainly be hard to take at these prices. But throw caution to the winds—innumerable Bostonians have gone before you and been delighted. There's piano music on weekends. ♦ Contemporary New England ♦ M-Sa 6PM-closing: 240 Commercial St (Atlantic Ave) Valet parking. Jacket recommended. Reservations recommended. 523.1126 ♿

19 Lewis Wharf Originally named for **Thomas Lewis**, native of Lynn MA, a canny merchant who acquired much of Boston's waterfront property after the American Revolution. In the mid-19th century, Boston's legendary clipper ship trade centered on this wharf. Ships carried off tea to Europe, and foodstuffs to be sold at exorbitant rates to prospectors during **California's Gold Rush** (eggs went for $10/ dozen; flour for $44/lb). The warehouse was built of Quincy granite between 1836–1840, attributed to **Richard Bond**, and renovated in the late '60s by **Carl Koch and Associates**, at which time the graceful gabled roof was replaced with an unwieldy mansard one. The building now houses residential and commercial units. To the right stretches an attractive harborside park. The **Boston Croquet Club** rents a portion and sets up their wickets—a genteel sight that brings home how long gone the city's seafaring era really is. One story claims that **Edgar Allan Poe**'s tale *The Fall of the House of Usher* was inspired by events that took place on the wharf's site in the 18th century. Two lovers, a sailor and another man's wife, were trapped by the angry husband in their rendezvous, a hidden tunnel underneath the Usher house. When the structure was torn down in 1800, 2 skeletons locked in embrace were discovered behind a gate at the foot of the tunnel steps.

Set back at the **Boston Harbor** end of Lewis Wharf—where old fallen-in wharf structures look ready for a harbor burial—is the popularly acclaimed **Boston Sailing Center**, which offers a variety of sailing and racing lesson packages as well as captained harbor cruises aboard 23- to 30-foot sailboats. Numerous membership plans are available. Boats also embark on day sails among the **Boston Harbor Islands** and on overnight trips to such destinations as **Provincetown, Martha's Vineyard, Newport**, and **Block Island**. The center acts as broker to arrange more extensive charters. ♦ Fees. Daily 9AM-sunset, May-1 Nov. 54 Lewis Wharf. 227.4198

As you walk back toward Atlantic Ave, there are some fine views of the city. A funny one features only the busts of the buildings downtown, their bases blocked from view by the long line of **Commercial Wharf** across the way.

North End

20 Giacomo's ★★$$ The open kitchen is close —but not too close, which means you're enveloped in tantalizing, spicy-sauce aromas, but you don't leave this cozy bistro drenched in olive oil and smoke. The grill's the thing here—meaty swordfish or tuna steaks arrive succulent and smoky from the charcoal flame, and grilled chicken and sausage are a fine duo. Try linguine with *frutte di mare*, a house specialty. Not content with the standard choice of white or red sauce, they've created *Giacomo* sauce— a feisty combination of the 2. The unfinished brick walls and refinished wood floors—signs of unwanted gentrification throughout the North End—are OK in owner **Jack Taglieri**'s unpretentious place. Spiffier than the average North End trattoria, Giacomo's doesn't overdo it. A handsome tin-stamped ceiling, oils on wood of Rome and Venice, and black-and-white caffè curtains add warmth and comfortable character. ♦ Italian ♦ M-Sa 5:30-10:30PM; Su 5-10PM. 355 Hanover St. 523.9026

21 St. Leonard's Church Peace Garden (1891, William Holmes) With tamed clumps of flowers and statuary that are spotlit at night, this is more like a garden center than a garden. But when there's an open gate leading to an open space in a crowded neighborhood like the North End, people can't resist wandering in. And this is a cheery spot, especially when decked out with lights at Christmastime. Planted at the close of the Vietnam War and maintained by the Franciscan Fathers, the garden endows the architecturally unremarkable church with some distinction. Two shrubs were brought over from the altar on the Boston Common where Pope John Paul II celebrated Mass. St. Leonard's was the first Italian church erected in New England. ♦ Daily 8AM-12:30PM. Mass Tu 6:30PM-closing; Sa 3-6PM. Hanover St at Prince St. 523.2110

22 Nuovo Boutiques are not a North End priority, but **Cynthia Byrne** and **Pat Guerrero**'s Italian clothing store for men and women adds a mod-ish accent to Hanover St. **Importano, Adriano, Georgiou, Adolpho** fashions are sold here, plus Byrne's own line. There's flamboyant fake gem-stone jewelry, perky hats, cotton and linen co-ordinates. Like everything else in the North End, the focus here is more on men, particularly of the peacock variety. ◆ M-Th 11AM-8PM; F-Sa 11AM-10PM; Su by chance. 354 Hanover St. 227.3445

23 St. Stephen's Church (1804, **Charles Bulfinch**; restored 1965, **Chester F. Wright**; National Register of Historic Places) Located at Hanover St's bend, on its sunny side, is Bulfinch's sole remaining church. He trans-formed what was a commonplace early meet-ing house (1714) called the **New North** into an elaborate, harmonious architectural composi-tion, for which the congregational society in

North End

residence paid $26,570. **Paul Revere** cast the bell that was hung in the church's belfry in 1805. Although Bulfinch was usually drawn to English architecture, Italian Renaissance cam-paniles also inspired him in this work—an ar-chitectural foreshadowing of the North End's future ethnic profile. The dramatic tower crowds to the front of the wide-hipped facade, a bold counterpoint to the subtle Federal archi-tectural gestures inside. Notice especially how the windows and column styles metamorphose as they move toward the gracefully curving ceil-ing. Most of the woodwork is original, including the pine columns. The 1830 organ was restored by **Charles Fisk** of Gloucester MA, a famous American organ conservator. In 1862, the **Catholic Diocese of Boston** bought the church to serve the North End's enormous influx of Irish immigrants, renamed it St. Stephen's, added a spire, raised the entire building 6 feet, and moved it back 16 feet to install a chapel un-derneath. **Rose Kennedy, JFK**'s mother, was christened here. In 1965 **Richard Cardinal Cushing** launched a successful campaign to renovate and restore the church to Bulfinch's design, respectfully returning the edifice to its original level and streetside prominence. ◆ Daily 8AM-5PM. 24 Clark St (Hanover St) 523.1230

24 Ristorante Lucia $$ The food is pretty good, featuring dishes from Abruzzi. One pasta dish reproduces the Italian flag with a white-cream, red-tomato, and green-pesto sauce. The walls are covered with takeoffs on Italian master-pieces. Upstairs is Lucia's best feature: the opulent pink-marble barroom, whose ceiling is painted with replicas of scenes from the **Sistine Chapel**. Note the tasteful touch the indiscreet **Michelangelo** omitted: undergarments resem-bling diapers and swaddling clothes. ◆ Italian ◆ M-Th 4:30-11PM; F-Sa 11:45AM-11PM; Su 1-11PM. 415 Hanover St (Charter St) Valet parking evenings. 367.2353

Drawing by Charles Shields

How to Eat a Lobster

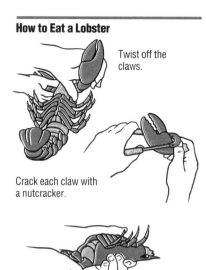

Twist off the claws.

Crack each claw with a nutcracker.

Separate the tailpiece from the body by arching the back until it cracks.

Bend back and break the flippers off tailpiece.

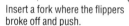

Insert a fork where the flippers broke off and push.

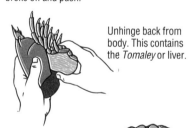

Unhinge back from body. This contains the *Tomaley* or liver.

Open the remaining part of the body by cracking sideways. Good meat here.

The small claws are excellant eating. The meat can be sucked out.

25 Davide ★$$$ The interior is bordello-esque, right down to the overstuffed, half-moon, red-velvet banquettes and the overheated color scheme. **Victor Grossi**, the maître d', oozes Mediterranean charm and could have been called up from central casting. This is no place for a namby-pamby evening—bring a group that can live up to the melodramatic setting. The menu changes seasonally (uncommon in the North End); try the duck served in a port sauce flavored with figs, risotto with seafood, or pan-fried bass with lemon-caper butter.
♦ Italian ♦ Daily 5-11PM. 326 Commercial St. Valet parking. Jacket recommended. Reservations required. 227.5745

26 Bay State Lobster Company The East Coast's largest retail and wholesale seafood operation, this 70-year-old business' biggest draw is the live lobsters customers can buy on the spot for tonight's dinner or have shipped by UPS to anywhere in the US (except in summer). Perhaps you'd like some additional companions on your flight home? Bay State also sells fish of all kinds, shellfish, and all the trimmings, as well as the company's own clam and fish chowders and lobster pies. Any of these items can also be packed for traveling. As you might guess, it's a madhouse here at times.
♦ M-W 9AM-5:30PM; Th 8AM-6PM; F 7AM-6PM; Sa 7AM-5:30PM; Su 7AM-1PM; Christmas Eve 5AM-5PM (the biggest sales day of the year) 379 Commercial St. No credit cards. 523.7960

27 Paul Revere Mall (1933, **Arthur Shurcliff**) Laid out in 1933, this tree-shaded park could have been plucked from Italy. It offers residents a comfortable cushion of space in their jam-packed quarter, and sightseeing pilgrims a pleasant passage from **St. Stephen's** to the **Old North Church** looming up ahead on **Salem St**. This modest, slightly scruffy park has more personality than any of Boston's grander spaces. Though it isn't very old, it has a very lived-in look. Also called the *Prado*, the mall's brick walls and paving carve out a reposeful realm where all generations of North Enders cheerfully converge. There's often a serious game of checkers or cards going on among the elders while perambulators are wheeled past, kids play, and dogs race about. The bronze equestrian statue of **Paul Revere** (1935, **Cyrus**

E. Dallin**) towers near the Hanover St edge, giving the young park a historical stamp. Hard-working, pragmatic artisan that he was, not to mention unremarkable in physique, Paul Revere wouldn't recognize himself in this dashing figure. On some of the side walls, plaques commemorate North Enders' contributions to their city. The mall ends at **Unity Street**; cross and enter the gate leading into the courtyard behind **Old North**. On the way, look for the **Clough House** (1715) at **No. 21** Unity. **Ebenezer Clough** lived here, one of the **Sons of Liberty, Boston Tea Party Indians**, and a master mason who laid the bricks for the church. The courtyard itself occupies the former site of **No. 19** Unity, which **Benjamin Franklin** bought for his 2 widowed sisters. ♦ Hanover-Salem Sts

28 The Old North Church (Christ Church) (1723, **William Price**; National Historic Landmark) Called the *Old North Church* by nearly everyone, this is the oldest church building in

Boston and the second Anglican parish founded in the city. Architect Price, a local draftsman and print dealer, emulated **Christopher Wren** quite nicely in this brick edifice. Coping with a tiny site in cramped quarters, Price gave the church needed stature and eminence by boldly attaching a 175-foot 3-tiered steeple. It was one of New England's earliest. What points to the sky today, however, is the 1955 replica of **Charles Bulfinch**'s 1806 replacement of Price's 18th-century original, the first 2 toppled by hurricanes. The weathervane on top is the original one, made by Colonial craftsman **Deacon Shem Drowne**. The 8 bells that ring from the belfry were cast in 1744 by **Abel Rudhall** of Gloucester, England, and range in weight from 620-1545 lbs. Their inscription recalls long-extinguished aspirations: *We are the first ring of bells cast for the British Empire in North America, Anno 1774*. The oldest and sweetest-sounding church bells in America, they have tolled the death of every American President since **George Washington** died in 1799. When he was 15, **Paul Revere** and 6 friends formed a guild to ring the bells.

Years later, Revere starred in the celebrated drama that has enveloped this landmark building with enduring legend, though a lot of the facts are cloudy. On the night of 18 April 1775, Revere rode on horseback to warn the **Minutemen** at **Lexington** and **Concord** of the approaching British troops. And as Revere arranged before departing, or so the story goes, **Robert Newman**, Christ Church's sexton, hung signal lanterns in the belfry to alert the populace that the British were on the march. Although a number of other messengers, including **William Dawes**, rode out into the towns, Paul Revere has eclipsed them all in fame. **Henry Wadsworth Longfellow** can take the real credit for Revere's glory; spellbound by the nearly forgotten tale, he wrote the inaccurate but entertaining poem *Paul Revere's Ride*, published in the *Atlantic*

Monthly in 1861. Every year, on the eve of **Patriots' Day**, descendants of Revere or Newman hang lanterns in the church belfry to commemorate that spring night. An unresolved controversy, however, concerns whether this is the real Old North Church, or whether the **Second Church** on **North Square**—nicknamed *The Old North*, which was burned by the British—truly held the leading role in the events on the eve of the American Revolution. If this theory is ever proven, it will cause a major rerouting of the **Freedom Trail**, so no one is rushing to verify it. No matter what the truth is, a sad and genuine chapter in Christ Church's past was the divided loyalties of its Episcopalian congregation; once the Revolution ignited, the church was closed until 1778 because of the tensions unleashed between Patriot and Tory parishioners.

The white church interior shimmers with light entering through pristine glass window-

panes. It's too bad there's never a chance to enjoy the church's unusual serenity and architectural clarity in solitude. Originally owned by parishioners, with brass plaques indicating which was whose, the high box pews were designed to hold the warmth of hot bricks and coals during the winter. Look for the Revere family pew—**No. 54**. Inscriptions worth reading abound in the church and on the walls of the **Washington Memorial Garden** in back; many offer interesting slants on Colonial Boston. The clock ticking reassuringly at the rear of the gallery was made by a parishioner in 1726; it's the oldest still running in an American public building. The brass chandeliers, also gifts, were first lighted on Christmas Day 1724—with candles, of course, not the current lightbulbs. To the right of the apse, a reproduction of a

1790 bust of George Washington rests in a niche. When **General Lafayette** returned to Boston in 1824, he noticed this bust and said, *Yes, that is the man I knew, and more like him than any other portrait.* Before leaving the church, look for the tablet on the left side of the vestibule, which identifies 12 bricks set into the wall. These were taken from a cell in **Guildhall** in **Boston, England**, where **William Brewster** and other **Pilgrims** were held after they were caught attempting to flee that country in 1607. In 1923, the mayor of Boston, England, sent the bricks on Christ Church's 200th anniversary as a gesture of friendship.

To the left as you exit is a curious museum and gift shop amalgam, housed in a former chapel that was built in 1917 to serve the North End's tiny community of Italian-speaking Protestants now vanished. In front of the street entrance, notice the amusing, stout little columns resting on the pair of lions' backs. Inside, look for the *Vinegar Bible*, a gift of **King George II** in 1733 and nicknamed for its famous typo: on one page heading, the *Parable of the Vinegar* appears instead of the *Parable of the Vineyard*. Tea retrieved from the boots of a **Boston Tea Party** participant is also on display. There are lots of silly, fun things to buy here too, from spice gumdrops and maple sugar candy to copies of Longfellow's poem to Wedgwood china decorated with the church's image.

Behind the church on both sides are charming small gardens nestled among clusters of nearby residences. Inmates of **Charlestown**'s old state prison made the ironwork. In early summer, the courtyard of the **Washington Memorial Garden** is awash in the fragrance of roses. Among its many commemorative tablets, one intriguingly states, *Here on 13 Sept. 1757, **John Childs**, who had given public notice of his intention to fly from the steeple of Dr. Cutler's church, performed it to the satisfaction of a great number of spectators.* Said Childs did indeed leap from on high, strapped to an umbrellalike contraption that carried him safely for several hundred feet.

Old North Church

Cross **Salem St** and look back at the church. Ever since its completion, the Old North has towered over the swath of red brick that makes up the North End's fabric. The church's Colonial neighbors are gone now, but since the newer buildings don't exceed 5 stories, you can still get a vivid image of the early 18th-century landscape. Unlike the **State House**, for instance, the Old North has not been overwhelmed by 20th-century urbanism. Historical talks are offered by staff ad hoc. ♦ Daily 9AM-5PM. Closed Thanksgiving and Christmas. 193 Salem St. 523.6676

28 Hull Street Leading up the hill from the Old North and abutting the **Copps Hill Burying Ground**, this one of the North End's most attractive streets. It was named after Boston's first mintmaster, **John Hull**, who coined the city's famous *pine-tree shillings* and had an estate that encompassed this neighborhood. ♦ Salem-Snowhill Sts

29 44 Hull Street (c. 1800) Located across from the Hull St entrance to **Copp's Hill Burying Ground** is, indisputedly, the narrowest house in Boston, one window per floor at the street end, squeezing up for air between its stout companions. An amusing tale claims that this house was an act of revenge, built solely out of spite to block the light and view of another house behind. In truth, this is a lonely survivor of the breed of modest dwellings called *ten footers*, depicted in old prints of Colonial Boston-town. This picturesque dwelling is 9 feet 6 inches wide, to be precise. A floral wrought-iron fence on the left leads to its charming entry. ♦ Salem-Snowhill Sts

30 Copp's Hill Burying Ground (1659) Another of Boston's wonderful outdoor pantheons, Copp's Hill not only offers a connoisseur the finest gravestones in Boston, but also some of the best views in the city of its most elusive feature—the waterfront. From this promontory you can see down to the boat-clogged Boston Harbor and over to **Charlestown** and its **Naval Yard**, where the venerable warship *Old Ironsides*, the U.S.S. *Constitution*, is docked—look for its rigging. This cemetery was established when **King's Chapel Burying Ground** got too crowded. Once an Indian burial ground and lookout point, Corpse Hill, as it is also known, has accommodated more than 10,000 burials including 1000 blacks. In Colonial days, black Bostonians settled in the North End in what was called the *New Guinea* community, at the base of Copp's Hill. A granite pillar marks where lies **Prince Hall**, black antislavery activist, Revolutionary War soldier, and founder of the Negro Freemasonry Order.

Sexton Robert Newman, who flashed the signals from Old North Church—and was imprisoned by the British for so doing—is buried here. And the formidable dynasty of the **Puritan Mathers**, churchmen and educators—Increase, his son **Cotton**, and Cotton's son **Samuel**—reside in a brick vault near the **Charter St** gate. (Increase was awarded the first doctor of divinity degree conferred in America.) During the Revolution, **British generals** directed the shelling of Bunker Hill from Copp's Hill and their soldiers used the gravestones for target practice—as you can still discern. Look for **Capt. Malcolm**'s bullet-riddled marker. His patriotic epitaph particularly incensed the soldiers: *a true son of Liberty/a friend to the Publick/an enemy to oppression/and one of the foremost/in opposing the Revenue Acts on America*. Copp's Hill legend tells of 2 tombs that were stolen here: interlopers ejected the remains of the graves' rightful owners, whose names were carved over with those of the thieves for future burial. ♦ Snowhill St (Charter-Hull Sts)

30 Copp's Hill Terrace After your scrutiny of the Puritan view of death, head downhill to this graceful plaza set into the sloping hill, beleaguered by neglect and vandals. It's still a wonderful architectural progression, most frequented by the youngest and oldest neighborhood residents. Near this site on Commercial St below, the

Great Molasses Flood occurred on 15 January 1919. A 4-story tank containing 2 $\frac{1}{2}$ million gallons of molasses burst, releasing a lavalike 50-foot torrent that destroyed buildings, killed 24 people, and injured 60. It took a week to clear the streets after the explosion, and a sticky-sweet aroma clung to the neighborhood for decades. Some North Enders claim they can still smell molasses from time to time in the heat of summer.

31 Pizzeria Regina ★$ In Boston, everybody but everybody knows the city's most famous (not best) pizza-pie joint: the North End Regina's. There are 7 or so Regina offspring around the city, but why not go right to the source, where it all began 45 years ago? Besides, some of the children are a little slick and unreliable, and none have their parent's comfortable, well-worn charm. This is brick-oven pizza of the thin-crust, oily variety. Customers from New York and Florida fly home with as many as 7 or 8 pizzas. It's a little tricky finding the curved corner building Regina's calls home; any North Ender can point you in the right direction. ♦ Pizza/takeout ♦ Daily 11AM-midnight. 11 $\frac{1}{2}$ Thatcher St (Washington St) No credit cards. 227.0765. Also at: Faneuil Hall Marketplace. 227.8180; 8 Holyoke St, Harvard Sq, Cambridge. 864.9279

Boston is full of an odd species of public *square*—a street intersection that is named after somebody—but the North End has an especially large supply of them. Most are named for Italian public figures, war heroes, and the like: **Joseph S. Giambarresi Square, Arthur A. Sirignano Square, Gus P. Napoli Square** to name a few.

Reverend Samuel Mather's home (long gone) on Moon St formerly belonged to a sea captain, who is remembered in history as the man put in the stocks on Boston Common in 1673 for *lewd and unseemly conduct*. The captain's crime: kissing his wife on their doorstep after returning from a 2-year voyage—unspeakable behavior, indeed, in Puritan times.

Pasta Varieties

Agnolotti		**Linguine**	
Bucattini			
Capellini d'angeli		**Manicotti**	
		Pappardelle	
Conchiglie		**Penne**	
		Ravioli	
Farfelle			
Fettuccine		**Rigatoni**	
Fusilli		**Rotelli**	
Gnocchi			
		Tagliatelli	
Lasagne		**Tortellini**	

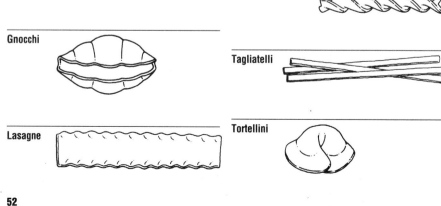

32 Oasis Cafe ★$ If you aren't in the mood for marinara, hop off the Italian express at this casual, comfy little café, where the order of every day is American homestyle cookery: meatloaf, BBQ-pork platter, cajun catfish, burgers, corn bread. The Oasis signature offering is its roast of the day, which can be accompanied by real mashed potatoes if you like. Every day there's an Oasis fritter too, either fruit or vegetable. Everything's homemade right down to the salad dressings. Be ready for whopping portions. Come hungry and have dessert—key-lime pie maybe. You'll dine to the tune of '30s and '40s jazz in a pink-and-black Art Deco setting. When you leave, find where **Endicott** intersects **North Margin St** at odd, appealing **Alfred Wisniski Square**. Looking down Endicott St toward downtown from here, you get one of the North End's few unimpeded views. So near and yet so far, as the cliché says, skyscrapers tower beyond the green barrier of the **Central Artery**— but here you are in another world entirely. ♦ American/takeout ♦ Tu-Sa 11:30AM-10PM; Su 11AM-3PM. 176 Endicott St (Alfred Wisniski Sq) 523.9274

33 Salem Street Running between **Cross** and **Charter** streets, this intimate, bustling street was dominated in the 19th century by the millinery and garment businesses owned by Jews who settled in this area. Now butcher shops, eateries, markets, and other businesses serving basic neighborhood needs are found along this narrow stretch. Great produce markets are tucked into tiny shopfronts, many with no signs and most with men who *serve* all customers— North Enders or not—with the same brusqueness, so don't let their ways prevent you from getting something good to eat. Most of the women you see lugging parcels are returning from this street; here one gets a glimpse of daily North End goings-on. From the southern end of the street you get a great view of the trucks and cars creeping along on the elevated **Central Artery**—enjoy your pedestrian freedom.

33 North Bennet Street School Founded in 1881 by **Pauline Agassiz Shaw**, this school originally helped North End immigrants develop job skills. No longer a social service agency, the school offers classes in furniture-making, carpentry, piano tuning, violin-making and restoration, bookbinding, jewelry-making, and watch repair, and other fields. Its graduates are trained in traditional craftsmanship and respected throughout New England. ♦ 39 N. Bennet St (Salem St)

34 Bova Italian Bakery *Fabuloso!* An Italian bakery that's open every hour, every day! If ever you suffer from insomnia, why not discover what the North End's like at 4 in the morning, when nary a tourist or car blocks your way, and get some fresh bread and pastries in the bargain at the **Bova** family's corner shop. For 70 years, Bova's been baking all its goods right on the premises. ♦ 24 hrs. 134 Salem St (Prince St) 523.5601

34 A. Parziale & Sons Bakery This is a businesslike shop, and its business is to make lots of great bread. The place is bursting with it. The Parziale family sells 1000 loaves a day of French bread alone. But why not stick to Italian varieties and try a handsome loaf of *Scali, Bostone*, or fragrant, rich raisin bread? Great *pizzelles* and anisette toasts, too. ♦ Bakery ♦ M-Sa 9AM-6PM. 80 Prince St (Salem St) 523.6368

35 Brook Farm Restaurant ★$ Not a name you'd expect to find in the North End, but this is very much a neighborhood hangout. It's a pleasant and unpretentious eatery, more spacious than most local spots, with wooden café chairs and tables and a wonderful counter for those who prefer to dine perched on stools. The weekday breakfast special is a tasty deal and the juice is fresh-squeezed. For lunch, there are salads, soups, burgers, and sandwiches served on bread from neighborhood bakeries. No din-

ner. No restrooms. It's hectic here on weekends. ♦ American/takeout ♦ Daily 7AM-3PM. 116 Salem Pl (Baldwin St) No credit cards. 720.3550 &

36 L'Osteria Ristorante ★★$$ *Every bite a delight*, say owners **Nicky** and **Lina DiPietrantonio**, and that's not the inflated claim it sounds. **Marge**, one of the waitresses, says she follows Nicky wherever he goes because the food's so good. It would be easy to overlook this unassuming spot, but go in for a warm welcome and well-prepared homestyle Northern Italian fare made from the freshest ingredients. Not a lot of elbow room here. ♦ Italian ♦ M-Th noon-10PM; F-Sa noon-11PM; Su 4-10PM. 109 Salem St (Parmenter St) Reservations recommended. 723.7847

37 Boston Public Library, North End Branch (1965, **Carl Koch and Associates**) Come by when the library is open to inspect one of the wonders of the North End: a remarkable 14-foot-long plaster model-diorama of the **Doge's Palace** in **Venice**. This clever creation was the consuming passion of **Henrietta Macy**, who taught kindergarten in the North End before moving to Europe. After she died in Venice, her handiwork was presented to the library. Painted settings and dolls enacting 16th-century scenes were added by **Louise Stimson** of Concord MA. As for the building, architect Carl Koch's attention to Italian-American cultural heritage has tempered and transformed the coldness of 1960s modernism into an extraordinary neighborhood addition. The library's atrium is cobbled like an Italian piazza, with plants and a small pool. Umbrellalike concrete vaults supported by 9 columns form a fascinating roof mass, raised to create a clerestory that illuminates the library interior. The brick exterior is punctuated by colored glass ceramics, adding festive notes to an otherwise drab streetscape. ♦ M-W 10AM-6PM; Th noon-8PM; F 9AM-5PM. 25 Parmenter St (Salem-Hanover Sts) 227.8135

Restaurants/Clubs: Red   **Hotels:** Blue
Shops/Parks: Green   **Sights/Culture:** Black

38 Polcari's Coffee Polcari's has been a fragrant North End fixture since 1932. In addition to his fine selection of coffees, congenial **Ralph Polcari** stocks more than a hundred spices from all over the world, sold by the ounce. Innumerable other specialty items fill every inch of shelf and floor space: chamomile flowers, *ceci* (dried chick peas), Arborio rice, flax seed, carob and vanilla beans, pine nuts, braided garlic, bunches of oregano. Polcari's wares are the stuff of alchemy in everyday cooking. ◆ M-Sa 8AM-6PM. 105 Salem St (Parmenter St) 227.0786

39 Fratelli Pagliuca's ★$$ There's decidedly nothing fancy about the **Pagliuca** brothers' very popular place. **Joe, Freddy**, and **Felix** changed the name from **Sabatino's**, but everything else is the same. A goodly number of locals eat here, Monday and Tuesday especially, as do businesspeople who know their way around the North End. This is satisfying, stick-

North End

to-the-ribs Northern Italian red-sauce cuisine served up in a family atmosphere. Favorites include the chicken-escarole soup, Chicken marsala, and sweet roast peppers with provolone and sausage, which come in large portions for reasonable prices. Don't look for the basic 4 food groups here: pasta and meat, not veggies, get priority. ◆ Italian ◆ M-Th 11AM-10PM; F-Sa 11AM-10:30PM. 14 Parmenter St. Reservations recommended F-Su. 367.1504

40 Mottola Pastry Shop Armando Mottola has been baking since he was 9 years old and his brother bakes here, too. In addition to cookies, cannolis, and other traditional pastries, the Mottolas turn out a wonderfully rich rum cake—the weight-watcher's nemesis. Another specialty is Armando's black-and-white cake made to look like a volcano—there's surely someone or some occasion it will suit perfectly. ◆ M-Th 8AM-6PM; F-Sa 8AM-7PM; Su 8AM-1PM. 95 Salem St. 227.8365

40 Giorgio's $ *Every pizza weighs a minimum of two pounds*, says a sign in the window, a promise that will scare some while luring others who like a hefty pie. Judging by the enormous slices, not to mention blimplike calzones (*one-pound minimum*), Giorgio's keeps its promise. What's really special about this popular pizzeria is the simple sauce, sweet with crushed ripe tomatoes and oil only; the wide selection of fresh toppings; and the owners, **Albert** and **Steven Giorgio** and their mother, **Lillian**. The Giorgios are very friendly, family-oriented people—Albert's wristwatch sports a photo of his 3 sons—who like to get acquainted with their customers. Try to sit by the window overlooking the street. ◆ Pizza/takeout ◆ Daily 10AM-8PM. 69 Salem St. No credit cards. 523.1373

41 La Piccola Venezia ★★$ Forget decor, forget romance, forget trendy angel-hair pasta concoctions—there's a whole slew of other reasons to frequent this no-frills spot. First, the hearty Italian home-cooking that runs the gamut from familiar favorites—lasagna, spaghetti with meat sauce, sausage cacciatore—to hard-to-find, traditional Italian fare like tripe, gnocchi, polenta, *baccala* (salt cod), and *scungilli* (conch). Second, everything's cheap and arrives in hefty portions, so when your wallet's light but your appetite's immense, this place is perfect. Third, it's noisy, it's hectic, it's tacky, it's bursting with people, but La Piccola Venezia is perpetually cheerful. Unlike many touristy North End spots peddling fake ambiance and tarted-up cuisine, everything here is exactly what it seems. And finally, look who's dining with you. Among the tourists are a lotta locals, many who've been coming to **John** and **Jimmy**'s place for a decade or more. ◆ Italian ◆ Daily 11:30AM-9:45PM. 63 Salem St. No credit cards. 523.9802

41 Dairy Fresh Candies If you like sweets, it's impossible to pass by without stopping in, and once you're inside, it's dangerous. Those who suffer from chocoholism will tremble at the sight of loose chocolates of every sort, including massive chunks of the plain-and-simple sinful stuff, and gorgeous packaged European assortments. The entire confection spectrum is here, including hard candies, old-fashioned nougats, and brittles to break teeth on. But the amiable **Matara** family, in the retail and wholesale business for over 30 years, goes way beyond candy: they've got Italian cakes and cookies, jams, dried fruits, nuts, edible seeds, exotic oils and extracts, vinegars, antipasti, pastas, cooking and baking supplies, and more—an extravaganza of delicacies. You can assemble a wonderful gift box here. *Thank you, stay sweet*, says the handlettered sign by the door. ◆ M-Th 8AM-6PM; F-Sa 8AM-7PM; Su 10AM-5PM. 57 Salem St. 742.2639 (dial RI.CANDY)

42 Maria's Pastry Shop What's a *pasticceria* without a display of marzipan in fruit and animal shapes, lurid with food coloring? Maria's has that popular almondy-sugary confection, and plenty more. Butter, anise, and almond scent the air, and through the kitchen door you can see women taking cookies out of the oven. Try Maria's *Savoiardi Napolitani*, lemon-frosted *anginetti*, or intriguing *moscardini ossa di morta* (which really do resemble bones). The *sfogliatelli* are great—creamy, citrony, and not too sweet. ◆ M-Sa 7AM-7PM; Su 7AM-1PM. 46 Cross St. 523.1196

Enrico Caruso loved the North End. When he came to Boston, he often ate at a restaurant that no longer exists, called the **Grotta Azura**, on Hanover St. A famous story about Caruso tells how the tenor wasn't able to cash a check at a neighborhood bank because he had no acceptable identification. Caruso launched into *Celeste Aida*, immediately delighting and convincing the skeptical bank manager.

Avoid the common mistake of calling the North End *Little Italy*, the nickname for New York City's Italian district.

Restaurants/Clubs: Red   Hotels: Blue
Shops/Parks: Green   **Sights/Culture:** Black

43 Purity Cheese Company Four people make all the marvelous ricotta and mozzarella sold fresh daily in this unobtrusive shopfront. It's easy to miss unless you glance in and spot the giant, pungent wheels of Parmesan and tubs of olives. Grating cheeses, pastas, oils, and big serving bowls are available also. **Vito Cucchiara**'s father began the business in 1938, and the operation is as unfussy as ever. Cheese, cheese, and more cheese of the highest caliber—that's why people from all over come here. It smells delicious inside. ◆ Tu-Sa 8AM-5PM. 55 Endicott St (Cross St) 227.5060 &

43 Pat's Pushcart ★$$ The decor here is nothing to speak of, but neither is that of most Italian family kitchens putting out good food for a hungry horde—which is what this place is like. And it too, is on the noisy side. On the outside, the Pushcart looks like a dive. Inside, it's packed with North Enders and anyone else wily enough to track down this great dining spot. Entrees are basic, tasty, and cheap. ◆ Italian ◆ Tu-Sa 5-10:30PM. 61 Endicott St (Cross St) 523.9616

The North End consists of 100 acres, 70% of which is housing.

Bests

Robert Levey
Restaurant Critic, *The Boston Globe*

Hottest ticket in town is for the daring cuisine at **Biba**.

Jasper's and **L'Espalier** remain superb and satisfying destinations among the deluxe independent restaurants.

Delicious, pampered hotel dining at **Aujourd'hui, Julien, Le Marquis de Lafayette, Seasons**, and the **Plaza Dining Room**.

In Chinatown, search out the dim sum at the **Golden Palace** or the **Imperial Tea House**. For yummy storefront fare, head for **Chau Chow Seafood**.

Top honors in trendy café dining go to **Olive's** in Charlestown, **Hamersley's Bistro** in the South End, and **Davio's Cafe** in Brookline.

Try **rocco's** or **Bnu** for casual Theater District nibbling.

And if you've come to town to hunt down seafood, stroll over to **Legal Sea Foods** in the Boston Park Plaza Hotel or **Skipjack's** off Copley Square.

Nostalgia buffs might still want to enjoy the ambiance of the glittering **Ritz-Carlton Dining Room** or the Continental elegance of **Locke-Ober**.

Chris Pullman
Design Manager, WGBH Boston (Public Broadcasting)

The third Sunday of October every fall is the Head of the **Charles Regatta**, an amazing spectacle of rowing (one boat leaves the starting line every 10 seconds from 9AM-4:30PM) and schmoozing. (THE social event for the East Coast college crowd.) Best places to watch are **Magazine Beach** (the launch site), the **Weeks Bridge** near Harvard, and the sharp curve near the **Cambridge Boat Club**.

The most interesting food in Cambridge is at the **Harvest** restaurant. Conceived by Ben Thompson (architect of Faneuil Hall and founder of Design Research), the place feels comfy and unpretentious, like it's been there forever, and serves imaginative seasonal concoctions. Great bread. Not cheap.

The **Gardner Museum** is a funky treasure trove of stuff (from Rembrandts to personal letters) collected by Isabella Stewart Gardner early in this century. The centerpiece is a magnificent 3-story courtyard with seasonal plantings. In the middle of January leaning out of the balcony into this space is a great refreshment. The little restaurant serves a nice lunch. It's minutes from the **MFA (Museum of Fine Arts)**.

Try weiner schnitzel, pan-fried potatoes, and spinach at **Locke-Ober**; insist on a table downstairs.

Walk from the **Hatch Shell**, down the **Esplanade** along the **Charles River** to **Cambridge**, and back the other side (or take the **Red Line** back from **Harvard Square**). At Harvard visit the **Fogg Museum, Houghton** (rare book) **Library**, and **Carpenter Center** (Corbusier). Then

North End

have lunch at **Bartley's Burger Cottage** on Mass Ave.

In Cambridge, start at the Harvard Square T stop and walk down **Brattle Street** through the shops and into the residential area (wonderful Colonial and Richardson houses) as far as you have time for. Take a different route back.

Gordon Hamersley
Owner/Chef/Restaurateur

Best Little Theater—**New Ehrlich Theatre** at the Boston Center for the Arts

Best Clothes Store—**Alan Bilzerian**—great clothes and terrific service, especially for me because I wear *real* clothes 3 times a year.

Best elegant New England dining—**Jasper's** restaurant; wonderful modern New England food. Casual, expensive elegance.

East Coast Grill—Inner beauty hot sauce! Speaks for itself.

Best walk—From **Charlestown** to the **South End**. You walk through everything imaginable.

Esplanade—Great place to run the dog and occasionally myself.

Best view—**Fenway Park**—any night in July and August.

Best flowers—**South End Flowers**—personalized service, beautiful arrangement.

Biba—for lunch overlooking the garden—try the great breads.

Most exciting driving is in Boston; like bumper cars with questionable insurance.

Wilson Farms—Outside Boston—Best thing about New England is being part of the constantly changing seasons—Boston's proximity to great and varied country activities. Within a half hour one can do so many terrific things: fish, ski, swim, surf, ride horses, work farms (pick your own).

Best little restaurant—**Hamersley's Bistro**.

Waterfront/Fort Point Channel

Newcomers to Boston have often heard of its great maritime past, and are surprised to discover how elusive the waterfront is. Hills that once overlooked **Boston Harbor** were leveled long ago, and the shoreline, for centuries Boston's lifeline, has been sheared from the city's core by Atlantic Avenue, the Central Artery, and modern buildings. But it takes only a little perseverance to cross this manmade divide to see where Boston began. An urban treasure, the waterfront is vibrant with light and hue, the constant motion of water and air. The history of the neighborhood's heyday is recorded in street and wharf names, captured in grand old buildings getting a new lease on life. The harbor itself, long the nation's most polluted, is about to undergo a massive clean-up. Once complete, the harbor's sprinkling of more than 30 islands will have the sparkling setting they deserve. The **Boston Harbor Islands**—from little **Gallops**, **Grape**, and **Bumpkin** to big **Peddocks** and **Thompson**—entice visitors with picturesque paths, beaches, and views of the city.

In Colonial times, young Boston looked to the Atlantic Ocean for commerce and prosperity. Throughout the 17th, 18th, and 19th centuries, profit-minded Bostonians industriously tinkered with the shoreline, which originally reached to where **Faneuil Hall** and **Government Center** are today, once the **Town Dock** area. Citizens built piers, shipyards, warehouses, and wharves extending ever farther into the sea, until the shoreline resembled a many-tentacled creature reaching hungrily for its nourishment: trade. The ocean brought profitable European and China trade and established the city's legendary merchant princes. One of Boston's most glorious moments was the clipper-ship era of the 1850s, when the harbor horizon was alive with masts and sails.

Boston's liaison with the sea began to suffer toward the turn of the century as rails and roads replaced sea routes and manufacturing supplanted maritime

Waterfront/Fort Point Channel

Take the **T** to the **Government Center** stop (**Green** and **Blue Lines**) and cross **City Hall Plaza** to the right of **City Hall**, descending the steps behind City Hall to **Congress St**, crossing to **Faneuil Hall Marketplace**, and continuing straight to **Christopher Columbus Park**—the *walk-to-the-sea* route. Or, the **Aquarium T** stop on the **Blue Line** brings you directly to the waterfront, to the right of the park. And the **South Station** stop (**Red Line**) brings you to the edge of the **Leather District** and **Fort Point Channel**.

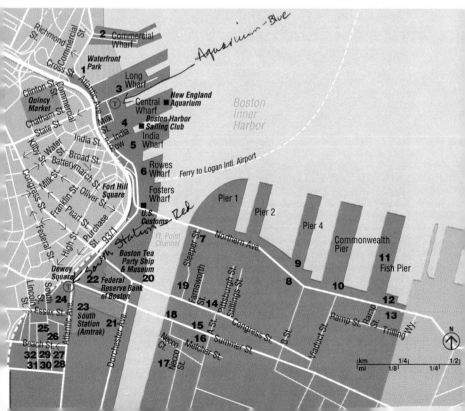

trade, fishing, and shipbuilding. The abandoned child of this union, it languished for decades until the late '60s, when the city began to reclaim it. Now the waterfront is gradually being resurrected, its connections to the heart of Boston reforged. The workaday harbor activities that remain have shifted elsewhere, primarily to **Charlestown** and **Fish Pier** in **South Boston**.

Today Boston is reinterpreting the waterfront's role as a place for leisure, luxurious residences and offices, pleasure boats, and waterside restaurants and hotels. Excursion and commuter boats depart from numerous wharves for the Boston Harbor Islands, **Nantucket, Martha's Vineyard, Provincetown** on **Cape Cod, Cape Ann**, and **South Shore** communities. *Harborwalk*, the pedestrian route along the waterfront, is lengthening; it will ultimately stretch from the **Charlestown Navy Yard**, where *Old Ironsides* is docked, to **Fort Point Channel**, eventually linking with walks along the **Charles River**—a total of more than 20 miles. For now, one great stroll begins at **Christopher Columbus Park** and **Commercial Wharf**, proceeds past the **New England Aquarium** and around sumptuous **Rowes Wharf**, crosses over the channel via the **Northern Avenue Bridge** into the Fort Point Channel area where Fish Pier and the **Children's** and **Computer Museums** are located, then doubles back past **South Station** to end with a brief meander in the little **Leather District**.

Fort Point Channel and the Leather District aren't part of the historic waterfront per se, but are natural companions because they, too, reveal facets of Boston's workaday life. Built up during the late 19th century, the Fort Point Channel neighborhood was the center for Boston's fishing, shipping, warehousing, and manufacturing industries; during the same era, the

Waterfront/Fort Point Channel

garment and raw leather goods industries thrived in the Leather District. In both atmosphere and architecture, these 2 neighborhoods, like the waterfront, are acquiring new vitality as galleries, restaurants, and shops move in, following the trail of artists and other urban pioneers. Walking the entire length of this far-flung neighborhood at one time is an ambitious undertaking, but definitely can be done if you're not with children; it's a great Boston experience.

1 Christopher Columbus (Waterfront) Park

(1976, **Sasaki Associates**) This friendly park opened a window to the sea and drew Bostonians back to where their city began. In fact, the park was built to complete the *walk-to-the-sea* that starts at **City Hall Plaza** at **Government Center**, proceeds through **Faneuil Hall Marketplace**, then passes under the **Central Artery** to end by the water. A handsome trellis promenade—short on greenery—crowns the park's center, with huge bollards and an anchor chain marking the seawall. The park offers views of the harbor and wharves, and a sociable scene. From morning until late-night, this versatile oasis hosts sea-gazing, ledge-sitting, sunning, frisbee-throwing, dog-walking, and romantic rendezvous. Watch planes take off across the harbor at Boston's **Logan International Airport**, and the steady boat traffic. On a summer afternoon, sit and read amid the grove of honey locust trees, or in the **Rose Fitzgerald Kennedy Garden**, fragrant with her namesake blooms. Tourists' children unleash pent-up energy clambering over ship-shaped timber play structures, with international lines forming for the tiny slide. **Quincy Market** is just a 5-minute walk away; pick up some treats and picnic with the breezes rustling by.

2 Commercial Wharf (1834, **Isaiah Rogers**; renovation of east section 1969, **Halasz and Halasz**; renovation of west section 1971, **Anderson, Notter, Feingold**) When Atlantic Avenue sliced through the waterfront in 1868, the rugged building of Quincy granite and Charlestown brick was sadly split in 2. Now the western half is home to **Michael's Waterfront Pub and Library**, and the larger eastern half houses offices and upscale apartments with enviable views. Architect Rogers also designed Boston's famed **Tremont Hotel**, long gone, the nation's first luxury overnight digs. If you walk to the wharf's end, you'll see ramshackle buildings, relics of days gone by. Now pleasure boats in the adjacent yacht marina crowd the pier and clamor for attention.

2 The Boston Sail Loft $ Strange as it seems in a seaside city, there aren't many restaurants in Boston where you can sit and look out at the water. This is one of them. Longtime residents fondly recall its predecessor, a rundown, quiet hole-in-the-wall called **The Wharf**. But things change; even if this is now a hopping touristy spot on the happy-hour trail, you get a nice view of **Boston Harbor** along with your oversize portions of decent seafood. Over in Cambridge another Sail Loft looks across a busy street to the **Charles River** (One Memorial Drive, 225.3888). ♦ American/Seafood ♦ M-Tu 11:30AM-10PM; W-Sa 11:30AM-11PM; Su noon-10PM. No tank tops. 80 Atlantic Ave. 227.7280 ⑤

Restaurants/Clubs: Red   Hotels: Blue

Shops/Parks: Green   **Sights/Culture: Black**

2 Cherrystone's $$ The food is pretty commercial, but the spacious dining rooms—especially on the 1st floor—are okay in a casual country club way. For a change, the nautical theme hasn't been overdone; in fact, the mounted book illustrations of fish are charming. There's lots of surf and some turf. The restaurant's location is its biggest asset—plenty of **Boston Harbor** and **Christopher Columbus Park** to see, with the neighboring wharves, **North End**, or **Faneuil Hall Marketplace** to choose from for a post-prandial stroll. A commercial parking lot is located next door. ◆ Seafood ◆ M-F 11:30AM-2:30PM, 5-10PM; Sa 5-10PM; Su 4-10PM. 100 Atlantic Ave (Commercial Wharf) Reservations recommended. 367.0300 ᕼ

3 Long Wharf (1710; National Historic Landmark) Boston was already America's busiest port when farsighted **Captain Oliver Noyes** constructed this wharf, the city's oldest. It originally extended from what is now **State Street** far out into then-**Town Cove**, creating a dramatic half-mile avenue to the farthest corners of the world. It was the Logan Airport of its day, where even the deepest-drawing ships could

Waterfront/Fort Point Channel

conveniently unload exotic cargoes on the pier lined with warehouses. Painter **John Singleton Copley** played here as a child, where his mother ran a tobacco shop. Landfill and road construction demolished most of the wharf by the 1950s, but the restoration of its remaining buildings and the arrival of the **Long Wharf Marriott Hotel** have made it a destination once more. Walk to the spacious granite plaza at the wharf's end for fresh air and lovely views.

On Long Wharf:

Long Wharf Marriott Hotel (1982, Cossutta and Associates) $$$ It's certainly pleasant to stay here at the city's edge in rooms surveying the lively waterfront, with **Christopher Columbus Park** next door, the **New England Aquarium** one wharf over, and the **North End** *ristoranti* and **Faneuil Hall Marketplace** mere minutes away. Many of the 400 rooms have good views—make sure yours does—and 2 luxury suites have outside decks. The Concierge Level offers premium services; general amenities include a business center, an indoor swimming pool, other exercise facilities, and a game room. The hotel has a couple of counts against it as a waterfront neighbor, however: it rudely crowds what should have remained a generous link in the *Harborwalk*, and the architects' attempt to mimic waterfront warehouses and the lines of a ship has resulted in an awkward, aggressively bulky building. The Marriott's red-garbed doormen are a striking sight. An appealing 19th-century fresco depicting **Boston Harbor** is mounted in the lobby upstairs. Relax by a window in the ordinary lounge named **Rachael's**; there is also the formal **Harbor Terrace** restaurant and a more casual café. ◆ 296 State St (Atlantic Ave) 227.0800, 800/228.9290; fax 227.2867

The Chart House (c. 1763; renovation 1973, **Anderson, Notter, Feingold**) $$$ A simple and solid brick warehouse, the waterfront's oldest, called the **Gardiner Building** was recycled for this chain restaurant. Inside, rustic bricks and beams recall the building's former life. Steak, prime rib, and seafood are the ticket, with children's plates available. Lots of stories circulate about the building's history—some possibly true—claiming it was called *Hancock's Counting House* because **John Hancock** had an office here, and that tea was stored here prior to the **Boston Tea Party**. When closed for the night, the sealed shutters outside convey a snug sleepytime look. The free valet parking is a great boon in a neighborhood born long before the days of autos. ◆ Seafood/American ◆ M-Th 5-11PM; F 5PM-midnight; Sa 4:30PM-midnight; Su 3-10PM. 60 Long Wharf. Complimentary valet parking. 227.1576

Custom House Block (1847, Isaiah Rogers; renovation 1973, **Anderson, Notter, Feingold** National Historic Landmark) Before his writing career finally freed him from ordinary pursuits, **Nathaniel Hawthorne** worked as a customs inspector in this building, which stored goods awaiting duties assessment. The renovated structure has an imposing granite facade and a picturesque north face, and now accommodates offices, apartments, a chandlery, and a boat-design firm.

4 Central Wharf (1816, **Charles Bulfinch**) In the early 19th century, Boston was rebounding economically from the American Revolution and becoming a booming seaport once more. The brilliantly daring developer **Uriah Cotting** formed the **Broad Street Association** of businessmen to modernize the dilapidated disorderly waterfront. With architect Bulfinch designing, the association created broad streets flanked by majestic 4-story brick-and-granite warehouses, and built this wharf and **India Wharf**. A seamen's chapel was also located here. Only a fragment of Central Wharf remains, with a handful of its structures stranded forlornly on the opposite side of the expressway.

On Central Wharf:

New England Aquarium (1969, **Cambridge Seven**) School kids and plenty of adults hurry eagerly across the expansive plaza, pausing to spot the harbor seals in their year-round outdoor pool (watch for **Rigel** the seal, who barks *hi!* like a parrot), then on inside to the aquarium's spectacular attraction: a 3-story 40-foot-diameter tank swirling with fish, sea turtles, sharks. The only lighting is the aquarium's illuminated displays and exhibit tanks: murky underwater ambiance. Visitors walk up the ramp winding around the central tank, transfixed by the constantly circling parade of flashing fins, spiky teeth, waving tails, opaque eyes. Watch for the divers who feed the fish 5 times a day, only after the sharks have otherwise dined. If you climb to the very top where the diving platform and lighting are, the mystery will disperse—so don't. Rewinding back down, check out the walls opposite the tank, inset with aqua-

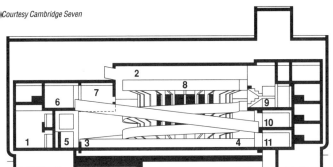

1. Lecture Room
2. Projection Area
3. Lobby Area
4. Gift Shop Area
5. World of Water
6. Fresh Water
7. Children's Aquarium
8. Giant Ocean Tank
9. Cold Marine
10. Temperate Marine
11. Tropical Marine

riums containing fascinating aquatic inhabitants. At the tank's base, smelly but endearing penguins stand at attention or zip about a shallow pool, barking noisily. Next door floats the **Discovery Theater**, where you can see the ever-popular dolphin and sea lion shows. On the outdoor plaza, summertime snack stands draw steady business. Don't miss the kinetic sculpture *Echo of the Waves*, nicknamed the *Whale*, which can move for hours without repeating the same pattern. The work of **Susumu Shingu**, the sculpture dampers to control its movement during high winds. The boxy concrete aquarium is now like a sea creature grown too big for its shell—during the next 5-or-so years, it will move into a new waterside home at Dry Dock No. 5 in the **Charlestown Navy Yard**. A model in its day, the aquarium plans a fabulous renaissance. ♦ Admission. M-Tu 9AM-6PM, W-Th 9AM-8PM (free admission 4-8PM), Sa-Su and holidays 9AM-7PM, 1 July-Labor Day; M-W 9AM-5PM, Th 9AM-8PM (free admission 4-8PM), F 9AM-5PM, Sa-Su and holidays 9AM-6PM, day after Labor Day-30 June; noon-5PM, 1 Jan. Central Wharf (Milk-Atlantic Sts) Recorded information 973.5200 ♿

New England Aquarium Whale Watching
Since the aquarium considers whales another aquatic exhibit, it takes the public 25 miles due east from Boston to visit the extraordinary mammals at **Stellwagen Bank**, a rich feeding ground. During the 5- to 6-hour voyage (round-trip), aquarium naturalists tell whale tales and describe other marine life en route. Sometimes whales come right up to the boat and let out a blow right into passengers' faces and cameras—a moment too exciting to ruffle even the most fastidious person's feathers. Whales frequenting New England coastal waters include humpbacks, finbacks, and right whales. In 1987, 2 blue whales, the largest creatures ever to live on earth, were sighted off Cape Cod. Dress warmly in layers—even in summer—and bring waterproof gear, rubber-soled shoes, and sunscreen. The boat leaves from Central Wharf and offers a full-service galley. Children under 3 aren't permitted on board. Call for times and reservations. ♦ April-October; Fee; reservations by credit card, payment in cash only. Recorded information 973.5277 ♿

5 India Wharf (Begun 1805) The other major result of the **Broad Street Association**'s 19th-century scheme to revamp the waterfront. India Wharf was once a half-mile stretch of piers,

stores, and warehouses designed by **Charles Bulfinch**. The last vestiges of the proudly handsome structures were levelled to make room for the upstart **Harbor Towers**.

On India Wharf:

Harbor Towers (1971, **I.M. Pei & Partners**) Whereas Boston's historic waterfront buildings stretched like fingers into the harbor, waves lapping among them, these towers aren't so

Waterfront/Fort Point Channel

interested in the maritime scene. The standoffish pair is more intrigued by the sky. In their day, the 40-story interlopers brought dramatic new style and scale to this part of town. Originally somewhat alienating, the towers have acquired a kind of folk appeal, like the **Pru** in **Back Bay**, partly because newer buildings more brazen and far less clever have pushed their way in—such as **International Place** across the street. The Harbor Towers are more exciting to live in than to look at; residents enjoy stunning views. **David von Schlegell**'s stark sculpture composed of 4 folded planes, *India Wharf Project* (1972), stands at the edge of the harborside terrace. The flat surfaces clad in stainless steel also ignore the harbor and reflect what's happening above instead. The human hustle-bustle and colorful disorder this wharf once knew has been replaced by lonely silent forms. But you won't find it gloomy here, just introspective—like the sea's occasional gray foggy face.

Boston Harbor Sailing Club Sail in the harbor and among the islands that once witnessed stirring arrivals and departures of Boston's majestic clipper ships. In a city famous for its exclusive clubs, this is not a club per se, but rather a 16-year-old private enterprise offering sailing classes taught by experts. The one-week courses are very popular, attracting novices from all over. Properly certified visitors can rent boats from a fleet of 80 ranging in length from 26 to 39 feet. ♦ Daily 8:30AM-10PM, May-Oct. 72 East India Row. 523.2619

Last year the **Port of Boston** handled a total of 21.1 million tons of cargo—95% of which was bulk tonnage, mainly fuel products received and discharged.

By 1995, 54% of Boston's population will consist of ethnic groups that are now considered minorities.

6 Rowes Wharf (1987, **Skidmore, Owings & Merrill**) A resplendent 6-story arch frames water and sky, luring pedestrians from Atlantic Avenue to the water's edge, where a copper-domed pavilion is a festive afterthought, like a boutonniere. Many Bostonians consider this grand red-brick complex—luxury condos, offices, shops, 38-slip marina, and hotel—the best addition to Boston in years. The 15-story development was built on the 1760s **Rowes** and **Fosters Wharves**. Many don't even realize it's new, because unlike **Harbor Towers**, Rowes Wharf looks backward in time. The ornamental overkill borders on kitsch, but the building is generous, capable of grand gestures. It has further privatized the waterfront, yet Rowes Wharf gives back to Bostonians things worth having: the heroic arch, an observatory, open space, a splendid *Harborwalk* extension leading past enormous yachts, and best of all, a new entry to the city via the water shuttle that zips between **Logan Airport** and Rowes. This speedy journey is worth taking for its own sake, sans baggage, to enjoy the most picturesque approach to Boston and see the flipside view through the monumental portal. It's not a cheap thrill, but do it once.

Airport Water Shuttle

The **Airport Water Shuttle** departs from Rowes Wharf and the Logan Airport dock. The trip, dock-to-dock, takes 7 minutes, with hotel courtesy buses and **Massport** buses operating on the airport dock side to and from the terminals.

Tickets are sold on board. ♦ Fee; elders, children at reduced rates, infants free. M-F 6AM-8PM, every 15 min; Sa-Su, national holidays noon-8PM, every half-hour. Closed Thanksgiving, Christmas, Independence days. Shuttle info and 24-hr Massport ground transportation 800/23-LOGAN

On Rowes Wharf:

Boston Harbor Hotel $$$$ The 230-room hotel's public spaces are tranquil and attractively dressed in warm woods, pearly grays, and subdued burgundies, companionable textures and tapestry patterns. Cove lighting adds a subtle glow and paintings by Massachusetts artists decorate the 1st and 2nd floors. Pay more for a room where you can gaze out at **Boston Harbor** instead of peering across the elevated expressway at the **Financial District**. In its **Magellan Gallery,** the hotel houses a largely undiscovered treasure: a private collection of early maps and charts depicting New England and Boston. Owned by **The Beacon Companies,** developers of the Rowes Wharf complex, the display includes Virginian **Captain John Smith**'s 1614 map of the New England coast, the first ever produced, which later guided the Pilgrims to Plymouth. Another fascinating map (1625, **Sir William Alexander**) records **The Council of New England**'s scheme to turn the region into an elite association of English estates, ultimately overturned by competition from the Massachusetts Bay Colony and support for the Puritan cause.

Pretty **Harborview Lounge** with its comfortable furnishings is a wonderful place to have a drink and watch the sun set to harp or piano music. A Sunday breakfast buffet is accompanied by a live trio, high tea is served Monday-Saturday, a dessert buffet is offered every evening, and a bar dinner menu on weekdays. Inquire about live music and dancing on weekends. Away from the water, overlooking empty sidewalks, **Rowes Wharf Bar** is unfortunately placed but blissfully quiet. The hotel's amenities include a posh health club and spa with a pristine 3-lane lap pool, 24-hour room service, nonsmokers' and handicapped-equipped rooms, and pet services from counseling to catnip. A year-round airport water shuttle, indoor parking, and marina slips are available. ♦ Deluxe ♦ 70 Rowes Wharf (Atlantic Ave) 439.7000, 800/752.7077; fax 330.9450 &

Within Boston Harbor Hotel:

Rowes Wharf Restaurant ★★$$$ The views are so splendid it would be easy not to care much about what's on one's plate. But in fact, the hotel has lavished attention on the roomy restaurant's cuisine. Chef **Daniel Bruce** hails from New York's **"21"** and **Le Cirque**, not to mention Venice and Paris ports-of-call. A blend of regional American and seafood specialties—such as a trio of fish with triplet sauces, bouillabaisse, crabcakes—are served with finesse amid a sophisticated rendition of the obligatory nautical theme, with fabric-covered walls and lush carpeting soaking up wayward sound. Come back for brunch, when a string quartet and red-flannel corned beef hash (prepared with beets) are standards. Look for **Dr. Robert Levine**'s 6-foot replica in mahogany, teak, and lemonwood of the renowned 1851 clipper ship *The Flying Cloud*.
♦ New American ♦ M-Th, Su 6:30-11AM, 11:30AM-4PM, 5:30-10PM; F-Sa 6:30-11AM, 11:30AM-4PM, 5:30-11PM

Rowes Walk Cafe ★★★$$ During spring and summer, weather permitting, enjoy lunch, cocktails, or dinner on the patio outside of the **Harborview Lounge**. The kitchen is outdoors, too, so the menu is simple; but the setting is gorgeous and you don't have to dress up.
♦ Café ♦ Daily 11:30AM-10PM, wk after Memorial Day-Labor Day &

Fort Point Channel

Most Bostonians have yet to stumble upon this fascinating place, and those who love the neighborhood hope that won't change too soon. This no-nonsense neighborhood exposes some of the city's practical inner workings. Slender Fort Point Channel is now all that divides the original **Shawmut Peninsula** from **South Boston**, once a far-off neck of land. In the 1870s, the **Boston Wharf Company** cut the channel and erected warehouses on the South Boston side to store lumber, sugar, coal, imported fruit, wool, raw pelts, and ice. **Commonwealth Pier** and **Fish Pier** were built on landfill, the second becoming the center of the Boston fishing industry. By the 1890s, the area was the major transfer point for raw materials fueling most New England industries, and was bursting with wharves, machine shops, iron foundries, glassworks, wagon factories, soap producers, brickyards, printing trades. Business boomed through the early 20th century, then slackened as the fishing and wool industries, shipping, and manufacturing declined. The construction of the **Central Artery** further isolated Fort Point, speeding the area's decline.

Artists rediscovered the neighborhood in the '70s, creating a SoHo-like atmosphere that early on earned the district the affectionate nickname *NoSo*, short for North of South Boston. Now more than 300 artists belong to the **Fort Point Arts Community**, the largest community of visual artists in New England. Headquartered at **249 A Street**, an artists' cooperative, FPAC sponsors several open studio weekends annually. A few pioneering galleries and museums moved in as well, then creative and service industries.

The **World Trade Center** and the massive **Boston Design Center**, the latter New England's major showroom facility for the interior design trade, have

Waterfront/Fort Point Channel

comfortably settled in now too. What port activity remains in Boston is located along Northern Avenue and at Fish Pier, home of the **New England Fish Exchange**. Mega-development of the vacant **Fan Pier** nearby—a defeated proposal for a city-in-a-city that's sure to resurface—would transform the neighborhood, a potentially scary prospect. But for now it's great fun to poke around the revival and rubble, still full of the old waterfront district's industrial flavor and vitality. Look for the Boston Wharf Company's architecturally inventive warehouses on Summer and Congress streets. Trucks and tractor-trailers rule the roads in this part of town. Back across the channel, skyscrapers spread like weeds; here low-rise buildings and empty lots let light flood in. Unfamiliar vantage points make the city's skyline seem a fresh find.

For such a tiny waterway, the Fort Point Channel bridges offer a remarkable survey of mechanical engineering. Each operates differently: the creaky **Northern Avenue Bridge**—soon to be replaced by a fixed bridge—is a trussed rolling bridge that swivels 90 degrees on a single axis to clear the channel for ships; the **Congress Street Bridge** has a giant counterweight to drive a large gear system that lifts up the bridge; and the **Summer Street Bridge** is engineered to slide sideways out of the way on rails built on piers.

At the **Black Falcon Cruise Terminal**—located across from the **Boston Design Center** (from Summer St, turn left into the Marine Industrial Park)—you can watch the exciting arrivals and departures of majestic *Cunard* and *Royal Viking* cruise ships, recalling heady days when transatlantic crossings transported Americans to their European adventures. The terminal was named in memory of the shipsmen killed when the *Black Falcon* freighter burned and sank at the **South Boston** pier.

Restaurants/Clubs: Red   Hotels: Blue
Shops/Parks: Green   **Sights/Culture:** Black

7 Venus Seafoods in the Rough ★★$ Look for the splashy red-and-yellow banner and the giant flashing arrow, right by the Northern Avenue bridge. Owners **Susan Chused-Still** and **Maggie McNally** serve inexpensive and delicious shack-style seafood cuisine, but with flair and consideration for health-conscious diners—you can even get a green salad here. Fish and seafood of all kinds are fried, boiled, grilled, and steamed. Order a classic New England clambake with all the fixings, or one of the nightly grilled fish specials. Out-of-staters—Maryland and Maine crabs—star in the autumn **Venus Cosmic Clambake**. Dine casually at picnic tables under the giant heated tent, with a wonderful view juxtaposing lobster boats and the city skyline. A great place for parties and familes. The hours vary; call ahead. ♦ Seafood ♦ Tu-Su 11:30AM-9PM, mid Apr-Oct. Closed November-mid April. 88 Sleeper St (Northern Ave) No credit cards. 426.3388 ♿

8 Our Lady of Good Voyage In addition to regular weekend Masses, an annual *Blessing of the Animals* service is held at this humble little chapel. ♦ 65 Northern Ave. 542.3883

Waterfront/Fort Point Channel

9 Anthony's Pier 4 ★$$ There are better places to go in Boston for an expensive seafood dinner, but Anthony's is worth a visit once to experience a big-time restaurant formula that keeps 'em coming, and coming, and coming. Owner **Anthony Athanas**, an Albanian immigrant, started out as a shoeshine boy, built a restaurant, and wound up ruling a fiefdom of 5 gigantic seafood houses. After an inevitable wait—no reservations accepted—enjoy towering popovers, raw oysters or clams, steamed lobster or simply cooked seafood, and end with Indian pudding or a dessert soufflé. The wine list may be New England's biggest and best. The colonial-nautical motif is milked for all it's worth, but they needn't have gone to the trouble: big views of Boston Harbor steal the show. No quiet corners here, where as many as 3000 meals a day are served. Take a look at the *Wall of Respect*—make that *Walls*—crammed with photos of Anthony and the **Pope**, Anthony and **John F. Kennedy**, Anthony and **Frank Sinatra**, Anthony and **Liz Taylor**, Anthony and **Gregory Peck**.... ♦ Seafood/American ♦ M-F 11:30AM-11PM; Sa noon-11PM; Su 12:30-10:30PM. 140 Northern Ave (Pier 4) Valet parking. Jacket required and tie preferred for main dining room at dinner; no jeans or sneakers. 423.6363 ♿

10 Commonwealth Pier/World Trade Center Excursion boats depart from this pier for **Provincetown, Martha's Vineyard, Nantucket**, the **Harbor Islands**, and other points. The beflagged and somewhat fascist-appearing World Trade Center accommodates all kinds of enormous functions. Across the street from its lower main entrance, a pedestrian walkway winds to the elevated **Viaduct Street**, a little-known route that offers unusual spacious cityscapes. Behind lies hectic **Fish Pier**; in another direction looms the Postmodern **Boston**

Design Center and giant **Boston Edison** with its towering stacks; on the right is Boston's southern flank. Continue *straight* on Viaduct's sidewalk until you reach Summer St, then turn right. But on the way, before it's gone from view, look back for the best view of the World Trade Center's monumental pomp and circumstance.

11 Fish Pier Two long arcaded rows housing fish-related businesses stretch more than 700 feet out onto the water, with the heroic **New England Fish Exchange** dominating the far end. The century-old building's arch is crowned with a wonderful carved relief of **Neptune**'s head, with more fabulous fishy ornamentation above. No longer the center of New England's—let alone America's—fish industry, Boston's catch keeps shrinking, with more and more fish brought in by trucks, not boats. But the venerable fish auction still starts up every morning around 6:30, presided over by exchange president **Marie Frattollilo**. It's well worth setting the alarm for 5 to arrive by 6 and watch the buyers haggling over that day's cod, hake, pollack, etc, sold right off the boats and rushed to refrigerated trucks.

11 No-Name ★★$ Once upon a time it had one, but the No-Name sure doesn't need one now. The hungry hordes all know where to find this big-business restaurant: in the right-hand building of **Fish Pier**, just past the arcade's first curve. The dinnertime line out the door helps point the way; don't fret at the sight—you may meet some amusing fellow diners. No-Name opened in 1917 and dished up from the crack of dawn onward for fishermen and pier workers. Enlarged to accommodate the tourists, businesspeople, and locals who have joined the old crowd, No-Name has kept its hole-in-the-wall look right down to the concrete floor. Hope for a table in the back overlooking the pier and the boats that brought your dinner. Sitting elbow-to-elbow at boisterous communal tables, fill up on *chowdah* and big portions of impeccably fresh fried seafood, boiled lobster, broiled fish, fish o' the day, delicious homemade pie. No reservations. Expect to wait in line. ♦ Seafood ♦ Daily 11AM-11PM. 15 1/2 Fish Pier (Northern Ave) No credit cards. 338.7539

12 Jimmy's Harborside ★$$ The waterfront's *Old Faithful*, Jimmy's has been in business since 1923, starting out as a 9-stool joint serving **Fish Pier** workers and fishermen. The cavernous seafood house's dated decor shows a refreshing lack of interest in fads. Notice the funky fish mosaics and neon on the facade. Showcased in walls of glass, the views are among the waterfront's most colorful, with big boats docked close by. The reliably fresh seafood is at its best in simpler preparations. Try the chowder; Jimmy's earned the title *Home of the Chowder King* from the late owner **Jimmy Doulos**' shining moment in the '60s, when he was invited to bring his great fish chowder to Washington DC, pleasing the palates of **John F. Kennedy** and members of Congress. Jimmy's son is in charge now, but politicians and other celebs still crowd in with tourists and regulars.

While waiting for a table, have a drink at **Jimmy Jr**, the boat-shaped bar. ♦ Seafood/American ♦ M-Sa 11:30AM-9:30PM; Su noon-8PM. 242 Northern Ave (Fish Pier) Valet parking. Jacket preferred; no jeans, sneakers, T-shirts at dinner. Reservations recommended. 423.1000 ♿

JIMBO'S

13 Jimbo's Fish Shanty ★$$ Geared toward the family trade, casual Jimbo's is run by the **Doulos** family, who own **Jimmy's Harborside** across the way. Jimbo's has a trains-and-hobos decor, and children are delighted to find 3 train sets zipping on overhead tracks. No harbor views, but lower prices for chowder, basic seafood, pizzas, salads, burgers, and other no-frills American food. Children's plates available. The restaurant's tiny newsletter-menu advises visitors to check out the **New England Aquarium** *for a close look at the seafood on the hoof.* ♦ Seafood/American ♦ M-Th 11:30AM-9:30PM; F-Sa 11:30AM-10PM; Su noon-8PM. 245 Northern Ave (Fish Pier) Valet parking at Jimmy's Harborside. 542.5600 ♿

13 Daily Catch ★$$ An offspring of the popular **North End** hole-in-the-wall, this larger place is just as redolent with garlic and serves the same great seafood, although the original has much more personality. Try one of the many variations on the calamari theme; the owners love to turn people on to their favorite seafood. ♦ Seafood ♦ M-Th 11:30AM-9:30PM; F-Sa 11:30AM-10:30PM; Su 5-9:30PM. 261 Northern Ave (Fish Pier) No credit cards. 338.3093. Also at: 323 Hanover St, North End. 523.8567; One Kendall Sq, Cambridge. 225.2300

14 Boston Fire Museum This chunky little granite-and-brick firehouse has its own street sign and is now owned by the **Boston Sparks Association**. Unfortunately, inadequate funding keeps the museum unfinished and inaccessible to the public, but the 1891 building's quite an attractive presence on the street with its tawny and red-brick hues and ornate touches. ♦ 344 Congress St (Farnsworth St)

14 Mobius Mobius is both the **Mobius Performing Group** of 18 artists and multimedia gallery and performance space on the 5th floor in a former leather-sole manufacturing building where other artists can also present their work. The founding group works in performance, installation, sound art, new music, film, video, dance, and intermedia. Works-in-progress are presented frequently. Performances change just about every weekend; call for times or to alert staff for wheelchair assistance. ♦ Admission varies. 354 Congress St. 542.7416

Mattress companies were once located on **Sleeper St** in the Fort Point Channel neighborhood.

Restaurants/Clubs: Red Hotels: Blue
Shops/Parks: Green Sights/Culture: Black

15 Entrée ★$ Frequented by local architecture offices, this stylishly sparse high-end cafeteria-style lunch spot serves great coffee, delicious soups, chowders, salads like smoked trout plate, sandwiches, hot and cold entrees like peppered flank steak, delectable desserts. Everything's made on the premises, including from-scratch morning muffins. ♦ New American/takeout ♦ M-F 7:30AM-4:30PM. 274 Summer St. 338.8850

16 Hav A Bite $ Local artists, factory workers, and businesspeople always sniff out the good

Waterfront/Fort Point Channel

eating deals, and this very basic, unpretentious luncheonette is on their list. It's big and clean and serves up good basic food cheap: subs, sandwiches, burgers, pizzas, chili dogs, gyros, fried-clam plates. Beer, too. While the rest of the city's asleep, get a hearty breakfast with lots of good grease to jumpstart your day. Walk up **Melcher Street** to see its gracefully curving warehouses. ♦ American ♦ M-F 5AM-5PM; Sa 5AM-noon. 324 A St (Melcher St) No credit cards. 338.7571 ♿

17 The Channel A cavernous raucous rock 'n' roll club that has played host to the **Neville Brothers, The Wailers, ThirdWorld**, one of **Roy Orbison**'s last shows, **Deborah Harry, The Georgia Satellites, The Bad Brains, Skid Row, Graham Parker**. Different nights feature local musicians, new and alternative music, with weekends focusing on national and international bands. Sundays are heavy-metal nights. Several dance floors and bars, snacks sold. Big acts draw big crowds, which sometimes get a little rough, so heads up. Minimum age 21, but most Sunday nights are designated for the 18+ crowd. Bring ID. Paid parking. ♦ Cover varies. Daily 8PM-closing; call for shows. 25 Necco St. Recorded information 451.1905

17 Necco Place Next door to **The Channel**. Every night a different kind of music's on the plate here, whether it be DJ-driven, an acoustic showcase, local light rock 'n' roll bands, blues, or international music. Sunday features national acoustic shows called *Acoustic Images*. An intimate setting for 200 people max; large windows overlook the channel and there's a dance floor, not to mention bargain snacks. Minimum age 21. Bring ID. ♦ Cover varies. Tu-Sa 7:30PM-closing; call for shows. One Necco Pl. 426.7744

18 Weylu's ★$$ Better-than-average Mandarin, Szechuan, and Cantonese Chinese food where you'd least expect it—far across the channel from **Chinatown**—with views of Boston's southern skyline. Traditional and innovative dishes mingle on the menu and are courteously served in a large modern setting. Luncheon specials daily. To the left of Weylu's entrance, stairs descend to a block-long arcaded path that ends at Congress St. Since Summer St is elevated and Congress St isn't, this is a convenient passage between the 2, and also overlooks the **Fort Point Channel**. ◆ Chinese/takeout ◆ M-Th 11:30AM-10:30PM; F 11:30AM-11:30PM; Sa 12:30-11:30PM; Su 12:30-10:30PM. 254 Summer St. 423.0243

▲▲▲▲▲▲▲
The
Children's
●●●●●●●
Museum
◆◆◆◆◆◆◆

19 The Children's Museum A 40-foot-tall milk bottle, one of Boston's most beloved landmarks, marks this popular spot on **Museum Wharf**. Built in the '30s and donated to the museum in 1977 by the **H.P. Hood Company**, the wooden bottle has been an outdoor refreshment stand ever since. (If filled, the bottle would hold 50,000 gallons of milk and 860 gallons of cream.) Kids adore this lively participatory museum located in a former wool warehouse. Whatever your age, a visit here will revive that urge to touch and get

into things, even if you restrain yourself and just watch. In ongoing exhibitions for toddlers to 14 year olds, kids may dress up in vintage duds in **Grandmother's Attic**, scramble on the 2-story **Climbing Sculpture**, learn personal health and well-being in **Mind Your Own Business**, exercise vocabulary and spelling skills at **The Ark in the Attic**, hang out in the **Clubhouse**, investigate what daily life is like in an authentic, reconstructed Japanese silk-merchant's home from **Kyoto**, Boston's sister city. A big, engaging new exhibition called **The Kid's Bridge** addresses Boston's multicultural heritage, and sensitive issues such as discrimination and prejudice. Every visit to the museum can be different, with frequent new exhibitions, special events, and performances. The **Resource Center** offers educational mate-

1 Ahead to the Past
   (Grandmother's House)
2 Waves & Vibrations
3 Raceways
4 Giant's Desk Top
5 Garage
6 El Mercado del Barrio
   (Superette)
7 Mind Your Own Business
8 What If You Couldn't...?
9 Ark in the Attic

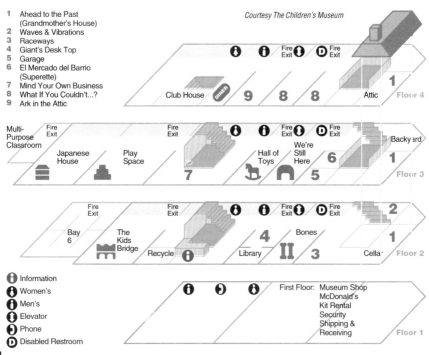

Courtesy The Children's Museum

rials and services to parents and teachers. **RECYCLE** sells industrial raw materials discarded by local factories—sold in bulk, dirt-cheap, cash only. **The Children's Museum Shop** is an unbeatable source for unusual gifts, toys, and books. Museum director **Ken Brecher** and his staff work with local neighborhoods on a variety of cultural events, so this is the place to find out about all sorts of family activities going on around Boston. ♦ Admission; reduced admission F 5-9PM. Tu-Th, Sa-Su 10AM-5PM; F 10AM-9PM. Open M during Boston school vacations and holidays. 300 Congress St (Museum Wharf) Recorded information 426.8855 &

19 McDonald's $ Adjacent to the **Children's Museum**, a special entrance also opens directly into the museum. The standard Mc-fare, but a cut above in decor and plenty of tables. If you're with kids, you're sure to end up here. ♦ M-Th 6:30AM-8PM; F 6:30AM-9PM; Sa 7AM-7PM; Su 8AM-6PM. 316 Congress St. No credit cards. 482.1746 &

19 The Computer Museum A remarkable repository of technologies past and present, this is the only museum in the world devoted entirely to computers. Forget those graceless terms—*nerd*, *hack*, *dweeb*—computer *companions* are made here, the museum says. Whether you're computer-literate or -leery, more than 60 interactive exhibitions chronicle computers and their role in society. Walk through a spectacular 20-times-larger-than-life 2-story computer model that

demonstrates how a personal computer functions, complete with 25-foot-long keyboard, 108-square-foot color monitor, and 6-foot-tall floppy disks. **Robert Macauley**, writer and illustrator of *The Way Things Work* and other delightfully reassuring show-and-tell-style books, illustrated the **Walk-Through-Computer Exhibit**. Hands-on exhibitions let visitors *paint* pictures, compose melodies, create programs, simulate aircraft flight, design a house or car, remodel their faces. Visit the amusing **Animation Theater**, and **Smart Machines Gallery** starring more than 25 robots. Vintage military, space, and commercial computers are on view; so is *Spacewar!*, the first interactive computer video game (1962). Ride the massive glass-enclosed elevator overlooking the **Fort Point Channel**. The techy gift shop even sells chocolate *chips*. The museum's waterfront setting makes sense, since Boston's economy is now as dependent on high tech as it once was on seafaring. ♦ Admission; reduced admission F 5-9PM. Tu-Th, Sa-Su 10AM-5PM; F 10AM-9PM. 300 Congress St (Museum Wharf) 426.2800 (human voice), 423.6758 (computer voice) &

Waterfront/Fort Point Channel

20 Boston Tea Party Ship and Museum The Boston Tea Party took place near here on Griffin's Wharf, long gone—its site now landfill on Atlantic Ave between Congress St and Northern Ave. On a cold December night in 1773, angry Colonists dressed as Mohawk Indians boarded ships and heave-hoed 340 chests of costly British tea into the harbor to protest the tax imposed on their prized beverage. A *cuppa* was a costly commodity in those times. Moored alongside the **Congress Street Bridge** is the *Beaver II*, a Danish brig resembling one of the 3 Tea Party ships and sailed here in 1973. Visitors help reenact the fateful December event. For kids, it's an adventure to climb about the 110-foot working vessel, listen to costumed guides, and finally toss a bale of tea defiantly over the side—the fact that it's roped to the ship

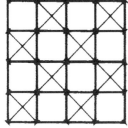

Courtesy The Computer Museum

and hauled back up again doesn't lessen the thrill. On the adjacent pier, the little museum contains exhibitions, films, ship models, and memorabilia, with printed information available in 7 languages. Tax-free tea is served at all times. ♦ Admission. Daily 9AM-dusk. Off Congress St Bridge (Atlantic Ave) 338.1773

21 U.S. Postal Service-South Postal Annex
Boston's general mail facility looks like a '20s ocean liner berthed alongside the channel. Always open, this is the mail processing hub for the Boston Division, with more than 1.2 million square feet of space and 12 miles of conveyors. Groups of 10 or more, minimum age 13 or 8th grade, can take a guided tour of the automated and mechanized facility and see how employees sort a daily average of 9 million pieces of mail with the help of optical character readers, letter-sorting machines, bar-code sorters, and other sophisticated equipment. Call to arrange a tour at least one week in advance. ♦ Free. Tours Tu-F Jan-Nov. 25 Dorchester Ave. 654.5081

22 Federal Reserve Bank of Boston (1977, **Hugh Stubbins & Associates**) Whether one

Waterfront/Fort Point Channel

thinks this building is shaped like an old-fashioned washboard, goal posts, or radiator, its shimmering aluminum-sheathed form is remarkably visible from many vantage points. The bank's art gallery on the ground floor is an alternative space where nonprofit New England-based artists and arts organizations mount 6 professional-level exhibitions annually. A performance series is held in the adjacent auditorium on weekdays, September-December and March-June. Call for program information. Free group tours of the bank's operational departments are offered Monday-Thursday, 9AM and 10:30AM, and visitors leave with souvenir packets of shredded money. Individual bank tours offered by appointment only, generally on Friday. ♦ Art gallery M-F 10AM-4PM. 600 Atlantic Ave. Recorded gallery information 973.3453, tours 973.3451/3463

23 South Station (1899, **Shepley, Rutan, and Coolidge**; National Register of Historic Places) When construction on South Station at **Dewey Square** was completed in 1900, it was the world's largest railroad station, holding that title for many years. And by 1913, handling 38 million passengers a year, it was the busiest station in the country—even topping New York's Grand Central Station. In peak year 1907, 876 trains plied the rails on weekdays. The majestically sprawling 5-story edifice, its shapely curved facade adorned with a 9-foot-wide clock surmounted by a proud eagle, proclaimed Boston's important place in the world. In its heyday, the station's comforts included a theater screening newsreels and **Our Lady of the Railways Chapel**. But when airplanes, trucks, and autos eclipsed trains, the station slid into decrepitude. Eventually, most of it was demolished except the handsome headhouse, and in the '60s that nearly gave up the ghost, too.

Now South Station's aggressive eagle has something worth lording over. Respectful restoration and intelligent planning have made the terminal an exciting destination once more, with pushcart vendors, a food hall, coffee bar, newsstand, bank, and other services to lure pedestrians from nearby streets. Look for the old tin ceilings and beautiful carved details. More than 200 commuter trains and dozens of **Amtrak** runs come and go on the busiest travel days. With a bus station nearby and the **Red Line** subway conveniently on site, travelers are linked to the rest of Boston and suburbs. Plans are afoot to turn the station into a major transportation center. ♦ Summer St-Atlantic Ave

The Leather District

Like the **Fort Point Channel** area, this tiny appendage to the **Financial District** has a businesslike personality and lots of integrity. You can cover the entire 7-block neighborhood in one half-hour stroll. When Boston's **Great Fire of 1872** swept clean more than 60 acres, it wiped out the city's commercial and wholesale center, including the dense leather and garment district concentrated here. But slowly businesses rose from the ashes and built sturdy new warehouses and factories, most along Lincoln and South streets, some Romanesque in style and quite distinguished. Except for a few leather firms, the leather warehousing industry long ago departed for other countries. In the '70s, artists and urban pioneers began to move in, followed by art galleries, shops and services, and restaurants. The neighborhood's new identity is still in the making. Arty attempts to update and upscale the neighborhood are like dressing up a business suit with a Day-Glo tie.

24 The Essex Grill ★$$ On the 1st floor of the former **Hotel Essex**, now spiffed up as the **Plymouth Rock Building**, the big dining room looks across at trains idling in the **South Station** yards and fronts a major street, so diners can survey the urban scene. Nicely prepared seafood dominates the menu, including freshwater varieties. Also on the 1st floor is the high-ceilinged, airy **Essex Bar**, a throwback to another era with wonderfully fussy columns and drapes. The old Hotel Essex, built about the same time as South Station, was a traveler's haunt, and it's easy to imagine the days when both rail-weary and raring-to-go travelers came and went from here, baggage in tow. As you come or go, look for the handsome old clocks in the lobby. There's also a popular takeout place on the premises that serves an eclectic menu and delivers locally; call for hours. ♦ Seafood ♦ M-F 7AM-10PM; Sa noon-10PM. 695 Atlantic Ave (Essex St) Reservations recommended for lunch. 439.3599, takeout 439.9365

NKADINKADO®

25 **Inkadinkado** Most Bostonians have yet to discover this captivating wholesale/retail shop purveying inexpensive trinkets and toys, though many are familiar with its biggest seller: clever rubber stamps of animals, buildings, cartoons, patterns, names, and hundreds of other designs—practical and outrageous—all manufactured right on the premises. Custom-orders taken, too. And if rubber stamps aren't your thing, for peanuts you can get a plastic Hula girl, chocolate cow, lobster-claw-shaped harmonica, blinking Christmas-bulb earrings with matching necklace, itsy-bitsy plastic ants and creepy bigger bugs, a l'il fridge inches high stocked with food-shaped desk supplies, palm-tree-shaped pens, plus all sorts of stationery, cards, handmade jewelry, mugs, wind-up toys—the whole kit and kaboodle of eccentric doodads. Inkadinkado sometimes sells from a pushcart at **Faneuil Hall Marketplace**, and a mail-order catalog is available. ◆ M-F 8:30AM-6PM; Sa 10AM-5PM, Oct-Dec; call for other Sa hrs. 105 South St (East-Beach Sts) 426.3458

25 **John Gilbert Jr. Co.** Established in 1830, this great spirits shop is Boston's oldest. It began as a purveyor of fancy groceries and delicacies; the ancient store ledgers are fascinating for their flowery penmanship alone. In addition to fine wine and beers, all kinds of liquid treasures are sold. ◆ M-Sa 9AM-6:30PM. 107 South St. 542.8900

25 **Cecil's on South Street** ★$$ Located in the 1888 **Beebe Building**, friendly Cecil's warms up its exposed bricks-and-beams interior with vivid Caribbean-style posters, fish statues, mobiles, ceiling fans, decorated wooden booths, and background jazz. The Colombian chef orchestrates an interesting rapprochement of Mexican and Latin, Caribbean, Italian, and American dishes at lunch, with a dinnertime focus on excellent Cuban-Latin cuisine. Try *ropa vieja, pollo borracho, pargo al ajillo*, or turkey potpie. Full bar. ◆ International/American/takeout ◆ M-Th 7AM-9:30PM; F 7AM-11PM; Sa 5-10PM. Closed mid June-Labor Day. 129 South St (East-Beach Sts) Reservations recommended at dinner. 542.5108

26 **Bromfield Gallery** Boston's oldest artist-owned cooperative gallery exhibits work ranging from Realist to abstract and conceptual art, displaying prints, paintings, photographs, and other media by a stable of a dozen-or-so artists. Shows change frequently: individual, group, invitational, and juried. ◆ Tu-Sa 10AM-5:30PM. 90 South St (East-Beach Sts) 451.3605

26 **Ware on Earth** The showroom for **Pot Specialists, Inc.**, local importers, this shop sells containers and planters from Thailand, Malaysia, Greece, Italy, China, and other countries. Some of the striking vessels are one-of-a-kind or antique, and some are enormous—such as antique Greek oil drums. Prices start very low and keep climbing. ◆ M-F 11:30AM-5:30PM. 104 South St (East-Beach Sts) 451.5995

27 **Interior Resources** Jonathan Diamond travels extensively to buy objects from throughout the world for residential and corporate interiors. His showroom is an eclectic presentation of contemporary and traditional home furnishings, decorative accessories, and antiques. It's fun to browse through while gallery-hopping in the neighborhood. ◆ Tu-F 11AM-6PM; Sa 10AM-5PM; and by appointment. 745 Atlantic Ave (Entrance Beach-South Sts) 542.5797

28 **Howard Yezerski Gallery** A bright, inviting gallery that strives to be a little offbeat and untraditional. It shows contemporary painting, sculpture, and photography by established and emerging artists from the USA and Europe, with a core group of 20-plus artists and guest exhibitors including **Natalie Alper, Domingo Barreres**, and **Paul Shakespear**. ◆ Tu-Sa 10AM-5:30PM. 186 South St (Beach-Kneeland Sts) 426.8085

28 **Harcus Gallery** Looking like it strayed from New York's SoHo, Harcus specializes in contemporary and major 20th-century painting, sculpture, graphics, and furniture. Gallery art-

Waterfront/Fort Point Channel

ists include **Philip Pearlstein, Pat Steir, Kenneth Noland, Beverly Pepper, Anthony Caro, Frank Gehry, Alex Katz, SherrieLevine**. ◆ Tu-Sa 9:30AM-5:30PM. 210 South St (Kneeland St) 262.4445

29 **Thomas Segal Gallery** Look for the signature clock. The 2nd-floor gallery mounts contemporary painting, sculpture, works on paper, photography, and ceramics by internationally and nationally known artists and local rising talent: **Olivia Parker, Jo Sandman, Nancy Haynes, Jannis Kounellis, Ed Ruscha, Mary Heilmann, David Ortins, Stephen Westfall, Catherine Lee**, to name a few. Modern masters exhibited include **Cy Twombly, Miquel Barcelo, Donald Judd**, and **Sol LeWitt**. Two concurrent exhibitions change every 4-6 weeks. ◆ Tu-Sa 10AM-5:30PM. 207 South St (Beach-Kneeland Sts) 292.0789

29 **Robert Klein Gallery** An important destination for photography collectors, this 5th-floor gallery exhibits, appraises, purchases, and sells stunning international 19th- and 20th-century photographs, many rare. More than 150 photographers are represented, including **William Henry Fox Talbot, Diane Arbus, Ansel Adams, Robert Mapplethorpe, Eugene Atget, Edward Weston, Richard Avedon**, and **Man Ray**. Special offerings have included **Lucien Aigner**'s limited-edition *Einstein Portfolio*. ◆ Tu-F 10AM-5:30PM; Sa noon-5PM. 207 South St (Beach-Kneeland Sts) 482.8188

The scientific name of the humpback whale, *Megaptera novaeangliae*, means *big-winged New Englander*. The whale's low whistlelike sound is so intense that—at certain depths—it can be heard across the globe.

Restaurants/Clubs: Red Hotels: Blue
Shops/Parks: Green **Sights/Culture:** Black

30 The Blue Diner ★$ There's no place else like it in Boston. Straddling this corner since 1947, the bluer-than-a-bluebird diner was carefully refurbished a few years ago, keeping its old character but acquiring a new sheen. A wonderful hangout—unfortunately, a *lot* of people think so—the diner has its original working *Seeburg* sound system, with *Wall-o-Matic* selectors at every booth—2 plays per quarter let you listen to a parade of vintage 45s: **Elvis, Aretha Franklin, Jerry Lee Lewis, Louis Armstrong**. Formerly a workingperson's haunt, the Blue Diner hasn't lost its old clientele, just gained a wider following. To the requisite rib-sticking diner fare—the daily *Blueplate Specials*

Waterfront/Fort Point Channel

include meatloaf, roast turkey and homemade gravy, and franks and beans—owner **Don Levy** has added imaginative grilled seafood items, Mississippi BBQ, vegetable fritters, vegetarian offerings. Unlike the average diner, all the food is *real* here—no mixes—right down to the maple syrup and magnificent mashed potatoes. The French fries are from scratch too. The Blue Diner starts the day early, as any respectable diner should, with hearty breakfasts. It's considering a 24-hour operation. Order a cup of coffee to go; it comes in a great Blue Diner-motif paper cup. ♦ Diner/American ♦ M-W 7AM-11PM; Th-Sa 24 hrs; Su 7AM-10PM. 178 Kneeland St (South St) 338.4639

31 Loading Zone ★$$ Located in a former warehouse (renovated by **SITE Projects Inc.**) and run by **Don Levy**, who also owns the ever-popular **Blue Diner** a few strides away, this is a barbecue pit with art gallery aspirations. The food is pretty good—not great—with best bets including the pulled pork (entree or sandwich), smoked-beef brisket, babyback ribs, BBQ chicken, Killer Chili, sweet-potato chips, onion rings. Or come for a down-home breakfast complete with grits. But the Zone's truly distinctive draw is its artful tables: each glass-topped shadow box holds the creation of a local artist. Come in off-hours so you can tour the tables, which range from funny to whimsical to outrageous to arresting. Eventually these tables will be auctioned and a new round commissioned. ♦ Barbecue ♦ M-W 11AM-11PM; Th-F 11AM-midnight; Sa 10AM-midnight; Su 10AM-11PM. 150 Kneeland St (Lincoln-South Sts) Reservations recommended Th-Sa nights. 695.0087 &

Chowder got its name from *chaudière*, the French word for cauldron, in which Canada's early Breton settlers simmered their fish soups.

32 F.C. Meichsner Company *The* source for binoculars, telescopes and accessories, barometers and ships' clocks, and replicas of old telescopes—the best optics for your money. Founded in 1916, this family-owned and -operated business is the only East Coast establishment that can fix and repair all makes and models of binoculars and telescopes. ♦ M-F 9AM-6PM; Sa 10AM-4PM. 182 Lincoln St (Beach-Kneeland Sts) 426.7092

New England Clam Chowder

(Serves eight as a main course)

10 pounds quahogs in the shell

scraps of onion, celery, thyme and bay leaf (optional)

$1/4$ pound smoked bacon or salt pork,
    cut in small ($1/4$ inch) dice (see Note)

2 medium onions,
    cut in medium ($1/2$ inch) dice (2 $1/2$ cups)

2 bay leaves

1 tablespoon chopped fresh thyme

2 tablespoons unsalted butter

5 or 6 red or white new potatoes,
    roughly cut in $1/2$-inch dice

2 cups heavy cream

freshly ground black pepper

2 tablespoons chopped fresh parsley

For Serving:

common crackers

cream biscuits

clam fritters

1. Scrub the quahogs thoroughly and place in a large pan with 2 cups water and any scraps of onion, celery, thyme and bay leaf you may have around. Cover and place on high heat until the quahogs are steamed completely open.

2. Pour off liquid and reserve. Remove the clams from their shells; roughly chop (about $3/8$-inch pieces); set aside. Carefully pour the liquid (about 3 cups) through a fine strainer; set aside.

3. Slowly render the bacon or salt pork in a soup pot until slightly crisp. Add the onions, bay leaves, thyme and butter. When the onions are translucent, add the potatoes and the broth from the quahogs. Simmer until potatoes are cooked (about 12 minutes).

4. Add the chopped clams and cream and simmer 5 minutes more. Season to taste with pepper and add chopped parsley. Ladle into soup plates or cups. Serve with common crackers, cream biscuits and clam fritters.

Note: Salt pork is traditional, but I prefer the smoky flavor the bacon imparts.

Jasper White's Cooking From New England

Boston sailor-historian **Samuel Eliot Morison** wrote: *A summer day with a sea-turn in the wind. The Grand Banks fog, rolling in wave after wave, is dissolved by the perfumed breath of New England hayfields into a gentle haze, that turns the State House dome to old gold, films brick walls with a soft patina, and sifts blue shadows among the foliage of the Common elms. Out of the mist in Massachusetts Bay comes riding a clipper ship, with the effortless speed of an albatross.*

The Boston Harbor Islands

Whether basking in summer heat or silvery winter light, the harbor islands offer wonderful respite from city crowds and new perspectives on Boston's connection to the sea. Thirty islands dot the inner and outer harbors, a number of which belong to the **Boston Harbor Islands State Park** and are reached by ferries departing from **Long Wharf** or **Rowes Wharf**. Privately operated, the ferries charge fees and most go to **Georges Island**, the hub of the chain, where free water taxis transport visitors to 5 other islands. The **Department of Environmental Management** (DEM) and the **Metropolitan District Commission** (MDC) work together to manage state-owned islands. (The agency in charge is listed after the island name.)

It's easy to forget these delightful sanctuaries exist, so close but seemingly so far; they were created more than 20,000 years ago when melting glaciers raised the ocean's waters several hundred feet. Georges Island (MDC) is dominated by **Fort Warren** (1834-1860), massive 19th-century granite fortifications where Confederate soldiers were imprisoned during the Civil War. (A famous local legend tells of a young southern woman who slipped into Fort Warren to join her imprisoned Confederate husband. Caught in their escape, he was killed and she was executed as a spy. Thereafter, her ghost has appeared from time to time, roaming the fort, dressed in the black mourning gown that has given her the name the *Lady in Black*.) Guided tours and programs are offered by state park staff 6 months of the year. The 30-acre island is the perfect place for a picnic overlooking the distant cityscape, and has restrooms, an information booth, and a first-aid station. Sixteen-acre **Gallops Island** (DEM) also has picnic grounds, a pier with a large gazebo, shady paths, meadows, and remnants of a WWII maritime radio school. **Lovell Island** (MDC), 62 acres large, offers the only supervised swimming beach—though you'd probably prefer to do no more than wade a bit until the harbor is cleaned up—a picnic area with hibachis and tables, camp sites, and a system of walking trails through meadows, saltmarsh, dunes, and woods; a great destination for birders. One of the harbor's biggest islands, 188-acre **Peddocks** (MDC) also has picnic and camping areas and the remains of **Fort Andrews** occupying its **East Head**. Because the **West Head** is a protected salt marsh and wildlife sanctuary, access beyond recreational areas is restricted to organized tours or by permission of park staff. Tranquil **Bumpkin Island** (DEM) offers trails to an old children's hospital ruins and stone farmhouse, and its rocky beach is popular for fishing. Wild rabbits and raspberry bushes proliferate. Some campsites are available. **Grape Island** (DEM), named for the vines that grew here in Colonial times, feeds many birds with its wild bayberries, blackberries, and rose hips. Come here for birding, picnicking, camping, and meandering. Rugged **Great Brewster Island**'s (DEM) 23 acres afford splendid views of **Boston Light** on **Little Brewster**, the country's oldest lighthouse, and the outer harbor, but can only

be reached by private boat. The lighthouse on Little Brewster began blinking away on 14 September 1716. Destroyed by a 1751 fire, rebuilt, destroyed by the evacuating British in 1776 and rebuilt again, Boston Light is visible 27 miles out to sea, powered by two 1000-watt bulbs installed behind a 5-ton lens consisting of 336 glass prisms, bent into light beams that flash every 10 seconds. One of only 6 lighthouses in the country that are still manned, the 89-foot lighthouse has been threatened with automation—forestalled for now with the help of one fan, Mass. senator **Edward Kennedy**. The first lightkeeper, **George Worthylake**, drowned with his family when his boat capsized on the way back to Little Brewster in 1718. **Benjamin Franklin** wrote a poem on the tragedy. The names of the present and former keepers are etched on island rocks. Owned by the **Thompson Island Education Center**, 157-acre **Thompson Island** is open on a limited basis for guided tours, hiking, picnicking, educational programs, and conferences—you must call ahead. The center provides boat transportation to the island. It's important to remember that *no fresh water* is available on Gallops, Lovells, Bumpkin, Grape, or Great Brewster Islands—be sure to bring your own. Day-use permits are required

Waterfront/Fort Point Channel

for large groups; permits also required for camping and for alcohol consumption on some islands. ♦ For information or to obtain permits: MDC islands, 727.5290; DEM islands, 740.1605; Thompson Island Education Center, 328.3900. ♿ on Georges, Bumpkin, Thompson Islands

Friends of the Boston Harbor Islands
is a nonprofit organization dedicated to preserving the harbor islands' natural and historic resources. The group helps out on the islands and sponsors year-round public education programs, *living history* tours, and special boat trips. ♦ Information 523.8386

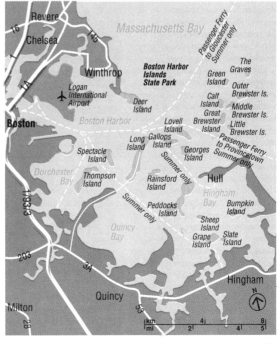

Financial District/ Downtown

Boston's most on-the-go neighborhood is its bustling retail core and financial district, bounded by the Boston Common to the west, the Central Artery and waterfront to the east; Government Center and Faneuil Hall Marketplace to the north, and Chinatown and the Theater District to the south. A bumper crop of skyscrapers have grown here in recent decades, celebrating the city's economic good health and transforming the skyline. The revitalized Downtown Crossing shopping area is cheerfully chaotic with pedestrians, pushcarts, and outdoor performers, luring shoppers to the internationally famous Filene's Basement and dozens of other stores and boutiques.

History's imprint is here as well: important Freedom Trail stops like the Old State House, Old South Meeting House, and Globe Corner Bookstore impart a vision of revolutionary-era Main Street. The Customs House Tower, State Street Block, and surviving wharf buildings designed by Charles Bulfinch speak of early wealth from the sea. Come during weekday work hours, when everything is open and in full swing. Walk along the profusion of twisty, tiny Colonial lanes that have turned into busy arteries shadowed by architectural giants, creating windy, dark New York City-style canyons. Businesslike street names—Water, Milk, State, Court, Broad, Federal, School—tell of the neighborhood's no-nonsense character. Numerous commercial palaces bear carved or fading traces of their original names, reflecting past lives.

From the city's earliest days, State Street was Boston's business artery, the most prestigious and spacious in town. Called King Street until the Revolution, State St stretched 800 feet from the Old State House to Long Wharf, the noble pier that once served as the city's highway to the sea. Where State intersects Washington Street was the epi-

center of Boston's commercial and financial life. Alas, State has lost its eminence, but many of its buildings bespeak former glory.

An old Indian trail, Washington St is now the major downtown commercial way. Always an important thoroughfare, it was the only road in the 17th and 18th centuries that ran the full length of Boston, linking the Old State House with the town gate at the neck of the **Shawmut Peninsula**. The street was renamed to honor **George Washington**'s visit to the city in 1789. Today, it becomes seedy beyond Temple Place as it heads toward the shrinking red-light district, the infamous **Combat Zone** (not a good place to be at night). Chockablock Washington is interesting, however, from beginning to end, with great streetscapes down the **Ladder Block** side streets toward the Common. Much of the existing Washington St area was built after the Great Fire of 1872, which leveled 65 acres bounded by Washington, Broad, Milk, and Summer streets, destroyed the heart of major New England industries, and left thousands without jobs. Many buildings still show scars and burns from the conflagration, which stopped just short of a number of Boston's historical treasures. Although the neighborhood was rapidly rebuilt, its residents had fled and commercialism took over. Boston's publishing and newspaper concerns flourished along **Newspaper Row** where Washington meets State and Court streets, and insurance, banking, retail, garment, manufacturing, and other industries stuck by their roots. The famous **Parker House** hotel and **Locke-Ober** restaurant also held on in the face of change, and to this day remain oases of gentility and aristocratic good living.

Economically, Boston was a Sleeping Beauty from 1895 until around 1965, so its building boom prince came late. Early skyscrapers are in short supply, but Boston does have its pleasing peculiar **Customs House Tower**, Art Deco **Batterymarch Building** and post office, lithe and lovely **Winthrop Building**. *If it ain't broke, don't fix it* is the Yankee credo; Bostonians have always had a talent for re-

Financial District/Downtown

cycling old structures. The city's fiscally conservative streak even influences new architecture. Unlike Chicago, for example, where buildings shoot up to the sky unimpeded, Boston prefers a more modest scale for its towers, so they politely accommodate older neighbors. Developers are subjected to stringent regulations and reviews. Some new buildings are dressed to the nines in decoration, but many are quite plain, even dowdy. It's as if the city is just getting used to its growing cosmopolitan stature and doesn't quite know how to dress the part.

The Financial District/Downtown neighborhood is large, but easily walked from any subway station in the area: **Park St** (**Red** and **Green Lines**), **State** (**Orange Line**), **Washington/Downtown Crossing** (**Red** and **Orange Lines**), **South Station** (**Red Line**), and **Government Center** (**Green** and **Blue Lines**) (the last 2 are just beyond this neighborhood's boundaries). The Park Street and Washington/Downtown Crossing stops are most convenient to the downtown shopping area; one block apart, either station can be reached from the other via an underground passage. The Government Center and State stops are near history and finance, and the South Station stop is just beyond the neighborhood's southeastern edge.

The first map compiled, drawn, engraved, printed, and published in America was of New England, produced in 1677 by Boston's first printer. The crude woodcut was prepared for **Hubbard**'s *A Narrative of the Troubles with the Indians in New England.*

1 Old State House (1712-1713, builder **William Payne**; rebuilt 1748, after gutted by fire; alterations 1830, **Isaiah Rogers**; restoration 1882, **George A. Clough**; restoration 1910, **Joseph E. Chandler**; National Historic Landmark) This lovable brick building, nicknamed the *Temple of Liberty*, has stubbornly survived centuries of tumult and transformation, witnessing more than its share of dramatic moments in local and American history. The structure is so remodeled and restored that its parts date from many eras. Situated at the head of State St, Old State originally commanded a clear view to the sea and in the mid-18th century became the political and commercial center of the **Massachusetts Bay Colony**. Its 1st floor was a merchants' exchange, with the wheels of government turning on the floors above. Even the site occupied an important place in the town's history, for the earliest Boston market square was located here, as were the stocks, pillory, and whipping post used to mete out 17th-century Puritan justice. In 1713, the building started life as a meeting place used by the British Crown's provincial governor, then later became the seat of the Commonwealth's new government after the Revolution sent the British packing once and for all. The ceremonial balcony at the State St end overlooks the site, marked by a star within a circle of cobblestones, where on 5 March 1770 frightened British soldiers fired on a large, angry mob of Bostonians, killing former slave **Crispus Attucks** and 4 others in the **Boston Massacre**. From this same balcony, the **Declaration of Independence** was first read to Bostonians on 18 July 1776. Every year since, the Declaration has been read from the same spot on the Fourth of July. **John Hancock** was inaugurated at Old State as the first governor under the new state constitution. And when **George Washington** visited Boston in 1789, he surveyed the great parade in his honor from here. But the monument's future was threatened after the new **State House** was built on **Beacon Hill**. The fantastical cavorting lion and unicorn on the elder edifice's gable, emblems of the hated crown, were frowned upon and removed. Old State eventually became a jack-of-all trades building, used and abused as a firehouse, commercial center, newspaper office, and, for a decade, Boston's City Hall.

The outcast's cause was championed just in time in 1881, when a private nonprofit organization called the **Bostonian Society** organized

Financial District/Downtown

to restore the building and preserve the rich history it had witnessed. Ever since, the society has called Old State home and maintained a marvelous museum featuring changing and permanent exhibitions on the Revolutionary era, maritime history, and other important chapters in the city's life. The Old State House's history is chronicled too. Paintings, portraits, figureheads, ship models, military and domestic artifacts, and other treasures tell the tale of this city quite well. The hook from which **John Brown**'s body hanged is on view, for instance; so too, is the coroner's report on Crispus Attucks. Look for the fabulous old commercial signs, such as the famous Blue Ball, which hung over the shop of **Benjamin Franklin**'s father; and for **Fitz Hugh Lane**'s painting *View of Boston Harbor*. A lovely spiral staircase leads to where inaugurations, daily government, and momentous meetings took place. For those who want to dig deeper, the society's splendid library across the street on the 3rd floor of 15 State St comprises more than 6000 volumes and 1000 maps and architectural plans, plus rare manuscripts and broadsides. The library also owns more than 10,000 Boston views in photographs, prints, watercolors, and drawings. Another great resource is librarian **Philip Bergen**, who holds much of Boston's history right in his head. Happily, the Old State House has flourished under the society's care. Unicorn and lion now prance with pride, copies elevated to the original animals' lofty perches. Another testament to the building's resilience: the presence of the State St subway station tucked underneath. For hours, check across the way at the **Visitor Center**. ♦ 206 Washington St (State St)

In 1772, the first stagecoach to New York departed from in front of the **Old State House**.

A bookshop once stood near the **Old State House**, where the first Bibles printed in America were sold, and where **Edgar Allan Poe**'s first volume of verse was published. No copies sold, a first blow among the many that darkened Poe's view of life.

Old State House

1 Visitor Center, National Park Service
Located across the way from the **Old State House**, the center is operated by the **Boston National Historic Park Service**, which is comprised of 8 historic sites: the Old State House, **Old South Meeting House, Faneuil Hall, Paul Revere House, Old North Church, Bunker Hill Monument, Charlestown Navy Yard**, and **Dorchester Heights**. In addition to offering information about these places, including a brief film, the center's staff of park rangers and volunteers answers questions about Boston and the entire National Park system. Find out about tours, many of which start from here. Pick up free **Freedom Trail** maps and pamphlets about all kinds of places, activities, events. The center also sells books and souvenirs. *Important*: Well-kept restrooms, water-fountains, and telephones are available here, public conveniences hard to come by in Boston. There are places to sit and rest weary bones. ◆ Daily 9AM-5PM, Jan-May, Sep-Dec; daily 9AM-6PM, June-Aug. Closed Thanksgiving, Christmas, New Year's Day. 15 State St (Washington-Devonshire Sts) 242.5642 &

2 Exchange Place (1889-1891, **Peabody and Stearns**; restoration and tower addition 1981-1984, **WZMH Group**) Opinions vary wildly about this blending of old and new. Actually, all that remains of the original **Stock Exchange Building** is a 60-foot segment of its worthy granite facade on the State St side, now arrogantly engulfed by the glassy tower. From some vantage points, its dark reflective surfaces shimmer interestingly, but overall the new building is, well, tacky. A handsome restored marble staircase is the atrium's incongruous centerpiece. This was the site of the historic **Bunch of Grapes Tavern**, located at the head of **Long Wharf** during the 19th century. A favorite watering-hole for patriot leaders before the Revolution, the tavern reputedly served the best bowl of punch in Boston. ◆ 53 State St (Congress-Kilby Sts)

3 75 State Street (1988, **Graham Gund Associates**) Some love and some hate this unabashedly gilded and gaudy showpiece. It simply refuses to be ignored on the skyline. The lobby looks like an example of tender loving care gone too far, with its plethora of patterns, types of marble, fancy fixtures—but the vast atrium lets in plenty of pure unadulterated light. ◆ Kilby St

4 Richards Building (c. 1859) In a neighborhood dominated by solid and substantial granite, this stunning cast-iron-front building has a much more frivolous demeanor. The lavishly arcaded facade was made in Italy and assembled in Boston. ◆ 114 State St (Merchants-Chatham Rows)

4 Cunard Building (1901, **Peabody and Stearns**) The boldly inscribed name on this Classical Revival building recalls another bright moment in Boston's past. The building was once the headquarters for the famous **Cunard Steamship Line**, which pioneered transatlantic steamship routes. Boston was proud to beat out New York City as the first American city to enjoy the innovative service. Nautical motifs aplenty—crowned Poseidon heads, anchor-and-dolphin lighting stanchions, a wave like ornamental

band—add an adventurous air to an otherwise sober structure. ◆ 126 State St (Merchants-Chatham Rows)

5 Board of Trade Building (1901, **Winslow and Bradlee**) This elaborate, urbane building has aged well. Its allegorical figures and vigorous stone carvings hearken to seafaring days gone by, especially the galleons rushing forward into the viewer's space. ◆ 131 State St (Broad-India Sts)

6 Custom House Tower (1837-1847, **Ammi Young**; tower addition 1913-1915, **Peabody and Stearns**) A preposterous marriage of convenience between a Greek Revival temple dating from one century and a 30-story tower plunked on top of it during the next originally appalled many Bostonians. After all, the proud Customs House was once the focal point of the thriving waterfront. Situated at the base of State St, the important Colonial route that once led from the **Old State House** and neighboring financial establishments out onto the wharves, the original Customs House was mammoth to begin with, each of its 32 Doric columns a single 42-ton shaft of Quincy granite. As the 20th century progressed and skyscrapers sprouted in other cities, Boston was mired in an economic slump. The federal government forked over the funds for the tower addition, which at 495 feet became the city's first—for a long time, only—skyscraper. It took awhile, but Bostonians have become very attached to their peculiar landmark, now a familiar friend. No matter how many new structures crowd the

skyline, the steadfast tower is the most memorable silhouette, its refurbished clock aglow at night. The little 25th-floor observation balcony is still a great place to scan the harbor and Financial District, and the lobby beneath the original building's rotunda—skylit until the tower leapt on top—deserves a look. Unfortunately, the interior is off limits for now until the building's fate is decided. The city bought the Customs House Tower from the federal government in 1987 and the plan is to open offices and possibly a sports museum or museum of the City of Boston, but the building remains shut during the funding scramble. ◆ State St (India St)

During the '60s and '70s, all 4 clock faces on the neglected **Custom House Tower** told different times. When installed in 1916, the 4-sided marble-and-bronze clock was the largest in the US. Its dials are 22 feet across, the minute hand 13 feet 8 inches long, and the clock numerals each a yard high. **Boston Edison Co**. restored the clock as a gift after the city bought the building in 1987. The wooden hands were replaced with aerodynamically molded hands made of a plastic composite used on Trident submarines and the space shuttle, then covered with 23 carat gold leaf to improve their visibility. Also in 1987 a new tradition was inaugurated: the Custom House Tower countdown to midnight on New Year's Eve, punctuated by laser displays and fireworks.

7 State Street Block (1858, Gridley J. Fox Bryant) One of the architects for the **Old City Hall** on School St, not to mention **Boston City Hospital** in the South End and the **Charles Street Jail** on Cambridge St, industrious Bryant also built a number of large granite warehouses that once extended to the harbor. Only one fifth of its original length, amputated to make way for new roads, this massive granite block looks proudly stern, as if admonishing: *Don't try to chop off any more of me!* Look for the big granite globe squeezed under the arched cornice facing the **Custom House Tower**. The mansard roofs were added later. ♦ 1 McKinley Sq (State St)

Within the State Street Block:

Tatsukichi and Club 189 ★★$$ Its unremarkable looks are deceiving, since this is one of Boston's superior and authentic Japanese restaurants. Explore the enormous sushi selection. Try teriyaki, sukiyaki, *kushiage* (skewers threaded with meats and vegetables, then batter-fried) or *shabu shabu,* the pot-cooked dinners for 2. Twenty percent of the menu is raw fish, and many uncommon entrees will pique an adventurous eater's curiosity. If you'd like privacy for your party, request a tatami room. Tuesday-Saturday nights, friendly **Jim Mullen** runs the bar. Upstairs is **Club 189**, Boston's only *kara-oke* (bottle club), where regulars—mainly Japanese businessmen—buy and store their drinks by the bottle. The club is open Monday-Saturday, 8PM-closing; there's a cover charge. It can get lively

Financial District/Downtown

here, with people singing and dancing to piano music. A tip for those driving: park all day at **200 State St**. Shop, eat, then get your parking ticket validated at Tatsukichi—but be out by midnight. ♦ Japanese ♦ M-F 11:30AM-2PM, 5-10PM; Sa 5-10PM; Su 5-9:30PM. 189 State St (Surface Artery) Reservations recommended. 720.2468

Newspaper Row, Boston's version of London's Fleet Street, once dominated the end of Washington St near the **Old State House**. In addition to newspaper publishers, booksellers plied their trade in this neighborhood. For close to a century, *The Boston Globe*, founded in 1872, occupied the site where the 42-story **Devonshire** building now stands. The Boston *Journal* was on the north corner of Water St and the Boston *Traveller* opposite the **Old South Meeting House**. At the south corner of Milk St at **No. 322-328 Washington, Gridley J. Fox Bryant's Boston Transcript Building** (1873) still stands, as does **Peabody and Stearns' Boston Post Building** (1874) next door at 17 Milk, which coincidentally inhabits the site of **Benjamin Franklin**'s birthplace. Born in 1706 to **Josiah** and **Abiah Franklin**, he was the youngest of the ten surviving children in an impressive brood of 17, and he became America's first ambassador to France. Benjamin was christened at the Old South Meeting House preceding the current 1729 structure. The extravagant cast-iron facade decoratively registers that fact, enshrining a Franklin bust.

Dockside $ At one of Boston's most popular sports bars, fans tune in 7 TVs and 2 big screens to watch the games. Dockside has been named one of the country's top 10 sports bars by *Sport* magazine. Better known for its drinks, rah-rah decor, comradery, and celebrity customers than cuisine, Dockside serves bar food basics like pizzas, BBQ, burgers. The full menu is available until 11PM, with snacks sold until midnight. One memorable night, **Jack Nicholson** tended bar. Sports stars often drop by, including **Larry Bird, Marvin Hagler**, assorted **Bruins**, and visiting players, so many fans bring autograph books. ♦ American ♦ Daily 11AM-2AM. 183 State St (Surface Artery) 723.7050

8 Central Wharf Buildings (1816-1817, **Charles Bulfinch**) On the opposite side of the Central Artery, Central Wharf concludes at the harbor's edge. The humble but handsome row of 8 brick buildings lingering here between India St and the elevated expressway are all that remain of the 54 designed by Bulfinch, which extended nearly 1300 feet to where the **New England Aquarium** now stands. All of the buildings originally opened onto the water, to receive goods from the ships parked right out front. ♦ 146-176 Milk St (India St)

9 Flour and Grain Exchange Building (1893, **Shepley, Rutan, and Coolidge**) This commercial castle brings a surprising fillip of fantasy to the hardnosed Financial District. The conical roof of the exchange's curvacious corner is bedecked with pointy dormers that look like a crown. Architect **H.H. Richardson**'s influence is palpable in this design by his successors, who also built the impressive **Ames Building** on Court St. Look for the extraordinary cartouche adorned with an eagle straddling a globe and cornucopias spilling fruit and coins. The exchange was built for the Chamber of Commerce and once housed a large trading hall on the 3rd floor. Now architects hold court within. Don't bother to visit the lobby; the original was renovated into oblivion. With its lanterns and scattering of trees, the building's triangular plaza is an oasis in this unexpectedly quiet corner of the city. ♦ 177 Milk St (India St)

10 Mrs. Fields Cookies Ultrarich, chewy, and chocolately cookies bring a steady stream of sweet-toothed customers to Mrs. Fields', one of 700 shops in the national chain. Choose from the rich repertoire of chocolate-chip varieties, or try oatmeal raisin or cinnamon sugar. Brownies and muffins too. ♦ M-F 8AM-7PM; Sa 11AM-7PM; Su 11AM-6PM. 264 Washington St (Water St) 523.0390 ♦ Also at: 426 Washington St (in Filene's) 357.9727; Copley Pl. 536.6833; Marketplace Center at Faneuil Hall, 200 State St. 951.0855

10 Merchants Wine & Spirits This former bank now secures a liquid treasure. One of the city's finest wine and spirits shops, Merchants offers unusual vintages as well as inexpensive drinkable monthly specials. Rare cognacs and superior Burgundies are a specialty, and there's a large California section. Tastings are held regularly in the old bank vault at the back, its walls still lined with safety deposit boxes. A blooming cheese department sells superb cheeses from small New England farmsteads, plus imports. Merchants publishes a very informative, chatty newsletter. ◆ M-F 9AM-6:30PM; Sa 10:30AM-5:30PM. 6 Water St (Washington-Devonshire Sts) 523.7425

11 Winthrop Building (1893, **Clarence H. Blackall**; National Register of Historic Places) Boston's first building with a steel skeleton instead of load-bearing masonry walls, the slim Winthrop slips gracefully into a tapering lot. Conceived by one of Boston's more adventurous architects, the gently curving building flows between Spring and Water streets. Its golden airiness and dressy decoration, especially on the lower levels, delight the eye. Architect Blackall's Chicago training was a fantastic boon to Boston. He designed a number of majestic theaters and other public buildings. Among Boston's other early steel-frame office buildings are this charming pair nearby: **Cass Gilbert's Brazer Building** of 1896 and **Carl Fehmer's Worthington Building** of 1894, standing side-by-side at **27** and **33 State St.** ◆ 276-278 Washington St (Spring Ln-Water St)

Within Winthrop Building (around corner, facing Water St):

Caffè Paradiso $ Another spin-off of a favorite North End meeting place, the caffè sells quick Italian treats to take away (counters, no tables). In addition to steaming cappuccino, espresso, and Italian beverages, they carry savory calzones, pizzas, quiches, cannoli, and delicious desserts, including a popular hazelnut truffle torte. ◆ Italian/takeout ◆ M-Sa 6AM-5PM. 3 Water St (Washington St) No credit cards. 742.8689 ᴋ Also at: 255 Hanover St. 742.1768; 1 Elliot Pl, Harvard Sq, Cambridge. 868.3240

12 The Globe Corner Bookstore (c. 1718; renovation and rear addition 1828; restoration 1960-1964, Francis N. Cummings, Jr; National Register of Historic Places) This prized relic of Colonial Boston is quite comfortably ensconced on its corner site. The red-brick, gambrel-roofed house was built for Thomas Crease, who opened Boston's first apothecary shop within. In 1828, Timothy Carter, a bookseller, took over and installed printing presses and opened the Old Corner Bookstore on the 1st floor. Thus was inaugurated the building's long career as the locus of Boston's publishing industry and literary life. Here Ticknor and Fields published

works by Harriet Beecher Stowe, Dickens, Tennyson, Browning, Thoreau, Hawthorne, Thackery, Julia Ward Howe, and Emerson, helping establish a native literature. Gregarious Jamie Fields in particular gained respect as counsel, friend, and guardian to authors, and was especially loved as an innovator who believed authors ought to be paid for their pains! Here too, The Atlantic Monthly was founded and rose to cultural eminence. The Boston Globe's downtown offices once occupied the building, whose preservation the newspaper ensured by opening its namesake bookstore in 1982. The current shop sells a wealth of works on New England and books by regional authors, plus a fine selection of guidebooks and world travel information on a floor also devoted to maps, globes, atlases. You can always find unusual cards, calendars, cookbooks, and marvelous children's books. ◆ M-Sa 9AM-6PM; Su noon-6PM. 3 School St (Washington St) 523.6658. Also at: 49 Palmer St (travel only) Harvard Sq, Cambridge. 497.6277

13 Brookstone The brainchild of engineer Pierre de Beaumont, a frustrated hobbyist who sought specialized tools that weren't available, Brookstone is a specialty store that stocks more than 1000 well-made, practical, and sometimes pricey tools and gifts. The inventory focuses on unusual, hard-to-find items and includes shop and gardening tools, small electronics, housewares, personal care items, exercise and sports equipment, indoor and outdoor games, desk items, travel and auto-

Financial District/Downtown

motive accessories. De Beaumont started Brookstone as a mail-order catalog business, then launched the innovative retail system used in the 95 Brookstone stores nationwide. It works this way: each store is like a giant 3D catalog, with information cards accompanying all displayed goods. Customers pick up and examine whatever interests them, fill out order forms and present them at the desk, then wait for purchases to be delivered by conveyor belt. Mail-order catalogs are available too. ◆ M-Sa 9:30AM-7PM; Su noon-5PM. 29 School St (Tremont-Washington Sts) 742.0055 ᴋ Also at: Copley Pl. 267.4308; Faneuil Hall Marketplace. 439.4460

After the **Boston Massacre**, **John Adams** and **Josiah Quincy** bravely undertook the legal defense of the accused soldiers. Although both men were staunch patriots, they were dedicated to obtaining fair trials for the unfortunate defendants. Seven of the 9 were acquitted; 2 were branded on the hand for manslaughter.

The Vault, formally known as the **Coordinating Committee**, is a powerful, elite advisory group of influential business leaders who represent business interests in setting Boston's public agenda. The group was founded in 1959 by a **Lowell** and a **Coolidge** to help revitalize the city's financial state. When the Vault speaks, mayors, legislators, and other public officials listen.

14 Kirstein Business Branch (1930, **Putnam and Cox**) A branch of the **Boston Public Library**, Kirstein specializes in noncirculating business and financial references. It's located off the beaten trail on a pedestrian lane connecting School and Court streets. An interesting feature of the building is its Georgian Revival facade, which replicates the central pavilion of daring **Charles Bulfinch**'s architecturally innovative (for America) and financially disastrous **Tontine Crescent** residential development, built on Franklin St (1793-94) and demolished in 1858. It was this speculative real-estate scheme's failure that cost Bulfinch his inheritance, and turned him from an architect by choice into one by necessity. Several blocks away, part of Franklin St still follows the footprints of the vanished Tontine's curve. ♦ M-F 9AM-5PM. 20 City Hall Ave (School St-Pi Alley) 523.0860

14 Pi Alley Probably named for the printer's term *pi*, meaning spilled or jumbled type. As the story goes, type would spill from printers' pockets as they went to and from a popular colonial tavern located at the alley's end. A less common account claims the alley is actually *Pie* Alley, named for the tavern's popular pies.

15 Hungry Traveller $ Across from the **Kirstein Business Branch**, tucked into a quiet street behind **Old City Hall**, is an ideal cafeteria-style eatery for early-bird eggs and bacon, or a quick cheap sandwich. Five or 6 hot entrees are prepared daily, plus salads and soups. Hang back until you know what you want, because once

Financial District/Downtown

the no-nonsense counterhelp spot you, they'll demand your order. A lot of people come here —tourists and on-the-job Bostonians—and the staff likes to keep things moving. ♦ American/takeout ♦ M-F 6AM-4PM. 29 Court Sq (Pi Alley) No credit cards. 742.5989 &

16 Rebecca's Cafe $ Popping up all over Boston are these popular offspring of the original Rebecca's restaurant on **Beacon Hill**. The made-from-scratch hot entrees, salads, sandwiches, pastas, soups, pastries, and dreamy desserts are winning more and more fans. ♦ Café/takeout ♦ M-F 7AM-8PM; Sa 8AM-6PM. 18 Tremont St (Court St) No credit cards. 227.0020 & Also at: 112 Newbury St. 267.1122; 65 JFK St, Harvard Sq, Cambridge. 661.8989

17 King's Chapel (1749-1754, **Peter Harrison**; National Historic Landmark) The original 1688 chapel stirred Bostonians' ire, since it was the city's first place of worship for Anglicanism, the official Church of England that had driven Puritans from their homeland. The plain wooden structure was built at the behest of **Sir Edmund Andros**, the royal governor who took the reins when the Massachusetts Bay Colony charter was revoked—just one early link in the long chain of events leading to the Revolution. To avoid interrupting services, the substantial Georgian chapel of Quincy granite standing

today was actually erected *around* the original building, which was dismantled and heaved out the windows of its replacement. If King's Chapel seems squat, that's because the elaborate steeple Harrison envisioned atop its square tower was never built; funds ran out. But in one splendid finishing touch, the facade was embellished with a portico supported by Ionic columns. The harmonious Georgian interior has weathered the centuries well. Its pulpit is the oldest still in use in America on the same site. The pew dedicated to early royal governors' use later accommodated **George Washington** on his Boston visits, and other American worthies. Slaves sat in the rear gallery on the cemetery side, and condemned prisoners sat to the right of the entrance for a last sermon before being hanged on the **Common**. After the Revolution, once the British and Loyalists had evacuated Boston, the chapel was converted around 1789 into the first American Unitarian church. Some of the rich presents given to the earlier chapel by **William** and **Mary** of Britain are still in use, but most are now displayed at the **Boston Athenaeum**. One of the church's other treasures is **Paul Revere**'s largest bell, which he called *the sweetest bell we ever made*. Come hear the resonant Charles Fisk organ, a replica of the church's 1756 original; every Tuesday, free musical recitals begin at 12:15PM; every Wednesday, an organ prelude commences at noon, with worship service at 12:15PM. On Thursday, free readings of poetry in *the King's English* start at 12:15PM. No tours offered, but guides are on hand to answer questions during summer months. ♦ Tu-Sa 10AM-4PM, May-Oct; Tu-F 10AM-2PM, Sa 10AM-4PM, Nov-Apr. 58 Tremont St (School St) 523.1749 &

Adjacent to King's Chapel:

King's Chapel Burying Ground Boston's earliest town cemetery's first resident was **Isaac Johnson**, who owned the land and was buried here in 1630. So many Boston settlers so quickly followed suit that some wag noted, *Brother Johnson's garden is getting to be a poor place for vegetables*. A pleasant neighbor today, the church next door was erected on land seized from the burying ground. Burials continued until 1796, although a gravedigger complained in 1739 that King's and 2 other local graveyards *were so fulled with dead bodies that they were obliged oft times to bury them four deep*. As in other Boston cemeteries, grave markers were moved about to accommodate newcomers, an unsettling practice that caused **Oliver Wendall Holmes** to complain: *the upright stones have been shuffled about like chessmen and nothing short of the Day of Judgment will tell whose dust lies beneath. . . Shame! Shame! Shame!* The Burying Ground's inhabitants include governors **John Winthrop** and **John Endicott**. On the chapel side, look for the 1704 gravestone of **Elizabeth Pain**, who supposedly bore a minister's child and probably was **Nathaniel Hawthorne**'s model for **Hester Prynne** in *The Scarlet Letter*. Also buried here is Sons of Liberty courier **William Dawes**, who rode through the night just as bravely as **Paul Revere**, but didn't have the posthumous good fortune to be lionized in a **Longfellow** poem. And for a sample of the Puritans' pessimistic stance on the snuffing of life's candle, look for **Joseph Tapping**'s stone. Stone rubbings are *not* allowed. ◆ M-Sa 8:30AM-3:30PM &

18 Omni Parker House $$$ Boston's genteel dowager hotel proclaims itself *the choice of legends since 1854*, and it's true: US presidents and celebrities of every stripe, from **Joan Crawford** to **Hopalong Cassidy**, have made themselves at home here. The Parker House is the oldest continuously operating hotel in America and represents the success story of Maine native **Harvey D. Parker**, who came to Boston with less than a dollar and became its leading hotelier. Rebuilt numerous times, the current structure dates to 1927. Attracting a business-oriented clientele, the Parker House offers 541 rooms on 14 floors, including handicapped-equipped rooms and nonsmokers' floors. A concierge is in attendance in the lobby, plus there's a computerized concierge system. Paid valet parking is available. Not too long ago, Boston's *old lady* hotel had some hard times and became shabby, but she has been lovingly restored and is luxuriant again, her centerpiece lobby clad in original oak woodwork with carved gilt moldings. Starting around 1855, the famous erudite **Saturday Club** met at the Parker House on the last Saturday of every month, its circle including many of the American literary and intellectual luminaries of the 19th century like **Hawthorne, Whittier, Emerson, Longfellow**. A spinoff group founded *The Atlantic Monthly* in 1859, a literary magazine that has enjoyed unflagging prestige. During one long Boston visit, the high-spirited, sociable **Charles Dickens** stayed at the hotel and joined the club's congenial gatherings, often fixing gin punch for his pals. The sitting-room mirror before which Dickens practiced his famous Boston readings now hangs on the mezzanine. On a more historical note, just 10 days before assassinating **Abraham Lincoln**, actor **John Wilkes Booth** stayed at the Parker House while visiting his brother **Edwin**, also an actor, who was performing nearby. John spent some time practicing at a nearby shooting gallery. And it was from the hotel's **Press Room** that JFK announced his candidacy for US president. **Parker's Bar** is known for its classic martini; try one with hors d'oeuvres, which are complimentary 5-7PM. By the way, the famous secret recipe for the soft Parker House roll was first created here (they bake 1308 of the fragrant rolls each day), as was the tasty but very unpielike Boston cream pie. Both are available in the restaurants and to take out. ◆ 60 School St (Tremont St) 227.8600, 800/THE-OMNI; fax 227.2120 &

Within Omni Parker House:

Parker's Restaurant ★★$$$ With vaulted ceilings and high wing-backed chairs, the restaurant is tranquil, roomy, and timeless. The good, reliable American cuisine—accompanied by those famous rolls—is undeservedly overlooked in Boston's frenetic dining scene. A harpist strums during the award-winning Sunday brunch, and piano music drifts in from **Parker's Bar** Monday-Saturday. ◆ American ◆ M-F 11:30AM-2:30PM, 5:30-10PM; Sa 5:30-11PM; Su 10:30AM-2:30PM. Valet parking (fee) Jacket preferred at lunch, required at dinner. Reservations recommended &

Café Tremont $ A sunny street-level spot offering splendid people-watching, the café serves moderately priced American fare and good desserts. This is a wonderful place for breakfast because even though the food isn't remarkable, it's fun to watch the city start up for the day from this busy corner. Lots of politicians and publishing people breakfast here. The takeout bakery features Parker House rolls, Boston cream pie, and other delicious favorites like chocolate mousse cake and fruit tarts. ◆ American ◆ M-F 6:30AM-2:30PM; Sa-Su 7AM-4PM. Reservations recommended at lunch &

The Last Hurrah! Bar and Grill ★$$ The place looks dated but that's the point—the walls are plastered with political memorabilia nostalgically harking back to when **Old City Hall** down the street was in full swing. And speaking of swing, the locally renowned

Financial District/Downtown

Winniker Swing Orchestra plays music ideal for dancing on Saturday from 7PM, attracting a loyal happy-feet crowd that's nicely diverse in age and background (there's no cover). There's also a swing brunch on Sunday. Monday-Friday, a DJ spins Top 40 hits and requests from 6PM. You can dine as well as drink here, but the food is nothing special. The bar is popular with the **State House** and **City Hall** sets. ◆ American ◆ M-F 11:30AM-1AM; Sa noon-2PM, 4PM-1AM; Su 11:30AM-2PM, 4PM-midnight. Reservations recommended &

Harvey Parker insisted on achieving culinary heights in his dining room, and was committed to satisfying even the most jaded appetite among Boston's prosperous, often-plump Victorians. One 11-course banquet ran this route: oysters, green-turtle soup, baked cod in claret sauce, leg of mutton, ham in champagne sauce, partridges with truffles and jelly, mayonnaise of chicken, sweetbreads, compote of pigeons, mongrel goose, aspic of oysters, snipe, blue-billed widgeon, yellow-leg and black-breasted plover, woodcock, black duck, bird-nest pudding, calf's foot and Madeira jellies, charlotte russe, mince, squash, lemon and apple pies, pears, oranges, peaches, walnuts, almonds, and raisins, coffee and olives.

Restaurants/Clubs: Red   Hotels: Blue
Shops/Parks: Green   **Sights/Culture:** Black

19 Old City Hall (1865, **Gridley J. Fox Bryant** and **Arthur Gilman**; renovation 1969-1970, **Anderson, Notter Associates**; National Historic Landmark) Replaced by modern **City Hall** at **Government Center**, this empress dowager is an exuberantly ornamental artifact of a more flamboyant era. The days when colorful Boston politicos like **James Michael Curley** held sway are long gone; retired in 1969, the old hall is no longer in the thick of things. For many visitors, it's a surprise to discover this French Second Empire edifice tucked away from the street. Still graced with ample arched windows and an imposing pavilion, the building has been sadly stripped of its magnificent interiors to accommodate offices and a restaurant. The exterior, however, is a great act of preservation. On either side of the entrance stand **Richard S. Greenough**'s statue of **Benjamin Franklin** (1855) and **Thomas Ball**'s of **Josiah Quincy** (1879), Boston's second mayor, who built **Quincy Market** and served as president of **Harvard College**. Franklin's likeness was the first portrait statue in Boston. Embedded in the sidewalk in front of the hall's cast-iron fence, look for **Lilli Ann Killen Rosenberg**'s appealing 1983 mosaic called *City Carpet*, which commemorates the oldest public school in the US. (Rosenberg lets you review your ABCs—in Boston, *G* is for *Grasshopper*, a few long hops away atop **Faneuil Hall**.) Erected near this site in 1635, the **Boston Public Latin School** gave School St its name and contributed influential alumni to American history books, including

Franklin, **John Hancock, Charles Bulfinch, Charles Francis Adams**, and **Ralph Waldo Emerson**. The school is now located near the **Fenway**. Rosenberg also created the mosaic located on the wall side of the subway's outbound Green Line platform in **Park St Station**, offering a delightful pictorial account of Boston history. ♦ 45 School St (Tremont-Washington Sts)

Within Old City Hall:

Maison Robert ★★★$$$$ The colorful political wheelings and dealings of Old City Hall belong to the past. But at Maison Robert, deals are still made, love affairs launched, marriages proposed, and other momentous occasions celebrated. For nearly 20 years, the superior French restaurant has made a happy home in the old hall. Inside Maison Robert, look for the brick vaulted ceilings and distinguished old doors, vestiges of the building's original interiors. **Ann** and **Lucien Robert** offer fine classic dishes, such as lobster bisque, rabbit sausage, country pâté, Dover sole, rack of lamb, and wondrous *tarte tatin* and crème brûlée. (Lucien recently was honored by the French Government with the *Chevalier du Merite* award for his contributions to French culture.) Upstairs is *Bonhomme Richard* (Poor Richard, in honor of **Franklin** and his famous almanac), the beautiful formal dining rooms with butternut wood-

work overlooking the **King's Chapel Burying Ground**; downstairs is the less fancy, very inviting **Ben's Cafe** (★★★$$$). It, too, was named for Franklin, and serves somewhat lighter and less expensive dishes. The Roberts' daughter **Andrée** skillfully undertakes the duties of chef. For private parties of 10-12 people, ask about dining in the **Vault**, the original City Hall vault. Maison Robert holds monthly wine-tasting dinners (put your name on the mailing list); and on the first Friday of each month hosts *The French Table* prix-fixe dinner, starting at 7:30PM with an apperitif social hour before. As many as 80 attend, native speakers and novices alike (reservations required). When spring comes, café tables and umbrellas appear on the lovely outdoor terrace, and the garden blooms again, signaling the return of a delightful dining spot. ♦ French ♦ M-F noon-2:30PM, 5:30-9:30PM (café), 6-10PM (upstairs); Sa 5:30-10:00PM (café), 6-10:30PM (upstairs); Su open for private parties and some holidays; inquire. Valet parking (fee) Jacket and tie required upstairs. Reservations recommended. 45 School St (Tremont-Washington Sts) 227.3370

20 Boston Five Cents Savings Bank (1926, **Parker, Thomas & Rice**; addition 1972, **Kallmann and McKinnell**) Adding on to a sedate Renaissance-style bank, the architects —who also designed the new **Boston City Hall** —created a dynamic building that's clearly as hard at work as its occupants. The remarkable addition has no secrets: its 5-story colonnade and enormous beams conduct their structural functions in plain view, and a glass curtain wall exposes all that goes on inside the bank. Big as it is, the building gracefully adapts to a tricky site and has earned its place in one of Boston's most historic quarters. The little park out front offers breathing space from Washington St crowds, and good views of the nearby Globe Corner Bookstore and the Old South Meeting House. ♦ 10 School St (Washington St)

21 Old South Meeting House (1729, **Joshua Blanchard**, builder; National Historic Landmark) After the **Old North Church** in the **North End**, this is Boston's oldest church—a traditional New England brick meeting house fronted by a solid square wooden tower that blossoms into a delicate spire. When nearby **Faneuil Hall**'s public meeting space grew too cramped, Bostonians congregated here for momentous town meetings peppered with fiery debate, to prepare for the coming Revolution and plan events like the **Boston Tea Party** of 1773. That cold December night, which Boston loves to remember, more than 5000 gathered at Old South to rally against the hated tea tax.

Old South Meeting House

South Association ever since. Step inside to experience Old South's restful simplicity. Because the British stripped the interior, only the upper-tiered galleries are authentic; teen-age boys, servants, slaves, and the town's poor once sat here. The award-winning permanent multimedia exhibition, *In Prayer and Protest: Old South Meeting House Remembers*, includes walls that talk, tapes of Boston Tea Party debates, a scale model of Colonial Boston, profiles of famous churchgoers, and artifacts. The museum shop sells unusual cards and souvenirs like penny whistles, quill pens, and soldier's dice made from musket balls. *Middays at the Meeting House*, an excellent series of monthly concerts and weekly lectures on American history and culture, runs October-April. Events are free with museum admission. In addition to hosting educational programs and performances, Old South still holds its place in Boston political life as the site for pub-lic debates, forums, and announcements of candidacies for office. During July and August, re-creations of 18th-century Boston town meetings are staged every Saturday at 2PM in **Boston Five Cents Savings Plaza** across the street, and bystanders are encouraged to participate. Tours for groups larger than ten are arranged with 2 weeks' advance notice. Out-side on the corner is Boston's largest and pret-tiest flower stand. ♦ Admission. Daily 10AM-4PM, Nov-Apr; daily 9:30AM-5PM, May-Oct. 310 Washington St (Milk St) 482.6439 ﾖ

Within Old South Meeting House (around corner, facing Milk St):

Financial District/Downtown

Goodspeed's Old South Branch In Old South's basement is a department of **Goodspeed's Book Shop**, purveyors of antiquarian books since 1898. One step in the door, and you'll sniff the unmistakable smell of old books. Goodspeed's sells and buys books on all subjects and does appraisals for institutions, estates, and government agencies, as well as individuals. Pick up a rare tome, or browse among the bargain book tables. They also carry maps. The main Goodspeed's is located at 7 Beacon St, 523.5970. ♦ M-F 9AM-5PM; Sa 10AM-3PM. (Closed Saturday, Jul-Sep) 2 Milk St (Washington St) 523.5970

Three ships filled with tea to be taxed were anchored at **Griffin's Wharf**, and the royal governor refused Bostonians' demands that the tea be sent back to England. **Samuel Adams** gave the signal igniting the protest that turned Boston Harbor into a teapot. During the British occupation, Redcoats struck back at the patriots by using their revered meeting place for the riding school of **General *Gentleman Johnny Burgoyne***'s light cavalry, complete with offic-ers' bar. By the time the British evacuated, the church was in a sorry state. The congregation finally moved back in, then decamped in 1875 to the **New Old South Church** in **Copley Square**. Among Old South Meeting House's early con-gregation members were **Phyllis Wheatley**, a freed slave and one of the first published black poets, **Elizabeth Vergoose**, a.k.a. *Mother Goose,* and patriots **James Otis, Samuel Adams**, and **William Dawes**.

Barely escaping destruction by the Great Fire of 1872, Old South was then nearly demolished to make way for commercial businesses. But Bostonians, including **Julia Ward Howe** and **Ralph Waldo Emerson**, contributed funds to purchase and restore the historic property, which has been maintained and operated as a national monument and museum by the **Old**

The first regularly issued American newspaper, *The Boston News-Letter*, was published in Boston in 1704.

Restaurants/Clubs: Red   **Hotels:** Blue
Shops/Parks: Green   **Sights/Culture:** Black

79

22 Rudi's ★$ Downstairs in this gourmet café, people flock for good morning coffee and croissants and light meals to go. Upstairs, more elaborate fare is served: personal-size pizzas, pastas, stuffed chicken breasts, wine and beer. Rudi's is also known for its sophisticated cakes, truffles, and other desserts. ♦ Café/takeout ♦ Downstairs takeout: M-F 7AM-5:30PM; Sa 9AM-4PM. Upstairs café: M-F 7:30AM-3:30PM; Sa 9AM-3PM. 1 Milk St (Washington St) 542.8660. Also at: 71 Summer St. 482.5544; 279 Newbury St. 536.8882

22 Blazing Salads $ This cheap quick-eats place serves all sorts of salads—chicken, tuna, Greek, niçoise, crabmeat, tabbouleh, to name a few—with lots of pita bread. Or try a tuna melt, chicken Oriental, steak teriyaki. Breakfast is offered until 11AM, and a piano plays from noon on. It's usually crowded here, but the efficient staff keeps traffic humming along. ♦ American/takeout ♦ M-F 7:30AM-6:30PM; Sa 7:30AM-4PM. 330 Washington St (Milk-Franklin Sts) No credit cards. 338.9614, 426.0864

23 Woolworth's Right in the thick of things is the very large, familiar granddaddy department store where you can purchase all kinds of inexpensive handy items and oddball gifts. Too bad the old lunch counter is no more, replaced by a Burger King. ♦ M-Sa 9:30AM-6:45PM; Su noon-5:45PM. 350 Washington St (Franklin St) 357.5353 & Also at: 633 Mass Ave, Central Sq, Cambridge. 876.7214

24 Bromfield Street This brief little street was once the location of Revolutionary hero **Thomas**

Financial District/Downtown

Cushing's residence, where the Massachusetts delegates to the first **Continental Congress** assembled, among them **Samuel** and **John Adams** and **Robert Treat Paine**. Today Bromfield is one of Boston's more interesting, lively commercial streets, packed with small establishments specializing in cameras, antiques, collector's coins and stamps, jewelry, watches, pens, not to mention pawn shops. Some great old buildings reside here, too, such as **Nos. 22** and **30** of 1848 and the **Wesleyan Association Building** at **No. 36** of 1870, all of granite.

24 Sherman's It's an unlikely spot for a department store, but once people discover Sherman's, they come back often for last-minute gifts, travel items, and housewares. In addition to major appliances and office equipment, Sherman's sells cameras, calculators, electronics, luggage, TVs, telephones, small appliances, cookware, jewelry, and miscellany for the manse. They also carry a number of items in other electrical currents, and arrange all shipping—including custom's —to foreign destinations. ♦ M, Th 9AM-6:30PM; Tu-W, F-Sa 9AM-5:30PM. 11 Bromfield St (Tremont-Washington Sts) 482.9610

25 Bruegger's Bagel Bakery $ Ten varieties of excellent bagels—Boston's best—are baked throughout the day at this family business, and are never more than 3-4 hours old. Bruegger's own factory also produces 8 different cream

cheeses to spread on top. If you want a more filling meal, try a sandwich-on-a-bagel accompanied by freshly made soup. Its decor is fast-food basic, but the restaurant is neat and clean, with plenty of seating. ♦ Bagels/takeout ♦ M-Sa 7AM-6PM; Su 8AM-5PM. 32 Bromfield St. No credit cards. 357.5577 & Also at: 636 Beacon St. 262.7939; 83 Mt Auburn St, Harvard Sq, Cambridge. 661.4664

26 Bromfield Pen Shop Accustomed to cheapo, use-and-abuse disposable pens? Wander into this little shop, gaze upon gleaming rows of new and antique pens, and reconsider your choice of writing instrument. What might that handsome handful of a lovingly restored Bakelite pen do for one's prose! In addition to standard brands such as Parker and Sheaffer, Bromfield carries Mont Blanc, Lamy, Pelikan, Yard-O-Led of England, S. T. Dupont, Waterman, Omas of Italy, even delicate glass pens. And plenty of ink varieties, of course. Engraving is free. The best store of its kind in New England, Bromfield Pen attracts customers from all over the country, including author **Jimmy Breslin** and playwright **Arthur Miller**, plus a plethora of local politicians, media, medical, literary, and legal types. Longtime manager **George Salustro** is not only expert at reconditioning or repairing customers' trusty old pens, he's a charmer, too. And he won't shame you if you decide what you *really* need for now is the same never-fail inexpensive pen used by Boston meter maids. The shop also stocks art supplies. If you have a nice old pen to sell, George might be interested. ♦ M-F 8:30AM-5:30PM; Sa 10AM-4PM. 39 Bromfield St (Tremont-Washington Sts) 482.9053 &

26 J.J. Teaparty Quality Baseball Cards A city that's passionate about sports in general and baseball in particular is the perfect place for this business. The tiny storefront, often crowded with wheeling-and-dealing kids, is owned by **Peter Leventhal**, whose father runs the coin shop with the same name one door away. Leventhal buys and sells mostly baseball cards, but also some for football, basketball, and hockey. He's got cards from the '50s and '60s, including Hall of Famers-that-were and -to-be. Unusual items crop up, like turn-of-the-century tobacco cards. Collectors can pick up the latest series by Score, Topps, Fleer, and others. ♦ M-F 10AM-5PM; Sa 10AM-4PM. 43 Bromfield St (Tremont-Washington Sts) 482.5705 &

26 J.J. Teaparty Coin Numismatists take note: for more than 30 years, owner **Ed Leventhal** has bought and sold coins at Bromfield St's premiere coin shop. Both casual collectors and serious investors come by to drop some coins of their own for proof sets, mint sets, and bullion coins like the American Eagle and Canadian Maple Leaf. ♦ M-F 9AM-4:30PM; Sa 9AM-2PM. Closed July-August. 51 Bromfield St (Tremont-Washington Sts) No credit cards. 482.2398

27 Province House Steps From Province St, mount the weathered steps that once led to the gardens of **Province House** (1679), the luxurious official residence of the royal governors of

Massachusetts Bay. Renamed **Government House** after the Revolution, the mansion was inhabited until 1796. Here **General Gage** ordered the Redcoats to Lexington and Concord; here, too, **General Howe** ordered his men to flee after **George Washington** and his troops managed to fortify Dorchester Heights, aiming big guns at the British. Years later, **Nathaniel Hawthorne** wrote about Province House, now a decaying tavern and inn, in *Twice-Told Tales.* Nary stick nor stone remains of the mansion except these steps. Up on the left, the modest Marliave is dressed up with bits of wrought iron and balconies. ◆ Bosworth St

27 Café Marliave $$ This restaurant has stood on its corner for so long—more than a century—that many Bostonians forget it exists. Then again, a cadre of loyalists keeps coming back. The Italian-American cooking is nothing to swoon over, but it's good and reasonably priced, with plenty of dishes to choose from. The same family has run the place for 60 years or so. The café sits high above the street, at the top of the Province House steps; dine on the 2nd floor by the windows and become part of the streetscape. ◆ Italian-American ◆ M-Th 11AM-9PM; F-Sa 11AM-10PM. 10 Bosworth St (alley off Province St) 423.6340

28 Tremont Temple (1895, **Clarence H. Blackall**) The fanciful Venetian stone facade made of 15 delicate shades of terra cotta that turns into a temple at the top incongruously fronts an office and church complex. It gets curiouser and curiouser with the added adornment of several elaborate balconies. The building stands on the site of the famous **Tremont Theater**, where illustrious 19th-century thespians, performers, lecturers, and politicians—including **Abe Lincoln**—enthralled the public. ◆ 88 Tremont St (School-Bromfield Sts)

Going to the Movies

Boston and Cambridge offer plenty of movie houses for first-runs, but there are a number of places to go for more unusual and international offerings. Call to find out about current programs, admission prices, discounts. Daily papers are best for first-run movie information; check the *Calendar* in *The Boston Globe* on Thursday and the *Boston Phoenix* on Fridays for special, foreign, and

revival films and series, including those shown at local colleges, universities, and libraries.

Boston Public Library Free movie series in a comfortable theater attracts the entire spectrum of Bostonians. A great place to satiate an urge to see all of **Katherine Hepburn**'s or **Cary Grant**'s classics or to see **Eugene O'Neill**'s plays brought to the screen, or other ever-popular greats. ◆ Rabb Lecture Hall, Copley Sq. 536.5400

Boston Video and Film Foundation Screenings of local, national, and international work by independent filmmakers. ◆ 1126 Boylston St. 536.1540

Brattle Theatre A very highly regarded independent repertory movie house offering classic Hollywood and foreign films, independent filmmaking, new art films, staged readings, and other performances. Different categories of double features offered most nights. ◆ 40 Brattle St, Harvard Sq, Cambridge. 876.6837

Ciné Club at the French Library A popular ongoing series of recent and classic French films, screened in a lovely setting. ◆ 53 Marlborough St. 266.4351

Coolidge Corner Theatre An innovative program of classic and contemporary local, national, and international films screened in a great old theater that was recently rescued from the spectre of gentrification. Animation and cartoon festivals and other special events. ◆ 290 Harvard St, Coolidge Cr, Brookline. 734.2500

Harvard-Epworth Series From silent movies with piano accompaniment to more recent art films. ◆ Harvard-Epworth Church, 1555 Mass Ave, Cambridge. 354.0837

Harvard Film Archive Repertory and contemporary international cinema. ◆ Carpenter Center for the Visual

Arts, 24 Quincy St, Cambridge. 495.4700

Institute of Contemporary Art Wonderful movies come to the ICA's tiny but very pleasant auditorium. Palestinian and Israeli films and an Argentinian film series have been screened here. Always worth investigating the schedule. ◆ 955 Boylston St. 266.5152

The Museum of Fine Arts The MFA regularly screens interesting alternative films from foreign to ethnic to documentary and avant-garde in **Remis Auditorium**. Japanese or Italian films might be on the plate, or **Ingrid Bergman**'s movies made in Sweden before she became a Hollywood star. Many films are shown here for the first time in this country. ◆ 465 Huntington Ave. 267.9300, ext 454

The Wang Center for the Performing Arts The **Classic Film Series** brings old and not-so-old favorites to this former movie palace's fabulous big screen, with live jazz beforehand in the lobby. ◆ 270 Tremont St. 482.9393

In addition to the Boston Public Library, a number of area libraries regularly screen free films, often as part of themed series. Libraries include: the **Brookline Public Library**, 361 Washington St, 730.2368; **Wellesley Free Library**, 530 Washington St, 235.1610; West End Branch Library, 151 Cambridge St, 523.3957; **Central Square Branch Library**, Pearl and Franklin Sts, Cambridge, 498.9081; **Mt. Auburn Branch Library** (children only), 64 Aberdeen Ave, Cambridge, 498.9085.

Restaurants/Clubs: Red   Hotels: Blue
Shops/Parks: Green   **Sights/Culture: Black**

29 Orpheum Theatre (1852, **Snell and Gregerson**) Originally called the **Music Hall**, the worldly Orpheum has seen a thing or 2. It housed the fledgling **New England Conservatory** and witnessed the **Boston Symphony Orchestra**'s debut concert in 1881. The **Handel and Haydn Society** performed here for years. **Tchaikovsky**'s first piano concerto had its world premiere here, **Ralph Waldo Emerson** and **Booker T. Washington** lectured, and **Oscar Wilde** promoted a **Gilbert and Sullivan** operetta. Vaudeville shows took a turn too. In the early 20th century, the theater was extensively altered, becoming Boston's first cinema, then later reverted back to a performance space. **The Opera Company of Boston** made its home here before moving to Washington St. Today, the Orpheum books rock concerts. ♦ Hamilton Pl (enter from Tremont St, between Bromfield-Winter Sts) No credit cards; to charge, call Ticketron. Recorded info 482.0650

30 Barnes & Noble Discount Bookstore A big general bookstore specializing in reduced-price bestsellers, discounted paperbacks and hardbacks, plus publishers' overstocks. It also sells children's books, magazines, board games, cards, local maps, and classical and jazz records, tapes, CDs. ♦ M-F 9:30AM-6:30PM; Sa 9:30AM-6PM; Su noon-5PM. 395 Washington St (Winter-Bromfield Sts) 426.5502 & Also at: 603 Boylston St, Back Bay. 236.1308

31 Filene's (1912, **Daniel Burnham and Company**) One of 18 stores in New England and New York, Filene's is a full-service department

store selling fashions and accessories for men, women, children, and the home. Formal, casual, and career clothing carry designer and major brand labels. The **Gift Gallery** stocks fine crystal, sterling, porcelains, and other specialty merchandise. Founder **William Filene** opened his first retail business in 1881. Filene's was the first—and probably only—department store to have a zoo on its roof, with a baby elephant flown in from Bangkok, plus lions, monkeys, and other wild animals. Sixty thousand children visited the zoo before it was demolished by the same hurricane that toppled **Old North Church**'s steeple in 1954. The distinguished but grubby terra-cotta face of Boston's popular department store is going to get a good scrubbing, and the drab 1972 addition just may get a makeover to make it a worthy escort for the original. The Chicago-style building boasts a grand corner clock. ♦ M-Sa 9:30AM-7PM; Su noon-6PM. Downtown Crossing, 426 Washington St (Summer St) 357.2100 &

In the 1840s, Italian émigré **Lorenzo Papanti**'s illustrious dance academy was located on **Tremont St** near **King's Chapel**. Here Papanti introduced the waltz to America, dancing the very first with socialite **Mrs. Harrison Gray Otis, Jr.**, in the opulent ballroom that boasted the nation's first dance floor on springs. Instantly, even the properest of *Proper Bostonians* couldn't get enough of this fad.

Downstairs in Filene's:

FILENE'S BASEMENT

Filene's Basement Far surpassing the fame of its parent store (the companies are now separately owned), the Basement opened in 1908, America's first off-price store. You can enter its 2 shopping levels from Filene's proper, or belowground from the **Downtown Crossing** subway station (**Red** and **Orange Lines**). There are now 26 Basements in 8 states, but the original is unsurpassed. Legends abound about this place and the determined do-or-die shoppers that regularly make it their mission to snag the best buys here. Many a quickie adulted course has been offered locally on how to *do* the Basement and come away flushed with success, laden with uncostly treasures. The simple formula: perseverance, skill, and dumb luck. Every day, trailers replenish the vast supply of overstocks, clearances, samples, and irregulars sold at 20-60 percent less than fine department stores. The inventory includes designer-label and bargain clothing and accessories for men, women and children, and housewares of all kinds. Retail stock is regularly featured from prestigious stores like Saks, Brooks Brothers, Bergdorf Goodman, and Neiman Marcus. Strike it lucky and you might come away with a steal of a wedding dress, or a winter coat, business suit, evening attire, luggage, lingerie, diamond ring, goosedown comforter, fine linen. Many fabulous finds come at end-of-season. On the lower level, there's also a designer boutique for women.

The Basement's famous automatic markdown system works this way: after 14 selling days on the floor, merchandise is reduced 25 percent; after 21 days, 50 percent; after 28 days, 75 percent. After 35 days, whatever is unsold goes to charity. If you find something after the 35 days, go to the *charity desk* and write a check directly to one of the organizations listed on the Basement's charities list. Crowds gather on the legendary Big Sale days, when the Basement opens early. Try to flip through a local Sunday paper, since many sales begin Monday. If you watch, you'll see how veterans work the room; you'll also see neat piles and racks of clothing and goods reduced to colorful chaotic heaps, and glassy-eyed, overstimulated novices escaping to the upper levels in defeat. And word has it, a monstrous Basement wrong will soon be righted: a dressing room will finally be installed in the women's departments, ending the awkward necessity to strip down to one's skivvies in public; the men's departments were already equipped. Conveniently, the Basement does have a return policy. ♦ M-Sa 9:30AM-7PM; Su noon-6PM. 542.2011, 348.7934 & (enter from Filene's, use elevator)

32 Jordan Marsh A stiff competitor to **Filene's** across the way, Jordan's is also an upscale comprehensive department store, part of a long-established Northeast chain. You'll find the whole kit and kaboodle here: clothing for men, women, and children, jewelry, shoes, cosmetics, housewares, home furnishings, and so on. Try the bakery's blueberry muffins. *A tradition since 1851*, as its slogan says, Jordan's began as a small, high-quality dry-goods establishment founded in Boston by **Eben Dyer Jordan** and partner **Benjamin L. Marsh**. It too, has a discount basement store, but not in the same big-bargain league as famous Filene's Basement. ♦ M-Sa 8:30AM-7PM; Su noon-6PM. Downtown Crossing, 450 Washington St (Summer St) 357.3000 ⓖ

33 Locke-Ober ★★★$$$ The winds of change may howl through Boston, but—with one exception—they've barely whispered at this bastion of Brahmin traditions. After trying his hand at numerous occupations, including taxidermy and barbering, **Louis Ober**, a French Alsatian, opened **Ober's Restaurant Parisien** in 1875 in this tiny residential alley. In 1892, **Frank Locke** opened a winebar next door that vied with Ober's establishment in masculine grandeur. Within 5 years, Ober left the business and Locke died. Ober's successors then combined the 2 restaurants and their founders' names, an ingenious partnership that has flourished tastefully to this day. For nearly 100 years, the downstairs **Men's Cafe** was reserved for gentlemen; escorted ladies were admitted only on New Year's Eve and on the night of the **Harvard-Yale** game. (Incidentally, if Harvard lost, the nude painting of **Yvonne** in the 1st-floor barroom was draped in black.) But one fateful day, modern times came knocking, and this hallowed enclave reluctantly began admitting women. Since 1974, both sexes have enjoyed its Victorian splendor, tried-and-true rich Yankee-European cuisine, and perfectly discreet—if not exactly friendly—black-tie old-world service. Who knows—you may share the dining room with stars of stage and screen, not to mention political heavies like the **Kennedy** family, and those ubiquitous Harvard students who come from across the Charles River to toast their graduations.

The famous downstairs is all dark-wood splendor, the hand-carved bar agleam with German silver, but the revamped and gilded upstairs is nice also. Private dining chambers are available

for a fee. You'll see plenty of loyalists, mostly male, sitting in their customary places and dining on delicious old favorites like oysters, lobster Savannah, steak tartare, filet mignon, Dover sole, roast-beef hash, rack of lamb, calf's liver, Indian pudding, baked Alaska. Follow their example and keep to the time-tested selections. After solicitously notifying the regular clientele well in advance that more—gasp!—change was in the works, Locke-Ober recently introduced healthful new dishes to the ancient menu. The café's lock-shaped sign, by the way, was inspired by one that adorned Locke's original establishment. Women aren't encouraged to wear slacks here. ♦ New England/European ♦ M-Sa 11:30AM-2:30PM; 5:30-10:30PM; Su 5:30-10:30PM. Winter Pl (Winter St) Valet parking after 6PM. Jacket and tie required. Reservations recommended. 542.1340

34 Fanny Farmer A Boston classic, this shop has been selling chocolates, fudge, and other candy, ice cream, and nuts on this site for more than 50 years. It is part of the huge national chain named for **Fanny Merritt Farmer**, Boston's legendary cookbook author. Among other innovations, Fanny introduced the level measurement system that revolutionized food preparation. The company also owns all rights to Fanny's immensely popular cookbook, *The Boston Cooking School Cookbook*, which the shop also sells. ♦ M-F 9AM-6PM; Sa 10AM-6PM; Su noon-5PM. 130 Tremont St (Winter St) 542.8677 ⓖ Also at: 288 Washington St. 542.7045

Financial District/Downtown

35 Cathedral Church of St. Paul (1820, **Alexander Parris**; National Register of Historic Places) Most of Boston's old buildings mingle comfortably enough with their modern neighbors, but dignified St. Paul's looks uncomfortable sandwiched between 2 towering commercial structures—as if wondering what happened to the spacious rural town of its day. Once surrounded by handsome homes, the Episcopalian cathedral is now situated in Boston's workaday district. The church is a simple temple of gray granite, Boston's first example of Greek revival architecture. The massive sandstone Ionic columns supporting its porch add proud conviction to a stretch of street that can use it. Architect Parris, the avid practitioner of the Greek Revival style, also designed **Quincy Market**, with stone carving by **Solomon Willard**, creator of the **Bunker Hill Monument**. If the temple's tympanum looks strangely blank, that's because the bas-relief figures intended for it were never carved—another example of a Boston building where ambitious aspirations exceeded funds. Visit the starkly impressive interior, which was revised somewhat by architect **Ralph Adams Cram** in the '20s. There's a noon service Monday-Friday, but no tours. ♦ M-Sa noon-5PM. 138 Tremont St (Temple-Winter Sts) 482.5800 ⓖ (enter through side entrance)

36 Santacross Distinctive Shoe Service In business since 1917, this shop will heal your footware woes. All work is done on the premises. Santacross does walk-in repairs, shoeshines, reheeling, and handbag repairs too. Orthopedic shoes are a specialty. ♦ M-Sa 8AM-5PM. 16 Temple Pl (Tremont-Washington Sts) 426.6978 ♿ Also at: 35 High St, 737.2010

37 Stoddard's Open since 1800, the country's oldest cutlery shop sells plenty of other invaluable items too: row upon row of nail nippers—who'd ever think so many kinds existed!—pocket knives, corkscrews, clocks, manicure sets, mirrors, magnifiers, binoculars, brushes, shaving brushes, scissors, lobster shears, fishing rods and lures, and almost anything else that could possibly come in handy. A great source for practical presents, Stoddard's is also one of a handful of places remaining where cutlery is sharpened by hand, the only way to give blades their proper edge. An expert grinder works upstairs, giving scissors and such a new lease on life. ♦ M-Sa 9AM-5:30PM. 50 Temple Pl Tremont-Washington Sts) 426.4187 ♿ Also at: Copley Pl. 536.8688

SUPER HERO UNIVERSE Stores

38 Superhero Universe III As the name suggests, the whole comic book cosmos is covered here at the largest store of its kind in the state, selling comics and collectibles based on Superhero characters, including T-shirts, watches, ornaments, keychains. Comics range from good ol' **Archie** to *adult.* Manager **Steven Atherton** is almost always on hand to help customers track down their favorite heroes. ♦ M-Sa 10AM-7PM; Su noon-6PM. 41 West St (Tremont-Washington Sts) 423.6676 ♿ Also at: 1105 Massachusetts Ave, Harvard Sq, Cambridge. 354.5344

39 Brattle Book Shop Both foreign and domestic bibliophiles find their way to this humble-looking establishment. Not only is the Brattle one of America's few remaining urban-based bookshops of its kind, it's also the successor to the country's oldest operating antiquarian bookshop (founded in 1825). For a good part of this century, the Brattle was run by the late and very literary **George Gloss**, originally a fruit peddler who once exchanged a bunch of grapes for a paperback **Dickens** novel, and who truly earned the nickname *the Pied Piper of book lovers.* One time, Gloss drove a covered wagon through the city, tossing free books to passersby. His worthy successor and son **Ken** now runs the place, having worked here since age 5. The 3-level shop holds every sort of used and rare book imaginable, with fine selections on Boston and New England, and a wealth of autographs, photo albums, and other ephemera. The helpful staff are expert book sleuths. The resilient Brattle has risen from the ashes of 2 big fires and relocated numerous times; may it long enjoy its present happy home. Many a treasure has passed through these portals, such as a well-read copy of *The Great Gatsby,* given by **F. Scott Fitzgerald** to **T.S. Biot**, which contained Fitzgerald's misspelled inscription and Eliot's annotations. Don't overlook the racks of bargain books set up outdoors when the weather allows. The Brattle does appraisals, often for free. ♦ M-Sa 9AM-5:30PM. 9 West St (Tremont-Washington Sts) 542.0210, 800/447.9595

39 Cornucopia ★★★$$ A gleaming jewel in a tarnished setting, Cornucopia is located on an old commercial street that is beginning to revive. It's a treat to step into this pretty place, appointed with handpainted café tables, **Charles R. Mackintosh** bar stools, muted colors and lighting. The clientele generally looks equally well designed. All seating is pleasant, but the skylit and trellised mezzanine is especially nice. The New American cuisine borrows liberally from international cooking styles. Menus change monthly, featuring dishes like pumpkin tortelloni, duckling galantine, lamb chops marinated in goat's milk with couscous, sautéed salmon with Pernod cream sauce. There's a café menu too. Nice touches include the long appetizer roster and wine recommendations paired with each dish. Chef **Ross Cameron** is a stickler for seasonal ingredients, and sometimes cooks with tomatoes and herbs fresh from his rooftop garden.

Beneath Cornucopia's dressed-up facade lies history: this 3-story townhouse, described as *Mrs. Peabody's caravansary* by **Nathaniel Hawthorne**, was home to the **Peabody** family from 1840-1854. In the rear parlor, Hawthorne married his beloved **Sophia**, the Peabody's youngest daughter, and **Mary Peabody** wed **Horace Mann**, the founder of American public education. In the front parlor, headstrong and brilliant **Elizabeth Peabody** opened Boston's first bookstore selling foreign works. Eldest daughter Elizabeth was a fervent abolitionist, pioneer for kindergartens in America, and the model for the formidable **Miss Birdseye** in **Henry James'** novel *The Bostonians.* Here, with **Ralph Waldo Emerson**, Elizabeth published *The Dial,* the quarterly journal of the Transcendentalists. And each Wednesday, local ladies came to hear journalist **Margaret Fuller's** Conversations, landmark lectures in the history of American feminism. ♦ New American ♦ Tu-Th noon-9:30PM; F noon-10PM; Sa 5:30-10PM. 15 West St (Tremont-Washington Sts) Reservations recommended. 338.4600 ♿

Restaurants/Clubs: Red **Hotels:** Blue
Shops/Parks: Green **Sights/Culture:** Black

40 City Cassette Drop in and hear the latest dance, rap, club, and house music on cassettes—plus CDs, 12-inch vinyls, music videos, and a big selection of used 45s of all kinds. **John DiMeo**, the knowledgable owner, will help you find what you like and will search out special and obscure requests. He sells recordings that haven't yet gotten—or may never get—airplay, so if you hear something you like, snap it up. A young urban and suburban crowd comes here, often armed with boomboxes and portable tape players, ready to hit the streets with their purchases blaring. ♦ M-Sa 10:30AM-7PM; Su 12:30-6PM. 36 West St (Tremont-Washington Sts) 426.7970

41 Opera House (1928, **Thomas Lamb**; National Register of Historic Places) Now the home of the **Boston Opera Company**, whose artistic director is the renowned **Sarah Caldwell**, the theater was first named the **B.F. Keith Memorial Theatre** to honor the show-biz wizard who coined the term *vaudeville* and was one of its biggest promoters. Keith introduced the concept of continuous performances of high-quality variety acts suitable for family viewing, to contrast with the lowlife entertainment offered at **Scollay Sq**'s notorious **Old Howard** theater. Keith owned a chain of 400 such theaters, after which early movie *picture palaces* were modeled. More recently, this one was called the **Savoy Theatre**. The Baroque terra-cotta facade is best seen from **Avenue de Lafayette** across the way. The lobby and auditorium are the worse for wear, but their decadent splendor is impressively dramatic, perfect for opera. It's easy to imagine what a thrill it was to come here during the theater's heyday. Call for information on performances; the Metropolitan Opera performs at the Wang Center, by the way. ♦ 539 Washington St (Ave de Lafayette) 426.5300 & (enter from Mason St; ushers are trained to assist)

Next to the Opera House:

Paramount Theatre (1932, **Arthur Bowditch**) Take note of the marvelous sign. This Art Deco delight is begging for a fresh start.

41 The Hub Club (1989; interior, **Tamarkin Techler Group**) Adopting Boston's famous nickname, *the Hub*, this relative newcomer is a hot spot for evenings on the town. The 3-story dance club's severe black facade and urbane lighting contrast starkly with the effulgent opulence of the adjacent **Opera House**. The Hub Club's music roster aims to be progressive, rotating regularly to satisfy eclectic music tastes. Anyone 18 and older is welcome on Wednesday; all other nights, the minimum age is 21. Thursday features an after-work jazz series with R&B offered later on, attracting a somewhat older professional crowd. Friday is international night, often showcasing reggae, dance rock, or Afro-pop bands. A DJ spins American and international dance tunes on the 2nd floor and creative dress is encouraged, attracting a more flamboyant younger set. And Saturday draws a dressier crowd for a weekly house party hosted by a DJ from WXKS—*KISS* —108FM. There's a full bar, of course, but no dinner menu. Buffets are sometimes offered. A favored setting for social events and private parties, the club witnesses its share of raucous

good times, with people outrageously costumed and swinging from ropes and such. Sit out the sets or bop until you drop, dress up or dress down—it's do as you please here. Everything is subject to change, so call ahead for programs and times. ♦ Admission varies. W, F-Sa 9:30PM-2AM; Th 5:30PM-2AM. 533 Washington St (Ave de Lafayette) Validated parking at Lafayette Pl. 451.6999 &

42 Lafayette Hotel $$$$ The Lafayette's 500 rooms and suites on 16 floors are far more sumptuous and traditional in decor than the hotel's severely impersonal exterior implies. In fact, this hotel is one of the best-kept secrets in Boston, since many don't anticipate finding such stellar accommodations in this part of town. Guest services include concierge, parking, multilingual staff, same-day laundry and valet services, indoor swimming pool and exercise equipment, and sun terrace. Swiss chocolates appear not only in guestrooms, but in a monstrous bowl located at the registration desk. The 19th floor offers Swiss Butler service, and there are handicapped-equipped rooms plus 2 nonsmokers' floors. Contemporary works by Swiss émigré artists adorn **Cafe Suisse**, an informal restaurant serving Swiss specialties, New England cuisine, and light dishes. The hotel is the anchor to the adjoining **Lafayette Place** shopping complex, which houses a beauty salon, newsstands, drugstores, and many retail shops. (Built in the early '80s, this complex has not been successful and plans are afoot to metamorphose and enlarge the whole shebang as the future **Boston Crossing**—in case you

Financial District/Downtown

wonder why that name appears on signs in the area.) ♦ 1 Ave de Lafayette (Washington-Chauncy Sts) 451.2600, 800/621.9200; fax 451.0054 &

Within Lafayette Hotel:

Le Marquis de Lafayette ★★★★$$$$
Local gastronomes deem dinner here a sublime experience. Master chef **Louis Outhier**, one of France's finest, oversees the French cuisine combining tradition and innovation, which has garnered enthusiastic kudos from local and national publications. The hushed gray dining room with banquettes and choice, understated decorations is an appropriate—if somewhat somber—backdrop to the subtle, seductive dishes: quail soup with quail egg, foie gras and truffles, lobster fricassee, duck breast in brandy sauce, salmon in puff pastry, *crème de cassis* cake, calvados mousse (the dessert selection is particularly stunning). In addition to the à la carte array, 2 or 3 clever prix-fixe tasting menus are offered, changing seasonally. ♦ French ♦ M-Sa 6-10:30PM. Complimentary valet parking. Jackets required. Reservations recommended &

The Lobby Bar A pleasant low-key bar beneath a 2-story atrium, the Lobby Bar offers a luncheon buffet, complimentary cocktail-hour hors d'oeuvres, international coffees and teas. Weekday evenings feature piano and vocal entertainment, with dancing on Saturday evening. ◆ Daily 11:30AM-2:30AM &

43 Winmill Fabrics Bostonians from all walks of life frequent this fabric store for its huge selection of sample cuts and remnant pieces of all kinds. Home decorating fabrics are sold at less-than-wholesale prices. Winmill has plenty of Spandex, the current big seller, and the complete line of Vogue patterns. Service is great; the owner is on the floor at all times. If you haven't a particular sewing project in mind, a visit to Winmill will inspire you. ◆ M-Sa 9AM-6PM. 107-111 Chauncy St (Ave de Lafayette) No credit cards. 542.1815

44 Slesinger's Fabric Store When the do-it-yourself urge strikes, dust off the sewing machine and come to **Jack Laven**'s emporium of bargain fabrics for bridal, drapery, upholstery, home-sewing, and craft projects. Search for the perfect stuff among discontinued decorator fabrics, leftover lots of woolens, cotton, challis, silk, and more. Notions are a real steal here. Laven also sells muslin and canvas to artists. Lycra Spandex is popular these days, he says, and the shop is especially busy at Halloween. His father-in-law, a woolen jobber, began the business; Jack himself started out in Boston's garment district more than 4 decades ago, at age 23. He's usually on the job about 7AM, and

Financial District/Downtown

lets early-bird shoppers in. ◆ M-Sa 9:30AM-6PM. 30 Chauncy St (Summer-Bedford Sts) 542.1805 &

44 Windsor Button Shop Buttons galore and a whole lot more, including sewing notions, trims, and craft supplies. Fifty years ago, Windsor opened as a buttons-only business, and it still has an extraordinary inventory of attractive, unusual, whimsical, and eccentric buttons to adorn any attire. If you're missing a hard-to-find button, match it here. Also in stock: rickrack, ribbons, rhinestone tiaras, zippers, felt, embroidery thread, crochet yarn, sequins, masks, veils, hatboxes, parasols, pompoms, fabric paint, bridal trimmings, braid, beads, boas, and just about everything else in the galaxy of home sewing. ◆ M-Sa 9:30AM-6PM. 36 Chauncy St (Summer-Bedford Sts) 482.4969 &

45 Procter Building (1897, **Winslow and Wetherell**) On sunny days, it's bathed in light and the perch for many pigeons. Every day, the little Jersey-cream-colored building is an orchestra of ornament crowned by a tiaralike cornice. Shells, birds, flowers, garlands, cherubs, urns, and more parade across the curving facade. ◆ 100-106 Bedford St (Kingston St)

46 Church Green Building (c. 1873) This fine addition to the city's stock of 19th-century granite mercantile buildings is named for **Church Green**, the triangular intersection of **Summer, Lincoln, High**, and **Bedford** streets, which in turn was named for a lovely church designed by **Charles Bulfinch** that once stood here. Just another example of how history haunts many Boston place names. Behind this structure rises red-roofed **99 Summer St**, a 1987 interloper by **Goody, Clancy & Associates** that tries mightily to fit in. Across the way is the brand-new **125 Summer St** by **Kohn Pederson Fox**, lurking behind an eclectic row of commercial facades now belonging to No. 125. A swath of old streetscape has been nicely preserved, but the huge modern tower bursting from its midst is a little eerie in contrast. ◆ 105-113 Summer St (Bedford St)

46 Bedford Building (1875-1876, **Cummings & Sears**; renovation 1983, **Bay-Bedford Company**; National Register of Historic Places) Red granite, white marble, and terra cotta romance well on the Ruskin Gothic-style facade. The proud building lost its original clock, but recently got a new stained-glass one that's particularly striking at night, the work of Cambridge artisan **Lynn Hovey**. ◆ 99 Bedford St (Lincoln St)

47 Boston Airline Center This is a handy walk-in center—*no phone number*—where you can make on-the-spot reservations or pick up tickets for airlines, including American, Continental, Delta, Northwest, PanAm, United, TWA, and USAir. ◆ M-F 9AM-5PM. 155 Federal St (High St) &

47 United Shoe Machinery Building (1929, **Parker, Thomas, and Rice**; National Register of Historic Places) Now renovated and renamed *The Landmark*, Boston's first Art Deco skyscraper takes giant steps back to form a handsome ziggurat crowned by a pyramid of tiles—a majestic architectural physique. At street level, look for the fine cast-metal storefronts set into limestone. Rude new buildings shove against this proud tower, which recalls the era when shoes were big business in Boston. ◆ 138-164 Federal St (High St)

48 One Winthrop Square (1873, **William Ralph Emerson** and **Carl Fehmer**; renovation 1974, **Childs, Bertman, Tseckares Associates**) **Ralph Waldo Emerson**'s nephew is responsible for several vigorously unconventional Boston structures, including the **House of Odd Windows** on Beacon Hill and the **Boston Art Club** in Back Bay. In this collaborative effort, Emerson's influence dominates in the eccentric mixing of architectural motifs. Originally a dry-goods emporium and then a publishing plant, the building has been adapted to offices. Out front, where trucks once loaded up with newspapers, is now an attractive park with **Henry Hudson Kitson**'s bronze of **Robert Burns** briskly striding along, walking stick in hand and collie at his side. ♦ Devonshire-Otis Sts

Off Winthrop Sq:

Winthrop Lane Opening onto the right-hand side of the square (if you're facing **One Winthrop**), this short-and-sweet brick lane would be unremarkable except for the florist and **Boston Coffee Exchange** shops at one end, and an imaginative work of public art called *Boston Bricks: A Celebration of Boston's Past and Present* by **Kate Burke** and **Gregg Lefevre** (1985). The artists have inset dozens of bronze brick reliefs amid the lane's bricks from its start to its finish. Each relief tells a significant, interesting, or entertaining piece of Boston's story. Have fun trying to figure out what's what. Some images and references are quite familiar: the **Customs Tower, Boston Common**'s cows, the **Boston Pops**, the city's ethnic groups, the Underground Railroad, the **Boston Marathon** and the **Red Sox**, whale watching, rowers on the **Charles River**, swans in the **Public Garden**, an amusing representation of the notorious Boston driver. Others may keep you puzzling awhile. Collectively, the clever bricks present a good likeness of the city. ♦ Enter from Devonshire St

49 Dakota's ★★$$$ Hailing from Dallas, the masculine-looking restaurant located on the 2nd level has barely unpacked its bags but is already doing big business in Boston, attracting the briefcase crowd at lunchtime and theater clientele in the evening. In fact, there's a special before-and-after-theater menu, and you can leave your car while attending the performance. The menu's focus is on American grill with a Southern accent. Many dishes are good and colorfully presented: try the calamari, venison-sausage quesadillas, onion rings, gulf seafood chowder, tortilla soup, roast chicken, lamb chops. Desserts are intensely rich, and the freshly made breads pleasantly fragrant. It's fun to sit in the elevated bar area and overlook the fast-paced dining room, although the clientele is rather homogenous. The restaurant is spiffed up with marble, ceiling fans, Roman shades, and club chairs. A pianist plays 6PM-closing, Wednesday-Saturday. Dakota's inhabits a new 21-story office tower called **101 Arch**, which incorporated the facade of **34 Summer St**, an 1873 commercial palace. (Visitors sometimes have trouble locating the restaurant, but the Summer St entrance is well marked.) ♦ American ♦ M-F11:30AM-3PM, 5:30-10:30PM; Sa 5:30-10:30PM. 101 Arch (Summer St) Complimentary valet parking after 5:30PM on Summer St side. Reservations recommended. 737.1777

Where **Winter** meets **Summer** at **Washington St** is the center of Boston's urban mall, called **Downtown Crossing.** Other than delivery trucks, the narrow bricked streets are for pedestrians only—thank goodness. From the business day's start to finish, shoppers and people heading to and from work stride along briskly, sometimes stopping to browse among clusters of sidewalk vendors or to listen to street musicians.

49 The Society of Arts and Crafts at 101 Arch A new satellite of the nonprofit crafts organization headquartered at **175 Newbury St** in Back Bay (266.1810), this educational outreach gallery on the 2nd level in 101 Arch is the first step toward establishing **The Craft Museum of Boston**. (The hope is that the museum's opening will coincide with the prestigious society's centennial in 1997.) The Arch St gallery showcases contemporary works-for-sale in a variety of media by society member artists, plus works on loan from museums and private collections, and rotating exhibitions of crafts by distinguished and emerging artists. The gallery's 1200-square-ft space is subsidized by **Metropolitan Life Real Estate Investments**. In addition to bringing crafts to the center of the city—a part of town that can always use color and creativity—the gallery is a great place to purchase exceptional, interesting objects like jewelry, glass, ceramics, small furniture. ♦ M-F 11AM-7PM. 101 Arch St (Summer St) 345.0033 ₺

50 Lauriat's Part of a chain throughout New England and New York, this bookstore caters

Financial District/Downtown

to the general public. It features a large sea-and-sailing section. ♦ M-Th 9AM-7PM; Tu-W, F-Sa 9AM-6PM. 45 Franklin St (Hawley St) 482.2850 ₺ (rear entrance) Also at: 20 Charles St. 523.0188

51 The London Harness Shop Rest assured you'll find only the finest in very proper gifts for travel, home, office, and personal use, tastefully arrayed amid the shop's gleaming old wooden fixtures. The oldest operating retailer in the country, the shop has done business in this general location since the 1700s. **Benjamin Franklin** was among the early shoppers, and traveled with London Harness trunks. Honor momentous occasions—weddings, graduations, christenings—or get yourself something indispensable that will last forever. Perhaps a wooden box with **Fenway Park** hand-painted on it, or an illuminated globe, or a chess set, or an umbrella that will stand up to Boston's gusty winds. Clocks, candlesticks, luggage, wallets and accessories, scarfs, photo albums, jewelry boxes, briefcases, book ends, desk sets, old prints and maps, and more—all the appurtenances for a civilized existence. ♦ M-F 9AM-5:30PM; Sa 10AM-5PM. 60 Franklin St (Washington-Arch Sts) 542.9234

The side streets linking **Tremont** and **Washington** streets are the rungs in what are called the *Ladder Blocks.*

52 Hole in the Wall $ One of the district's tiniest tidbits of real estate, this diminutive deli manages to turn out a huge assortment of breakfast and lunch items to go. You'd be hard-pressed to think of a hot or cold sandwich that isn't served here (okay, so there's no peanut butter), not to mention the salads, soups and stews, egg combos, burgers, and snacks. Owner **Benny Yanoff** and his family run the place at top speed. Join the line at the outside counter, or step inside to watch how skillfully counter staff on duty dart past each other in close quarters. It was a passerby's chance remark—*Look at that hole in the wall*—that gave the 12x4-foot eatery its apt appellation. With brown bag in hand, take a moment to examine **Richard Haas**' trompe l' oeil mural across the street, painted on the back of **31 Milk St**, which portrays a cutaway of the actual facade. Haas also painted the well-known architectural mural on the **Boston Architectural Center** in Back Bay. ♦ Takeout ♦ M-F 5AM-4PM. 24 Arch St (Milk-Franklin Sts) 423.4625 ♿ Also at: 125 Summer St, 345.0515/9229

53 International Trust Company Building (1893, **William G. Preston**; enlarged 1906; National Register of Historic Places) **Max Bachman**'s allegorical figures **Commerce** and **Industry** adorn the **Arch St** side, while **Security** and **Fidelity** are ensconced on **Devonshire St**, adding a fanciful representation of business rectitude modern buildings sorely lack. This edifice incorporated the remains of a building partly destroyed by Boston's terrible 1872 fire. ♦ 45 Milk St (Arch-Devonshire Sts)

Financial District/Downtown

54 Milk Street Cafe ★$ Downtown shoppers and Financial District denizens love this crowded cafeteria, and many a politician stops in for dairy kosher, vegetarian home-style cooking that includes muffins and bagels, soups, pizzas, pastas, quiches, salads, and sweet treats. Breakfast and lunch, only. ♦ Café/takeout ♦ M-F 7AM-2:30PM (during daylight savings); M-F 7AM-3PM (rest of year) 50 Milk St (Devonshire St) 542.FOOD/2433 (recorded menu) Also at: 125 Summer St, 345.0515/9229; 101 Main St, Kendall Sq, Cambridge. 491.8287

55 Designers' Clothing Should you opt to blend in with the business crowd, this is a good source for men and women's professional attire (mostly men's). Tailored clothing from designer lines is discounted 30-60%, and everything is first quality, no irregulars. ♦ M-F 9AM-6PM; Sa 9:30AM-5PM. 161 Devonshire St (Milk-Franklin Sts) 482.3335 ♿

56 First National Bank of Boston (1971, **Campbell, Aldrich & Nulty**) An ungainly brown tower with a big belly that has earned an apt and famous nickname: *The Pregnant Building*. The bank operates the marvelous **Bank of Boston Gallery** on the 36th floor, well worth a visit, which displays the bank's own collection and exhibitions ranging from fine arts to architecture, design, and furniture. The curator,

employed by the bank, often organizes collaborative shows with Boston-area institutions, museums, and schools. The gallery overlooks gorgeous cityscapes and harborscapes too. Several other retail galleries are just 4 blocks away, on **South St**. ♦ Free. M-F 9AM-noon, 2-5PM. 100 Federal St (Franklin St) 434.4297 ♿ (Congress St side)

57 Post Office Square Another of Boston's many triangular *squares*, this is one of the busiest and most visually exciting pockets in the city. Surrounded by worthy buildings, including the Art Deco post office and telephone company headquarters, it swings open to offer wonderful views of the city's densest blocks where new and old exist cheek by jowl. For instance, a new edifice by **Kohn Pederson Fox** at **101 Federal St** has merged with handsome 60-year-old **75 Federal**, and their union has resulted in one of Boston's most interesting interior public spaces. (Be sure to look inside and out at No. 75's spectacular Art Deco elevators.) At the heart of the square, a new grassy park will soon carpet an underground garage. ♦ Congress-Pearl Sts (Water-Franklin Sts)

57 Angell Memorial Plaza At the triangle's tip opposite the post office. Dedicated to **George Thorndike Angell**, founder of the Massachusetts Society for the Prevention of Cruelty to Animals and the American Humane Education Society. A sculpture of a small pond and its inhabitants is located in the middle of a brick circle inset with reliefs of birds, beasts, bugs, et alia—a very sweet assemblage. Look for Angell's wise words: *Our humane societies are now sowing the seeds of a harvest which will one of these days protect not only the birds of the air and beasts of the field but also human beings as well.* Looming near the pond is the fountain designed by **Peabody and Stearns** as a watering place for horses in 1912.

57 John W. McCormack Post Office and Court House (1930-1931; **Cram & Ferguson** with **James A. Wetmore**) A commanding Art Deco building with plenty of crisp ornament and vertical window ribbons, the post office has a nicely weathered gray facade with interesting lines. Even the grates are special. The architects later designed the old **John Hancock** building in Back Bay, with its famous flashing weather beacon, and the nearby **New England Telephone Headquarters Building** at **185 Franklin St**. ♦ Congress St at Post Office Sq

58 New England Telephone Headquarters Building (1947; **Cram & Ferguson**) The Art Deco throwback occupies its place with pride, but its best features are inside: first, the mural circling the lobby; and second, the re-creation of inventor **Alexander Graham Bell**'s garret located off the main lobby. **Dean Cornwell**'s frenzied and colorful mural (1951) is *really* something—**Norman Rockwell**-esque eyefuls. Called *Telephone Men and Women at Work*, the 160-foot-long, action-packed painting depicts 197 life-size figures in dramatic groupings. It lionizes not only Bell and other telephone pioneers, but also employees on the job, and those risking life and limb in the face of disaster to keep those calls coming. Cornwell was an old hand at this sort of thing, creating murals honoring steelworkers, pioneers in medicine, various states' history, etc. Bell's lab is a painstaking replica of his original studio at **109 Court St** in old **Scollay Sq**, where he electrically transmitted the first speech sounds over a wire on 3 June 1875. (The following March, in a different lab, Bell succeeded in sending not just sounds but intelligible words, when he issued his famous line: *Mr. Watson, come here, I want you.*) The studio was saved from demolition, dismantled, eventually brought here in pieces and rebuilt. On display are models, telephone replicas, drawings, references, and historic artifacts, plus a wonderful diorama of the view of Scollay Sq from Bell's window. Pamphlets about Cornwell's creation and Bell's garret are usually available. ♦ Free. M-F 8:30AM-4PM. 185 Franklin St (Congress-Pearl Sts) 743.9800 ♿ (enter from Franklin St)

59 **State Street Bank & Trust Company** (1966, **Hugh Subbins and Associates, F.A. Stahl and Associates, Le Messurier Associates**) The bank is directly across the street from the **New England Telephone** building. Take the elevator one flight down and visit the **Concourse Art Gallery**. About 4 shows are mounted each year on art and architecture, often in collaboration with local nonprofit groups like the **Boston Architectural Center** and the **Massachusetts Horticultural Society**. The bank owns a fine maritime folk art collection and 19th-century maps and charts. Works by city youth are shown every summer. ♦ Free. M-F 9AM-5PM. 225 Franklin St (Pearl-Oliver Sts) 654.3938 ♿

60 Hotel Meridien $$$$ (1922, R. Clipston Sturgis; reuse and tower addition 1981, Jung/Brannen Associates, Inc., and Pietro Belluschi) The Old Federal Reserve Bank has been happily preserved as part of this prestigious European hotel, located in the heart of the Financial District. It's an easy walk to many popular attractions as well as the Theater District. The former bank adjoins One Post Office Sq, a 41-story tower. French chocolates and a daily weather report appear bedside nightly in each of the Meridien's 326 accommodations. Rooms are contemporary in decor, while the lobby and public spaces feature restored original architectural details. Because a glass mansard roof was plunked on top of the old structure to add additional floors, many rooms feature sloping glass walls with electric drapes, offering great views. Suite No. 915 is especially popular; so are the loft suites. Fifteen rooms are handicapped-equipped, and one floor is reserved for nonsmokers. There's a posh health club called Le Club Meridien on the 3rd floor, featuring pool, whirlpool, sauna, exercise equipment; and a full-service business center complete with foreign currency exchange. Amenities include multilingual staff, valet parking, 24-hour concierge and room services, express laundry and dry cleaning. Paid parking is offered in the 400-car garage. Because the hotel is owned by Air France, it is often associated with major French cultural events in Boston, such as those hosted

by the **French Library** and **Alliance Française**. ♦ 250 Franklin St (Oliver-Pearl Sts) 451.1900, 800/543.4300; fax 423.2844 ♿

Within Hotel Meridien:

Julien ★★★$$$$ Named for Boston's first French restaurant, which opened on this same site in 1794, Julien draws a predominantly business clientele. Yet the restaurant's lofty refined splendor and haute nouvelle cuisine make it a good choice for a serious evening out. Acclaimed French chef **Olivier Roellinger** consults with Julien's resident chef **Anthony Ambrose**, combining fresh native ingredients with French creativity in dishes like duck glazed with Caribbean-spiced caramel, pomegranate seeds, and watercress, or salmon with vintage Madeira and cardamon. Desserts are inspired, and the wine list exceptional. The menu is à la carte, with a Taste of New England 4-course prix-fixe dinner available, as well as a prix-fixe

Financial District/Downtown

business lunch. Julien is located in the high-ceilinged hall that once served as the bank's Members Court, or board room. Vast as the dining room is, tables are generously spaced and diners settle into Queen Anne wingback chairs, promoting privacy and conversation. The **Julien Bar**, resplendent with gilded coffered ceilings and wonderful carved details, provides background piano music. Look for the pair of **N.C. Wyeth** murals portraying **Abraham Lincoln** and **George Washington**. The bar once served as the reception room for the bank's governors. ♦ French ♦ M-F noon-2PM, 6-10:30PM; Sa 6-10:30PM; Su 11AM-2PM. Complimentary valet parking. Jacket and tie required at Julien; no blue jeans allowed at Julien Bar. Reservations recommended

. . . which American city can point to so many lovely, queer, and compelling names for its streets as Boston? Beacon, Batterymarch, Pinckney, Tremont, Hereford, Salutation, Merchant's Row, Cornhill, Brick Alley, and Sun Court Street, for example. And who else lives where Winter runs forever into Summer, and Water is always on the verge of turning into Milk?

Author **David McCord**

Restaurants/Clubs: Red   Hotels: Blue
Shops/Parks: Green   **Sights/Culture:** Black

Café Fleuri ★$$$ Situated beneath the 6-story atrium in **One Post Office Sq**, connecting to the hotel, the airy and open café features moderately priced brasserie-style cuisine, and is popular for business breakfasts and lunches, and the spectacular, belly-bludgeoning Sunday brunch. In addition to the regular à la carte menu, a special buffet is offered on Friday and Saturday nights, when you can also dance to a jazz quartet. The buffet themes change regularly, and focus on a particular cuisine: from the French West Indies, Provence, or Brazil, for example. *Attention all chocoholics*: starring on Saturday afternoons the café puts on the sumptuous all-you-can-eat Chocolate Bar buffet, a truly hedonistic, decadent display of cakes, pies, tortes, fondues, mousses, cookies, brownies. ♦ Café ♦ M-Sa 7-11AM, 11:30AM-2:30PM, 6-10:30PM; Su 7-11AM, 2 brunch seatings 11AM and 1PM, 6-10:30PM. Valet parking. Reservations recommended

61 Liberty Square Where **Water, Kilby**, and **Batterymarch** streets meet, you'll find another of Boston's quaintly misnamed *squares* squeezed into a busy block. This one is multipurpose: it commemorates angry Bostonians' destruction on 14 August 1765 of the British Stamp Tax office that was located here (a year later, England repealed the Stamp Act); it was formally named in 1793 in a gala ceremony honoring the French Revolution, complete with extravagant feasting and 21-gun salute, and is dominated by **Gyuri Hollosy**'s memorial to the Hungarian Revolution of 1956, dedicated in

Financial District/Downtown

1986. For those who love old urban pockets lingering in modern cities, Liberty Sq is a treat, surrounded by 19th-century businesslike buildings that reveal curious and delightful details if you take time to notice. The old street pattern's turns and angles provide interesting vistas.

61 Appleton Building (1926, **Coolidge and Shattuck**; renovation 1981, **Irving Salsberg**) A powerful, austere Classical Revival edifice named for **Samuel Appleton**, a Boston insurance magnate. The building's most expressive gesture is its generous curve to accommodate converging streets on **Liberty Sq**, its best side. (Be sure you're on that side, since the **Milk St** facade is far less interesting.) All else is measured, pragmatic, restrained—just right for the industry it housed. But the more you study the Appleton, the more inventive it appears, especially its syncopated window patterns and entrance facade friezes depicting a violinmaker, carpenter, glassblower, sculptor, draftsman, and other artisans. Peek into the elliptical lobby with its elegant gilded ceiling. ♦ 110 Milk St (Oliver-Batterymarch Sts)

62 Bakey's ★★$ This upscale delicatessen with full bar serves all sorts of sandwiches for lunch and supper, plus an extensive Continental breakfast. Bakey's amusing logo of a man asleep on an ironing board indicates imagination at work. The story is, owner **George Bakey** once found his father in this pose, ensconced on the family ironing board. Bakey's has 2 very pleasant dining rooms—one called *the Snug*, named for the room women retired to when it wasn't considered proper for the sexes to mingle in bars. George has gone all out in his establishment's decor: wooden bars and booths imported from England (be sure to notice the Snug's snug little square bar), antique lighting, Oriental rugs, fresh linen and flowers. Be forewarned, *smoking isn't allowed* anywhere. Every evening, **LuAnn** plays the piano from 5PM-closing. ♦ American/deli ♦ M-F 7AM-8PM. 45 Broad St (Water St) 426.1710 ♿

62 Broad Street Indefatigable developer **Uriah Cotting** led his **Broad Street Association** in many ambitious 19th-century urban redevelopment schemes, of which Broad Street itself was but one byproduct. Laid out around 1805 according to **Charles Bulfinch**'s plans, the street quickly became a handsome commercial avenue to the sea, bordered by many Federal-style Bulfinch buildings. A scattering of these still stand among more recent but distinguished structures such as **No. 50** (1863). With its many low-rise buildings, Broad St is one of the neighborhood's most open, sunny spots. A historical note: **Francis Cabot Lowell**, one of Cotting's partners, developed a power loom in a Broad St store that ultimately revolutionized American textile manufacture.

62 Sakura-bana ★★$$ The name means *cherry blossom*. Sushi is the house specialty—as you might guess if you notice the poem by the entrance extolling *sushi rapture*—and you can even order *sushi heaven*, a sampler of more than 2 dozen varieties of sushi and sashimi. If you order à la carte, you can be as daring or timid as you wish, staying with salmon, tuna, and mackerel, or exploring exotica like flying fish roe and sea urchin. The daily *bento* (lunch box) specials served with soup, salad, rice, and fruit are also good choices. For dinner, try seafood *teppan yaki*, broiled with teriyaki sauce and served on a sizzling iron plate. Not only is this trim and tidy restaurant's cuisine outstanding, its prices are reasonable and portions generous. Lots of Financial District workers regularly queue up for lunch. ♦ Japanese ♦ M-F 11:30AM-2:30PM, 5-11PM; Sa 1-10PM; Su 5-11PM. 57 Broad St (Milk St) Reservations recommended for dinner. 542.4311

63 The Architectural Bookshop Owned by the **Boston Society of Architects**, who recently bought and renovated this 1853 granite warehouse (now called the **Architects' Building**), the bookshop has one of the country's largest selections of books and publications on local, national, and international architecture, and related fields such as architectural practice, theory and history, esthetics and criticism, interior design, landscape, preservation. Also noteworthy are the architectural stationery, posters, guidebooks, magazines, and unusual gifts. If you're intrigued by any aspect of the built world, something here will strike your fancy. ♦ M-F 9AM-6PM. 50 Broad St (Milk St) 951.0696

64 Sultan's Kitchen $ Located in a remnant of **Charles Bulfinch**'s 19th-century **Broad St** development, this self-service restaurant cooks up fresh and delicious renditions of Middle Eastern and Greek favorites for the lunch crowd: kabobs, grape leaves, Greek salad, baba ghanouj, egg lemon chicken soup, falafel, tabbouleh. Try the cool, crisp Sultan's salad or rich *tarama* salad made with fish roe. If too many dishes tempt you, order one of the sampler plates. ♦ Turkish/takeout ♦ M-F 11AM-5PM. 72 Broad St. 338.7819/8509 (recorded menu) &

65 Country Life ★$ For Boston's most complete vegetarian dining experience, sample Country Life's ample all-you-can-eat lunch, brunch, and dinner buffets. Absolutely no dairy, meat, refined grains, or refined sugar sneak into any of the dishes. Substitutes include soy milk and cheeses made from nuts. The inventive menu changes daily—with a new one printed each month—featuring soups like garbanzo dumpling, lentil, and Russian potato; entrees like stir fries, lasagna, enchiladas, and vegetable potpie; and always an interesting choice of vegetables. Desserts, too. Everything is self-serve and the decor is neat but plain; emphasis is entirely on hearty, healthy food. ♦ Vegetarian/takeout ♦ M 11:30AM-3PM; Tu-Th 11:30AM-3PM, 5-8PM; F 11:30AM-2:30PM; Su 10AM-3PM, 5-8PM. 112 Broad St (Surface Artery) No credit cards. 350.8846/8625 (recorded menu) &

66 Nara ★$$ Lawyers, brokers, bankers, et alia, favor this cozy, private little place located along an alley. One might easily miss Nara altogether, so watch for the Japanese lanterns and red awnings. Sushi-lovers find happiness in the extensive selection, and others can sample tempura, teriyaki or *katsu* entrees, or savory Korean treats like *bool goki*. A family-run restaurant, friendly Nara is crowded by day, quieter by night, but always enjoyable. ♦ Japanese/Korean/takeout ♦ M-F 11:30AM-2:30PM, 5-10PM; Sa 5-10PM. 85 Wendell St (Broad St) Reservations recommended. 338.5935

Visitors take note of a pressing 1930s measure. Says Ch. 11, Sec. 272: *No person other than a registered voter of the city of Boston shall take seaworms within the limits of the city, except that this prohibition shall not apply to a person taking for his own use and not for purposes of sale not more than ¹/₂ pint of seaworms in any one day.*

67 Chadwick Lead Works (1887, **William Preston**) An unsightly elevated highway ramp barrels past its front door, but this forceful rustic structure easily holds its own on the Financial District fringe. Its architect also created the former **New England Museum of Natural History** in Back Bay, now the upscale **Louis, Boston** clothing store. Handsome 3-story arches with a graceful ripple of spandrels are topped by a marching row of little windows and a bold parapet. A gargoyle glares from one corner, and other grotesques and dragony lizards cling to the facade. At the back is the square shot tower, inside which molten lead was poured from the top, cooling into shot before reaching the bottom floor. The lead works was built by its president, **Joseph Houghton Chadwick**, once described as *Lead King of Boston.* ♦ 184 High St (Batterymarch St and Leman Pl)

68 Batterymarch Building (1928, **Henry Kellogg**) Named for the street it adorns, which was once part of military companies' marching route from **Boston Common** to now-leveled **Fort Hill**, this heroically optimistic Art Deco assemblage is wonderful to behold in the midst of a district becoming ever more crowded and shadowed by impersonal modern giants. The 3 slender towers linked by 3rd-story arcades undergo a truly marvelous transformation as they push through the crowded block to the sky: their dark brown brick at ground level gradually lightens in color until a glowing buff at the top, as if bleached by sunlight, the one commodity always in short supply in con-

Financial District/Downtown

gested downtowns. Under the handsome entrance arches, look for the charming reliefs of boats, trains, planes, stagecoaches, clipper ships. Unlike the heavy-handed gilding of nearby **75 State St**, this building's discreet touches of gold enhance rather than bedizen its fine form. ♦ 60 Batterymarch St (Franklin St)

Bests

Charles Laquidara
Radio Announcer, WBCN Radio

Fenway Park—Watching a ballgame in the greatest park in baseball. The awful food and condiments are bearable. An experience not to be missed—for the whole family.

Davio's restaurant—Newbury Street—Great food, service, and atmosphere; reasonable prices; formal and fine downstairs—with formal and fun upstairs.

Cloud 9 Limousine—A classy, fun way to move through the city in style and security.

Boston Garden—New president, new look, new attitude, old charm.

Watching the students move into Boston in the fall—the hustle, the bustle, the lost looks as the newcomers try to figure out our drivers, our language, our streets.

Chinatown/Theater District

This checkered neighborhood's story has had many acts, characters, triumphs, and tribulations, the plot now thickening at a quickening pace. For within this geographically awkward and angular fringe of the city converge—sometimes collide—the following principal dramatis personae:

Theater District: Now clustered near **Tremont** and **Stuart** streets, Boston's Rialto originally extended much farther—a glittering, glamorous mecca that brought all the big names to town. Beginning in the '20s, Boston was a tryout town for Broadway-bound plays. However, vaudeville faded, cinema outstripped theater in popularity, the suburbs eclipsed the city, and great houses like the **Wilbur** and the **Majestic** deteriorated. Roofs leaked, walls crumbled, paint and plaster peeled, and the shadow of the wrecking ball loomed. But Boston's boom-town days have rescued a number of theaters: the Wilbur is repaired, the **Shubert** refurbished, the Majestic resuscitated. The **Colonial** forges on with new vigor. Other houses cling to life or remain dark, awaiting an angel; there's reason to hope.

Combat Zone: A sleazy so-called adult-entertainment district concentrated on lower **Washington Street**, the Zone thrived during the '70s, as home to the X-rated **Pussycat Cinema, Goodtime Charlie's,** the **Glass Slipper,** the **Naked i,** and dozens of other seamy strip joints, peep shows, porn shops. Development pressures are strangling the Zone, shrunk from 30-plus establishments in 1986 to only a few today. Shady sorts still hang out here, so it's unsafe at night, but the Zone's carnal carnival days are over; its days are numbered, period.

Chinatown: It's official entry is a massive ceremonial gateway on **Beach Street**, but pedestrians approach this closeknit residential/commercial quarter from every which way. Bounded by **Kneeland**, Washington, and **Essex** streets and the **Central Artery**, the 4-block-long neighborhood is known for its exotic restaurants and shops, family-oriented character, and hospitality. Cramped it may be, but Chinatown's always full of activity, festive with subtitled signs and banners, pagoda-topped phone booths, shop windows piled high. Popular events are **Chinese New Year**

Chinatown/Theater District

The subway stations most convenient to the neighborhood are the **New England Medical Center** and **Chinatown** stops, (both on the **Orange Line**), and the **Arlington** stop (**Green Line**). The **Park Street** stop (**Red** and **Green Lines**) and the **Boylston** stop (**Green Line**) are also within easy walking distance.

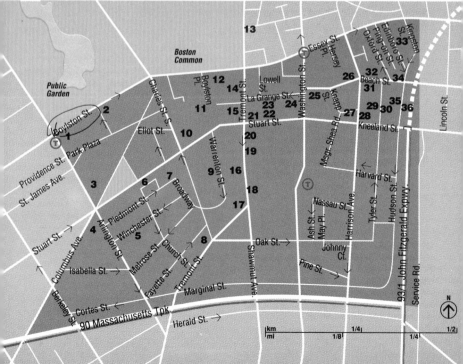

and the **August Moon Festival**, when local martial arts groups don dragon costumes and dance through the streets amid exploding firecrackers and crowds of celebrants. Jammed into dense blocks are 150-200 restaurants—many open as late as 4AM— bakeries, gift and curio shops, and markets selling live poultry, fresh fish, vegetables. What remains of the textile and garment industry, once Chinatown's economic mainstay, is located where **Harrison Avenue** intersects Kneeland. **Tyler Street** is showiest, with some flamboyant storefronts, while Beach St offers the real workaday scene. As you stroll, look right and left.

A community at a crossroads, Chinatown is struggling to preserve its ethnic character. The first Chinese came to Boston soon after the Revolution; subsequent China trade brought workers to the seaport, but a permanent community wasn't established until 1875. With the liberalization of immigration laws in the mid '60s, Chinatown ballooned, but then lost half its land to highway expansion, downtown encroachment, and the New England Medical Center. The population has swelled to more than 7500, with Vietnamese, Laotians, and Cambodians increasing the ethnic composition. Bursting at the seams, demoralized by the decaying Zone and lack of affordable housing, troubled by refuse-strewn streets, Chinatown's future looked grim until recently; now the Neighborhood Council has created a plan to control Chinatown's destiny and reap a fair share of whatever benefits future development may bring.

New England Medical Center (NEMC): Founded in 1796 as **The Boston Dispensary**, NEMC is the oldest health care institution in New England and the teaching hospital for **Tufts University School of Medicine.** NEMC is comprised of a medical center for adult patients, the **Floating Hospital for Infants and Children**, the **Pratt Diagnostic Clinic**, and various research, treatment, and diagnostic services.

A dénouement to the neighborhood drama may be the proposed urban megadevelopment called the **Midtown Cultural District** (boring name for a lead player!), a 2-square-mile mixed-use community of office towers, department stores, hotels, restaurants, clubs, retail and cultural space that would

Chinatown/Theater District

encompass **Park Square**, the Theater District, the Zone, and **Downtown Crossing**. It would serve as the catalyst for restoring historic theaters, ensuring Chinatown's prosperity and NEMC's growth, and boosting downtown nightlife. And one unsavory character would be eliminated in the process—the troublemaking Zone. Whatever the story's outcome, this neighborhood will remain the source for great performances in gorgeous old theaters, vibrant comedy club acts, authentic Chinese culture and cuisine, and new sophisticated restaurants perfect for a night on the town.

1 The Heritage on the Garden (1987, **The Architects Collaborative**) One of Boston's more accommodating new architectural presences is this mixed-use complex of retail and commercial space and luxurious residential condos. A number of high-powered shops and restaurants are located on the Heritage premises, albeit with confusingly varied addresses, including **Sonia Rykiel Boutique**, 280 Boylston St, 426.2033; **Waterford Wedgwood**, 288 Boylston St, 482.8886; **Maud Frizon**, 292 Boylston St, 426.4723; **Yves Saint Laurent Rive Gauche**, 304 Boylston St, 482.6661; **Escada**, 308 Boylston St, 437.1200; **Hermès**, 22 Arlington St, 482.8707; **Doubleday Book Shop**, 99 Park Plaza, 482.8453. ♦ 300 Boylston St (Arlington St) &

Within The Heritage on the Garden:

Biba ★★★★$$$ Boston's wild about Biba, the adventurous inspiration of Boston-born and trained chef **Lydia Shire**. Shire rose to eminence through stints at several renowned local restaurants, then left for California. Thankfully, she has returned and opened this restaurant bubbling over with *joie de vivre*. Daring Shire experiments with international cooking styles and her innovations parade onto the menu. Appetizers and entrees are intermixed so diners may choose any combination suiting their fancy. Marvelous flatbread arrives hot from the Indian tandoori oven in the corner. The menu changes frequently, but early surprises have been fried boned quail with parsnip chips, calf's brains with crisp-fried capers, green-tea duck with ginger-and-scallion pancakes, maple-and rum-smoked salmon, wood-roasted chicken, and sour-cherry ice cream with chocolate cake and *something crunchy*. New York architect **Adam Tihany** designed the restaurant, a quirky ensemble of styles. But the 2nd-floor dining room's best feature is big views of the **Public**

| Restaurants/Clubs: Red | Hotels: Blue |
| Shops/Parks: Green | Sights/Culture: Black |

Garden lagoon. Service at Biba is spotty, but is always good-natured. The restaurant gets pretty noisy—don't plan on *sotto voce* confidences. If upstairs is booked, despair not—mix and match a delightful eccentric repast from the bar menu downstairs. The sultry ground-floor bar, decorated with a **Robert Jessup** mural depicting well-fed people, is where many stylish singles find each other. You don't have to look designed, however, to feel comfortable upstairs or down. ♦ International ♦ M-Th, Su 11:30AM-2:30PM, 5:30-9:30PM; F 11:30AM-2:30PM, 5:30-10:30PM; Sa 5:30-10:30PM. 272 Boylston St (Arlington St) Valet parking except Su during day (fee) Reservations required for dining room. 426.7878 &

The Spa

The Spa at the Heritage The public can come to this ultrachic and expensive European-style spa/health club/salon for pampering body, skin, and hair care treatments, including 6 kinds of massage, facials, body wraps, and manicures. You can also take aerobics classes for a fee. But workout facilities and the 3-lane lap pool under vaulted ceiling are limited to members or guests of member hotels. Plenty of special packages with the works are available, some

Chinatown/Theater District

including hotel accommodations and food. **Schwartz/Silver Architects** designed the pristine interior, collaborating with artist **Stephen Knapp**. The same owners operate the equally elite **Le Pli** in Harvard Sq, Cambridge, 868.8087. ♦ 28 Arlington St (Boylston St-Park Plaza) Spa 426.6999, salon 482.2424

PASTAVINO

Pastavino ★★$$ The name sounds Italian and the cuisine is trattoria-style, but this sleek newcomer is actually an American import of a French-based restaurant group. At least the dramatic decor comes from Italy—and those seeking a great plate of pasta will be content with the selection of more than a dozen kinds, plus daily specials such as *scamponi alla griglia* (grilled jumbo shrimp with olive oil and garlic sauce). Good salads too. Pumpkin-yellow tablecloths glow under myriad tiny electric stars set into the black ceiling, their glimmer reflected on the cloudy granite floor. Mirrored walls turn the dining room into a galaxy, but make some diners self-conscious. Pastavino offers superb, extensive takeout cuisine for breakfast, lunch, and dinner from **Bottega**, a separate shop on the premises with a few café tables. Once the weather warms up you can eat out front on a small plaza. ♦ Italian ♦ Pastavino: M-Th 5:30-10PM; F-Sa 5-11PM. Bottega: M-F 7AM-9PM, Sa 8AM-9PM, Apr-Sep (approx);

M-F 7AM-7PM, Sa 8AM-7PM, Su 9AM-9PM, Oct-Mar (approx). 91 Park Plaza. Valet parking weekends (fee) No jeans. Reservations recommended. Pastavino 482.0010; Bottega 482.0200 &

2 Four Seasons $$$$ Watch them come and go in the lovely **Public Garden** from the hotel's rooms and restaurants. Ask for a room with *the* view, this grand hotel's grandest offering. Public and private spaces are expansive. Among the celebrities who have stayed in the posh Presidential Suite are **Bruce Springsteen, Glenda Jackson, Christopher Plummer, Luciano Pavarotti, Leonard Bernstein**. A special Four Seasons asset is its friendly and solicitous staff. Exceedingly civilized, the hotel's concern for niceties gives a Boston visit extra sheen: every crib comes with a teddy bear, kids get bedtime milk and cookies and kits with cameras or magic tricks; the concierge distributes duck food for those voracious quackers across the way; and the restaurant packs picnic baskets. For joggers, the hotel offers running shoes and maps with trails starting from its entrance. There are 288 accommodations on 8 floors, with handicapped-accessible and nonsmokers' rooms available, and amenities feature concierge services, 24-hour room service, same-day laundry and 24-hour valet and pressing services, valet parking, business services. The health spa has a lap pool, Jacuzzi, sauna, on-call trainers. Although it lacks historic charm, the Four Seasons is a serious rival to the celebrated **Ritz-Carlton**, a block away. ♦ Deluxe ♦ 200 Boylston St (Arlington St) 338.4400, 800/332.3442, 800/268.6282 (Canada); fax 426.9207 &

Within Four Seasons:

Aujourd'hui ★★★$$$$ An ultrarefined setting for an elegant meal, nicest while light lingers in the **Public Garden** beyond. Reserve a windowside table. Chef **Mark Baker**'s acclaimed seasonal menu is complemented by the lengthy international wine list. Recent offerings: pumpkin-and-smoked-scallop bisque; broiled oysters with crab gratin and Ossetra caviar; hunter's plate with pheasant, mountain squab and axis deer; rosemary-roasted rack of lamb with hard cider; Chinese barbecued salmon with black-radish turnip cakes; chocolate-almond soufflé. Special dishes have reduced calories, sodium, and cholesterol. For a cozier party, reserve one of 2 private dining rooms. Professionals working and dining against the clock can reserve what's called a *Business Priority Lunch,* with arrival and departure times established beforehand (451.1392). Theatergoers also pressed for time may opt for the prix-fixe, pretheater menu. ♦ New American ♦ M-Th 7-11AM, 11:30AM-2:30PM, 6-10:30PM; F 7-11AM, 11:30AM-2:30PM, 5:30-11PM; Sa 7AM-noon, 5:30-11PM; Su 7-10:30AM, 11:30AM-2:30PM; 6-10PM. Valet parking (fee) Jacket and tie required at dinner. Reservations recommended. 451.1392, 338.4400 &

In Boston, the first black representatives to sit in any state legislature did so in 1866.

The Bristol Lounge ★★$$ Pick one of the discreetly positioned clusters of chairs and sofas for your conversation, accompanied by lunch, afternoon tea, cocktails, before- and after-theater supper and desserts. A children's menu is offered. Pianists provide classical music and soft jazz afternoons and evenings. Friday and Saturday evenings, 9PM-midnight, the Bristol sets out a lush prix-fixe Viennese dessert table. A fireplace warms things up during the winter. ♦ New American ♦ M-Th 11AM-midnight; F 11AM-2AM; Sa 11:30AM-2AM; Su 11:30AM-midnight. Reservations recommended for lunch &

Adesso Owners **Rick Grossman** and **Françoise Theise** are retail pioneers, dedicated to discovering and introducing the best up-to-the-moment furniture and lighting to America from France, Italy, West Germany, Holland, Austria. Some from America too. Called *new classics* by the owners, these pieces are smashing in any setting. Often they are architect-designed and available only to the trade in other cities. Adesso ships all over the world and produces newsletters and catalogs. ♦ M-W, F-Sa 10AM-6PM; Th 10AM-8PM. 451.2212 &

3 Boston Park Plaza Hotel & Towers $$$
Steps away from the theaters and one block from the **Public Garden**, this 1927 hotel has nearly 1000 rooms, more than 80 of which are located in the Plaza Towers atop the main hotel. Decor and room sizes vary considerably. At higher rates, the Towers offer more luxurious quarters, concierge, Continental breakfast, and other personalized services. Ask for a room on high overlooking the Public Garden. The Plaza offers individual voice-mail for every room; a weight room; free privileges at the nearby elegant **The Spa at the Heritage**, including pool and sauna; 24-hour room service; nonsmokers' floors; pharmacy. You can check out and order breakfast via video. On the premises are major airline ticket offices, a travel agency, and a ticket agency for sports, theater, and concert events. Within or adjacent to the Park Plaza are restaurants and lounges, including the peerless **Legal Sea Foods**. **Swans Lobby Lounge**, where **Liberace** began his career, serves tea and pastries and offers a full bar, with piano music after 4PM. The longtime hit *Forbidden Broadway*, a 45-minute cabaret spoofing current and vintage Broadway hits, is performed in the **Terrace Room**. ♦ Admission to *Forbidden Broadway*, shows Tu, F 8PM; Sa 7, 10PM; Su 3, 6PM. 64 Arlington St (at Park Plaza) 426.2000, 800/225.2008; fax 426.5545

Restaurants/Clubs: Red Hotels: Blue
Shops/Parks: Green **Sights/Culture: Black**

Legal Sea Foods ★★$$$ *If it's not fresh, it's not Legal.* The **Berkowitz** family lives up to their slogan every day in their restaurant fleet, the seafood starships of the Hub. This one's the flagship. Observe the long and patient lines—it's hard to believe the Legal empire began as a single, lowly fish-and-chips joint fewer than 20 years ago. Now an endless menu offers all the fruits of the sea, always superior and flapping-fresh. First, choose your fish, then decide on broiled, grilled, fried, stuffed, sautéed, steamed, pan-blackened, Cajun-style, even unusual Chinese recipes devised for Legal's by visiting chefs from China's Shandong province. The fish chowder could double for wallpaper paste in consistency but wins hordes of fans—including US presidents—as do the smoked salmon and bluefish pâté. And this is one place where it's always safe to eat raw clams and oysters—every batch is tested at an in-house laboratory. The extraordinary, extensive wine list lives up to the menu. *But be forewarned*: Legal's is not the place for lingering conversa-

Chinatown/Theater District

tion. There are no reservations, so you can easily cool your heels interminably; the loudspeaker incessantly barks out names; the dining rooms are noisy and jammed; and the policy is to bring food when ready, not necessarily when your companions receive theirs—still, superb seafood is worth some concession. When you require your brain food yet can't endure a mob scene, Legal's smaller café/takeout operation next door is the answer. The seating here is snugger than in the restaurant, but the café offers almost the same menu plus full bar, and operates a little faster. And if the café is too full, get dinner-to-go. ♦ Seafood ♦ M-Th 11AM-10PM; F-Sa 11AM-11PM; Su noon-10PM. 35 Columbus Ave (Park Sq) Restaurant 426.4444, café/takeout 426.5566 & Also at: Copley Pl. 266.7775; 5 Cambridge Center, Kendall Sq, Cambridge. 864.3400

Legal Sea Foods Cash Market The gargantuan Legal Sea Foods enterprise has yet another giant offshoot: this one-stop gourmet shop featuring a fish counter stocking at least a dozen kinds of fresh fish—from the same supplier used by the restaurant. Pick up live lobster packed to travel, whatever fish you wish, famous Legal chowder, pâtés, cheeses, crackers, salads, soups, sauces, condiments, marinades, coffees and teas, chocolates, etc, etc. Even Legal's own cookbook. The liquor department sells 600 wines, cold beer, and a full liquor selection. The Berkowitz family covers all the bases. But don't expect bargains. ♦ M-Sa 9AM-9PM; Su noon-6PM. 15 Columbus Ave (Park Plaza) 426.7777 &

Ben & Jerry's Ice Cream This franchise exclusively sells the populist entrepreneurs' popular ice cream, shipped fresh from their Vermont factory. Heath Bar Crunch is the biggest favorite, with all flavors available in sundaes, shakes, cones, ice-cream cakes, and between brownies and cookies. Coffee and muffins baked on the premises are sold in the morning until they run out. The shop is easy to miss; it's around the corner from Legal Seafoods. ♦ M-F 7:30AM-11PM; Sa 11AM-11PM; Su noon-11PM. The Statler Office Building at 20 Park Plaza (Charles St So-Arlington St) No credit cards. 426.0890 &

4 Park Plaza Castle (1891-1897, **William G. Preston**; National Register of Historic Places) The imposing granite *Castle*, as the eyecatching landmark is universally known around Boston, was built as an armory for the **First Corps of Cadets**, a private Massachusetts military organization founded in 1741 and commanded at one time by **John Hancock**. The Victorian fortress was a social center for prominent Bostonians in the late 1800s, and its luxurious clubby interior was the site for billiards, imbibing fine wine, and for the popular Cadet Theatricals. The corps now operates a private military museum in **Back Bay**. With its lofty hexagonal tower, turrets, crenellated walls, lancet windows, and drawbridge, the Castle is ready for medieval-style combat, but fulfills much calmer

Chinatown/Theater District

functions as an exhibition and convention center owned by the **Boston Park Plaza Hotel & Towers**. Bostonians flock to the annual **Crafts at the Castle** sale held here in early December and sponsored by **Family Services of Greater Boston**. Among major recent exhibitions was the famous **Names Project** display of quilt panels made by friends and family in memory of AIDS victims. Next door to the Castle is the **Back Bay Racquet Club**—built in 1886 as **Carter's Ink Factory**—which boasts an impressive terra-cotta-and-brick facade. ♦ 130 Columbus Ave (Arlington St) For events info, call Boston Park Plaza Hotel & Towers and request sales office: 426.2000 & (Columbus Ave entrance)

5 Bay Village A snippet of 19th-century Boston that's difficult to find by car and easy to miss on foot. Take a 15-minute stroll along **Piedmont, Church, Melrose**, and **Fayette** streets for the flavor of this insular nook. The tight cluster of short streets bordered by diminutive brick houses was mostly laid out during the 1820s and 1830s. Many of the artisans, housewrights, and carpenters who worked on fashionable **Beacon Hill**'s prestigious residences concurrently built their own small homes in Bay Village. The neighborhood's residents once encompassed other colorful professions: sailmakers, paperhangers, blacksmiths, harness and ropemakers, painters, salt merchants, musical instrument makers, cabinetmakers. **Edgar Allan Poe** was born in a lodging house in the vicinity in 1809; his parents were actors in a stock company playing nearby. Because

it's so close to the Theater District, Bay Village gradually acquired a bohemian flavor and spillover nightlife. Off Fayette St, look for brief **Bay St** with its single house, a concluding punctuation mark.

6 Suntory ★★$$$ Surely Boston's showstopping Japanese restaurant, Suntory provides 3 elegant settings for 3 distinctive dining styles. Superb sushi is composed at the 1st-floor sushi bar. The 2nd-floor Shabu-Shabu Room is named for its special offering: Japanese-style hot-pot with seafood or beef and vegetables cooked in copper pots filled with steaming broth. Other traditional dishes like tempura, teriyaki, and sukiyaki are highlighted on this menu, and do-it-yourselfers can opt for the unusual *ishiyaki*, which entails broiling your own raw seafood or beef on a hot stone brought to the table. Or ascend to the Teppan-Yaki Room on the 3rd floor, where *teppan* chefs dazzle with dramatic preparation and grilling of mixed seafood, meats, and vegetables on cooking surfaces set into the tables. For the best fun, order a multicourse dinner and watch the acts unfold. The restaurant is the first in a new chain owned by the giant corporation **Suntory Limited**, makers of the signature beer. ♦ Japanese ♦ M-Th 11:30AM-2PM, 6-9:30PM; F-Sa 11:30AM-2PM, 6-10PM; Su 5:30-9PM. 212 Stuart St (Charles St So) Valet parking at dinner (fee) No jeans, shorts, sneakers. Reservations recommended. 338.2111, 423.4060 &

7 57 Park Plaza Hotel/Howard Johnson $$ Smack dab in the middle of this neighborhood, the hotel has 350 rooms on 24 floors, 2 restaurants and a bar, an indoor heated pool, sauna, sundeck, room service, and free on-premises parking with direct access to the hotel. Handicapped-equipped rooms available. ♦ 200 Stuart St (Charles St So) 482.1800, 800/HOTEL 57; fax 451.2750 &

8 Beacon Hill Skate This is where you can rent or purchase roller skates to whiz along the **Esplanade** bordering the **Charles River**, or, in winter, ice skates to skim over the **Public Garden** lagoon while it's vacated by ducks and Swan Boats for the season. (Skates available lagoon-side too, through this shop.) Skateboards too. ♦ M-Sa 11AM-6PM; Su 11AM-5PM; closed Christmas, New Year's Day, Thanksgiving. 135 Charles St So (Warrenton-Tremont Sts) 482.7400

9 Nick's Entertainment Center Another fixture on Boston's entertainment scene, Nick's has 3 parts: the popular **Nick's Comedy Stop**, a club featuring local and national comics; a cabaret theater; and an Italian restaurant called **Giancarlo's**. Many people opt for the special package that includes dinner in the restaurant and one of the shows. Tickets are also available at **Bostix**. ♦ Admission. Box office: daily 10AM-9PM. Nick's Comedy Stop: M-Th 8:30PM; F-Sa 8, 10, 11:30PM; Su 9PM. Cabaret theater: Th-Sa 8PM, Su 7:30PM. Giancarlo's: Tu-Su 5-10PM. 100 Warrenton St (Charles St So-Stuart St) No tank tops. Reservations with credit card payment. 482.0930

STUART STREET — PARKING — WATER TANKS — BOYLSTON PLACE — BOYLSTON STREET

9 Charles Playhouse, Stages I, II, III

(1839-1843, **Asher Benjamin**; renovation, 1957-1966 **Cambridge Seven**; National Register of Historic Places) The Theater District's oldest playhouse began life as a church and today is a rental facility for private productions, all managed separately. Playing on Stage I is *Nunsense*, an unholier-than-thou farce that's a local hit. On Stage II, *Shear Madness* has played for more than a decade, and is likely to go on as long as new visitors come to town. It's already made the *Guinness Book of World Records*. The comedy-whodunit, set in a Boston beauty salon, often stars good local professional actors. An eccentric concert pianist who lives upstairs is bumped off, and everybody has a motive. Boston police officers enlist the audience to find the culprit, with the solution changing nightly and new improvisations, local color, and topical humor added continually. Stage III is home for **The Comedy Connection**. ♦ Stage I seats 399; box office M 10AM-4PM; Tu-F 10AM-8PM; Sa 10AM-9PM; Su noon-5PM; shows Tu-F 8PM; Sa 6, 9PM; Su 3PM. Stage II seats 196; box office daily 10AM-last show; shows Tu-F 8PM; Sa 6:30, 9:30PM; Su 3, 7:30PM. 74-76 Warrenton St (Charles St So-Stuart St) Cash only at box office. Stage I 426.6912; Charg-Tix 542.8511. Stage II 426.5225; Charg-Tix 542.8511

Within Charles Playhouse, Stage III:

The Comedy Connection Attracting the 21-30 crowd, especially college students, this well-established stand-up comedy cabaret books headliner acts Wednesday-Sunday, with new or established talent launching new material scheduled for Monday and Tuesday. Full bar and bar food are served throughout shows. If you charge your tickets in advance, seats will be reserved for you; if you pay cash, you can reserve seats the day of the performance. Eighteen year olds admitted Sunday-Thursday and for first show Friday-Saturday. ♦ Admission. Shows M-Th 8:30PM; F 8:30, 10:30PM; Sa 7, 9, 11:15PM; Su 8:30PM. Credit cards accepted in advance; cash only at door. 391.0022; Charg-Tix 542.8511 ♿

The 900,000-square-foot **Massachusetts State Transportation Building** is warmed in winter by the heat generated by lights, computers, photocopiers, coffee machines, and 2000-or-so employees. The heat is recycled by an innovative energy-recovery and storage system with heat pump/chillers and an insulated tank for storing 750,000 gallons of water. In the summer, the same system runs in reverse and cools the complex.

10 Massachusetts State Transportation Building

(1983, **Goody, Clancy & Associates**) The architects recognized that this farflung office complex for state transportation agencies, occupying an entire city block, was an unprecedented disruption in a diverse and scattered low-rise neighborhood. With the participation of local business, cultural, and neighborhood groups, the architects created a building that exerts itself to relate to the surrounding streetscapes and activities, and incorporates an interior pedestrian mall with shops and restaurants to draw that vitality inward. The result isn't an architecturally exciting building, but a well-intentioned one. Across the street from the entrance, in a motley little greenspace, stands one statue Boston could do without. **Moses Kimball**'s hero-worshipping homage to **Abraham Lincoln** portrays the President as the *Great Emancipator*, anointing a kneeling former

slave, with the inscription *A Race Set Free/A Country At Peace/Lincoln Rests From His Labors* (1879). From today's vantage point, many find the work paternalistic and demeaning. ♦ 10 Park Plaza

Within the Massachusetts State Transportation Building:

rocco's ★★★$$$ There's no better prelude or finale to an evening at the theater than dinner here. Or come add a dash of drama to an otherwise uneventful night. Painted murals, enormous arches, flamboyant draperies, and artful props give rocco's a fantastic stagestruck look perfect for this part of town. **Kevin Schopfer** created the decor, **Julia Matheson Roe** painted the Rococo-inspired ceiling frescoes. Dining here is like joining in a perpetually improvised performance, always festive and fun—this is a happenin' place in the best sense. Owners **Patrick** and **Jayne Bowe** deserve an ovation for letting collective imaginations run wild. Dine café-style and less expensively on appetizers and wine, or indulge more extravagantly, like the lush, fleshy figures overhead. The eclectic cuisine tours the world with wonderful results: pizzettas, venison goulash, rack of lamb, paella, Thai stir-fry, Peking duck, Jamaican stew. Desserts are equally versatile. The extensive use of fabric means you can talk as well as gawk. ♦ International ♦ M-W 11:30AM-2:30PM; Th-F 11:30AM-2:30PM, 5:30-11:30PM; Sa noon-3PM, 5:30-11:30PM; Su noon-3PM. Reservations recommended. 5 Charles St So (Boylston-Stuart Sts) 723.6800 ♿

Bnu ★★$$ The café's owners have managed to create a charming niche in the vast transportation complex, with frescoes and ornament projecting the pleasing illusion of an Italian piazza. Bnu serves the freshest ingredients prepared simply and deliciously, in dishes like pizzettas with a changing collection of toppings; fettucine with saffron-cream sauce and grilled mussels; veal stew with lemon, cloves, and bay leaves on a bed of polenta; linguine with Parmesan, grilled shrimp, broccoli, pine nuts, roasted red pepper, and garlic; cannoli with sweet herbed ricotta and roasted almonds. The salads are also noteworthy. By-the-glass specials of beer and wine are offered. If you have a performance to catch, let the maître d' know beforehand and relax. ◆ Northern Italian ◆ M-W 11:30AM-9:30PM; Th-F 11:30AM-11PM; Sa 5-11PM; Su 5-9PM. 123 Stuart St (Charles St So-Tremont St) Reservations recommended. 367.8405 &

Joyce Chen ★$$ A famous local chef, Chen's restaurant is both fancier and pricier than most other Chinese restaurants in the neighborhood. This isn't the place to seek exotic new tastes—the tiny nondescript places are much better for that—but to enjoy reliable Mandarin and Szechuan dishes in comfort. Popular choices include General Gau's chicken, lobster with ginger and scallions, Peking duck. On weekdays, there's a fixed-price luncheon buffet.

Chinatown/Theater District

◆ Chinese/takeout ◆ M-W 11:30AM-9:45PM; Th-F 11:30AM-12:45AM; Sa noon-12:45AM; Su noon-9:45PM. 115 Stuart St (Tremont St) Valet parking (fee) Reservations recommended for 5 or more. 720.1331, for deliveries call TAKEOUT & Also at: 390 Rindge Ave, Fresh Pond, Cambridge. 492.7373

11 Boylston Place Located off **Boylston St** along **Piano Row**, this pedestrian cul-de-sac reputedly was where football was born in 1860, when a student of **Mr. Dixwell's Private School** organized the first game. The rubber sphere used for a ball is in the **Society for the Preservation of New England Antiquities**' collections. Enter via a fanciful arch replete with theatrical and local allusions. At the end of Boylston Pl, a pedestrian passage leads through the **Transportation Building** to **Stuart St**, a handy shortcut.

On Boylston Place:

Zanzibar One of the city's most popular dance and party spots is this 2-story, tropical para-

dise-themed playhouse, with soaring palm trees, Caribbean-motif architecture, ceiling fans, spacious dance floor. A DJ spins a mix of Top 40 and rock 'n' roll floorburners for an upscale crowd, generally ranging in age from mid 20s to mid 40s. There's a full bar, but no food except for private events. At the moment, Zanzibar is where concierges at local hotels send guests to kick up their heels. No one under 21 admitted. ◆ Cover. W-Su 8PM-2AM. 1 Boylston Pl (Off Boylston St, Charles St So-Tremont St) Valet parking on weekend (fee) Jacket and tie required. 451.1955 &

Sweetwater Café $ When you want to be casual and anonymous, try this laid-back, cheap-eats place for big portions of Tex-Mex and bar food like nachos, tostadas, burritos, BBQ beef, and super-hot buffalo wings. There's a bar on the 2nd level, but the downstairs is quieter, with booths. Two juke boxes crank out tunes, one stocked with old 45s. You can eat outdoors in nice weather. ◆ American ◆ M-W noon-1AM; Th-Sa noon-2AM. 3 Boylston Pl (Off Boylston St, Charles St So-Tremont St) 357.7027

The Tavern Club Since 1887, this exclusive club, only recently open to women, has resided in 3 quaint brick row houses dating from early-to mid-19th century. The Theater District location is appropriate, since for generations the club has been famed for its private performances of outrageous plays starring club members. ◆ 4-6 Boylston Pl (Off Boylston St, Charles St So-Tremont St)

12 Boylston Street The slice of Boylston St facing the **Boston Common** was once known as *Piano Row* for its concentration of piano-making and music-publishing establishments—enterprises in which music-loving Boston led the nation during the 19th and early 20th centuries. The businesses occupied—some still do—several handsome buildings that are physical expressions of the city's traditional high esteem for music: until recently, the **Wurlitzer Company** resided at No. 100 with its elegant, elaborate storefront, designed by **Clarence H. Blackall** and also home to the distinguished **Colonial Theatre**; the **Boston Music Company** moved to 172 Tremont St after a century at No. 116; the **Steinert Piano Company** is located at Beaux-Arts-style No. 162 by **Winslow and Wetherell**, 1896; No. 154-156 is the **E.A. Starck Piano Company Building**; and **Vose and Sons Piano Company** occupies No. 158-160. While you're on this stretch of Boylston, look for the **Little Building**, No. 80, a 1916 commercial edifice designed by Blackall's firm with a Gothic-influenced terra-cotta facade. Step inside and take a look at Little's arcaded lobby decorated with silly-charming murals of Boston history. Then cross **Tremont St** to see No. 48, the eye-catching Ruskinian Gothic **Young Men's Christian Union** of 1875, by **Nathaniel J. Bradlee**, listed on the National Register of Historic Places. A few steps farther is the **Boylston Building**, No. 2-22, an 1887 edifice listed on the **National Register of Historic Places** and the work of **Carl Fehmer**, architect of numerous important Boston office buildings and homes, including the grandiose **Oliver Ames Mansion** on **Comm Ave** in **Back Bay**.

12 Colonial Theatre (1899-1900, **Clarence H. Blackall**; interior decoration, **H.B. Pennell**) The most gloriously grand theater in Boston, the Colonial is also one of the handsomest in the country. The play may disappoint, but the Colonial, never. Actually, this is a very un-Colonial-style structure, a 10-story office building with a theater tucked in. The Colonial brims with classical ornament, ebulliently gilded and mirrored, with glittering chandeliers, lofty arched ceilings, sumptuous frescoes and friezes, allegorical figures—all the ruffles and flourishes imaginable. Yet the theater is also intimate and comfortable, with excellent sight lines and acoustics. Brilliant Blackall's other local credits include the nearby **Wilbur** and **Metropolitan** (now the **Wang**) theaters, as well as the **Winthrop Building** downtown. Thankfully, Blackall and Pennell's masterpiece has been spared the ups, downs, and indignities of many ravaged Boston theaters, and has been lovingly preserved. Built expressly for legitimate theater, the Colonial continues to book major productions, often musicals, many on the way to Broadway. In the theater's 90-odd years, **Flo Ziegfeld**, **Irving Berlin**, **Rodgers and Hammerstein**, **Bob Fosse**, and **Tommy Tune** have launched shows here; **Ethel Barrymore**, **Frederic March**, **Helen Hayes**, **Katherine Hepburn**, **Henry Fonda**, **Fred Astaire**, **Eddie Cantor**, **W.C. Fields**, **the Marx Brothers**, **Will Rogers**, **Danny Kaye**, and **Barbra Streisand** have all trod the boards. Those lucky enough to find their way deep into the backstage recesses discover a wealth of history and memorabilia from past productions. Half-price fares offered for handicapped persons and one companion. ♦ Seats 1658. Box office M-Sa 10AM-6PM; Su noon-6PM; open until 8PM performance days. 106 Boylston St (Tremont St) 426.9366 ら

13 The Boston Music Company Open for 105 years, the august music emporium purveys New England's largest selection of sheet music and books on music. One glance inside tells you this shop's an oldie but goodie. Its clientele encompasses music lovers and musicians, professional and amateur, who seek anything from choral pieces to the latest rock 'n' roll hit. Boston Music is proud of its enormous collection of music-related gifts, like its cases of music boxes ranging to $5000 or so. A musical instrument department sells traditional and late electronic instruments. Boston Music is also an educational music publisher, distributing its titles throughout the world. It's owned by

Hammerstein Music and Theatre Corp., owned in turn by the estate of the legendary **Oscar Hammerstein**. ♦ M-F 9:15AM-7PM; Sa 9:15AM-6PM. 172 Tremont St (Charles St So-Tremont St) 426.5100. Also at: 57 JFK St, Harvard Sq, Cambridge. 497.1567

14 Jack's Joke Shop *Yes, We Have Warts!* a shop notice reads. Pick out your latest disguise at owner **Harold Bengin**'s wholesale/retail emporium for tricksters. Or make an unforgettable impression with a unique gift from an inventory topping 3000 different items, including backward-running clocks, instant worms, garlic gum, sneeze powder, and ever-popular gross-outs like severed heads, fake wounds, and worse. Open in Boston since 1922, the oldest shop of its type in the US, Jack's is definitely one of the city's more colorful institutions. Halloween is the shop's biggest selling season, naturally, but kids and adults stream in throughout the year for jokes, tricks, magic, novelties, complete costumes, masks, wigs, beards, flags of all countries, oddities galore. Even New York visitors exclaim over the selection. Bengin and his staff clearly get a kick out of this business. ♦ M-Sa 8:30AM-5:30PM. 197 Tremont St (Boylston St) No credit cards. 426.9640 ら

15 Emerson Majestic Theatre (1901-1903, **John Galen Howard**) Originally famous for its musicals and opera performances, the extrava-

Chinatown/Theater District

gantly ornate, beaux-arts-style Majestic was bought by a movie-theater chain in the '50s that slapped tacky fake materials on top of marble and Neoclassical friezes. **Emerson College** rescued the theater in 1983, spent several million dollars on renovations, and intends to spend more until the Majestic lives up to its name once again. Today, under Emerson's wing, the Majestic is a multipurpose performance center for nonprofit groups, including **Dance Umbrella**, **Boston Lyric Opera**, the **New England Conservatory**, and **Emerson Stage**. Patrons favor the Emerson Majestic for its sense of excitement and inclusion with performers; performers favor the theater for its rococo high style and fine acoustics—but grumbling is growing over the cramped orchestra pit. This was Boston's first theater with electricity incorporated into the building's design. ♦ Seats 859. Box office daily 10AM-4PM during shows. 219 Tremont St (Boylston-Stuart Sts) 578.8727

The **Colonial Theatre**'s opening day, 20 December 1900: an extraordinary blockbuster production of *Ben-Hur* was launched in which 4 hydraulic lifts were used to raise a dozen horses from below stage for the show's dramatic chariot race. Hitched to Roman chariots, the horses galloped toward the audience on treadmills built into the stage, a thrilling spectacle that won accolades from reviewers. After opening night, *The Boston Globe* enthused: *Nothing So Beautiful, Pictorially and Mechanically, Ever Seen Before on a Boston Stage.*

16 Shubert (1908-1910, **Hill, James, and Whitaker**; National Register of Historic Places) The refined Shubert, with its graceful marquee, is part of the famous chain, but has a fine reputation in its own right among actors and audiences. **Kathleen Turner** heated up the town in **Tennessee Williams'** *Cat on a Hot Tin Roof*. The illustrious **Sir Laurence Olivier, John Barrymore**, and **John Gielgud** performed here; so did **Sarah Bernhardt, Mae West, Humphrey Bogart, Ingrid Bergman, Cary Grant, Helen Hayes**. You have to squeeze in here a bit. Greatly discounted tickets are offered to handicapped persons and one companion.
◆ Seats 1680. Box office M 10AM-6PM during shows; Tu-Sa 10AM-8:30PM during shows; Su noon-6PM if performance scheduled. 265 Tremont St (Stuart St) 426.4520 ⟨&⟩

17 The Tremont House $$ Billing itself as *Boston's Affordable Alternative*, the Tremont House takes the name of Boston's first grand hotel, long gone, and fills the shoes of the former **Bradford Hotel**, where '50s big bands played. Offering 281 rooms on 15 floors, including handicapped-equipped and nonsmokers' rooms, the newly renovated hotel caters to the theater crowd, both performers and spectators. Casts often stay here, and special packages, including tickets, are available. Amenities include room service and valet parking with charge. Sharing the building is **Stage Deli**,

Chinatown/Theater District

where theater stars and fans alike flock. The hotel's brass Elks Club doorknobs are a clue: the hotel was built in 1926 as the national headquarters for the **Benevolent and Protective Order of Elks**, which explains why the public spaces are so grand. ◆ 275 Tremont St (Stuart St) 426.1400, 800/228.5151; fax 482.6730 ⟨&⟩ Within Tremont House:

Stage Deli of New York ★$ Glitzy and frenetic, this New York-style delicatessen is doing its best to satisfy the cravings of deli-starved Boston with provisions trucked in fresh from the Big Apple. Stage is known for its corned beef and pastrami, humongous hot entrees, and sky-high sandwiches fit for Dagwood, including more than 2 dozen named for local and national celebrities. Tackle the **Larry Bird** Triple Decker, the **Raymond Flynn** Reuben, the **Chet and Natalie** Triple Decker, named for Boston's husband-and-wife TV anchor team. Dive into knockwurst and sauerkraut, stuffed cabbage, potato pancakes, blintzes, apple strudel, New York-style cheesecake. Somewhat more modest sandwiches are offered for less courageous appetites. Celebrities from whatever shows are in town drop in all the time; their particular deli addictions sometimes make it into a local gossip column. ◆ Deli/takeout
◆ M-Th 11AM-11PM; F 11AM-1AM; Sa 7:30AM-1AM; Su 8AM-10PM. 523.3354 ⟨&⟩

Restaurants/Clubs: Red   Hotels: Blue
Shops/Parks: Green   **Sights/Culture: Black**

NYC Jukebox and VHF This is one club with 2 rooms and 2 DJs playing 2 different kinds of music. In one room, Bostonians can shake, rattle, and roll to '50s and '60s dance music; in the other, a younger crowd flocks to watch Top 40 videos on dozens of TV screens. There's a full bar, but no food. No one under 21 admitted.
◆ Cover. NYC Jukebox: Th-Sa 8PM-2AM. VHF: F-Sa 8PM-2AM. Casual attire, but no T-shirts, tank tops, or sweats. 542.1123 ⟨&⟩

Roxy Swank and sophisticated, the Roxy puts on the Ritz with spinning mirrored balls splashing light across the big dance floor. Swing music performed by the 14-piece **White Heat Swing Orchestra**—accompanied by a jazz vocalist—alternates with contemporary dance hits spun by a DJ. The **Roxy Dancers**, a 6-member act, put on a stage show twice nightly. Many come to the Roxy for romance, and some find it: one couple met and later married here, their *I do*'s followed by White Heat playing the lovers' favorite song. Full bar, no food. On Saturday parties of 2 or more can reserve seats in the special balcony section overlooking the dance floor and stage—the Roxy Regency—with dessert buffet included.
◆ Cover. Th-Sa 8PM-2AM. 279 Tremont St (Stuart St) Jacket required, no jeans or sneakers. 227.7699 ⟨&⟩

18 The Wang Center for the Performing Arts (1925, **Blackall, Clapp and Whittemore**, et al.; expansion 1982, **Jung, Brannen**; National Register of Historic Places) It's worth the ticket price to whatever performance you can catch here just to see inside this former motion-picture cathedral. Predating New York City's **Radio City Music Hall**, this mammoth entertainment palace was considered the *wonder theater of the world* when it opened in the Roaring Twenties, built to pack in huge crowds 4 times daily for variety revues and first-run movies. An architectural extravaganza, the 7-story theater boasts a succession of dramatic lobbies—concluding with the 5-story Grand Lobby—bedecked with Italian marble columns, stained glass, bronze detailing, gold leaf, crystal chandeliers, florid ceiling murals. In the theater's early days, billiards, ping-pong, card parties, and other games in 4 ornate lobbies occupied the crowds until the next show started. First called the **Metropolitan Theater** then later the **Music Hall**, it was renamed for a major benefactor in 1983 and renovated to accommodate a variety of performing arts, including opera, ballet, and Broadway musicals. The Wang now has one of the largest stages of any theater in the world. For plays, try hard to get down-front center seats in the orchestra, where sight and sound are best. The Wang's

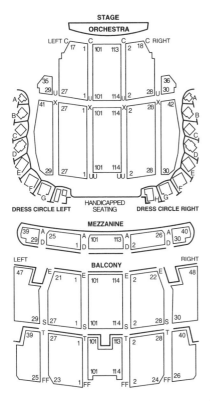

STAGE
ORCHESTRA

LEFT C ———— C   C ———— C RIGHT
17 | 1 | 101 | 113 | 2 | 18

35 / 29 | 27 | 1 | 101 | 114 | 2 | 28 | 36 / 30

41 | X | 27 | X | 101 | 114 | X | 2 | 26 | X | 42

29 | 27 | 1 | 101 | 114 | 2 | 28 | 30

101 | 114
39 / G | HANDICAPPED | H / G
DRESS CIRCLE LEFT | SEATING | DRESS CIRCLE RIGHT

MEZZANINE
39 / 29 | 25 | 101 | 113 | 26 | 40 / 30

LEFT | **BALCONY** | **RIGHT**
47 | E | 21 | 1 | E | 101 | 114 | E | 2 | 22 | E | 48

29 | S | 27 | 1 | S | 101 | 114 | S | 2 | 28 | S | 30

39 | T | 27 | 1 | T | 101 | 113 | T | 2 | 28 | T | 40

101 | 114
25 | FF | 23 | 1 | FF | FF | 2 | 24 | FF | 26

Young at Arts educational outreach program for the Boston community involves children in the visual and performing arts through workshops, performances held in Wang's lobbies, and an annual art contest; subsidized tickets are available and many events are free. Call to inquire. The theater also brings back a hint of its past history with a classic film series shown on one of the world's largest screens. The **Boston Ballet** makes its home here, and famous visiting performers such as the **Alvin Ailey American Dance Theater** and the **Bolshoi Ballet Academy** visit frequently. Further restoration to come will bring back more of the Wang's former splendor while updating its facilities and theater technology. And the unfortunate statues will get new heads. ◆ Seats 4200. 270 Tremont St (Stuart St) Info 482.9393; Ticketmaster 931.2000 ♿

19 Wilbur Theatre (1914, **Clarence H. Blackall**; National Register of Historic Places) This distinguished Colonial Revival theater has witnessed its share of dramatic debuts, including the pre-Broadway production of **Tennessee Williams**' *A Streetcar Named Desire* starring **Marlon Brando** and **Jessica Tandy**. Another of Boston's Blackall treasures, the Wilbur endured dark days and decay, its nadir a brief stint as a cabaret that flopped. But the lights are on again: the proud theater has rebounded, newly restored. The modestly sized fan-shaped house has been renovated to accommodate Off Broadway-style productions. Recent smash runs were *Steel Magnolias* and **A.R. Gurney**'s *Love Letters*. Look up at the facade and note the 3 theatrical masks—grinning, grimacing, agape—above the upper windows. Half-price

fares offered for handicapped persons and one companion. ◆ Seats 1200. Box office M-Sa 10AM-6PM; during shows M 10AM-6PM, Tu-Sa 10AM-8PM, Su noon-6PM. 246 Tremont St (Stuart St) 423.4008 ♿

21 Zoots On Thursday, Friday, and Saturday nights, from 9PM-1AM, this casual club features live music: R&B, blues, country, zydeco, rock, rockabilly—just about anything except hard rock and polka bands. The type of crowd

Chinatown/Theater District

on the dance floor varies with the music, but anyone can come in and feel comfortable. Unlike the other nightclubs nearby, jeans are just fine here. The jukebox has a little of everything—**Frank Sinatra** to **Paula Abdul**—and there's cable TV for sports. Barfood is served. ◆ M-Sa 4PM-2AM. 228 Tremont St (Stuart St) 451.5997 ♿

22 Montien ★★$$ A solid favorite with theatergoers, businesspeople, and staff from the nearby medical complex. Montien offers all the classic favorites like *pad Thai*, *satay*, and curries, plus unusual specials like *kat-thong-tong*, a crisp pastry shell filled with ground chicken, onions, corn, and coriander with sweet dipping sauce. Tamarind duck and fried squid are superb. The hot-and-spicy set will find their pleasure, as will palates preferring subtler sensations. Service is respectful and prompt, so you'll make that curtain. ◆ Thai/takeout ◆ M-Sa 11:30AM-11PM; Su 4:30-11PM. 63 Stuart St (Tremont St) Reservations recommended for large parties. 338.5600 ♿

Arkansas Congressman **Wilbur Mills**, former chairman of the powerful **House Ways and Means Committee**, met his political downfall in the shape of stripper **Fanne Fox**, with whom he cavorted on stage at the racy **Pilgrim Theatre** in the Combat Zone, December 1974.

The first American labor organization was founded 18 October 1648 by Boston shoemakers.

22 **Jacob Wirth** ★$$ (1844-1845, **Greenleaf C. Sanborn**; National Register of Historic Places) Amid the whirl of Boston's dining fads and fashions, this aged establishment plods along unwaveringly on its own steady course. Bratwurst, knockwurst, sauerbraten, sauerkraut, accompanied by heady, specially brewed dark beer—Jacob Wirth has been offering up the same hearty traditional German fare in the same bowfront row house since its doors opened in 1868. All the furniture and fixtures—globe lighting, brass rails, dark paneling—are original. Even the waiters' attire looks vintage. It's easy to step into the past here; in fact, that's the reason to come. The cavernous beer hall is a great place to bring a crowd and sample the long list of beers. Those in your party with big appetites might attempt the German boiled dinner: pig's feet, pork roast, ribs, and cabbage. Food service stops after 10PM Monday-Thursday, after 10:30PM Friday-Saturday. Sing along with piano music from 7:30PM-midnight on Friday. The restaurant provides 2 free hours of parking at the adjacent lot for diners. ◆ German ◆ M-W 11:30AM-11:30PM; Th-Sa 11:30AM-midnight. 37 Stuart St (Tremont-Washington Sts) 338.8586 &

23 **Downtown Cafe** ★$$ *Everything from Scratch* is the promise of this endearing hole-in-the-wall located at the edge of the Combat Zone's last battleground. Step from alleylike, shabby La Grange St into the snug 11-table café, and you'll feel welcome. The bohemian surroundings feature ever-changing, whimsical decorations like dangling Mardi Gras beads, bric-a-brac, copper pots, local artists' work. Chef and owner **Daniel Holmes** offers one of Boston's most inventive menus, with lots of daily specials and plenty of beverages and wines to choose from. He features sirloin, chicken, salmon, and pleasing pasta renditions, plus potato pancakes, soup and salad combos, homemade blintzes, omelets, and more. You're encouraged to eat dessert here. Holmes uses hard-to-find ingredients and pays homage to every holiday and special occasion with seasonal treats. A neighborhood pioneer, he is doing his best to preserve the area's rich character in the face of massive urban redevelopment. ◆ New American/International ◆ M 5PM-closing; Tu-Sa 11AM-closing; Su noon-closing. 12 La Grange St (Tremont-Washington Sts) Reservations recommended. Credit for $25 and up. 338.7037

24 **Hayden Building** (1875, **H.H. Richardson**; National Register of Historic Places) An overlooked, modest-size office building that isn't one of **Richardson**'s finer works, but does display his characteristically vigorous Romanesque Revival approach. Unfortunately, the building has been put to demoralizing uses and poorly maintained. It patiently awaits better

days at the head of **La Grange St**, once a thriving mercantile stretch with hatters, tailors, shoemakers, and such. From the '60s until recently, La Grange was caught in the midst of the Combat Zone and its once-reputable appearance was shamefully besmirched. Today, La Grange is slowly reviving as the Zone collapses. ◆ 681 Washington St (La Grange St)

25 **Hong Kong Cuisine** $ The same people own the nearby **Golden Palace**, renowned for its dim sum, and you can savor identical tasty mouthfuls every day 8:30AM-3:30PM. The entrees are also good and authentic, such as the Chinese-sausage rice pot, salt-and-pepper squid or shrimp, roast duck, seafood pot, Peking-style pork chops. Appetizers include a great Chinese parsley-and-fish soup, shrimp-dumpling soup, and beef *satay*. This restaurant draws a mostly Asian clientele, so many off-the-menu choices are available for those who want to investigate. Don't expect much in the way of decor. ◆ Chinese/takeout ◆ Daily 8:30AM-11PM. 27-29 Beach St (Washington St-Harrison Ave) No credit cards. 451.2006

26 North End Fabrics Not only do they have the largest selection of fake fun-furs around—great for a come-as-you-were-half-a-million-years-ago party—but just about everything else in the way of fabrics one could possibly want: wool challis, velvets and velveteen, Thai silk, drapery and upholstery materials, bridal and theatrical fabrics, handkerchief linen, imported lace, odd bolts and remnants, notions—you name it. Professional dressmakers, designers, and home sewers all frequent this shop, around now for more than 30 years. ◆ M-Sa 9AM-5:45PM. 31 Harrison Ave (Beach-Essex Sts) 542.2763

27 **Dong Khanh** $ Come to this clean and bright eatery for fast food Vietnamese-style, including more than a dozen great noodle-soup dishes. The *bi cuon* (meat rolls) are very tasty; so are the fish in spicy soup and assorted BBQ meats with vermicelli. Be daring and try a *durian* juice drink, made from the Southeast Asian fruit that looks like a hedgehog and smells like rotting garbage, but has plenty of fans for its flavor. Lots of other intriguing drinks too. ◆ Vietnamese ◆ Daily 9AM-10PM. 83 Harrison Ave (Beach-Kneeland Sts) No credit cards. 426.9410

28 **Maxim's House** ★$ Tiny Maxim's shows its muscle with tremendous Vietnamese cuisine. Dip cold and crispy spring rolls in spicy peanut sauce, then try *banh xeo*, Vietnamese crêpe stuffed with little morsels of meat and vegetables, or fiery stir-fried chicken with chili peppers and lemon grass, or spicy fried squid, or any of 200 or so other inexpensive dishes. Beer and wine are served. Maxim's is owned by a Saigon dentist who came to Boston and started out selling eggrolls from the back of a station wagon. ◆ Vietnamese ◆ M-Th 9AM-11PM; F-Sa 9AM-midnight; Su 9AM-11PM. 84-86 Harrison Ave (Beach-Kneeland Sts) 451.5282

Theater tickets sell out well in advance and those available float among the different agencies, so shop around by phone.

29 Carl's Pagoda $$ Yes, there is a Carl, and many diners rely on his judgment when it comes to ordering. Carl is like a potentate ruling his personal fiefdom. But even if he's not there, a great meal can be had with tomato soup, lobster Cantonese style, clams in black-bean sauce, superb steamed fish, special steak. A shrimpy little place it is, but Carl's is one of the few Chinatown restaurants with tablecloths. ♦ Chinese/takeout ♦ M-Th, Su 5PM-midnight; F-Sa 5PM-1AM. 23 Tyler St (Beach-Kneeland Sts) Reservations recommended on weekends. No credit cards. 357.9837

30 Golden Palace ★★$ Many Chinatown eateries are so innocuous looking that they're easy to miss, but not this one—it has the fanciest facade around. The Palace's main attraction is excellent dim sum—perhaps Boston's best—served daily 9AM-3PM. There's no menu; when the carts roll up, simply select whatever tidbits strike your fancy in the sea of little plates loaded with dumplings, fried and steamed pastries, noodle dishes. Try *har gao* (shrimp dumplings), sparerib in black bean sauce, steamed *bao* (meat-filled buns), *shu mai* (pork dumplings), or more adventurous items like tripe and curried squid. This sprawling place—aglitz with reds, golds, pinks, and painted and carved dragons—is a noisy neighborhood favorite. People come to eat, not unwind, so service is hurried and atmosphere minimal. But the dim sum is piping hot, and the regular menu offers loads of superior dishes, including abalone and squab treatments. ♦ Chinese/takeout ♦ Daily 9AM-11:30PM. 14-20 Tyler St (Beach-Kneeland Sts) Reservations recommended for 10 or more. 423.4565

You'll notice many Chinatown restaurants have posted signs in Chinese specifying other available dishes that aren't listed on the menu. These are aimed at the neighborhood clientele. Delectable treats, homestyle dishes, and scary food apparitions—to the unaccustomed palate—are often listed this way. If you don't speak Chinese, it will be difficult in some restaurants to find out exactly what these mystery offerings are. For some, it's fun to take the plunge and try off-menu offerings, for others it may be too terrifying. And to avoid MSG, which does crop up in a lot of Chinatown cooking, tell your server you don't want any in your meal.

Restaurants/Clubs: Red   **Hotels**: Blue
Shops/Parks: Green   **Sights/Culture**: Black

31 Lucky Dragon $ Many of Boston's top chefs, including **Jasper White**, favor this place for dinner in Chinatown. Try watercress with oyster sauce, *chow foon* plates, Singapore rice sticks, fried bean cake with shrimp, seafood hot pot, beef with string beans, hot and spiced squid—there's a daunting list of possibilities. Bring your late-night cravings for good Chinese food here. ♦ Chinese ♦ Daily 11:30AM-3:30AM. 45 Beach St (Harrison Ave) Reservations recommended. 542.0772

31 Viet Restaurant ★$ The vast menu reels off dozens of tempting Vietnamese and Chinese dishes—but stick with Vietnamese fare the first time around, which is among Boston's best. Good choices include Vietnamese salad, lemon grass chicken, crunchy seafood salad with mint and basil, noodle soups, Vietnamese stew, wedding duck (steamed, roasted whole duck—order in advance). Great lunchtime specials. Beer and wine served. ♦ Vietnamese/Chinese ♦ M-Th 11:30AM-11PM; F 11:30AM-1AM; Sa 10AM-1AM; Su 10AM-11PM. 25-27 Tyler St (Beach-Kneeland Sts) 350.6615, 338.1791

32 Chau Chow Seafood ★★$ Definitely the Chinatown gem, this very busy, very basic place does great things with all sorts of seafood: crab with ginger and scallions, steamed sea bass and flounder, fried noodles with seafood and vegetables, salted jumbo shrimp in the shell, baby clams in black-bean sauce, sea-

food *chow foon*. Pork, beef, chicken, and duck dishes abound, all excellent. Sample stir-fried watercress, Swatowese dumplings, soup with sliced fish and Chinese parsley. Beer is served. Understandably, there's always a long line for dinner. ♦ Chinese/takeout ♦ 52 Beach St (Harrison Ave) M-Th 10AM-2AM; F-Sa 10AM-4AM; Su 10AM-1AM. No credit cards. 426.6266

33 Dynasty $$ A big-time kind of restaurant, Dynasty has lots of mirrors and golden columns and offers good Cantonese dishes: pan-fried spiced shrimp, chicken with cashews, clams in black-bean sauce, and steamed sea bass and gray sole, to name a few. And it stays open nearly round the clock. ♦ Chinese ♦ Daily 9AM-4AM. 33 Edinboro St (Essex St) 350.7777

33 Moon Villa $ A hangout for hungry night owls, Moon Villa is by no means the romantic place it sounds, but does serve family-style Cantonese dishes while the rest of the city snoozes. For dim sum, however, you have to come during the day. The waiters would make Frankenstein seem friendly. ♦ Chinese/takeout ♦ Daily 11AM-4AM. 15-19 Edinboro St (Essex St) 423.2061

34 Imperial Tea House ★$ Right at the gateway to Chinatown, this noisy, cavernous restaurant is a good choice for its 2nd-floor dim sum parlor, where a fleet of carts laden with arrays of little treats—pork dumplings, shrimp balls, bean curd, stuffed meat buns, braised chicken's feet, etc, etc—whiz past packed tables. Just point to your selection and it's whisked onto the table. Always mobbed, the tearoom attracts a fascinating mixed clientele. There's usually a short wait. Downstairs, order traditional Cantonese dishes from the regular menu. ♦ Chinese/takeout ♦ Daily 9AM-1AM. 70-72 Beach St (Edinboro St) Reservations recommended for large parties at dinner. No credit cards. 426.8439

35 Ho Yuen Ting ★$ People don't flock to this no-frills eatery for ambiance or decor, but for delectable Cantonese seafood specials like lobster with ginger, salted and spiced squid, shrimp with spicy sauce, or stir-fried sole and vegetables served in a crunchy edible bowl made of batter-fried fish bones. Also recommended: pork-and-watercress soup and fish-stomach soup with mushrooms or sweet corn. This is a good place to explore the unknown. The restaurant's located below street level, so be on the lookout or you'll pass right by. Another branch is located a couple blocks away on **Beach St**. ♦ Chinese/takeout ♦ M-Th, Su 11:30AM-9:30PM; F-Sa 11:30AM-10:30PM. 13A Hudson St (Beach-Kneeland Sts) No credit cards. 426.2316

36 New House of Toy $ It takes some guess-work—or fluency in Chinese—to decide what to order here, but a lot is very good. The dim sum tea brunch features nearly 60 varieties. Try to get the English version of the special menu on the window, which supplements the regular roster of dishes. Sample the steamed oysters in

Chinatown/Theater District

black-bean sauce, bean curd with shrimp and scallops, scallops in *satay*, short rib in spiced sauce, the sizzling platters. Frogs' legs aficionados will rejoice. ♦ Chinese ♦ Daily 9AM-10PM. 16 Hudson St (Beach-Kneeland Sts) 426.5587

Clubs

Read *The Boston Globe Calendar* on Thursday and the *Boston Phoenix* on Friday for information on the local club/music scene. A selection:

Boston

Axis Music changes nightly and includes progressive, punk, funk, heavy metal, hard rock, live bands, alternative dance tunes, DJ music. On Sunday, Axis connects with **Citi** next door for gay night; enter through Citi. ♦ 13 Lansdowne St, Kenmore Sq. 262.2437

The Black Rose Irish music and Irish fare, with plenty of great beers and ales on tap. ♦ 160 State St, Faneuil Hall Marketplace. 742.2286

The Channel A noisy, huge place with multibars and dance floors and a big stage for strong local and national acts—rock, reggae, world music. Fledgling local bands, too. Next door is **Necco Place**, 426.7744, a promising new club that's still shaping its identity. The smaller, more hospitable listening room features light rock and acoustic, rock, reggae, blues, jazz. Good sound system. ♦ 25 Necco St, Waterfront. 451.1905 (concert line)

The Hub Club A tripledecker club, one of the city's most popular, with a variety of music from old soul and

funk to international, reggae, progressive rock, late-breaking dance music. ♦ 533 Washington St, Downtown. 451.6999

NYC Jukebox and VHF Oldies but goodies in one room decorated with old jukeboxes and a '54 Ford; rock videos in the other. ♦ Tremont House, 275 Tremont St, Theater District. 542.1123

Paradise Rock Club One of Boston's best places to see national and international groups in concert. New Wave and rock are the mainstay at the Paradise, but it also books jazz, folk, blues, country. Get tickets in advance. ♦ 967 Comm Ave, Kenmore Sq. 254.2052/2053

The Plaza Bar An elegant cabaret-style setting where local and national entertainers perform jazz, pop, blues. Reservations recommended; jacket and tie required. ♦ The Copley Plaza Hotel, 138 St. James St, Back Bay. 267.5300

The Rat (Rathskeller) Boston's first New Wave club is an environmental disaster, but has a star-studded history of supporting local garage bands who've made it big, including **The Cars**, **The Police**, the **Talking Heads**, the Go Gos. The club books high-quality local and touring rock bands, up to 4 a night, 3-4 nights a week. ♦ 528 Comm Ave, Kenmore Sq. 536.2750

The Roxy Big band swing and contemporary dance music in a swank setting; jacket required. ♦ Tremont House, 279 Tremont St, Theater District. 227.7699

Wally's Café The little red schoolhouse of jazz features young musicians, often from Berklee, and is also a pleasant neighborhood bar. Founded nearly a half-century ago by owner **Joseph Walcott**, tiny Wally's is family-run and a Boston institution. ♦ 427 Mass Ave, South End. 424.1408

Zanzibar A tropical playpen extremely popular for dancing with a decked-out crowd. Jacket and tie required. ♦ 1 Boylston Pl, Theater District. 451.1955

Cambridge

Cantab Lounge Lots of dancing, and a lot of fun late Saturday night. Rock, blues, and jazz by local bands. ♦ 738 Mass Ave, Central Sq. 354.2685

Cantares Latin American salsa and merengue for dancing; regular blues jams. Mexican and Spanish cuisine. ♦ 15 Springfield St, Inman Sq. 547.6300

Man Ray An arty bar with progressive New Wave and rock; connected to **Campus**, a predominantly gay jukebox joint. ♦ 21 Brookline St, Central Sq. 864.0400

Nightstage Features only *signed* people (with record contracts). The club books rock, blues, zydeco, jazz, folk, country, international—a wide variety of great bands. A spacious medium-size room built expressly for music, with tables, understated decor, and orderly ambiance. ♦ 823 Main St, Central Sq. 497.8200

Passim Little coffeehouse below street level owned by **Bob** and **Rae Anne Donlin**; music added in '71. Encouraged local folk and bluegrass groups, made lots of loyal friends like **Tom Rush** and **Suzanne Vega**. National and local acoustic performers. Unpretentious. No liquor license, but a light menu with coffees, teas, cider. By day, a gift shop and café. ♦ 47 Palmer St, Harvard Sq. 492.7679

The Plough and Stars A rowdy, neighborly little Irish bar with Guinness, Harp, and Bass on tap, good pub-style food, live Irish, blues, country, and bluegrass music that attracts a cross section of Cantabrigians: artists, plumbers, writers, scholars, carpenters, students. Too small for dancing, barely enough room for the band, good-natured crowd. ♦ 912 Mass Ave, Central Sq. 492.9653

The Regattabar An upscale club that showcases nationally known names in jazz. Dress nicely. ♦ Charles Hotel, 1 Bennett St, Harvard Sq. 876.7777

Ryles You can often get a table in this casual, comfortable, quietish club booking top local and national jazz groups on 2 floors. ♦ 212 Hampshire St, Inman Sq. 876.9330

T.T. the Bear's Place Several new and established local bands are booked each night in this homey rock 'n' roll club. Sunday features a DJ dance format. ♦ 10 Brookline St, Central Sq. 492.0082

Western Front A long-lived club offering rasta, reggae, ska, funk, Latin, jazz, Jamaican music—it often showcases native local musicians. Lots of loyal regulars dance up a storm here. The Front has collaborated with **New York City**'s **Knitting Factory** to bring in great progressive jazz acts. ♦ 343 Western Ave (out of Central Sq). 492.7772

Other Neighborhoods

Green Street Station Entertainment includes open jams, rock and rockabilly—a casual neighborhood place to hear up-and-coming new bands every night of the week. A lotta dancing. **George** is *the shepherd* of the place. ♦ 131 Green St, Jamaica Plain. 522.0792

Harper's Ferry This dependable club boasts a horseshoe-shaped bar and big dance floor, and emphasizes blues and R&B and lots of favorite local bands, plus some out-of-towners, nationals, too. They give unknown new bands a first shot on Monday night. Wednesday and Sunday are open-mike nights for blues and R&B. ♦ 158 Brighton Ave, Allston. 254.9743

Johnny D's Restaurant and Music Club A laid-back club that's very popular with locals. Blues, R&B, zydeco, ska, folk, reggae, world beat. Local bands and newcomers, too. Dancing. ♦ 17 Holland St, Davis Sq, Somerville. 776.9667

Tam O' Shanter Universally called *The Tam* and as well known for its homey, tasty dinners and brunches as its music. A general R&B club with a touch of rock 'n' roll and Dixieland once in a while. Live music every night, dancing, tap revues. ♦ 1648 Beacon St, Brookline. 277.0982

Bests

Susan Berk
President, Uncommon Boston, Ltd.

Shopping for bargains at the 3rd-floor loft of **Charles Sumner**, Newbury Street. Designer clothing at 50-75 percent off.

Massage with Maureen at **M.J.N. at Harringtons**

Drinking a tasty, nonalcoholic beer, Clausthaler, at **Champions**, the sports bar at the Marriott Copley Place Hotel, co-owned by Bob Woolf, the sports attorney, and filled with Bruins, Red Sox, and Celtic memorabilia, T-shirts, autographs, photographs, etc.

Eating the delicious *lite* clam chowder at **Legal Sea**

Foods, Boston Park Plaza Hotel, made without cream or butter.

When it's time for a break on Beacon Hill, head for the **Coffee Connection** for the best cup of decaffeinated coffee and a bran muffin.

The lectures, happenings, and events at the **Victorian Society in America**, on Beacon Street.

The guided walks through **Mount Auburn Cemetery** conducted by the Friends of Mount Auburn Cemetery (547.7105). Learn about literature, history, horticulture, and bird-watching.

Museum of Fine Arts. The best place in town not only for art, but also for music, movies, and lectures all under one roof.

Barbara Krakow
Art Dealer

A baseball park in the heart of the city—**Fenway Park**—and the Red Sox. And a hot dog an inning.

Boston Film Festival—an opportunity to eat popcorn nonstop for days and, incidentally, role play as film critic.

Great to bike or walk—from the **Museum of Science** along the Memorial Drive side of the Charles River to the **Larz Anderson Bridge**, and back along the Storrow Drive side of the Charles, passing MIT, Harvard, BU, the Hatch Shell, Beacon Hill, and, in parallel view on the river, the college crew teams and the sailboats.

Chinatown/Theater District

A Swan Boat ride in the center of the extraordinarily beautiful **Public Garden**.

Advanced fashion for the head, hand, and body:

Frank Xavier, Newbury Street

Body Sculpture, Newbury Street

Alan Bilzerian, Newbury Street

Skinner's jewelry auctions at the **Ritz-Carlton Hotel**

Restaurants: Those where the chef and owner are one in the same. The quality of the food is consistently high, the menus change often, and, of great importance, the idiosyncrasies of their patrons are graciously attended to without the blink of an eye.

Allegro, Waltham

Biba

East Coast Grill, Cambridge

Hamersley's Bistro

Harvard Street Grill, Brookline

Icarus

Jasper's

Olive's, Charlestown

And then those favorites with the owners always on the premises:

On the Park

Michela's, Cambridge

St. Cloud

Sol Azteca

Back Bay

Back Bay is Boston's sumptuous centerpiece of illustrious institutions and architecture, and hundreds of boutiques and galleries. The best place in Boston for extravagant shopping sprees and leisurely promenades, Back Bay attracts a stylish international crowd that's as fun to look at as any of **Newbury Street**'s artful windows. An animated set, Back Bay is also a comfortable, compact neighborhood of broad gracious streets bordered by harmonious 4- and 5-story Victorian townhouses. Its residents are well-to-do families and established professionals, footloose young people and transient students, for whom the **Public Garden** is an outdoor living room and the **Charles River Esplanade** a grassy waterside backyard.

In the 19th century, Boston's wealthy old guard and brash new moneymakers together planted this garden of beautiful homes and public buildings, creating a cosmopolitan, Parisianlike quarter wrapped in an aura of privilege and prosperity. This lingering mystique has tricked even some Bostonians into believing Back Bay is one of the city's oldest neighborhoods, when it's really one of the youngest. What began as Boston's wasteland was transformed into its most desirable neighborhood by a spectacular feat of urban design.

In the 1850s, Boston boasted a booming population and exuberant commercial growth. Railroads and manufacture supplanted the sea as the city's primary source of capital. The nouveaux riches were hungry for spectacular domiciles, but the almost-waterbound city was already overcrowded on its little peninsula. The problem: where to get land? In 1814, a mile-and-a-half-long dam had been built from the base of **Beacon Hill** to what is now **Kenmore Square** to harness the

The **T** stops in and most convenient to Back Bay are **Arlington**, **Copley**, **Prudential**, and **Hynes Convention Center/ICA** (all **Green Line**). Just outside the neighborhood, **Park Street** (**Red** and **Green Lines**), **Boylston** (**Green Line**), **Back Bay/South End** (**Orange Line** and also a railway station), and **Symphony** stops are handy, too. From Back Bay, access to the **Mass Pike** is easy.

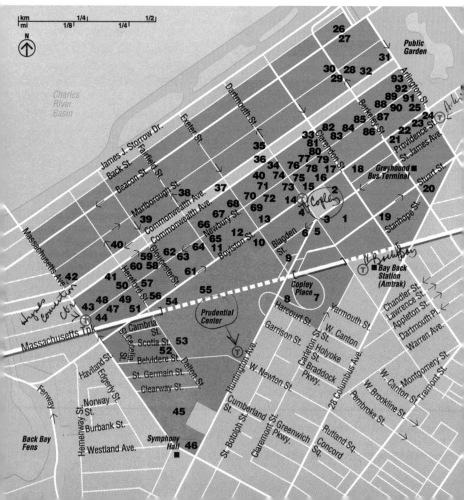

Charles River's tidal flow and power a chain of mills. The scheme failed, and the acres of water trapped by the dam became a stagnant, stinking, unhealthy tidal flat called *Back Bay* that Bostonians longed to eradicate. This became the unlikely canvas that developers clamored to fill with daring urban design schemes. To accomplish this, land had to be reclaimed from the sea by a fantastically ambitious landfill program.

Inspired by **Baron Haussmann**'s Parisian boulevard system built for **Emperor Louis Napoleon**, architect **Arthur Gilman** proposed Back Bay's orderly layout. Starting at the Charles River, the principal east-west streets are **Beacon Street, Marlborough Street, Commonwealth Avenue, Newbury Street**, and **Boylston Street**, all bisected by 8 streets named alphabetically from **Arlington Street** to **Hereford Street**. Sixteen-foot public alleys interlace these blocks and provide access to the rear of buildings, originally for service and deliveries. Gilman's rational grid remains a startling departure from old Boston's labrynthine tangles.

In 1857, the gigantic landfill wave began its sweep across the marshland block by block, from Arlington St at the Public Garden's western edge toward the **Fenway**. As soon as a single-family lot was ready, another architectural beauty debuted. By the time the wave subsided in 1890, 450 acres and more than 1500 new buildings had been added to the 783-acre peninsula. Gone was the loathsome eyesore; in its place a charming neighborhood of the same name. Completed in just 60 years, Back Bay is an extraordinary repository of Victorian architectural styles, the most outstanding in America. As an urban design scheme, it was surpassed in its era only by **L'Enfant**'s plan for Washington DC.

The newborn Back Bay instantly became Boston's darling, a magnificent symbol of civic pride and the city's coming of age. No Puritan simplicity or provincialism here—affluent Boston had learned how to stage a good show, from **Copley Square**'s lofty cultural aspirations to Commonwealth Ave's architectural revue starring fancy brickwork, stained glass, cut granite, gaggles of gargoyles, ornate ironwork, and other European conceits. In Back Bay's golden hours, the city's leading financiers, authors, industrialists, artists, architects, and legendary Brahmins lived here. But as the city's economy soured late in the 19th century, the ostentatious single-family dwellings were gradually converted to more modest use.

Back Bay

Though Back Bay's shining moments as a residential district faded after the Great Depression, the neighborhood has resiliently adapted to 20th-century incursions of shops, offices, apartments, and condominiums.

1 John Hancock Tower

(1972–76, **I.M Pei & Partners**) When towering new edifices invade historic neighborhoods, they often try to gain public acceptance with lame gestures—by aping local architectural modes or bribing with street-level shops, skimpy parks, or outdoor art. The John Hancock Tower makes no such insincere overtures. It's cool, aloof, inscrutable, with its own singular style. And that's why more and more Bostonians have grown fond of this skyscraper—New England's tallest—as the years pass. A glass rhomboid 62 stories high, its shimmering surface acts as **Trinity Church**'s full-length mirror while reflecting the constant shifts of New England weather. The tower's crisp form is mesmerizing from all angles, whether you glimpse the broad faces or razor-blade edges.

It's amazing the John Hancock Tower has become so popular, considering its rocky start. When first erected, inadequate glass was used in its sheathing and the windowpanes randomly popped out due to wind torquing, raining onto the square below. Sidewalks were cordoned off to protect pedestrians. All 13 acres of 10,344 glass panels were replaced, and are now continuously monitored for visible signs of potential breakage. Making matters worse, a later engineering inspection revealed that the building was in danger of toppling, which required reinforcing its steel frame and installing a moving weight on the 58th floor to counter wind stress. Once Bostonians could walk by the tower without flinching, they began to notice what a dazzling addition to the Boston skyline it is. It has become a gift to the city, beautifully wrapped.

For stunning views that will put all of Back Bay and Boston into perspective, visit the **John Hancock Observatory** on the 60th floor.

Binoculars are already zeroed-in on some of the city's most famous sights. The taped narrative *Skyline Boston* by the late architectural historian **Walter Muir Whitehill** is wonderful not only for his vast knowledge, but for his Proper Bostonian accent. There's also a little sound and light show about Boston in 1775—with a 20-foot topographical model of the city when all its hills were in place and Back Bay was its watery old self. ♦ Admission. M-Sa 9AM-11PM, Su 10AM-11PM, May-Oct; daily noon-11PM, Nov-Apr (Observatory open until 11PM, but last tickets sold at 10:15PM) 200 Clarendon St (St. James Ave-Trinity Pl) 247.1977 ♿

2 Copley Square Once called *Art Square* for the galleries, art schools, and clubs clustered round, the square's modern name honors **John Singleton Copley**, Boston's great Colonial painter. Copley Sq began as an unsightly patch created by the disruption of Back Bay's grid by 2 rail lines. After the **Museum of Fine Arts** opened its doors there, the square blossomed. (The museum stood where the **Copley Plaza Hotel** does today until the institution moved to its current address in the **Fenway** and its old residence was demolished.) **Trinity Church** and the **Boston Public Library** were spectacular additions, and the presence of numerous ecclesiastical and academic institutions nearby, including the **Massachusetts Institute of Technology** and the **Harvard Medical School**, enhanced the square's reputation—in Bostonians' minds—as the Acropolis of the New World. The square's latest look (1989, **Dean Abbot**) is

Back Bay

pleasant, but fails to satisfy Bostonians' century-old dreams of a magnificent public space.

2 Trinity Church (1872–77, **H.H. Richardson**; west porch and tower peaks 1890s, **Shepley, Rutan & Coolidge**; chancel 1938, **Charles D. Maginnis**; restoration, 1974–81 **Shepley, Bulfinch, Richardson & Abbott**; National Historic Landmark) Approach **Copley Square** from any direction, and your eyes will be

drawn to this grandiose French-Romanesque-inspired edifice. It is one of the great buildings in America. Be sure to go inside! The century and more that has passed since Trinity Church first graced the city has taken nothing from its power to fascinate. Like a wise and tolerant elder, Trinity offers a model of urbane dignity and grandeur that has never been equalled in Boston. The church converses most with the old **Boston Public Library** across the way, another handsome building that knows how to live.

H.H. Richardson was at the summit of his career when he designed Trinity Church. In the 1860s, its leaders decided to move the parish from Summer Street (downtown) to the Copley Sq site. In retrospect their decision seems prescient; one of Boston's great conflagrations destroyed the Summer St building in November 1872. In March of that year, 6 architects had been invited to submit designs for the new Trinity. Thirty-four years old at the time and a New York City resident, Richardson had already contributed one admired piece to the emerging Back Bay fabric, the **First Baptist Church** (then called **New Brattle Square Church**) under construction on Clarendon St.

Trinity's cruciform church's fluid massing is an inimitable Richardson tour de force, especially the leaping exterior colonnade. To contend with the awkward triangular site, Richardson designed the great square tower as the central element. Assisting Richardson with the tower was apprentice **Stanford White**—later of **McKim, Mead & White**, the Boston Public Library architects. The church's ageless vitality comes from the tension between Richardson's powerful vision of the whole and his spirited treatment of its parts. Elegant bands of red sandstone hold the coarse granite's brute force in check. Inside and out, the church is richly polychromatic in wood, paint, glass, and stone—another Richardson signature. With the aid of 6 assistants, most notably young **Augustus Saint-Gaudens, John La Farge** decorated the majestic interiors: look for his 12 frescoes on the vaulted ceilings beneath the tower, 103 feet above the nave. La Farge orchestrated production of the stained-glass windows, among them vividly glowing creations of his own—look for the lancet windows on the west wall in particular—and some jointly executed by **Edward Burne-Jones** and **William Morris and Co**. The interior resembles a gigantic tapestry woven in intricate patterns of opulent gold and medieval tones. Trinity's finest moment comes

Trinity Church

Trinity Church Windows

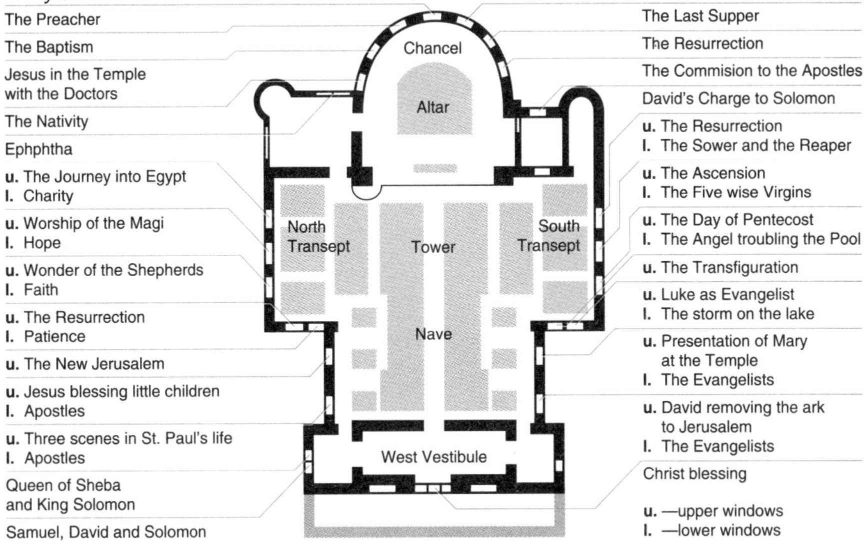

The Preacher
The Baptism
Jesus in the Temple with the Doctors
The Nativity
Ephphtha
u. The Journey into Egypt
l. Charity
u. Worship of the Magi
l. Hope
u. Wonder of the Shepherds
l. Faith
u. The Resurrection
l. Patience
u. The New Jerusalem
u. Jesus blessing little children
l. Apostles
u. Three scenes in St. Paul's life
l. Apostles
Queen of Sheba and King Solomon
Samuel, David and Solomon
Chancel
Altar
North Transept
Tower
South Transept
Nave
West Vestibule
The Last Supper
The Resurrection
The Commision to the Apostles
David's Charge to Solomon
u. The Resurrection
l. The Sower and the Reaper
u. The Ascension
l. The Five wise Virgins
u. The Day of Pentecost
l. The Angel troubling the Pool
u. The Transfiguration
u. Luke as Evangelist
l. The storm on the lake
u. Presentation of Mary at the Temple
l. The Evangelists
u. David removing the ark to Jerusalem
l. The Evangelists
Christ blessing
u. —upper windows
l. —lower windows

at Christmastime, when the church is filled with candlelight and carols during a special annual service.

Outside, Augustus Saint-Gaudens added a fine flourish: on the church's northeast corner stands his dramatic depiction of **Phillips Brooks**, the Copley Square Trinity's first rector, the Episcopal Bishop of Massachusetts, and author of *O Little Town of Bethlehem*. A somber, shrouded Christ stands behind the orating preacher. It was daring Brooks who convinced his congregation to move to the new frontier of Back Bay. Saint-Gaudens died before his design was sculpted; assistants completed the statue in 1910, which was set into a marble canopy by McKim, Mead & White. Step into the cloistered colonnade to your left that overlooks a pretty enclosed garden with its much humbler statue of **St. Francis of Assisi**. Free half-hour organ recitals offered Friday 12:15PM. Tours by arrangement. ♦ Daily 8AM-6PM. 206 Clarendon St (Copley Sq) 536.0944

After graduating from Harvard College in 1859, **Henry Hobson Richardson**, a Louisiana native, headed for Paris and launched into architectural studies at the **Ecole des Beaux Arts**. Returning to America 7 years later, H.H. quickly advanced his energetic individualistic style, creating works at once robust, monumental, and picturesque. He began his practice in New York, then moved to Boston after winning the **Trinity Church** commission. As Trinity's resplendent interior illustrates, H.H. liked to pull out all the stops, enlisting celebrated artists and sculptors to collaborate on the decoration of his buildings. He designed houses, churches, schools, libraries, hospitals, public buildings, bridges, railroad stations, even furniture, echoing the prolificity of his predecessor—architect **Charles Bulfinch**—but winning far greater fame. Richardson built in and around Boston, in numerous Massachusetts cities and towns, and throughout the northeast, leaving a grand architectural legacy. Whatever its size or setting, a Richardson building commands attention.

3 The Copley Plaza Hotel $$$$ (1912, **Clarence Blackall** and **Henry Hardenberg**) The empress dowager of Boston's hotels, the Copley Plaza enshrines the mature, full-flowered Back Bay. It not only draws business and international guests, but also lovers of grand epochs gone by. Designed by Blackall and Hardenberg, the latter, architect of the **Plaza Hotel** in New York and the **Willard Hotel** in Washington DC, this Italian Renaissance Revival has endured well. A pair of gilded lions

guard the entrance. Take a walk through the glittering lobby with its mirrored walls and a painted sky hovering over the registration desk —glorious overkill. The current owner recently renovated all 393 rooms into period style. Every year, the fabulous ballroom becomes a fantasyland for the debutante cotillion in June. Corner suites overlook Copley Square and Trinity Church. Nonsmokers' rooms and 8 rooms designed for handicapped persons are available. Multilingual staff; 24-hour room service; small pets allowed. ♦ Deluxe ♦ 138 St. James Ave (Trinity Place-Dartmouth St) 267.5300, 800/225.7654; fax 247.6681 ♿

Within The Copley Plaza Hotel:

The Plaza Dining Room ★★★$$$$ Dine in British Empire magnificence under a barrel-vaulted ceiling, attended by a well-trained battalion of captains, waiters, and busboys. US presidents **John F. Kennedy** and **Jimmy Carter** ate here, so have many movie stars. This unabashedly opulent dining room is as gilded, polished, and stately as Boston's most famous grandes dames. And under the new and gifted Alsatian chef **Philipe Reiniger**, the costly European cuisine has finally begun to attain the heights of its setting. The encyclopaedic wine list is one of the city's finest. Piano music streams in from the foyer. ♦ French ♦ Tu-Sa 6-10PM. Valet parking. Jacket and tie required. Reservations required

The Plaza Bar ★★★$$ Collect yourself on posh leather lounges under the Edwardian bar's handsome coffered ceiling. Cabaret-style enter-.tainment—jazz, pop, blues—features local and national entertainers. **Alfred Fiandaca** created the staff's attire. Hors d'oeuvres served 5-6PM. ♦ Cover. M-Sa 5PM-2AM. Jacket and tie requested. Reservations recommended for shows ♿

Copley's Restaurant and Bar ★★$$ An atmospheric, clubby place for reasonably priced but fashionable cuisine with a New England accent. There's a bar lounge at the back. On a cold afternoon, retreat to this wonderful high-ceilinged setting, where enormous draped windows overlook Copley Square. ♦ American ♦ Daily 6:30AM-3PM, 5-11PM ♿

4 Boston Public Library (1888–95, **McKim, Mead & White**; National Register of Historic Places) To fully justify its title, *the Athens of America*, Boston demanded a splendid public library that would set an example for the nation. After all, America's first free municipal library supported by public taxation opened in Boston in 1854. In its every detail, architect **Charles Follen McKim**'s coolly serene Italian Renais-

sance Revival edifice enshrines and celebrates learning. A *Palace for the People* was what the library's trustees had in mind, and that's precisely what McKim's firm achieved. The library's decoration and design brought together the most magnificent crew of architects, artisans, painters, and sculptors ever assembled in the US until that time. Materials alone reflect the nothing-but-the-best attitude of its creators; for instance, a palette of more than 25 different types of marble and stone was used. Sadly, years of neglect and an awkward shift of functions from the old building to the addition have diminished much of the library's original glory. (Today the addition holds the library's general collections and the **McKim Building**, as it is now called, houses research collections.) However, an attentive tour uncovers treasures.

Flanking the **Dartmouth St** entrance are massive bronzes of 2 seated women personifying *Art* and *Science* (1911, **Bela Pratt**), their pedestals carved with the names of artists and scientists. Prickly wrought-iron lanterns bloom by the doorways—startlingly Halloweenish. Look at the library parapets carved with the names of important people in the history of human culture. There are 519 names in all; the carvers mistakenly repeated 4. When one local newspaper reported that McKim, Mead & White had

amused themselves by working the firm's name into the first letters in 3 of the panels, enough taxpayers were incensed that the architects had to erase their clever acrostic.

Pass through the bronze portals and enter the main entrance hall. Everywhere you turn there are more inscriptions, dedications, names of the forgotten great and zealous benefactors. Brass intarsia of the zodiac signs inlay the marble floor; look up at the intricate mosaic ceilings. Climb the grand staircase of tawny Sienna marble past the noble pair of lions to the enormous contemplative Arcadian allegories by **Puvis de Chavannes** (artist of the poetic murals in the **Hotel de Ville** in Paris), which decorate the 2nd-floor gallery. Adjacent is **Bates Hall**, a cavernous reading room 218-feet long with a barrel-vaulted ceiling 50-feet high. To the right is the former **Delivery Room**, where Bostonians waited for their requested books to arrive, transported from the stacks by a tiny train hidden from view.

In the library's remotest reaches on the 3rd floor resides one of Boston's forgotten treasures: the **Sargent Gallery**. Few people ever find their way up the gloomy stairs to this poorly lit place, yet **John Singer Sargent** considered this gallery the artistic apex of his career. He devoted 30 years to planning the historical murals—their theme is Judaism and Christianity—and designing the entire hall where they were placed. The gallery wasn't quite complete when he died in 1916. The somber murals are tragically faded, but deserve attention. Also on the 3rd floor is a gallery mounting frequent exhibitions and the **Cheverus Room** housing library treasures such as the **Joan of Arc Collection**.

The most satisfying way to end any trip to *the BPL*—the library's nickname—is to visit its peaceful central courtyard with reading in hand. (If you don't qualify as a borrower, bring your own.) Follow the example of other Bostonians and pull a chair between the sturdy stone columns of the cloister, modeled after the **Palazzo della Cancelleria**'s in Rome. Landscaping is gentle—just a few trees, a reflecting pool and fountain, some plantings. Even on a rainy day this is a restful place to read; just pull your chair under the protective vaults. One-hour tours depart from the lobby at the Dartmouth entrance. ♦ Free. Tours Sa 11AM. Enter at Dartmouth St (Copley Sq) 536.5400

4 Boston Public Library Addition (1972, **Philip Johnson**) When the Boston Public Library outgrew **McKim, Mead & White**'s palatial structure, this annex was added. In materials and monumentality, Johnson's addition echoes the original BPL, but it's a cold, stark place. The interior connection between the new and old buildings is circuitous—you reach the old from the new by turning left just beyond the entry turnstiles, and following a corridor past **Louise Stimson**'s appealing dioramas to an innocuous door leading to McKim's building. Nevertheless, Bostonians use the BPL addition like mad; here the stacks are open, so there's immediate access to the books. Exhibitions are held regularly in the lofty central space. In the basement is a comfortable theater, where a free film series offers weekly screenings. Many homeless people come to the showings; the library is one of the city's few places truly hospitable to all Bostonians. The **Access Center** on the **Concourse Level** is dedicated to serving handicapped patrons, offering special equipment and materials. Given the local restroom shortage, don't forget that there are large restrooms in the basement here as well as telephones. ♦ M-Th 9AM-9PM; F-Sa 9AM-5PM. 666 Boylston St (Dartmouth-Exeter Sts) 536.5400 &

5 Westin Hotel, Copley Place $$$$ One of Boston's many major chain hotels, the Westin has 804 rooms and suites on 36 floors, with good views to be had above the 11th floor and 2 specialty suites on the 36th floor. Some floors are designed for handicapped persons and non-smokers. The hotel calls itself *The Gateway to Copley Place*, which sure isn't Oz, but does offer shops aplenty for the shop-until-you-drop crowd. Hotel amenities: 24-hour room service; bilingual concierge; valet parking; health club with indoor pool; car rental desk; expansive lounge with comfy, overstuffed furniture; and several restaurants. Small pets are allowed—leave the Newfoundland home and bring little old Fluffy. ♦ 10 Huntington Ave (Dartmouth St) 262.9600, 800/228.3000; fax 424.7483 &

Within the Westin Hotel:

Turner Fisheries ★$$ Much prettier than most Boston fish houses, this softly lit, spacious restaurant is also *quiet*. You can enjoy conversation along with absolutely fresh, simply prepared seafood. The clam chowder has been elevated to the citywide annual **Chowderfest**'s Hall of Fame. For a quick light meal, there's an oyster bar, or sit in the lounge and order the smoked bluefish appetizer. ♦ Seafood ♦ Daily 11AM-1AM. Reservations recommended. 424.7425 &

6 House of Siam ★$ Though tucked in an inconvenient block across Huntington Ave from the Westin Hotel, Copley Place, this little pink haven is worth seeking out as an inexpensive respite from Back Bay's complacent costliness. The duck and other standard dishes are excellent; try chicken or beef typhoon sautéed with bamboo shoots, minced hot chili, garlic, and basil. ♦ Thai/takeout ♦ M-Sa 11:30AM-3PM, 5-10PM; Su 11:30AM-3PM. 21 Huntington Ave. 267.1755

7 Copley Place The largest private development in Boston's history and the largest mixed-use single-phase complex in the United States, Copley Place covers 9.5 acres of land and air rights above the **Mass Pike**, includes 3.7 million square feet of space, is the size of 2500 *average* American homes or 822 football fields, and equals in size more than 2 John Hancock Towers. It includes 2 hotels, over 100 upscale shops and restaurants, an 11-screen cinema, four 7-story office buildings, 1400 parking places, and 104 residences. Walkways and pedestrian bridges lead from the complex to the hotels and to the **Prudential Center** complex. In Copley Place's central atrium, 1000 gallons of water per minute cascade over **Dimitri Hadzi**'s 60-foot-high water sculpture made of more than 80 tons of travertine and granite.

Well! Needless to say, the genesis of this giant created a furor that hasn't entirely abated. Plunked down at one corner of **Copley Square**, Copley Place, unfortunately, has become a formidable barrier to the neighboring South End. But as bland, anonymous, and prefab-looking as the exterior is, many people say Copley Place could have been much worse. Inside, it's marble, marble everywhere, and hardly a bench to sit on. You're meant to come with laden pockets, ready to empty them in shops identical to those in many other cities, with a few exceptions. By and large, stick to Newbury St unless the weather is bad, because although prices are exorbitant there too, it's much more genuinely Boston. ♦ Mall, M-F 10AM-7PM; Sa 10AM-6PM; Su noon-5PM. 100 Huntington Ave (Dartmouth St) 375.4400 (info desk) &

8 Boston Marriott Copley Place $$$ This massive 38-story complex rode into town in the early '80s with the **Copley Place** megadevelopment. Since that's next door, there's plenty of shopping and movies only seconds away. The highest-up of the 1146 rooms and suites offer nice views. All are furnished in Queen Anne-style, with color cable TV and individual climate control. Many rooms are designed for handicapped accessibility; 4 floors are for nonsmokers. Two levels of executive rooms cost more and include breakfast, private

lounge, and special concierge service. A waterfall gushes in the 4-story atrium. The hotel is also connected to the **Prudential Center** and **Hynes Convention Center** by an enclosed footbridge. Other features: 24-hour room service, valet parking, valet service, travel agency, indoor swimming pool, health facilities, barber and beauty shops, meeting facilities and business services, exhibit hall, and Boston's largest ballroom. The hotel is directly above the **Mass Pike**. ♦ 110 Huntington Ave (Exeter St) 236.5800, 800/228.9290; fax 236.5885 &

9 Copley Square Hotel $$ One of Boston's oldest, this modestly sized 1891 hotel is a Back Bay bargain and attracts an international clientele. It has a pleasantly low-key, informal European style. Nothing fancy. All 150 rooms and suites—varying a lot in size—feature individual climate-control, closet floor safes, windows you can open. Only some have private baths. Economy rooms available. For a small fee, use the nearby **Westin Hotel**'s health facilities. Coffeeshop, lounge, rooms for nonsmokers, inexpensive adjacent parking, and airport limo available. ♦ 47 Huntington Ave (Exeter St) 536.9000, 800/225.7062; fax 267.3547

Within the Copley Square Hotel:

The Cafe Budapest ★★$$$ Serenaded by violin and piano, propose marriage, celebrate an anniversary, or toast true love in the intimate, old European bar with alcoves for 2. For more than 25 years, Budapest's has been the most romantic restaurant in Boston—but be *sure* to request the tiny blue or pink dining room. Contrary to common opinion, lovers usually have perfectly good appetites—may even need extra fuel—and Budapest's Central European cooking is certainly rich, hearty comfort food, albeit elegant. Perennial favorites are the chilled tart-cherry soup, *wiener schnitzel à la Holstein*, veal *gulyas*, and *sauerbraten*. The homemade pastries include extraordinary strudels, of course. Hungarian wines are served. The pianist and strolling violinist perform Tuesday-Saturday. The presence of flamboyant proprietor **Edith Ban**, dressed in white, only enhances the mood. ♦ Hungarian ♦ M-Th noon-10:30PM; F-Sa noon-midnight; Su 1-11PM (dinner served all day) Jacket and tie required. Reservations required. 266.1979

10 Boylston Street Unlike human-scaled Newbury St with its continual retail diversions or Comm Ave with its architectural ones, it seems like a *loooong* walk from one end of Boylston to the other. But the street has been revamped over the last decade and now offers new shops and restaurants among its imposing historic, cultural, and religious institutions. Once an unkempt stretch bordering Boston's railyards, Boylston is becoming fashionable.

Back Bay

America's first **marathon** and one of the oldest annual sporting events in the country has been run every year since 1897, except in 1918 because of WWI. The Boston Marathon is run on the third Monday in April every year, which is Patriots' Day in Mass and a day off from work for many. Walls of enthusiastic fans form early on both sides of the heroic, hilly route, which begins in **Hopkinton** and ends in front of the **John Hancock Tower** in **Copley Sq**, **Back Bay**, home of the race's major corporate sponsor. The famous course's most challenging moment is **Heartbreak Hill** in Newton. Boston's unpredictable weather and wind can be friend or foe to the runners: in 1967, it was snowing on the morning of the race, while in 1976 the temperature at the start was 96 degrees. The **Boston Athletic Association** has organized the race since its inception, when 15 runners started and 10 finished. Women were officially admitted to the race in 1972. In 1990, more than 9000 runners participated, with more than $350,000 awarded in prize money. Every year, thousands of volunteers including doctors, nurses, and running-club members operate water stations and offer first aid and encouragement. Kids eagerly hold out cups of water, hoping for takers.

The first long-distance telephone call was made from Boston to **New York City** on 27 March 1884.

Restaurants/Clubs: Red   **Hotels:** Blue
Shops/Parks: Green   **Sights/Culture:** Black

10 The Lenox Hotel $$ When the Lenox opened in 1900, it stood alone in the midst of railroad tracks. That year, the *Boston Sunday Post* said the Lenox would *scrape the sky and dally with the gods*. In its heyday, **Enrico Caruso** stayed here. Later, like its city, the Lenox hit hard times. But fully refurbished today, this small hotel's 220 soundproof rooms line spacious corridors and have rocking chairs and settees, walk-in closets, and your choice of Oriental, 2 types of Colonial, or French Provincial decor. The Green Colonial and the corner Oriental with working fireplaces are favorites. Some rooms are for nonsmokers. Long popular with guests on a budget, prices are moving up as the **Saunders** family spruces up the vintage hotel. But a genuine personal touch is still present. Amenities include valet service, valet pay parking, and baby-sitting. Pets can stay. **The Lenox Pub & Grill** on the premises serves hearty, casual pub fare downstairs and grilled entrees upstairs. ♦ 710 Boylston St (Exeter St) 536.5300, 800 225.7676; fax 267.1237

Within the Lenox Hotel:

Diamond Jim's Piano Bar All night long, it's one great big friendly, spontaneous sing-a-long at Diamond Jim's, where locals and visitors feel free to come in and pitch their pipes when they're in the mood and have the courage. Regulars are dubbed the **Lenox Singers**. On the second Wednesday of every month, there's a sing-off judged by local celebrities. **Tom Selleck, Leonard Bernstein, Guy Lombardo, Frank Fontaine**, and assorted **Metropolitan Opera** stars have shown up here. No food—that would only vex the vocal chords. ♦ M-F 5PM-1:30AM, Sa 5:30PM-1:30AM

11 J.C. Hillary's ★$$ It's a little nondescript, but well-established and nicer-looking than the other Back Bay restaurants of its ilk. Respectable burgers and bar food, seafood and pasta at reasonable prices, and a full bar. ♦ American/takeout ♦ M 11:30AM-11PM; Tu-Th 11:30AM-midnight; Sa 11:30AM-12:30AM; Su 11AM-11PM. 793 Boylston St (Fairfield St) Valet parking evenings. Reservations recommended weekends. 536.6300

11 The Famous Atlantic Fish Company ★$$ Long on selections and better priced than many seafood houses in Boston, this is a reliable choice for a casual meal. Fried-clam lovers will be particularly content. At lunchtime, they guarantee that your meal will arrive within 12 minutes after ordering or it's on the house, so there's always a crowd of time-is-money professionals. ♦ Seafood ♦ M-Th 11:30AM-10:30PM; F-Sa 11:30AM-11:30PM; Su 11:30AM-10PM. 777 Boylston (Exeter-Fairfield Sts) 267.4000 &

11 Buddenbrooks Booksmith This shop boasts that it's the only place in the world where you can buy the illustrated first edition of *Paradise Lost* and a mass-market edition at the same time. True or not, old and new mingle nicely here; the ancients get the handsome cases in the antiquarian section at the back, where books of all kinds jumble together in polite mayhem. Finds include first and early illustrated editions of children's books. Creaky wooden floorboards and disorderly displays add to the proper bookstore mood. Buddenbrooks stocks more than 50,000 titles and will special order. Open 364 days a year, they close only for Thanksgiving and donate all Christmas receipts to charity. ♦ M-F 8AM-11:30PM; Sa-Su 9AM-11:30PM. 753 Boylston St (Exeter-Fairfield Sts) 536.4433

11 Boston Chicken ★$ Queue up with the lunchtime crowds for the best take-out chicken we've ever tried; it's roasted slowly in a brick-fired rotisserie to seal in a secret marinade. The result is well worth the wait. ♦ M-Th, Su 11AM-10PM; F-Sa 11AM-11PM. 745 Boylston St (Exeter-Fairfield Sts) 859.0015

12 Dunkin' Donuts Pick up a good reliable cup of coffee to go. ♦ Takeout ♦ Daily 6AM-midnight. 715 Boylston St (Exeter-Fairfield Sts) 267.7153

13 Morton's of Chicago ★$$ The restaurant's stock of prime-grade dry-aged beef is flown in fresh from Chicago daily. One of a chain of 10 restaurants, Morton's has an unusual practice: in place of menus, a cart rolls out laden with raw slabs of steak, veal, lamb chops, even an unhappy live lobster, and the waiter does a show-and-tell. Some find it disconcerting saying hello to their dinner-to-be. But nobody quibbles with the restaurant's fabulous way with steak, especially the 24-ounce porterhouse, Morton's hallmark. Come famished enough to eat a side of beef, a flock of chickens, a school of fish—even the baked potatoes are behemoths. There are some smaller cuts of meat for smaller eaters, but that's relative here. Crowds of businesspeople mean a lot of power eating's going on. Morton's is located in what Bostonians have nicknamed *The Darth Vader Building*, a modern building so awful it's the architectural equivalent of a bad haircut—odd-looking and sticking out in the wrong places. ♦ Steakhouse/American ♦ M-F 11:30AM-2:30PM, 5:30-11PM; Sa 5:30-11PM; Su 5-10PM. 1 Exeter Plaza (Boylston St) Valet parking. Jacket and tie required. 266.5858 &

Radio in Boston

America's 7th-largest radio market, Greater Boston tunes in daily to more than 60 stations offering enormous variety, but with heavy emphasis on popular music. The influx of college students influences the local market, and various college stations offer the most progressive and experimental programming—constantly changing with the students.

FM Commercial Stations

WAAF	107.3	Current rock 'n' roll
WBCN	104.1	New and old album rock
WBOS	92.9	Album classics, jazz, some New Age
WCRB	102.5	All classical
WFNX	101.7	Current album rock, emphasis on alternative music
WMJX	106.7	Easy-listening adult contemporary
WODS	103.3	Oldies all the time
WROR	98.5	Adult contemporary—familiar hits, familiar artists
WXKS	107.9	Top 40, up-tempo mainstream
WZOU	94.5	Same as above

FM College Stations

WERS	88.9	Folk, jazz, reggae, show tunes—the Emerson College station is the city's oldest, over 40 years old
WHRB	95.3	Classical, bluegrass, blues, folk (Harvard University)
WMBR	88.1	Local New Wave, jazz, classical R&B (Massachusetts Institute of Technology)
WMFO	91.5	Jazz, blues, R&B, women's, reggae, local and world music, etc. (Tufts University)
WRBB	104.9	R&B, jazz rock (Northeastern University)

WZBC	90.3	Eclectic experimental rock you won't find in most music stores, jazz, country (Boston College)

FM Public Broadcasting

WBUR	90.9	National Public Radio news, classical, jazz, folk music (owned by Boston University, but run independently)
WGBH	89.7	Classical music and jazz, varied music weekends, news programming (the GBH stands for Great Blue Hills)
WUMB	91.9	Folk, acoustic music (owned by University of Massachusetts but run independently)

AM Commercial Stations

WADN	1120	Folk music and international news (from BBC)
WBZ	1030	Popular music and banter
WEEI	590	All news, Celtics games
WHDH	850	All talk, Patriots games
WILD	1090	Operates sunrise to sunset only, urban R&B
WKKU	1510	All country, Bruins games
WNTN	1550	Spanish and ethnic programming (Newton)
WORC	1310	All country (Worcester)
WRKO	680	All talk (featuring the infamous Jerry Williams), Celtics games
WUNR	1600	All Spanish by day, ethnic mix nights and weekends (Brookline)
WXKS	1430	Big bands

New Old South Church

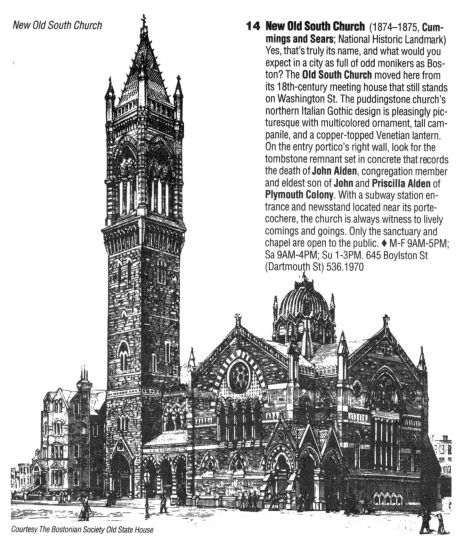

Courtesy The Bostonian Society Old State House

14 New Old South Church (1874–1875, **Cummings and Sears**; National Historic Landmark) Yes, that's truly its name, and what would you expect in a city as full of odd monikers as Boston? The **Old South Church** moved here from its 18th-century meeting house that still stands on Washington St. The puddingstone church's northern Italian Gothic design is pleasingly picturesque with multicolored ornament, tall campanile, and a copper-topped Venetian lantern. On the entry portico's right wall, look for the tombstone remnant set in concrete that records the death of **John Alden**, congregation member and eldest son of **John** and **Priscilla Alden** of **Plymouth Colony**. With a subway station entrance and newsstand located near its porte-cochere, the church is always witness to lively comings and goings. Only the sanctuary and chapel are open to the public. ♦ M-F 9AM-5PM; Sa 9AM-4PM; Su 1-3PM. 645 Boylston St (Dartmouth St) 536.1970

13 Glad Day Bookstore The only one of its kind in New England, this bookshop stocks a comprehensive selection of gay and lesbian literature, including foreign-language titles. Magazines, cards, calendars, CDs, LPs, cassettes, and videos are also sold. Special orders are welcome. Just outside the bookstore is a heavily used community bulletin board. Located on the 2nd floor, the bookstore can be reached by the steps or a cramped elevator—too small for many wheelchairs. ♦ M-Sa 9:30AM-11PM; Su, holidays noon-9PM. 673 Boylston St (Dartmouth-Exeter Sts) 267.3010

13 Le Grand Café ★$ Casual and hectic, this café's bistro menu features specialty egg dishes, fresh soups, grilled luncheon sandwiches, and rotisserie and pasta entrees. Breakfast on homemade muffins and yogurt in the sunny front alcove. ♦ American ♦ M 7:30AM-6PM; Tu-Sa 7:30AM-10PM; Su 9AM-6PM. 651 Boylston St (Dartmouth-Exeter Sts) 437.6400

Next to New Old South Church:

Copley Square News **Max** has run this newsstand—where you can get periodicals in English, Spanish, French, Italian, and German as well as flowers—for 61 years. ♦ M-Sa 3AM-6:30PM. 262.1477 (a pay phone; Max will answer)

15 Bromer Booksellers No dusty musty old bookshop this. A stop on the treasure-seeking trail of the serious browser and buyer only, and *not* for casual page-thumbers, this impeccable 2nd-floor gallery displays rare books of all periods. Earnest collectors themselves, **Anne** and **David Bromer** sell literary first editions, private press and illustrated books, books in finely crafted bindings, and rare children's books. The couple is internationally recognized as the major dealers in miniature books—less than 3 inches in both dimensions—on all subjects, such as a miniscule *New Testament* written in shorthand and published in 1665, or *Mite*, a late-1800s English compendium of funny nonsense, or *The Language of Flowers*, printed in Japan in 1980. ♦ M-F 9:30AM-5:30PM; Sa 9:30AM-4PM. 607 Boylston St (Dartmouth St) 247.2818

16 Back Bay Bistro ★$$ A Parisian like neighborhood bistro of a fancier sort, but one where you'll feel comfortable whether nibbling on appetizers or feasting on full-course meals. The pâtés and smoked items are homemade and change daily, as does the interesting parade of entree specials. There's a generous list of wines available by the glass. The salmon-pink dining room is low-key and agreeable, and so are the staff: the dining room manager once gave her own skirt to a regular customer who had spilled soup on hers and had to give a presentation after lunch. After dinner on a clear night, walk across **Copley Square** to the **Hancock Tower**, and ride up to the observatory to see illuminated Boston compete with the stars. ◆ French/takeout ◆ M-Th 11:30AM-2:30PM, 5:30-10:30PM; F 11:30AM-2:30PM, 5:30-11PM; Sa 5:30-11PM; Su 5:30-10PM. 565 Boylston St (Clarendon-Dartmouth Sts) 536.4477 ㅊ

17 Mr. Leung's ★★$$$ A world apart from the formica tabletops and slapdash service of Chinatown, this suave, black lacquer-box restaurant theatrically presents upscale Szechuan-Cantonese dishes to a well-heeled clientele. Taking the stage under tiny ceiling spotlights are a smashing rendition of Peking duck for 2, grape-cluster sea bass, *shrimp soong,* and fish in wine sauce. You can order the old standbys here too, *moo shi* pork and all, but they come quite dear. On weekends, dim sum brunch is served. ◆ Szechuan-Cantonese/takeout ◆ M-F, Su noon-3PM, 6-10PM; Sa noon-3PM, 6-11PM. Su noon-3PM. 545 Boylston St, lower level (Clarendon-Dartmouth Sts) Valet parking evenings. Jacket required. Reservations required. 236.4040

18 500 Boylston St (1988, **John Burgee** and **Philip Johnson**) Called *a sort of box covered with architectural clothes* by *Boston Globe* architecture critic **Robert Campbell**, 500 Boylston is an overblown, outscaled complex that houses fancy shops and offices. Its famous architects must have lost interest during the project—the building is unimaginative kitsch that bullies Boylston St and turns a cold shoulder to its perenially inviting neighbor, **Trinity Church**. The bowling-ball spheres and urns along 500's parapets look ready to topple. Philip Johnson was the architect of the **Boston Public Library Addition**, and Johnson and Burgee designed **International Place** near South Station in the Financial District, another graceless building that dismays many Bostonians. Even though local citizens tried to stop it, 500 went up. Boston's learning a lesson from this one. ◆ Clarendon St

Within 500 Boylston (entrance also on Clarendon St):

Skipjack's ★$$ This Art Deco-and-neon restaurant with underwater motif looks like what it is: an upstart rival to Boston's venerable seafood establishments. The favorite seafood emporium of many younger Bostonians, Skipjack's purveys 33 different types of seafood—including many Pacific varieties like Hawaiian Mahi-Mahi. The new kid on the block draws long lines and gets very hectic; if you feel daunted when you arrive, you can opt for a takeout dinner. Or phone in an order—Skipjack's delivers in Boston, Cambridge, and Brookline. Live jazz with Sunday brunch. ◆ Seafood/takeout ◆ M-W, Su 11AM-10PM; Th-Sa 11AM-11PM. Valet parking evenings. Takeout 536.4949, restaurant 536.3500 ㅊ Also at: 2 Brookline Place, Brookline. 232.8887

19 Hard Rock Cafe $$ The crowds of tourists and teens piling up under a fake rock facade inscribed *Massachusetts Institute of Rock* should clue you in: here's Boston's new addition to the famous chain of restaurants where rock 'n' roll is family fare. There's no live music here, as anyone in the know knows—just eardrum-pummeling recordings of old hits that accompany a menu of surprisingly good bar food starring burgers and BBQ. The rock 'n' roll theme plays itself out all over: the bar's shaped like a Fender Stratocaster guitar; stained-glass windows honor **Elvis Presley**, **Jerry Lee Lewis**, and **Chuck Berry**; and a function room wall is covered with bricks taken from the demolished **Cavern Club** in **Liverpool, England**, where the **Beatles** got their start. Like all

of its Hard Rock siblings, Boston's café overflows with its share of memorabilia: **Roy Orbison**'s autographed Gibson, **John Lennon**'s original scribblings for *Imagine*, an Elvis Presley necklace, and a cavalcade of objects belonging to other stars. But really, why come here unless you like din with your dinner, or want to personally experience a legendary marketing coup, or have a young friend who's hot on the idea. ◆ American ◆ Daily 11AM-2AM. 131 Clarendon St (Stuart St) 424.7625 ㅊ

Adjacent to the Hard Rock Cafe:

Hard Rock Merchandise This shop peddles *the Hard Rock Experience* so you can take a piece of it home in the form of T-shirts, hats, pins, sweatshirts, jackets, etcetera, etcetera. ◆ M-W 10AM-midnight; Th-Sa 10AM-1AM; Su 11AM-midnight. 267.7655 ㅊ

20 GRILL 23 & Bar ★★$$$ (1929, **Densmore, Le Clear, and Robbins**) A sea of white linen, mahogany paneling, bankers lamps, and burnished brass give GRILL 23 quite a gentlemanly demeanor—the ideal setting for a festive but seemly occasion. During the week you'll see many more wheeling-and-dealing Boston professionals than tourists here. Famous for its savoir-faire with red meat, especially the perfectly aged and charbroiled 18-ounce New York sirloin, the restaurant turns out splendid seafood and poultry too. The old-fashioned American practice of topping off hearty fare with equally hearty sweets is bolstered in a dessert list featuring good old apple pie, New York cheesecake, and Indian pudding. Come famished. With few rugs on its wooden floors and an open kitchen, the cavernous dining room gets very noisy. For more subdued ambiance, try Sunday brunch when the menu is equally sumptuous (brunch isn't served July and August). GRILL 23 is located in the renovated **Salada Tea Building**; on your way out be sure to look for the fantastic bronze doors at the **Stuart St** entrance. Cast from Englishman **Henry Wilson**'s design, they depict exotic scenes from the tea trade and won a silver medal at the 1927 Paris Salon. Elephants and solemn human figures protrude dramatically in bas-relief from the doors and their carved stone setting. ♦ American ♦ M-Th noon-2:30PM, 6-10:30PM; F noon-2:30PM, 6-11PM; Sa 6-11PM; Su 11:30AM-3PM, 6-10PM. 161 Berkeley St (Stuart St) Jacket and tie recommended at dinner. Reservations recommended. 542.2255

21 Berkeley Building (1905, **Codman & Despredelle**) Stand on the opposite side of the street to get a full view of this striking Beaux-Arts-inspired office building's spectacular cornice and colorful banners waving above. Clad in enameled terra cotta, the steel frame supports 5-story towers of glass edged in sea-foam green. There's only one elegant embellishment of gilt —the facade is dressy enough. The Parisian architect Despredelle taught design classes

Back Bay

across the street, where the **Massachusetts Institute of Technology School of Architecture** was once located. ♦ 420 Boylston St (Berkeley St)

22 Malben's Gourmet Years before Bostonians collectively went wild over deluxe and designer foodstuffs, Malben's was stocking its shelves with fancy imported treats. It's not as glossy as Boston's newer gourmet grocers, but it still reels in crowds and takes calls from as far away as New Zealand. Malben's ships, too. Browsers come not only to ogle the cornucopia of jams, mustards, cheeses, caviar, cookies, candies, oils, honeys, teas, gourmet gifts, etc, but also to graze at the deli, bakery, hot foods, and produce counters. Gather all the fixings for a fair-weather picnic, including the wicker basket and wine, and head for the **Public Garden** up the street. Come back for a traditional plum pudding at holiday time. ♦ M-F 6AM-6PM; Sa 9AM-6PM. 384 Boylston St (Arlington-Berkeley Sts) 267.1646 &

Now condominiums, for many years **40 Hereford St** was the site of **Fanny Merrit Farmer**'s cooking school, founded in 1902. Farmer's *The Boston Cooking-School Cookbook* was a smash hit, and her books still grace kitchens all across America. It was Farmer who introduced modern measurements, such as the teaspoon, to American cooking.

23 Women's Educational and Industrial Union (1906, **Parker, Thomas and Rice**; restored 1973, **Shepley, Bulfinch, Richardson & Abbott**) Floating above this local institution's decorative entry is a gilded swan: WEIU chose this symbol for a logo because the union was launched in 1877, the same year the **Swan Boats** settled in the **Public Garden**'s lagoon. A small group of women established WEIU to further employment and educational opportunities and to help the elderly, disabled, and poor. In 1891 **Julia Ward Howe** became the first president of the Traveler's Information Exchange, which began as a secret underground organization for women travelers, unaccompanied by men, to share information. Today, men participate in all WEIU programs. In 1926, **Amelia Earhart** found a job as a social worker through WEIU's career services program; her application was noted *Has a sky pilot's license???*

The genteel retail shop run by this private social service organization is a favorite with Bostonians, particularly at holiday time. Staffed by WEIU's friendly volunteers, the store is filled with handmade articles of all kinds, books and toys for children, knitting and craft supplies, stationery and wrapping papers, and a wealth of household treasures. Be sure to visit the consignment shop on the upper level where great finds often surface. ♦ M-F 10AM-6PM; Sa 10AM-5PM. 356 Boylston St (Arlington-Berkeley Sts) 536.5651 &

24 Shreve, Crump & Low In the event of a wedding, *The Boston Herald* gossip columnist **Norma Nathan** always writes that *a little silver something* is being sent from this renowned institution. Since 1800, innumerable Brahmin brides have registered at Shreve's, and countless marriages have been launched with jewelry, crystal, sterling, and china purchased from the city's jeweler of choice. You can also pick up your favorite new baby's little silver cup here, order personalized stationery, or peruse exclusive New England items. Also famous, the antiques department displays 18th- and 19th-century English and American furniture and prints; China-trade furniture and porcelain; English, Irish, and American silver. Service is assiduous and expert. Outside, the Art Deco facade is discreetly ornamental and stylized; inside, notice the handsome columns and silvered ceiling. ♦ M-Sa 9:30AM-5:30PM. 330 Boylston St (Arlington St) 267.9100

Iconoclastic, eccentric art lover **Isabella Stewart Gardner**, founder of her namesake museum, once lived at **152 Beacon St** with her husband **John**. In that grand mansion, demolished long ago, *Mrs. Jack* began stockpiling the fabulous art collection that soon cried out for a museum all its own. After her husband died, Isabella moved in 1902 to her Venetian palace on the **Fenway**, imperiously requesting that the city never allow the number 152 to be used on Beacon St again. She got her way, of course.

Restaurants/Clubs: Red **Hotels:** Blue
Shops/Parks: Green **Sights/Culture:** Black

Courtesy Arlington Street Unitarian Universalist Church

Wing. The institute's library collection of more than 8000 volumes and 40 periodicals and newspapers is open to the public, though only cardholders may check out materials. Language programs and film series, exhibitions, and other cultural events are also offered.

In the entrance hall, look for the framed chronicle of an amusing episode in the Boston branch's recent history: in 1985, **Senator Robert Dole** wrote to the institute, inviting Goethe to join the **Republican Senatorial Inner Circle**—a group of party donors—and to attend a special meeting of the Circle. Of course, while the institute named for him is alive and well, one can't say the same for **Johann Wolfgang von Goethe**, 1749-1832. The director of the institute, **Dr. Hans Winterberg**, sent *a telepathic response* to Dole's invitation, with Goethe stating: *Although once well off, I do not own anything anymore and will surely be excused from contributing to the Republican Fund.... In any case, I would be delighted to be 'spiritually' present.* The confusion persisted, and a number of national papers and magazines carried the story of Dole's embarrassingly untimely offer. ♦ Offices: M-F 9AM-5PM. Library: W, F noon-6PM; Th noon-8PM; 1st Sa of every month 10AM-4PM. 170 Beacon St (Arlington-Berkeley Sts) 262.6050

27 The Gibson House Facades can only reveal so much; here's your best chance to peer into private Back Bay life. Three generations of Gibsons lived in decorous luxury in this Victorian residence, one of Back Bay's earliest. It

Back Bay

was built for **Catherine Hammond Gibson** and bequeathed nearly a century later to the **Victorian Society in America** by her grandson **Charles**, to be made into a museum enshrining his family's life and times. Not much to look at on the outside, inside is a wonderful 6-story repository of perfectly preserved Victoriana. The Gibsons' ghosts would be quite content to wander through their beloved dim rooms (sunshine was considered common then), still crowded with the ornaments, overstuffed furniture, fixtures, keepsakes, and curios they amassed and passed down to one another. The tour takes you into the kitchen, laundry, and other service areas so you get a full upstairs-downstairs portrait of daily life at the Gibson's. ♦ Admission. Groups of 12 or more by appointment only. W-Su 2-5PM, May-Oct; Sa-Su 2-5PM, Nov-Apr. Tours 2, 3, 4PM. Closed all major public holidays and some religious holidays. 137 Beacon St (Arlington-Berkeley Sts) 267.6338

25 Arlington Street Unitarian Universalist Church (1861, **Arthur Gilman**; National Register of Historic Places) This church's most striking feature is its shapely tower, inspired by **St. Martin's-in-the-Fields** in London. The first building erected in Back Bay, this simple brownstone structure was quite conservative in style—as if unsure of its leadership role in storming the mud flats. The outspoken minister **William Ellery Channing** served here for many years; his statue just across the way in the **Public Garden** keeps watch still. A staunch abolitionist, Channing invited **Harriet Beecher Stowe** and **William Lloyd Garrison** to address his congregation. During the Vietnam War, the church was active in the peace movement. **Rev. Kim Crawford-Harvie** now ministers here; Sunday attendance has skyrocketed since her arrival. Inside, look for the numerous Tiffany windows. Call for an appointment. ♦ 351 Boylston St (enter at Arlington St) 536.7050

26 Goethe Institute, German Cultural Center (1909, **Ogden Codman**) New England's branch of the Munich-based institute inhabits an Italian Renaissance revival built by Boston financier **Eben Howard Gay** to house his formidable Chippendale and Adams furniture collection, parts of which are now in the **Museum of Fine Arts**, where Gay donated the **Chippendale**

28 Marlborough Street A peaceful shady residential street in the midst of urbane Back Bay, Marlborough St is humbler than Comm Ave, but has aged nicely. Many families live in the well-kept townhouses adorned with tidy little gardens, and students share the blocks nearer Mass Ave. Every 14 July, Marlborough is blocked off near the **French Library** for the annual **Bastille**

Day celebration, an evening of dining, music, and dancing that Bostonians enjoy with French flair—as if Lafayette never left.

28 First Lutheran Church (1959, **Pietro Belluschi**) Entering from Berkeley St, enjoy a quiet moment in the small landscaped courtyard nestled against the modest brick church. ♦ 299 Berkeley St (Marlborough St) 536.8851

29 First and Second Church (1867, **William Robert Ware** and **Henry Van Brunt**; 1971, **Paul Rudolph**) In 1968, Ware and Van Brunt's First Church burned down, but the conflagration spared some remnants that Paul Rudolph ingeniously incorporated into this hybrid, built under the combined auspices of the First and Second churches. Rudolph is best known for **Yale University's School of Art and Architecture** in New Haven CT. Even using coarse striated concrete—the brutal material that is his trademark—Rudolph creates poignant connections with the ruined fragments, particularly the square stone tower and rose window. ♦ M-F 9AM-3PM, June-Aug (call first); M-F 9AM-5PM, Sep-May. 66 Marlborough St (Berkeley St) 267.6730

30 The French Library in Boston Ever since the dashing young **Marquis de Lafayette** won over Bostonians' hearts, the city has had a special fondness for all things French. If you're walking on Marlborough St and overhear a conversation in French—a common occurrence—the speakers could be walking to or from The French Library, Boston's center for French language and culture since 1946. The

Back Bay

library today holds more than 45,000 books on a great many topics, and hundreds of cassettes, records, and periodicals. A special treat are its collection of *bandes dessinée*, comic books for mature readers, which offer a good workout in idiomatic and colloquial French. You may borrow books only if you're a member. The library offers language lessons and hosts an annual **Bastille Day** celebration, lectures, exhibitions, wine tastings, concerts, children's activities, and many other events. There's a cozy reading room and an intimate theater where French films are regularly screened. Whether to ponder Sartre, flip through a travel guide, get a quick phrase translation, or ask anything at all about *La Belle France*, this is the place to come. ♦ Tu, F-Sa 10AM-5PM; W-Th 10AM-7PM. 53 Marlborough St (Berkeley St) 266.4351

31 Commonwealth Avenue This expansive, ruler-straight street was the major clue that the new Back Bay wouldn't resemble Boston's mazelike older districts. Modeled after grand Parisian boulevards, Comm Ave—its undignified, unpunctuated nickname—was the first of its kind in America, setting a chic French example for the rest of Back Bay to follow; in fact, the **French Consulate** is located at No. 3. Comm Ave and is 240 feet wide, with a 100-foot central mall that **Winston Churchill** deemed one of the world's most beautiful. The avenue is shaded with elms and planted with statues memorializing both the famous and forgotten. May visitors are lucky, arriving when the magnolias are in bloom. This Victorian promenade was once the place for the fashionable to stroll and be seen. Today a more casual collection of Bostonians ambles along, including plenty of dogwalkers and young matrons wheeling infants. The block after block of handsome buildings were once aristocratic townhouses, but now house luxury condos, apartments, businesses, and institutions. Unfortunately, a number of homes bear the indignity of having suburban roofdecks and unsympathetic stories tacked on, ruining many a graceful roofline. The boulevard's northern, sunny side was the most desirable residential stretch in Back Bay, and many showplaces remain. Comm Ave starts to run out of charm when one nears Mass Ave and Kenmore Sq beyond, however, so linger longest up the street.

31 Harbridge House (1860, **Arthur Gilman**) In 1893, Boston's grande dame and arts patron **Mrs. J. Montgomery Sears** combined No. 12 Arlington St, one of Back Bay's earliest homes, a formidable 5-story French-Italian style mansion, with No. 1 Commonwealth Ave, creating a small palace to house her famous art collection and music room. Pianist **Ignace Paderewski** and violinist **Fritz Kreisler** visited Mrs. Sears here, as did **John Singer Sargent**, who executed a portrait of his patron and her daughter at home. Gilman also designed the Arlington Street Church down the block. ♦ 12 Arlington St (Comm Ave)

32 Baylies Mansion (1912, **Thomas and Rice**) Textile industrialist **Walter C. Baylies** moved to Boston, married into a wealthy family, and promptly metamorphosed into a full-fledged Brahmin. He tore down an 1861 house to build this showy Italianate mansion, adding a fabulous Louis XIV ballroom for his daughter's debut. A site for glittering society events, the room did its stint of civic service too: during World War I, bandages were rolled here. Cohabiting with the large Baylies entourage was the family's pet squirrel, who reportedly snacked on the costly draperies. Since 1941, this has been the home of the **Boston Center for Adult Education**. Many of the mansion's original ornament and interior finishes remain untouched. ♦ 5 Comm Ave (Arlington-Berkeley Sts)

33 First Baptist Church (Church of the Holy Bean Blowers) (1871, **H.H. Richardson**) Henry Hobson Richardson was just starting to flex his creative muscles when he won the commission for this puddingstone church (originally called the **New Brattle Square Church**) in a competition. Its marvelous campanile springs into the air to create one of Back Bay's most striking silhouettes. The belfry's frieze was modeled in Paris by **Frédéric Auguste Bartholdi**, sculptor of the **Statue of Liberty** (Bartholdi had a way with drapery), and its scenes depict the sacraments of baptism, communion, marriage, death. Some of the sculpted faces supposedly belong to famous Bostonians, including

Hawthorne, Emerson, and Longfellow. Protruding proudly from the corners, the angels' trumpets won them the irreverent nickname, *The Holy Bean Blowers.* Come at sunset to admire their profiles etched crisply against a darkening sky. Unfortunately, the original congregation disbanded and funds ran out, so Richardson's lofty plans for the church interior never came to be. ◆ M-F 9AM-4PM. Service Su 11AM. 110 Comm Ave (Clarendon St) 267.3148

34 **Hotel Vendôme** (corner building 1871, **William G. Preston**; main building 1881, **J.F. Ober**; renovation 1971–1975, **Stahl Bennett**) You'd think the marsh-bottomed Back Bay would sag under the weight of this magnificent monster. For 100 years, the Vendôme reigned as Boston's most fashionable hotel, the only one where **Sarah Bernhardt** would deign to lay her weary head. **General Ulysses S. Grant, President Grover Cleveland, John Singer Sargent, Oscar Wilde, Mark Twain**, and countless other worthies stayed here. The Vendôme boasted unheard-of luxuries: it was the first public building in the city to have electric lighting (1882), powered by a plant **Thomas Edison** designed; and every room had a private bathroom, fireplace, and steam heat. Inevitably, the Vendôme's heyday passed and it became a rundown white elephant. In the 1970s, the hotel's interior decor was obliterated during renovation, and a terrible fire destroyed portions of the roof and building. Now a condominium complex, the hotel has accepted its comedown as gracefully as possible. To the left at **Dartmouth St** is Preston's original structure, forced to play a supporting role to Ober's enormous addition on the right. The duo's conjoining marble facades ripple with opulent ornamentation. ◆ 160 Comm Ave (Dartmouth St)

35 **Ames-Webster House** (1872, **Peabody and Stearns**; enlarged 1882, **John H. Sturgis**; restoration 1969, **CBT**) This mansion was built for railroad tycoon and US congressman **Frederick L. Ames**, its massive pavilion and porte-cochere added 10 years later. The exterior is impressive enough, with fine wrought-iron gates, a 2-story conservatory, monumental tower, and commanding chimney. But inside is the extraordinary grand hall bedecked with elaborately carved oak woodwork. The theatrical staircase ascends toward the skylit stained-glass dome, past murals by French painter **Benjamin Constant**. There's a compact jewel of a ballroom, celery-green-and-gilt and delicately proportioned, particularly its *heavens,* the balcony where musicians played. The house is now used for private offices and, unfortunately, is rarely accessible to the public. ◆ 306 Dartmouth St (Comm Ave)

The **John Hancock Tower** required the largest order of structural steel ever—32,000 tons—for a New England building. The tower rests on an 8^{1}/2-foot-thick reinforced concrete mat that's supported by 3000 H-shaped piles driven into bedrock 160 feet below street level.

Commonwealth Avenue and **Massachusetts Avenue** are most often referred to by their breezy nicknames: *Comm Ave* and *Mass Ave.*

36 **Wiliam Lloyd Garrison Statue** (1885, **Olin L. Warner**) Boston's famed abolitionist (1805-1879) looks as though he'd been intently reading when the artist interrupted and asked him to pose; Garrison suggests a man taut with energy, feigning relaxation, stretching back in his armchair with his books and papers hastily stuffed underneath. His profile is memorable. The fiery inscription *I am in earnest—I will not equivocate. I will not excuse. I will not retreat a single inch, and I will be heard!* expresses all of Garrison's unquenchable conviction and is from the inaugural manifesto of *The Liberator,* a journal he founded and edited. ◆ Commonwealth Mall (Dartmouth-Exeter Sts)

37 **Admiral Samuel Eliot Morison Statue** In **Penelope Jencks'** statue, the sailor and historian (1887-1976) is seated on a rock by the sea, binoculars in hand, dressed in oilskins with a jaunty yachting cap on his head. Notice the coppery lichen on his stony perch, and the sandcrabs on the beach below. Smaller rocks are inscribed with quotes from his books, such as *Dream dreams then write them/Aye, but live them first.* Across the street is the exclusive **St. Botolph Club**, to which Morison belonged. ◆ Commonwealth Mall (Exeter-Fairfield Sts)

38 **Algonquin Club** (1887, **McKim, Mead & White**) It would be hard to find a haughtier facade in the city than this one, with its overblown frieze and projecting pair of falcons. But the Italian Renaissance Revival palace, built for a private club, certainly catches the eye with its self-confident, flamboyant architectural maneuvers. ◆ 217 Comm Ave (Exeter-Fairfield Sts)

Back Bay

38 **First Corps of Cadets Museum** This one's for military history buffs. Established in 1726, the **First Corps of Cadets** is one of America's oldest military organizations. Members have served in most US wars and conflicts. The corps began as bodyguards to the royal governors of the Province of Massachusetts Bay. **John Hancock** served as colonel in 1774. The museum holds examples of most arms in existence, dating back to **King George II**. Many weapons and memorabilia were brought back from action by corps members. Flags, uniforms, drums, and paintings also. Free 2-hour tours offered by appointment only. ◆ 227 Comm Ave (Exeter-Fairfield Sts) 267.1726

Boston is often even windier than *Windy City* **Chicago**—for proof, just stand near the **John Hancock Tower** or traverse the **Christian Science International Headquarters** plaza on a breezy day.

In 1972, Boston mayor **Kevin White** bailed the **Rolling Stones** out of jail to keep a date at **Boston Garden**.

39 267 Commonwealth $$ This intimate Victorian hotel is owned—and was restored—by **Bob Vila**, former host of *This Old House*, a popular public TV series. An 1880 brownstone that was once a single-family residence, No. 267 is broken up into five 1-bedrooms and 4 studios, with high ceilings, handsome woodwork, marble or handcarved fireplaces, and kitchenettes. The studio rooms actually feel grander since they weren't divided to create sitting rooms. Room No. 7 was the master bedroom and overlooks Comm Ave and its mall, as does No. 5. The penthouse room is a contemporary addition with modern furnishings. About half the guests are corporate relocations; many are affiliated with hospitals. Opera, ballet, and music stars often stay here. Laundry facilities in the building; weekly rates available. Though credit cards aren't accepted, the hotel will bill companies. ♦ Fairfield-Gloucester Sts. No credit cards. 267.6776

40 Nickerson House (1895) Architects **McKim, Mead & White**'s last Back Bay residence offers one monumental gesture in the sweep of its bulging granite bowfront. The building is a model of chilly restraint, but enjoyed a brief fling as the site of 2 of Boston's most lavish debutante balls, held by **Mrs. Pickman**, wife of the second owner, for her daughters. ♦ 303 Comm Ave (Gloucester-Hereford Sts)

41 Burrage Mansion (1899, **Charles E. Brigham**) Cherubim and griffins and gargoyles, oh my! Not all Bostonians were willing to surrender their highfaluting aspirations to fit Back Bay's decorous

Back Bay

mold. Certainly not **Albert Burrage**; his theatrical limestone mansion simultaneously pays homage to the **Vanderbilts**' Fifth-Avenue mansions and the French château **Chenonceaux** on the Loire. A multitude of strange carved figures peer down from and crawl across the facade's excess of ornament. Burrage once cultivated orchids in the splendid glass-domed greenhouse at the rear. The mansion is now home to the **Boston Evening Clinic**, founded in the '20s by **Dr. Morris Cohen**, a self-taught immigrant, to provide health care services for those who work all day. Peek inside to see how enthusiastically the interior competes with the exterior, particularly in the sculpted marble staircase and abundant embellishments. ♦ 314 Comm Ave (Hereford St)

42 Oliver Ames Mansion (1882, **Carl Fehmer**) The original owner was head of the Ames Shovel Manufacturing Company, president of the Union Pacific Railroad, philanthropist, owner of the Booth Theatre in New York, and a Massachusetts governor. Clearly, a lion like Ames would command Back Bay's biggest mansion. **H.H. Richardson** prepared a sketch for the house, but apparently it was rejected and Fehmer took over. Take a good look at the frieze panels of putti and floral ornament; they portray the activities that occurred in the rooms behind. Now an office building, the mansion was the longtime headquarters of the National Casket Company. ♦ 355 Comm Ave (Mass Ave)

43 Newbury's Steak House $ A user-friendly, well-worn neighborhood steak house, and one of the few Back Bay joints where you can comfortably bring children. It has its detractors, who consider it drab and dull, but it's a reliable fixture in Back Bay's here-today-gone-tomorrow landscape. *The Boston Globe* columnist **Mike Barnicle** is a vocal fan. London broil is a good choice here and there's a salad bar. Roast beef, chicken, fish, and burgers round out the menu. ♦ American ♦ Daily noon-midnight. 94 Mass Ave (Comm Ave-Newbury St) 536.0184

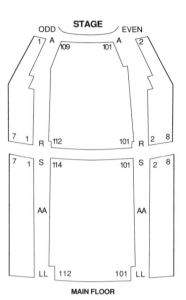

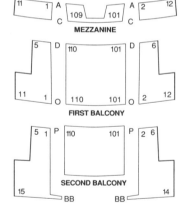

44 Berklee Performance Center Associated with the highly regarded **Berklee College of Music**, the center hosts popular performances of all types of contemporary music, especially jazz and folk. Call for performances and times. Cash only at box office. ♦ Admission. Box office M-Sa 10AM-6PM. 136 Mass Ave (Boylston St) 266.1400, recorded concert info 266.7455

45 Christian Science International Headquarters (original church 1893–94, **Franklin J. Welch**; addition 1903–06, **Charles E. Brigham with Solon S. Beman, Brigham Coveney and Bisbee**; Administration Building,

Colonnade Building, Sunday School 1968–73, **I.M. Pei andPartners** and **Cossuta and Ponte**) It's easy to overlook the little acorn from which this gigantic oak grew: the original Romanesque Christian Science Mother Church, which founder **Mary Baker Eddy** called *our prayer in stone*, is now dwarfed by a behemoth extension soaring to a height of 224 feet. This Renaissance basilica bears the weight of its towering dome like giant Atlas holding the world upon his shoulders. Designed to seat 5000, the basilica boasts one of the world's largest pipe organs, a 13,595-piped **Aeolian Skinner** manufactured locally. Located on what was the outer edge of respectability, in the midst of tenements and crowded residential blocks, the old and new church clung together until I.M. Pei's master plan carved out a great swath of 22 acres, populating its core with monumental church administration buildings.

Strategically flanking the mother church like Secret Service agents are the 28-story **Church Administration Building**; fan-shaped **Sunday School**; and the low-slung **Colonnade Building**. They surround a vast public space dominated by a 670-foot-long, 100-foot wide reflecting pool rimmed with red granite, a pleasant feature with a hidden agenda: to cool water from the air-conditioning system. The circular fountain at one end is as dull as an empty dish when shut off, but when gushing on hot days, it becomes a hectic playground and contributes a badly needed note of spontaneity to this austere over-planned setting. With rows of manicured trees, flowerbeds, and water, the plaza is a popular lunchtime spot. But in the winter, the wind can whip through here fiercely, treating the office tower as a sail.

To one side of the church is the **Christian Science Publishing Society** building, offices for the well-regarded *Christian Science Monitor*, founded in 1908 and now published in 30 languages. Inside, look up at the 2 extraordinary glass globe lanterns suspended from the lobby ceiling; one lights up to tell the time, the other the date. Follow signs to the fabulous **Mapparium**, a vividly colored stained-glass globe 30 feet in diameter, traversed by a glass bridge. Since glass doesn't absorb sound, you can stand at one end and send whispered messages echoing eerily across the way to a partner. Made of more than 600 kiln-fired glass panels, the Mapparium is illuminated from without by 300 lights. Designed by the building's architect, **Chester Lindsay Churchill**, the globe was completed in 1932 and has not been altered since. It's outdated, but all the more interesting for its pre-World War II record of political boundaries. Free ongoing 10-minute tours of the Mapparium and free guided tours of the Mother Church and extension. ♦ M-Sa 9:30AM-3:30PM. Mass Ave-Huntington Ave. 450.2000

Back Bay, wrote American writer **Lewis Mumford**, *is a geographic area, a historic monument, and a cultural symbol; there are even moments when the Back Bay might almost be identified as a state of mind.*

46 Horticultural Hall (1901, **Wheelwright and Haven**; National Register of Historic Places) Founded in 1829, the **Massachusetts Horticultural Society** holds the nation's oldest annual spring flower show here. It is a spectacular event, but has bloomed too large for the exhibition hall. The society launched America's school-gardening movement, which now brings gardening studies into many Boston public schools, and spreads the love of growing things via its traveling Plantmobile exhibits. In addition to operating the world's largest independent horticultural library, the society publishes a fine magazine and runs a gift shop selling seeds, books, and prints. You can even call for free advice. The society's dignifiedly decorative building—which it now shares with other organizations—makes a striking-looking couple with **Symphony Hall** across the street. ♦ 300 Mass Ave (Huntington Ave) 536.9280

47 Newbury Street As toney as streets come, Newbury St is slightly less so toward Mass Ave, although its less fashionable stretch has acquired a youthful exuberant panache. With the third highest rents in the US, coming in behind **Beverly Hill's Rodeo Drive** and **Palm Beach's Worth Ave**, Newbury St aspires to commercial heights. Partake of the lively Saturday scene. A blend of **New York's Columbus** and **Madison** avenues, this is the only street in Boston where you'll feel underdressed just strolling along. Newbury St pays homage to *the beautiful look*; in addition to the boutiques and galleries, there are dozens of hair *designers*, tanning and facial salons, modeling studios.

Back Bay

(Newbury St boasts 64 hair salons in the 8 blocks between Arlington St and Mass Ave.) For those who seek something else, there's art, literature, antiques, and costly geegaws galore, plus a thriving café society. The only item in short supply here is a bargain.

47 360 Newbury Street An early-1900s warehouse designed by **Arthur Bowditch** was recently metamorphosed into a dramatic iconoclast by architect **Frank O. Gehry** with the assistance of **Schwartz/Silver Architects**. No. 360 towers over the Mass Ave-end of Newbury St. Viewed from the Mass Pike and from many Back Bay angles, the building is a challenging, alert, eye-catching presence. Its brash projecting struts, canopy, and cornice make it appear scaffolded and still in process, as if the building hasn't quite decided what to be yet. Step into the bank-breaking splendor of the lobby on the Newbury St side.

Building on Back Bay landfill required special engineering considerations. For example, **Trinity Church**'s massive tower weighs 90 million pounds and rests on 2000 wooden piles set in a 90-foot square. Atop the piles are 4 granite pyramids 35 feet square and 17 feet tall, which support the tower's 4 corner piers. Because the pilings are made of wood and must be submerged in water to prevent dry-rot, the water-table level is constantly checked through a hatch in the subbasement.

Within 360 Newbury Street:

Tower Records/Video Calling itself *the largest record store in the known world*, this enormous multilevel emporium is one of a chain of 54 stores in the US, London, and Japan, and sells LPs, 45s, CDs, cassettes, cassette singles, and videos. They cover all the music bases, but this isn't the place to come for unconventional, hard-to-find recordings. You can purchase tickets to most concerts in person at the **Ticket Master** counter. A lot of late-night socializing goes on here. ♦ Daily 9AM-midnight. 360 Newbury St (Mass Ave) 247.5900

48 **Johnson Paint Company** Look for the famous sign with bright multicolored stripes and real gold leaf. For more than 50 years, the Johnson family's business has occupied this former carriage house, where horses owned by wealthy Back Bay residents once slept. In addition to selling good old-fashioned paint products—they've carried the same lines of paint since 1936—the store is a fixture in the fine art community, stocking what the staff refers to as *fancy painting stuff* such as brushes imported from 5 countries, easels, tables, pads, powdered pigments, art books. If you have a tricky wall color to match, try Johnson's: renowned city-wide, the color mixer has worked here for more than 30 years and is better than a computer at matching samples. Classes run continually on faux painting, glazing, gilding, and other techniques. You can even buy a T-shirt with the store's gaily-colored emblem. ♦ M-F 8:30AM-5:30PM; Sa 8:30AM-1PM. 355

Back Bay

Newbury St (Hereford St-Mass Ave) 536.4244/4838/4065, 266.5210 &

48 **Avenue Victor Hugo Bookshop** Just a glance in the window reveals what a treasure trove this used bookstore is. Row upon row of 9-foot-tall bookshelves—be ready for some stretching on tiptoe—are crammed with used books in 250 subject areas, ranging in price from 25-cent paperback romances to $200 limited editions. Put yourself in a nostalgic mood browsing through the used periodicals dating from 1854 to present. There's some new fiction, comic books, a great card and postcard selection, old maps, vintage sheet music. Prowling the premises is **Feet**, the store's lordly cat—*All used bookstores should have one*, says owner **Vincent McCaffrey**. ♦ M-F 9AM-9PM; Sa 10AM-8PM; Su noon-9PM. 339 Newbury St (Hereford St-Mass Ave) 266.7746

49 **Trident Booksellers & Cafe** ★$ Calling itself *Boston's alternative bookstore*, Trident sells some fiction, but is particularly strong in Jungian psychology, acupuncture, poetry, Eastern religions, Buddhist, women's, and metaphysical works. Crystals, incense, scented oils, tarot cards, bonsai trees also on sale. The little café is a popular neighborhood meeting place for a broad spectrum of Bostonians, who come for its no-fuss, down-to-earth, tasty menu of homemade soups, sandwiches, bagels, croissants, rib-sticking desserts like carrot cake, plus a variety of coffees and cappuccino. Poetry readings are held every Sunday, 4:30-6PM, and are free (donation requested). ♦ American ♦ M-F 9AM-11PM; Sa 10AM-11PM; Su noon-9PM. 338 Newbury St (Hereford St-Mass Ave) 267.8688 &

😊 Newbury Comics

49 **Newbury Comics** This oddball store started as a comic-book outpost, then branched into anything music related. They still sell comics here, including interesting ones aimed at adult readers, but Newbury's eccentric inventory now encompasses independent label and import music in CDs, cassettes, records; music and comic T-shirts; music videos; music-related books; portable *music makers* and accessories; posters; biker-style jewelry; and bizarre novelties. College students flock here for hard-to-find recordings. ♦ M-Sa 10AM-9PM; Su noon-7PM. 332 Newbury St (Hereford St-Mass Ave) 236.4930 &

49 **John Fleuvog** If your feet want to make a particularly eccentric fashion statement, don a pair of Fleuvog's clunky Munster Platforms fit for Frankenstein; or the Bump, a style fit for L'il Abner; or the Superpoint line that looks lethal to the toes; or the Doctor Marten's incredibly blocky styles. English-made in plenty of leathers and colors, with crests and bows and buckles and tapestry, these shoes are ready for action of some sort. ♦ M-Sa 11AM-7PM; Su 1-6PM. 328 Newbury St (Hereford St-Mass Ave) 266.1079

49 **Nostalgia Factory** *The Eye Shall Never Rest* is the credo of this gallery bursting with old collectibles and ephemera. Owners **Rudi** and **Barbara Franchi** scour fairs, flea markets, and England to come up with their ever-changing assortment of rare posters, early postcards, political buttons, antique signs, soda-pop art, English royalty souvenirs, old advertising, and memorabilia of all kinds. A browser's delight, yes, but the gallery also portrays more serious changing attitudes and trends: a fascinating display of magazine advertising from the '20s through the '50s chronicled products once considered safe and now banned or warned against, such as cigarettes, asbestos shingling, and lead paint. ♦ Sa 11AM-7PM; Su noon-6PM. 324 Newbury St (Hereford St-Mass Ave) 236.8754

In Boston, a *place* is an alley and a *square* is a street intersection. The city has a confusing proliferation of squares—some constituting entire neighborhoods.

49 Boston Architectural Center (1967, **Ashley, Myer & Associates**) This bulky concrete block of a building has turned out to be an unexpectedly amiable addition to Back Bay. Don't let the structure's contemporary look fool you; it houses a century-old school of architecture, the BAC, which began life in 1889 as a free atelier run by the **Boston Architectural Club**, where deserving youth were given drawing lessons. The BAC is unique in America today for requiring its students to work full-time as fledgling architects while taking classes at night from an all-volunteer faculty. The inviting, glass-sheathed ground floor is a public space for student work and art and architecture exhibitions.

On the building's exterior west wall, New York artist **Richard Haas** painted one of his best murals (1977) and it's become a Back Bay landmark. This 6-story-high architectural trompe l'oeil is a cross-sectional view of a French Neoclassical palace in the Beaux-Arts style. Look for the mural's teasers: the shadow of a man against a corridor wall; a foot disappearing through a closing door; and a man appearing in a doorway on his way up to the top of the rotunda. ◆ Gallery M-Th 9AM-9PM; F-Sa 9AM-5PM; Su 11AM-5PM. 320 Newbury St (Hereford St) 536.3170

50 Genji ★$$ One of Boston's trailblazing Japanese restaurants, Genji has long been an attractive presence at the less fashionable end of Newbury St. Named for a 12th-century Kyoto nobleman, the restaurant offers theatrical *teppan* (tabletop cooking) upstairs, and an excellent sushi bar downstairs. Also available downstairs are traditional dishes such as teriyaki, and colorful *bento* dinners handsomely served in compartmentalized black-lacquer boxes. Thanks also to its gracious service and tranquillity, Genji has shown unusual staying power on a flighty street. Artist **Alejandro Sina** created the delicate neon art in the windows that looks like luminous pick-up sticks. ◆ Japanese ◆ M-Th noon-2:30PM, 5:30-10:30PM; F-Sa noon-2:30PM, 5-11PM; Su 12:30-3:30PM, 5-10PM. 327 Newbury St (Hereford St) Reservations required on weekend. 267.5656

51 Institute of Contemporary Art (ICA) and Engine and Hose House Number 33 (1885–1886, **Arthur H. Vinal**; fire station renovation 1971, **Arrowstreet**; police station renovated 1975, **Graham Gund Associates**) A police station and fire station once shared this building, designed by city architect Vinal, but the police eventually moved next door and the ICA moved in after Graham Gund handsomely restored its half. Inside the Romanesque-style shell are multilevel galleries and a 140-seat theater for the ICA's mixed-media exhibitions, films, and performances in the visual arts. Established in 1936, the museum has no permanent collection and is famous for its eclectic, sometimes uneven, but always interesting array of work by known and unknown artists. One-of-a-kind in Boston, the ICA aims to be a research and development laboratory for new ideas. As you head over to the entrance, you'll see the firemen on the job, taking a break from time to time to watch the colorful crowd on the trendy

art trail. The ornate turret tower on the Hereford St side is still used for drying fire hoses. ◆ Admission. W, Su 11AM-5PM; Th-Sa 11AM-8PM; free Th 5-8PM. 955 Boylston St (Hereford St) 266.5152. Limited wheelchair access; call first

51 Division Sixteen $ Located in a former police station, this sleek Art Deco restaurant is a popular spot with students and youngish singles seeking same. At night there's inevitably a wait, and the horrendous din and clatter will drown out any conversation unless you insist on a booth in the back. But there is a reason to come here: monster portions of reasonably priced, decently prepared casual food, such as sandwiches, salads, omelets, burgers, nachos, and the like. The shoestring fries are made from scratch. On a weeknight, better still a rainy one, this place goes well with an evening at one of the movie theaters nearby. ◆ American ◆ Daily 11:30AM-1:30AM. 955 Boylston (Hereford St) 353.0870 ♿

52 Back Bay Hilton $$$ A stone's throw from the Hynes Convention Center, this rather nondescript 25-story Hilton caters assiduously to the business traveler. All 335 rooms are soundproofed, with small bathrooms, bay windows you can open, and calm decor, and many have balconies. Amenities include a year-round swimming pool; access for a daily usage fee to a Fitcorp® health facility on site; 24-hour room service; 24-hour parking garage; meeting and banquet rooms; nonsmokers' floors. In addition to a lounge, there's an upscale nightclub. ◆ 40 Dalton St (Belvidere St) 236.1100, 800/874.0663 ♿

Back Bay

Within Back Bay Hilton:

Boodle's of Boston ★★$$$ A sillier name for such an earnest grill room would be hard to find. The English decor is a little ponderous and hotel-ish, but perfectly appropriate to the main business at hand: expertly grilling massive cuts of meat over a variety of hardwoods such as sassafras and hickory. Seafood and vegetables take many a pleasant turn on the grill here too, and there are oyster dishes galore. You can dress up the simple entrees by choosing from 20 butters, sauces, and condiments. Good beer selection and good service. ◆ Steak house/American ◆ Daily 7-10:30AM, 11:30AM-2:30PM, 5-11PM. Reservations recommended for dinner. 266.3537 ♿

The Boston area's 65 **colleges** and **universities** enroll approximately 250,000 students and contribute $5 billion or so annually to the local economy. Every fall, the tide of incoming students swells the Greater Boston-area population, accounting for 9 percent. More than 32,000—graduates and undergraduates—arrive at **Northeastern University**, 28,500 at **Boston University**, 17,300 at **Harvard University**, 14,500 at **Boston College**, 10,800 at **University of Massachusetts-Boston**, and 9300 at the **Massachusetts Institute of Technology**, to name just a few.

Restaurants/Clubs: Red   Hotels: Blue
Shops/Parks: Green   **Sights/Culture:** Black

53 Sheraton Boston Hotel & Towers $$$
Here's where sports teams stay, with one staffer solely dedicated to their needs and wants. The 1250-room hotel abuts the **Hynes Convention Center**, which conventioneers can enter without ever going outdoors. A business-service center handles word processing, copying, and other office functions. One of the twin 29-story towers offers 4 floors that are a minihotel-within-a-hotel, with quieter rooms, butler service, and a VIP lounge. One of the 7 butlers is named *Snow White*, and truly resembles that raven-locked heroine. Every December, the **Bill Rodgers' Jingle Bell Run**—a *fun run*—is sponsored by the hotel to benefit the **Special Olympics**, and about 4000 people participate, wearing Christmas regalia. Get a room up high for good views of the **Christian Science International Headquarters'** geometries or the **Charles River**. A number of floors are dedicated to nonsmokers and handicapped persons. Small pets allowed. Other amenities: 24-hour room service; indoor/outdoor pool; health club with Jacuzzi; beauty salon and barber. ◆ 39 Dalton St (Boylston St) 236.2000, 800/325.3535; fax 236.1702

Within the Sheraton Boston Hotel & Towers:

The Mass. Bay Company ★$$ Come here when you can't tolerate the lines or prices at Boston's high-profile, celebrity seafood houses. Specialties include award-winning clam chowder, salmon and trout smoked on the premises, fish grilled over mesquite charcoal. A big plus: they take reservations, not the common prac-

Back Bay

tice with the city's fish emporiums. ◆ Seafood ◆ Daily 5:30-10:30PM. Reservations recommended. 236.8787 &

54 **John B. Hynes Veterans Memorial Convention Center** (1988, **Kallmann, McKinnell & Wood**) Known simply as *the Hynes*, this functions facility is not open to the public, although it's easy to slip in for a peek. Cross to the opposite side of Boylston St to study the Hynes' impressive honest facade and ground-floor loggia, then look inside at the magnificent main rotunda. Unlike many of Boston's newer buildings, the Hynes is much admired. Built by the architects of Boston's unusual **City Hall**,

the convention center picks up the mantle from Boston's 19th-century architectural masterpieces up the street. The building is so conciliatory toward its surroundings that it's easy to forget it can handle a convention of 22,000. Bankers, dentists, lumbermen, teachers—even the **Association of Old Crows** pass through the handsome portals. ◆ 900 Boylston St (Gloucester St) 424.8585, 954.2000 &

55 **Prudential Center** (1959–1960s, **Charles Luckman and Associates** and **Hoyle, Doran, and Berry**) Home of the insurance giant, the *Pru* is a dowdy complex, unloved by many and the worse for wear. It houses 6 million square feet of offices, apartments, hotels, and stores in a network of elevated blocky buildings and windy plazas, parts of which appear eerily abandoned to the ravages of time. But when the sprawling 27-acre Prudential Center was plopped down here in the '60s, it covered up the unsightly Boston & Albany rail yards, introduced a new scale to Back Bay, and stirred high hopes for a rejuvenated modern Boston. It's worth a visit to grasp the '60s radical concept of American urban renewal. The Pru is due for a major overhaul during the next 10 years; with luck, the complex will get a brighter image.

Once the city's tallest skyscraper, the inelegant 52-story **Prudential Tower** has been outraced to the heavens by its rival, the sleek **John Hancock Tower**. Still, many Bostonians have grown fond of the homely Pru Tower. Take an elevator up to the **Skywalk**, the observation deck on the 50th floor, and see what's happening for miles around. The Skywalk offers the only unobstructed 360-degree view of Boston. Or enjoy the view with a drink at the **Top of the Hub**. (Don't bother with a meal; the restaurant is just further proof that penthouse restaurants don't live up to their aerial heights.) At Christmastime, an enormous tree with strange-colored lights is illuminated on the plaza in front of the tower, facing Boylston St. ◆ Admission to Skywalk. M-Sa 10AM-10PM; Su noon-10PM. 800 Boylston St (Gloucester St) Entrance also on Huntington Ave. 236.3318 &

Back Bay landfill operations chugged along 24 hours a day, with as many as 3500 carloads of gravel transported daily from **Needham**, 9 miles distant, on a railroad built for that purpose.

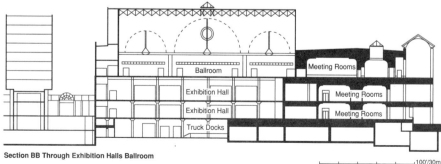

Section BB Through Exhibition Halls Ballroom

`|————————————————|100'/30m`

John B. Hynes Veterans Memorial Convention Center

Courtesy Kallmann, McKinnell & Wood

56 The Cactus Club ★$$ The American southwestern motif has gotten so out of hand, it's parody—intense aqua galore, Georgia O'Keeffe-esque skulls, a buffalo over the bar—but as the big, high-ceilinged rooms fill up, the design assault recedes. Beneath this garishly cheerful disguise lurks a fern bar. The nouvelle Southwestern cuisine highlights ribs, grilled fish and meats, pastas, barbecue, and the like, far better than you'd expect, with surprising accents such as fresh coriander and chipotle peppers. If you have a penchant for swimming in fishbowl-size glasses, you'll like the drinks. This has become a popular hangout for a youngish crowd. The restaurant inhabits the handsome **Tennis and Racquet Club** building (1904), which has a splendid gate in its lobby that prevents access to upstairs offices after hours. ♦ Southwestern ♦ M-Sa 11:30AM-3:30PM, 5-11PM; Su 11:30AM-4PM, 5:30-11PM. 939 Boylston St (Hereford St) 236.0200

57 Steve's Greek & American Cuisine ★$ Lots of locals, students, and conventioneers from the nearby Hynes come to this cheerful restaurant whose owner, **Steve Kourtidis**, says, *It's our pleasure to serve the people*. On one side is the takeout operation, on the other the pleasant plant-entwined dining room overlooking Newbury St. It sometimes gets smoky here from cigarettes. The menu features Greek and Middle Eastern favorites—moussaka, grape leaves, baklava, shish kebabs—and burgers and omelets. ♦ Greek American/takeout ♦ M-Sa 7:30AM-9:30PM. 62 Hereford St (Newbury St) No credit cards. 267.1817

58 Echo ★$$$ The minimalist white-on-white

dining room is the perfect foil for elegant attire. It often seems as if a striking cast of extras were assembled to add panache, even in the more casual café downstairs. Upstairs, the Mediterranean-inspired seasonal menu is restrained and modern—eggplant timbale, roasted *poisson*, grilled duck—although cream finds happy fulfillment in mousses and crème brûlée. Downstairs, the café offers bar food and light meals; sit on the terrace in nice weather. Still a newcomer, Echo is quickly developing the hip, insouciant style Newbury St denizens like best. ♦ New American ♦ M-Th 11:30AM-10PM; F-Sa 11:30AM-11PM; Su 11AM-10PM. 279A Newbury St (Gloucester St) 236.4488

59 L'Espalier ★★★★$$$$ It is this refined and sophisticated establishment that started Boston's restaurant revolution in 1978, yanking the city out of its doldrums into a new era of posh cuisine. **Frank McClelland**, acclaimed successor to the original owner, leans a bit more toward contemporary American cuisine using native products these days, but dinner at L'Espalier is as rarefied and highfalutin an event as ever. Set in a stately 1873 townhouse, the stunning dining rooms will satisfy your whim to experience Back Bay's heyday. The prix-fixe menu includes surcharges for its most precious offerings. Squab and fig salad, grilled partridge, fricasee of Maine lobster, duck breast coupled with foie gras; every dish is tenderly treated, gorgeously presented in modest—sometimes overly so—portions. Service is exceedingly proper. ♦ French ♦ M-Sa 6-10PM. 30 Gloucester St (Newbury St-Comm Ave) Valet parking. Jacket and tie recommended. Reservations required F-Su. 262.3023

60 Casa Romero ★$$$ The prices are steep, though there's compensation in the picturesque dining rooms brightened with hand painted tiles and Mexican handicrafts. And a number of dishes are outstanding: avocado soup, *mole poblano*, *puerco adobado* (pork with smoked chilies), and *flan al Cognac* are a sampling. Enter from Gloucester St at the side alley that

Back Bay

runs between Comm Ave-Newbury St. ♦ Mexican ♦ M-Th, Su 6-10:30PM; F-Sa 5-11PM. 30 Gloucester St. Reservations recommended. 536.4341

61 The Pour House Restaurant and Lounge $ When Back Bay's aura of prestige and privilege gets too rich for your blood, this very basic place is a good antidote. Recently remodeled and expanded, The Pour House has managed to hold onto its pleasingly plain atmosphere, even though it's pink now and has a new compact-disc jukebox. There's a wealth of good cheap bar food to be had here: Philly steaks, burgers, Mexican plates—plus daily specials like shepherd's pie, American chop suey, liver and onions. Come in the morning and order *the piglet* breakfast from **Margie**, a very nice woman who's had regulars chasing after her for years. ♦ American ♦ M-F 7AM-1AM; Sa-Su 8AM-1AM. 909 Boylston St (Gloucester St) No credit cards. 236.1767 ₺

In 1913, excavations for the **New England Life** building at **501 Boylston St** and a subway station, now **Arlington**, uncovered 65,000 sharpened wooden stakes, which archeologists concluded belonged to an ancient fish weir that New England aborigines may have used between 2000 and 3600 years ago.

Restaurants/Clubs: Red	**Hotels:** Blue
Shops/Parks: Green	**Sights/Culture:** Black

61 Gyuhama ★$$ One of Boston's best sushi bars, Gyuhama is the only place in town serving lobster sashimi—a spectacular presentation that's not for the faint-hearted since the lobster pieces may still be twitching when served! Less daring choices include delectable sukiyaki. The basement dining room is intimate, though a trifle seedy. There are always many Japanese diners, a testament to the fastidiously fresh and imaginatively prepared food. In fact, Gyuhama lures so many regulars that it can have a cliquey air. Dine early or be prepared for a wait. ♦ Japanese ♦ M-Th noon-2:30PM, 5:30-10:30PM; F-Sa noon-2:30PM, 5:30-11:15PM; Su noon-2:30PM, 5-10PM. 827 Boylston St (Gloucester-Fairfield Sts) 437.0188

62 Fine Time Antique Timepieces The owners are experienced timepiece dealers and specialize exclusively in buying, selling, restoring, and appraising fine vintage wristwatches and antique pocket watches, such as Patek Philippe, Rolex, Vacheron, Hamilton Watch Company, Cartier, Waltham. Even authentic Mickey Mouse alarm clocks. No reproductions here—just the splendid real tick-tockers. ♦ Tu-Sa 10:30AM-5:30PM. 279 Newbury St (Gloucester St) 536.5858

62 Rudi's $ Though overpriced, Rudi's is popular for its tasty ready-to-go gourmet concoctions: salads, breads, sandwiches, soups, entrees, pastas. The homemade truffles are truly luxurious and so are some of the French pastries and desserts. Mornings, you'll see lots of people on the way to work toting a Rudi's bag that holds their precious croissant and café. The interior

Back Bay

has a few tables—no table service—and should be a whole lot nicer, but the patio is pleasant. ♦ Café/takeout ♦ Daily 7:30AM-8PM. 279 Newbury St (Gloucester St) 536.8882. Also at: 1 Milk St. 542.8660; 71 Summer St. 482.5544 (both in the Financial District)

62 Davio's ★★$$$ Still young and evolving, Davio's features Northern Italian cuisine with continental finesse. The romantic, jewel-box restaurant is a favorite with Back Bay residents. The kitchen makes its own pastas and sausage, and lavishes attention on soups, seafood, venison, and veal. The wine list includes some costly Italian venerables. At the informal café upstairs, snack on fashionable pizzas and pastas at lower prices. There's a little terrace out back for fair-weather dining. ♦ Italian ♦ Café: M-F 11:30AM-3PM, 5-11PM; Sa-Su 11:30AM-11PM. Dining room: M-Sa 11:30AM-3PM, 5-11PM; Su 5-11PM. 269 Newbury St (Fairfield-Gloucester Sts) Valet parking evenings. Reservations recommended in dining room. 262.4810

63 Maximilian Beaded, leather, woven, tapestry, bejeweled, from discreet to showy, classically or iconoclastically shaped, all handbags are produced by small European manufacturers, introduced to America by Maximilian. None are sold in department stores, and once a manufacturer starts mass-producing, their wares are discontinued here. Some manufacturers are more than 200 years old; one company used to make sword cases for musketeers, but when that market dried up it began turning out handbags instead. Prices range from reasonable to breathtaking. ♦ Daily 11AM-6PM. 268 Newbury St (Fairfield-Gloucester Sts) 859.1414

64 Beacon Guest Houses $ Mostly tourists and foreign visitors take advantage of these inexpensive pension-style accommodations. The office screens guests and provides single and double efficiencies (twin beds only) for brief or long-term stays in converted Back Bay townhouses. In the winter, this address is the only building in operation; in the summer, others open. The rooms have no telephone, TV, maid or room service, but all have private bath and kitchenette with some utensils, and linens and towels. ♦ 248 Newbury St (Fairfield-Gloucester Sts) 266.7276, 262.1771 (M-F 8:30AM-5:30PM) 266.7142 (evenings, weekends, holidays)

64 Ciao bella $$ It's nice to have lunch alone at the bar, looking out at Newbury St. In the evening, the dressy dining room draws a chic clientele. Dabble in the appealing selection of appetizers, like *involtini di melanzani* (stuffed eggplant), then turn to pasta or a simple meat dish like the *coletta di vitello*. In nice weather, dine alfresco on the patio. ♦ Italian ♦ M-W 11:30AM-11PM; Th-F 11:30AM-11:45PM; Sa 11:30AM-4:30PM, 5:30-11:45PM; Su 11:30AM-3:30PM, 5:30-11PM. 240 Newbury St (Fairfield St) Valet parking Th-Sa in winter, Tu-Sa rest of year. Reservations recommended F-Su. 536.2626

65 Vose Galleries of Boston The 5th generation of Voses now run this art gallery. Established in 1841, it's the oldest continuously run gallery in America. More than 29,000 paintings have passed through Vose Galleries since 1896. The Voses specialize in 18th-,19th-, and early 20th-century American painting, and they've sold paintings to nearly every major American museum. They frequently show works by the **Hudson River School, Luminists, American Impressionists**, including **Childe Hassam** and **John Henry Twachtman**, and the **Boston School**. At the turn of the century, a Vose agent returned from France with a full-length male nude by **Géricault**. High-minded **Seth Vose** decided to cut off the improper lower portion and sold the torso to the wife of the **Museum of Fine Arts**' president. Fifty years later, Vose's descendants came upon the unseemly portion in their basement and gave it to the MFA, where it was joined to the previously donated upper portion, thus making the poor man whole again. ♦ M-F 8AM-5:30PM; Sa 9AM-4PM. 238 Newbury St (Exeter-Fairfield Sts) 536.6176

Back Bay's flowering coincided with a tremendous increase in the number of Bostonians. In 1800, Bostontown's population was fewer than 25,000. In 1825, it was 58,277. In 1850: 136,881. In 1988 greater Boston's population topped 2.2 million.

Restaurants/Clubs: Red   Hotels: Blue
Shops/Parks: Green   **Sights/Culture:** Black

65 Wenham Cross Antiques Up on the 2nd floor, Irma and Emily Lampert, mother and daughter, preside over an inviting one-room shop full of folk charm and delightful country antiques: handpainted furniture, primitive paintings, hooked rugs, quilts, and samplers, iron banks and wooden pull toys, mottoed plates, Majolica and Quimper pottery. The cupboards and tabletops are never, ever bare. ♦ M-Sa 10AM-5PM. 232 Newbury St (Exeter-Fairfield Sts) 236.0409

66 Eastern Accent Tabletop and desktop items, most imported from Japan, are displayed against a vivid chartreuse backdrop. Lovely twirly-glass pens, surrealist cutlery, cast-iron and concrete clocks, artful bowls and teapots, clever jewelry, texturous writing papers reflect the store's motto, *living with design*, and the Japanese precept that the functional should be well-made. Other straightforward materials include stainless, celluloid and Bakelite, natural porcelains, silk, anodized aluminum. ♦ M-Sa 11AM-6PM. 237 Newbury St (Fairfield St) 266.9707

67 Newbury Pizza $ Get a thick-crusted, topping-laden, zesty, and inexpensive slice of pizza here —the kind you have to fold over to stuff in your mouth fast enough. Newbury Pizza also sells subs, salads, and old favorites like spaghetti and meatballs. Believe it or not, this pizzeria serves fruit cups, and has an attractive, very unpizzeria-esque decor complete with wall sconces. ♦ Pizza/takeout ♦ M-Sa 11AM-10PM; Su 1-10PM. 225 Newbury St (Exeter-Fairfield Sts) No credit cards. 536.9451

Zoe

68 Zoe Gallery Zoe exhibits work by contemporary Boston-area and internationally known artists such as Shelley Reed, David Kelley, Emmett McDermott, Mary Sherwood, Darryl Zeltzer, Louis Risoli, James Hansen ♦ M-Sa 10AM-6PM. 207 Newbury St (Exeter-Fairfield Sts) 536.6800 &

69 Harvard Book Store Café ★$$ Independently operated, the shop and café have enjoyed a happy marriage here. The café's new American cuisine borrows from international ethnic dishes and recently reached new heights under the direction of one of the café's new managers, **Moncef Meddeb**, the former owner and chef *extraordinaire* who created the stellar **L'Espalier**, another Back Bay institution. Prices at the café are reasonable for Back Bay and the clientele has a strong international streak. There's something deeply satisfying about dining in the midst of stacks of books; if you're alone, pick one up and linger awhile. Don't settle for a table in the back dining room, with its bookless dull decor. On a summer day, the outdoor café is a fine place to relax and watch waves of shoppers flow by.

The bookstore keeps abreast of the latest literary currents, and offers out-of-print and second-

hand book searches. It publishes a monthly newsletter reporting on new titles, two author series it coordinates with the **Boston Public Library**, and another series at a sister bookstore, sans café, in Cambridge: the **Harvard Book Store**, 1256 Mass Ave, Harvard Sq, 661.1515. ♦ New American ♦ Shop and café: M-Th 8AM-11PM; F-Sa 8AM-midnight; Su noon-11PM. 190 Newbury St (Dartmouth-Exeter Sts) 536.0095 (store) 536.0097 (café) &

70 Exeter Street Theatre Building (1885, H.W. Hartwell and W.C. Richardson; restaurant renovation 1975, Childs, Bertman, Tseckares, Casendino) Once Boston's oldest continuously operating theater, the Exeter Street Theatre was the Proper Boston woman's favorite haunt for many years. It was run by a cultivated and business-minded woman, who shunned the racy Hollywood fare that shocked her discriminating clientele and instead booked edifying foreign films. Unfortunately, the old theater's wonderful interior was renovated out of existence. The Victorian gem of granite and brownstone was built as a temple for the **Working Union of Progressive Spiritualists**, but today a steady stream of Materialists visits the **Conran's** home-furnishings emporium, which replaced the theater and got its own name up in lights. Grafted onto the building is the glass extension to **Friday's**, a watering-hole and pickup joint for young working people and tourists that features a grotesquely huge menu and frenetic atmosphere. A schlocky place where *Life is a Beach* T-shirts abound.

Back Bay

Within Exeter Street Theatre Building:
Conran's Habitat Part of the retail chain. ♦ M, W 10AM-9PM; Tu, Th-F 10AM-7PM; Sa 10AM-6PM; Su noon-5PM. 26 Exeter St (Newbury St) 266.2836

71 Nielsen Gallery Nina Nielsen has run this gallery for more than 25 years, and exhibits contemporary works by Joan Snyder, Jake Berthot, Harvey Quaytman, Jane Smaldone, and Profirio DiDonna (his estate) from a roster of roughly 20. Nielsen isn't a trend-chaser; she looks for artists—many young, awaiting their first break—whose work expresses highly personal viewpoints, often spiritual, whom she sticks with and nurtures. She'll also show work by famous 20th-century artists such as Jackson Pollock and David Smith. Nielsen likes what she likes and has many clients who feel the same. She doesn't shy away from making one of her big interests apparent: the continuum of spiritual substance in art. Says Nielsen about purchasing art: *Buy for love after talking to knowledgable people.* If you give the gallery's staff advance notice about visitors in wheelchairs, they are happy to assist. ♦ Tu-Sa 10AM-5:30PM. 179 Newbury St (Dartmouth-Exeter Sts) 266.4835

For all Back Bay's French influences, its street names are aggressively Anglophile.

71 Marcoz Something splendid always graces the show windows. Marcoz occupies 2 handsomely preserved floors of a Victorian townhouse, a wonderful setting for decorative merchandise from the 18th–early 20th century. The hard-to-find accent pieces are imported from England or France, or purchased from New England estates. Knowledgable and friendly, Mr. Marcoz will tell you all about whatever strikes your fancy, be it the 17th-century Madonna and child processional figures, 19th-century French *boule de petarque* (boccie-style ball), exquisite engravings, ivorine and sterling-silver napkin rings, desktop inkwell, pocket watch, furniture, or other singular finds. Designers call from Toronto to Palm Beach. ♦ M-Sa 10AM-6PM. 177 Newbury St (Dartmouth-Exeter Sts) 262.0780

71 The Society of Arts and Crafts Stop in here for a special something handmade and one-of-a-kind. The oldest nonprofit craft association in America, operating since 1897, the society promotes established and up-and-coming craftspeople by putting their wares before the public. All work is selected by jury: jewelry, ceramics, glass, quilts, weaving, wood, collages, leather, clothing and accessories, and furniture—the last is always especially noteworthy. Exhibitions are held on the 2nd floor; recent shows included one on whimsy called *Eraserheads, Fishsticks and the Wizards of Ozone*, and another called *American Furniture*. A satellite gallery is located in the Financial District at 101 Arch St, 345.0033. ♦ M-Sa 10AM-5:30PM. 175 Newbury St (Dartmouth-Exeter Sts) 266.1810

Back Bay

71 Pucker Safrai Gallery More than 20 years in the business, this gallery displays local and international contemporary artists' graphics, paintings, sculptures, and porcelains. They also carry modern masters such as **Chagall**, **Picasso**, and **Hundertwasser**. Israeli art is a specialty, with works shown by **Samuel Bak, David Sharir, Shraga Weil**. ♦ M-Sa 10AM-5:30PM. 171 Newbury St (Dartmouth-Exeter Sts) 267.9473

71 Monhegan An ideal source for wedding gifts of the pampering, homey kind: cozy wool blankets, throws hand-woven in New England, European and domestic custom and handmade linens, cedar chests, even some sweaters. Colors and textures are soft and alluring. You can purchase a gift here that will make a new baby feel very welcome in this world. This store draws a lot of repeat business as customers keep adding to the comforts of home. ♦ M-Sa 10AM-6PM. 173 Newbury St (Dartmouth-Exeter Sts) 247.0666

Boston has long endured the reputation of prudery. A 19th-century etiquette pamphlet advised: *The perfect hostess will see to it that the works of male and female authors be properly separated on her bookshelves. Their proximity unless they happen to be married should not be tolerated.*

72 La Ruche The perfect source for whimsical house gifts, La Ruche is best known for trompe l'oeil and painted furniture and lampshades, and Italian and French faience. They also carry flora- and fauna-shaped mugs, teapots, and jars; lovely French ribbon; garden ornaments; unusual glasses; linens; lamps; tapestry pillows; and other decorative wares. Potpourri scents the air. ♦ M-Sa 10AM-5:30PM. 174 Newbury St (Dartmouth-Exeter Sts) 536.6366

72 The Copley Society of Boston The oldest art association in America, the nonprofit society was founded in 1879 to promote access to art, particularly new European trends, and to exhibit the work of its members and other artists of the day. Members **John Singer Sargent** and **James McNeill Whistler** showed their work in society galleries. In 1905, the society mounted **Claude Monet**'s first American exhibition, a controversial event, and in 1913 **Marcel Duchamp**'s *Nude Descending a Staircase* was shown here, creating an enormous furor. Today the society has more than 500 committee-selected members from across the country and around the world, though most come from New England. It operates 2 floors of galleries, with individual artists renting space upstairs and an ongoing members' show downstairs. The society no longer is in the vanguard, having gotten somewhat mired in tradition. Its shows are uneven in quality. But work by noted and rising artists is often on view, so it's worth investigating what's on the walls. ♦ Tu-Sa 10:30AM-5:30PM. 158 Newbury St (Dartmouth-Exeter Sts) 536.5049

73 Boston Art Club (1881, **William Ralph Emerson**) This artful assemblage is the work of **Ralph Waldo Emerson**'s clever nephew, also creator of the fascinating **House of Odd Windows** on Beacon Hill. Emerson let loose his entire artillery of architectural forms and ornament on the Queen Anne-style facade: from every angle, there's something peculiar or interesting to see. **Copley Square High School** now occupies the building. ♦ 270 Dartmouth St (Newbury St)

74 London Lace A bit of fine old lace is a lovely thing indeed. This 2nd-story shop is as snowy and bright as its goods. Owner **Diane Jones** travels to England, Ireland, and Scotland to collect restored antique lace curtains, table and bed linens dating from 1860-1920, and reproductions. She also imports new lace made from original Victorian patterns on 100-year-old Scottish looms. ♦ M-Tu, Th-Sa 10AM-5:30PM; W 10AM-7PM. 167 Newbury St (Dartmouth-Exeter Sts) 267.3506

74 Kitchen Arts A wonderful resource for cooks, both expert and far-from, you can pick up any kitchen tool your culinary sleight-of-hand requires. The emphasis here is on performance, not pretty-to-look-at gifts; these wares are ready to go to work immediately—slicing, dicing, decorating, coring, chopping, cracking, grinding, whatever. Kitchen cutlery and knife sharpening are sub-specialties. ♦ M-Sa 10AM-6PM; Su noon-5PM. 161 Newbury St (Dartmouth-Exeter Sts) 266.8701

74 Du Barry $$ Don't expect French cooking worthy of accolades here, but this quiet, old-fashioned restaurant is a Back Bay landmark nonetheless, family-owned and operated since 1936. The owners are French, and their son is responsible for the classical and provincial cuisine. Dine out back on the terrace. Back Bay residents are loyal to this place, and it attracts its share of students, professionals, movie stars. ◆ French ◆ M-Sa noon-2:30PM, 5:30-10PM; Su 5:30-9:30PM. 159 Newbury St (Dartmouth-Exeter Sts) Reservations recommended for 4 or more. 262.2445

75 Papa Razzi ★★$$ An inviting, busy Italian trattoria complete with wood-burning pizza oven, Papa Razzi's menu leans toward rustic Northern Italian dishes with California overtones. Chef **Rebecca Matarazzi** hails from Beverly Hills' famous **Prego**, and her hearty fare includes an array of splendid crispy-crusted pizzas, polenta with grilled Italian sausages, and bountiful antipasti and pastas. ◆ Italian ◆ Daily 11:30AM-2AM. 271 Dartmouth St (Newbury-Boylston Sts) 536.9200

76 Body Sculpture This gallery of contemporary jewelry and accessories represents a regular group of more than 20 artists who work in media such as metal, polyester resin, acrylics, silicone, stones, precious metals, clay, and silk. Hundreds of white drawers are filled with off-beat jewelry perfect for art-to-wear lovers. No diamond tennis bracelets here. Five to 6 shows each year. ◆ M-Sa 10AM-6PM. 127 Newbury St (Clarendon-Dartmouth Sts) 262.2200

76 Autrefois Antiques Another time, says the name: 18th- and 19th-century France is captured here in fine imported hardwood furnishings such as armoires, tables, chairs, chandeliers, and mirrors. Other epochs and origins also creep in. The biggest shipments of new merchandise arrive in the spring and fall. The expert owners will do on-site restoration and adapt old furnishings for modern needs; updating lighting is their specialty. ◆ M-Sa 10AM-5:30PM. 125 Newbury St (Clarendon-Dartmouth Sts) 424.8823. Also at: 130 Harvard St, Brookline. 566.0113

77 Goods Lingerie Bostonian women love this shop for its pretty and sensual array of silk, lace, and cotton lingerie and feminine items for the boudoir. Labels include Sabath-Row, Christian Dior, and Hanro of Switzerland. The collection of hair ornaments is exquisite—those with short hair will be tempted to let it grow. ◆ M-W, F-Sa 10AM-6PM; Th 10AM-7PM. 123 Newbury St (Clarendon-Dartmouth Sts) 536.7860

77 Alpha Gallery The best free shows in town are often here. A family affair, the gallery is owned by **Alan Fink**, managed by his daughter **Joanna**, and shows work by his wife **Barbara**

Swan and son **Aaron Fink**—both of whom merit the attention. Alpha exhibits 20th-century and contemporary American and European painting, sculpture, and prints. Distinguished artists shown here include American painters **Milton Avery, Bernard Chaet, Fairfield Porter**; Europeans **Mimmo Paladino** and **Georg Baselitz**; Massachusetts realists **Scott Prior** and **Gregory Gillespie**; and gifted young artists such as **T. Wiley Carr**. Over its 2 decades-plus, Alpha has mounted major exhibitions of work by **John Marin, Max Beckmann, Stuart Davis**, and **Picasso**'s complete Vollard Suite. ◆ Tu-Sa 10AM-5:30PM. 121 Newbury St (Clarendon-Dartmouth Sts) 536.4465

78 Serenella Women come to this small, friendly boutique to invest in luxurious, classical, timeless clothes that will serve them well for years. The emphasis is on European designer daytime wear, with some accessories and shoes. Owner **Ines Capelli** does all the buying, and is always on the lookout for styles that are just right for her regular customers. ◆ M-Tu, Th-Sa 10AM-6PM; W 10AM-7PM. 134 Newbury St (Clarendon-Dartmouth Sts) 262.5568

RICCARDI

78 Riccardi The latest exemplars of European fashion rendezvous at Riccardi. All of the clothing, for men and women, is made in Italy, but designs and influences come from throughout Europe. Even the store's facade looks Italian.

For women, designs by **Ann Demeulemeester**, Belgium; **John Galliano**, England; **Martine Sitbon**, Paris; **Sybilla**, Madrid. For men, **Byblos, Fugiwara, Moschino**, and **Panchetti**, all Italian. Shoes and accessories are multinational too. An entire department is devoted to sporting wear. The staff is always up-to-date and informative on fashions. This is certainly one of Boston's most worldly shops; they even accept JCB, the major Japanese credit card. ◆ M-Tu, Th-Sa 10AM-6PM; W 10AM-7PM. 128 Newbury St (Clarendon-Dartmouth Sts) 266.3158

78 Judi Rotenberg Gallery Rotenberg is very dedicated to her 20-or-so artists, both established and emerging, who include **Joseph Solman, Marianna Pineda, Bert Yarborough**. Rotenberg and her father **Harold** also show here. ◆ M-Sa 10AM-6PM. 130 Newbury St (Clarendon-Dartmouth Sts) 437.1518

79 Rebecca's Cafe $ Everything is made fresh daily at this gourmet takeout place, a satellite of the original Rebecca's at 21 Charles St on Beacon Hill. Lines form all day for homemade muffins and scones, fresh salads, hot entree specials, and the spectacular desserts and pastries the kickoff Rebecca's made famous. The chocolate-mousse cake and the fresh-fruit tarts are pure pleasure. There are a few tables at the back. ◆ Café/takeout ◆ M-Sa 7AM-9PM; Su

8AM-5PM. 112 Newbury St (Clarendon-Dartmouth Sts) No credit cards. 267.1122. Also at: 18 Tremont St. 227.0020; 290 Main St, Kendall Sq, Cambridge. 494.6688; 65 JFK St, Harvard Sq, Cambridge. 661.8989

80 Bargain Box/Surprise Box Quality Clothing & Collectibles Upstairs at the Bargain Box, gently used clothing—mostly for women, but some for men—is donated or consigned, much of superior and designer quality. Many a discarded treasure is discovered here. Some accessories, too. Downstairs, the Surprise Box is more of a mishmash of antique and second-hand silver and glassware, bric-a-brac, crafts, painted furniture, handmade stuffed animals, silver, dried flower arrangements, and baskets. Both shops are run by the **Junior League of Boston, Inc.**, a nonprofit women's organization dedicated to promoting community volunteerism. ♦ M-F 10AM-6PM; Sa 11AM-6PM. 117 Newbury St (Clarendon-Dartmouth Sts) 536.8580

80 Cuoio Pronounced *coyo*, the name means *leather* in Italian. For women only, this store showcases fashionable leather boots and shoes, lots imported from Italy, and accessories such as jewelry, hats, and fabulous hair ornaments. Many smart styles aren't available elsewhere in the city. ♦ M-Sa 10AM-6PM; Su noon-5PM. 115 Newbury St (Clarendon-Dartmouth Sts) 859.0636. Also at: 170 Faneuil Hall Marketplace. 742.4486

80 Isabelle Collins of London The British owner concentrates on country furniture and

Back Bay

decorative arts from the British Isles and Ireland, with some finds from Scandinavia. Linens, embroideries, majolica, dairy utensils, and kitchenware too. ♦ M-F 10AM-6PM; Sa 10AM-5PM. 115 Newbury St (Clarendon-Dartmouth Sts) 266.8699

81 David L. O'Neal Antiquarian Booksellers, Inc. Antiquarian bookseller for more than 25 years, O'Neal's concentrates on fine and rare books from the 15th century to present—including first editions in literature—many with superior bindings or leatherbound in sets. Many works have remarkable printing, typography, illustrations. Original, historical, and decorative American and European prints from the 16th-19th century are also displayed. First-edition **Jane Austen** works, **Nathaniel Bowditch**'s wonderful navigation book, **James Fenimore Cooper**'s rare, anonymous first novel, **Cotton Mather**'s psalter, **Shelley**'s *Prometheus Unbound*—a mere sampling of what many come to covet. Appointments are encouraged. An illustrated catalogue is available. ♦ M-Sa 9AM-5PM. 234 Clarendon St (Newbury St-Comm Ave) 266.5790 &

Boston was the first American city to establish a police department.

Restaurants/Clubs: Red   **Hotels:** Blue
Shops/Parks: Green   **Sights/Culture:** Black

82 Trinity Church Rectory (1879, H.H. Richardson; National Register of Historic Places) The massive arched entry bellows the name of the rectory's masterful architect, H.H. Richardson, who designed its parent **Trinity Church** at Copley Square. The building's surface is vigorously alive with twisting flowers and ornament. A 3rd story was, unfortunately, added by HHR's successor firm after his death. ♦ 233 Clarendon St (Newbury St)

83 New England Historic Genealogical Society Many an aspirant to the lofty branches of some illustrious Yankee family tree has zeroed in on this private, nonprofit research library, the oldest of its kind in the nation and the first in the world. The mission: to plumb the past, to root out those roots. Housed in a former bank, NEHGS was founded in 1845 and now holds 200,000 volumes and more than a million manuscripts dating to the 17th century. NEHGS is dedicated to the study and preservation of family history, with records and histories for all US states and Canadian provinces, plus Europe. There's no better place to try to entangle one's heritage with that of the **Adams**, the **Cabots**, the **Randolphs**, and other American Olympians. What would caste-conscious Boston do without it? NEHGS has more than 11,000 members with access to its archives. Visitors pay a half- or full-day research fee. ♦ Fee. Tu, F-Sa 9AM-5PM; W-Th 9AM-9PM. 101 Newbury St (Berkeley-Clarendon Sts) 536.5740

Unusual Libraries

The following is but a sampling.

American Jewish Historical Society ♦ 891.8110

Appalachian Mountain Club Library ♦ 523.0636

Boston Athenaeum ♦ 227.0270

Bostonian Society Library ♦ 720.3285

Francis A. Countway Library of Medicine ♦ 732.1000

Educational Resources Information Center at Boston Public Library ♦ 536.0200

The Endowment for Biblical Research Collection, Boston University ♦ 353.3724

The French Library ♦ 266.4351

Goethe Institute ♦ 262.6050

John F. Kennedy Library ♦ 929.4500

Massachusetts Historical Society ♦ 536.1608

Massachusetts Horticultural Society Library ♦ 536.9280

The New England Historic Geneological Society ♦ 536.5740

Society for the Preservation of New England Antiquities (SPNEA) ♦ 227.3960

State Library of Massachusetts ♦ 727.2590

Swedenborgian Library ♦ 262.5918

Just about everyone—Bostonians included—becomes confused by Back Bay's profusion of *Copleys*: among them, the **Copley Plaza Hotel**, not to be confused with the **Copley Square Hotel**, and **Copley Square**, not to be confused with **Copley Place**.

84 **John Lewis, Inc.** Swinging in the window, wave upon wave of silver strands lure passersby into this serene 1876 brownstone, where veteran Newbury St proprietors **John** and **Louise Lewis** design jewelry in workrooms located on the premises. Working with solid precious metals and natural stones, the couple turns out a glittering array of imaginative designs. Some are simple, pure expressions of rich materials and careful workmanship. Others are more intricate, such as the Lewis' line of Victorian-inspired jewelry with its panoply of cherubim, scrolls, flowers, and bows. ◆ Tu, Th-Sa 10AM-5PM; W 10AM-7PM. 97 Newbury St (Berkeley-Clarendon Sts) 266.6665 ⅋

84 **Haley & Steele** It's fun to rifle—gingerly, of course—through the flat files crowded with prints of all kinds. The gallery focuses on 18th- and 19th-century prints in scores of categories, including botanical, sporting, architectural, military, New England maritime, birds, historical, and genre. The custom frame shop specializes in painting conservation and French line matting, and has served local artists since 1899. A print from Haley & Steele's will add a handsomely proper accent to any setting. ◆ M-F 10AM-6PM; Sa 10AM-5PM. 91 Newbury St (Berkeley-Clarendon Sts) 536.6339

84 **Café Florian** ★$ A Hungarian émigré opened this sidewalk café 30 years ago, and it has always held onto a bit of European flavor. The food isn't special, though the pastries are nice. Sip wine by the glass and survey the posh Newbury Street scene while guiltlessly eavesdropping on conversations in foreign languages. Entertain yourself counting how many different designer shopping bags pass by in a quarter-hour. There's live music on Friday and Saturday nights. ◆ Café ◆ M-Th 9AM-11PM; F-Sa 9AM-midnight; Su 10AM-10PM. 85 Newbury St (Berkeley-Clarendon Sts) 247.6600

84 **Martini Carl** The **Ventola** family's boutique stocks sophisticated European apparel for men and women ranging from very casual to very dressy, with all the requisite accessories. The designer and private labels emphasize rich fabrics and leathers, superb tailoring, and enduring styles. ◆ M-Tu, Th-Sa 10AM-6PM; W 7:30PM. 77 Newbury St (Berkeley-Clarendon Sts) 247.0441

85 **Gallery NAGA** Run by the **Newbury Associated Guild of Artists**, a cooperative of 28 local artists, the gallery mounts interesting exhibitions of contemporary painting, sculpture, photography, and prints by the known and unknown. Director **Arthur Dion** likes to bridge the division between fine art and craft, and shows furniture, ceramics, and glass. Exhibitors have included **Henry Schwartz, James Gemmill, Irene Valincius**; furniture designers **Tom Loesser** and **Judy McKie**. The gallery occupies a generous swatch of space—1400 square feet—in the **Church of the Covenant**, whose progressive congregation gives art a boost by keeping rents low, from a mandate to minister to the city. ◆ Tu-Sa 10AM-5PM. Closed mid July-Labor Day. 67 Newbury St 267.9060

85 **Church of the Covenant** (1867, R.M. Upjohn; National Register of Historic Places) A Gothic Revival **Tiffany** treasure-house, with the largest collection of the stained-glass master's work in the world: 43 windows, some 30-feet high, and clerestories too. Especially noteworthy is the sanctuary lantern with 7 angels. It was designed by Tiffany's firm for the Tiffany Chapel exhibited at the **Columbian Expositon of 1893** in Chicago, then installed here. Also, look for the last remaining **Welte** pipe organ in the country, a 5-keyboard, manual 4500-piped instrument, which can be heard during the church's fall and spring organ recital series. The church has a long history of giving generously to the community; it also founded the **Back Bay Chorale** and the **Boston Pro Arte Chamber Orchestra**, which perform regularly here and at **Harvard University**. ◆ Tu-Sa 9AM-noon, Jan-Apr, Nov-Dec; Tu-Sa 9AM-5PM May-Oct. 67 Newbury St (Berkeley St) 266.7480

86 **Louis, Boston** (1863, William Gibbons Preston) Until the **New England Museum of Natural History** moved to its current site straddling the Charles River and changed its name to the **Boston Museum of Science**, it was jammed into this French Academic structure. The museum was one of Back Bay's pioneers. When it vacated, part of moving-day chaos included lowering a stuffed moose from an upper-story window, a scene captured in a photograph that the museum now prizes. **Bonwit Teller** then resided here for decades until Louis, the city's astronomically priced clothier, took over and gave the building a much-needed restoration. There are

3 floors dedicated to men's apparel, one to women's—everything's of exceptional quality. The building's splendid isolation makes it appear even more magnificent than it is. Inside, it's enjoyably spacious for browsing. ◆ M-Tu, Th-Sa 10AM-6PM; W 10AM-8PM. 234 Berkeley St (Newbury-Boylston Sts) 965.6100 ⅋

Within Louis, Boston:

Cafe Louis ★★$ Louis' café deserves a special visit. High-ceilinged, furnished with lacquered bamboo chairs and tapestry banquettes, this pleasant nook echoes the store's sunny palette, but in a warm butterscotch. You can enter at the café's main entrance off the parking lot, but why not stroll through the store, past $1000 sweaters and $200 scarfs. The menu marries Italian and French flavors. Indulge in seductive pastries, smoked fish, or French toast ordered by the slice in the morning; antipasto for 2 or a sandwich handsomely composed and garnished for lunch; or a splendid slice of cake with tea in late afternoon. You can dine outdoors at tables on the cement landing, though the view of the parking lot and the New England Life Building across the way isn't exactly breathtaking. A small gourmet shop offers prepared and packaged treats of all kinds to go. The café's major flaw: it closes much too early. ◆ Café/takeout ◆ M-Tu, Th-F 7:30AM-6PM; W 7:30AM-8PM; Sa 10AM-6PM. 266.4680

87 Alan Bilzerian In Bilzerian's striking display windows, it's the dramatic clothes that create the mood—needing few props, they speak for themselves. A native of Worcester MA, Bilzerian started out with a college student clientele 2 decades ago, then began selling to rock stars. Now Bilzerian's is the local name in fashion best known outside of Boston. In fact, New Yorkers with the fashion world at their feet still make special trips, and lots of celebrities drop in when in town—**Cher** and **Mick Jagger** among them. The art-to-wear fashions, accessories, and shoes for men and women feature the work of European and Japanese designers: **Yohji Yamamoto, Rei Kawakubo, Dries van Noten, Issey Miyake, Katharine Hamnett, Rifat Ozbek, Jean Paul Gaultier, Azzedine Alaia, Romeo Gigli**, to name a few. Complementing the other collections, Bilzerian designs for men, and his wife, **Bê**, designs for women. Of course, outlandishly stylish wear commands outlandishly high prices. ♦ M-Tu, Th-Sa 10AM-5:30PM; W 10AM-7PM. 34 Newbury St (Arlington-Berkeley Sts) 536.1001 & The staff will carry wheelchairs up the stairs; once inside, there's an elevator to the 2nd-floor women's department

88 Romano's Bakery & Sandwich Shop $ The Back Bay needs all the unpretentious, reliable places it can get, and this little 40-seater is one of the good ones. Casual and cafeteria-style, Romano's has won a dedicated clientele with its fragrant fresh muffins, bagels, Danish, and croissants in the morning—the busiest time—homemade soups, quiches, sandwiches, and tantalizing desserts later on. You can also get cappuccino and espresso. The serving people

Back Bay

are a lively and efficient crew. ♦ Café/takeout ♦ M-F 7AM-6PM; Sa 7:30AM-5PM; Su 10AM-5PM. 33 Newbury St (Arlington-Berkeley Sts) No credit cards. 266.0770

Boston's Best Views

Aside from the obvious **John Hancock Tower** and **Prudential Tower** vantage points, great views can be had from the **John F. Kennedy Library and Museum**; riding on the **Red Line** across **Longfellow Bridge**, between the **Kendall Sq** and **Charles St** stops; driving across the **Tobin Bridge**, walking along elevated **Viaduct St** on the **South Boston** side of **Fort Point Channel**; relaxing in the **Ritz Bar** across from the **Public Garden**, skimming across **Boston Harbor** on the **Airport Water Taxi**, which you can take to and from **Rowes Wharf**; gazing seaward or Bostonward from many of the **Boston Harbor Islands**; on Boston Harbor cruises; in the **Skyline Room Cafeteria** at the **Museum of Science**, straddling the **Charles River Dam**; at the public 16th-floor observation deck in the **Traffic Control Tower** at **Logan International Airport**; at the **Bay Tower Room** restaurant; at **Seasons** restaurant in the **Bostonian Hotel**, overlooking **Faneuil Hall**; at the **Spinnaker Italia**, a revolving rooftop lounge and restaurant in the **Hyatt Regency Cambridge**, and from **Copps Hill** in the **North End** and **Bunker Hill** in **Charlestown**.

Restaurants/Clubs: Red   **Hotels:** Blue
Shops/Parks: Green   **Sights/Culture:** Black

88 29 Newbury ★$$$ A few too many snobby waiters have been encountered here, but 29 still draws a hip clientele and the food is often imaginative and health-conscious. The somewhat subterranean-feeling dining room is treated like an art gallery, with monthly openings. Come in nice weather, when you can join the eclectic crowd on the sidewalk patio. The Sunday brunch earns raves. ♦ New American ♦ M-Th 11:30AM-5PM, 5:30-11PM; F-Sa 11:30AM-5PM, 5:30PM-midnight; Su noon-4PM, 5-9PM. 29 Newbury St (Arlington-Berkeley Sts) Reservations recommended. 536.0290

89 Emmanuel Church (1862, **Alexander R. Estey**; enlargement 1899, **Frederick R. Allen**) Its uninspired rural Gothic Revival architecture doesn't do justice to this Episcopal church's lively, creative spirit. Dedicated since the 1970s to *a special ministry through art*, the church organizes a variety of music and cultural events. A Bach cantata, performed professionally, accompanies the liturgy every Sunday, September-May, drawing crowds. Jazz celebrations are held periodically. ♦ 15 Newbury St (Arlington-Berkeley Sts) 536.3355

Within Emmanuel Church:

Leslie Lindsey Memorial Chapel (1920–1924, **Allen and Collens**) This Gothic chapel was erected by **Mr. and Mrs. William Lindsey** as a memorial to their daughter, **Leslie**, who with her new husband was bound for a European honeymoon on the ill-fated *Lusitania*. Some time after the boat sank, Leslie's body supposedly washed ashore in Ireland, still wearing her father's wedding gift of diamonds and rubies; they were sold to help pay for her memorial. The chapel is sometimes called the *Lady Chapel* for its marble carvings of female saints. Architects Allen and Collens were already nationally renowned for **Riverside Church** in New York.

90 Charles Sumner A head-to-toe boutique, Sumner carries great imported and American women's designer apparel—by **Donna Karan, Valentino, Gianfranco Ferre, Missoni, Koos van den Akker, Isaac Mizrahi**, and others—plus shoes, handbags, makeup, hosiery, jewelry, gloves, hats. In 1985, new owners **Brit d'Arbeloff** and **Anita Chilen** took over an old establishment, which had become an off-puttingly snobby shoppe, and turned Sumner into a welcoming place to go for truly wonderful things. The enthusiastic salespeople try hard to work with customers and make them feel at home. Be sure to investigate **Sumner's Loft** on the 3rd floor for tremendous bargains on last season's sale merchandise. ♦ M-Tu, Th-Sa 10AM-5:45PM; W 10AM-7PM. 16 Newbury St (Arlington-Berkeley Sts) 536.6225

90 Barbara Krakow Gallery Don't pass this 5th-floor gallery by. That's hard to do anyway because there's an eye-catching marble bench carved with enigmatic messages by **Jenny Holzer** on the sidewalk out front. Krakow has been in the art-selling business for nearly 30 years and is now at its pinnacle. Highly respected, she's called the Queen of the Scene. Krakow's gallery is possibly Boston's most important, and she directs its prestige to numerous worthy causes. Many of the most significant nationally and internationally known contemporary artists are shown here, among them Holzer, **Agnes Martin, Cameron Shaw, Jim Dine, Donald Judd, Michael Mazur, Claudia Hart** Despite the superstars on its walls, the gallery is a very hospitable, unpretentious place. Krakow combines sure taste with a willingness to take risks —showing work by high school kids, for example, or Boston artist **Jerry Beck**'s bedroom made from styrofoam. ♦ Tu-Sa 10AM-5:30PM. 10 Newbury St (Arlington-Berkeley Sts) 262.4490

91 Skinner, Inc. (Above Burberry's) Founded in 1962, Skinner's is the fifth largest auction gallery in the US, and New England's foremost. Skinner's exhibitions and auctions are free and fascinating fun—even if you come just to observe. A form of live theater, auctions began as a tasteful way to conduct bankruptcy, and evolved into a lively marketplace for collectors of all kinds. The auctioneer's voice and gavel command buyers from all over. Just watching people handle the suspense of bidding is a study in human nature. Skinner's holds more than 60 previews and auctions annually in 15 specialty categories, such as American furniture and decorative objects, toys, fine jewelry, musical instruments, holiday gifts. Unlike museums, the art and objects sold can be examined at close range, with specialists on hand to answer questions. Highlights from select auctions are on view in Skinner's gallery. Auctions are held at the **Ritz-Carlton** and at Skinner's main gallery in **Bolton MA**, about a 45-minute drive outside Boston. Call to find out what's in store. ♦ M-F 9AM-5PM; Sa only for previews, call for times. 2 Newbury St (Arlington St) 236.1700 ᷂

92 Domain It's fun to prowl through this mecca of home embellishments, a fantasy habitat for a menagerie of antique, traditional, and designer pieces; not commonplace or conventional. The aim here is to mass-market one-of-a-kind-looking furnishings. A multitude of quirky accessories crowd in with the beds, tables, sofas. Textures, colors, patterns, and styles veer crazily in all directions. ♦ M-Sa 10AM-6PM; Su noon-5PM (call for later hours in the summer). 7 Newbury St (Arlington St) 266.5252 ᷂

When Back Bay was built, old families with money were already entrenched on **Beacon St**, and claimed new lots as it was extended, especially on the water side. Families with old names but no money took over **Marlborough St**, the new rich built their grandiose digs on **Comm Ave**, and the middle- and upper middle-class settled on **Newbury** and **Boylston** streets.

93 Ritz-Carlton Hotel $$$$ (1927, **Strickland and Blodget**; addition 1981, **Skidmore, Owings & Merrill**) The oldest Ritz-Carlton in the country, the hotel's reputation for luxury, elegance, superlative service, and all the little niceties proper Bostonians love so well has never slipped. The elevator attendants, for example, wear white gloves. The understated edifice perfectly expresses the fastidious courtesies and traditions of its inhabitant. There's nothing flashy or eye-catching about this building, except for its parade of vivid blue awnings. But it has become a timeless, steadfast fixture on the street, exactly the position the Ritz-Carlton occupies in the city.

The Ritz's 278 rooms and suites are simply and traditionally appointed in European style. Rooms have safes and locking closets, all windows open, and 41 suites have wood-burning fireplaces. Request rooms with views of the **Public Garden**. Rooms for nonsmokers and handicapped persons are available. You can bring your pet if it's leashed. The Ritz has a small health club and guests have complimentary access to the fancy spa at **The Heritage** a block away. Other amenities: 24-hour room service, valet parking, same-day valet laundry, multilingual staff, babysitting, concierge, barber, shoeshine stand. If that's not enough, the staff *will provide anything legal.* ♦ Deluxe ♦ 15 Arlington St (Newbury St) 536.5700, 800/ 241.3333; fax 536.1335

Within the Ritz-Carlton:

The Ritz Lounge ★★★$$ While a harpist

thrums soothingly in the corner of this quiet, lovely drawing room on the 2nd floor, sit in a high-backed chair and nibble tiny sandwich triangles, fruit tarts, and scones with jam, sipping perfectly brewed tea. A tea dance is held every Thursday from 5:30-8:30PM and there's dancing every night after 8:30PM. ♦ Café/tea ♦ Daily 11:30AM-12:30AM (cocktails); 11:30AM-4PM (lunch); 3-5:30PM (tea). Jacket and tie required evenings; no denim or running shoes

The Ritz Bar ★★★★$$ On a snowy evening, the gorgeous view of the **Public Garden** from this cozy street-level bar is a page out of a storybook. Inside, there's no entertainment, just plenty of welcome serenity and a crackling fire on the hearth. The bar is famous for its perfect martinis; ask for the special martini menu, which featured 13 varieties at last count, including the **James Bond**. Boston mystery writer **Robert B. Parker**'s fictional sleuth **Spenser** has quaffed many a beer here. Lunch is served, except on Sunday. ♦ M-Sa 11:30AM-1AM; Su noon-midnight

The Ritz Cafe ★★$$$ With views of Newbury St, quiet vanilla decor, and cordial service, the café offers respite during a hectic day. When you've had it with the world, come here for a restorative touch of civility. Since you can't see the **Public Garden** from here, the

Ritz's prized honorary possession, it's been reproduced in a mural. Weekdays, many of Boston's business heavy-hitters breakfast here, with an eye on the commercial street scene. At night, the café also caters to the after-theater crowd. Children may order from a special menu. ♦ American ♦ Daily 6:30AM-2:30PM, 5:30PM-midnight. Jacket and tie required evenings; no denim. Reservations recommended at lunch

The Ritz Dining Room ★★★$$$$ Every day, new Hub restaurants open—but there will *never* be another Ritz. The 2nd-floor dining room is the hotel's showpiece, with cobalt-blue Venetian crystal chandeliers, gold-filigreed ceiling, regal drapery, and huge picture windows overlooking the **Public Garden**. There's no better place for wedding proposals, anniversaries, momentous occasions. Piano music and an occasional harpist add to the spell. Timeless classics such as rack of lamb and châteaubriand for 2 commune with a few more stylish offerings on the menu. But the chef introduces innovations very carefully; the old-guard patrons would rise up in arms if Boston cream pie and other old-time favorites were seriously challenged. Entrees low in sodium, cholesterol, and calories are available; so is a children's menu. Fashion shows are held every Saturday, and chamber music accompanies the fabulous Sunday brunch. ♦ French ♦ M-Th noon-2:30PM, 5:30-10PM; F-Sa noon-2:30PM, 5:30-11PM; Su 10:45AM-2:30PM, 6:30-10PM. Jacket and tie required. Reservations required

Bests

Robert B. Parker
Pearl Productions

Seasons in the **Bostonian Hotel**

Rarities in the **Charles Hotel**

Hamersley's Bistro

The Harvest

roccos

Legal Sea Foods

Fenway Park

Boston Garden

Le Pli Health Club

The **Charles River**

Museum of Fine Arts

David Breashears
Filmmaker and Himalayan Mountaineer

A Brief Walking Tour of Boston

I like to introduce visiting friends to Boston with a brief 2- to 3-hour walking tour, given my limited tolerance for this kind of thing. I begin my tour with a view of the city from the **John Hancock Tower** observation deck. This is very important, as Boston's geography can easily befuddle even the most seasoned traveler—local residents, too. While there, take time to view the beautiful illuminated diorama on display,

which provides the first-time visitor with a brief, relevant historical background of the city.

Upon descending and leaving the Hancock tower, visit **Trinity Church** just a few steps away, a masterpiece of 19th-century American-Romanesque architecture designed by Henry Hobson Richardson. Many of Richardson's other fine buildings can be seen elsewhere in the metropolitan area. Before entering the church, observe the stunning juxtaposition of architectural styles: the featureless, sky-blue Hancock (or slate blue-gray, if the day is overcast) enters the earth without a whisper, while the richly textured Trinity warmly embraces the ground in earth tones. Once inside, you'll find a charming sanctuary of stained glass and carved wood, and a magnificent organ to be heard during Sunday services.

Cross a block over from Boylston St to **Newbury St**, where a multitude of shops and restaurants suit all tastes, with numerous galleries displaying the work of local artists. Walking against traffic, you'll soon arrive at the **Boston Public Garden**. Verdant in summer, the picturesque garden provides a respite from street traffic and sidewalk bustle and a chance to rest the feet. If small children are included in your party, visit the bronze **ducklings** modeled after the feathered protagonists of Robert McCloskey's famed *Make Way for Ducklings* tale (they're near the corner of Beacon and Charles streets).

On **Beacon Hill** across from **Boston Common** sits the State House; on the opposite side of Beacon Street is Augustus Saint-Gaudens' bas-relief of **Robert Gould Shaw** and the heroic black regiment he commanded. At the back of the **State House** find **Mt Vernon St**, erstwhile home of Boston's most prestigious families, abolitionists, industrialists, and philanthropists alike. This area best represents old Boston. Visitors from certain areas of London will feel they never left home.

At the base of Mt Vernon, turn right and walk down **Charles St** with its functioning gaslights and many antique shops. At its end, look for the pedestrian entrance to the **Longfellow Bridge** with its matching sets of *salt and peppers shaker* towers. Stop at the first tower and take in the view of **Boston's skyline;** once again, the contrast between old and new is striking. Beacon Hill appears superimposed against towering modern structures.

Returning, descend from the bridge to an elevated walkway sloping downward to the **Esplanade**. Proceed upriver past the **Hatch Shell** of Arthur Fiedler and July 4th renown. With a summer breeze the sailboats should be numerous, tacking back and forth on the Charles River. Sit down and enjoy the view of Cambridge across the way, then return to Boston proper via another elevated walkway, the unmistakable dusty-pink **Fiedler Footbridge**, which deposits you near the Public Garden. Your walking tour now over, it's time for a meal or an invigorating cup of tea in the **Ritz-Carlton Tea Lounge**—proper dress required. Or, if your party is more casual, seek out one of the outdoor cafés along Newbury St.

According to a 1701 Boston law that's still alive and kicking, **Paul Revere** could have been hauled in by the local police for speeding on his midnight ride from Boston to **Lexington**. The law states *no person having the care of a horse or other beast of burden shall drive, or ride. . . at a greater rate of speed than 7 miles per hour in a public street.*

David Rose
Director, The Institute of Contemporary Art

A proper visit to Boston should involve walking. The kind you usually do when visiting older European cities. A good idea would be to begin with a walk through the **Back Bay**. Save **Newbury Street** and its shopping for last, instead start with a walk down **Marlborough Street** and back by **Commonwealth Avenue**. I'm constantly amazed by the beauty and variety of the stream of 19th-century brownstone facades. A walk along the **Esplanade** at sunset is quite something, though it's almost better to walk along the **Cambridge** side (near **MIT**) so that you get Boston in the background. The **Freedom Trail** and **Black Heritage Trails** are remarkable and worth the time of adults as well as children.

During any season, with the possible exception of deep winter, a leisurely stroll through the **Public Garden** will renew your appreciation of **Olmsted**'s genius, and renew your dedication to fight for intelligent urban design wherever you come from.

For religious experiences, there are 2 in this city that rank with the world's greatest. The first is a visit to **H.H. Richardson**'s masterpiece, **Trinity Church**. Arguably one of the 10 most beautiful buildings in the United States, it has the power and subtlety of all great art. The second is a visit to **Fenway Park**, the home of one of the few real, truly transcendent unadulterated American experiences available for a reasonable price. And since the **Red Sox** are all about faith and suffering, even if you hate baseball you gain an unparalleled understanding of the Boston psyche.

When you finally do a shopping trip to Newbury Street, the one store not to miss is Boston's claim to fame: **Alan Bilzerian**. A small men's and women's store, it is as close to an art gallery as a clothing store ought to be. Great design standards, somewhat pricey, and that wonderful feeling that you've actually found just what you've been looking for.

When I check out Boston artists represented in the contemporary gallery scene, I put on my walking shoes and check out **Zoe Gallery**, **Akin Gallery**, **Howard Yezersky**, and **Gallery Naga**. Other important galleries like **Barbara Krakow**, **Thomas Segal**, **Mario Diacono**, and **Portia Harcus** mix Boston art with a larger dose of national and international artists. All are sophisticated and easily worth your time and probably an investment of more tangible resources as well. As in many major American cities, the gallery scene follows the available real-estate market, and as such is somewhat scattered about. Don't be discouraged, however, as this whole group of galleries can be visited easily in a leisurely Saturday morning and afternoon.

As far as museums are concerned, I have my obvious biases, but you essentially can't go wrong. Clearly, you should visit the **ICA**. You could spend an hour or a week at the **MFA (Museum of Fine Arts)** and feel fine about the way you used your time. The **Gardner** is not to be missed, and the **Fogg** is a connoisseur's delight.

Finally, if you have a spare day, take the time to drive 50 minutes south on Route 3 to **Plimouth Plantation**. *Back to the Future*'s got nothing on this place. It's such an authentic 17th-century village, it's almost surreal. Pure *Twilight Zone* and a great way to cap a visit to these parts

Benjamin Thompson
President, Benjamin Thompson & Associates, Architects

To understand Boston and its architecture, walk around this pedestrian city and see—besides the well-scaled streets and finely detailed buildings—how the city's site defines and explains what it is and has been. Boston is a peninsula pointed at the sea. Today's plan emerges with great clarity from the organic irregularity of its origins. Walking around, it tells you many things.

Start at **Arlington Street** (the logical *A* of an alphabetic **Back Bay** grid) at the edge of the **Boston Garden** and **Common**. Sheep once grazed on this rural backside of the original town. Make your way up **Beacon Hill** via **Boylston Street** to the gold-domed **State House** on the ridge, and look east toward the harbor. Fanning out in a bold arc around the base of the hill are the waterfront piers, where settlement and commerce started, working their way up the hill. (Still on the inner streets of Beacon Hill are lovely brick townhouses, quiet streets, elegant **Louisburg Square**—an 18th-century urban miracle.) You can make your way to the water by various routes. Down Beacon Hill to **City Hall** and through **South Market Street** to **Waterfront Park** takes you along the scenic *Walk to the Sea*, terminating at **Long Wharf** and the adjacent **New England Aquarium**. (Here, the **Chart House** is a good bet for an atmospheric waterfront dinner.)

In Colonial days Long Wharf was Boston's deepwater pier, receiving British goods and unwelcome troops; at **Dock Square**, its watery landing place for small boats, old **Faneuil Hall** was built as the first city market. In 1825, to serve a growing city, **Quincy Market** was

Bests

built on landfill and **Atlantic Avenue** became the pierhead edge of the harbor, facing east to the great ocean beyond.

Here you have 2 choices. You can turn south on Atlantic, reaching the new **Rowes Wharf** (where a commuter boat will whisk you to **Logan Airport**), then cross the **Northern Avenue Bridge** to **South Boston**, an emerging warehouse district whose first visible attraction is the imaginative **Children's Museum**. Pick up a lobster dinner or a lunch of steamers or oysters at the **Dockside Restaurant** at the end of the bridge along the channel (outdoor seating in season).

Or you can travel north on Atlantic Avenue along the piers (which continue to be reclaimed for apartments and offices and restaurants and people) on a route that runs to the mouth of the **Charles River**. When this gets dull, loop back through the colorful **Little Italy** of the **North End** and reemerge at **Faneuil Hall Marketplace**. Pause for drinks at the **Marketplace Café** on **North Market Street** next to the **Flower Market**, watching the people stream by. Or try **Brasserie Les Halles** upstairs for good French food and special views. Watch the activity in the marketplace from south windows, or **Haymarket** from the north windows of the dining room.

Because landfill progressed so neatly from east to west, Back Bay is a chronological history of architecture, from the French Academic and Italianate forms near **Arlington St** to Georgian Revival toward the **Fens**. With each block, time advances.

Kenmore Square/Fenway

This piece of Boston befuddles even Bostonians, who regularly scramble references to **Fenway Park** (the nationally known ballpark), the **Fenway** (a parkway), the **Fens** (part of the park system designed by **Frederick Law Olmsted**), and **Fenway**, the district containing all 3. Also part of Fenway is **Kenmore Square**, a student mecca, and **Longwood Medical Area**, a dense complex of world-renowned medical and educational establishments—including **Harvard Medical School**—that's a city unto itself. Unlike **Beacon Hill** or **Back Bay**, Fenway lacks a cohesive personality, and its indeterminate boundaries are a constant source of confusion to visitors and residents alike. But it's worth navigating the helter-skelter Fenway to find its main attractions: the **Museum of Fine Arts** and **Isabella Stewart Gardner Museum**; **Symphony Hall**; Frederick Law Olmsted's famous **Emerald Necklace**; and, of course, Fenway Park, home of the **Red Sox**.

Fenway was the last Boston neighborhood built on landfill, and only emerged after the noxious and loathsome **Back Bay Fens** was imaginatively rehabilitated by Olmsted. Like the original Back Bay—stagnant tidal flats that metamorphosed into the city's most fashionable neighborhood—the Back Bay Fens was considered an unusable part of town, a stinking, swampy mess that collected sewage and runoff from the **Muddy River** and **Stony Brook** before draining into the **Charles River**. The prob-

lem worsened after Back Bay was filled in and the Fens' unsanitary state became a concern for the city. A group of commissioners formed to address the Back Bay Fens drainage problems and simultaneously develop a park system for Boston, an idea that gained momentum in the 1870s. Co-creator of **New York City's Central Park** and founder of the landscape architecture profession in America, Frederick Law Olmsted was called in as consultant and ultimately hired in 1878 to fix the Fens and create the **Boston Park System**. His ingenious solution involved installing a tidal gate and holding basin, and using mud dredged from the refreshed Fens to create surrounding parkland. Developers quickly recognized the neighborhood's new appeal, and it was *Westward-ho!* once again for overcrowded Boston.

The transformed Fens became the first link in Olmsted's Emerald Necklace, the most important feature in the **Boston Park Department**'s plan for a city-scaled greenspace network, the first of its kind in the nation. Instead of a New York-style central park (inappropriate given Boston's topography), Boston wanted a system of open spaces throughout the city, offering breathing room to residents. This meshed perfectly with Olmsted's noble esthetic and social ideals for landscape architecture. He envisioned interconnected parks, recreation grounds, boulevards, and parkways that would not only beautify the environment and enhance public health and sanitation, but also direct urban expansion, population density, and local economy. Boston and Olmsted were ideally matched: city officials appreciated not only his talents and civic-mindedness, but also his interest in solving practical problems through landscape design.

Attracted by Olmsted's lovely park and succeeding Emerald Necklace links, numerous cultural, medical, educational, and social institutions began relocating in the Fenway area. Boston's devastating downtown fire of 1872 and advances in public transportation also encouraged many to move. During the 1890s and early 1900s, the **Massachusetts Historical Society**, Symphony Hall, **Horticultural Hall**, **New England Conservatory of Music, Simmons College**, Museum of Fine Arts, and Harvard Medical School were built. Another neighborhood pioneer was **Fenway Court**, the fashionable residence where **Isabella Stewart Gardner** installed the magnificent personal museum of art that now bears her name. Since then, other institutions have followed the same trail; **Northeastern University** and **Boston University** (B.U.) now dominate the district. Fenway's resident educational and medical institutions have played the largest role in shaping its contemporary character. Today, the Fenway/Kenmore Square area claims a huge concentration of college students and young adults. It has the lowest median age of all Boston neighborhoods and a transient feel. Originally an extension of prestigious Back Bay with fine hotels, offices, and shops, Kenmore Sq is now largely geared toward its student population with plenty of fast fooderies and cheap-eats delis, good ethnic restaurants, clubs, record shops, and the like. The square's famous landmark is the **Citgo Sign** straddling the **B.U. Bookstore**. The sign's pulsating light patterns are particularly arresting when seen from the bridges spanning the Charles River, or reflected waveringly on the water.

The **Symphony** and **Hynes Convention Center/ICA** subway stops (**Green Line**) are on the **Back Bay** edge of this neighborhood; the **Kenmore Sq** (**Green Line**) stop puts you in the middle of the club and student scene and is minutes away from **Fenway Park**, as is the **Fenway** stop (**Green Line**). The **Ruggles/Museum** stop (**Green Line**) is most convenient to the **MFA** and the **Isabella Stewart Gardner Museum**. From the **Longwood** (**Green Line**) stop, you can walk to the **Longwood Medical Area**. After the Kenmore Sq stop, the **B Line** to **Boston College** makes frequent stops aboveground on **Comm Ave** (along **Boston University**'s campus), and the **C Line** to **Cleveland Circle** does the same on **Beacon St**; don't confuse these 2 lines (all **Green Line**), which residents and visitors alike often do.

Restaurants/Clubs: Red   Hotels: Blue
Shops/Parks: Green   **Sights/Culture**: Black

1 Symphony Hall (1900, McKim, Mead & White; National Register of Historic Places) Deep-pocketed Brahmin philanthropist and amateur musician **Henry Lee Higginson** founded the **Boston Symphony Orchestra** (BSO) in 1881, and wanted his creation's new home to be among the world's most magnificent. The hall's enduring fame stems not from its restrained Italian Renaissance style, however distinguished, but rather from its internationally distinguished acoustics, which have earned Symphony its nickname as a *Stradivarius* among concert halls. Symphony is the first concert hall in the world to be built according to an acoustical formula, the work of **Wallace Sabine**, an assistant professor of physics at **Harvard University** and one of the first to probe the scientific basis of acoustics. The hall is basically a bell-shaped shell built to resonate glori-

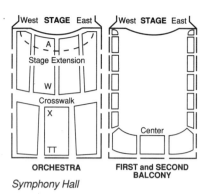

Symphony Hall

(diagram labels: West **STAGE** East; West **STAGE** East; A; Stage Extension; W; Crosswalk; X; TT; ORCHESTRA; Center; FIRST and SECOND BALCONY)

ous sound to astound the ears; the eyes matter less (physical comfort, too; the seats are rather hard). Directed by **Seiji Ozawa**, the BSO remains one of the world's preeminent orchestras. It is in residence at Symphony Hall from October-April; from July-August it performs at **Tanglewood**, an open-air theater in western Mass. The hall is also home to the beloved **Boston Pops**, conducted by Hollywood composer and Oscar-winner **John Williams**, which performs from May to mid-July at Symphony Hall. (The seats are removed from the main floor, replaced by tables and chairs, and food and drink are served.) Williams' predecessor was the late renowned **Arthur Fiedler**, who wielded the baton for more than 50 years. No one should miss the chance to experience orchestra and hall together, a delight music-loving Boston has always cherished. The **Handel & Haydn Society**, America's oldest continuously active performing arts organization, performs here too, as do many other local, national and international groups. The hall also

Kenmore Square/Fenway

holds a magnificent 5000-pipe organ. Subscriptions are available. To reserve and charge seats for BSO or Pops performances, call Symphony-Charge 266.1200. Bargain alert: same-day, one-per-customer discounted seats for BSO performances are available on Tu, F, and Sa. The line forms near the box office Tu and Sa from 5PM, and from 9AM on F. ♦ Seats 2625. Box office M-Sa 10AM-6PM; through intermission on concert evenings. 301 Mass Ave (Huntington Ave) 266.1492 &

2 Thai Cuisine ★$$ After a concert at **Symphony** or a foreign film at the **MFA**, dine on good Thai dishes, fiery or delicate, in this little 50-seater located right behind **Symphony Hall**. The owner has opened several other Thai restaurants in Greater Boston, all highly regarded. Go the spicy route with *kang liang* (peppered shrimp soup) or *gai pud gra prao* (chicken, onion, and chili), or try more subtle tastes like *tom you koong* (soup with shrimp, lemon grass, lime, and chili), steamed whole fish, Thai seafood combination, or the selection of curries. It's sometimes a little hurried here. ♦ Thai/takeout ♦ M-Th 11:30AM-3PM, 5-10PM; F-Sa 11:30AM-3PM, 5-10:30PM; Su 5-10PM. 14A Westland St (Mass Ave) 262.1485 &

3 Bangkok Cuisine ★$ A favorite with students and people working nearby, Boston's oldest Thai restaurant is still turning out great beef and chicken *sate*, *duck choo chee* (curry), *pad Thai*, whole fried bass with chili sauce, and Thai bouillabaisse, which features assorted tender seafood served in a puffed pouch. The long, narrow dining room empties and fills quickly, but service is sometimes desultory so allow extra time if you have a concert or movie ahead. ♦ Thai/takeout ♦ M-Sa 11:30AM-3PM, 5-10:30PM; Su 5-10:30PM. 177A Mass Ave (Norway St) 262.5377 &

4 The Huntington Theatre Company (HTC) at Boston University Theatre Acclaimed HTC, the professional company-in-residence, puts on 5 plays annually at this charming 1925 Greek Revival theater. HTC's focus is both classic and contemporary, like *The Piano Lesson*, **Shakespeare**, and musicals like *Candide* and *Animal Crackers*. Discounts offered for senior citizens and students; subscriptions available. ♦ Seats 850. 264 Huntington Ave (Mass Ave) Ticket info 266.3913 & (call in advance)

5 Jordan Hall at the New England Conservatory of Music (NEC) (1901; hall 1904, **Wheelwright and Haven**; National Register of Historic Places) Smaller and more intimate than **Symphony Hall**, Jordan is also an acoustically superior concert hall, ideal for chamber music. It belongs to the NEC, established in 1867 as the first music college in the country and internationally renowned today for its undergraduate and graduate music programs. In addition to hundreds of NEC concerts, many free and most held during school months, Jordan accommodates a number of musical groups, including the **Juilliard Quartet, Tokyo String Quartet, Boston Symphony Chamber Players, Cantata Singers, Carlos Montoya**, and the **Boston Chamber Music Society**. The hall was funded by **Eben Jordan**, founder of the **Jordan Marsh** department stores ♦ Box office M-F 10AM-6PM; Sa noon-6PM. 30 Gainsborough St (Huntington Ave) Cash only; no reservations by telephone or mail. Program info 536.2412 & (call in advance)

6 Greater Boston YMCA $ Mainly students and tourists stay in this 50-room Y; 10-day maximum visit, and you must be at least 18 years old with a picture ID and luggage to stay. Two of 3 floors are for men, the other's coed. Single and double rooms available, all share baths. Children can stay with a parent. Breakfast is free, as is use of the gym, indoor track, pool, and sauna. There's a cafeteria-style restaurant and laundry facilities on the premises. Smoking is allowed everywhere. A modest key deposit is required. Reserve 2 weeks in advance by mail; walk-ins accepted daily after 12:30PM. ♦ Office M-Sa 6AM-6PM. 316 Huntington Ave (Gainsborough St-Opera Pl) 536.7800

The **Boston Symphony Orchestra**'s first concert was held 22 October 1881 in the Music Hall, since demolished. That season's ticket demand: 83,359 persons attended 20 concerts and 20 rehearsals.

Restaurants/Clubs: Red	**Hotels:** Blue
Shops/Parks: Green	**Sights/Culture:** Black

7 Boston International American Youth Hostel (AYH) $ There's no cheaper lodging available in the city, and it's near the **Museum of Fine Arts**. Offering 150 rooms in the winter and 220 in the summer, the hostel accommodates men and women of all ages in dormitory style, with 6 bunks per room, separated by sex. Every floor has showers and bathrooms, and the building houses laundry facilities plus 2 kitchens with utensils. Sleeping bags are *not* allowed; you can rent a sleep sheet for a modest fee and deposit. The hostel fills up quickly from May until fall. The fee is lower if you're a member of AYH, and you can join on the spot. Bikes and packs can be stored securely on the premises. No alcohol allowed, no smoking except in one public room, and there's a 3-night limit per 30-day period. ♦ Reservations are recommended; you can only reserve by mail, not by telephone, but walk-ins are accepted for 25 percent of the beds nightly. Cash only. Daily 7AM-11AM; lockout 11AM-2:30PM; open again 2:30PM-midnight (*no* admittance after that) 12 Hemenway St (Haviland St) 536.9455

8 Looney Tunes A good source for serious and dilettante collectors of used and out-of-print jazz, classical, and rock records, some rare. The store also sells movie and Broadway sound tracks, comedy, country, blues, and opera LPs and 45s, plus *cut-outs*, CDs, cassettes, videos. A few new items, too. They also buy. ♦ M-Sa 10AM-9PM; Su noon-6PM. 1106 Boylston St (Hemenway St) 247.2238 ᕫ Also at: 1001 Mass Ave near Harvard Sq, Cambridge. 876.5624

8 Soft Rock Cafe ★$ Inexpensive and elegant fare served in a restful, subtle setting. Try bourbon French toast, omelets, fresh muffins, and steamed hot chocolate for breakfast, smoked turkey and avocado on homemade mini-baguette, lamb brochettes, Green Goddess salad, and tasty daily specials for lunch. Great coffee, too. An ideal spot for a light early supper or leisurely Sunday brunch. ♦ Café ♦ M-F 7AM-7PM; Sa 9AM-3PM; Su 11AM-3PM. 1124 Boylston St (Hemenway St) 424.1789

9 The Massachusetts Historical Society (1899, **Edmund March Wheelwright**; National Historic Landmark) The first historical society founded in the New World (1791), the society largely operates as a research center for the study of American history and is only surpassed by the **Library of Congress**. The focal point is the library, which contains some 3200 collections of manuscripts and several hundred thousand books, pamphlets, broadsides, maps, early newspapers, and journals, including **Governor John Winthrop**'s and the **Adams** family's papers, **Paul Revere**'s accounts of his famous ride, 2 copies of the Declaration of Independence—one written in **John Adams**' hand, the other in **Thomas Jefferson**'s—and a staggering quantity of other such treasures. The society's rare book collection includes most of the important early books printed in America or about its discovery and settlement. Government, politics, women's history, slavery, the China trade, railroads, science and technology—the breadth of topics addressed is immense. The society also owns prints, engravings, furniture, antique clocks, personal belongings, and several hundred works of art. The first map produced in British North America, an 18th-century Indian archer weathervane by **Deacon Shem Drowne** (maker of **Faneuil Hall**'s grasshopper), a list of Americans killed in the **Battle of Concord**, and Jefferson's architectural plans for **Monticello** are among the items it preserves. Free guided tours are given if requested in advance. Having enumerated all these virtues, here's the catch: to use the library, you must pass muster as a *serious* pursuit with a *serious* and *worthy* pursuit. ♦ Free. M-F 9AM-4:45PM. 1154 Boylston St (Charlesgate E) 536.1608 ᕫ

10 The Museum of Fine Arts, Boston (MFA) (1909, **Guy Lowell**; addition 1966-1970, **Hugh Stubbins and Associates**; addition 1976, **The Architects Collaborative**; West Wing 1981, **I.M. Pei & Partners**) The MFA first exhibited upstairs at the **Boston Athenaeum** on **Beacon Hill**, then moved in 1876 to its own ornate Gothic Revival **Copley Sq** quarters, since demolished. In 1909, the museum made the trek out to the newly fashionable Fenway area along with numerous other pioneering public

institutions seeking more spacious sites than Boston proper could offer. The MFA now resides in an imposing if dull Classical Revival edifice, with a majestic colonnade on the Fenway side and a temple portico on the **Huntington St** side flanked by 2 big wings. Standing in the front courtyard is a statue of a mounted Indian gazing skyward, appealing for aid against the white man's invasion. **Cyrus Edwin Dallin**'s *Appeal to the Great White Spirit* won a gold medal at the 1909 Paris Salon and attracted many admirers when erected here in 1913, but looks quite odd in this ordered setting today.

The museum's somber starkness ends abruptly indoors, where an embarrassment of riches begins, much of which was acquired through the generosity of wealthy Victorian Bostonians committed to creating a truly cosmopolitan cultural repository. The MFA is one of the country's greatest museums and deserves repeated exploration. Begin with a dose of familiar sights and historic local names and faces in the American collections. The MFA owns more than 60 works by **John Singleton Copley**, including his portrait of **Paul Revere** (whose artistry as a silversmith is on display

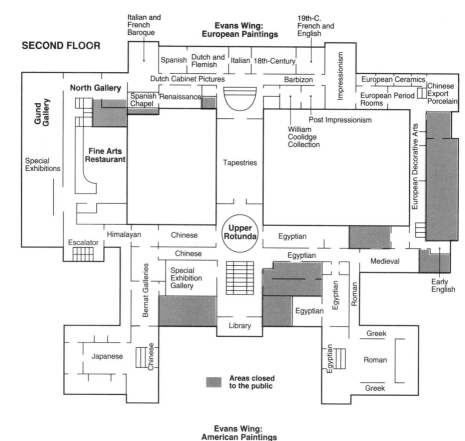

SECOND FLOOR

Italian and French Baroque

Evans Wing: European Paintings

19th-C. French and English

Spanish | Dutch and Flemish | Italian | 18th-Century

Impressionism

Dutch Cabinet Pictures

Barbizon

European Ceramics

European Period Rooms

Chinese Export Porcelain

North Gallery

Spanish Chapel | Renaissance

Gund Gallery

Special Exhibitions

Fine Arts Restaurant

Post Impressionism

William Coolidge Collection

European Decorative Arts

Tapestries

Upper Rotunda

Himalayan | Chinese

Egyptian

Escalator

Chinese

Medieval

Special Exhibition Gallery

Egyptian

Early English

Bernat Galleries

Egyptian

Roman

Library

Egyptian

Japanese | Chinese

Egyptian

Greek

Roman

Greek

Areas closed to the public

Evans Wing: American Paintings

FIRST FLOOR

20th-Century American and European

Ladies Comm. Gallery

American Folk Paintings

Japanese Garden

American Impressionism | American Masters

19th-C. Landscape and Genre

Copley and His Contemporaries

American Federal

Foster Gallery

20th-C. Works on Paper

Early 20th-C. American

Karolik Collection

Oak Hill Rms

19th-C. American

Special Exhibitions

Watercolors

Seminar Room

American Neoclassicism and Romanticism

English Silver

Remis Auditorium

Museum Shop

American Modern

18th-C. European Boston

Forsyth Wickes Collection

18th-C. French Art

Café

Courtyard

WEST WING ENTRANCE

C. Brown Gallery | Carter Gallery

Lower Rotunda

Mummies

18th-Century American Furniture

Slide Library

Escalator

Members' Room

Torf Gallery

Pre-Columbian | American Silver

Information Center

Islamic

Prints Drawings Photography

Egyptian

Prints

Indian

Musical Instruments

Near Eastern

S.E. Asian

Japanese

HUNTINGTON ENTRANCE

Greek

Korean

Etruscan

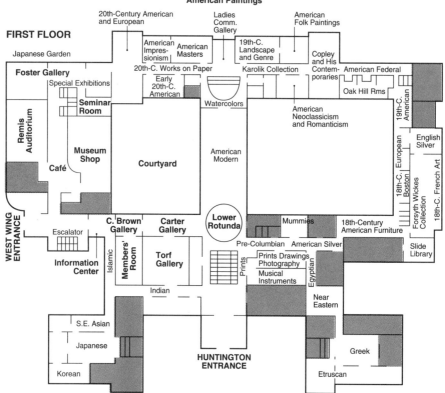

Courtesy Museum of Fine Arts

elsewhere, including his famous Liberty Bowl), and paintings by local boy **Winslow Homer, Gilbert Stuart, Edward Hopper, John Singer Sargent, Fitz Hugh Lane, Mary Cassatt, James McNeill Whistler, Thomas Eakins**. Holdings range from native New England folk art and portraiture to the **Hudson River School, American Impressionists, Realists, Ash Can School,** and New York's **Abstract Expressionists**. The **Department of American Decorative Arts and Sculpture** is particularly noteworthy for its pre-Civil War New England products, and includes furniture, silver, pewter, glass, ceramics, sculpture, and folk art; the collection progresses from the rustic functional creations of early colonial times to the elegant pieces popular in the increasingly prosperous colonies. The **Department of Twentieth-Century Art** is a Johnny-come-lately, emphasized only since the '70s, but does include **Jackson Pollock, David Smith, Robert Motherwell, Helen Frankenthaler, Morris Louis, Joan Miró, Adolph Gottlieb, Georgia O'Keeffe**.

The MFA owns superb works from all major developments in European painting from the 11th-20th centuries, with a particularly rich representation of 19th-century French works. Victorian Bostonians loved French painting, eagerly exhibiting the Impressionists while they were still awaiting acceptance in their own country. On display in the **Evans Wing** galleries are more than 40 **Monets** and more than 150 **Millets**, including his best-known painting, *The Sower*, works by **Corot, Délacroix, Courbet, Renoir, Pissarro, Manet, van Gogh, Gauguin, Cézanne**. Other celebrated artists shown in this wing are **van der Weyden, Il Rosso, El Greco, Rubens, Canaletto, Turner, Picasso**.The MFA's extraordinary collection of Asiatic art—the largest under any one museum roof—features one of the greatest Japanese collections in existence, important objects from China, India, Southeast Asia. (Before you leave the MFA grounds, be sure to visit **Tenshin-en-Garden of the Heart of Heaven**, on the museum's north side—a contemplative Japanese garden designed by garden master **Kinsaku Nakane**.) The **Egyptian and Ancient Near Eastern Art** galleries are a favorite with kids—they have mummies!—and are also treasure troves of jewelry, sculpture, and other objects from throughout Asia's western regions. The MFA's array of Old Kingdom sculpture is equaled only by the **Cairo Museum** because the MFA and **Harvard University** jointly sponsored excavations in Egypt for 40 years. And it is apt that the *Athens of America* boasts a superb representation of ancient Greek, Roman, and Etruscan objects, including bronzes, sculpture dating from the 6th-4th centuries BC, and vases painted with fascinating figures and vignettes by some of the greatest early Greek artists.

Other highlights: the **Department of European Arts** features a collection of antique musical instruments like lutes, clavichords, harps, and zithers, replicas of which are often played in special MFA concert programs. The **Department of Textiles** displays an international collection of tapestries, batiks, embroideries, silk weavings, costume materials and other textiles. The Boston area was the capital of the textile industry in the late 19th century, and the MFA was the first museum in America to elevate textiles to the status of art. Its collection ranks among the world's greatest. Spanning the 15th century to today, the **Department of Prints and Drawings** has particularly outstanding 15th-century Italian engravings and19th-century lithography, many works by **Dürer, Rembrandt, Goya**, the **Tiepolos**, the **German Expressionists**, **Picasso**'s complete *Vollard Suite*, the **M. and M. Karolik Collection of American Drawings and Watercolors** from 1800-1875, a growing collection of original photographs, and still more.

Special exhibitions are mounted in the modern light-filled West Wing, where you'll find the **Fine Arts Restaurant, Galleria Café, Cafeteria** and **Museum Shop**. Many Bostonians make special trips just to visit the latter for its wonderful selection of books, prints, children's games, cards and stationery, reproductions of silver, jewelry, glass, textiles, and other decorative items aplenty. The MFA's excellent film, concert, and lecture series are held in the West Wing's **Remis Auditorium**. Also in the neighborhood is the **School of the Museum of Fine Arts** and the **Massachusetts College of Art**.
♦ Admission (reduced when West Wing only is open); members and children under 16 free; reduced admission for senior citizens. Entire museum: Tu, Th-Su 10AM-5PM; W 10AM-10PM; free W 4-6PM. West Wing only: Th-F 5-10PM. Closed 1 Jan, 4 July, Labor Day, Thanksgiving, 24-25 Dec. Free guided tours: Tu-F 11AM, 2PM; Sa 11AM, 1:30PM. Free introductory walk in Spanish 1st Sa of every month

Kenmore Square/Fenway

11:30AM. 465 Huntington Ave (Museum Rd) Limited paid parking available off Museum Rd. Handicapped parking near West Wing entrance. 267.9300, recorded info for weekly schedules 267.9377, daily schedules 267.2973, TTY/TDD 267.9703; concerts, lectures, film info 267.9300 ext 306 &

Within the Museum of Fine Arts:

Fine Arts Restaurant ★★$$ The food is unexpectedly good, with special themed menus playing off the current high-profile exhibition. For *Monet in the '90s*, a sandwich called the Grainstack and an entree called Water Lily were among the offerings. A popular place for brunch. ♦ New American ♦ Tu, Sa 11:30AM-2:30PM; W-F 11:30AM-2:30PM, 5:30-8:30PM &

Galleria Cafe ★$ Refuel for another foray through the galleries over cappuccino or wine and light meals, fruit, cheese, or desserts at the informal open café. ♦ Café ♦ Tu, Sa-Su 10AM-4PM; W-F 10AM-9:30PM &

Cafeteria $ If you're with children, this is the best option for a quick meal, and there's rarely a wait. ♦ American ♦ Tu, Sa-Su 10AM-4PM; W-F 10AM-8PM. Lower level &

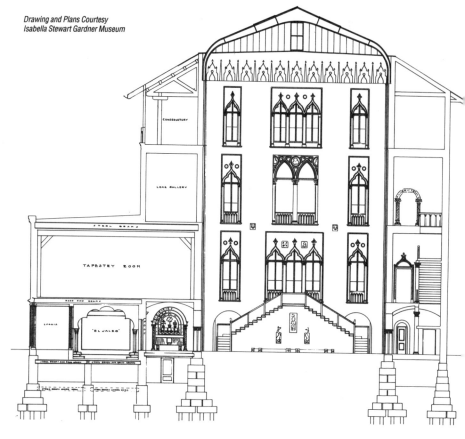

Drawing and Plans Courtesy
Isabella Stewart Gardner Museum

11 Isabella Stewart Gardner Museum (1902, **Willard T. Sears**) On New Year's Eve 1903, **Isabella Stewart Gardner** held a glorious gala-

Kenmore Square/Fenway

to-end-all-galas to unveil her private art collection in its opulent new **Fenway Court** home. No one could pass up this event, including those who typically snubbed flamboyant Isabella. Fifty **Boston Symphony** musicians played a Bach chorale, and when the crowd caught sight of the now-famous flowering palace courtyard, a collective gasp was followed by awed silence. Admirers and detractors alike were wowed by Gardner's resplendent array of paintings, sculpture, tapestries, *objets d'art* in their dazzling setting. An admiring **Henry Adams** wrote: *As long as such a work can be done, I will not despair of our age....You are a creator and stand alone.* It's hard to imagine inhabiting such a place as Fenway Court, but Gardner settled right in, describing it after 20 years of residence as *very nice, very comfortable, and rather jolly.* Upon her death in 1924, her will officially turned the mansion into a museum and stipulated the demanding terms of its operation: all is to remain *exactly* as it was upon her death, or else all shall be sold and the proceeds given to **Harvard University**. (That accounts for the very idiosyncratic, hodgepodge manner in which the works of art are displayed—Gardner's personal predilections at

THIRD FLOOR

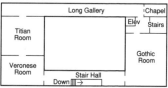

SECOND FLOOR

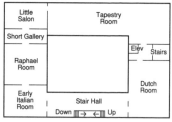

GROUND FLOOR

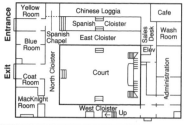

Restaurants/Clubs: Red   Hotels: Blue
Shops/Parks: Green   Sights/Culture: Black

work into perpetuity!) Until recently, the museum director lived rent-free in Gardner's own lush apartment; the most liberal reinterpretation of her will to date was to transform these 4th-floor living quarters into office space, a controversial move.

For countless Bostonians and visitors, Gardner's museum has no equal, and many return again and again for another heady dose of her compelling creation. As was true in her lifetime, the museum's great appeal is in the total impression it creates. In a series of singular stage-set galleries—the Veronese Room, Gothic Room, Dutch Room, Titian Room—look for **Botticelli, Manet, Raphael, Rembrandt, Rubens, Matisse, Sargent, Titian, La Farge, Whistler**. Nearly 2000 objects are on display, spanning more than 30 centuries, with emphasis on Italian Renaissance and 17th-century Dutch masters. (Be sure to look for the **Blue Room** display of Gardner's correspondence with her distinguished friends.) Objects from different periods and cultures are liberally intermixed in the eclectic manner she favored. But on 18 March 1990, the most devastating day in the museum's history, terrible empty spaces were created on the walls. Thirteen uninsured paintings and artifacts valued at $200 million were stolen by 2 thieves disguised as policemen in what the *Boston Herald* dubbed *the Heist of the Century*. The most famous work, *The Concert*, by **Jan Vermeer**, cost Gardner $6000 at an 1892 auction in Paris; it is now priceless. The illustrious art historian **Bernard Berenson**, befriended by Gardner when he was a **Harvard College** student, sometimes advised her on what to buy, and counseled her to purchase 2 works by Rembrandt, *The Storm on the Sea of Galilee* (his only known seascape) and *A Lady and Gentleman in Black*, both stolen. In gentler times, Gardner often acted as her own security guard.

With its soft light, cloudy pink walls, picturesque balconies, quiet fountain, and fragrant fresh flowers and plantings supplied by the museum's own greenhouse, the 4-story courtyard is one of Boston's most serene and beloved places. It is composed of authentic architectural and decorative elements collected by Gardner from throughout Europe as well as Egypt. From September-June, chamber or classical music concerts are held 3 times weekly in the **Tapestry Room**; call for times (fee included with admission). ♦ Admission: members and children under 12 free; reduced admission for elders and students. Tu noon-6:30PM (July-Aug noon-5PM); W-Su noon-5PM; free W. Closed national holidays. Free guided tour Th 2:30PM. Private tours require 3-4 wks advance notice. 280 The Fenway. 566.1401, recorded concert info 734.1359 ♿ (limited because of narrow spaces; museum provides wheelchairs that fit everywhere)

Within the Isabella Stewart Gardner Museum:

The Cafe at the Gardner ★$$ Open the same hours as the museum, the café serves excellent lunches like quiches, salads, sandwiches, and desserts, and a full English tea starting at 3:30PM, Tuesday-Friday. Weather permitting, dine on the outdoor terrace overlooking the museum gardens. ♦ Café ♦ ♿ (limited because of narrow spaces; museum provides wheelchairs that fit everywhere)

Mrs. Jack's Palace is among the finest private house museums in the world, and *Mrs. Jack* was the larger-than-life **Isabella Stewart Gardner** (1840-1924), a charismatic, spirited, and independent New Yorker who married into Victorian Boston's high society, but never bowed to its conventions. Many proper Bostonians forever dismissed her as a brash outsider, but Isabella didn't give a hoot—a passionate woman, she loved the spotlight. She delighted in upstaging her critics and creating a stir with outrageous behavior and amusements, but with a regal awareness of her lofty social stature. Among her many pleasures were art, literature, and music, and she surrounded herself with a circle of the most fashionable talents of her time. But most of her tremendous energy went toward acquiring fabulous art objects, often with her husband, John, from old masters to sculpture, textiles, ceramics, furniture, metalwork, architecture. When her posh Back Bay mansion on Beacon St became too small for her treasures, Gardner and her husband started planning in earnest for a museum. After his death in 1898, she forged on and built **Fenway Court**, a 15th-century Venetian-style palazzo that proudly towered alone in the midst of the unfashionable Fenway. While Fenway Court was under construction, Gardner was always on the scene directing and often got into the action—climbing on scaffolds to mix and daub the paint to her liking on the courtyard walls, for instance. She was accompanied by a trumpeter who summoned workmen when she wanted to confer with them: one note for the architect, another for the plumber, and so on. Anyone ignoring the summons was fired. In the showplace Gardner enshrined her

Kenmore Square/Fenway

collections and held court among them, blurring the distinction between residence and museum in an extraordinary, idiosyncratic way. Her personal mementoes mingle with the works of art. Signs of her presence remain—a table set for tea, for instance—as if she were in the next room. A 19th-century woman, prevented by gender from the prestige and power she was suited for by temperament, Gardner found in her museum the stage, cultural forum, artistic medium, and professional avocation denied her by her times. Look for the plaque she first affixed over the door in 1900, giving her home its official name. Then find the seal designed for her achievement, carved in marble and set into the museum facade's brick wall, which bears her motto, *C'est mon plaisir*, and a phoenix, symbol of immortality. **Henry James** thought she resembled *a figure on a wondrous cinquecento tapestry*. **John Singer Sargent**'s portrait of Gardner stirred a scandal when it was first unveiled in 1888 at the private all-male **St. Botolph Club**, to which husband John belonged. Isabella had posed bare-armed in a clingy décolleté gown, which so shocked proper Bostonians that her husband became infuriated, threatened to horsewhip any gossipers, and forbade the picture to ever again be publicly displayed. But you can see it now through untitillated 20th-century eyes at Isabella's museum, where it finally found its niche in 1924.

12 The Best Western Boston $$ Smack dab in the middle of the **Longwood Medical Area**, the economical hotel attracts many guests connected with Longwood in one way or another, but is open to all and is among the city's more affordable options. The **Museum of Fine Arts** and **Isabella Stewart Gardner Museum** are nearby, and it's just 15 minutes to **Back Bay** via the Green Line. Nonsmokers' and handicapped-accessible rooms available; there is a restaurant on the premises as well as room service. The hotel is connected to a galleria of fast-food shops, a health club, and other services. ♦ 342 Longwood Ave (Brookline Ave) 731.4700; fax 731.6273 &

13 Steve's Ice Cream Popular with just about everybody, Steve's sells super-rich, creamy ice cream in lots of different flavors—some exotic—with all kinds of *mix-ins* mashed into the ice cream to order. Sundaes, ice creamsodas, milkshakes, and all that jazz. ♦ M-Th 11:30AM-11PM; F-Sa 11:30AM-midnight; Su noon-11PM. 95 Mass Ave (Newbury St) 247.9401 & Also at: Faneuil Hall Marketplace. 367.0569; 31 Church St, Harvard Sq, Cambridge. 354.9106

13 Oceanic Chinese Restaurant ★$ It would take hundreds of visits to exhaust this versatile restaurant's enormous menu. In addition to unadventurous old favorites like spareribs and spring rolls, Oceanic serves unusual specialty seafood items, including shark's fin and shredded duck soup, whole fried sole, abalone with tender vegetables, clams with black-bean sauce, various seafoods with ginger and scallions. Treats that don't hail from the sea are

Kenmore Square/Fenway

crisp roasted duck, spicy Szechuan dishes, and sizzling hot pots. The restaurant is a trifle fancier than the average Chinatown eatery, but replicates that neighborhood's estimable authentic cuisine—for that's where Oceanic's owners and staff started out. ♦ Chinese/takeout ♦ Daily 11:30AM-1AM. 91 Mass Ave (Comm Ave-Newbury St) 353.0791 &

14 The Eliot Hotel $$ Located on the edge of Back Bay, this is a convenient place to stay. Just 94 rooms on 9 floors, the modest-size 1927 hotel is privately owned and attracts international visitors, conventioneers, visiting professors. It's one of the city's best buys. The top 4 floors were recently renovated, and the overall ambiance is quiet and old-fashioned. There's no restaurant on the premises, but Continental breakfast is served daily in the lobby. Nonsmokers' rooms and pay parking available. ♦ 370 Comm Ave (Mass Ave) 267.1607; fax 536.9114

The alphabetic street-naming of **Back Bay** (**Arlington**, **Berkeley**... **Hereford**) continues in **Fenway** on the opposite side of Mass Ave with **Ipswich**, **Jersey**, and **Kilmarnock** streets.

Restaurants/Clubs: Red	Hotels: Blue
Shops/Parks: Green	Sights/Culture: Black

14 The Eliot Lounge and Cafe $ The famous sports bar is unofficial headquarters for the **Boston Marathon**, before and after which the place is mobbed for days. Gregarious bartender and running guru **Tommy Leonard** lends a willing ear to whomever feels like chatting. Leonard is a good buddy of the daytime bartender over at the **Bull & Finch** on **Beacon Hill**, with whom he has raised thousands of dollars for good causes. The comfortable friendly bar attracts all kinds, and students flock in for once-a-week DJ dancing. The café serves down-to-earth fare like chili, pizzas, sandwiches, hamburgers. ♦ American/takeout ♦ M-Sa 11:30AM-1:15AM; Su noon-1:15AM. 370 Comm Ave (enter from Mass Ave) Lounge 262.1078, café 421.9169

15 Miyako ★★$$ The downstairs restaurant's humble appearance is deceptive, since Miyako produces beautifully prepared and presented Japanese food that tastes terrific. Expert sushi cutters create a grand selection of sushi and sashimi; some exotic kinds aren't listed on the menu, so ask. The tempura dishes and sukiyaki are excellent, and there are lots of intriguing appetizers to try. It's often busy here, but the wait staff is always gracious. ♦ Japanese/takeout ♦ M-Th noon-2:30PM, 5:30-10:30PM; F-Sa noon-2:30PM, 5:30-11PM; Su 5:30-10PM. 468 Comm Ave (Charlesgate W-Kenmore St) Reservations recommended on weekends. 236.0222

16 Bruegger's Bagel Bakery $ Stop in for a cup of coffee and a very fresh, delicious bagel with one of Bruegger's own cream-cheese spreads. Lots of varieties. ♦ Bagels/takeout ♦ M-Sa 7AM-7PM; Su 8AM-7PM. 636 Beacon St (Raleigh St) No credit cards. 262.7939. Also at: 32 Bromfield St. 357.5577; 83 Mt. Auburn St, Harvard Sq, Cambridge. 661.4664

17 The B.U. Bookstore You won't have trouble locating this store, since blinking away atop it is Kenmore Sq's famous landmark, the **Citgo Sign**. **Boston University**'s bookstore is the largest in New England, with 3 floors of books to browse among. In addition to textbooks for BU and several other local educational institutions, there's a great selection of current and backlist hardcover and paperback books: bestsellers, cookbooks, children's books, classics, hobbies, gardening, law, women, history, politics—the works. The store sponsors frequent events, including author signings and children's story readings. And beyond books, this 6-story department store includes specialty shops selling clothing and accessories, chocolates, stationery, housewares, office supplies, flowers, electronics and cameras, and more. A travel agent, too. If you're in the square with time to spare before the **Red Sox** game, this is the place to dawdle. ♦ M-F 9:30AM-7PM; Sa 10AM-6PM; Su noon-5PM. 660 Beacon St (Comm Ave) 267.8484 &

Within the B.U. Bookstore:

Cafe Charles ★$ There are plenty of places to grab a quick bite in Kenmore Sq, but few as serene as this pretty café tucked far from the madding crowd. Soups, sandwiches on French bread, muffins, cappuccino, and desserts, including an excellent hazelnut torte, are served. Bring a book and relax at a table, or watch the non-stop activity on the streets below from the windowside marble counter. The café overlooks the last mile marker for the Boston Marathon. A good place for conversation, it attracts BU's students, faculty, president, and local residents; most Bostonians haven't discovered it. The café is open the same hours as the bookstore, but closes approximately one hour earlier. ◆ Café/takeout ◆ 2nd fl. ♿

Atop the B.U. Bookstore:

Citgo Sign The 60-square-foot double-sided sign with its 2 miles of red, white, and blue neon tubing dates from 1965, its pulsating delta controlled by computer. An immediate Pop Art hit, the sign inspired one filmmaker to create a short film called *Go, Go Citgo*, in which the sign did its off-and-on routine to music by the **Monkees** and **Ravi Shankar**, an Indian sitarist. But the sign was turned off during the energy crisis of the '70s, and almost torn down in 1982. Fortunately, the public quickly stood up for its favorite commercial icon. **Arthur Krim**, a Cambridge resident, college teacher, and member of the **Society for Commercial Archeology** (which works to preserve urban and roadside Americana like neon signs, diners, gas stations), helped lead the fight to save **Kenmore Sq**'s illuminated heartbeat from the scrap heap. Happily, Oklahoma-based Citgo agreed to keep the sign plugged in and maintained.

18 Kenmore Club It's really 3 clubs in one, interconnected so one admission applies to all. **Narcissus** is largest, a bilevel disco club with glitzy mirrors and lights; and then there's **Celebration** and **Lipstick**, which offers a little more in the way of rock 'n' roll. DJ-played Top 40 music is featured throughout, with Latin night on Sunday and heavy metal on Wednesday in Narcissus. Occasionally, special shows with live bands are scheduled. Thursday night is college night, although the crowd is young every night. Full bar; no food served. Only those 18 and older admitted. ◆ Cover. Daily 8PM-

2AM. 533 Comm Ave (Beacon St) No sneakers, T-shirts, jeans, hats, workboots, sweatshirts or collarless shirts for men. 536.1950 ♿

19 Nuggets The first store of its kind in the area, Nuggets sells new, used, rare, and out-of-print records, CDs, tapes, 12" disco singles. The focus is on rock, but you can find jazz, reggae, blues, and more. ◆ M-Sa 10AM-10PM; Su 11AM-6PM. 482 Comm Ave (Kenmore-Beacon Sts) Credit accepted for purchases $15 and over. 536.0679

19 Rathskeller (The Rat) ★$ The Rat is one of the very few clubs in town serving up good music and good food. It's not much to look at, to say the least, but the Rat was Boston's first New Wave club. It has boosted many local groups and was the first Boston club to headline the **Cars, Police, Talking Heads**, and **Go Gos**. The club books high-quality local and touring rock bands, up to 4 a night, 3-4 nights a week, and they usually go on at 9:30PM. On weekends, you can listen for free to bands playing on the balcony. There are 2 bars serving cheap drinks, pinball, video, and a great jukebox. Chef **James Ryan**'s secret sauce slathered on slow-cooked ribs has elevated him to celebrity status, and made this joint a favorite hangout for anyone with a taste for BBQ. Lots of musicians, big stars and unknowns, have enjoyed Ryan's ribs, chicken, crisp French fries and onion rings, salads, coleslaw, cornbread, sweet-potato pie—some struggling performers have even done stints in the kitchen. A generous guy, Ryan cooks for homeless friends as well as the hungry well-to-do. For admittance to the club, not the restaurant, you must be 21 or older unless a special all-ages show is scheduled. ◆ American/BBQ ◆ Cover for club. Daily

Kenmore Square/Fenway

11AM-2AM; restaurant open until 10PM. 528 Comm Ave (Beacon St) No credit cards. 536.2750 ♿ restaurant only

20 Pizzeria Uno $ Ever-popular with students and the baseball crowd for decent deep-dish pizza. ◆ Pizza/takeout ◆ One Kenmore Sq (Comm-Brookline Aves) 262.2373 ♿ Also at: 731 Boylston St. 267.8554; Faneuil Hall Marketplace, 423.5722; 22 JFK St, Harvard Sq, Cambridge. 497.1530

21 Howard Johnson/Kenmore $$ Just beyond Kenmore Sq on **Boston University**'s campus, this bustling HoJo's is convenient to **Fenway Park** and western Boston. Also near **Back Bay**, lots of tour groups stay here. An older but well-kept hotel, it has 180 rooms on 7 floors—including an executive section with larger rooms and VCRs, complimentary coffee and newspaper—plus restaurant, lounge, indoor pool. Nonsmokers' rooms and free parking available. ◆ 575 Comm Ave. 267.3100, 800/654.2000; fax 267.3100 ext 40

The **Boston Red Sox** were originally called the **Pilgrims**, but were renamed for the color of the players' stockings by owner **John Taylor** in 1907.

22 Photographic Resource Center (PRC)

(1985, **Leers, Weinzapfel Associates/Alex Krieger Architects**) One of the few centers for photography in the country (located below street level, entry on the left-hand side), this nonprofit arts organization leases space from **Boston University** and houses 3 galleries for photography exhibitions and a nonlending photography library. PRC's intelligent award-winning design evokes the mechanical process of photography, its manipulation of light, and mediation between art and technology—particularly in the architects' use of industrial materials and glass. The exhibitions emphasize new and experimental photography from the US and abroad; popular recent shows were *Locomotion*, a historical study of movement in photography, and *Constructed Spaces*, with architectural references. Check local papers or call to find out about frequent lectures/slide presentations; **Aaron Siskind, Mary Ellen Mark, John Baldessari,** and **Lucas Samaras** have also spoken here. Everything is open to the public. PRC publishes a monthly newsletter and the quarterly journal *VIEWS,* and offers educational programs. Call in advance to arrange a tour. ♦ Admission. Tu-W, F-Su noon-5PM; Th noon-8PM. 602 Comm Ave (Blandford St) 353.0700 &

23 Mugar Memorial Library of Boston University (BU)

Few outside the BU community know about this library's marvelous and massive **Department of Special Collections,** dedicated to scholarly research but also open to the public. The Mugar owns and exhibits rare books, manuscripts, and papers pertaining to hundreds of interesting people, famous and not, from the 15th century onward (the 20th-century archives are particularly strong). The

Kenmore Square/Fenway

3rd-floor **King exhibit room** displays documents from the archives of BU alumnus **Dr. Martin Luther King, Jr.** The library also boasts a huge holding of **Theodore Roosevelt**'s and **Robert Frost**'s papers and memorabilia. The collections include journalists, politicians, mystery writers, film and stage actors and actresses, musicians. Browse a while and you'll encounter **Frederick Douglass, Bette Davis, Florence Nightingale, Albert Einstein, Tennessee Williams,** original cartoons of **Little Orphan Annie** and **L'il Abner, Irwin Shaw, Arthur Fiedler, Eric Ambler, Walt Whitman, Michael Halberstam, Rex Harrison, Fred Astaire, Abraham Lincoln** Call the BU Administration Office to find out about tours, 353.2318. ♦ M-F 9AM-5PM. 771 Comm Ave (St. Mary's St) 353.3696 &

A. Bartlett Giamatti, the late baseball commissioner, former **Yale University** president, and eloquent ardent baseball fan praised **Fenway Park** as *a place of weird angles and distances and beautiful ricochets.* He also said something baseball **Red Sox** fans can relate to: *Somehow the Sox fulfill the notion that we live in a fallen world. It's as though we assume they're here to provide us with more pain.* When, oh when, will Boston fans implore, will the Red Sox win the **World Series** again?

24 Paradise Rock Club

This club and adjacent **M-80** are beyond the neighborhood's borders, but shouldn't be overlooked because they are 2 of Boston's best places to see national and international groups in concert and to dance. Other than for scheduled performances, the Paradise is only open on Saturday night 10PM-2AM for dancing with DJ. New Wave and rock are the mainstays, but the Paradise also books jazz, folk, blues, country. **The Buzzcocks, Rickie Lee Jones, U2, Tower of Power, The Scorpions, Nick Lowe** have all appeared here. Doors open at 8PM for shows; sometimes two are scheduled per night. Get tickets in advance, since few if any are available for popular groups on the day of the shows. Full bar. Minimum age requirements vary by shows. By subway, take the B Line to the Pleasant St stop. ♦ Admission. Box office M-F noon-6PM; Sa 3-6PM. 967 Comm Ave (Pleasant-Babcock Sts) Sa night dancing: no jeans or sneakers. Cash only at the door, credit accepted at box office and bar. Recorded info 254.2052/2053; Ticketmaster 931.2000

24 M-80

A new European-style club where DJs spin dance music, with live entertainment from time to time. Many international exchange students seek this club out, which is jammed on some nights. Full bar; no food served. You must be 21 or older. ♦ Cover. W-Th 10PM-2AM; F-Sa 11PM-2AM. 969 Comm Ave (Pleasant-Babcock Sts) No jeans or sneakers. 254.2054

25 Savoy French Bakery

Go out of your way to sample the fantastic apple-and-almond, apricot, chocolate, plain, and other croissant varieties baked by Savoy. One owner was trained by a French baker; the baked goods are classic French. Equally delicious are the decorative fresh-fruit tartlets and minicakes like hazelnut *frangipane.* They bake all kinds of cookies—try the traditional French *palmier,* nicknamed *elephant's ear*—and breads, including baguettes, *batards,* and *petit pain.* Truffles, too, and some lunch items. ♦ Tu-F 7:30AM-6:30PM; Sa 8AM-6:30PM; Su 8AM-2PM. 1003 Beacon St (St. Mary's St) No credit cards. 734.0214 &

26 Sol Azteca

★★$$ Dinner begins with some of the best piquant salsa and chips to be had in Boston, and progresses to marvelous Mexican fare like mole *poblano,* chiles *rellenos,* enchiladas *verdes, camarones al cilantro, puerco en adobo.* With the meal, enjoy excellent sangria or Mexican beer; afterward, try coffee flavored with cinnamon and the great coffee-flavored flan. The rustic dining rooms are gay and festive with hand-painted tile tables and handicrafts. Family-owned and operated, this is one of Boston's older Mexican establishments, but it never seems to lose its flair. ♦ Mexican ♦ M-Th 6-10:30PM; F-Sa 5:30-11PM; Su 5-10PM. 914A Beacon St (Park Dr) Reservations accepted M-Th only. 262.0909 &

27 Stitches and HooDoo BBQ $$ The well-established comedy club offers local and national headliners, plus an R-rated hypnotist on Tuesday. Dinner and show packages are available; the restaurant joined the act recently and serves rib-sticking spicy fare. There's no dress code for either Stitches or HooDoo, and the clientele is diverse. Park for free in an adjacent lot. You must be 18 or older Sunday-Thursday, 21 or older Friday-Saturday. ◆ BBQ/takeout ◆ Club shows: Tu-Th 9PM; F-Sa 8:30, 10:30PM; Su 9PM. Restaurant daily: 11AM-2AM. 835 Beacon St (Miner-Munson Sts) Reservations recommended Sa. Ticketmaster 931.2000; or charge tickets at club 424.6995 (after 11AM), HooDoo 267.7427 (BOS.RIBS) &

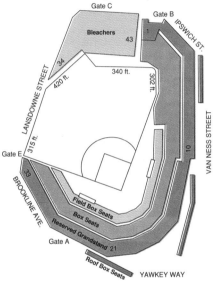

28 Fenway Park Home of baseball's 1990 American League Eastern Division Championship **Red Sox**, Fenway Park is the country's smallest major-league ballpark—capacity 34,000—so fans are thrillingly close to the players. **Carl Yastrzemski, Ted Williams, Dwight Evans, Roger Clemens** have all dominated the diamond. **Babe Ruth** made his debut as a **Red Sox** pitcher at **Fenway Park** on 11 July 1914. He was later traded—not one of the team's smarter moves. The park is a block west of Kenmore Sq but easy to find; just join the throngs pouring out of the Kenmore Sq and Fenway subway stations before every game, or look up for the lights. Built in 1912 and rebuilt in 1935, Fenway Park is a classic, dating from the golden age of baseball design, with plenty of quirks that only enhance its battered charm. Its green grass is still real green grass. Its idiosyncratic shape is the result of an awkward site, since the surrounding lots weren't for sale when the ballpark was embedded in the city. One of the park's famous landmarks is the notorious *Green Monster*, the 37-foot-high

cement wall at left field that has destroyed many a batter's hope for a short easy homer. And a gustatory institution are **Fenway Franks**. Even if baseball leaves you unmoved, come for the show—just sitting among Boston's demanding, impassioned, extremely vocal fans is fun. The ballpark opens 1½ hours before game time. Tickets are available on a first-come, first-served basis to a reserved alcohol-free zone. Ask about special youth, elder, and family discounts available for designated dates. Souvenirs are sold on all sides of the park (look for the amazing **Souvenir Shop** across from the ticket office) and vendors both legal and illegal and ticket scalpers do brisk business. Before and after the games, crowds flock to the **Cask 'n Flagon** sports bar at 62 Brookline Ave, 536.4840, among other neighborhood watering holes. ◆ Ticket office M-F 9AM-5PM. 4 Yawkey Wy (Lansdowne-Van Ness Sts) To charge call 267.1700; recorded info 267.8661 & (special section)

29 Citi This mammoth dance club holds up to 1500 people for a rotating roster of music: at the moment, Wednesday features urban house music and hip-hop funk, Thursday international, Friday house and contemporary dance music, Saturday Top 40 and progressive, and Sunday floorburner dance music. Citi packs in a mixed early-20s clientele, except on Sunday night, when patrons are primarily gays and lesbians. Full bar, but no food served. On Wednesday, those 19 and over are admitted; all other nights you must be at least 21. There's almost always a line, but unless it's very late everyone gets in eventually. Sunday and concert nights, no dress code. All other nights, no sneakers, jeans, or athletic wear. Men

should wear dress slacks, dark shoes, and collared shirts. ◆ Cover, cash only. W-Th 10PM-2AM; F-Su 9PM-2AM. 15 Lansdowne St (Brookline Ave-Ipswich St) 262.2424 &

29 Axis Music changes nightly and includes progressive, punk, funk, heavy metal, hard rock, live bands, alternative dance tunes, DJ music. On some nights, you must be at least 21 years old to be admitted, on others 18 or 19; call to inquire on minimum ages and shows. Creative dress is encouraged; *When in doubt, wear black* is the club's advice. On Sunday, Axis connects with **Citi** next door for gay night; enter through Citi. ◆ Cover. Tu, F-Sa 10PM-2AM; W-Th, Su 9PM-2AM. 13 Lansdowne St (Brookline Ave-Ipswich St) 262.2437 &

In 1827, under the name of **Edgar A. Perry**, a destitute **Edgar Allan Poe** did a stint as a soldier at the fort still standing on **Castle Island**. His famous tale *The Cask of Amontillado* is based on a story he heard during his tour of duty, about how 10 years earlier 2 officers fought a duel over a game of cards. One was killed. Friends of the deceased officer got revenge by capturing the killer and sealing him alive behind a brick wall. The story was considered apocryphal until 1905, when a skeleton clothed in a military uniform was discovered behind a brick wall.

29 Venus de Milo Look for her statue above the entrance, sporting a neon hula-hoop. The club strives for a dark Gothic Renaissance decor, its youngish urban crowd dancing to hip-hop, house, and funk music. Wednesday is gay night, Thursday is rock, and Friday and Saturday feature regular dance music. You must be 21 or older unless it's a special 18-and-over night. ♦ Cover, cash only. 7 Lansdowne St (Brookline Ave-Ipswich St) No athletic wear, baseball caps, workboots. 421.9595 &

29 Jillian's Billiard Club Get behind the 8-ball at one of 39 tournament-quality billiard, pocket billiard, and snooker tables. Darts, shuffleboard, table tennis, backgammon, chess, batting cage, ping pong games, video games, and wide-screen TVs, too. You pay by the hour for your play. Basic appetizers, beer, and wine are served. After 8PM, only those age 18 and over admitted. ♦ M-Sa 11AM-1AM; Su noon-1AM. 145 Ipswich St (Lansdowne St) No hats, sleeveless shirts, sweats, cutoffs. 437.0300

30 Buteco ★$ Don't be put off by the shabby facade; good food lurks inside. With Latin music pulsing in the background, a diverse, youngish clientele—lots of regulars—packs the tiny dining room to enjoy plates piled with spicy Brazilian dishes: *mandioca* (fried cassava root with carrot dipping sauce), hearts of palm salad, black-bean soup, *picadinho a carioca* (beef stew with garlic), *vatapa a Baiana* (sole baked in coconut milk, served on shrimp with peanut paste), *churrasco* (mixed grill). Weekends only, while it lasts, order *feijoada*, the Brazilian national dish, a hearty stew with black beans, pork sausage, beef, collard greens, and orange. Plenty of noise and comradery here. ♦ Brazilian ♦ M-Tu, Su 5:30-10PM; W-Th noon-4PM, 5:30-10PM; F noon-4PM, 5:30-11PM; Sa 5:30-11PM. 130 Jersey St (Queensbury St-Park Dr) Reservations recommended on weekends. 247.9508 & Also at: 57 W. Dedham St. 247.9249

(1878-1895, **Frederick Law Olmsted**; National Historic Landmark) Ponds and parks strung together by parkways form Boston's prized Emerald Necklace, which on maps dangles from **Boston Harbor** as from around a neck. Executed for the **Boston Park Commission**, Olmsted's design for an interconnected park system totaled more than 2000 acres of open land when complete, its main artery the 5-mile-long Emerald Necklace. The largest continuous green space through an urban center in the country, the Necklace traverses a number of communities and is adorned with 5 major parks—**Back Bay Fens**, **Muddy River Improvement**, **Jamaica Park**, **Arnold Arboretum**, and **Franklin**

Kenmore Square/Fenway

Park—which are connected by the **Fenway**, **Riverway**, **Jamaicaway**, and **Arborway** parkways. Olmsted's Necklace was further embellished by joining with two existing gems, the **Boston Common** and **Public Garden**. The **Charles River Esplanade** is often considered an additional strand as well, although it wasn't built until 1931, long after Olmsted's death. Actually, there's a lot of confusion among Bostonians themselves about what belongs to the Emerald Necklace, and what the names of all its pieces are. Unfortunately, the Necklace has broken and is missing links as well (which the city plans to mend), most importantly the never-realized **Columbia Road** extension by which Olmsted intended to link Franklin Park with **Marine Park** in **South Boston**. The only way to see the entire Emerald Necklace at one time is to drive its length along the parkways, but the twisting and confusing route will offer frustrating fleeting glimpses of greenery and water, not at all the restful communion with nature Olmsted had in mind. Instead, pick a fair-weather day and jog, bicycle, walk, even horseback-ride a segment of the park system. Bring a book, binoculars, frisbee, picnic lunch. The necklace is dotted with benches, fields to sun in, shady copses.

The Emerald Necklace starts at the **Boston Common** (**1**), proceeds through the **Public Garden** (**2**), then continues along **Commonwealth Avenue Mall** (**3**) to **Charlesgate** (**4**), the original connection Olmsted forged between the Mall and **Back Bay Fens** (**5**) where the **Muddy River** entered the **Charles River Estuary**. But Charlesgate's open wetlands were largely destroyed when elevated overpasses to **Storrow Drive** were built during the '60s. Despite this plundering, the necklace still joins tenuously with the Back Bay Fens, Olmsted's first contribution. Named for the marshlands of eastern England, the Fens originally embodied its designer's love for picturesque, misty, and idyllic English rural landscapes. Dredging, draining, and landscaping rescued the Fens from its reeking mudflat past—Olmsted considered the project as much a sanitation improvement as a park—and made way for tranquil saltmarsh meadows. The damming of the Charles River in 1910 changed the water from salt to fresh, destroying Olmsted's original scheme. Years of neglect and incursions of elements and functions he never intended have taken their toll also. Yet the park is still a pleasant spot to loll on the grass and wander among willows, dogwoods, lindens, hawthornes. The **Victory Gardens** planted during WWII, the spectacular **Rose Garden** behind the **Museum of Fine Arts**, as well as an athletic field, have settled in to stay. Thankfully, one original Fens feature has survived unscathed: the puddingstone bridge where **Boylston St** crosses the river is a poetic charmer, designed in 1880 by Olmsted's good friend **H.H. Richardson**. A cautionary note: don't linger in the Fens after dark, and never stray into the stands of tall reeds that grow as high as 13-14 feet.

The **Muddy River Improvement** (**6**) is the next ornament, although its connection to the Fens via the Riverway was obliterated by construction of the former **Sears Roebuck** building, now slated to become a science/technology complex. A little perseverance returns you to nature, to a meandering riverside park that looks in places like leftover wilderness, with riding/walking/running paths, graceful small bridges, placid ponds, lush untamed plantings. The Improvement—unpoetically named for the clean- and spruce-up job it accomplished—widens at a section now called

Olmsted Park, where **Leverett, Willow,** and **Wards Ponds** are. And then one arrives at **Jamaica Park (7)**, its centerpiece the largest freshwater pond in Boston. Fringed by a pretty tree-shaded promenade lit by gas lanterns, where walkers and joggers go round and round, **Jamaica Pond** is popular for sailing, rowing, and fishing. **Edmund Wheelwright** designed the decorative 1913 boathouse and gazebo, where refreshments are sold. Jamaica Pond was once surrounded by farms and summer estates in the late 19th century when **Jamaica Plain** was considered the country, and Boston's wealthy escaped here.

From Jamaica Pond the Jamaicaway leads to the world-renowned **Arnold Arboretum (8)**, which belongs to the **Boston Park System** but is administered by **Harvard University**. An arboretum—from the Latin word *arbor*, meaning tree—is a specialized form of botanical garden. **Charles Sprague Sargent**, a gentleman landscape gardener and the arboretum's first director for more than half a century, collaborated with Olmsted in 1878 to design this living museum of trees, named for its first big donor, a merchant and amateur horticulturist. Both Olmsted and Sargent envisioned a scientific *plein air* museum that would also be a de-

lightful picturesque park.

Linked to the arboretum by the arborway, the Emerald Necklace's massive pendant is **Franklin Park (9)**, named for **Benjamin Franklin**. The Boston Park System's masterpiece and one of Olmsted's 3 greatest parks, Franklin Park's design expresses his precept that the natural world offers the ideal antidote to dehumanizing urban living. Within this 500-acre tract straddling **Dorchester, Jamaica Plain,** and **Roxbury,** Olmsted preserved and enhanced existing natural features, leaving as much as possible untamed and bucolic. He envisioned a place where all classes of Bostonians would mingle peacefully, reaping restorative physical and psychological benefits from nature. Franklin Park is a great green swath of rolling hills, broad fields and meadows, with hickory, hemlock, locust, oak, tulip trees, and myriad other plantings, and enormous boulders and manmade park ornaments fashioned from Roxbury puddingstone. But because the park is 4 miles from the heart of Boston and tricky to reach, it never got the popularity it deserved and languished from the '40s until recently. And like the Fens, changes and additions have been made that spoil the integrity of Olmsted's original plan. But if Franklin

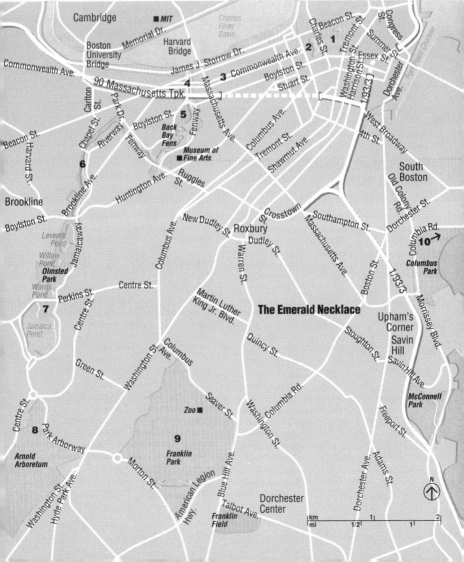

Park is not a perfect emerald, it's still a gem, a sanctuary from the city where one can walk, jog, picnic, birdwatch, play golf or pickup baseball, watch the annual September **Kite Festival**, attend the August **West Indian Carnival** and other festivals, visit the zoo undergoing radical improvements, and generally let loose a little. The park's 18-hole course, designed by **Donald Ross**, a renowned golf-course architect, has been newly refurbished. No private country-club atmosphere here; city residents come together to play on the par-70 course, the country's second-oldest

---

When **Frederick Law Olmsted** found his professional niche at age 35, the notion of creating public parks was still fresh. Once he discovered his calling, Olmsted sped into a long career focused on designing healthful, beautiful settings offering respite from cities and everyday life. Today he is lauded as the creator of landscape architecture as a profession and an art in America. Born in Hartford CT in 1822, Olmsted apprenticed on farms, studied scientific agriculture and civil engineering, and did stints as a clerk, ship's hand in the China trade, farmer, writer, newspaper correspondent, head of the Red Cross, and publisher before his professional turning point in 1857. That year he was appointed superintendent of an enormous new park planned for New York City: **Central Park**. The following year, he won the design competition for the park with architect **Calvert Vaux**, who became his frequent collaborator. Ultimately, political wrangling and the city's rigid grid defeated both Olmsted and his ambition to create a park system for New York; he was dismissed as landscape architect in 1878. In 1869, Olmsted had begun consulting to the **Boston Park Commissioners** on plans for a park system for the city. He eventually was put in charge of designing the entire **Boston Park System**, and moved home and office from New York to Brookline in 1883; his address, 99 Warren Street, which he called **Fairsted**, is now a National Historic

Kenmore Square/Fenway

Site. In addition to parks, Olmsted and his firm designed residential communities and home sites. In addition to Central Park and the Boston Park System, his most famous projects include **Prospect Park** in **Brooklyn**, the **South Parks** in **Chicago**, **Belle Isle Park** in **Detroit**, the **United States Capitol** grounds, and the **Stanford University** and **Princeton University** campuses. His last 2 major works were the site plan for the **World's Columbian Exposition** of 1893 in **Chicago**, and **George W. Vanderbilt's Biltmore** estate in **Asheville NC**. Dedicated to preserving areas of natural beauty for public enjoyment, Olmsted also headed the first commission in charge of **Yosemite Valley**, which became the country's first national park, and helped establish the **Niagara Reservation**, which he planned with Vaux. Said Olmsted: *The park should, as far as possible, complement the town. Openness is the one thing you cannot get in buildings. Picturesqueness you can get. Let your buildings be as picturesque as your artists can make them. This is the beauty of a town. Consequently, the beauty of the park should be the other. It should be the beauty of the fields, the meadow, the prairie, of the green pastures, and the still waters. What we want to gain is tranquillity and rest to the mind.* Olmsted retired in 1895 and died in 1903. His successor firm, headed by his 2 sons, continued to dominate the profession until WWII.

municipal golf course. Although it will take time for Franklin Park to shake its unfair poor reputation, it's actually one of the city's safer parks. Don't linger after dark or stray into the overgrown areas, but do enjoy an oasis that Bostonians are beginning to appreciate anew.

The necklace breaks after Franklin Park, but should have led via **Columbia Road** through **Upham's Corner** and on to **Marine Park (10)**. Lack of funds kept Columbia Road from becoming the spacious green boulevard Olmsted intended; perhaps someday. On **City Point** in South Boston, Olmsted created Marine Park's **Pleasure Bay** by linking the **City Point Battery** to **Castle Island**. The island's prominent feature is an 1801 star-shaped fort built of Quincy granite, the last in a line of successors to the first fort built here in 1634 under **Governor John Winthrop**'s authority to defend tiny Boston-town. During the Revolution, a subsequent fort served as headquarters for the British troops and gave refuge to local Tories. As the Revolution heated up, the island became the British naval garrison. From here, the Redcoats made frequent forays to Boston for provisions, antagonizing the Americans. And from here the British evacuated at last when **General George Washington**'s men trained guns on the island from **Dorchester Heights**. The fort has played a role, though far less prominent, in several wars since then. Now its role is strictly pacific. An enormously popular bathing, boating, and fishing spot when it opened in 1891, Marine Park no longer draws crowds, eclipsed long ago by suburban beaches. But the sea breezes and harbor views are worth an outing, and here you can look at the shiny bellies of the big jets as they descend to **Logan International Airport**. It's best to drive here; there's always plenty of parking.

Now missing from the Emerald Necklace, **Charlesbank** was a pioneering neighborhood park designed by Olmsted in the 1890s that bordered the Charles River near **Massachusetts General Hospital**. The park was intended to alleviate the unhealthy overcrowding suffered by residents of the **West End**, a multilayered ethnic neighborhood that was largely wiped out by urban renewal in the '60s. Charlesbank featured America's first free open-air gymnasiums, long demolished, with one for men and another for women and children. The city's first playgrounds were located in the park, part of the new playground movement sweeping the country, and so were America's first sandboxes, called *sand courts*. Today Charlesbank is mostly buried under a tangle of roadways.

Two of the most popular Emerald Necklace attractions are: **The Arnold Arboretum** Built on the old **Benjamin Bussey** farm, the arboretum has more than 4000 woody plants, trees, shrubs, and vines, collected on expeditions throughout the world. Olmsted interlaced its acreage with walks and drives offering a pleasant progression through meticulously sited plantings. Arboretum plant-hunters have searched unknown provinces of China and Tibet, explored Borneo, Japan, and the Americas to bring back rare finds. The arboretum is the focal point of a favorite annual event, **Lilac Sunday**. Azaleas, magnolias, and fruit trees burst forth in full glory, too. Along the **Chinese Path**, some rarer older Asian specimens are planted, including the **Dove Tree** from China, a magical sight in spring when its creamy white bracts flutter like wings. Wind your way up to one of several promontories for splendid views. Maps for self-guided walking tours can be obtained in

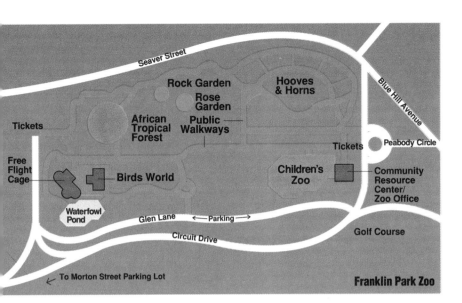

Franklin Park Zoo

the **Visitor Center**, where you can also find out about year-round events, workshops, classes, and exhibitions. The shop offers New England's largest selection of books on horticulture and other items. Guided walking tours or bus tours can be arranged for a fee; call tour coordinator in advance, 524.1718. ♦ Free (voluntary contributions welcomed) Daily dawn to dusk. Visitor Center: M-F 9AM-4PM; Sa-Su 10AM-4PM. Shop hours: Tu-Su 10AM-4PM. 125 Arborway, Jamaica Plain. Recorded info on what's in bloom 524.1717. Plant questions answered M-Tu 1-3PM, general info 524.1718. ᕙ (driving permits for elders and handicapped available for slow-speed touring)

Franklin Park Zoo (1989; Huygens, DiMella, Shaffer and Associates) The 70-acre zoo's main attraction is the domed **African Tropical Forest** pavilion, the largest in North America, with sculpted cliffs and caves, waterfalls, wooden footbridges, and lush African vegetation. The 3-acre environmental exhibit is home to gorillas—meet **Vip, Gigi, Kiki, Kubandu,** and **Bobby**—leopards, forest buffalo, bongo antelopes, dwarf crocodiles, 3-inch scorpions, and exotic birds. One of the stars is 17-year old **Camille**, a shy 500-pound pygmy hippo, whom you can watch tiptoeing in her lagoon. There are 75 species and 250 specimens in all, with no cages and almost imperceptible barriers between looked-ons and onlookers. Before the pavilion opened, local rock climbers clambered over the cliff walls to make sure the gorillas would stay on their side of the moat. Exhibits educate the public on the international crisis of human destruction of African and South American rain forests. When it's cold outdoors, come soak up some warm tropical mist. The exhibit's ecosystem creates periodic rainstorms and rainbows. The zoo also features a **Children's Zoo** with a petting barn, where kids learn about New England farm animals. The **Hooves and Horns** section stars zebras and camels, including **Becky** the dromedary. In **Birds' World**, visitors can see and touch more than 50 species of birds in the Chinese-pagoda birdhouse and free-flight cage, which dates from the zoo's 1913 opening. Like Franklin Park, the zoo was nearly abandoned from the '60s until recently; now it's enjoying a renaissance. Plans are afoot to add more pavilions and other wondrous attractions. Some elephants would be nice ♦ Admission; discount for elders, uniformed military, children 5-18. Daily 9AM-5PM, May-Oct; daily 9AM-3:30PM, Nov-Apr; free Tu noon-5PM. Closed Christmas and New Year's Day. Franklin Park Rd (off Blue Hill Ave) 442.2002 ᕙ

Boston's men and women in green on foot and horseback, the **Park Rangers**, direct all kinds of activities throughout the Boston Park System: historical strolls and tours, children's story readings and learning activities like *Horse of Course*, about a day in the life of a Park Ranger horse, nature walks through the **Arnold Arboretum**, birdwatching along the **Muddy River**, a bicycle tour of the **Emerald Necklace**, fishing on

Kenmore Square/Fenway

Jamaica Pond, an architectural exploration of **Commonwealth Ave**, and more. Some events require reservations; all are free. For information, call the **Boston Parks and Recreation Department**, 725.4505; or the **Boston Park Rangers**, 522.2639.

During the summer, recreational and educational programs are planned for kids and young people throughout the **Boston Park System**, including golf clinics and instruction at **Franklin Park**, *Sox Talk* with **Red Sox** players at neighborhood parks, sailing on **Boston Harbor** and **Jamaica Pond**. Outdoor concerts and theater performances, too. Call the **Parks and Recreation Activities Eventline** for daily updates on what's going on, 725.4006. Boston parks are officially closed from 11:30PM-6AM.

A legislative proposal in 1912 sought to tax any bachelor older than 35 if he couldn't prove he was *unfit for matrimony*. The proposal failed.

A number of exotic animals made their American debuts in Boston: the white bear was first exhibited here on 18 January 1733, the lion on 26 November 1716, the leopard on 2 February 1802; the camel was first imported here on 2 October 1721, the Guernsey cattle in 1831, and the mule on 26 October 1785.

Jeff Brewer
Inventor

One of my Boston favorites is **Sunday Views**—picturesque vistas of the city that can be seen from cars during leisurely drives in off-hour traffic times. It's best to prowl the city this way on early Sunday mornings, or late Sunday or Monday for night views.

Particularly recommended in the night category is the **Tobin Bridge** (coming into Boston from the north, with a beautiful view over the harbor of the city in tiny twinkling light). Also at night, the approaches to **Kenmore Square** along **Brookline Avenue** or **Commonwealth Avenue** provide excellent views of Boston's famous **Citgo Sign**.

Another good night view, and a spectacular sunrise scene, is from the **Mass Turnpike** inbound just after the Allston tollbooth. **Memorial Drive** inbound along the Charles River is good day or night, but as always, choose a time when there is practically no traffic. (People who use these routes for commuting will find my commentary ludicrous.)

Entering the city from the south by way of the **Southeast Expressway** has some excellent features. Don't fail to note the **Dorchester Gas Tank**, one of Boston's great driving landmarks; its paint swooshes are the work of Corita, a leftwing nun and '60s artist. As you enter the city, just before getting onto the Central Artery, you will go through the **Dewey Square Tunnel**, one of the first tunnels ever made with entrances and exits underground, and a glimpse of Boston's future as the same engineers prepare a longer version to replace the fantastic view you are about to see.

As you exit the tunnel, you suddenly are propelled upward onto a flying freeway skirting Boston's **Financial District**. The fabulous **Custom House Tower** is to the left, along with Boston's wonderful maze of 19th- and

Bests

20th-century commercial buildings; to the right, the new **Rowes Wharf** complex and **Boston Harbor**. It's almost like a helicopter ride through the heart of the city, and equally spectacular in the morning or night. A fine ending to this mini-tour is to take the **Storrow Drive exit**—a kind of roller-coaster ride through a maze of steel support girders that is thrillingly featured in a short film about Boston at the **Museum of Science's Mugar Omni Theater**. Then take the lovely drive along the river back out of town.

Michael Dathe
Landscape horticulturist and designer

Boston is home to 2 of the finest garden parks in the United States. Blending horticultural diversity and landscape design with historical prominence, the **Arnold Arboretum** in **Jamaica Plain** and the **Mt Auburn Cemetery** in **Cambridge** are havens for gardeners, artists, scientists, historians, and general browsers of the out-of-doors.

The 265 acres of the Arnold Arboretum form the crown jewel of Boston's **Emerald Necklace**. Founded in 1872 as an educational and research facility, the arboretum is a living museum of woody plant material. Its staff endeavor to grow all the trees and shrubs

hardy in the North Temperate Zone. Bordering the arboretum's main walkway, plant families are loosely laid out in their naturally occurring sequence of evolution, with most specimens labeled. Also on the grounds are an **herbarium**, the **Dana greenhouses**, the **Larz Anderson Bonsai Collection**, and the oldest and third-largest **lilac collection** in North America (call for public-access information).

The Jamaica Plain site is one of the arboretum's 3 physical locations. The other 2 are the **Gray Herbarium** at **Harvard University** in Cambridge and the **Case Estates** in **Weston** MA. The Gray Herbarium contains more than one million noncultivated plants. Especially well documented are woody plants of the North Temperate Zone and plants of eastern and southeastern Asia. In addition to providing nursery space for the arboretum, the Case Estates contain perennial gardens, ground-cover plots, display beds, a display area for suburban trees, and gardens maintained in cooperation with the Hosta Society and the Massachusetts Chapter of the American Rhododendron Society.

The Mount Auburn Cemetery is the oldest and most important garden cemetery in America. Opened in 1831, its design ideas and system of avenues and footpaths laid out so as to enhance the existing landscape mark the cemetery as the beginning of the naturalistic public park style of gardening in this country. The 170 acres are a well planted, maintained, and labeled collection of woody plant material. Into this setting, the cemetery's architectural styles, sculptures, chapels, and final resting place of so many prominent Americans blend to effect a place of distinction.

For those staying longer in the Boston area, an enjoyable day trip is to drive to the **Garden-in-the-Woods** on Hemenway Rd in **Framingham** MA, run by the New England Wildflower Society. The 45-acre botanical garden offers an excellent representation of New England wildflowers and offers a succession of lovely blooming phases from early spring until fall.

Jane Thompson
Urban Planner, Benjamin Thompson & Associates, Architects

To experience the dense intellectual activity of the **Boston-Cambridge area**, you can drive along the river on Storrow Drive from downtown Boston, past **Boston University** (with **Northeastern University** just inland), crossing over the **Harvard Bridge** where **MIT**'s domed citadel rises on the Cambridge banks of the **Charles River**. Continue up Memorial Drive, past MIT's dorms and halls, until you reach the unmistakably Georgian presence of **Harvard University**, flanking both sides of the river at the Anderson Bridge. On the south (Boston/Allston) bank is the **Harvard Business School** and **athletic stadium**; on the Cambridge side along J.F. Kennedy Street are residential houses and the **J.F. Kennedy School of Government**, forming gateposts to **Harvard Square**.

Harvard Square, of course, is not a square but a mammoth crossing, with cars sluicing through this town center past the gates of Harvard. It is best to stop and explore **Harvard Yard** on foot, enjoying the choreographic patterns of students and bikes intersecting on tree-shaded paths. It is the ensemble that counts here—brick, ivy, elms, statuary, bike racks, grass, against a backdrop of diverse building styles in harmonious scale.

Architecture of note on the campus:

Boylston Hall and **Emerson Hall** (renovations 1959-1961, designed by Benjamin Thompson); **Carpenter Center** (1963, Le Corbusier); **Arthur M. Sackler Museum** (1986, Stirling/Wilford); **Gund Hall-Graduate School of Design** (1969, John Andrews, Anderson and Baldwin); **Harvard Law School Faculty Office Building and Administration Building** (1969, Benjamin Thompson & Associates); **Harkness Common and Graduate Center** (1950, The Architects Collaborative)

To experience Cambridge at the heart of Harvard Square, proceed back to the head of **Brattle Street**, where a workaday assortment of shops is elevated by the sparkling glass **Design Research building** (1969, Benjamin Thompson & Associates). Now an expansive **Crate & Barrel** store, this sparkling prism, at the corner of Story and Brattle streets, is the centerpiece of *architects' corner*, 4 buildings that achieve uncommonly civilized relationships of height, scale, and material. (Three were designed by architects for their own offices—J.L. Sert, The Architects' Collaborative, Earl Flansburg and Associates.) In the next Brattle Street block is the **Harvard Graduate School of Education** (1971, Benjamin Thompson & Associates) followed, a block beyond, by the **Loeb Drama Theater** (1959, Hugh Stubbins). Thereafter the street becomes residential, a stately corridor of Colonial, Victorian, and modern homes (including that of H.W. Longfellow) extending west for a dozen blocks.

After wandering along Brattle and its side streets, you may want to turn back to the square to find a watering spot. Try **The Harvest** restaurant (behind Crate & Barrel), good for anything from a homemade soup lunch to an elegant wild game dinner or drinks on the patio.

Best bets around Harvard Square:

A noon-hour picnic on a sunny spring day in **JFK Park** or on the river banks—get choice takeout fare from **The Harvest Express** in the passageway at 44 Brattle Street.

The funky Bogie revivals at the **Brattle Theater**; the real and experimental art of the Loeb Drama Center; a browse through the world-spanning periodicals (serious and racy) at the **Harvard Square news kiosk**.

The exquisite *glass flowers* at the **Peabody Museum**; the elegant collections of the **Fogg Museum**; art in the galleries and in the visible studios (*pancakes in the window*) at the **Carpenter Center Of Visual Arts**.

Tea and pastry at the **Blacksmith House**; cocktails on the tree-shaded patio of The Harvest restaurant, followed by a dinner of robust (café) or elegant (dining room) cuisine in the ultimate Cambridge *high casual* environment.

Boston's land area is 46 sq miles; the Greater Boston land area is 1100 sq miles. Boston has 790 miles of streets, 47 miles of waterfront, 15 miles of beaches, 349 bridges, 8 historic or preservation districts, and 8 major medical research centers.

Males make up 48% of Boston's population, females 52%. Whites are 61% of the population, Blacks 25%, Asian 5%, Hispanic 7%, other 1%. The median age of Bostonians is 28.8.

Margaret Reeve
Publications Director, SCI-Arc

Harvard Bridge, Charlestown Navy Yard—great views of the city.

Boston Athenaeum, Houghton Library—wonderful collections, great ambiance.

BSO, Jordan Hall, Sanders Theatre—beautiful spaces, great music.

Café Pamplona, Iruña, The Grolier Book Shop—retain original flavor of Cambridge.

Bromfield Pen Shop, Windsor Button Shop, Jewelers Building—real retail shops with knowledgeable and pleasant service people.

Harvard Square, Au Bon Pain, Cafe Florian, Il Dolce Momento—people watching.

Sandy Pond in **Lincoln** and **Lake Waban, Wellesley**—good for early spring or fall walks. **DeCordova**, Sunday afternoon outdoor concerts.

Ars Libri, Harrison Ave; fantastic collection of rare and architecture books; **Sessa's** and **Gino's Davis Square**, Somerville, fabulous Italian grocery and greengrocer; **Stellina's, Watertown**, great Italian food, nontrendy atmosphere.

The Caterer, Medford—great-tasting, great-looking food for parties.

Michael Webb
Architecture Critic

Louisburg Square on a winter's night, when snow blankets the cars and transports you back to Brahmin Boston in its heyday.

Faneuil Hall Marketplace—Ben Thompson's vision

Bests

created a great people place—in contrast to the sterility of City Hall Plaza.

Children's Museum—If you don't have kids, borrow one for the afternoon and relive the joys of childhood.

John Hancock Tower—A high rise whose elegance compensates for the eyesores. Best seen from across the Charles River.

The 5th-floor reading room of the **Boston Athenaeum**—scholarly research in a setting of neo-classic splendor.

Rapid transit—Given the congestion and the homicidal drivers, it's just as well that Boston has America's best subway system.

Cambridge old and new—Where else could you find Alvar Aalto, Le Corbusier, and James Stirling in such a mellow context?

The **John F. Kennedy Library**—I.M. Pei's building is worth the trip, but it's the images of the president and his slain brother that reach out and grab you.

The emerald perfection of village greens—In **Harvard, Lexington, Falmouth**, and **Cohasset**—a 19th-century dream of a past that never was.

Martha's Vineyard out of season—Ideally on a cold spring day, when the white clapboard houses seem fresh minted.

South End

The South End is not a destination for sightseers, but rather for urban explorers who like to stray from tourist tracks and make their own discoveries. Enticements include block after block of undulating Victorian bowfronts, intimate residential parks, vibrant streetlife, out-of-the-ordinary shops, and more unusual restaurants of excellent quality than **Back Bay**. Yet the South End is often overlooked, separated from central Boston and neighboring Back Bay by railroad tracks and the **Copley Place** and **Prudential Center** developments.

The South End is one of Boston's most diverse neighborhoods—racially, economically, ethnically, and religiously. Rich variety exists within this square mile. The South End is the largest Victorian row house district extant in the US and is listed on the National Register of Historic Places. After a brief flowering as a genteel enclave, the neighborhood became home to Boston's immigrant populations. Today the South End still exudes port-of-entry flavor: various blocks are predominantly Lebanese, Irish, Yankee, Chinese, West Indian, Black, Greek, or Hispanic. Boston's largest gay population resides here. Over the last 20 years, young middle-class professionals, mainly white, have moved in, gentrifying patches of this crazy quilt. The neighborhood also has a bohemian side, attracting visual artists, architects, writers, performers, designers, craftspeople, musicians.

Like Back Bay, the entire South End rests on landfill. The neighborhood was originally marshland bordering **Washington Street**, which was once a narrow neck that linked the peninsula crowded by young Boston to the mainland. By the mid-19th century, upwardly mobile Bostonians wanted fashionable new quarters. From 1850-1875, the South End emerged as speculators filled in blocks of land and auctioned them off. Unlike Back Bay, there was no grid or grand plan. Whereas Back Bay is French-inspired and cosmopolitan in style, the South End follows more traditional English patterns. To attract buyers, developers created London-style residential parks like **Worcester, Union**, and **Chester** squares, oases loosely linked by common architecture. Less haphazard in plan than Boston's oldest neighborhoods, the South End still has a transitional, unpredictable feel.

Most convenient to the South End are the **Back Bay/South End (Orange Line)** and **Massachusetts Avenue (Orange Line)** subway stops; the **Prudential** and **Symphony** (both on the **Green Line**) stops are beyond the neighborhood's borders but mere minutes away on foot. **Amtrak** also stops at **Back Bay/South End**, as well as at **South Station**

The South End rose and fell from grace in less than a decade, eclipsed by glamorous Back Bay and the allure of streetcar suburbs. By 1900, prosperous Bostonians had abandoned their handsome row houses, which were then divided into multiple units and lodging rooms to accommodate waves of immigrants and working-class families. Industries and businesses sprang up. **Boston City Hospital** was founded in the 1860s, the oldest institution on **Hospital Row**, a dense cluster of university and municipal medical buildings located near the **Roxbury** border. The South End also became the largest lodging-house district in the US, gaining a reputation for dens of vices and unsavory pursuits. Finally declared a federal urban renewal area in 1965, the South End was rent apart by drastic development, which set the stage for pell-mell gentrification in the '70s and '80s.

The neighborhood endures, changeable and fascinating as ever. Residents and community groups take active parts in healing old wounds—the new **Southwest Corridor Park** is but one attractive result. Although the neighborhood fabric has been torn by insensitive institutions and neglect, many buildings and blocks are being recycled and renewed. Visit in late morning or early afternoon, when the streets are safest and liveliest. Explore **Columbus Avenue** and **Tremont Street** for the greatest concentration of good shops and restaurants. Walk in tiny **Rutland Square** or tranquil **Union Square**, both hugged by carefully restored residences. Stroll along **Chandler, Lawrence**, and **Appleton** streets, lined with smaller-scale, appealing brick houses. From block to block, architecture changes from down-in-the-dumps to resplendently restored. And with each block you'll sense the presence of different populations, such as the black community to the south, Middle Easterners and Armenians along **Shawmut Avenue** to the east.

1 Southwest Corridor Park (1977, **Roy B. Mann**, landscape architect) Where an ugly gash once slashed the South End, a curling ribbon of attractive parkland now wanders. In the '70s, more than 100 acres of housing in the South End and adjoining **Roxbury** and **Jamaica Plain** were demolished to make way for a highway project. Community protests killed that plan, but the blight remained, a sore spot awaiting healing. At last, 52 acres of this area were reclaimed for parkland to reknit divided neighborhoods. More than a decade in the making, the park is just becoming a real part of the city. Twenty-three architecture and engineering firms worked with more than 15 community groups to chart the course of the new green trail. The result: 4.7 miles of walkways and bike paths dotted with tot lots, street-hockey rinks, basketball and tennis courts, and graced with young trees and plantings. An adjunct project, the community-run **Southwest Corridor Farms**, manages 13 acres, providing

plots and training to urban gardeners. The lauded fingerlike park is as narrow in spots as 60 feet, and as wide in others as a quarter mile, and points all the way to **Franklin Park**, the **Arnold Arboretum**, and **Forest Hills Cemetery**. Starting behind **Copley Place**, stroll as far west as your fancy takes you, and see how intensely used the well-loved park has become by all ages, all races, all economic groups.

The park is just one piece of the controversial, enormous, near-800-million-dollar **Southwest Corridor Project** still under way, which also involved relocating and depressing Boston's old elevated **MBTA Orange Line** and constructing 9 new rapid transit stations. Two are in the South End: **Back Bay/South End** station is a well-crafted structure designed by **Kallmann, McKinnell and Wood**, extending from Dartmouth St across from the park's beginning to Clarendon St. In its heroic navelike concourse vaulted by huge wooden arches and illuminated by clerestory windows,

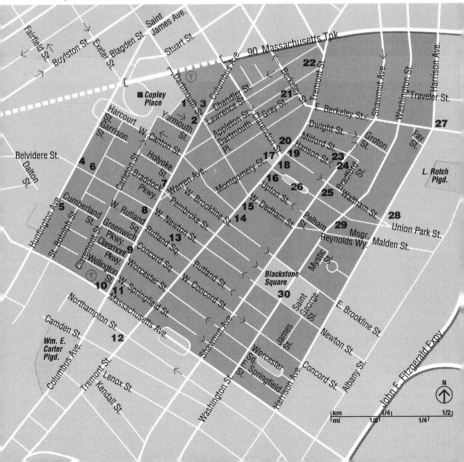

Back Bay/South End Rapid Transit Station
Courtesy Kallmann, McKinnell & Wood

the station recalls the grandeur of Victorian railway stations. The **Massachusetts Avenue** subway station, by **Ellenzweig, Moore and Associates**, is a sleek, sinuous brick, glass, and aluminum structure located where the park intersects Mass Ave. The Southwest Corridor Project is also creating development parcels along this route that are intended to revitalize neglected Boston neighborhoods by providing employment and development opportunities for those communities. ♦ Park begins at Dartmouth St (Huntington-Columbus Aves)

2 Street The gracious owners have interior design and retail backgrounds, and Street is the culmination of their professional dreams. Stark and SoHo-like, the shop has an outstanding array of men's and women's clothing and accessories for all ages. Colors, shapes, and textures are striking. **Gary Marotta** and **Thom Lapan** look for interesting experimental pieces, offering frequently changing lines from Madrid, London, Amsterdam, Montreal, Paris. The background music and artwork by local artists change often too, to suit the moment. A café on the premises serves cappuccino, espresso, Italian sodas, and a daily dessert. ♦ M-F 11AM-8PM; Sa 10AM-8PM; Su noon-6PM. 130 Dartmouth St (Huntington-Columbus Aves; behind Copley Pl) 266.1121 ♿

2 Tent City (1988, **Goody, Clancy & Associates**) The construction of affluent **Copley Place** across the way was the catalyst that brought black community activists to this site to protest the South End's gentrification, forcing Boston to alter plans for a parking lot and build affordable community-responsive housing instead. The result is a gentle addition to the neighborhood. One-quarter of the units in the cheerful patterned-brick complex of apartments and row-houses are market-rate, one quarter are for low-income residents, and one-

South End

half are for moderate-income residents. The biggest surprise is the name, which preserves the political moment when the activists set up tents here, an early episode in the wave of tent cities to come as the lack of affordable housing and the homelessness crisis have worsened in Boston and cities across the country. ♦ Dartmouth St (Huntington-Columbus Aves; behind Copley Pl)

In the **Back Bay/South End** subway station lounges a statue of **A. Philip Randolph** (1889-1979), founding president of the **Brotherhood of Sleeping Car Porters**. Many of these porters, who were black, worked at the former Back Bay railway station and settled in the South End (and **Roxbury**), helping stabilize the struggling neighborhood and establishing the core of its strong black community.

Back Bay's allure remains so powerful that the dividing line between it and the South End is constantly disputed. New residents and businesses often try to push the boundary in order to claim a Back Bay address.

3 Chef Chandler's Commonwealth Grill
★★$$ Once a dining-car chef on the old New Haven railroad, **Willard Chandler** also made the rounds in a number of Boston taverns and clubs before winding up in his latest digs. The new place is far bigger and fancier than his previous hangout round the corner, but Chandler just keeps doing what comes naturally—cooking up enormous affordable portions of lip-smacking spicy food. His blackboard roster of Cajun, Caribbean, and Creole dishes goes swooningly on and on: seafood file gumbo, Cajun meat pie, crawfish bisque, jambalaya, BBQ rack of lamb, BBQ ribs, Chandler's bayou steak, catfish with hush puppies and pompano sauce, praline cheesecake, sweet-potato, pecan, and key-lime pies. Alligator, goat, and swamp-turtle soup too. Even the side dishes are forces to be reckoned with, like rich delmonico potatoes and nutmeg squash. Chandler's portion control policy: *When you can't get anything else on the plate, that's a portion.* If your eyes are bigger than your stomach, you're in trouble. Don't wear tight clothes. And be prepared—everything heats up once the nighttime crowds arrive. A jazz trio plays on Monday, 8-11PM. The lounge stays open until 2AM every night. ♦ Cajun/Creole ♦ M-Sa 6-11PM; Su 4-9PM. 111 Dartmouth St (Columbus Ave) Reservations recommended. No credit cards. 353.0160 ♿

3 Tim's Tavern $ Once **Chef Chandler** decamped for his new place on **Dartmouth St**, many people forgot about Tim's as a dining possibility. However, the tavern's management certainly didn't forget, and Tim's remains a great place to get a good pub-style repast. It's very funky, but a bargain. Give Tim's a try for one of the best cheap steaks in town. Although the tavern is always busy, there's usually no wait. ♦ American ♦ M-Sa 11:30-midnight. 329 Columbus Ave (Dartmouth St) 247.7894 ♿

3 The Claddagh $ This Irish pub offers just the sort of filling, unfussy food you'd expect to find in a neighborhood bar. You're best off with burgers, chicken, stews, and other straightforward items. Walls are adorned with Irish family crests. Quieter on weeknights, the Claddagh becomes boisterous on weekends, often hosting sing-alongs. A new room has been renovated for live music. The same owners operate **The Black Rose**, 160 State St, Faneuil Hall Marketplace. 742.2286; and **The Purple Shamrock**, 1 Union St, Faneuil Hall Marketplace. 227.2060—both extremely popular and cast from the same mold. ♦ Irish-American/takeout ♦ Daily 11:30AM-12:30AM. 335 Columbus Ave (Dartmouth St) 262.9874

4 The Colonnade Hotel $$$ Recently renovated and well located, this 300-room hotel's amenities include 2 restaurants, an outdoor rooftop pool, a fitness room, indoor parking, a multilingual staff, 24-hour room service, same-day valet service (fee), foreign currency exchange. Handicapped-equipped and non-smokers' rooms available. If the hotel's service is anywhere near as delinquent as the public relations department, a stay here will have its irritations. ♦ 120 Huntington Ave (W. Newton St) 424.7000, 800/962.3030; fax 424.1717 &

5 The Midtown Hotel $$ A well-kept secret, this 2-story 159-room hotel is older and far less fashionable than the numerous luxury hotels located nearby, and also much less expensive. It's frequented by families, tour groups, and businesspeople. Rooms are spacious and there's free parking, 24-hour laundry service, an outdoor pool with a lifeguard (in season), and a multilingual staff. Children under 18 stay with parents for free. Winter packages are available on request. **Seiyoken**, a Japanese restaurant, is located on the premises. ♦ 220 Huntington Ave (Mass Ave) 262.1000, 800/343.1177; fax 262.8739 &

6 St. Botolph Street Stroll down this pleasant stretch of street, which **New York City**'s Ash Can School painter **George Benjamin Luks** portrayed in *Noontime, St. Botolph*, on view in the **Museum of Fine Arts**. Look for the **Musician's Mutual Relief Society Building** at 52-56, an 1886 commercial hall designed by **Cabot and Chandler** that was renovated and suitably ornamented for the society's use in 1913. Separated by stone lyres beneath the cornice are composers' names. At the **Cumberland St** intersection is an attractive former schoolhouse, dating from 1891, converted to condominiums in 1980 by **Graham Gund Associates**.

6 St. Botolph Restaurant ★$$ A neighborly restaurant in a charming 19th-century townhouse, St. Botolph's is a Sunday good choice for its 4-course prix-fixe brunch featuring muffins, Bloody Mary or screwdriver, appetizer, coffee, entree, and dessert. The casual street-level café—complete with bar and jukebox—offers bistro fare, with a full range of appetizers, grilled pizzas, sandwiches, pastas, risottos, soups, salads. Dinner only is served in the upper-level main dining room, where smoking is not allowed. The restaurant is named for the street named in turn for Boston's patron saint, also the namesake for **Boston, England**—a contraction of *St. Botolph's town*. ♦ New American/takeout ♦ Café: daily 11:30AM-midnight. Main dining room: M-Th, Su 5:45-10:30PM; F-Sa 5:45PM-midnight, 99 St. Botolph St (W. Newton St) Reservations recommended for dinner. 266.3030

In 1951, during his first semester as a doctoral student at **Boston University**'s **School of Divinity**, the **Reverend Martin Luther King, Jr.**, took a room on **St. Botolph St**. He then moved to more spacious quarters nearby on **Mass Ave**.

7 Charlie's Sandwich Shoppe ★★$ All night, **Christi Manjourides** stays up baking pies and muffins. At 5AM, sons **Chris** and **Arthur** arrive and get ready for a day at the grill. Then regulars begin drifting in after 6, anticipating a gentle morning start with counter-side conversation over coffee and Charlie's famous breakfast platters such as cranberry pancakes or a Cajun omelet with spicy sausage. Family-run for more than 50 years, this unpretentious luncheonette is a melting pot, attracting anyone with an appetite for hearty breakfasts and lunches. At communal tables, designer suits mingle with blue jeans and work boots, celebrities mix with folks struggling to get by. Relax among the awards, accolades, and smiling photos taken since opening day in 1927. Stoke up on blueberry French toast, cheeseburgers, Greek salad, turkey hash, frankfurts and beans, fried clams, hot pastrami on a bulky roll, sweet-potato pie. It feels great to hang out here, although there are often hungry people waiting impatiently by the door. Charlie's welcomed famous black musicians like **Duke Ellington** in the '40s, a period when blacks were barred from most Boston restaurants. ♦ American ♦ M-F 6AM-2:30PM; Sa 7:30AM-1PM. 429 Columbus Ave (Braddock Pkwy-Holyoke St) No credit cards. 536.7669

8 Union United Methodist Church (1877, A.R. Estey) Designed by the architect of **Emmanuel Church** in Back Bay, this Gothic Revival creation has the gracious proportions and picturesqueness of a rural parish church. Rather than reaching for the sky, it reaches out

South End

to those who approach on foot. ♦ 485 Columbus Ave (W. Newton St)

There have always been large active **gay** and **lesbian communities** in Boston. For the most current information about activities, events, organizations, clubs, services, etc, an excellent source is the **Glad Day Bookshop** in Back Bay, 673 Boylston St, 2nd fl, 267.3010. They carry all available literature and periodicals, including the *Gayellow Pages* (Northeast Edition), with listings for Boston and Provincetown; as well as *The Guide*, a monthly about gay travel, entertainment, politics, and sex, published in Boston. The staff is friendly and knowledgeable about the Boston scene. Other tabloids to pick up (often in the **South End, Back Bay**, or **Beacon Hill**) are *Bay Windows* and the *Gay Community News*. The **Gay Pride March** held early each summer is the gay community's most political and festive event of the year, with tens of thousands of marchers and bystanders lining the parade's route through the heart of Boston.

Restaurants/Clubs: Red   **Hotels:** Blue
Shops/Parks: Green   **Sights/Culture:** Black

9 Divine Decadence Taking its name from the movie *Cabaret*, this shop offers a delightfully diverse array of American, South American, and European home furnishings and accessories dating from 1900 to yesterday, with occasional earlier pieces. The focus is on unusual investment-quality items that epitomize their era—whether a kicky shoe-shaped '20s chair from a defunct Boston shoe store, a fully-functioning '40s jukebox, or '80s desk with neon. Some collectibles are commonplace items from a distant decade that have become treasures with time, others are the work of renowned designers like **Charles Eames**. It's always fun to come back, since you never know what owner **Richard Penachio** will chance upon next. Prices range widely, because there are lots of wonderful small items like clocks, tableware, and mirrors. Pennachio updates and combines some items into artful new creations. When you leave the store, look up **Claremont Pk** for a nice view of the **Christian Science Mother Church**'s dome. ♦ Tu-F noon-6PM; Sa 11AM-6PM; Su noon-5PM (closed Su Memorial Day-Labor Day). 535 Columbus Ave (Claremont Pkwy) 266.1477 ♿

10 Skippy White's Skippy doesn't want his record shop to be like all those soulless mall-type music stores. He's been in business for more than 30 years, and stocks thousands of unusual old and new albums as well as cassettes, 12"s, and CDs. Sure, it's the CD age and records are going the way of the dodo, but Skippy thinks some music just sounds better on vinyl. He has a great collection of gospel records, plus rhythm and blues, reggae, rap, jazz, soul, and lots of vintage singles and LPs. If you don't know the title you're hunting for, hum a few bars and Skippy can probably locate it. Step in the door, and it's instantly clear why people come here from all over. Credit accepted for $25 and up. ♦ M-W 9AM-6PM; Th-Sa 9AM-8PM. 410 Mass Ave (Columbus Ave-St. Botolph St) 266.1002 ♿ Also at: 555 Mass Ave. Central Sq. Cambridge. 491.3345

In the middle of the day on 19 May 1780 it became nearly completely dark in most of New England, causing many to fear the Day of Judgment had arrived. That **Dark Day** has never been explained, although it's hypothesized that the pollution from burning coal fires, or possibly ash and smoke carried over from huge forest fires in the Great Lakes region, was the cause.

Albert Schweitzer played the organ in the **All Saints' Lutheran Church** on **W. Newton St.**

11 Harriet Tubman House (1974, **Don Stull Associates**) Named for the *Moses of the South*, who was herself a runaway slave and Underground Railroad organizer, this iconoclastic complex greets the street with spirit and purposefulness. It's home to the **United South End Settlements**, a social service organization responsible for vital community programs. The architect deserves applause for doing a lot with a little budget. Incidentally, the house stands on the site of one of Boston's famous great jazz clubs, **The Hi Hat**, which burned down. ♦ 566 Columbus Ave (Mass Ave) 536.8610

12 Piano Craft Guild (c. 1853; reuse 1972, **Gelardin/Bruner/Cott** with **Anderson, Notter Associates**) When new, the Chickering piano factory was reputedly the second-largest building in the US. The surprisingly graceful industrial structure is enlivened by a sprightly octagonal tower, and was renovated in 1972 for artists' studios and living spaces. Visit the 2-story gallery showing works by residents. This was one of the first and largest mill conversions in the state, an early example of the creative lengths Boston artists have gone to in obtaining affordable housing. ♦ F 6-9PM; Sa-Su 2-6PM. 791 Tremont St (Northampton-Camden Sts) Recorded info 437.9365

13 Rutland Square (c. 1865-1875) One of the South End's most intimate oases is this shady, slim elliptical park bracketed by 2 rows of 3-story bowfronts. A number of facades break from the neighborhood pattern of warm red brick, and instead are prettily painted and detailed in light colors. Only one block long, the square is so small that its fenced-in park hardly seems a place for actual play; rather, it's a lovely sliver of greenspace in which residents can contemplate. ♦ Rutland St (Tremont St-Columbus Ave)

14 Villa Victoria (1969-1976, **John Sharratt and Associates**) This housing complex is a local success story. A largely Puerto Rican community not only participated in every stage of its development, but also collaborated with the architect so that residents' cultural values and traditions would be expressed with dignity. While the complex is by no means beautiful, given limited funds, it has its own strong identity. Located in a former church with a splashy mural adorning the facade, the **Jorge Hernandez Cultural Center** is a vibrant creative outlet that hosts events of all kinds: jazz, theater, music, and dance, most featuring Latino performers. ◆ Bounded by Tremont St-Shawmut Ave, W. Brookline-W. Dedham Sts. Cultural center info 262.1342

15 Buteco II $ An easy-going hole-in-the-wall (its name is Portuguese slang for *joint*) that serves authentic Brazilian dishes like *mandioca frita* (fried cassava root with carrot sauce), *moqueca de peixe* (fish in spicy coconut sauce), and—weekends only—the popular feijoada (black-bean stew with sausage, dried beef, pork, rice, collard greens, and orange). Some traditional Spanish dishes are offered too. The lively restaurant attracts a large South American clientele. ◆ Brazilian/Spanish ◆ M-Th 11:30AM-10PM; F-Sa 11:30AM-11PM; Su 5:30-10PM. 57 W. Dedham St (Tremont St-Shawmut Ave) Reservations for 5 or more. 247.9249 ᪶ Also at: 130 Jersey St, Kenmore Sq. 247.9508 (live music and Brazilian-only cuisine here)

16 Hamersley's Bistro ★★★★$$$ Bistro-style restaurants offering simpler full-bodied fare have become very popular in Boston, and **Gordon** and **Fiona Hamersley**'s snug Federal storefront is one of the most appealing. In the exposed kitchen, Gordon and his crew don baseball caps and deftly turn out favorites inspired by French country cooking—golden roast chicken, sirloin with mashed potatoes, bouillabaisse, cassoulet—as well as more adventurous flights of fancy like roasted salmon with oysters, bacon, and hollandaise sauce, or a marvelous grilled mushroom-and-garlic sandwich on country bread. Sunday is a day of rest for Gordon, with a slightly different and lower-priced evening menu. In the summer, the menu features more Mediterranean dishes. The wine list changes seasonally to suit the food. The tiny dining rooms are black-and-white simplicity—heated up by the blazing red bar—and cozily filled with an interesting assortment of neighborhood people, surburan visitors, artists, actors, musicians, architects, and the like. ◆ New American/Mediterranean ◆ M-Sa 6-10PM; Su 6-9PM. 578 Tremont St (Clarendon-Dartmouth Sts) Valet parking M-Sa (fee) Reservations recommended, especially F-Su. 267.6068 ᪶

16 Tremont Ice Cream $ Just the kind of place everyone wants in their own neighborhood, this casual and cheap eatery serves homestyle dinerlike food made on the premises. Sidle up to the 6-stool counter or grab a booth. A great choice for breakfast pancakes and French toast, the restaurant also serves clam chowder and makes soups fresh daily, plus basic sandwiches and salads. The ice cream comes from a dairy in Middleton MA. ◆ American/takeout ◆ Tu-Sa 6AM-6PM; Su 8AM-6PM. 584 Tremont St (Clarendon-Dartmouth Sts) No credit cards. 247.8414

17 St. Cloud ★★★$$$ **Rebecca Caras**, creator of a local caravan of signature cafés, named this sleek chic spot for the twin-towered former residence hotel next door, the **St. Cloud Hotel** by **Nathaniel J. Bradlee** (1870), who designed many South End row houses. (The hotel's fash-

ionable French flats were forerunners to the apartment houses that soon spread like weeds in American cities.) In her enterprises, Caras consistently tries hard to please and succeeds here too, with satisfying cosmopolitan entrees like pumpkin ravioli filled with ricotta and prosciutto, rack of lamb, roast pheasant with apple sauce, chicken and potato dumplings, almond-raspberry cake. Light fare is available too, so prices vary widely. This is a sophisticated yet comfortable setting, enhanced by murals, soft jazz, soft evening lighting. With windows on 3 sides, St. Cloud is light and airy by day, attentive to the street scene beyond. The staff is exceptionally considerate; one diner suffering from a cold asked for chicken soup—not on the menu—and received a delectably soothing bowl along with heartfelt sympathy. Happily, the restaurant stays open later than most in town, and the bar is a lively late-night rendezvous. ◆ New American ◆ M-Sa 11:30AM-3PM, 5:30PM-midnight; Su 11AM-4PM; 5:30PM-midnight. 557 Tremont St (Clarendon St) Valet parking after 5:30PM and Su brunch (fee) Reservations recommended. 353.0202 ᪶

18 Zigzag Artful, sleek, streamlined, and witty modern furniture comfortably inhabits a Victorian bowfront. Owner **Michael Bojanowski** shows his work and that of local designers like **José Pascual** and **Shadi**, with pieces by international designers sneaking in. Pieces are mainly of steel, aluminum, and wood, with some upholstered. Even the most understated spartan chairs are comfortable as can be. ◆ Tu-Sa 11AM-5PM. 558 Tremont St (Clarendon St) 482.5504

18 Water Cafe $ When it comes to service, this Greenwich Village-style café epitomizes nonchalance. However, the chichi sandwiches—salmon and boursin, turkey and brie, mozzarella and sundried tomatoes, etc—are among

South End

the best in town. Dinner recipes are drawn from all over the map and feature fresh local food. Everything seems spur-of-the-moment here, so who knows what you'll find on the menu—Maine crabcakes, mussels risotto, linguini puttanesca, and Thai beef with green curry have put in appearances. A special brunch menu is offered Saturday and Sunday. ◆ New American/takeout ◆ M-Tu 8AM-4PM; W-F 8AM-4PM, 5:30-10:30PM; Sa 9AM-3PM, 5:30-10:30PM; Su 9AM-3PM. 560 Tremont St (Clarendon St) No credit cards. 350.8915

18 Odeon David Christina crisscrosses the US for one-of-a-kind accessories for men, women, and the home. The boutique's current and vintage selections include reconditioned antique telephones, hand-carved Kenya soapstone, wrought-iron candlesticks, jewelry ranging from rhinestones to avant-garde, amusing housewares, rayon shirts and boxer shorts, great socks. This shop defies categorization, but it does have a West Coast flair. ◆ M-Sa 10:30AM-6:30PM; Su noon-5PM. 562 Tremont St (Clarendon St) 542.4412

Chona

19 Chona One glance at the striking windows tells you something interesting is up. A spirited new store for men's and women's fashions, Chona emphasizes clothing as entertainment and shopping as a fun experience. The wonderful-looking clothes are colorful, contemporary, and reasonably priced, blending familiar labels with local designers' lines. Chona also stocks accessories galore: belts, jewelry, ties, boxer shorts. It's impossible not to like a place where the sales help is so friendly, and the dressing rooms so inviting. ♦ M-F 11AM-7PM; Sa 10AM-6PM; Su noon-5PM. 540 Tremont St (Hanson St) 482.6803

19 Capriccio piu ★$ Occupying 2 floors in a Victorian townhouse, this neighborhood favorite's delicious homestyle fare includes lots of grilled vegetables, fritters, small pizzas, pastas of all shapes and sizes with great sauces, Venetian-style salt cod, risottos, and cornmeal-eggplant-mozzarella cakes. The menu changes every few months to please the regulars. The decor—pale-stucco walls, black-and-white floor, and banquettes—suggests a stage set for an Italian piazza scene. ♦ Italian ♦ Daily 5-11PM. 550 Tremont St (Waltham St) Reservations required for 5 or more. 338.6252

20 Boston Center for the Arts, Cyclorama (1884, **Cummings and Sears**; National Register of Historic Places) Since 1970, the Boston Center for the Arts (BCA) has owned, operated, and organized art and cultural events at the Cyclorama complex. The central building's beautiful shallow steel-trussed dome was built to house a novel tourist attraction: a 400x50-ft cyclorama mural of the *Battle of Gettysburg* by

South End

Paul Philippoteaux, now exhibited elsewhere in the US. Other chapters in the adaptable building's life: it served as a skating rink; a track for bicycle races; a gymnasium and work-out ring for boxers where Boston's famous prizefighter **John L. Sullivan** fought; **Alfred Champion**'s garage, where he invented the spark plug; and flower market from 1923-1968. The Cyclorama now hosts annual art and antiques shows, flea markets, the Sugarplum Circus at Christmastime, and other large events. The attractive kiosk out front was originally a cupola atop a **Roxbury** building designed by **Gridley J.F. Bryant**, architect of **Old City Hall**, the original **Boston City Hospital** building, and other Boston landmarks. In addition to housing the **New Ehrlich Theatre**, the BCA rents out a small theater space called **The Leland Center**, and holds programs and recitals of the **Community Music Center** in the **Black Box Theatre**—all in the Cyclorama's lower levels. To return is the **Boston Ballet**, which will move its performance and rehearsal spaces onto the BCA grounds. ♦ 539 Tremont St (Berkeley-Clarendon Sts) 426.5000 &

Within the Cyclorama:

New Ehrlich Theatre A nonprofit resident theater company dedicated to the developmen of Boston theater artists, New Ehrlich offers approximately 6 productions a year of classic and modern works. It runs the NEWorks program of readings, workshops, and world premieres of plays by Massachusetts playwright The theater also directs a conservatory from which it often draws company members. Ticket prices are very low for Boston. ♦ Seats 147. Box office Tu-F 2-6PM and 2 hrs before curtain. Tickets also available at Bostix. Lowe level. Recorded info 482.6316 &

Adjacent to the Cyclorama:

Mills Gallery Housed by the **Boston Center for the Arts**, the gallery exhibits far-ranging work by regional contemporary artists in the beginning or middle of their careers, with emphasis on experimental media such as computer art. Some performance pieces and installations are also shown. Most shows feature 2 or more artists and change frequently. The gallery is located in the **Tremont Estates Building**, which also contains 50 studios for visual artists chosen by the BCA board, plus offices for theater and dance groups. ♦ Tu-W, F-Sa noon-4PM; Th noon-7PM. 549 Tremont St (Berkeley-Clarendon Sts) 426.8835 & (will assist)

21 Berkeley Residence Club $ Run by the YWCA, this 200-room residence for women combines features of a hotel, dormitory, and old-fashioned rooming house. The clientele is an interesting mix: tourists, students, working and professional women, some settled in long term. Rooms are tiny—just the basics—with some doubles available. Each well-kept bathroom is shared by 13-16 women. Stay by the night or longer, paying by the week. There's a library, sitting room, laundry room, TV room, and pretty outdoor courtyard. The dining roor serves 2 full meals a day (extra charge), with takeout available. Conveniently located, the residence is affordable and secure. Inquire about the rules, which aren't excessive and protect residents. The 2nd floor has a less restrictive policy on gentlemen callers. To stay here, you must pay an immediate nominal fee for temporary membership. No children or pets. ♦ 40 Berkeley St (Appleton St) 482.885(

22 Icarus ★★$$$ A South End pioneer quartered in a former jazz club, Icarus is eclectic in decor and cuisine in an interesting, sophisticated way. The mood is muted and relaxed. A statue of winged Icarus beneath a cool ceiling band of neon surveys the 2-tier dining room, where a diverse clientele enjoys chef/co-owne **Chris Douglass**' seasonal inspirations: polenta with wild mushrooms and thyme, lobster in ginger-cream sauce on homemade noodles, grilled tuna with wasabi and sushi, pork loin with mango and jalapeño salsa, caramel-apple tart, cherry-chocolate-chunk ice cream with icebox cookies. The lengthy wine list is superb ♦ New American ♦ M-Th 5:30-10PM; F-Sa 5:30-11PM; Su 11AM-3PM. 3 Appleton St

(Berkeley-Tremont Sts) Valet parking W-Sa (fee) Reservations recommended F-Su. 426.1790

23 Cedars Restaurant $ All the food is cooked every day by **Elias Aboujaoude**, an owner who lives in the building. A very informal place, Cedars serves great hummus, tabouleh, and kibbie. Its owners and those of **Nadia's Eastern Star** a block away are related, and both places are consistently popular for tasty, affordable meals. ♦ Lebanese/takeout ♦ Daily 5PM-midnight. 253 Shawmut Ave (Milford St) Reservations required for 10 or more. No credit cards. 338.7528

24 Nadia's Eastern Star $ Some unstylish eateries manage to hold their own quite nicely in the increasingly fashion-conscious South End. For more than 20 years, friendly, faithful Nadia's has catered to hearty appetites with good Lebanese fare like hummus, *kufta*, shish kebabs, garlic chicken, stuffed cabbage leaves. For a sampling, order a combination plate. Nadia's keeps late hours, so remember it if you're hungry and the city's other kitchens have shut down for the night. But you can't sneak in liquor anymore. ♦ Lebanese/takeout ♦ Daily 5PM-1AM. 280 Shawmut Ave (Milford-Hanson Sts) No credit cards. 338.8091 ♿

25 East Meets West To Go A marvelous bakery for breads, muffins, pastries, and desserts like the ultrarich chocolate crater cake and chocolate chubby cookies (ignore the name and chomp away). Mainly for takeout, the bakery does have a couple of tables and sells some lunch items, coffee, and sodas. Cakes to order, too. ♦ Daily 7AM-7PM. 312 Shawmut Ave (Union Park) No credit cards. 482.1015 ♿

26 On the Park ★★$$ A bright, sunny, friendly spot with windows all around, the café is a few strides away from the South End's prettiest greenery. It serves homemade breads and satisfying dishes like shepherd's pie made with real mashed potatoes, stews, potpies, fresh fish, tasty desserts. Sunday brunch is down-home-style, with a few highfalutin' treats like Bellinis. The art on the walls comes from local artists and Newbury St galleries, and changes each month. Regulars and word-of-mouth keep the café's 30 seats filled. Reservations are not taken; there's sometimes a 10-15 minute wait. ♦ American ♦ M-Th 5:30-10:30PM; F 5:30-11PM; Sa 9AM-3PM, 5:30-11PM; Su 9AM-3PM. 315 Shawmut Ave (Union Park) 426.0862

26 Union Park Square (1851-1860) The first square to be finished in the South End remains one of its most special places. The elliptical park enclosed by an iron fence is lush and shady, with fountains and flowers. It's bordered by big brick townhouses dating from the neighborhood's brief shining moments before Back Bay became *the* place to lay one's welcome mat. The handsome houses and perfect park commune harmoniously in their own little world. Regrettably, gauche modern hands have tacked on unsightly extra stories here and there, marring an otherwise splendid composition. ♦ Tremont St-Shawmut Ave

27 Medieval Manor What to say about this inexplicably popular and long-running themed theater/restaurant? Well, simply this: an evening here involves a 3-hour, gargantuan eat-with-your-fingers fixed-price feast of sorts, and bawdy musical comedy starring singing wenches, oafs, strolling minstrels, and a sexist Lord of the Manor. More than enough said. The whole thing's participatory, which means you can get into the action if you so choose—joined by many others from the typically vocal audience. Students pack the place. Believe it or not, vegetarians can join the orgy too, with 48 hours' advance notice. Parties of 4-8 recommended, and no party of more than 12 is accepted if all male, all female, or all Harvard. There are more numbers-related rules; call to inquire. The best—possibly only —way to get here is by car: take the Southeast Expressway south to Albany St exit; turn right onto E. Berkeley St. ♦ Admission. Call for show times. No jeans or T-shirts. Reservations required. 246 E. Berkeley St (Albany St) 423.4900

28 Ars Libri Out of the way and hidden on the 3rd floor in a nondescript converted factory now occupied by architects, designers, and dancers, Ars Libri is renowned nationally and internationally for the country's largest comprehensive inventory of rare and out-of-print books and periodicals about the fine arts, including architecture and photography. Here's where one might encounter all of **Francisco da Goya**'s *Los Caprichos*; drawings by **Albrecht Dürer**; a complete set of *Pan*, the stunning journal of the German *Jugendstil*; an extremely rare edition of *La Prose du Transsibérien*, an extended poem illustrated by **Sonia Delaunay**, or any number of other cherishable works. The owners buy and sell out-of-print and rare scholarly works, exhibition catalogs, print portfolios, and books with original graphics dating

from the 16th century onward. The shop is quiet, since most business is conducted via subject-oriented catalogs sent to universities, libraries, museums, and individuals. **Machado Silvetti** designed this collector's sanctuary. ♦ M-F 9AM-6PM; Sa 11AM-5PM. 560 Harrison Ave (Waltham St) No credit cards. 357.5212 ♿ (by arrangement)

The South End's changeable nature means that many shops and restaurants come and go, and those that stay often keep ad hoc hours. The best approach is to call ahead when possible, be prepared for occasional disappointment, and be alert to interesting new finds.

Adding to Boston's perpetual names confusion, this is actually the *New* South End, since the original South End was located in what is now the **Financial District/Downtown** area.

Restaurants/Clubs: Red	Hotels: Blue
Shops/Parks: Green	Sights/Culture: Black

Architectural Elements of a Typical Boston Townhouse

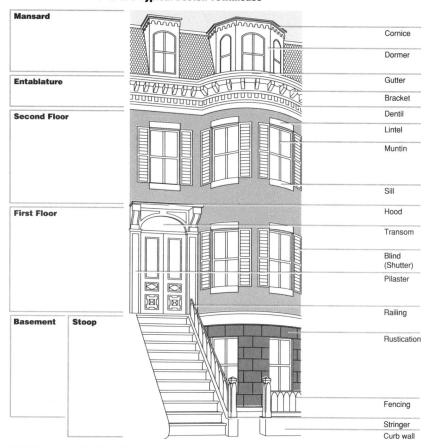

Mansard

Entablature

Second Floor

First Floor

Basement | Stoop

Cornice

Dormer

Gutter

Bracket

Dentil

Lintel

Muntin

Sill

Hood

Transom

Blind (Shutter)

Pilaster

Railing

Rustication

Fencing

Stringer

Curb wall

29 Cathedral of the Holy Cross (1867-1875, **Patrick C. Keeley**) An unexpected sight along

South End

a sadly rundown stretch of Washington St is this heroic Gothic Revival elephant, designed by the architect of **St. Patrick's Cathedral** in New York City. New England's largest church, and the largest Catholic church in the country when it was built, the cathedral recalls an era when Irish Roman Catholic immigrants were a dominant presence in the South End. (The needs of this burgeoning population had already resulted in a prior Keeley-designed church, the imposing white granite **Church of the Immaculate Conception** [1861] at 761 Harrison Ave at Concord St, an unusual design worth a look.) The Roxbury puddingstone cathedral accommodates 3500. It's still the principal church of the **Archdiocese of Boston**, but is now used mainly for special occasions, such as when the **Pope** came to call in 1979. The front vestibule's arch contains bricks rescued from a Somerville convent burned during anti-Catholic rioting in 1834. As is true of so many Boston ecclesiastical edifices, the intention was to surmount the 2 towers with spires, but that never happened.
♦ Washington St (Union Park St)

30 Blackstone and Franklin Squares Divided by Washington St, both squares were built in the 1860s, but originated in an 1801 plan to which **Charles Bulfinch**, then chairman of Boston's Board of Selectmen, was a major contributor. Although they have lost a lot to time, the squares' original grandeur remains palpable. Look for the brownstone houses overlooking Blackstone Sq on **W. Newton St**, once exemplars of architectural elegance, and project yourself into the neighborhood's genteel past. At **11 E. Newton St** (St. James-Washington Sts) stands the **Franklin Square House** apartments for the elderly. Built as the **St. James Hotel** in 1868, the lumbering French Second Empire building was considered the South End's poshest hotel, even equipped with 2 steam-powered elevators. At the height of the hotel's brief eminence, **President Ulysses S. Grant** stayed there. ♦ Washington St (Blackstone Sq at W. Newton St; Franklin Sq at E. Newton St)

Busing in Boston

On 21 June 1974, **US District Judge W. Arthur Garrity, Jr.**, ordered the immediate integration of the oldest school system in the country after finding that Boston had been maintaining separate and unequal systems, relegating black students to inferior schools.

The controversial **Boston School Committee** and city officials wouldn't act to redress the illegal segregation, so the federal court intervened. According to racial quotas established by Garrity, students were assigned to schools and bused across the city.

Thus began one of the most painful periods in Boston's history, the city that was a focal point of the Abolitionist movement and proudly proclaimed itself the *Cradle of Liberty*, the *Athens of America*. But Boston is a city of close-knit neighborhoods, the boundaries of which often demarcate strong racial and ethnic divisions. The nation watched while the notorious crisis played out in the media. **J. Anthony Lukas's Pulitzer Prize** winning bestseller *Common Ground* (1985) chronicles the busing saga through the eyes of 3 very different Boston families—the **Twymons**, the **Divers**, and the **McGoffs** —as they endured the tumultuous, angry days following Garrity's decision. A dense, riveting account of that era, *Common Ground* was shoehorned into a 4-hour TV miniseries that aired nationally in 1990.

Nearly 2 decades after Garrity's order, almost half of the city's approximately 60,000 students are bused. Reactions among busing supporters and detractors still run strong. Opinions vary on the results of the court's remedy: detractors claim it simply condemned all students to a mediocre education; supporters claim there was no other alternative, and that however traumatic busing was, it paved the way for more minority and parent participation in shaping the school system, and for the appointment of the first black school superintendent in Boston's history. Busing's impact still reverberates throughout the school system.

Bests

Cynthia Hadzi, Exhibitions Coordinator
Dimitri Hadzi, Professor Emeritus
Carpenter Center for the Visual Arts, Harvard University

Art things:

Galleries on **Newbury Street**, and Boston's version (tiny) of SoHo: **South Street**.

Art to be seen on the subways (**Arts on the Line** projects).

Sculpture collection on the **MIT** campus, Cambridge.

Check exhibitions at the **List Visual Arts Center, MIT**, and landscape around designed by *site specific* artists.

Carpenter Center for the Visual Arts at Harvard, only US building by **Le Corbusier**; exhibition program, and the **Harvard Film Archive** every evening.

The sculpture/fountain at **Copley Place**, Boston. The 60-foot-high stone work by **Dimitri Hadzi** is a central meeting point—a boon for photographers, and wedding groups!

Bookstores:

Brattle Book Store—best in Boston.

Goodspeed's near the State House—quite unique.

Harvard Book Store Cafe on Newbury Street—good bookstore, good café, nice location.

Architecture:

The **MIT** campus—architectural masters.

Harvard (**Richardson** buildings—**Emerson Hall, Sever Hall; Corbu's Carpenter Center; Gwathmey's**

addition to the **Fogg** coming next year; **Stirling's Sackler Museum**).

Special things in Cambridge:

Brattle Street houses (always admired by European visitors).

Walking around **Mount Auburn Cemetery**, especially in spring—beautifully, naturally landscaped.

Fogg Art Museum—wonderful collection; also the **Sackler Museum** (great for Asian and Classical art); **Peabody Museum**—of course, the glass flowers, but *everything* else is also extraordinary: American Indian, South American cultures, etc.

The **Charles River**, good for walking if you can avoid joggers; on Sundays in summer, part of Memorial Drive is closed to traffic, so great for walkers, bicycles, etc.

Other ideas about Boston:

Looking at the elegant restored houses in the **South End**; restaurants that are special in that area: **Hamersley's Bistro; St. Cloud**.

The whole **Charlestown** area—smart renovations, the waterfront, new restaurants everywhere.

The **Gardner Museum** (of course), for concerts on Sunday afternoon, café.

The magnolia trees on **Marlborough Street** in the spring.

The **Arnold Arboretum** anytime.

Filene's Basement (obviously).

Restaurants (a quick list):

In Cambridge:

Dolphin Seafood on Mass Ave; marvelous fresh fish, simple place, cheap, popular.

Roka, a couple blocks from the Dolphin —terrific Japanese in fancy Euro-Japanese decor.

Casa Portugal—on Cambridge Street near Inman Square, simple Portuguese bistro run by small family;

South End

cheap and delicious, and authentically European.

Café China, also near Inman Square (Chinese/French).

East Coast Grill, in same area, very popular, yuppy, and noisy, but good food; the takeout operation next door is sometimes better (and quieter).

Green Street Grill behind Cambridge Post Office near Central Square—delicious, Caribbean-style bistro.

Excellent Chinese in Cambridge at **Changsho**, on Mass Ave between Harvard and Porter squares— large and elegantly architect-designed.

In Boston:

Ristorante Toscano on Charles Street.

Biba at the Heritage on the Garden—very trendy but good; chef **Lydia Shire**.

Brunch at **St. Cloud** in the South End.

Wonderful **Hamersley's Bistro**.

Bnu in the Transportation Building.

Espresso at the **Caffé Paradiso** in the North End Italian district, which is interesting to walk around in, but offers no good Italian restaurant!

The **Northeastern University Boathouse** is a new, deep-orange shingled structure that pays architectural homage to the river's older boathouses, especially Harvard's 2 from the turn of the century. Designed by **Graham Gund Associates**, the building has playful touches, such as oar-shaped balusters.

Radcliffe College

On Sundays during daylight-saving time, **Memorial Drive** on the **Cambridge** side of the river is closed to traffic from **Western Avenue Bridge** to **Eliot Bridge**, creating what is called **Riverbend Park**.

Fogg Museum

• On the **Cambridge** side of the river near **Harvard University** it's only a few minutes' stroll up JFK St to Harvard Sq's restaurants and shops.

• **Harvard**'s picturesque **Weld Boathouse** was built in 1909, designed by **Peabody and Strearns.**

• **John W. Weeks Bridge** is a graceful footbridge and the best place to watch the *Head-of-the-Charles Regatta.*

Eliot Bridge

1

Memorial Dr.

JFK St.

Harvard University

Anderson Bridge

Weeks Bridge

Harvard Stadium

Harvard University

• A special act of Congress was passed in 1911 to close the Charles River to navigation so that the **Anderson Bridge** could be built without a drawbridge. *To a father by a son,* a tablet reads; **Larz Anderson**, US ambassador to Belgium, gave the bridge in memory of his father, **Nicholas Longworth Anderson**, also a Harvard graduate. Oddly, the bridge is usually referred to locally by the son's name, not the father's.

Western Ave.

Hoyt Field

Western Ave. Bridge

Soldiers Field Rd.

River St.

River St. Bridge

2

3

• **Harvard University**'s first permanent boathouse, **Newell Boathouse**, dates from 1900 and was designed by **Peabody and Stearns**. It's a familiar sight, with red-slate walls and delicate finials. The boathouse is dedicated to varsity teams, who often train for the **US Olympic** team or England's famed *Henley Royal Regatta.* Harvard's famous passion for rowing began with the founding of the country's first boat club there in the 1840s. The oldest intercollegiate crew meet in the country is the annual **Harvard-Yale** competition, first held in 1854.

Cambridge St.

Above **Watertown**, about 8 miles upstream from the Harvard Bridge, the river is rated Class B (okay for swimming and fishing). But below Watertown, the basin is NOT swimmable.

■ *Bath House*

Magazine Beach

Boston Univ. Bridge

The **Boston Manufacturing Company**, formed in 1814 and led by blue-blood entrepreneurs **Francis Cabot Lowell, Nathan Appleton**, and **Patrick Tracy Jackson**, improved upon an existing **Waltham** dam, now known as the **Moody Street Dam**, and opened a mill alongside. The new textile mill was the first in America using water-powered looms to turn out cotton cloth and thread with unprecedented efficiency, and to include spinning and weaving in the same plant. The Waltham venture was a whopping success. Adjacent to part of the original company building is the **Charles River Museum of Industry**, Th-Su 10AM-5PM, 154 Moody St, 893.5410, with fascinating displays on the important manufacturing systems that helped industrialize America. Highlighted are machines and equipment developed or used by manufacturers along the Charles since the 1800s, including a paperbag-making machine, timepieces, steam-powered fire engine, and more.

On the Boston side of the river, the subway stop handiest to the **Esplanade** is the **Charles** stop (**Red Line**). But within easy walking distance (only 5-6 blocks) are the **Arlington, Copley, Hynes Convention Center/ICA** stops (all **Green Line**); and **Back Bay/South End** stop (**Orange Line**). On the Cambridge side, the **Harvard Sq, Kendall Sq** (both Red Line), and **Science Park** (**Green Line**) stops are nearest the river.

N

km
mi

1/8   1/4   1/4   1/2

Charles River Basin

The Charles River Basin and its **Esplanade** laced with paths, playgrounds, lagoons, and lawns together form a lovely urban water park, the most spectacular section of the **Charles River Reservation**. Of all Boston places, the waterway is the most visually striking, with the Boston skyline on one side and Cambridge opposite. In this majestic, romantic setting, Bostonians congregate for promenades and rendezvous, outdoor concerts, picnics, jogging, bicycling, games, sailing, sculling, canoeing, and feeding the hungry ducks made famous in **Robert McCloskey**'s 1941 children's story *Make Way for Ducklings*. In fall and winter, the riverside is still and contemplative, and the Cambridge shoreline seems far away. But in spring and summer, the 2-mile-long Esplanade brims with activity from **Beacon Hill** to **Boston University**, and the river sparkles with white sails and ripples with sleek shells. As the days heat up, free evening concerts and dance performances draw crowds; the *pièce de résistance* is the traditional 4th of July **Boston Pops** concert, which attracts hundreds of thousands—a river of people that overflows the Charles' banks and bridges.

The lazy brown-green Charles casually zigs and zags, coiling left and right, even appearing at times to change its mind and turn back, before traversing an 80-mile course from **Hopkinton** to **Boston Harbor**—a distance less than 30 miles as the crow flies. In

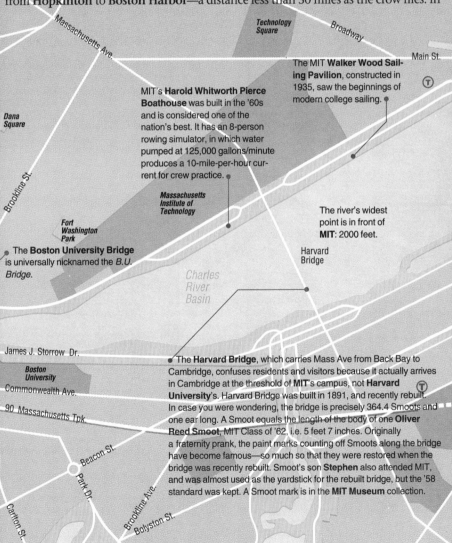

The MIT **Walker Wood Sailing Pavilion**, constructed in 1935, saw the beginnings of modern college sailing.

MIT's **Harold Whitworth Pierce Boathouse** was built in the '60s and is considered one of the nation's best. It has an 8-person rowing simulator, in which water pumped at 125,000 gallons/minute produces a 10-mile-per-hour current for crew practice.

The river's widest point is in front of **MIT**: 2000 feet.

The **Boston University Bridge** is universally nicknamed the *B.U. Bridge*.

The **Harvard Bridge**, which carries Mass Ave from Back Bay to Cambridge, confuses residents and visitors because it actually arrives in Cambridge at the threshold of **MIT**'s campus, not **Harvard University**'s. Harvard Bridge was built in 1891, and recently rebuilt. In case you were wondering, the bridge is precisely 364.4 Smoots and one ear long. A Smoot equals the length of the body of one **Oliver Reed Smoot**, MIT Class of '62, i.e. 5 feet 7 inches. Originally a fraternity prank, the paint marks counting off Smoots along the bridge have become famous—so much so that they were restored when the bridge was recently rebuilt. Smoot's son **Stephen** also attended MIT, and was almost used as the yardstick for the rebuilt bridge, but the '58 standard was kept. A Smoot mark is in the **MIT Museum** collection.

A new **Charles River Dam** was built 1974-1978, downstream from the old, and is one of the country's most powerful. The old dam remains permanently open. The new dam's 3 locks don't open for boats only; when enough migratory fish show up, they're given right of passage too. Many Charles River dams have special fishways installed.

The first ferry on the Charles began operating between the Boston and Charlestown peninsulas in 1631.

Luna and *Venus* are a pair of retired old tugboats that worked **Boston Harbor** for half a century. In 1936, *Luna* led an entourage of tugs that escorted the *Queen Mary* into New York Harbor on her maiden American voyage. **Hardie Gramatky's** classic tale *Little Toot* regales children with *Luna's* adventures.

Charlestown Bridge

93

Nashua St.

3

93 3/1

Charles River Dam

5

6
Science Park

The 1906 **Longfellow Bridge**, at first called the **Cambridge Bridge**, was renamed for poet **Henry Wadsworth Longfellow**. He often walked along its predecessor bridge, the **West Boston Bridge**, and wrote: *I stood on the bridge at midnight/As the clocks were striking the hour/And the moon rose o'er the city/Behind the dark church tower.* (The tower Longfellow refers to belongs to the **Charles Street Meeting House** on Beacon Hill.). The bridge is also nicknamed the *Salt and Pepper Bridge* for the shakerlike shape of its stone towers. The bridge bears the **Red Line** subway tracks, so commuters get great views of the river on both sides. Coming from Cambridge, the view is especially fine, with red-brick Beacon Hill rising up ahead.

Commercial Ave.

Northern Traffic Rte.

Charlesbank Playground

Mass. General Hospital

Main St.

Longfellow Bridge

Cambridge St.

African Meeting House

Embankment Rd.

Charles River Basin

Esplanade

Boston Common

Beacon St.

Public Garden

Charles St.

A particularly pretty spot along the **Esplanade** is **Storrow Lagoon**, enclosed by a slender outer island joined to the mainland by little stone bridges. The fingerlike island is a delightful detour, and children often sail model boats on the lagoon.

The **Union Boat Club** is America's oldest rowing club, founded in 1851; its boathouse was built at the turn of the century on Embankment Rd.

Built in 1940, using a German-patented concrete system, the **Hatch Shell** was designed by **Richard Shaw** and is one of Boston's great Art Deco pieces. To find out about free outdoor concerts at the shell during the summer, including the traditional **Boston Pops Esplanade Orchestra** series, check the weekly *Boston Globe Calendar*, published on Thursday.

The **Arthur Fiedler Memorial Footbridge** (1954), by **Shepley, Bulfinch, Richardson, and Abbott**, named for the famous Boston Pops conductor, is a sinuous pink structure of poured concrete connecting the Esplanade to Back Bay at Beacon St near Arlington St.

Huntington Ave.

Tremont St.

Shawmut Ave.

Washington St.

Harrison St.

When he was a musician with the **Boston Symphony Orchestra**, **Arthur Fiedler** instituted the first free outdoor concerts by BSO members for the public, and conducted **Esplanade Concerts** from 1929 until his death in 1979. Fiedler is fondly remembered in Boston as the illustrious conductor of the beloved **Boston Pops**; a highlight of his career was the 4th of July concert of '76, America's Bicentennial, complete with the traditional **Tchaikovsky's** *1812 Overture* featuring cannons and church bells. The annual 4th of July concert at the **Hatch Shell** continues to attract astounding numbers.

Columbus St.

general, the sluggish Charles is not an impressive river, shrinking to a mere stream in some places. But the Charles River Basin is the splendid lakelike section 9 miles long that progresses from **Watertown**, past **Harvard University** and the **Massachusetts Institute of Technology**, and on to the ocean. Here the Charles has been sculpted into a splendid urban waterway—in fact, a lot of the river is more manmade than natural.

The river got its name 15 years before the **Puritans** arrived, when explorer **Captain John Smith** sent early maps of New England home to **Charles Stuart**, aged 15 and future **King Charles I**, and asked him to give its prominent features good English names. From earliest days, the river was a vital economic asset. Throughout the 18th and 19th centuries, industries fueled by the Charles expanded from gristmills and sawmills to iron and paper products, leather, chocolate, spinning, and weaving. But intense industrialization polluted the river, and its estuary shrank from incessant landfilling. At low tide, the Charles in Boston was a malodorous eyesore bordering wealthy **Back Bay**, which is why that district appears to turn its back to the river.

In the early 1900s, a long crusade to make the lower Charles healthy and attractive gained momentum. Prominent Boston and Cambridge residents, including landscape architect **Charles Eliot** (colleague of **Frederick Law Olmsted** and founder of the **Trustees of Reservations**, a nonprofit conservation group) and philanthropists **Henry Lee Higginson** (founder of the **Boston Symphony Orchestra**) and **James J. Storrow** led the drive to build the **Charles River Dam** in 1908. This created the freshwater Charles River Basin, with an embankment popular for promenading extending from **Charlesgate West**, where the **Back Bay Fens** meets the river, to the old **West End**. In the early '30s, **Arthur A. Shurcliff**, landscape architect of **Colonial Williamsburg**, greatly embellished the embankment, designing the picturesque Esplanade and its lagoons with funding provided by Storrow's widow, **Helen Osborn Storrow**. In 1951, Boston's **Museum of Science** took up residence astride the Charles River Dam on the Boston-Cambridge boundary. In the early '50s, **Storrow Drive**, the frenetic autoway, was built on the original embankment and, ironically, named for **James J. Storrow**, the avid supporter of the park it shouldered aside. (Storrow Drive's counterpart, on the Cambridge side of the river, is **Memorial Drive**.)

1 Sports Museum of New England A diehard sporting town like Boston is the perfect place for this museum, which will eventually be moving from its riverside home to larger facilities because it's overflowing with photos, memorabilia, and artifacts of pro, college, and amateur sports. Life-size statues of **Larry Bird** and **Bobby Orr** in uniform are popular exhibits. Visitors can also select and watch not-so-great moments in sports annals on video. There's also a library room. Former **Celtics** star **Dave Cowens** is chairman of the museum board. Special requests for group tours accommodated. ♦ Admission; discounts for elders, children; children under 5 free. W-Su 11AM-5PM. 1175 Soldiers Field Rd (across from the WBZ station) Free parking. 787.7678 ♿

1 The Publick Theatre Boston's oldest resident professional theater company has been staging performances under the stars for more than 20 years, in cooperation with the **Metropolitan District Commission** (MDC). The company has put on classical plays and musicals, including **Shakespeare, Gilbert & Sullivan**, and *Man of La Mancha*—new shows, too. Very popular locally, the company's season runs late May-early September, with subscriptions available. Performances held weather permitting. You can write to the company for tickets at 52

Charles River Basin

Joy St, Boston 02114. Special discounts for families. Purchase tickets at the on-site outdoor box office after 7PM on performance nights, or charge by phone; tickets also available at **Bostix** and **Out of Town Ticket Agency**. ♦ Seats 200. Shows W-Su 8PM. Christian A. Herter Park, Soldiers Field Rd (across from the WBZ station) Free parking and picnic facilities. 720.1007; TDD 720.2789 ♿

2 Guest Quarters Suite Hotel Boston/Cambridge $$$ The site is inauspicious, right by the Mass Pike Cambridge/Allston exit, but the 310 accommodations on 15 floors are all 2-room suites, most with good views—request one facing the river. Each suite has 2 TVs, a wet bar and fridge, a fold-out sofabed in the living room, and a king-size bed in the bedroom. Some bi-level suites are available on upper floors. Guest Quarters provides complimentary van service to downtown Boston and Cambridge, an indoor pool, sauna, whirlpool, exercise room, and reasonably priced on-premises parking. Handicapped-accessible and non-smokers' suites too. For a fee, buffet breakfast is offered in **Scullers Grille**. Ask about the hotel's numerous special rates. ♦ 400 Soldiers Field Rd, Brighton (River St Bridge) 783.0090, 800/424.2900; fax 783.0897 ♿

Within Guest Quarters:

Scullers Jazz Club/Scullers Grille $$ A new and welcome addition to local nightlife is Scullers Jazz Club, a comfortable listening room that books local and national jazz and cabaret acts, with emphasis on vocalists. Only those 21 and older admitted; the crowd generally ranges from 28-45. Full bar and light fare like pâté and smoked salmon served. Meanwhile, at Scullers Grille, they're preparing great bouillabaisse and other seafood specialties for the dinner crowd. Dine with a river view. ♦ Seafood ♦ Club: Tu-W 8-11:30PM; shows Th-Sa 8, 10PM. Grille: Daily 5-10PM. 2nd fl. Low-priced on-premises parking. No jeans allowed and jackets required in both. Reservations recommended Th-Sa. 783.0811 ♿

3 Howard Johnson Cambridge $$ A modern high-rise in which most of the newly renovated rooms, 205 in all, have lovely views—ask to overlook the river, although the Cambridge skyline is nice too. This *HoJos* has an indoor pool, free parking, the **Bisuteki Japanese Steakhouse** and 2 other restaurants, and it's just a 10-15 minute walk to **Harvard Sq**. Nonsmokers' rooms available, and pets allowed. ♦ 777 Memorial Dr, Cambridge (River St-B.U. Bridges) 492.7777, 800/654.200; request fax at 492.7777

Charles River Basin

4 Hyatt Regency Cambridge $$$ A glitzy, glassy ziggurat-shaped structure, nicknamed the *Pyramid on the Charles*, the hotel has 469 rooms, some with outdoor terraces overlooking the river and Boston. The atrium rises 14 stories, with balconies, trees, fountains, even glass-cage elevators. The skylit health spa has an indoor pool, sauna, whirlpool, exercise room, and a sundeck overlooking the pool, plus retractable ceiling and walls. There's also an outdoor basketball court and playground. The hotel has adult's and children's bicycles for rent, so you can set off on a leisurely riverside journey. The Hyatt offers handicapped-acces-

sible and nonsmokers' rooms; valet and self-parking on premises; a special rate for a 2nd room when traveling with children; a special children's package; and a free shuttle van traveling to **Harvard** and **Kendall** squares, **Faneuil Hall Marketplace, Copley Sq**, and other locations. The hotel is popular with families and locals seeking a little weekend luxury, and the ubiquitous business and convention crowds. The Hyatt's 3 restaurants include one with a pleasant outdoor terrace facing the river. ♦ 575 Memorial Dr, Cambridge (Harvard-B.U. Bridges) 492.1234, 800/233.1234; fax 491.6906. ♿

Within the Hyatt:

Spinnaker Italia ★$$ Boston's one and only revolving rooftop lounge and restaurant lets you gaze upon the city's twinkling night skyline, stretching from the **Financial District** and **Beacon Hill** to **Back Bay** and the **Prudential Center**. The room spins like a lazy Lazy Susan. Spinnaker recently revamped its cuisine; while not as spectacular as the views, the Italian fare includes tasty pastas, gourmet pizzas, and entrees like *pollo arrosto*. From 9:30PM-closing daily, the restaurant serves cocktails and light food. ♦ Italian ♦ M-F 11:45AM-2:30PM, 6-9:30PM; Sa 6-9:30PM; Su 10AM-2PM, 6-9:30PM. On-premises parking is free for 2 hrs. No jeans, sneakers, T-shirts. Reservations recommended. 492.1234 ♿

Sally Ling's ★★$$$ For an excellent, extravagant gourmet Chinese dinner and a gorgeous view, there is only one choice in the Boston area. Fortunately, Sally Ling's prepares excellent and unusual Cantonese, Mandarin, and Szechuan specialties such as peony-blossom beef, minced chicken in lettuce with pine nuts, or lobster sautéed with ginger and scallions, a novel reprise of the perennial favorite. But for those who prefer authentic Chinese cooking without all the hoopla, Boston's **Chinatown** waits across the river, seemingly in another galaxy. ♦ Chinese ♦ M-F noon-2PM, 6-10PM; Sa-Su 6-10PM. 14th fl. On-premises parking is free for 2 hrs. Jacket required. Reservations required. ♿ Also at: 256 Commercial St, North End. 720.1188

5 Royal Sonesta Hotel Boston/Cambridge $$$ Ask for a room facing the river and look across at the gold dome of the **State House** gleaming above **Beacon Hill**. The hotel has 400 contemporary-furnished rooms on 9 floors, including nonsmokers' and handicapped-accessible rooms. It's near the **Museum of Science** and the new **Cambridgeside Galleria** featuring the locally famous **Lechmere** department store, **Filene's, Sears**, and a host of other stores and boutiques. From early June until

Each June, tens of thousands assemble along the banks of the Charles for the multicultural **Cambridge River Festival**, which features a colorful parade, singing, dancing, storytelling, face-painting, visual arts installations, vendors of exotic ethnic foods and crafts.

Restaurants/Clubs: Red   **Hotels**: Blue
Shops/Parks: Green   **Sights/Culture**: Black

mid September, the Sonesta operates a pontoon boat (capacity 15) for a narrated river tour, free to guests. The hotel also provides guests with free ice cream, bicycles, and cameras during the summer. Hotel recreational facilities include an indoor pool under a retractable roof. A courtesy van provides transportation to **Harvard** and **Kendall** squares and Boston. The hotel displays an excellent modern art collection with pieces by **Frank Stella, Andy Warhol, Robert Rauschenberg.** ◆ 5 Cambridge Pkwy, Cambridge (Charles River Dam) 491.3600, 800/SONESTA; fax 661.5956

6 Museum of Science A familiar sight is the museum's funky '50s silhouette above the Charles. Streams of families and fleets of school and tour buses arrive all day long. If you're with kids, you can be sure they'll have a great time. If not, you'll wish the crowds would thin and the decibels lower, but you'll still squeeze past many interesting exhibits. In the beginning, the museum was the **Boston Society of Natural History**, founded in 1830, then the **New England Museum of Natural History**, residing in an imposing French Academic edifice in **Back Bay**. In 1951, the museum moved to modern quarters on this site straddling the **Charles River Dam** and changed its name to reflect the forward-looking attitude that has

made it so innovative. The **Exhibit Hall**'s 400-plus exhibits date from 1830 to this minute, covering astronomy, astrophysics, natural history, humans and medicine, computers, physical sciences, and much more. All-time favorites are the *Plexiglas Transparent Woman* with light-up organs, the chicken hatchery with its active eggs, the world's largest **Van de Graaff** generator spitting 15-foot lightning bolts, a space capsule replica, the 20-foot-high model of Tyrannosaurus Rex. Newer exhibits include the **Human Body Discovery Space**, where children (or adults) ride a bike while a bike-riding skeleton mimics. Walk on the moon or fly over Boston at the **Special Effects Stage**. See how an ocean wave is made. The museum has 3 cafeteria-style restaurants, but the one to try is the **Skyline Room Cafeteria** for its captivating views—perhaps Boston's best—of Boston on one side of the Charles, Cambridge on the other, and boats passing through the dam below and cruising upriver. Explore the **Museum Shop**, one of the best around, which has a fantastic inventory of science-related projects, gadgets, toys, jewelry, books, T-shirts. Under former director **Bradford Washburn**, a world-renowned explorer, mountaineer, and mapmaker, the pioneering museum embraced modern science and the changing nature of museums. It became a flexible participatory place, providing exceptional educational programs to families, schools, and communities. Special events include the **Inventor's Weekend Exhibition**, held annually on **Thomas Alva Edison**'s birthday in February, when students' inventions—such as an automatic baseball card stacker—are exhibited along with adults'.

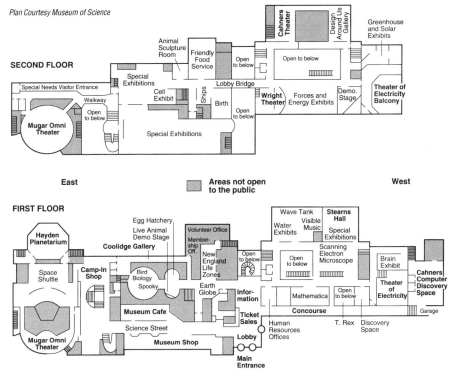

Plan Courtesy Museum of Science

SECOND FLOOR

Cahners Theater · Design Around Us Gallery · Greenhouse and Solar Exhibits · Animal Sculpture Room · Friendly Food Service · Open to below · Open to below · Special Needs Visitor Entrance · Special Exhibitions · Cell Exhibit · Lobby Bridge · Ships · Wright Theater · Forces and Energy Exhibits · Demo. Stage · Theater of Electricity Balcony · Walkway · Birth · Open to below · Mugar Omni Theater · Open to below · Special Exhibitions

East

Areas not open to the public

West

FIRST FLOOR

Wave Tank · Visible Music · Stearns Hall · Water Exhibits · Special Exhibitions · Egg Hatchery · Live Animal Demo Stage · Volunteer Office · Scanning Electron Microscope · Hayden Planetarium · Coolidge Gallery · Membership Off. · New England Life Zones · Open to below · Open to below · Brain Exhibit · Cahners Computer Discovery Space · Space Shuttle · Camp-In Shop · Bird Biology · Spooky · Earth Globe · Information · Mathematica · Open to below · Theater of Electricity · Museum Cafe · Ticket Sales · Concourse · Garage · Mugar Omni Theater · Science Street · Lobby · Human Resources Offices · T. Rex · Discovery Space · Museum Shop · Main Entrance

The museum is located near the **MBTA Science Park** stop on the Green Line. ♦ Admission; discounts for elders and children 4-14; children under 4 free 1-5PM Nov-Apr. (Separate admissions charged for **Charles Hayden Planetarium** and **Mugar Omni Theater**, with combination discount tickets available.) M-Th, Sa-Su 9AM-5PM, F 9AM-9PM, May-early Sep; Tu-Th, Sa-Su 9AM-5PM, F 9AM-9PM; free W 1-5PM, Nov-Apr. Closed Thanksgiving and Christmas. Science Park (Charles River Dam) Paid parking available. 723.2500, 523.6664; TDD 227.3235 &

Within the Museum of Science:

Charles Hayden Planetarium A 2-million-dollar Zeiss planetarium projector and state-of-the-art multiimage system create enthralling programs on what's happening in the heavens, such as the seasonal skies over Boston or phenomena like black holes and supernova. Special laser shows, too. Not recommended for children under 4. ♦ Admission; discounts for elders and children 4-14. Call for show times &

Mugar Omni Theater In New England's only OMNIMAX theater, a tilted dome 76 feet in diameter and 4 stories high wraps around you, and state-of-the-art film technology makes you feel surrounded by the images on the screen. The regularly changing films project viewers into locales like the Great Barrier Reef, China, inside the human body, outer space, or on a roller-coasterlike tour of Boston. Not recommended for children under 4. ♦ Admission; discounts for elders and children 4-14. Call in advance for show times; the shows are very popular &

The river's typical shade of murky green is not a sign of the pollutants present, but rather results from color seeping from vegetation in the wetlands as the river slowly winds past.

Recreation Along the Charles River

Since the late '70s, the Charles River has been steadily rebounding from severe abuse and pollution. The **Broadmoor Wildlife Sanctuary** of the **Massachusetts Audubon Society** is a 577-acre tract along the Charles in **Natick** and **Sherborn**, 280 Eliot St (Rt 16) S. Natick, 508/655.2296; here you can see the river environment in its most protected natural state. Travel by canoe to the wildlife sanctuary, where many say the waterway is its prettiest. The river's wetlands are home to wood ducks and mallards, great blue herons and great horned owls, wood warblers, ospreys, red-tailed hawks and white-tailed deer, red foxes, river otters, muskrats, minks, snapping turtles, and 30 or so fish species, including carp, northern pike, and large-mouth bass.

Sailing vessels bearing passengers and freight once plied the river, and later tugboats, tankers, and barges, but today recreational craft rule: canoes; sailboats; single and double shells,

Charles River Basin

fours and eights; and powerboats. The river is dotted with numerous boathouses and yacht clubs, many dating from the turn of the century.

Cape Cod Mercury, 15'   470, 17'

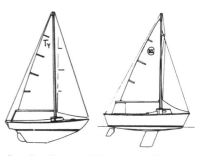

Cape Dory Typhoon, 18'   Barnegat, 20'

Sailboard, 12'   Laser, 13'

Sailing Community Boating is a nonprofit organization that offers sailing and instruction for all at the lowest possible prices. The program is cooperative, with experienced members teaching novices. Its fleet includes more than 100 sailboats, plus windsurfers. More than 40 years old, Community Boating is America's oldest and largest public sailing program. In addition to summer- and month-long memberships, a 7-day visitor membership is available, as are discounted programs for elders and youths. All kinds of special events and trips are planned. ♦ Located behind the Hatch Memorial Shell, 21 Embankment Rd (Charles St footbridge) 523.1038; TTY 523.7406 &

Canoeing/Rowing Over 60 of the Charles River's 80 miles can be canoed, although a few portages are required. The **Charles River Watershed Association**, a private nonprofit conservation group founded in 1965, publishes a **Charles River Canoe Guide** and the last Sunday in April sponsors popular races called **Run of the Charles**, with contestants furiously pad-

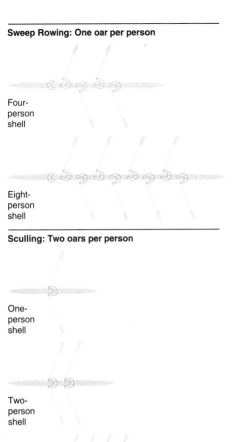

Sweep Rowing: One oar per person

Four-
person
shell

Eight-
person
shell

Sculling: Two oars per person

One-
person
shell

Two-
person
shell

Four-
person
shell

dling and portaging canoes around dams. For information, call 527.2799. You can rent canoes, kayaks, paddleboats, and rowing shells at the **Charles River Canoe and Kayak Center** at the **Metropolitan District Commission** (MDC) building at 2401 Comm Ave, Auburndale, 965.5110, on a spacious calm section of the river called the **Lakes District**. The center offers canoeing, kayaking, and rowing classes for all levels. Better still, begin your journey farther up the river and rent your vessel at **Tropicland Marine and Tackle**, 100 Bridge St, Dedham, 329.3777.

Rowing and the Charles have had a long romantic liaison. A single figure sculling gracefully over the river's surface is a common early-morning sight. So, too, are *eights*, crew boats with exhorting coxswains, which skim past then disappear beneath the next bridge. Four colleges, 2 prep schools, and 3 distinguished boat clubs maintain handsome boathouses on the river for their crew teams and scullers. The annual *Head-of-the Charles Regatta*, on the next to last Sunday in October, is the world's largest single-day regatta, the granddaddy of head-style racing in the US, and an amazing spectacle. More than 3000 male and female athletes from all over the world in almost 1000 boats represent 200-plus colleges, clubs, high schools, and other organizations, or just themselves. The course extends downstream of the **Boston University Bridge** to a half-mile above **Eliot Bridge**. This is not a head-to-head competition, but rather is computer-timed, with boats departing at 10- to 12-second intervals. For information on the Head-of-the-Charles, call 864.8415. For group or private rowing instruction, investigate **Community Rowing** at **MDC Daly Ice Rink**, Nonantum Rd, Newton, 868.4903. All rowers go out with coaches. Open to the public April-October, very reasonable fees charged on a monthly basis. Community Rowing organizes adaptive rowers' groups for all handicaps.

Bicycling Boston is not very hospitable to bicyclists, unfortunately. The safest and prettiest place to cycle in the city is along the **Charles River Embankment**, but don't try to reach racing speeds or you'll terrorize children, joggers, promenaders, and ducks. The most popular route is the **Dr. Paul Dudley White Charles River Bike Path** (a mouthful!), which covers 17.7 miles from the **Museum of Science** to **Watertown Sq**, then back along the **Cambridge** side of the river. For information on other trails, including those to **Provincetown** on **Cape Cod**, write or call the Department of Environmental Management, Division of Forests and Parks, Saltonstall Bldg, 100 Cambridge St, Boston 02202; M-F 9AM-5PM, 727.3180. Rent your wheels at **Community Bike Shop** in the South End, 490 Tremont St (E. Berkeley) 542.8623; or at **West End Bicycle Cellar**, 303 Cambridge St (Charles Circle—near MBTA Charles St stop), 227.4616. The **Boston Area Bicycle Coalition**, a Cambridge-based advocacy group for Greater Boston bikeriders, offers information on trails, rules of the road, rental and repair, etc, 491.RIDE. Both the **American Youth Hostel**

Charles River Basin

(AYH) 730.8AYH (recorded trip information), and the **Appalachian Mountain Club** on Beacon Hill, 5 Joy St, 523.0636, organize bicycling trips. Bikes aren't allowed on MBTA subways, must be boxed if transported on trains, and are allowed on most ferries; always ask.

Running and roller-skating Far and away the favorite places to run in Boston are the paths on both sides of the Charles. Roller-skating and skateboarding are popular here too; skates and boards can be rented from **Beacon Hill Skate**, 135 Charles St So, Theater District, 482.7400.

In the early 1900s, **canoeing** on the Charles was all the rage. In 1903, the metropolitan park police posted strict rules for canoeists—couples were forbidden to recline side by side in a canoe, and one couple was arrested for kissing—a story made much of in local papers at the time.

Cambridge

Across the **Charles River** from Boston is its intellectual, self-assured neighbor, Cambridge. Boston too, is crowded with campuses, but Cambridge exudes true college-town ambiance—even though it's Massachusetts' 7th-largest city. Many identify Cambridge with **Harvard University**, nearly as old as the city itself; for some it's prestigious **Massachusetts Institute of Technology** (MIT), which moved to Cambridge in 1916. The 2 giant institutions account for more than 26,000 students, hailing from nearly 100 nations. Harvard alone is the alma mater of 6 US presidents. Since WWII, Harvard and MIT, with government and industry support, have made Cambridge a world-renowned research center leading in the development of modern technologies, first focusing on military and aerospace industries, and later on fields such as artificial intelligence and genetic engineering. These partnerships have spurred the growth of related industries in Cambridge and beyond, creating Massachusetts' high-tech economy.

In 1630, **Newtowne** village was founded by the **Massachusetts Bay Colony**, led by **Governor John Winthrop**, as its fortified capital on the Charles River. The government seat budged from the Boston side of the river for only a few years before returning; the settlement took root regardless. In 1638, Newtowne was nostalgically renamed Cambridge, after the English university where many Puritans had been educated. That same year, the nation's first college, founded here 2 years earlier by the colony's Great and General Court, was named **Harvard College** to memorialize **John Harvard**, a young **Charlestown** minister who bequeathed his 400-volume library and half his estate to the fledgling school. And in 1639 the New World's first printing press was established in Cambridge, publishing the first American document, *Oath of a Free Man*. Nowhere else in the colony was permitted a press until 1674, so Cambridge became the earliest publishing center of the hemisphere, ensuring enduring prominence as a place of ideas.

The engine of academia drives the 6.25-square-mile city of 93,000 or so *Cantabrigians* (the name for a resident of Cambridge), half of whom are affiliated in some way with

the local universities. But that's by no means the whole story. Cambridge has traditionally been a place for progressive politics and lawmaking, where generations of residents have embraced issues such as antislavery, women's rights, the antinuclear movement and environmentalism, opposition to the Vietnam War and US foreign policy in Central America, and many other concerns. Others dismiss Cambridge as an uppity enclave of eggheads and bleeding-hearts, so strong is its reputation as a bastion of liberalism. But it's known for cultural diversity as well; it's full of people from somewhere else. Its cafés, bookstores, shops, and restaurants reflect a multicultural persona, a mélange of Yankee gentry, blue-collar workers, conservatives, liberals, immigrant newcomers, and long-established ethnic groups, which have coexisted well and less well over the years. They live in **Brattle Street** mansions, crowded tripledeckers, chic condos, former factory workers' homes, subsidized housing.

In 1846, the town officially became a city: **Old Cambridge** joined with the industrial riverside communities of **East Cambridge** and **Cambridgeport**. Today the city consists of distinctive neighborhoods in addition to famous **Harvard Square**, loosely defined as **Kendall Square, East Cambridge, Inman Square, Central Square, Cambridgeport, Riverside, Mid-Cambridge, North Cambridge, West Cambridge**. Even residents only know where 2 or 3 of these begin and end. **Mass Ave** runs the length of Cambridge, leading from the **Harvard Bridge** on the Charles through MIT's campus to Harvard Sq and northward. Travel by the **Red Line** subway to Cambridge's main attractions is fast and easy. (Street-parking is impossibly difficult, even worse than in Boston.)

It would take months to fully comb Cambridge, so most visitors head directly to Harvard Sq, *the Square*, the city's centerpiece and the heart of Old Cambridge, now losing its interesting layers to overdevelopment. But you can still sit in cafés and browse in bookstores, pretending to read while overhearing amazing conversations among an extraordinarily eclectic group. On a warm afternoon, watch all of Cambridge stroll by the **au bon pain** outdoor café. In summer, the Square's nighttime street life is constant, especially near **Brattle Square** (a tiny square-within-the Square) where outdoor entertainers hold forth every few yards. The Square boasts a galaxy of bookstores, catering to every interest, many open very late. Commercial landmarks are the **Harvard Coop, Out of Town News**, the **Tasty, WordsWorth, Elsie's Famous Sandwiches**, a travel agency advertising *Please Go Away Often*, genteel shops purveying the traditional Harvard look, or others selling the Harvard insignia plastered on anything and everything. Studenty cheap-eats abound; so do gourmet food shops, vintage and avant-garde clothing boutiques, housewares and furnishings stores. Experience the overwhelming aura of **Harvard Yard**, then walk up Brattle St, formerly **Tory Row**, and visit lovely **Radcliffe Yard.** You'll see plenty of historic edifices and some interesting modern architecture. The Square offers good theater, movies, and music in a variety of settings, plus Harvard's great museums. Along with MIT and other local colleges and institutions, Harvard hosts a long menu of lectures, exhibitions, symposia, and cultural and sports events throughout the academic year.

Take the MBTA **Red Line** to Cambridge: the **Kendall Square** station is nearest MIT and near **East Cambridge** (The **Lechmere** station on the **Green Line** is even more convenient to East Cambridge.) The **Central Square** station is in the heart of Central Sq and convenient to Inman Sq; the **Harvard Square** station is in the heart of Harvard Sq and convenient to parts of **North Cambridge** the **Porter Square** station is nearest to North Cambridge.

1 Harvard Square Not really a square at all; it's officially located where Mass Ave heading from Boston turns and widens into a big triangle, on which the landmark **Out of Town News** and MBTA Red Line station are located. On one side of this triangle are **Harvard Yard** and university buildings; on the other 2 lie commerce.

But to students and Cantabrigians, *the Square* always refers to the much larger area radiating from this central point, with most shops, restaurants, clubs, services, etc., concentrated on Brattle, JFK, and Mt Auburn streets, as well as lots of little sidestreets like Church, Plympton, Dunster, and that whimsical pair, Bow and Arrow streets. All around the Square, sidewalks are ever-crowded with students, professors, canvassers, protestors, businesspeople, entertainers—in fact, you can assume you're heading beyond the Harvard Sq area when the foot traffic starts to dwindle.

1 Cambridge Discovery Information Kiosk Located near the MBTA station entrance (main entrance opposite the **Harvard Cooperative Society**) is an information kiosk where you can

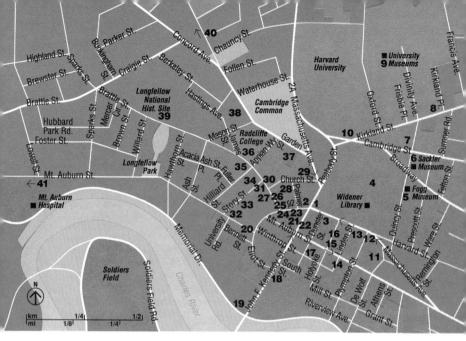

get bus and train schedules, maps, brochures, and a wealth of information on Cambridge, its universities, and attractions, including great self-guided walking tours to *Revolutionary Cambridge*, *East Cambridge*, and more. They sell a variety of guidebooks too, highlighting architecture, restaurants, history, Harvard University, the Square, etc. Some materials are free and some are sold for modest fees to pay the overhead of the nonprofit **Cambridge Discovery** organization, which operates and staffs the kiosk. Cambridge Discovery provides information on the city to both tourists and residents, offering guided group tours for a fee (from late June-Labor Day; inquire at booth for tour times), information packages, a news-letter, and school outreach programs. Many of the volunteers speak other languages and are ready for your questions. They have infor-mation on local lodging too. You can write Cambridge Discovery at P.O. Box 1987, Cam-bridge MA, 02238. ◆ M-Sa 9AM-6PM, Su

Cambridge

1-6PM, late June-Labor Day; M-Sa 9AM-5PM, Su 1-5PM, Labor Day-late June. 0 Harvard Sq (Mass Ave) 497.1630, administration office 497.1631 ⓖ

1 Out of Town Newspapers (National Historic Landmark) Busy from opening to closing, the newsstand—universally called *Out of Town News*—sells newspapers from every major American city and many large cities worldwide, plus a huge array of magazines. Maps, comic books, and Harvard T-shirts, too. Many a ren-dezvous is kept at the familiar ornate kiosk. If your craving for newspapers and mags isn't sated here, there's **Nini's Corner** across the way, next to the **Harvard Coop**. Nini's has lots of souvenirs and postcards, too.

Also nearby is **Dimitri Hadzi**'s 21-foot-tall sculpture *Omphalos*, Greek for *navel*, signifying the center of the universe. Generations of Harvard students and Cantabrigians have con-sidered the Square precisely that. ◆ M-Th, Su 6AM-11:30PM; F-Sa 6AM-midnight. 0 Harvard Sq (Mass Ave) No credit cards. 354.7777 ⓖ (rear entrance)

1 Out of Town Ticket Agency Down the main entry to the **Harvard Square MBTA Station**, look for the mezzanine-level window. Here you can purchase all kinds of tickets: sports events, popular concerts, plays, anything going on at **Boston Garden** from rock concerts to ice skating shows to **Bruins** and **Celtics** games, and special events. ◆ M-F 9AM-7PM. Harvard Sq MBTA Station, 0 Harvard Sq. Cash only. 492.1900; credit card service at ConcertCharg 497.1118

1 The Tasty $ A dozen stools, a counter where doughnuts recline on pedestals under plastic covers, a grill that keeps the place warm winter and summer—that's all there's room for in this closet-size sandwich shop, open since 1925. A remnant of old Harvard Sq before terminal trendiness set in, the Tasty serves round the clock. It's the only witness to the Square's brief hushed hours. ◆ 24 hrs. 2A JFK St (Brattle St) No credit cards. 354.9016

A statue of **Charles Sumner**, US senator and ardent abolitionist, is located between **Harvard Yard** and **Cambridge Common**. Sumner was severely beaten and left senseless by a Southern senator wielding a cane, and took more than 3 years to recover. **Anne Whitney** of Watertown first designed a statue of Sumner for an anonymous Boston competition in 1875. She won, but when the judges discovered the awardee was female, they gave the commission to a man instead. Finally, in 1903, when Whitney was 80 years old, this bronze version of her original work was unveiled.

3 Harvard University The first and foremost of the famed *Ivy League* schools was originally founded to train young men for the ministry. Harvard College moved from Puritanism to intellectual independence during the 18th and 19th centuries, and became a private institution in 1865. In the mid-19th century, the college became the undergraduate core of a burgeoning modern university, with satellite professional schools. Today Harvard University's 10 graduate schools are Arts and Sciences, Business Administration, Dental Health, Design, Divinity, Education, the John F. Kennedy School of Government, Law, Medical, Public Health. Harvard and its Cambridge surrounds are so entwined that it's hard to tell where town and gown begin and end. The university has some 400-odd buildings on 380 acres of land in the Cambridge/Boston area. Harvard's current endowment is $5 billion, give or take many millions, the largest of any university in the world. **Harvard Houses**, where students live after freshman year, dot the Square toward the river and include lovely Georgian-style brick residences with courtyards. Most memorable are the **River Houses**, best seen from the Charles.

The student-run **Harvard University Information Office** is located on the ground floor of **Holyoke Center**, plainly visible from the street. Maps, pamphlets, self-guided walking tours, and other materials (some free, some sold) on Harvard and area events can be picked up here. Events tickets are sold here, too. Get a free copy of the *Harvard University Gazette*, which lists events open to the public. Harvard students also offer free one-hour tours departing from the office

2 Harvard Cooperative Society Universally known as **The Coop**, pronounced like the chicken abode, the society was founded in 1882 by students angered at local coal merchants' price gouging. Their enterprise sold goods to faculty and students, and gradually blossomed into a full-fledged collegiate department store. The store is owned by its members: Harvard and MIT students, faculty, employees, and alumni. The Coop is best known for its 3 floors of books, including bestsellers, paperbacks, nonfiction, remainders, and textbooks; extensive record collection; New England's largest selection of posters; and anything and everything emblazoned with Harvard colors and *Veritas* seal. The clothing and footwear selection for men and women may not be the height of fashion, but there's a little of everything and frequent sales. The Coop sells housewares, sports equipment, radios and TVs, luggage, computers, typewriters, small electronics, cameras and accessories, lots of stationery products, and just about anything else a student or faculty member might hanker for, including snacks. Sidewalk sales are often set up in the rear alley, between the original Coop building and its annex. You can also find restrooms here, a Cambridge rarity. ♦ M-W, F-Sa 9:20AM-5:45PM; Th 9:20AM-8:30PM. 1400 Mass Ave (Brattle St) 492.1000 & Also at: MIT Coop, 3 Cambridge Ctr, Kendall Sq. 491.4230; Medical Center Coop, 333 Longwood Ave, Fenway. 731.5200; Downtown Coop, 1 Federal St. 536.1986

3 au bon pain $ The mass-produced croissants taste exactly that, but are okay if you're hungry. They also sell muffins, sandwiches, soups. The real reason to come here is to relax outside on the large terrace in nice weather and watch the incessant tide of humanity flow to and from the Square, day and night. Students of human nature won't find a better vantage point or more varied collection of people in Greater Boston. Singers, jugglers, musicians, promoters of causes often hold forth alongside the café. A local chess master regularly plays games against the clock for a small sum at one of the café's chess tables, attracting aficionados.

that give visitors a good general introduction to the university. ♦ Tours M-F 10AM, 2PM, Sa 2PM during academic year; M-Sa 10, 11:15AM, 2, 3:15PM, Su 1:30, 3PM during the summer. Holyoke Center, 1350 Mass Ave (Holyoke-Dunster Sts) 495.1573 &

In 1764, a predecessor to **Harvard Hall** burned down and the fire destroyed the college's 5000-volume library, then North America's largest. All of the book collection belonging to the college's benefactor **John Harvard** went up in smoke, except for a single volume borrowed by a student on the night of the fire. According to legend, the following day the student took the precious book to the president, who thanked the student profusely, accepted the book, then expelled the student for taking it without permission.

4 Harvard Yard (National Register of Historic Places) Always verdant and dappled with sun and shade, its great trees sentinels to the education of generations, Harvard Yard exudes an aura of privilege and prestige, the essence of the institution. But anyone is welcome to relax on its grassy lawns, although when late spring arrives the air becomes thick with lawn fertilizer and noisy with machinery as the university starts sprucing up for another commencement. Summer mornings are particularly tranquil here; early fall heralds the return of the students and faculty with their brisk, purposeful traffic to and from classes. Harvard's oldest buildings date from the early 18th century; its newest were built yesterday. From **Holyoke Center**, cross Mass Ave and enter the gate, within which stands the **Benjamin Wadsworth House**, an attractive yellow clapboard house, built in 1726, where Harvard presidents resided until 1849. It briefly served as **General George Washington**'s headquarters when he took command of the Continental Army in Cambridge in 1775. Walk through the yard (this western side is considered the *Old Yard*); to the left is Early Georgian **Massachusetts Hall**, the oldest university building of all and a National Historic Landmark, dating from 1718, where the president's offices are now. Patriot regiments were once housed here, and in several other buildings nearby. Opposite is **Harvard Hall** (1766); between the 2 halls is **Johnston Gate** (1889), the yard's main entrance, by **McKim, Mead & White**. Standing at attention by the gate is a bit of frippery, the tiny guardhouse

designed by **Graham Gund**. Next on the left is **Hollis Hall** (1763), where **John Quincy Adams, Ralph Waldo Emerson**, and **Henry David Thoreau** roomed. Beyond is **Holden Chapel** (1742; National Register of Historic Places), a High Georgian gem, complete with family coat of arms, once called *a solitary English daisy in a field of Yankee dandelions*, but tarnished through constant alterations. (The coat of arms originally faced Mass Ave, but was moved as the college's orientation turned from Mass Ave inward on the yard.) Next is **Stoughton Hall** (1804), designed by Harvard graduate **Charles Bulfinch**.

Opposite Johnston Gate on the right stands **University Hall**, on the National Register of Historic Places, designed by Bulfinch in 1815. It was this building that turned the yard into an academic enclave, instead of clusters of buildings facing outward. In front stands **Daniel Chester French**'s 1884 statue of **John Harvard** (French also sculpted **Abraham Lincoln** in the **Lincoln Memorial** in Washington DC). The statue is famous for the 3 lies set forth in its plaque stating *John Harvard, founder 1638*. It is the image of an 1880s Harvard student, not Harvard himself; Harvard was a benefactor, not a founder; and the college was founded in 1636. Nevertheless, the false John is nearly always surrounded by tourists and visitors. Although the light here is generally poor for photos, you'll probably have to swing wide of clusters of people posing. Every now and again, rival schools give the statue a decorative paint job.

Behind University Hall, in the *New Yard*, is **Memorial Church** (1931) with its soaring needle-sharp spire. By Harvard regulations, the church's wonderful **University Choir** only performs during religious services here. Installed in the church is a glorious organ, creation of the late **C.B. Fisk** of Gloucester and one of the greatest American instruments built according to Baroque principals. Many important international organists have vied to play on it. Looming opposite is massive **Widener Memorial Library**, across grassy **Tercentenary Theater**, where the university's commencements are held with every ruffle and flourish—even a Latin oration. As you head in that direction you'll pass Romanesque Revival **Sever Hall** on your left, designed by **H.H. Richardson** in 1878, a National Historic Landmark and one of his greatest buildings. Study its brilliantly animated and decorative brickwork. Alongside Widener are **Pusey Library**, located underground, where the university's archives and map and theater collections are stored, and **Houghton Library**, home to its rare books, portraits, and manuscripts, including the memorabilia and furnishings from **Emily Dickenson**'s Amherst home, and the single book remaining from John Harvard's library. Pusey often exhibits its selections from its theater collection on the 1st floor, and Houghton offers public displays of some of its treasures, with emphasis on fine book-making. Near **Lamont Library**, which is tucked in the corner, is a **Henry Moore** sculpture called *Four-Piece Reclining Figure*. ♦ Mass Ave-Quincy St

Harvard Historia

When Harvard University was young, well-heeled students who paid a higher tuition and gave the university a silver vessel were honored with the title *Fellow Commoners*. They sat at the dining hall's high table, where the ceremonial silver was placed, while poorer students were stuck *below the salt*, an appropriately medieval designation.

The original Harvard College was surrounded by cow yards; hence the name Harvard Yard.

Until 1693, Harvard College was the only college in this hemisphere.

Restaurants/Clubs: Red   Hotels: Blue
Shops/Parks: Green   **Sights/Culture:** Black

Harry Elkins Widener Memorial Library

(1913) A more triumphal and imposing entrance than Widener's would be hard to find, with its massive Corinthian colonnade and grand exterior staircase. Chilly-gray and austere, Widener is the patriarch in Harvard's family of nearly 100 department libraries campus-wide. It was named for **Harry Elkins Widener**, who went down with the *Titanic*; a plaque tells the story. The largest university library in the world, Widener's collection of books is only surpassed by the **Library of Congress** and the **New York Public Library**. It has 3.2 million volumes on more than 5 miles of bookshelves; the entire library system contains more than 11 million volumes, plus manuscripts, microforms, maps, photographs, slides, and other materials. Widener is open to the public, but access to its stacks is limited to the fortunate cardholders with Harvard affiliation or to those with special permission. In the resplendent **Harry Elkins Widener Memorial Room**, bibliophile and collector Harry's books are on display, including a *Gutenberg Bible*, one of only 50 remaining, and a First Folio of **Shakespeare**'s plays dated 1623, the first collected edition. Look for the dioramas depicting Cambridge in 1667, 1775, and 1936; and **John Singer Sargent** murals in the main stair hall. ◆ M-F 9AM-10PM; Sa 9AM-5PM, Su noon-5PM when school in session; M-F 9AM-5PM during school vacations. Harvard Yard. 495.4166 ♿

Drawing Courtesy Carpenter Center

5 Carpenter Center for the Visual Arts

(1963, **Le Corbusier**; National Register of Historic Places) Coolly surveying Harvard Yard across the way, the sculptural Carpenter Center is the only structure designed by Le Corbusier in North America. The iconoclastic concrete-and-glass form carries on an interesting dialogue with the sedate **Fogg Art Museum** next door, and other conservative architectural neighbors crowding round. Within is Harvard's department of visual and environmental studies. Carpenter orchestrates a rotating program of contemporary exhibitions in its 2 public galleries, lectures, and the wonderful **Harvard Film Archive** series. The center houses a film archive, photography collection, and studios. ◆ Lobby gallery: M-F 9AM-11PM; Sa 9AM-6PM; Su noon-10PM. 3rd fl Sert Gallery: Tu-Su 1-6PM. 24 Quincy St (Mass Ave-Broadway) 495.3251, recorded info on film showings 495.4700 ♿

Nathaniel Eaton was the first headmaster of the new, not yet named **Harvard College**, but was removed from office for severely beating students and feeding them poorly.

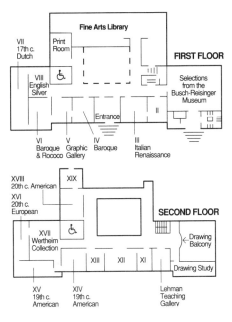

5 Fogg Art Museum

(1927, **Coolidge, Shepley, Bulfinch and Abbot**) Founded in 1891—Harvard's oldest museum—the Fogg's comprehensive collection represents most major artistic periods in the history of Western art from the Middle Ages to the present. Art galleries on 2 levels surround an Italian Renaissance courtyard modeled after a 16th-century canon's house. The Fogg's French Impressionist, British, and Italian holdings are especially strong; look for works by **Whistler, Rossetti, Géricault, Fra Angelico, Rubens, Ingres, Beardsley, Monet, Renoir, Picasso, Pollock**. Visit the **Wertheim Collection** on the 2nd floor. Also on the 2nd floor is a spectacular new addition to the Fogg: Harvard's first permanent gallery of decorative arts, which leisurely rotates displays of treasures from the university's vast collection of furniture, clocks, chests, Wedgwood, silver vessels, and other household goods bequeathed by Harvard alumni and others over 300 years' time. Probably the most famous item

Cambridge

is the **President's Chair**, a knobby, uncomfortable-looking triangular-seated chair made in England or Wales in the 16th century, and brought to Harvard by **Rev. Edward Holyoke**, president from 1737-1769. Since Holyoke (a portrait of whom seated in this chair was painted by **John Singleton Copley**), the President's Chair has supported every Harvard president during commencement ceremonies. The Fogg, by the way, sponsors great concerts in the courtyard during the academic year, from Renaissance Italian composers to **Gershwin**. ◆ Admission (includes **Sackler Museum**) reduced for elders, students; free under 18. Tu-Su 10AM-5PM; free Sa 10AM-noon. Free tours 11AM, 2PM, with admission. 32 Quincy St (Broadway) 495.9400 ♿

6 Arthur M. Sackler Museum (1986, **James Stirling**) Across Broadway from the **Fogg**, the Sackler is a relative newcomer to Harvard. Except for its brick stripes, interesting window arrangements, and touches of electric-lime paint, the chunky Postmodern building is quite ordinary looking. It was designed by British architect James Stirling, who aptly called Harvard's campus *an architectural zoo*. The Sackler houses ancient, Asian, and Islamic art, including the world's finest collections of ancient Chinese jades and cave reliefs and Chun-ware ceramics, and an exceptional collection of Japanese woodblock prints. Special exhibitions are also installed here, and the **Harvard University Art Museum Shop** is on the 1st floor. The very odd portal and pillar arrangement on the Sackler's upper facade facing Broadway marks where a skyway was to connect the Sackler and Fogg museums, but never materialized. ♦ Admission (includes Fogg Museum) reduced for elders, students; free for those under 18. Tu-Su 10AM-5PM; free Sa 10AM-noon. Free tours 1PM, with admission. 485 Broadway (Quincy St) 495.9400 &

6 George Gund Hall (1969-72, **John Andrews**) Home of the **Graduate School of Design**. The modern concrete building is notable for the striking nighttime silhouette created by its stepped-glass roof, beneath which design students visibly toil at their drawing boards late into the night. Within Gund is the **Frances Loeb Library**, which has architecture and urban design collections. On the first floor, look for changing architecture exhibits, and a small **Charette** store. ♦ Quincy St. 495.4731

7 Memorial Hall (1870-1878, **Henry Van Brunt** and **William R. Ware**; National Register of Historic Places) Just north of **Harvard Yard** looms this Ruskinian Gothic gargantua. Alive with colorful ornament, gargoyles, pyramidal roofs, and square tower, the cathedral-like hall has plenty of pomp and circumstance to spare. Designed by 2 Harvardians, the hall was built as a monument to university alumni who died in the Civil War—on the Yankee side, of course. You can see their names inscribed in the transept inside. Some of the stained-glass windows were produced in the studios of **Louis Comfort Tiffany** and **John La Farge**. Innumerable momentous events have occurred here—depending on one's perspective—from college registration and examinations to major lectures and concerts. ♦ Cambridge-Quincy Sts

Within Memorial Hall:

Sanders Theatre Celebrated painter **Frank Stella** and composer **John Cage** , as well as many other illustrious figures, have lectured in the richly carved wooden theater. Also appearing here are national performers such as the **Beaux Arts Trio** and local music groups, including the **Pro Arte Chamber Orchestra of Boston**, **Cantata Singers**, **Cecilia Society**, **Cambridge Society for Early Music**, and the festive annual **Christmas Revels**. Admission is charged for most events. ♦ Seats 1224. Recorded info 495.2420 & (Kirkland St entrance)

8 Adolphus Busch Hall Named for the famous beer baron, the noble hall with its carved heroes and solemn inscriptions was formerly the **Busch-Reisinger Museum**. It's now occupied by Harvard's **Center for European Studies**. Designed by a German architect and completed in 1917, the medievalesque edifice was built to house Harvard's Germanic collections. It was enormously expensive and is full of lavish detail. Originally lauding German culture, the hall and its purpose have been influenced by the World Wars and changes in international opinion toward Germany. Much of the former museum's 20th-century German art was collected during the rise of **Hitler**, when the works were declared degenerate, banned by the **Nazis**, and shipped to the States. Now at the **Fogg Museum**, the Busch-Reisinger's Renaissance, Baroque, and modern holdings will eventually be displayed in the new **Werner Otto Hall**, under construction behind the Fogg. Busch Hall will display medieval statuary, stained glass, metal, and other works not needing climate control. Overlooking the wonderful courtyard garden are carved stone heads taken from **Wagner**'s *Ring of the Nibelungen*. Sunday evening concerts are given on the famous Flentrop organ as part of the Fogg music series; a small fee is charged. Across **Kirkland St** from the hall is a Gothic Swedenborgian church, a little jewel. ♦ Courtyard: M-F 11AM-3PM. Collection: 1-5PM 2nd Su every month. Kirkland St (Quincy St) Concert info 495.4544

9 Museums of Natural History Sharing one roof are 4 separate **Harvard University** museums dedicated to the study of archaeology, botany, comparative zoology, and minerals. The most famous exhibition is the **Botanical Museum's Blaschka Glass Flowers** collection, handblown by **Leopold** and **Rudolph Blaschka** in Dresden, Germany, 1887-1936, using a process that was lost with their deaths. More than 840 plant species are represented, with a few irrevocably lost when shattered by sonic booms. Another odd exhibition is **Rosalba Towne**'s 19th-century series of paintings depicting every plant and flower mentioned in the works of **Shakespeare**. Particularly wondrous is the **Mineralogical and Geological Museums**' collection of gemstones, minerals, ores, and meteorites. Find the giant Mexican crystals.

The **Peabody Museum of Archaeology and Ethnology** is the oldest museum in this hemisphere dedicated to archaeology and ethnology, with treasures from prehistoric and historic cultures from all over the world. Founded in 1866 by **George Peabody**, many of the museum's displays were brought back from Harvard-sponsored expeditions. The Peabody's largest collections focus on North, Central, and South American Indian cultures. Visit the **Hall of the Maya**, and the newly renovated **Hall of the North American Indian**'s exhibition of some 500 artifacts, which were blessed in 1990 by **Slow Turtle**, chief medicine man of the **Wampanoags**. The exceptional comprehensive display includes objects from 10 or so different Indian cultures over 5 centuries, with some items brought back by the **Lewis** and **Clark** expedition (1804-1806), and features magnificent towering totem poles, peace pipes, a Plains Indian ceremonial outfit, warriors' longbows, and a bison skull with a symbol on its forehead representing the 4 winds.

Tracing the evolution of animals and man, the **Museum of Comparative Zoology** delights kids with its whale skeletons; a 180-million-year-old *Paleosaurus*, the 25,000-year-old Harvard mastodon; the giant sea serpent *Kronosaurus*; **George Washington**'s pheasants; the world's oldest egg, 225 million years old; and the largest known fossilized turtle shell. The museum also displays the *Coelacanth,* a fish thought to have been extinct for 70 million years until fishermen began to catch some live in 1938. Visit the museums' gift shop, a largely undiscovered treasure trove, delighted in by all ages. The Peabody Museum has a separate gift shop, also excellent. ♦ Admission (one fee for all 4) reduced for elders, students, and children 5-15; children under 5 free. M-Sa 9AM-4:30PM; Su 1-4:30PM; free Sa 9-11AM. 24 Oxford St (entrance also on Divinity Ave side) Peabody 495.2248, Botanical 495.2326, Mineralogical 495.4758, Zoology 495.2463. Recorded info 495.1910, admission info on all 495.3045 ₺ (inquire at admission desk)

9 Harvard Semitic Museum Founded in 1889, the museum participated in the first US archaeological expedition to the Near East that year, and the first scientific excavations in the Holy Land, 1907-1912. The museum closed during WWII and reopened in 1982; it now presents special exhibitions drawn from its archaeological and photographic collections, which include 28,000 photographs of 19th-century life in the Near East. ♦ Admission. M-F 11AM-5PM. 6 Divinity Ave (Kirkland St) 495.3123

10 Science Center (1973, **Sert, Jackson and Associates**) The largest building on Harvard's campus looks like a giant Polaroid Land camera to some eyes, with a complex and multiterraced exterior. Science buff alert: on the center's lower level you'll find **Harvard's Collection of Scientific Instruments**, a repository for scientific apparatus used for Harvard teaching and research in astronomy, surveying, physics, geology, electricity, navigation, and other subjects since approximately 1765. On view are telescopes, sundials, clocks, vacuum pumps, microscopes, early computing devices, and more, with additional devices donated to the university dating back to c. 1550. In front of the center is the cluster of rocks, the *Tanner Fountain*, always alluring to children when spraying jets of mist into the air. The fountain has timed cycles, turning off when there are high winds and emitting steam during the winter. On a sunny day, if you stand in the right place, you may see a rainbow hovering over the fountain. ♦ Kirkland St (Oxford St)

11 Cafe Pamplona ★$ The most European of Cambridge cafes, where patrons linger comfortably for hours drinking espresso and writing, reading, or engaging in conversation from the mundane to the supremely esoteric. Tiny Pamplona is in the lower level of a snug red house, with an outdoor terrace where people linger until midnight in the summer. The clientele is eclectic, leaning toward highbrow. In addition to teas and coffees of all kinds (try the mocha), Pamplona serves sandwiches, a special, and tamales for lunch; after 3PM and on Sunday, the menu strips down to one sandwich and garlic and gazpacho soups. Flans, parfaits, chocolate mousse, delightful little pastries too. (More restaurants near this edge of Harvard Sq are in **Central Sq/Riverside** pages 190, 191). ♦ Spanish/South American/Café ♦ M-Sa 11AM-1AM; Su 2PM-1AM. 12 Bow St (Arrow St) No credit cards. No phone on premises.

12 Harvard Book Store Open since 1932, this Cambridge institution and family business is a general-interest bookstore that emphasizes scholarly works and customer service. The store's particularly strong in philosophy, literary theory and criticism, psychology, black studies, women's studies, classics, books from university presses. People flock in for its great remainders selection and basement inventory of used paperbacks, hardcovers, and texts. It puts out a monthly newsletter. Owner **Frank Kramer** also operates the extremely popular

Harvard Book Store Cafe, 190 Newbury St, Back Bay. 536.0095/0097 (café), which has a more general-interest slant and serves good food to book browsers. ♦ M-Sa 9:30AM-11PM; Su noon-8PM. 1256 Mass Ave (Plympton St) 661.1515/1516 ₺ (street level only)

12 The Grolier Book Shop The nation's only all-poetry book shop was founded in 1927 as a rare-book store, then was converted to its specialty in 1982 by poetry-loving owner **Louisa Solano**. She bought the shop 16 years ago because she couldn't afford to continue buying book after book. Grolier has 14,000 poetry titles today, including books and cassettes on poetry, first editions, small press publications, little magazines. Solano cosponsors a poetry-reading series for nonpublished poets, hosts autograph parties about once a week from Sep-May, and keeps a mailing list and bulletin board going, as well as a photography gallery of poets/patrons portraits. Her shop is a formal and informal meeting place for poets, and has figured in manuscripts produced by local writing classes seeking unusual settings. (One story included a blow-by-blow account of a young woman's unsuccessful attempt to pick up a dreamboat at Grolier's.) Lots of visiting poets use Solano and her shop as an info center and sounding board. ♦ Tu-Sa 10AM-6PM. 6 Plympton St (Mass Ave-Mt Auburn St) 547.4648, 800/234.POEM

13 Briggs & Briggs Established in 1890, distinguished B&B is known for its stock of classical and popular sheet music and books. It also sells musical instrument accessories, stereo equipment, and classical, jazz, blues, folk, and world music on CDs, records, and tapes. ♦ M-Sa 9AM-6PM. 1270 Mass Ave (Plympton St) 547.2007 & (they offer assistance)

14 Harvard Lampoon Castle (1909, **Wheel-wright and Haven**; National Register of Historic Places) Cambridge's most whimsical building is home to the *Harvard Lampoon* offices, an undergraduate humor magazine that inspired the *National Lampoon* (no affiliation). *Poonies* have long been famous for their pranks, from stealing the Massachusetts State House's Sacred Cod in 1933, to hiring an actress in 1990 to hold a press conference and pretend she was **Marla Maples**, the alleged mistress of financier **Donald Trump**. Pick out the eyes, nose, mouth, and hat on the entrance tower. Atop is a statue of an ibis, frequently absconded by *Harvard Crimson* staffers. **William Randolph Hearst**, a former *Lampoon* business manager, donated the land. ♦ Mt Auburn St-Plympton St

Within Harvard Lampoon Castle:

Starr Book Shop An academic bookstore purveying antiquarian sets and scholarly works in literature, philosophy, classics, history, biography, general subject areas. Current reviewers' copies, too. Graduate and undergraduate students frequent the shop, which is owned and operated by the Starr family. ♦ M-Sa 10AM-

Cambridge

8PM; Su 2-6PM. 29 Plympton St (Mt Auburn St) 547.6864

15 Pangloss Bookshop Peruse used, out-of-print, and rare scholarly monographs in the humanities and social sciences, and literary magazines. Pangloss does book searches and special orders too. ♦ M-W, Sa 10AM-7PM; Th-F 10AM-10PM. 65 Mt Auburn St (Holyoke-Linden Sts) 354.4003

Early **Harvard College** had a brewhouse that supplied students and faculty with the popular Colonial beverage, then healthier than local water.

Restaurants/Clubs: Red **Hotels**: Blue
Shops/Parks: Green **Sights/Culture**: Black

15 Elsie's Famous Sandwiches $ There was indeed an Elsie, who retired at least a quarter century ago. Yet she'd probably find the food here quite familiar, for it never changes; young and old alike troop in for good fat sandwiches like the Turkey Deluxe, Roast Beef Special, hot pastrami, and 30 or so other sandwiches and subs. Don't look for french fries or any other fried foods, but you will find salads, and all the dressings are made right here. Bargain breakfasts in the AM. Munch away at a windowside counter, or brown-bag it and walk 5 minutes to the river. Harvard alumni recall frequent trips to Elsie's. ♦ Sandwiches/takeout ♦ M-Sa 7AM-1AM; Su 11AM-midnight. 71A Mt Auburn St (Holyoke St). No credit cards. 354.8781

16 Pizzeria Regina $ Another link in the famous **North End** chain, Regina's serves thin, crispy, oily pizza plus pasta dishes. Almost always busy, the restaurant is downstairs, carved names adorning every inch of the wooden booths, and the bar is upstairs. The original Regina's is at 11½ Thatcher St, North End, 227.0765. ♦ Pizza/takeout ♦ M-Sa 11AM-midnight; Su 2-11PM. 8 Holyoke St (Mass Ave-Mt Auburn St) No credit cards. 864.9279 & Also at: Faneuil Hall Marketplace. 227.8180; The Corner Mall, Downtown. 426.9256

16 Upstairs at the Pudding ★★★$$$ First, to set the stage: The Hasty Pudding Theatrical Building is home to the undergraduate **Hasty Pudding Club**, a dramatic society established in 1795 and renowned for its annual *Hasty Pudding Awards* to the Man and Woman of the Year. The celebrity recipients—**Lucille Ball, Cher, Kevin Costner, William Hurt, Meryl Streep** are past winners—are honored with parades through Cambridge in February, accompanied by male club members in female attire. The guest is then treated to an irreverant performance and comedic roast, and presented with a ceremonial pudding pot. Now, the dramatic twist: while Cantabrigians and Bostonians alike are regaled in the local papers with news of the club's exploits, many don't know about this restaurant serving Northern Italian and European cuisine, residing above the theater. Beneath high-vaulted ceilings and posters of old Hasty Pudding theatricals, amid forest green, crisp white, and romantic pink, enjoy a convivial repast spilling over with atmosphere, away from the Square's commotion. Upstairs at the Pudding offers a prix-fixe menu, except for Sunday brunch, of artful dishes like grilled quail on gnocchi, clams Florentine, risotto with shrimp, rack of lamb with black-olive butter, venison steak, roast *poussin*, Queen Mother's cake, Sicilian lemon cream with strawberry sauce. Many entrees are accompanied by a dramatic array of vegetables. The à la carte Sunday brunch is deliciously out of the ordinary. Definitely not a student stomping ground, except when Mom and Dad come to town; there is no dress code but most diners strive for a festive look. A parking garage is across the street. ♦ Northern Italian/European ♦ M-Sa 6PM-closing; Su noon-2:30PM. 10 Holyoke St (Mass Ave-Mt Auburn St) Reservations recommended. 864.1933 &

17 Schoenhof's Foreign Books, Inc. The late Andrei Sakharov dropped in to browse during one visit to Boston. Writer John Updike, Harvard economist John Kenneth Galbraith, and chef Julia Child have all shopped here, too. And soon after arriving in America, many of Boston's foreign residents and students immediately head to the understated shop located in the basement of **Harvard's Spee Club**. The reason: Schoenhof's is the best foreign bookstore in the country, with more than 30,000 titles—original works, not translations—representing 150 languages (other than English). Founded in 1856 by Carl Schoenhof to serve Boston's German community, Schoenhof's today is dedicated to bringing together people and books of all nationalities. Its 6 managers are all fluent in several languages and work together to select books with emphasis on history, philosophy, literature, literary criticism. The biggest selections are French, Spanish, German, Italian, and Russian. Schoenhof's also has a great department of references, records, and tapes for language learning. Children's books, too. The wholesale/retail store runs an extensive mail-order service worldwide and is tenacious at tracking down even the most esoteric special orders—a French book on termites or a $5000 German edition on Freud, for example. ♦ M-W, F-Sa 10AM-6PM; Th 10AM-8PM. 76A Mt Auburn St (Dunster-Holyoke Sts) 547.8855

18 Iruña ★$ Despite Harvard Sq's international population, most of its restaurants have an Americanized style. Not this little café tucked down a short alley. Iruña offers a relaxed and simple European ambiance, and good food that has earned it a devout clientele throughout its quarter century. The Spanish specialties are moderately priced and good: try the gazpacho, garlic soup, paella, Basque chicken, steak, potato omelet. Daily specials feature whatever's fresh, such as Cornish game hen or rabbit. Try the red or white sangria. In warm weather, there's a small outdoor patio for dining, but it's actually more pleasant inside, especially if you dine early. ♦ Spanish ♦ M-F 11:30AM-2PM; 6-10PM; Sa 1:30-10PM. 56 JFK St (Bennett-Mt Auburn Sts) Reservations recommended F-Sa. No credit cards. 868.5633

19 John F. Kennedy Memorial Park Often nearly empty of people and very well-maintained, the park is a big grassy blanket, wonderful for lounging. There's an interesting variety of trees, many still quite young, since the park was only completed a few years ago. It's behind the John F. Kennedy School of Government and The Charles Hotel, with the river just across the street. Look for the fountain with JFK quotes inscribed. ♦ JFK St-Memorial Dr &

20 Harvard Manor House $$ In the heart of the Square, the low-key friendly hotel has 72 rooms on 4 floors (avoid the 4th floor) and offers complimentary Continental breakfast and free parking on the premises. Lots of visiting parents, professors, and prominent guests of the nearby **John F. Kennedy School of Government** stay here. Despite the name, the hotel is privately owned and run. ♦ 110 Mt Auburn St (Eliot St) 864.5200; fax 864.2409 &

20 The Charles Hotel $$$ Harvard University guests and entertainment industry folk stay here, many long-term, and business travelers who like to be near the late-night liveliness of the Square. The hotel is also popular with writers and sponsors readings. Part of the **Charles Square** complex, which features shops, condominiums, a health club, and restaurants, the 299-room 10-story hotel offers many rooms overlooking the **John F. Kennedy Memorial Park** and the **Charles River**, with Shaker-style furniture, telephones and TVs in all bathrooms, and a patchwork down quilt on every bed. The King Charles minisuites have four-poster beds. Eighteenth-century quilts, New England antiques, and works by local artists enliven the hotel's main entry and halls. Handicapped-equipped and nonsmokers' rooms, 24-hr room service, concierge, multilingual staff, complimentary overnight shoeshine, valet parking and self-parking for fee available. Guests have complimentary access to the neighboring **Le Pli** health club's exercise equipment and pool (868.8087). Through special arrangement with nearby **Barillari Books**, you can order books by room service: on the telephone, key in the special number connecting to the bookstore and a bellman will pick up your selection. The hotel and Charles Sq jointly sponsor free jazz

concerts in the courtyard Wednesday, 6-8PM (depending on weather), late June-September, which attract hundreds. ♦ 1 Bennett St (Eliot St) 864.1200, 800/882.1818; fax 864.5715 &

Within The Charles Hotel:

Rarities ★★★$$$$ The subtle decor suits the sophisticated American cuisine, with soft piano music from the **Quiet Bar**. Named for a 1672 botanical book, the restaurant displays a collection of its prints. This is not a place to take dinner lightly; the food is too special and the wine list one of the best in town. The ambitious menu changes seasonally, with game and fresh seafood specialties. If you can handle it, the award-winning chocolate pâté dessert—a dense, rich cakelike brownie served in slices, doused with sauces—will satisfy the most intense chocolate craving. Sleek and chic it may be, but Rarities isn't too proud to feature a good old banana split, too. A private dining room for up to 16 can be reserved. ◆ American ◆ M-Sa 6-10PM. Jacket and tie required. Reservations recommended at all times ⬥

The Quiet Bar A prelude to dinner at **Rarities**, with pianists playing softly every night. Cozy and yes, quiet, this is a nice change and a far cry from the noisy student bars that predominate in the Square. Rarities desserts served. There's no dress code, although the clientele generally has a well-heeled look. The bar offers very good wines. ◆ Daily 4PM-1AM ⬥

Bennett Street Cafe ★$$ A pleasant place that a lot of locals have yet to discover, the 2nd-floor cafe overlooks a sunny courtyard and is always airy and open. The menu ranges from simpler offerings to more complex regional cuisine with international twists and turns. Doodle away between courses with the crayons provided on the paper table covering. There are 3 seatings for the popular Sunday buffet brunch: 11AM, 1 and 2PM. Come back early on a weekday and enjoy a tasty Continental breakfast before the Square wakes up. ◆ American regional ◆ M-Th, Su 6:30AM-10PM; F-Sa 6:30AM-11PM. Reservations recommended for 6 or more, and for Sunday brunch ⬥

The Regattabar The Charles Hotel pulled it off with panache: it gambled and launched a popular place to listen and dance to local and nationally acclaimed jazz acts. The **George Shearing Duo**, the **Milt Jackson Quartet, Gary Burton, Herbie Hancock, Ahmad Jamal, Pat Metheny, Herbie Mann**, the **Four Freshmen** have all performed in this comfy venue. Tickets for Friday and Saturday sell out fast, so plan a week in advance. Jazzophiles drive up from New York regularly to hear good jazz for reasonable prices. Hotel guests admitted free to all Tuesday-Thursday shows and any 11PM show after signing up with the concierge; all customers may purchase 1½ tickets and stay for both shows on one night. ◆ Tu-Sa 8PM-1AM. Shows Tu-W 9PM; Th-Sa 9, 11PM. Proper

Cambridge

attire required. Tickets sold by Water Music, Inc. 876.7777 ⬥

20 Shops at Charles Square The stark modern complex's numerous shops and restaurants include **Banana Republic, Crabtree and Evelyn, Giannino's Restaurant and Bar, Laura Ashley, Le Pli Health Club,** the **Narragansett, Papermint** and **Talbots**. Because it's a little out of the way, Charles Sq has attracted public attention very slowly, and businesses come and go. But it's worth a look and you can browse unhurried. The **Charles Sq Parking Garage** is open 24 hours. ◆ Shops M-F 10AM-7PM; Sa 10AM-6PM; Su noon-6PM. 1 Bennett St (Eliot St) ⬥

Restaurants/Clubs: Red
Shops/Parks: Green

Hotels: Blue
Sights/Culture: Black

Within Charles Sq:

Honore Jewelry A tantalizing inventory of antique, estate, Victorian, and contemporary jewelry and adornments, with a great selection of amusing and art pieces. There's no better place to find something rare, unusual, or exotic in a wide range of prices. ◆ M-F 10AM-7PM; Sa 10AM-6PM; Su noon-6PM. 497.7187 ⬥

21 Charrette Flagship of the national chain. Catering to design professionals, the sleek inventory includes top makers' and Charrette's own lines of great-looking fine art and office supplies, portfolios, framing and modeling supplies, drafting instruments, furniture, desktop-publishing software. The store is a magnet for the local architecture and design community, and students from the **Harvard University Graduate School of Design** (There's a small Charrette outlet at the **GSD** for emergencies). Charrette stocks 6000-8000 products, with 41,000 available at the warehouse. If you need something the store doesn't have, check out the thick Charrette catalog, and your purchase can sometimes be sent from the warehouse that same day. In addition, a spin-off enterprise called **Charrette Reprographics** specializes in the latest technologies for design professionals' presentations: located at 44 Brattle St, Harvard Sq, Cambridge, 495.0200; 1033 Mass Ave, Cambridge, 495.0235; and 184 South St, Waterfront, 292.8820. ◆ M-F 8:30AM-7PM; Sa 10AM-6PM; Su 1-6PM. 95 Mt Auburn St (JFK St) 495.0250. Also at: 45 Batterymarch St, Financial District. 542.1666; 777 Boylston St, Back Bay. 267.2490

22 Revolution Books Located in **The Garage**, a complex of funky stores and eating places, this independently-owned and-operated book shop has a progressive political focus that makes it perfectly at home in the Square. It stocks books and periodicals on revolutionary politics, including Marxist literature and works on Central America, Africa, women, Third World culture, geography, ecology, history, and will special-order. The store promotes the literature and politics of the **Revolutionary Communist Party USA**, and is part of the **Revolutionary Internationalist Movement**, but is not owned by either group. ◆ M-W, Su noon-6PM; Th noon-9PM; F-Sa noon-7PM. 38 JFK St (Mt Auburn St) 492.5443

22 The Coffee Connection ★$ Also in **The Garage**, this cafe is the Square's premier rendezvous for potent, fragrant fresh-roasted coffee, equally full-bodied conversation, and light meals. The food's okay; but the coffee's the thing here, all different kinds served all different ways. Most customers choose the superstrong *melior* brewing method; look around, and you'll likely see at least one frazzled student nursing a giant pot to cope with the course load. There's a coffee bar, but better still, sit at one of the tables on the upper level so you can watch who's coming and going, always an intriguing collection of characters. Weekday mornings and late afternoons are the café's quietest hours, but there's usually a line. You can also enter from **Dunster St**, up a short flight of stairs and to the left. Be forewarned: there are no restrooms on the premises! The retail operation sells 25-30 different award-winning coffees, excellent teas, and every kind of brewing paraphernalia imaginable. You can order by mail too. ♦ M-Th, Su 8AM-11PM; F-Sa 8AM-midnight. 36 JFK St (Mt Auburn St) 492.4881 ♿ Also at: Faneuil Hall Marketplace. 227.3821; Copley Pl, Back Bay. 353.1963; 97 Charles St, Beacon Hill. 227.3812

22 Catch a Rising Star Part of a national chain, the comedy club books big-name acts with national headliners. Monday and Tuesday are local comedy showcase nights, with nationally-known talent featured all other nights. Sandwiches, cold appetizers, and full bar available. (No smoking at tables; only at bar and open bay area.) It's first-come, first-served for seats, and all shows are for all ages. ♦ Cover. Shows M-Th 8:30PM; F 8:30, 11PM; Sa 7:30, 9:45PM, midnight; Su 8:30PM. 30B JFK St (Brattle-Mt Auburn Sts) Reservations recommended, especially weekends. Recorded info 661.9887, tickets 661.0167; Teletron 720.3450

22 Pizzeria Uno $ Always full of noisy students hungry for deep-dish pizza, but sometimes you can squeeze in for a filling, cheap meal. There's a bar downstairs. ♦ Pizza/takeout ♦ M-W 11AM-12:30AM; Th-Sa 11AM-1AM; Su 11:30AM-12:30AM. 22 JFK St (Brattle-Mt Auburn Sts) 497.1530 ♿ Also at: 731 Boylston St, Back Bay. 267.8554; Faneuil Hall Marketplace. 423.5722; 645 Beacon St, Kenmore Sq. 262.2373

23 Urban Outfitters Where all the chic-looking students and general under-30s crowd shop for the latest in men's and women's urban attire, fashion accessories, housewares, and a whole slew of trendy novelties. Lots of popular name brands and the store's own label. A bargain basement sells vintage clothing, too, popular in the Square. You can also enter the store from **Brattle St**, making this a convenient cut-through. ♦ M-Sa 10AM-10PM; Su noon-8PM. 11 JFK St (Brattle-Mt Auburn Sts) 864.0070. Also at: 361 Newbury St, Back Bay. 236.0088

24 Brattle Street Called **Tory Row** in the 1770s because its residents were loyal to **King George**. They resided in magnificent summer homes and country estates, spacious lands spilling over to the river's edge. In the summer of 1775, the Patriots under **George Washington** appropriated the homes. Today Brattle St is far more densely inhabited, but its sumptuous properties secure its reputation as one of the country's poshest streets. **H.H. Richardson** designed the **Stoughton House** at No. 90 in 1882. No. 159 is the **Hooper-Lee-Nichols House**, pieces of which date back to the 1600s, now headquarters of the **Cambridge Historical Society**. The society is open to the public on some afternoons and offers tours of Tory Row and the **Old Burial Ground**; call 497.1630 for information. **John Bartlett**, the Harvard Sq bookseller who compiled the famous *Bartlett's Familiar Quotations*, lived at No. 165, erected for him in 1873.

24 WordsWorth A lotta books and a lotta people all the time at the Square's busiest bookshop, where all books but text books are discounted. This is a full-service general book store with a fully computerized inventory system, developed by the owner and adopted by other bookstores, tracking 60,000-100,000 titles in 95 subject areas. WordsWorth publishes a newsletter and sponsors an excellent reading series. There's a fine children's section with its own staff, and a bountiful selection of greeting cards, calendars, and wrapping papers. *For the voracious reader.* ♦ M-Sa 8:30AM-11:30PM; Su 10AM-10:30PM. 30 Brattle St (Eliot-Mt Auburn Sts) 354.5201

25 Motto/MDF Side by side are 2 small shops with different wares, but the same distinctive esthetic. Both are owned and operated by **Jude Silver**, whose own art background influences her emphasis on modern, functional, and sophisticated creations by more than 100 primarily American artists and artisans. Motto sells abstract avant-garde jewelry of striking materials, textures, compositions, tones. They can suggest European élan, classical coolness, industrial efficiency, Southwestern warmth. MDF (**Modern Design Furnishings**) sells personal and home and office accessories, lamps, small furniture, men's jewelry—all fabricated from nontraditional materials in abstract designs. Brides-to-be can register at MDF, and both stores special-order, pack, and ship all over the world. ♦ Both shops M-F 11AM-7PM; Sa 10AM-6PM; Su noon-6PM. 17-19 Brattle St (Palmer St) Motto 868.8448, MDF 491.2789 ♿ (street level)

Cambridge

25 Cambridge Booksmith *Dedicated to the fine art of browsing*, its motto says, and indeed the store's relaxed ambiance and large inventory encourages communion with books. It caters to the student/professional crowd and stocks all the latest paperbacks and hardcovers, plus a good selection of remainders, books on tape, greeting cards and postcards, calendars, and more. Popular for fiction, history, philosophy. ♦ M-Sa 9AM-11:45PM; Su 10AM-11:45PM. 25 Brattle St (Eliot St) 864.2321

It was the building of bridges—particularly the **West Boston Bridge** of 1793 and the **Craigie Bridge** of 1909—that turned Cambridge into a city by opening direct routes to Boston.

26 Jasmine/Sola Jasmine sells moderately expensive women's clothing and accessories, many in unusual rich fabrics and striking styles, ranging from casual to dressy. The jewelry is always fun, much of it produced by independent and emerging jewelry makers. Sola sells men's and women's shoes, ranging widely in price, with some hard-to-find brands. **Sola Men** has a modest selection of great-looking men's clothing, often European in style. ♦ M-Tu, Sa 10AM-5:45PM; W-F 10AM-7:45PM; Su noon-6PM. 37 Brattle St (Eliot-Church Sts) 354.6043 &

26 J.F. Olsson On this spot for more than 80 years and in the Square since 1885, Olsson sells hand-crafted ornaments and gifts from Sweden, Germany, Italy, and other countries, handmade pottery, jewelry, figurines, all sorts of novelties and children's toys, miniatures, exquisite stationery, cards, and wrapping papers. The store fills up around holiday time. A great place for those who adore pretty little this and thats. ♦ M-Sa 10AM-6PM. 43 Brattle St (Church St) 876.0938 & (1st level only)

BRATTLE THEATRE

27 Brattle Theatre *Here's looking at you, kid.* 1990 marked the 100th anniversary of the one-of-a-kind Brattle. Independent movie house extraordinaire, the Brattle is struggling valiantly to preserve its identity in the midst of increasingly commercial Harvard Sq and an era of movie-chain monopolies. Recently renovated from top to bottom, retaining its rare rear-screen projection system (originally used on cruise ships), the Brattle is one of the country's oldest and few remaining repertory movie houses, offering classic Hollywood and foreign movies, independent filmmaking, new art films, staged readings, music concerts, and performing arts to a faithful following. If it doesn't look much like a movie house, that's because the Brattle opened as **Brattle Hall** on 27 January 1890, founded by the **Cambridge Social Union** as a place for literary, musical, and dramatic

Cambridge

entertainments. (One of the union's cofounders was poet **Longfellow**'s brother, **Reverend Samuel Wadsworth Longfellow**.) From 1948-1952, the **Brattle Theatre Company** occupied the Brattle and put on nationally acclaimed performances from **Shakespeare** to **Chekhov** with many notable stars, including **Jessica Tandy** and **Hume Cronyn**. It made a policy of hiring actors who were blacklisted during the US government's political witch hunts of the era. **Zero Mostel** was one of the blacklisted guest stars. The Brattle began running in the red, then was converted to an art cinema in 1953 by Harvard grads **Bryant Haliday** and **Cyrus Harvey, Jr.**, who together founded **Janus Films** and brought the first films of **Fellini, Antonioni, Bergman,** and **Olmi** to America. A local

Humphrey Bogart cult was born here in the '50s, when owners Harvey and Haliday screened neglected *Bogie* films during Harvard exam time, drawing college students and other fans in droves, who chanted favorite lines from *Casablanca* and competed for film attendance records. As the revived Bogey mystique spread across the country, a week-long Bogart series became an annual Brattle tradition. In a historic 1955 decision, the **Massachusetts Supreme Judicial Court** broke the state censorship law and ruled for the Brattle that the state commissioner of public safety cannot ban a movie on Sunday. The movie that caused the ruckus was the Swedish film *Miss Julie*. The Brattle has been operated since 1986 by **Connie White** and **Marianne Lampke's Running Arts** company, which features different categories of double features nearly every night. The general roster: Monday, film noir; Tuesday, author readings sponsored by nearby **WordsWorth** bookstore, independent filmmaking, or other arts activities; Wednesday, theme selections such as a particular director; Thursday, international films; Friday and Saturday, themes such as a particular style or content. Innumerable Cambridge-area movie lovers have assignations at the Brattle every single week, drawn by the attractive lineup and 2 shows-for-one-price admission. A free 2-month program lineup is available in front of the theater. Since the '60s, the movie house has shared its quarters with a variety of retail businesses. Call for screening times. ♦ Admission. Closed Christmas Day. 40 Brattle St (Eliot-Story Sts) Recorded info 876.6837 &

28 The Book Case The crowded window displays reflect this fun little shop's quirky personality. It's a bargain basement of used paperbacks and hardcovers in all subjects, plus a great mishmash of postcards, greeting cards, and doodads of all sorts, including miniatures, novelties, figurines, and whatnots. ♦ M-Sa 10:30AM-5PM. 42 Church St (Brattle St-Mass Ave) No credit cards. 876.0832 &

28 The Globe Corner Bookstore An outpost of the Boston original, this shop specializes in books, maps, and guides for New England and world travel, and also carries travel-oriented novelties, games, accessories. ♦ M-Sa 9AM-9PM; Su noon-6PM. 49 Palmer St (Church St) Credit accepted for $10 or more. 497.6277. Also at: 3 School St, Downtown. 523.6658

28 Passim ★$ One of America's oldest and best-known coffee houses is **Bob** and **Rae Anne Donlin**'s little below-street-level club, where they began featuring folk music around '71. Passim (Latin for *here and there*, and pronounced *PASS-im*, although just about everybody says *Pass-EEM*) is the only remaining commercial coffeehouse presenting live music in Boston and Cambridge. The Donlins have always been true-blue friends to local folk and bluegrass groups, and among those they helped boost to fame are **Tom Rush, Jackson Browne, Tracy Chapman, Suzanne Vega, Greg Brown, Nanci Griffith, Tom Waits, Patty Larkin**. The Donlins recently celebrated Passim's 20th anniversary with a special concert; many famous alumni returned to thank Bob and Rae Anne with music. The stalwart club has weathered well, and continues to showcase contemporary acoustic music, some traditional, too. Very unpretentious, with no liquor license, Passim seats 50. There's a light menu of soups, sandwiches, quiches, desserts, coffees, teas, cider. No smoking permitted (except daytime, in one section). By day, Passim is a combination cafe/gift shop. The admission prices are low; the club deserves lots of support. Call for performance schedule, which varies. Weekends feature a headliner with opening act, the latter usually new local talent. Seating is first come, first-served. ♦ Cover. Club shows: M-Th 8:30PM when scheduled; F-Sa 8, 10:30PM; Su 8PM when scheduled, winter only. Restaurant: Tu-Sa noon-4:45PM. Gift shop: Tu-Sa noon-5:30PM. 47 Palmer St (Church-Brattle Sts) 492.7679

29 First Parish Church and Old Burying Ground (1833, **Isaiah Rogers**) The wooden Gothic Revival church was partially funded by Harvard, in return for pews for students' use. Called *God's Acre*, the adjacent Old Burying Ground is where numerous Revolutionary War veterans—including 2 black slaves, **Cato Stedman** and **Neptune Frost**, who fought alongside their masters—and Harvard's first 8 presidents are buried. Many of the graves' metal markers were melted down for bullets. ♦ 3 Church St (Mass Ave)

Within First Parish Church:

Nameless Coffeehouse Located in the basement, the country's oldest free, volunteer-run coffeehouse is a neighborly venue where local folk musicians play. **Tracy Chapman** played here during her days as a Harvard Sq street performer. ♦ Free. Shows F-Sa 8PM. Zero Church St (Mass Ave) Recorded info 864.1630

The first full-size American book was published in Cambridge in July 1640. The first children's book was published the next year.

31 Design Research Building (1969, **Benjamin Thompson & Associates**) Now home to **Crate & Barrel**, Thompson built this architectural equivalent of a giant glass showcase for **Design Research**, the store he founded to introduce Americans to international modern design products for the home. His idea had wings and has spread all over the country, though less imaginatively. Thompson certainly knows how to display for interest, as a later project, **Faneuil Hall Marketplace**, attests. ♦ 48 Brattle St (Story St)

31 The Harvest ★★★$$$ Restaurants come and go frequently in the Harvard Sq area, but the excellent Harvest flourishes. Owners **Jane** and **Ben Thompson** (of **Benjamin Thompson & Associates**, architects of **Faneuil Hall Marketplace** and the **Design Research Building**, above) have hidden the restaurant from the street in a passageway alongside the **Crate & Barrel** store, so don't miss it! Although the decor needs sprucing-up, the Harvest has earned its lofty place in the local dining circuit with inventive seasonal entrees. The chef likes to experiment, creating all-original stocks and sauces, and the contemporary American

cuisine spotlights wild game and exotic fish specialties; in fact, the Harvest offers an annual international **Wild Game Festival** every February. The pastry chefs bake wonderful breads and desserts on the premises all night. The dining room's evening menu changes daily to take advantage of fresh native ingredients. More casual, **Ben's Cafe** offers less expensive but delicious regional American dishes, with its menu changing monthly. (Both café and main dining room offer the same menu at lunch.) A light bar menu is also served between lunch and dinner and after dinner hours. The Harvest's regular clientele is a rich Cambridge mix: faculty and international scholars, deans and university presidents, students and parents, writers, poets, and actors. On a summer night, it's delightful to dine in the courtyard. Evenings, especially Thursdays, the bar is crowded with unattached singles seeking same. ◆ New American ◆ M-Th 11:30AM-10PM; F 11:30AM-10:30PM; Sa noon-10:30PM; Su 11AM-10PM. 44 Brattle St (Eliot-Story Sts) Reservations recommended for dinner in dining room. 492.1115 ♿ (from Mt Auburn St)

31 The Harvest Express $ A separate shop at the same address as the Harvest restaurant, the Express serves delicious food to go, or to eat on the spot at minimal seating. A variety of dishes are always available, many Italian-influenced. Try the pasta *fagiole* soup, pasta salads, sandwiches, calzones, hot entrees. Express features numerous veggie dishes to please Cambridge's many vegetarians. The Harvest is known for its fabulous desserts, so Express always has tons of sweets to choose from like *Expresso* brownies, ginger-oatmeal cookies, various cakes, and lots of other squares and bars. ◆ Italian/takeout ◆ M-F 10AM-7PM; Sa 11AM-6PM; Su 11AM-5PM. 44 Brattle St (Eliot-Story Sts) 868.5569 ♿ (from Mt Auburn St)

31 Brattle House (1727; National Register of Historic Places) Belonged to **William Brattle**, a Tory who fled in 1774 and for whom the street is named. From 1840-1842, **Margaret Fuller** lived here; she was the feminist editor of *The Dial*. The house is now **Cambridge Center**'s headquarters. ◆ 42 Brattle St (Eliot-Story Sts)

32 Barillari Books A very spacious full-range bookstore that discounts all hardcovers and paperbacks except text editions, with an extensive fine arts, architecture, and photograpy department that includes history, monographs, and theory, plus good cookbook and children's book sections. Lots of newspapers, journals, and reviews too; pick up the morning paper and sit at the small outdoor patio, where cappuccino, espresso, imported Italian cookies and chocolates are served. Located off the beaten trail, Barillari is never crowded and you can peruse quite peacefully. Just west of the store is a shortcut through to **Brattle St.** ◆ M-Sa 8AM-midnight; Su 10AM-10PM. 1 Mifflin Pl on Mt

Auburn St (Eliot-Story Sts) 864.2400/3041/3414 ♿

33 Mandrake Book Store More than 40 years in business, Mandrake specializes in the social sciences and art, architecture, and design, selected and arranged with fastidious expertise. It's located near **Architects' Corner**, where a number of architects built their own quarters in the early '70s, architectural styles interacting quite amicably. ◆ M-Sa 9AM-5:30PM. Closed Saturday Jul-Aug. 8 Story St (Brattle-Mt Auburn Sts) No credit cards. 864.3088

34 Clothware A well-known small shop where it's fun to mix and match from carefully selected, uncommon women's attire, all made from natural fibers, especially cottons and silks. The designer lines, including a private label made by an original owner, focus on graceful, classic, and fun-to-wear styles. The lingerie selection is especially tempting. Some accessories, including jewelry, leggings and tights, wallets, scarfs, hats, handbags, lots and lots of socks, and more. The shop has regular sales, but this is not a place for bargain-hunting. ◆ M-W, F 10AM-6:30PM; Th 10AM-8PM; Sa 10AM-6PM; Su 1-6PM. 52 Brattle St (Story St) 661.6441

34 Blacksmith House Bakery Cafe ★$ *Under a spreading chestnut tree/The village smithy stands/The smith a mighty man is he/With large and sinewy hands. . .* The smithy in **Henry Wadsworth Longfellow**'s famous poem *The Village Blacksmith* lived in this old yellow house dating from 1811, the **Dexter Pratt House**. (A stone nearby commemorates the famous chestnut tree that once was.) For more than 45 years, the resident bakery has concocted delicious Viennese-style pastries, tortes like the famous Linzer and Sacher, coffeecakes, croissants, brioches, breads, and cookies. Special offerings are created for holidays, like the *bûche de Noel*. Buy treats from the bakery, or enjoy them at the café's outdoor patio or historic interior, with its quaint rooms and creaky floorboards. The café shares the bakery's kitchen and also serves sandwiches, salads, quiches, soups. The house now belongs to the **Cambridge Center for Adult Education**, which offers courses, lectures, seminars, films, and cultural activities. It rents to the bakery/café. ◆ Bakery/café/takeout ◆ Bakery: M-F 9AM-7PM; Sa 9AM-5PM. Restaurant: M-Sa 9AM-4:45PM (check hours during the summer, when they are often extended and include Su) 56 Brattle St (Story-Hilliard Sts) Credit accepted for purchases over $10. 354.3036 ♿

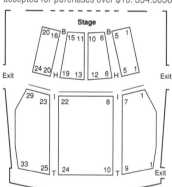

35 Loeb Drama Center/Harvard University (1959, **Hugh Stubbins and Associates**) The center is home to the prestigious **American Repertory Theatre** (ART), a nonprofit professional company affiliated with Harvard that presents new American plays, neglected works from the past, and unconventional interpretations of classics, and to the student **Harvard-Radcliffe Dramatic Club**. The ART has premiered works by **Jules Feiffer, Carlos Fuentes, Philip Glass, Marsha Norman, Milan**

Kundera, and **David Mamet**. The *Mainstage* series runs November-May, with some shows offered in the summer. The company's *New Stage Series* is presented at the **Hasty Pudding Theatre** on Holyoke St. The Loeb Center's main stage was the first fully flexible one in the country, easily converting into different stage styles. Frequent free student performances are also held in the experimental theater; information available at the box office. ♦ Seats 356. Box office daily 10AM-5PM; 10AM-8PM when performances scheduled. 64 Brattle St (Hilliard St) 547.8300 ⓑ (hearing aids available on request)

36 Radcliffe Yard Stroll through Radcliffe's pretty green centerpiece and notice the college's first building, **Fay House**, an 1806 Federal mansion. Radcliffe College was founded for women in 1879, named for Harvard's first female benefactor, **Ann Radcliffe**. It was Harvard's sister school until officially united in 1975, when the administrations were merged and equal admission standards adopted for men and women. Radcliffe remains an independent corporation with its own president, but its students share housing, classes, facilities, and degrees. Radcliffe's buildings include the stately **Agassiz House**, where the **Harvard Gilbert and Sullivan Players** put on operettas. The **Arthur and Elizabeth Schlesinger Library** has the most extensive collection in America of books, photographs, oral histories, and other materials on women's history, including manuscripts and papers belonging to famous women and organizations. Radcliffe's **Mary Ingraham Bunting Institute** is a highly regarded postdoctoral program for women scholars, writers, artists.

37 Christ Church (1760, **Peter Harrison**; National Historic Landmark) America's first trained architect, Harrison also designed **King's Chapel** in Boston. The **Apthorp House**, still standing surrounded by newer buildings just off Plympton St, was built for the first rector, **East Apthorp**. Its extravagance so shocked Puritans that they dubbed the house *The Bishop's Palace*, sparking a controversy so fierce that Apthorp quickly returned to England. Cambridge's oldest church, the former Tory place of worship served as barracks for Connecticut troops, who melted down the organ pipes for bullets during the Revolution. **George** and **Martha Washington** worshipped here in a special New Year's Eve service in 1775. **Theodore Roosevelt** taught Sunday school here while at Harvard. Like the Boston chapel, the gray-wood church's interior is simple and filled with light.

Now sadly scruffy and much diminished in size, **Cambridge Common** (1631) across from the church was the site of **General Washington**'s main camp from 1775-1776. At **Dawes Island** in the middle of Garden St heading toward Harvard Sq, look for the bronze horseshoes embedded in the sidewalk, marking **William Dawes**' ride through town on the way to warn the populace in Lexington with the famous cry *The British are coming!* They were given by his descendants as a Bicentennial gift. ♦ 0 Garden St (Appian Wy)

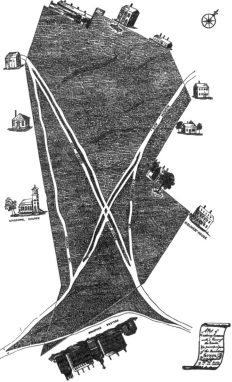

Cambridge Common

38 Sheraton Commander $$$ Near **Cambridge Common** and a short walk to the Square, this gracious old reliable has 176 understated but pleasant rooms on 6 floors. A complimentary *Wall Street Journal* is delivered to each room. Six *executive king* rooms include a sitting area, small dining area, canopied bed, and whirlpool bath. Hotel amenities include a fitness room, multilingual staff, concierge, business center, and complimentary valet parking. Handicapped-equipped and nonsmokers' rooms available. Live entertainment from Top 40s to jazz is offered nightly in the **16 Garden Street Cafe** lounge, and the **Brandywine** restaurant is on the premises. Prominent political guests

Cambridge

stay here. Free parking. ♦ 16 Garden St (Berkeley-Mason Sts) 547.4800, 800/325.3535; fax 868.8322 ⓑ

A shameful problem in Cambridge—worse than in Boston, if that's possible—is the lack of public restrooms. The **Harvard Cooperative Society** (the Coop) does a heroic job of maintaining 2 facilities that are in constant use. Otherwise, you can find restrooms in the larger restaurants, the **Charles Sq** shopping complex, **Harvard University's Widener Memorial Library**, and numerous other buildings belonging to the universities. Don't hesitate to check out any possibility, even if you're not a card-carrying student or customer, since the lack of facilities is a terrible discourtesy to visitors, and the Square's institutions and businesses will just have to cope.

Henry Wadsworth Longfellow

40 Harvard College Observatory Open to the public for **Observatory Nights**; an hourlong lecture-film program geared toward teenagers and older is followed by telescopic observing, weather permitting. For the *Sky Report*, a recorded update of astronomical information, call 491.1497. The domed pavilion is the only surviving element of the original building, 1843-1851, designed by **Isaiah Rogers**. It was built after the *Great Comet*'s appearance in 1843 sparked public interest in astronomy.
♦ Free. 3rd Th each month, 8PM. 60 Garden St (Madison St) North of Harvard Sq. 495.9059

41 Mount Auburn Cemetery Located on the Cambridge/Watertown line, the cemetery is worth seeking out for a sunny afternoon stroll and picnic, and fine birdwatching. Now one of its illustrious residents, **Henry Wadsworth Longfellow** called Mt. Auburn the *city of the dead*. Founded in 1831, the first garden cemetery in America, its 170 acres are verdant with unusual native and rare foreign trees and flowering shrubs. **Oliver Wendell Holmes, Isabella Stewart Gardner, Mary Baker Eddy,** and **Winslow Homer** are also among the 70,000 and more persons buried here. The cemetery introduced a new concept of interment in the US when it was founded. Before, colonial burial grounds were rustic graveyards where the dead were buried in an erratic fashion. Grave markers were frequently moved about and bodies, too, with the dead's remains even shuttled from one burial ground to another—Boston's cemeteries offer plenty of evidence of these casual practices. But with the creation of Mt. Auburn, the idea of commemorating an individual with a permanent, unencroachable burial place was instituted. A cult of memory took root in America, with personal gravesites becoming a new status symbol. Stop by the office and pick up maps for self-guided walks, either a horticultural tour of more than 3000 trees, most of which are labeled, or a tour of the cemetery's notable memorials. The **Friends of Mount Auburn** offers special walks, talks, and other activities. ♦ 580 Mt Auburn St. 547.7105 &

39 Henry Wadsworth Longfellow House (1759) During the Siege of Boston, 1775-1776, **George Washington** moved his headquarters from **Wadsworth House** near Harvard Yard to this stately Georgian residence, built by a wealthy Tory, **John Vassall**, who fled just before the Revolution. Longfellow rented a room here in 1837, then was given the house by his wealthy new father-in-law upon marrying heiress **Frances Appleton** in 1843. (She died here tragically years later, burned in a fire in the library.) Longfellow wrote many of his famous poems in this mansion, including *Hiawatha* and *Evangeline*. He lived here for 45 years, with prominent literary friends often gathered round. The house has been restored to the poet's period, with thousands of books from his library, plus many of his possessions. Vestiges of the spreading chestnut tree that inspired him were made into a carved armchair, on display, presented as a birthday gift from Cambridge schoolchildren. The home stayed in the Longfellow family until 1973, and is now operated by the **National Park Service** as a **National Historic Site**. It is one of only 5 in the country enshrining famous literary inhabitants (**Poe, O'Neill, Sandburg,** and **Hawthorne** are the others). Call to find out about special events, including children's programs, a celebration of Longfellow's birthday in February, outdoor poetry readings and concerts held on the east lawn in the summer. Half-hour tours are given throughout the day; reserve in

Cambridge

advance for groups. A bookstore offers almost all Longfellow books in print, plus books on his life, the literary profession, poetry, and more. Incidentally, the first poem to win national acclaim was **Henry Wadsworth Longfellow**'s *Song of Hiawatha*, published in Boston on 10 November 1855. ♦ Admission; free for those under 16 and over 62. Daily 10AM-4:30PM. Closed Christmas, Thanksgiving, New Year's Day. 105 Brattle St (across from Longfellow Park) 876.4491 & (staff will assist)

In 1778 and 1779, Massachusetts held the first **Constitutional Convention** at Cambridge's **Fourth Meeting House**. The resulting document is the oldest constitution still in use today, and was a model for the US Constitution.

Boston has always had a **sweet tooth**. For a century and a half, until just after WWI, New England cranked out all these treats: Charleston Chews, Necco Wafers, Mary Janes, Conversation Hearts, Sugar Daddies, Squirrels. Candy plants dotted Greater Boston: **Baker's** in Dorchester, **Schrafft** in Charlestown, **Bailey's** in Boston, **Necco**, **Squirrel**, and **Fanny Farmer** in Cambridge. The first chocolate mill opened in 1765 on the banks of the **Neponset River** in **Dorchester. Dr. James Baker** bought the plant in 1780, founding Baker & Co., Ltd., makers of baking chocolate. In Cambridge near MIT, rich aromas waft from the **New England Confectionary Company**, known as Necco, maker of the famous multicolored, multiflavored candy wafers. **Admiral Byrd** took 2.5 tons of Necco wafers to the North Pole. Necco was founded in 1901; one of the cofounders invented America's first candy-making machine. Today Necco makes more than a trillion wafers a year.

Restaurants/Clubs: Red   **Hotels**: Blue
Shops/Parks: Green   **Sights/Culture**: Black

Kendall Square

The closest T-stop to the **Massachusetts Institute of Technology** (MIT). Located in the **Kendall Square Station** on the Red Line is a 3-part kinetic musical sculpture by artist/inventor **Paul Matisse**, grandson of Henri. *The Kendall Band* is a musical trio comprised of 3 pieces titled *Pythagoras*, *Kepler*, and *Galileo*. Commuters crank wall handles on either side of the tracks and set large teak hammers into motion, which strike 16 tuned tubular chimes and produce melodious bell-like music—that's *Pythagoras*. Pull another handle a number of times, and a triple-headed steel hammer strikes an aluminum ring, producing a low F-sharp note—that's *Kepler*. *Galileo*'s mechanism makes rumbling, windlike music. In unison, they're a pleasing concert that soothes impatient T-riders. The work is part of the MBTA's *Arts on the Line* program, which has commissioned art for 23 Boston-area stations.

Massachusetts Institute of Technology (MIT)

MIT was founded in 1861 on the Boston side of the river by **William Barton Rogers**, a natural scientist. MIT's first president, Rogers envisioned a pragmatic institution fitted to the needs of an increasingly industrialized and mechanized America. The modest technological school, then called **Boston Tech**, moved to its current site in 1916, quite comfortable with its industrial surroundings. MIT has never aspired to Harvard's picturesque Olympian aura, but rather has focused on scientific principles as the basis for advanced research and industrial applications. Appropriately, the school's motto is *Mens et Manus*, Mind and Hand. Often referred to as *the factory*, MIT grew rapidly and played a significant role in scientific research with the onset of WWII; in hastily assembled laboratories, Harvard and MIT scientists developed the machinery of modern warfare. In peacetime, the same labs have produced instrumentation and guidance devices for NASA and nuclear submarines. MIT graduates have founded local, national, and international high-tech companies in the Greater Boston area. Today coeducational MIT has schools of Engineering, Sciences, Architecture and Planning, Management, Humanities and Social Science, and a very international identity.

For general information on MIT or to join one of the free student-guided campus tours, lasting just over an hour and offered weekdays at 10AM and 2PM, stop by the **Information Center**, open Monday-Friday 9AM-5PM, Rogers Bldg, 77 Mass Ave (near Memorial Dr), 253.4795. Arrange tours in advance if you're with a group.

The numbering system used to identify MIT buildings is but one hint of the institute's practical bent. Take a chance on getting lost for a bit in the domed Neoclassical **Rogers Building** at 77 Mass Ave with its factorylike maze of hallways and numbered office doors. Amble across the 150-acre campus weighted with monumental rugged architecture. Despite MIT's well-deserved image as the temple of high-tech, it gives the arts elbow room, too, and has several excellent museums as well as some superb modern architecture and public art. Admission to all is free. Call for times; many of the galleries close during the summer. The **MIT Museum** houses photos, paintings, scientific instruments, and artifacts representing themes and ideas related to the institute, and is located at 265 Mass Ave, 253.4444. The **Albert and Vera List Visual Arts Center**'s 3 galleries present the highest quality, most challenging art and design in diverse media by professional contemporary practitioners, 1st floor, Wiesner Bldg, 20 Ames St, 253.4680. If you're an old/young salt or trekking about with kids, visit the little **Hart Nautical Collections**' display of ships' models and plans representing vessels from all over the world, Rogers Bldg, 77 Mass Ave, 1st floor, 253.5942. If you still have time to spare, walk through *Strobe Alley*, a demonstration of high-speed stroboscopic equipment and photographs by the late **Harold E. *Doc* Edgerton**, Class of '27, also at No. 77 Mass Ave on the 4th floor.

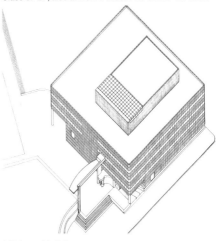

Weisner Building
Courtesy Pei, Cobb, Freed & Partners

MIT's **East Campus**, on the east side of Mass Ave, has an impersonal, businesslike look, particularly since new office and research buildings have sprouted around Kendall Sq since the early '80s. In the last few years, **Main St** at Kendall Sq has gotten a sprucing up, with the arrival of a major hotel and numerous cafés and restaurants serving the MIT population. And MIT has, fortunately, preserved a network of big greenspaces, where fine outdoor art can be found. In **Killian Court** behind the Rogers Bldg is **Henry Moore**'s *Three-Piece Reclining Figure* (1976). (Another Moore work, *Reclining Figure*, is located off Ames St between the **Whitaker Lab** and **I.M. Pei's Weisner Building Center for Arts &**

Media Technology). **Michael Heizer**'s sculpture *Guennette* stands opposite. Looming over Killian Ct is the **Great Dome**, MIT's architectural focus. From this grassy expanse, the view to the river and Boston beyond is magnificent (and the court and towering dome are splendid in Boston's eyes too). At **McDermott Court**, look for **I.M. Pei's Green Building Center for Earth Sciences** (1964). In front is the giant black-steel sculpture *La Grande Voile* (The Big Sail) designed by **Alexander Calder** as a wind baffle, helping the Green Building's revolving doors to work properly. Nearby is a 1975 black steel sculpture by **Louise Nevelson** called *Transparent Horizon*. At the end of Main St near the **Longfellow Bridge** is a small outdoor plaza adorned with a controversial new creation called *Galaxy* by sculptor **Joe Davis**. The focal point is a meteoritelike stainless-steel globe encrusted with strange topographic textures and patterns, clouds of steam billowing from below. The mysterious globe is ringed by 12 smaller ones that cast unusual illuminations at night. Picasso's *Figure découpée* (1963) stands in front of the **Hermann Building** at the far east end of campus. A 5-mile system of underground passages, the *infinite corridor*, connects the East Campus buildings.

The **MIT Press Bookstore** sells scholarly books and journals on engineering, computer science, architecture, philosophy, linguistics, economics, and more, 292 Main St, 253.5249; and the **MIT Coop**, scion of the Harvard Coop in Harvard Sq, is located at 3 Cambridge Ctr, 491.4230.

For a variety of dining options, visit the **One Kendall Square** development, a handsomely renovated factory complex.

It's home to **Goemon Japanese Noodle Restaurant,** specializing in oodles of noodle dishes and tempura, 577.9595; **The Woven Hose Cafe**, 577.8444, which serves great American homestyle cooking; the **Cambridge Brewing Company**, 494.1994, a comfortable pub/restaurant where you can sample the company's own beers and ales; and **The Daily Catch**, 225.2300, featuring seafood of all kinds, which has popular Boston siblings. Always crowded and noisy, another chapter of the famous local **Legal Sea Foods** empire serves all kinds of fresh fish just about any way you could imagine, 5 Cambridge Ctr, 864.3400. Accommodations can be had at the **Boston Marriott Cambridge** ($$$), 2 Cambridge Ctr, 494.6600.

MIT's **West Campus**, west of Mass Ave, has a more residential and relaxed atmosphere. Look for **Kresge Auditorium**, designed in 1955 by **Eero Saarinen**, unmistakable with its curving roof, one-eighth of a sphere, which rests on 3 abutments and floats free of

Cambridge

the auditorium structure beneath. Also by Saarinen, the exquisite interfaith **MIT Chapel** is illuminated by a skylight that focuses light on the altar and is surrounded by a small moat that casts reflections upward on the interior walls. **Harry Bertoia** designed the sculpture behind the altar. Sought after as a site for weddings, the cylindrical structure is topped by **Theodore Roszak**'s aluminum belltower and bell.

Under **MIT**'s orderly numbering system, a single room number fully identifies any location. In a typical room number, 7-111, for example, the number preceding the hyphen is the building number, the first number after the hyphen is the floor, and the last 2 numbers, the room. Buildings on the main campus east of the **Great Dome** (Building 10) have even numbers; those west of the dome have odd numbers.

Baker House
Courtesy MIT Museum and Samuel Chamberlain

Nearby is **Baker House,** a 1949 dormitory designed by **Alvar Aalto**. Its serpentine form cleverly maximizes views of the Charles.

East Cambridge

This multicultural community, predominantly Italian and Portuguese today, was once a prosperous Yankee enclave. In the 19th century, factories turning out glass, furniture, soap, boxes, woven hose, and other goods flourished along the Charles, and the **Quality Row** of fine townhouses sprung up. Then slowly, the riverside industries declined. After suffering through decades as a forgotten backwater, East Cambridge is now undergoing major urban renewal and development. Look for the magnificently restored **Bulfinch Superior Courthouse Building**, original site of the Middlesex County court system, now occupied by the **Cambridge Multicultural Arts Center** with its 2 galleries and theater.

Cambridgeside Galleria
Courtesy Arrowstreet Inc. Architects

A new addition to the neighborhood is the **Cambridgeside Galleria** on First St, where you'll find the **Lechmere** department store, a local institution where you can buy anything and everything for the home at bargain prices. **Filene's** and **Sears** are here too, along with many other shops and services. And nearby is pleasant **Lechmere Canal Park** with its lagoon and 50-foot geyser. Bostonians and Cantabrigians alike flock to **Michela's**, loved for innovative new Italian fare—consistently marvelous pastas and sauces made fresh daily by chef **Jody Adams**, 1 Atheneum St, 225.3366.

Central Square/Riverside

It's hard to tell where Harvard Sq ends and Central Sq begins, a sprawling area located straight down Mass ve toward Boston. Central Sq has been the section of Cambridge most resistant to gentrification, and claims the greatest concentration of international restaurants and interesting clubs. If you're seeking dining possibilities, **Cafe Sushi** offers a spectrum of sushi and sashimi, 1105 Mass Ave, 492.0434. **Dolphin Seafood** is a friendly little family place serving good and reasonably priced seafood, 1105 Mass Ave, 661.2937. **Roka** serves an extensive array of superior Japanese dishes and sushi, 1001 Mass Ave, 661.0344. Located off Mass Ave, **Cremaldi's** is a fabulous neighborhood grocery/café with European distinction, open until 7PM with tables inside and out, 31 Putnam Ave, 354.7969. For an inexpensive dinner of deep-dish pizza or calzones, try **Bel Canto**, 928 Mass Ave, 547.6120. **Lai Lai** is a good Chinese restaurant specializing in seafood entrees; jazz music on some nights, too, 700 Mass Ave, 876.7000. A sociable combination restaurant/club, **Middle East Restaurant** books interesting eclectic acts including jazz, local rock, blues, country, folk, Latin, etc, 472 Mass Ave 492.9181, 354.8238. **Mary Chung** is a modest-looking place with superb Mandarin and Szechuan specialties, 447 Mass Ave, 864.1991. Central Sq has lots of good Indian restaurants, the best of which is **India Pavilion**, 17 Central Sq, 547.7463.

Heading toward Boston down Main St, off Mass Ave, is **Al's Lunch**, a whimsical little storefront luncheonette serving tasty breakfasts and lunches, 901 Main St, 661.5810. Next door you'll find the best ice cream anywhere at **Toscanini's**—tell Gus we sent you, 899 Main St, 491.5877. For superb regional American cuisine visit the new **798 Main** restaurant at No. 798, 876.8444, one of the best restaurants to open in Cambridge in recent years and worth a special trip. The popular gourmet pizza/pasta chain **Bertucci's** has a spacious outpost at 799 Main St, 661.8356. For good, traditional homestyle Italian cuisine, try **La Groceria**, 853 Main St, 547.9258 or 876.4162. A little out of the way, but worth the effort, **Green Street Grill** (sharing space with old-timey **Charlie's Tap**) serves assertive flamboyant dishes with Caribbean influence in a funky setting, 280 Green St, 876.1655.

Evening entertainment in Central Sq centers on music of all kinds, with clubs ranging from neighborhood-casual to somewhat chic, but none demand the high style found in a lot of clubs across the Charles River in Boston. Starting off with the tiniest and rowdiest, stop in **The Plough and Stars**, 912 Mass Ave, 492.9653, an Irish pub with Irish beers on tap, pub fare, live Irish, blues, country, and bluegrass music. Hear rock, blues, and jazz by local bands and dance the night away at the **Cantab Lounge**, 738 Mass Ave, 354.2685. **T.T. the Bear's Place** is a homey rock 'n' roll club featuring new and established local bands, 10 Brookline St (off Mass Ave), 492.0082. An art-bar featuring progressive New Wave and rock dancing, **Man Ray** is at 21 Brookline St, 864.0400. Man Ray connects to **Campus**, a predominantly gay jukebox joint. Out of the way but worth the effort is a long-lived club known for reggae, rasta, Jamaican music, progressive jazz, and more, great for dancing, called the **Western Front**, 343 Western Ave (6 blocks off Mass Ave—don't walk at night), 492.7772. Cambridge's best-looking club, built expressly for music, is **Nightstage**, 823 Main St, 497.8200, which books rock, blues, zydeco, jazz, folk, country, international—a wide variety of great bands.

Central Sq has quite a few interesting shops, including a great old **Woolworth's**. Other finds are 2 old-fashioned gold-mine record shops, **Cheapo Records** at 645 Mass Ave, 354.4455, and **Skippy White's** at 555 Mass Ave, 491.3345. If you need a Swiss Army knife to take on a picnic, or innumerable other practical items, try **Central Surplus Store**, 433 Mass Ave, 876.8512. Cheap lodging is available at the **YMCA** (men only), 820 Mass Ave, 661.9622. Accommodations are customary Y-style: tiny rooms, shared baths, recreational facilities, some house regulations.

Inman Square

A 20-minute walk south on Cambridge St from Harvard Sq (or the same distance east on Prospect St from Central Sq), Inman Sq is a quieter residential district with a surprising array of great restaurants, both ethnic and American, and an outstanding club or 2. (It used to have many more, alas.) The square is slowly being gentrified, shedding much of its character as a family neighborhood with a variety of ethnic populations. It's definitely worth making a dinnertime journey here. Although renovated beyond recognition, the **S&S Restaurant** is an Inman Sq oldtimer and a neighborhood meeting place, serving traditional and gourmet deli-diner fare, 1334 Cambridge St, 354.0777. The nationally known and very popular—deservedly so—**East Coast Grill** will more than satisfy cravings for gourmet BBQ and great grilled fare, 1271 Cambridge St, 491.6568. Next door is **Jake & Earl's Dixie BBQ**, owned by East Coast Grill, which purveys simpler, cheaper, but also delicious BBQ and fixings to go, 1273 Cambridge St, 491.7427. **Cafe China** serves gourmet Chinese/takeout, 1245 Cambridge St, 868.4300. **New Korea House** is one of Greater Boston's best spots for delicious authentic Korean cuisine, 1281 Cambridge St, 876.6182. **Haveli** serves very good Indian dishes, 1248-1260 Cambridge St, 497.6548. For spicy Cajun/Creole cooking, try the local fixture, **Cajun Yankee**, 1193 Cambridge St, 576.1971. Come with a ravenous group to homey family-run **Casa Portugal** to enjoy heaping helpings of excellent Portuguese cuisine featuring great seafood and sausage specialties, 1200 Cambridge St, 491.8880. For after-dinner music, go to **Ryles**—a local favorite—a casual and comfortable jazz club booking top local and national acts, 212 Hampshire St, 876.9330; or **Cantares**, a Latin American restaurant that also features merengue and salsa dance music and blues jam sessions, 15 Springfield St (off

Cambridge St), 547.6300. For dessert, visit **Rosie's Bakery & Dessert Shop**, 243 Hampshire St, 491.9488. A 15-minute walk from Inman Sq is famous **Savenor's** gourmet market, 92 Kirkland St, 547.1765—where you can purchase just about any taste sensation, including buffalo steaks—frequented by Cambridge resident and chef Julia Child.

When railroads arrived in the mid 1800s, Cambridge ballooned into Massachusett's second most important industrial city. Its firsts in American commerce included a ladder factory, piano keys, galvanized iron pipe, reversible collars, waterproof hats, and mechanical egg beaters.

Restaurants/Clubs: Red   Hotels: Blue

Shops/Parks: Green   **Sights/Culture**: Black

North Cambridge

First, 2 pleasant dining prospects that really don't fit in the North Cambridge category, but should be included: **Chez Nous** is a tiny storefront dining room that demands a special trip for superb New French cuisine, 147 Huron Ave, 864.6670. Once you've located Huron Ave, come back the next day for brunch—delicious scones!—at folksy, well-worn **Pentimento**, 344 Huron Ave, 661.3878. Now northward: on Mass Ave toward Porter Sq, established in '55, **Chez Jean** offers tasty bistro-style French food, 1 Shepherd St, 354.8980. Stop in for enchiladas at **Mexican Cuisine**, 1682 Mass Ave, 661.1634, which shares space with a noisy bar and serves some of the best authentic Mexican food in Boston, particularly the seafood specialties. **Changsho** is a spiffy but noisy dining room with a big menu of Chinese dishes, 1712 Mass Ave, 547.6565. **Matsu-Ya** serves good Japanese and Korean dishes, 1790 Mass Ave, 491.5091. **Christopher's** is popular with locals for its pubby atmosphere and big menu of favorites, 1920 Mass Ave, 876.9180. For Lebanese and Greek cuisine and belly dancers, go to **Averof**, 1924 Mass Ave, 354.4500.

Mass Ave toward Porter Sq also offers interesting shopping, including international clothing boutiques, shops purveying natural foods and products, antiques. **Pepperweed** sells distinctive contemporary attire from American, Japanese, and European designers, 1684 Mass Ave, 547.7561. Particularly numerous are vintage clothing and accessories stores, including **Red-dog Antiques**, 1737 Mass Ave, 354.9676; the very eccentric **Arsenic and Old Lace**, 1743 Mass Ave, 354.7785; **Atalanta**, 1766 Mass Ave, 661.2673; and **Vintage Etc.**, 1796 Mass Ave, 497.1516. **Joie de Vivre** is a delightful shop selling unusual and artful trinkets, geegaws, and gifts, 1792 Mass Ave, 864.8188. This stretch of Mass Ave includes several excellent children's stores, including the **Children's Workshop**, 963 Mass Ave at Porter Sq, 354.1633. **The Music Emporium**, 2018 Mass Ave, 661.2099, sells old and antique stringed instruments, as well as acoustic and folk-related music and instruments.

For accommodations in convenient walking distance to both Harvard and Porter squares, try **Quality Inn-Cambridge** ($$). It's a basic cooky-cutter motel, but moderately priced with an outdoor pool and free parking, 1651 Mass Ave, 491.1000, 800/321.2828.

For more elegant digs, try **A Cambridge House** ($$) bed-and-breakfast inn, built in 1892 and listed on the National Register of Historic Places. Its 12 rooms are handsomely restored and decorated, and an elaborate breakfast is complimentary. At 2218 Mass Ave, 491.6300, 800/232.9989; fax 868.2848.

In Boston, Cambridge is often referred to as *across the river* .

Bookstores

Boston and Cambridge are internationally renowned meccas for booklovers; after all, both cities have treated the printed word reverentially since their founding days. When the Puritans arrived, books transported from England were among their most prized possessions. Boston's first English settler was **William Blaxton**, a loner whose idea of perfect companionship was communing with his enviable library of 200 or so volumes. Cambridge remains the true booklover's haven for its critical mass of shops clustered in **Harvard Square**, the bookshop capital of the East Coast if not the country. Together Boston and Cambridge bookstores can satisfy any interest. A sampling:

Harvard Sq, Cambridge (unless noted)

Asian Books Big selection of books on Asia and the Islamic and Arab worlds. ♦ 12 Arrow St. 354.0005

Robin Bledsoe and H.L. Mendelson Out-of-print scholarly works on art history, architecture, archaeology, city planning, graphic design, women artists, landscape architecture, decorative arts. New, used, and imported books on horses. ♦ 1640 Mass Ave. 576.3634

Grolier Book Shop The nation's only all-poetry book shop. See page 179 ♦ 6 Plympton St. 547.4648

The Harvard University Cooperative (The Coop) Harvard University's official bookstore, the Coop has several branches, including one at **MIT**. See page 175 ♦ 1400 Mass Ave. 492.1000

Harvard University Press Display Room Check out the latest Harvard University Press publications for sale, including the Loeb Classical Library. There's a bargain section too. ♦ 1354 Mass Ave, Holyoke Center Arcade. 495.2625

Kate's Mystery Books Over 10,000 new and used mysteries amid black cats galore. Also the hangout for the **Cadaver Club**, a loose association of local mystery writers. ♦ 2211 Mass Ave, No of Porter Sq. 491.2660

Mandrake Book Store Specializes in the social sciences and art, architecture, and design, selected and arranged with fastidious expertise. See page 186 ♦ 8 Story St. 864.3088

The MIT Press Bookstore Scholarly books and journals on engineering, computer science, architecture, philosophy, linguistics, economics, and more. ♦ 292 Main St, Kendall Sq. 253.5249

New Words Feminist bookstore, with books by and about women, records, T-shirts, posters, postcards. Nonsexist and nonracist books for kids a specialty. ♦ 186 Hampshire St, Inman Sq. 876.5310

Pangloss Bookshop Used, out-of-print, and rare scholarly books. See page 180 ♦ 65 Mt. Auburn St. 354.4003

Reading International General book shop carrying all the latest hardcovers and paperbacks, with a general academic slant, and a noteworthy periodical section. See page 185 ♦ 47 Brattle St. 864.0705/0706

Revolution Books Books and periodicals on revolutionary politics. See page 182 ♦ 38 JFK St. 492.5443

Schoenhof's Foreign Books, Inc. America's oldest and largest comprehensive foreign-language bookstore. See page 181 ♦ 76A Mt. Auburn St. 547.8855

Seven Stars New Age books, crystals, incense. ♦ 58 JFK St. 547.1317

Starr Book Shop Academic bookstore. See page 180 ♦ 29 Plympton St. 547.6864

WordsWorth The square's busiest book shop, where all books but textbooks are discounted. *For the voracious reader.* See page 183 ♦ 0 Brattle St. 354.5201

Boston

The Architectural Bookshop One of the country's largest selections of books and publications on architecture. Operated by the **Boston Society of Architects**. See page 91 ♦ 50 Broad St, Financial District. 951.0696

Ars Libri The country's largest comprehensive inventory of rare and out-of-print books and periodicals about the fine arts. See page 161 ♦ 560 Harrison Ave, South End. 357.5212

Avenue Victor Hugo Bookshop New and used paperbacks and hardcovers, magazines, comic books. See page 122 ♦ 339 Newbury St, Back Bay. 266.7746

B. Dalton Bookseller General-subject chain bookstore. ♦ Prudential Center Shopping Plaza, Back Bay. 437.1113

Barnes & Noble Giant bookseller of reduced-price books. Also, children's books, magazines, classical and jazz records, tapes, CDs. See page 82 ♦ 395 Washington St, Downtown. 426.5502. Also at: 607 Boylston St, Back Bay. 236.1308

Boston Cooks Cornucopia of cookbooks in hardcover and paperback, with many privately printed by organizations all over America. ♦ Faneuil Hall Marketplace. 523.0242

Brattle Book Shop The successor to America's oldest operating antiquarian book shop has 3 floors with a little bit of everything. See page 84 ♦ 9 West St, Downtown. 542.0210, 800/447.9595

Bromer Booksellers Rare books of all periods, literary first editions, private press and illustrated books, books in fine bindings, miniature and children's books. See page 114 ♦ 607 Boylston St. 2nd fl, Back Bay. 247.2818

Maury A. Bromsen Associates, Inc. Dr. Bromsen shows his specialties: rare Americana, Latin Americana, autographs and manuscripts, bibliography and reference works, fine arts (19th-century paintings and prints), exploration and discovery. Appraisals. By appointment only. ♦ 770 Boylston St (Prudential Ctr) Suite 23J, Back Bay. 266.7060

B.U. Bookstore A 6-story collegiate department store, as well as New England's largest bookstore. See page 144 ♦ 660 Beacon St, Kenmore Sq. 267.8484

Buddenbrooks Booksmith General book shop stocking more than 50,000 titles. Good antiquarian section. See page 113 ♦ 753 Boylston St, Back Bay. 536.4433

ChoreoGraphica A well-established used bookstore specializing in the performing arts, especially dance. Some reviewers' copies, too. It shares space with **Sher-Morr Antiques**. ♦ 82 Charles St, Beacon Hill. 227.4780

Glad Day Bookstore New England's only gay and lesbian full literature book shop. See page 114 ♦ 673 Boylston St. 2nd fl, Back Bay. 267.3010

The Globe Corner Bookstore A wealth of works on **New England** and books by regional authors; plus a fine selection of guidebooks and world-travel information. See page 75 ♦ 1 School St, Downtown. 523.6658

Goodspeed's Book Shop Purveyors of antiquarian books, maps, and prints since 1898. Goodspeed's sells and buys books on all subjects and does appraisals. From rare tomes to bargain books. See pages 15 and 79 ♦ 7 Beacon St, Beacon Hill. 523.5970. Also at: basement of Old South Meeting House, 2 Milk St, Downtown. 523.5970

Harvard Book Store Café Current and backlist hardcovers and paperbacks. Dine and read in the pleasant café. See page 127 ♦ 190 Newbury St, Back Bay. 536.0095

Priscilla Juvelis, Inc. By appointment, Juvelis purveys *livres d'artiste*, literary first editions, fine bindings, illustrated books, press books, fine art. ♦ 150 Huntington Ave, Back Bay. 424.1895

David L. O' Neal Antiquarian Booksellers, Inc. Fine and rare books from 15th-20th century. See page 130 ♦ 234 Clarendon St. 2nd fl, Back Bay. 266.5790

Pepper & Stern—Rare Books, Inc. Peter L. Stern and **James Pepper** specialize in first editions of American and English literature, mystery and detective fiction, rare cinema material, signed and inscribed books, autograph letters, manuscripts. ♦ 355 Boylston St. 2nd fl, Back Bay. 421.1880

Rizzoli Art and architecture, design, photography, current fiction and nonfiction, international and classical music. ♦ Copley Pl, Back Bay. 437.0700

Spenser's Mystery Bookshop and Marlowe's Used Books New and used mystery books, first editions, collectible paperbacks. ♦ 314 Newbury St, Back Bay. 262.0880

Traveldays Part of a new travel chain owned by Doubleday Book Shops Inc., with around 5000 titles plus maps, videos, globes, atlases, foreign-language guides. ♦ Copley Place, Back Bay. 247.2291

Trident Booksellers & Cafe *Boston's alternative bookstore.* Crystals, incense, scented oils, tarot cards, bonsai trees sold. The little cafe is a popular neighborhood meeting place. See page 122 ♦ 338 Newbury St, Back Bay. 267.8688

Cambridge

Waldenbooks Current paperbacks and hardcovers on general subjects. Chain store. ♦ 2 Center Plaza, Beacon Hill. 523.3044

Outside Boston

New England Mobile Book Fair Well worth a drive, this store is not mobile in the least—it's actually a huge warehouse stocking more than 800,000 books. Everything is discounted 20 percent, and there's a special mark-down section. Many titles are arranged by publisher—author/title reference books are available at the store. ♦ 82 Needham St, Newton. 527.5817, 964.7440

Big-leaguer of the Ivy League it may be, but **Harvard**'s buildings are largely minus the trailing greenery because of the plants' destructive effects on brick.

Other Neighborhoods

Close-knit communities with distinctive personalities, Boston's other neighborhoods seem quite separate from the core city. That makes sense; most of them developed independently before being absorbed by Boston. Even more than landfilling, annexation increased the city's size. An overcrowded seaport in 1850, by 1900 the metropolis had flung itself across a 10-mile radius and engulfed 31 cities and towns. Public transportation—horsecars, then electric trolleys—made it possible for people to live in *streetcar suburbs* within easy traveling distance to their workplaces. The expanding middle class and immigrant families began moving beyond old Boston, swelling the commuter ranks. There are many Boston neighborhoods, largely residential, with a smattering of important historical, recreational, and cultural attractions. Here are some.

Charlestown

The **North End** and this neighborhood stare at one another across the mouth of the **Charles River**. Now a small satellite that's rather tricky to get to—reached by crossing the **Charlestown Bridge** by car or on foot, departing by boat from **Long Wharf** in the summer, or riding an MBTA bus—Charlestown was actually settled one year before Boston, in 1629. Most of the harborside town was burned by the **British** during the Battle of Bunker Hill in 1775, then rapidly rebuilt as a flourishing port where wealthy captains and ship owners lived in grand mansions on the hillsides. The opening of the **Charlestown Navy Yard** brought jobs and prosperity throughout the 1800s-early 1900s, attracting waves of European immigrants while well-to-do families moved out. Charlestown was annexed to Boston in 1874. Maritime activities began shrinking and the Great Depression increased the neighborhood's economic woes. It deteriorated faster as the Navy Yard dwindled and was finally shut down by the federal government in 1974. Charlestown has been rebounding steadily, with the beautifully sited Navy Yard recycled for residential, office, retail, and medical research space. Many have recognized the charm of Charlestown's narrow colonial streets bordered by neat little residences. A predominantly white, Irish-American enclave since the turn of the century, Charlestown is still a family-oriented neighborhood entrenched in tradition where almost no minorities live. But young professionals have been moving in, and enormous change is afoot that will further open up this insular spot. One major event: in the next few years, the **New England Aquarium** will shed its old

Other Neighborhoods

shell at **Central Wharf** on Boston's waterfront and inhabit a new abode at **Dry Dock Number 5** on the Navy Yard's northern end, bringing millions of visitors, new businesses, and liveliness to the waterfront.

Its rigging visible from **Copp's Hill** in the North End, the USS *Constitution* is the oldest commissioned ship in the **US Navy**, maintained to this day by Navy personnel. She was launched 21 October 1797 in Boston, served in **Thomas Jefferson**'s campaign against the Barbary pirates, and won 42 battles in the War of 1812. She never lost an engagement. Nicknamed *Old*

Old Ironsides salutes the dawn, a US Navy tradition.

to-bottom tours, including the claustrophobic living quarters belowdeck. ♦ Admission; discounts for elders and children; special family rate. M-F 10AM-4PM, Sa-Su 9AM-5PM, winter; daily 9AM-5PM, spring and fall; daily 9AM-6PM, summer. 426.1812

Ironsides for her combat-proven wooden hull, not for any iron plating, the ship is permanently moored at **Constitution Wharf** in the Charlestown Navy Yard. (She makes one tour of the harbor every 4 July, called the *turnaround*, to weather evenly and to remain a commissioned warship.) Guides take visitors on top-

The enormous Charlestown Navy Yard was founded in 1800 to build warships and evolved over 170 years with increasingly sophisticated technologies to meet the Navy's changing requirements. A National Historic Landmark, the distinguished-looking Navy Yard is a physical record of American shipbuilding history. Among its interesting 19th-century workshops, barracks, and other structures: the **Ropewalk**—the last in existence—designed by **Alexander Parris** 1834-1836 and nearly a quarter-mile long, where all rope for the

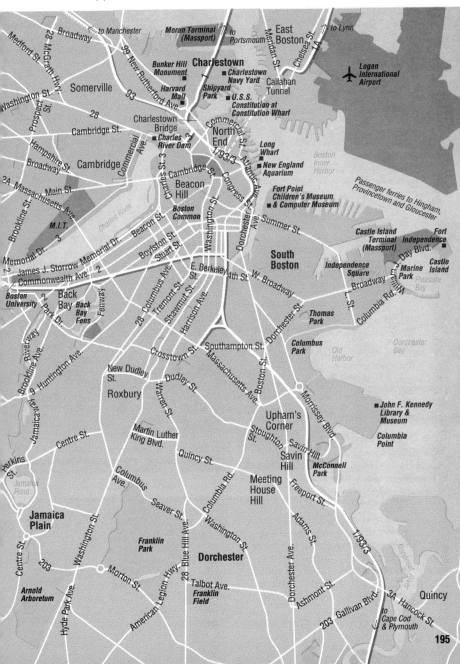

Navy was made for 135 years; **Dry Dock Number 1**, tied with a Virginia dry dock as the first in the US, and called Constitution dock because *Old Ironsides* was the first ship to dock here; the ornate **Telephone Exchange Building**, 1852; and the **Commandant's House**, an 1809 Georgian mansion. You can also board the USS *Cassin Young*, a World War II destroyer of the kind once built here. Originally a wood-and-metal shop, **Constitution Museum** displays original documents and other important artifacts from the historic vessel. Before leaving, visit **Shipyard Park** on the waterfront. Views of Boston are great. ♦ Free. Daily 9AM-5PM. 242.5611/5670

Every American schoolchild learns how the Battle of Bunker Hill was really fought on **Breed's Hill**, where **Solomon Willard**'s **Bunker Hill Monument** now points to the sky, visible from many Boston points. The hill rises from the midst of formal **Monument Sq** and its handsomely preserved 1840s townhouses. Climb the grassy slope to the monument, part of the **Boston National Historic Park**. The **Marquis de Lafayette** laid the cornerstone in 1825, visiting the US for the first time since his days as a dashing youthful hero. The monument was finally completed in 1843, and **Daniel Webster** orated at the dedication. The 220-foot obelisk of Quincy granite rises from the area where, 17 June 1775, **Colonel William Prescott** reportedly ordered his citizen's militia not to fire *till you see the whites of their eyes*. The **Redcoats** ultimately seized the hill, but suffered more than 1100 casualties, a devastating cost that boosted the colonists' morale. Every 17 June, the battle is reenacted. Climb 295 steps to the monument observatory for fine views; back at the bottom, notice the dioramas portraying the battle. **Boston Park Rangers** offer talks in the summer. ♦ Free. Daily 9AM-5PM (museum at monument base) 9AM-4:30PM (monument) Closed Thanksgiving, Christmas, New Year's Day. 242.5641

Leave Monument Sq and descend serene **Monument Ave** to **Main St**. If you visit the Bunker Hill Monument late in the afternoon and then dawdle, you can plan on a wonderful dinner at **Olive's** (★★★$$), Olivia and Todd English's European bistro-style restaurant at 67

Other Neighborhoods

Main St, 242.1999. Friendly, noisy Olive's is known for chef Todd English's creatively rustic dishes like savory tarts, bouillabaisse, spit-roasted chicken, butternut-squash ravollini; many items cooked in a wood-burning brick oven. Reservations accepted only for 6 or more, so get your name on the list very early—by 5:30PM. That likely means an early dinner, but it's the only way to ensure seating. If you have a wait, go to the c. 1780 **Warren Tavern** a few strides away for a drink and plenty of atmosphere, 2 Pleasant St, 241.8142. Named for the Revolutionary War hero **General Joseph Warren**, who died in the Battle of

Bunker Hill, the tavern also serves dinner if you can't get into Olive's. Or continue your sightseeing on Main St up **Town Hill** to **Harvard Mall**, National Register of Historic Places; the young minister **John Harvard** and his family lived near here. When Harvard died at 31, he bequeathed half his fortune and all his library to the college in **Cambridge** that took his name in thanks. At the mall's edge is charming **Harvard Sq**—not to be confused with the famous Cambridge square—and its modest mid-19th century dwellings. Leaving Charlestown, visit the **Charles River Dam Visitors Information Center** on the river, 250 Warren Ave, City Sq, 727.0059, for a 12-minute multimedia presentation explaining the Charles River Dam's operations: flood control, fish ladders, boat locks. Guided tours of the dam also, which has one of the mightiest pumping stations in the US.

South Boston

Expanded by landfilling since the 18th century, South Boston is now a peninsula of approximately 4 square miles, with broad beaches and parks. Founded in 1630 as part of **Dorchester**, it was largely undeveloped until annexed to Boston in 1804, with the first bridge to Boston built the next year. Then real-estate speculators arrived, and Yankee gentry built handsome wooden houses along **E. Broadway** and around **Thomas Park** on **Telegraph Hill**. With the building of bridges to Boston, railways, and growth of industry, the arrival of great numbers of Irish Americans at century's end established the tight-knit neighborhood known as *Southie* today. Lithuanians, Poles, and Italians also settled here. The wealthy merchants moved out as immigrants moved in and **Back Bay** became the latest magnet for fashion-seekers. Like **Charlestown** and **East Boston**, South Boston is a white enclave with a family focus and few minority residents. More than half the neighborhood population is of Irish ancestry, and a major local event is the annual St. Patrick's Day parade and festivities. Drive in for great views of the harbor and islands from **Day Blvd** and **Castle Island** at **Marine Park**. Visit star-shaped 1801 **Fort Independence** on the island (actually no longer an island), then walk along **Pleasure Bay**, designed by **Frederick Law Olmsted**. Near the fort is a statue of **Donald McKay**, who designed Boston clipper ships, including the famous *Flying Cloud*. Southie abuts the **Fort Point** artists' community, formerly an industrial and wool-processing area where the **Children's Museum** and the **Computer Museum** are now grand attractions. A popular Irish bar complete with priests is near the **Broadway T Station**: Amrhein's (★$), 80 W. Broadway and A Sts, 268.6189. Family-owned and run, 100-year-old Amrhein's has the oldest beer-pump system in Boston and the oldest hand-carved wooden bar in the country. People come from all over for great meat-and-potatoes meals, fabulous onion rings, and of course, beer.

The **L Street Brownies** are a famous **Southie** group of hardy seal-like souls, members of the **L Street Swimming Club** who swim year-round, taking an annual New Year's Day dip in the frigid Atlantic, an event always featured in the local papers.

Dorchester

If it weren't part of Boston, racially, ethnically, and economically diverse Dorchester would be an important Massachusetts city in its own right. Originally, it was even larger and included **South Boston** and **Hyde Park**. Dorchester is an area of intimate neighborhoods, like the close-knit **Polish Triangle**, or **Dudley**, home to Hispanic and Cape Verdean families. **Dorchester Avenue**, nicknamed *Dot Ave*, is the community's spine, with lots of ethnic and family-owned businesses: Irish pubs and bakeries are alongside Southeast Asian markets alongside West Indian grocers selling curries and spices. In 1630, the Puritans landed at *Mattapannock*, today called **Columbia Point**, and fearing Indian attacks, established homesteads near a fort atop **Savin Hill**. **Upham's Corner** was once known as **Burying Place Corner** for the cemetery founded there in 1633, the **Dorchester North Burying Ground**. Nearby is Boston's oldest standing house, the 1648 **Blake House**; both burying ground and house are on the National Register of Historic Places. Atop **Meeting House Hill** is the **Mather School**, the oldest elementary school in the nation, founded in 1639 as a one-room schoolhouse. From **Dorchester Heights**, now a National Historic Site with monument, **Patriots** commanded a clear view of the **Redcoats** during the Siege of Boston in 1776. Here **George Washington** and his men set up cannons, heroically hauled through the wilderness for 3 months by Boston bookseller-turned-general **Henry Knox**. The guns were trained on the British, powerful persuasion that convinced them to flee for good. ♦ Free. Daily dawn-dusk; park open year-round, monument open July-Aug (call for tours at other times) In Thomas Park off Telegraph St near G St. 242.5642

Dorchester was an agricultural community well into the 1800s. Gradually, rich Bostonians built country estates and summer residences on its southern hilltops. In the early 1800s, commercial villages grew up along the **Neponset River** and the waterfront. With the electric tram's inauguration in 1857, Dorchester became a suburb of Boston, annexed in 1869. Lovely Victorians are sprinkled throughout this neighborhood, but the best-known architectural style in Dorchester is its distinctive 3-family houses, called *three-deckers*, which became the rage in the early 1900s. But after WWII, the suburban ideal of single-family homes and shopping malls emerged, and Dorchester suffered from flight and neglect. It's still not a safe place to wander, but it's being rediscovered and improving its image. A sign of the neighborhood's vitality is the rejuvenation of the 1918 **Strand Theater** at Upham's Corner, a former movie palace restored as a grand venue for performing arts and community events.

The Boston Globe is headquartered at 135 Morrissey Blvd, 929.2653. Make an appointment for a free tour explaining how a major metropolitan daily gets printed every day, as *The Globe* has been for 114 years. The hour-long tours are scheduled Monday-Thursday, with a 15-minute film included. A favorite for more than 50 years, the **Venetian Garden** (★$), 1269 Mass Ave, 436.9327, is popular with *Boston Globe* employees as well as residents. The V.G. was recently renovated, but still serves great homestyle Italian-American cooking.

The **John F. Kennedy Library and Museum** (1977-1979, **I.M. Pei & Partners**) couldn't find a home in Cambridge and landed out on Columbia Pt, inconvenient for tourists but a dramatic site with glorious uninterrupted views of the ocean. The starkly magnificent library is the official repository of JFK's presidential papers and many personal belongings. The library archives contain all of his papers, classified and declassified, all of his speeches on film/video, and also **Robert F. Kennedy**'s senatorial papers. The museum displays 9 exhibitions on JFK and 2 on RFK, with tapes and videos. The library also possesses 95 percent of American writer **Ernest Hemingway**'s works and is sought out by scholars—2 of whom recently pieced together 2 previously unpublished short stories from his papers here. Also in the neighborhood is the **Bayside Exposition Center**, where major expositions and events are held. ♦ Admission; discounts for elders, children under 16 free. Daily 9AM-5PM. Closed Thanksgiving, Christmas, New Year's Day. Columbia Pt. 929.4500/4567 (recorded info)

Beer, or **ale**, was the favored Colonial beverage. During the 17th century, Boston ship crews were issued beer rations of more than a quart per day; Puritan minister **Richard Mather** recommended beer consumption along with fresh air and church-going; **Harvard College** operated its own brewery in its backyard. The right to brew was jealously guarded by Puritan leaders, who had the power to giveth and taketh away licenses, and readily did so when a brewer's beer was deemed inferior. The American Revolution interfered with beer production, and in 1789 the state exempted brewers from taxes for 5 years to *encourage the manufacture and consumption of strong beer*. National and statewide prohibitions during the 19th and early 20th centuries, and the growth of beer conglomerates, increasingly disrupted Bay State brewing. There wasn't a single working brewery in the state by the early '80s. But several excellent breweries have opened in the last few years.

Boston Beer Company The famous award-winning Samuel Adams Boston Lager is brewed here, plus Boston Lightship Beer, Samuel Adams Double Bock Beer, and others. One-hour tours and tastes at brewmaster James Koch's facility are given Thursday and Saturday, 2PM. ♦ 30 Germania St. 522.9080

Other Neighborhoods

Cambridge Brewing Company A brew-pub featuring its own Regatta Golden, Cambridge Amber, Charles River Porter, summertime Wheat Ale, and casual pub fare. ♦ 1 Kendall Sq. 494.1994

Commonwealth Brewing Company A brew pub serving a variety of its own creations, including Golden Ale, Boston's Best Burton Bitter, Classic Stout, Golden Export, and Famous Porter, plus pub cuisine. Ask about free tours. ♦ 138 Portland St. 522.8383

Mass. Bay Brewing Company Sample Harpoon Ale and other brews on hand. Forty-five-minute tours are given Friday and Saturday, 1PM. ♦ 306 Northern Ave (beyond Jimmy's Harborside). 574.9551

Those who harp on Boston's Puritan roots should take heed of the city's hedonistic streak: Bostonians eat more **ice cream** than residents of any other city in the country. New Englanders consume 23 quarts per person per year, compared to 15 quarts in the rest of the country. The fact that this is a student town keeps those statistics high. Storefronts peddling the rich, creamy treat are busy even in cold winter months. You could spend an entire day touring and sampling the enormous variety available; here's a list of some of the best.

Toscanini's Perhaps the very best, offering the most intriguing and authentic flavors, including Orange Chocolate Chip, Coffee Macadamia Nut, Gingersnap Molasses, Cardamom. Even plain ol' vanilla is spectacular. ♦ 899 Main St, Central Sq, Cambridge. 491.5877

Herrell's Ice Cream Founded by **Steve Herrell**, a former high school English teacher who originated then later sold **Steve's Ice Cream**, now a national brand. Many think Herrell has outdone himself in his new enterprise. Try Lemon Mousse or Chocolate Pudding or Vanilla with *smoosh-ins*—candies, nuts, and other treats smooshed into ice cream to order. ♦ 15 Dunster St, Harvard Sq, Cambridge. 497.2179. Also at: Longwood Galleria, 350 Longwood, Fenway. 731.9599

Steve's Ice Cream Try Coffee Oreo. Steve's is famous for *mix-ins* mashed in to order. ♦ 95 Mass Ave, Fenway. 247.9401. Also at: 31 Church St, Harvard Sq, Cambridge. 497.1067; Faneuil Hall Marketplace. 367.0569

Emack and Bolio's The originator of the Oreo Cookie flavor is also known for its Key Lime Pie, Chocolate Moose, and hand-rolled chocolate-dipped cones. ♦ 290 Newbury St, Back Bay. 247.8772. Also at: 1310 Mass Ave, Harvard Sq, Cambridge. 497.5362; 1726 Mass Ave, Cambridge. 354.8573

Ben & Jerry's Ice Cream Heath Bar Crunch is one of the most popular flavors offered by this Vermont-based chain. ♦ In the Boston Park Plaza Hotel & Towers (Charles St-Arlington St) Theater District. 426.0890

Other Neighborhoods

Brigham's In business since 1914, Brigham's invented jimmies, little chocolate sprinklings, which they offer free. March is cookies month, when Brigham's features the Girl Scout Mint Cookie flavor, contributing a percentage of sales to the Girl Scouts. The chain sells more than 2 million gallons of ice cream a year, 30-40 percent of which is vanilla. ♦ Prudential Center Shopping Plaza, Back Bay. 247.7448. Also at: 127 Tremont St, Downtown. 338.9180; 109 High St, Financial District. 338.7315

Dave's Homemade Oreo and Chocolate Chip are the faves here; people also love the Black Raspberry and Peach frozen yogurt flavors. ♦ 144 Newbury St, Back Bay. 262.5737

Jamaica Plain

JP to Bostonians. Originally part of neighboring **Roxbury**, Jamaica Plain was once fertile farmland. In the late 1800s, it became a summer resort for wealthy Back Bay and Beacon Hill residents, who drove their carriages along the tree-shaded **Jamaicaway** to pass the season at splendid estates surrounding **Jamaica Pond**—*The Pond*. On the other side of town, thousands of factory workers labored in JP's 17 breweries, all of which eventually closed. (A few years ago, **Boston Beer Company**, maker of the multiaward-winning Samuel Adams Lager Beer, moved to JP and offers guided tours, 522.9080.) In the 1830s, railroads began bringing well-to-do commuters who built Greek Revival, Italianate, and mansard residences; in the 1870s, streetcars brought the growing middle class. Today JP is one of Boston's most integrated neighborhoods. Lots of families live in its 3 square miles. The annual springtime **Wake up the Earth Day**, with its colorful parade down **Centre St** and all-day multicultural celebration, vividly expresses the community's diversity.

Centre St developed early as JP's main artery, and retains its small-town character. Along its bumpy, narrow length are good, cheap ethnic restaurants, bodegas, Irish pubs, mom-and-pop stores, and a slowly growing number of upscale establishments. Boston has few vegetarian restaurants, and one of the very good ones is macrobiotic **Five Seasons** (★$) at 669A Centre St, 524.9016, offering simply prepared, innovative international dishes. Read the paper over coffee and a treat at spacious and spare **Today's Bread** (★$), with its big windows on the street, wonderful croissants—try the poppyseed-and-cheese — muffins, desserts, quiches, salads, sandwiches. One of Boston's best Irish bars and a local institution is **Doyle's Braddock Cafe** (★★$), 3483 Washington St, 524.2345, with its famous clock logo. In a cavernous vintage setting full of memorabilia, try fine Irish coffee and Bloody Marys, abundant brunches, basic delicious food, and a variety of beers on tap. Some of the loveliest sections of **Frederick Law Olmsted's Emerald Necklace** are in or border JP: Jamaica Pond, the **Arnold Arboretum**, and **Franklin Park**. The city's last working farm is in JP: **Allandale Farm**, 259 Allandale Rd, 524.1531, open May-Christmas Day. As spring turns to summer turns to fall, you can buy plants, fruits, vegetables, apples, pumpkins, cider pressed on the premises, Christmas trees and wreaths. The farm has been operating on the old **Brandegee Estate** for more than 125 years.

A 1963 law makes it illegal, punishable by fine, for sports fans older than 16 to direct *any profane, obscene or impure language or slanderous statement at a participant or official in a sporting event.* As attendance at any sporting event will demonstrate, Boston's full of intrepid lawbreakers.

The **Mounted Unit** of the **Boston Police Department** first rode city streets in 1883, the longest continuous mounted unit in the country. Once more than 100 horses strong, the unit today has 20; the oldest horse, now retired, is 31-year-old **Prescott**, who put in 2 decades of loyal service.

Allston-Brighton

Polyglot Allston-Brighton is Boston's most integrated district, where Irish, Italians, Greeks, and Russians are joined by growing numbers of Asians, Blacks, and Hispanics. Most Bostonians associate this neighborhood with students from the local universities, large numbers of whom live here, convenient to both **Harvard University** and Boston schools. An agricultural community founded in 1635, the neighborhood later was the locale for huge stockyards, slaughter houses, and meat-packing operations serving the region, then became industrialized. Since WWII, there has been dramatic change led by the construction of the **Mass Pike**, which further split Allston from Brighton, already divided by railroad tracks. Allston-Brighton has developed in a haphazard way that makes it confusing to navigate, but it has many pleasant streets with nice old homes, apartment buildings, and a cozy feel. The neighborhoods have innumerable ethnic restaurants and markets, pubs, interesting shops, antique stores. A popular hangout is **Harper's Ferry**, 158 Brighton Ave, 254.9743, an established blues club.

Brookline

Actually, Brookline isn't part of Boston—although not for lack of Boston's trying. When the cramped city began busily annexing towns to solve its land crunch, independent-minded Brookline refused to be swallowed. It's home to an increasingly diverse ethnic population, and is a somewhat expensive place to live.

Coolidge Corner, where **Harvard** and **Beacon** streets meet, is a mini-Harvard Square with old-fashioned and new-fashioned establishments. The **Coolidge Corner Theatre**, 290 Harvard St, 734.2500, was recently saved from the development scourge by movie lovers, and offers interesting, intelligent vintage and contemporary films. A few blocks from the theater is **John F. Kennedy**'s birthplace (29 May 1917), 83 Beals St, now the **John F. Kennedy National Historic Site.** The Kennedys lived here until 1920. ♦ Admission; elders and children under 12 free. Daily 10AM-4PM. Closed Thanksgiving, Christmas, New Year's Day. 566.7937

An undiscovered gem in Brookline is the **Frederick Law Olmsted National Historic Site**, the rambling home and office named *Fairsted* by its owner, who was America's first landscape architect and founder of the profession in this country. Olmsted's successor firm practiced here until 1980, and the site archives include valuable plans, photographs, and other documentation of the firm's work. ♦ Free. F-Su 10AM-4:30PM. 99 Warren St. 566.1689

When you're hungry, try one of the excellent local delis, like **B & D Deli** (★$), 1653 Beacon St, 232.3727; or kosher **Rubin's** ($), 500 Harvard St, 731.8787 (on the Allston border). Have a casual, delicious dinner at the **Tam O'Shanter** (★$$), *The Tam*, which doubles as a club, 1648 Beacon St, 277.0982. Also casual, the **Harvard Street Grill** (★★$$$) offers a calmer, more refined setting and elegant New American cuisine like lobster terrine and watercress, grilled rack of lamb, pork loin with pistachios, 398 Harvard St, 734.9834. Parking, by the way, is not too bad in Brookline by day, but notoriously impossible overnight, when all visitors' cars on the street are subject to ticketing between 2-6AM. While on the subject of cars, the **Museum of Transportation** is also in Brookline and explores the cultural and sociological impact of the automobile on American society. Special exhibitions on other transportation topics too, such as German aviation. ♦ Admission; discounts for elders and children. W-Su 10AM-5PM. Carriage House, Larz Anderson Park, 15 Newton St. 522.6140

Other Neighborhoods

Day Trips

Boston is a wonderful place, yet it's fast and easy to leave when you want something different. In 1-4 hours, public transportation or auto can take you to the rocky beaches of **Cape Ann** or the dunes of **Cape Cod**, the green hills of the **Berkshires**, the beckoning mountains, lakes, and fall colors of **New Hampshire** and **Vermont**, **Maine**'s coastal villages and idyllic islands. And if Boston begins to seem too large an urban center, in one hour you can be in **Providence**, **Rhode Island;** if too small, in 5 hours you can be on the streets of **New York City**. Many New England spots have seasonal attractions, but don't let out-of-season put you off since those are often their nicest, quietest times. Cape Cod and the islands in winter, for example, have their own compelling moods. A great source for guidebooks on day trips and travel throughout New England—the world, for that matter—is **The Globe Corner Bookstore**, 1 School St, 523.6658; 49 Palmer St, Harvard Sq, Cambridge, 497.6277. Also, get a wealth of free information on Massachusetts places and events by calling or writing the **Massachusetts Office of Travel and Tourism**, 100 Cambridge St, Boston 02202, 727.3201, 800/447.6277. The following are destination ideas rather than itineraries; arm yourself with information on hours, admissions, and other nearby activities and attractions—or just head out with a good map or 2 and a spirit of exploration.

Arthur Krim, Society for Commercial Archeology

North/North Shore

Head north for clams, the best in the world. While on the quest, there's plenty more to see. Just north of Boston, the infamous **Saugus Strip** along Rte 1 is an eyesore to some and beloved by others for its miracle-mile-style roadside commercial signs and attendant establishments, vintage kitsch inspired by America's love affair with the auto. This stretch of Rte 1 is home base for several of America's biggest, gaudiest restaurants. A giant cactus sign and herd of life-size cattle heralds **Hilltop Steak House** (*The Hilltop*), home of red-meat-and-potatoes overeating, Rte 1 on southbound side, 233.7700; a Polynesian theme reigns at **Kowloon**, located across from The Hilltop on Rte 1 northbound, 233.9719; and for Chinese food in Disneylike ambiance, there's gargantuan **Weylu's**, Rte 1 northbound, 233.1632. As you ride along, keep an eye out for the **Leaning Tower of Pizza**; a miniature golf course with towering Tyrannosaurus rex, **The Ship**-shaped restaurant, and other quirky sights.

Of a different historical slant is the **Saugus Iron Works National Historic Site**, 244 Central St, 233.0050 (Main St exit), a reconstruction of the first integrated iron works in North America (1646). The site includes a furnace, a forge, 7 water-powered wheels, and a rolling and slitting mill. A well-kept Saugus secret is the **Breakheart Reservation**, 177 Forest St, 233.0834, a **Metropolitan District Commission** (MDC) park with 600 acres of oak, hemlock, pine-covered hills, 2 freshwater lakes, 10 miles of trails, and lots of birds.

Take Rte 1A from Boston to Rte 129 to **Marblehead**, a picture-postcard New England seaside town with early New World flavor and historical attractions, splendid views of the ocean, plus boutiques and good seafood restaurants. It's a perfect place for a leisurely day of walking and poking around. The **Old Town** section predates the American Revolution and boasts Federal-style sea captains' homes and neat cottages. For information, call the **Marblehead Chamber of Commerce**, 508/631.2868.

Salem, *the witch city*, is a short drive from Marblehead on Rte 114 to Rte 1A. The notorious witchcraft trials of 1692, one of the colony's most troubled chapters, caused 19 people to be hanged and one to be pressed to death before the hysterical Puritan populace regained reason. Pick up self-guided walking tour maps from the **Chamber of Commerce** at Old Town Hall on Front St, 508/

744.0004 (and any other tourist information you may need). Don't miss the **Salem Maritime National Historic Site**, 174 Derby St, 508/744.4323, where American maritime history is enshrined in the **Custom House, Derby House/Wharf, Bonded Warehouse, West India Goods Store**, and lighthouse. Explore 3 centuries of historic Salem at the **Essex Institute Museum Neighborhood**, comprised of library, museum, and 7 period houses, 132 Essex St (museum), 508/744.3390. Less critical to see, but beloved by kids, is the **Salem Witch Museum**, 19$^{1}/_{2}$ Washington Sq No, 508/744.1692. Visit the inspiration for **Nathaniel Hawthorne**'s novel, the *House of the Seven Gables* (1668), 54 Turner St, 508/744.0991; and the **Peabody Museum**, 161 Essex St, 508/745.9500, for its collections of maritime history, ethnology, natural history, and Asian export. If you don't want to direct your own steps, take the **Salem Trolley** tour, 508/744.5463.

Continue north on Rte 1A to **Beverly** for an afternoon of turn-of-the-century-style, Vaudeville-esque **Marco the Magi's Production of Le Grand David and His Own Spectacular Magic Company** at the **Cabot Street Theatre**, 286 Cabot St (for Sunday show, seats 750) or at the more intimate **Larcom Theatre**, 13 Wallis St (for Saturday show, seats 450), both 508/927.3677. The charming, masterful magician Le Grand David and his company enthrall with a bombardment of puzzlement and sleight-of-hand and quicker-than-the-eye fireworks of enchantment. For all ages, and there's nothing like it anywhere.

En route northeast from Beverly to Gloucester is **Manchester-by-the-Sea**, the first North Shore summer resort-by-the-sea, serving Proper Bostonians in the 1840s. The pretty-as-a-picture **Singing Beach** is a favorite for Boston day trippers. To avoid the parking

hassle, rise early and take a morning beach train on the **Rockport Line Commuter Rail** from **North Station** (227.5070). When you've had enough sunning, swimming, and clambering over rocks, it's a short pleasant walk into town for a bite to eat before the train ride back.

To drive **Cape Ann**'s rugged shore beside chilly, invigorating water, continue north on Rte 127 to **Gloucester**. You can also travel here via ferry from **Rowes Wharf** in Boston on **Mass Bay Lines**, 542.8000. The largest town on the North Shore, Gloucester was settled as a fishing colony in 1623 and is still an important port. Its famous landmark is **Leonard Craske**'s statue the *Gloucester Fisherman*, honoring the intrepid Gloucestermen who have died at sea. The fishing fleet is blessed annually, with attendant colorful festivities in late June. Whale watching excursions leave from here. A favorite pastime is eating fresh lobster. Visit the **Cape Ann Historical Association**, 27 Pleasant St, to see the stunning collection of 19th-century American painter **Fitz Hugh Lane**'s luminous views of **Gloucester Harbor** and islands. Perched on rocks overlooking the harbor is *Beauport*, the **Sleeper-McCann House**, 75 Eastern Point Blvd, 508/283.0800. Beauport was built 1907-1934 by architect/interior designer **Henry Davis Sleeper**, who greatly influenced contemporary tastes and style-setters, including **Isabella Stewart Gardner**. Within Beauport's conglomeration of turrets, dormers, and dovecotes are 18th- and 19th-century decorative arts and furnishings. Then on to the **Hammond Castle Museum**, 80 Hesperus Ave, 508/283.2080 (recorded info) and 800/649.1930. The medieval-style castle was the humble home (1929-1965) of inventor **Dr. John Hays Hammond, Jr.**, whose brainstorms included shaving cream, the car starter, electrified toy trains, the forerunner of stereophonic sound, the precursor to remote control—more than 437 patented inventions. Hammond's resplendent digs contain medieval furnishings, paintings, and sculpture. Monthly organ concerts are played on the 8600-pipe organ, the largest in a private American home. Tours given daily.

A short drive up Cape Ann from Gloucester is tiny **Rockport**, a fishing-turned-artists' colony that can be happily meandered in a day. (It's a dry town, by the way.) Parking is downright impossible in the center of town unless you arrive with the birds, so take the commuter train from **North Station** (227.5070) in Boston if you can—it's a very pretty ride. Rockport's light is particularly beautiful at day's end and in early spring and late fall. The **Toad Hall Book Store**, 51 Main St, 508/546.7323, is wonderful for old-time friendliness and

Day Trips

service and has a large selection on local geography, history, lore. Restaurants and shops are densely clustered on **Bearskin Neck** (where only misguided drivers venture), and it's easy to find whatever you want—from seafood to sandwiches for the beach to saltwater taffy and homemade fudge, plus galleries, artisans' wares, clothing and souvenir shops. The neck is plainly for tourists and avoided by residents except during off-hours and off-season, but you will find neighborhood-style places scattered among the too-cute establishments. A tranquil windswept haven and public park is the 68-acre **Halibut Point State Park and Reservation** (no swimming) off Gott Ave, 508/546.2997. An acclaimed annual event worth coming out for is the **Rockport Chamber Music Festival**, 508/546.7391.

Heading inland on Rte 133 from Gloucester is **Essex**, with more antique shops in a single-mile stretch than almost anywhere else in New England. Stop for sustenance at super-casual, rambling **Woodman's**, a North Shore favorite, where **Lawrence Woodman** first dipped clams in batter and deep-fried them in 1916. Come early or late to avoid huge family-time crowds, but the steamers, lobsters, clams, scallops, chowder, etc, are worth a wait. Nearby Ipswich, also prized for its clams and perhaps more so for its beautiful beaches, has more 17th-century houses than any other town in America. The **Crane Memorial Reservation** includes 4 miles of shoreline and excellent sandy beaches on **Ipswich Bay**. The old Crane residence—the **Great House**—hosts weekend concerts and art lectures during the summer and has gorgeous Italianate gardens with sea views.

Near the northeastern tip of Massachusetts, via Rte 1A No, is **Newburyport**, once a shipbuilding center and birthplace of the **US Coast Guard**. Stroll along the waterfront park, promenade, and through the restored commercial district, an enclave of 3-story brick-and-granite buildings. For many, the town has gone overboard gussying itself up for tourists, but it's a nice place to while away a few hours if you're in the mood for shopping, eating, and strolling.

One of Massachusetts' treasures is the **Parker River National And State Wildlife Refuge** on **Plum Island**, 508/465.5753, which offers unsullied beauty, refreshing sea air, glimpses of shy wildlife. From Newburyport, head back on Rte 1A to Rte 113 to **Newbury** and watch carefully for signs to Plum Island and the wildlife refuge. It's headquartered at the old Coast Guard lighthouse at the island's northern end. The 4662-acre refuge has 6 miles of sandy beaches, hiking trails, observation towers for spotting more than 300 bird species, salt- and freshwater marshes, sand dunes, surf fishing, nature-study hikes, cross-country skiing, beach plum and cranberry picking, waterfowl hunting, clamming. Come early on summer weekends because the refuge closes when its quota of 240 cars is reached, often by 9AM. It then reopens at 3PM, so if you're shut out early, spend the day in Newburyport and try again later. In late summer and autumn, the

Day Trips

marshland takes on rich, soft coloring and sunsets are breathtaking. The island really empties out after the summer.

Northwest of Boston is **Lowell**, America's first successful planned industrial complex and now a **National** and **State Historical Park**, Visitor Center, 246 Market St, 508/459.1000. Located at the confluence of the **Concord** and **Merrimack** rivers, Lowell was transformed from a sleepy agricultural village into an industrial powerhouse in 1822 by Boston merchant

Francis Cabot Lowell and fellow investors. Mr. Lowell's **Boston Manufacturing Company** had already successfully developed a textile mass-production system driven by water-powered looms in **Waltham**. Lowell (the town) first played a pioneering role in the American industrial revolution, gradually became a squalid environment after exploiting female mill workers and immigrants, slowly began to improve under labor reform movements, then floundered as the US economy shifted. Now revitalized by high-tech industries, its fascinating past has been preserved. Visitors today can tour the mill complexes, operating gatehouses, workers' housing, and a 5 1/2-mile canal system. Self-guided tour maps are available at the visitor center, including one for **Jack Kerouac**'s Lowell. Guided interpretive mill and canal tours are offered numerous times daily during the summer, reservations required. The **Lowell Heritage State Park Waterpower Exhibit** is open daily at 25 Shattuck St, 508/453.1950. The town is also the birthplace of **James Abbott McNeill Whistler**, 243 Worthen St, 508/452.7641. On view is 19th- and 20th-century American art, including works by Whistler.

Bostonians and visitors alike go beyond Massachusetts' northern border for fall foliage splendor, hiking, cross-country and downhill skiing, rock climbing, canoeing, shopping at factory outlet stores, tranquillity and natural beauty. To determine which places and recreational activities appeal to you most, contact the **New Hampshire Office of Vacation Travel**, 603/271.2666; the **Vermont Travel Division**, 802/828.3239; the **Maine Publicity Bureau**, 97 Winthrop St, Hallowell ME 04347, 207/289.2423.

Near Northwest

A few miles northwest of **Cambridge** on Rte 2A are **Lexington** and **Concord**, historic towns where the first military encounters of the American Revolution took place, also rich in literary history. Concord grapes were first cultivated here, as were ideas of **Emerson**, **Hawthorne**, **Thoreau**, and **Louisa May Alcott**. The most notable among many historic sites are the **Lexington Battle Green**—or **Common** (Visitor Center, 1875 Mass Ave, 862.1450). Here the first skirmish of the Revolutionary War broke out on 19 April 1775 between the Concord-bound British troops and **Colonial**

Cooking and Serving   **Lobster**
Fill a large pot with 1 quart water. Add 2 tablespoons salt and bring to a boil. Put lobsters in head first. Bring water back to boil. Lower heat, cover and simmer:

Weight	Cooking time	Feeds
1 1/4 lb	12 minutes	feeds 1
1 1/2-2 lb	20 minutes	feeds 1
2 1/2-3 1/2 lbs	25 minutes	feeds 2
4-5 lbs	30 minutes	feeds 3-4

Minutemen, alerted earlier by messengers on horse-back of the **Redcoats'** approach. (A reenactment of the Battle of Lexington is staged every April.) The second battle of the day was fought in neighboring Concord, where the citizen militia attacked and drove the British soldiers from **North Bridge**. **Daniel Chester French's** famous *Minuteman* statue now stands guard over the bridge. The **Minute Man National Historical Park** encompasses 750 acres in Concord, Lexington, and Lincoln, commemorating the start of the colonies' War for Independence. The park is a narrow strip running on either side of **Battle Rd** (a portion of Rte 2A). It begins beyond **Lexington Center** with the **Battle Road Visitor Center** located at one end, off Rte 2A on Airport Rd, Lexington, 862.7753; and the **North Bridge Visitor Center** on the other end, west of Monument St off Liberty St, Concord, 508/369.6993. Though interpretive films and information are on hand, you'll need a bit of imagination to conjure scenes of strife in this bucolic setting.

Concord's most precious asset—although sometimes not treated that way—is the **Walden Pond Reservation**, a **National Historic Landmark** open daily 5AM-dusk and located along Rte 126, 508/369.3254. The quiet pond is 62 glimmering acres nestled in 333 woody ones. The transcendentalist and free-thinking **Henry David Thoreau** lived and wrote alongside the pond 1845-1847, in a 10x15-foot hand-hewn cabin. Visitors to the reservation will find woods and pathways descending to smooth water, where sandbars slope to 100-foot depths. Bostonians delight in this gentle place, so it gets overcrowded and overworked as summer progresses, but slowly recovers during fall and winter—the best of all times for waterside contemplation.

Architecture enthusiasts inevitably make the trek to the **Gropius House** in **Lincoln**, 68 Baker Bridge Rd, 227.3956 (SPNEA). Follow Rte 2 W to Rte 126 So, and watch for Baker Bridge Rd. German architect **Walter Gropius** built the house in 1937, the first year after he came to America. His iconoclastic modern residence introduced the **Bauhaus** principles of function and simplicity to this country. The house's industrial quality derives from its components ordered from catalogs that supplied nonresidential buildings, a revolutionary architectural approach at the time. Gropius' residence includes furniture designed by him, **Marcel Breuer**, and others, and creates an extraordinary quality of place. The house is part of the **Society for the Preservation of New England Antiquities'** historic homes collection, and SPNEA offers excellent guided tours. Nearby, also in Lincoln, is the **DeCordova and Dana Museum and Sculpture Park**, Sandy Pond Rd, 259.8355. The castlelike museum shows work by mostly New England contemporary artists in its galleries and 35-acre sculpture park. July and August feature outdoor concerts on grounds that are even better than the collections. This is a gorgeous spot for a picnic and stroll any time of year.

West/Berkshires

The Mass Pike, a.k.a. I-90, heads west from Boston all the way to **New York State**, or choose the more northerly and scenic Rte 2, which also traverses the state. A popular destination west of Boston is **Old Sturbridge Village**, on US 20 off I-84, 508/347.5383. The living historic museum, encompassing more than 200 acres, re-creates an early 19th-century New England agricultural community. Its vintage displays include a clock gallery, folk art and portraiture, firearms and militia accouterments, a working farm, blacksmith, shoemaker, potter, cooper, gardens of culinary and medicinal herbs. Sturbridge features participatory activities and is perfect for a family outing.

The Berkshires refers to the westernmost part of Mass, a verdant region dappled with rivers, lakes, and gentle hills. It's a romantic and serene area with twin legacies: culture and leisure. For information, call or write the **Berkshire Visitors Bureau**, The Common, Pittsfield 01201, 413/443.9186 or 800/237.5747. From March-early April, you can see tree-tapping, watch sap reduce into real maple syrup, and savor the precious not-quite liquid product. Nestled within mountains, the Berkshires offers hiking, camping, biking, fishing, canoeing, fall foliage, skiing—and welcoming country inns to retire to after the day's activities. Head for the town of **Becket**, off Rte 2, the summer home of **Jacob's Pillow Dance Festival**, 413/243.0745, the oldest dance festival in the country, at which you can see performances by some of the world's most exciting companies. Picnic under the trees before a performance. Stay and/or dine nearby at the **Federal House**, 102 Main St (Rte 102) in Lee, 413/243.1824. Visit famous **Tanglewood**, summer home to the **Boston Symphony Orchestra**, Rte 183, Lenox, 413/637.1600 summer only (or in Boston call 266.1492). The lush 200-acre estate is a popular destination for a one-day trip from Boston; bring a picnic and dine *en plein air*. The world-renowned **Tanglewood Music Festival** is held here annually, July-August, and other events include the **Popular Artists Series** (throughout summer) and **Labor Day Weekend Jazz Festival**.

Not far from **Lee** and **Lenox** in the Berkshires is **Stockbridge**, a perfectly cast New England town known for its **Norman Rockwell Museum** on Main St, 413/298.3822; and for the landmark **Red Lion Inn**, also on Main St, 413/298.5545, which has been there since its beginnings as a hostelry in 1773. The well-preserved inn provides rural charm year-round with a lobby fireplace, a cat or 2, music from the grand piano, rockers along the front porch ideal for reading the Sunday paper. Just beyond Stockbridge is **Chesterwood**, 413/298.3579, the former studio and summer

residence of the prolific sculptor **Daniel Chester French**, who created **Abraham Lincoln's** famous image in the **Washington DC** memorial and the *Minuteman* statue in Concord, not to mention many works around Boston. Casts, models, tools, drawings, books, and French's personal belongings are displayed here. There's a garden and nature trail, too. North from here on US Rte 7/20 is **Williamstown**, home of **Williams College** and the **Sterling and Francine Clark Art Institute**, 225 South St, 413/

458.9545. The institute houses a wonderful collection from the 15th-19th centuries of paintings, drawings, prints, and antique silver. Detour on Rte 20 to the **Hancock Shaker Village**, 413/443.0188, a restoration of the Shaker community founded here in 1790. Twenty buildings have been restored, including a remarkable round stone barn. Shakers lived here until 1960.

South/South Shore

Before opting to leave Boston for more distant destinations, spend an afternoon island-hopping along the lovely local chain of **Boston Harbor Islands** (see page 67). Bostonians often lose sight of them, just beyond what was once the city's front door, and yet the islands offer bird-watching, hiking, picnicking, walking, and all sorts of other recreational activities. Enjoy cooling breezes on the boat rides to and from even on the sultriest summer days.

For an unusual architectural tour, from Boston take I-93 So to Rte 138 So, heading southwest inland to **North Easton. Oliver Ames**, manufacturer of the common shovel that helped build America—as well as a railroad tycoon and Mass governor 1887-1890, whose mansion is located at 355 Comm Ave in Back Bay—chose **Henry Hobson Richardson** to design numerous public buildings for North Easton, manufacturing home of the Ames shovel. In the course of 9 years, Richardson built a library, train station, civic center, and other buildings in his characteristic Romanesque-rugged masonry style, with other major artisans playing important roles. (Richardson's friend and occasional collaborator, **Frederick Law Olmsted**, designed the complementary **North Easton Common**.) The result: a sampler of late 19th-century civic architecture that vividly portrays Richardson's ideas.

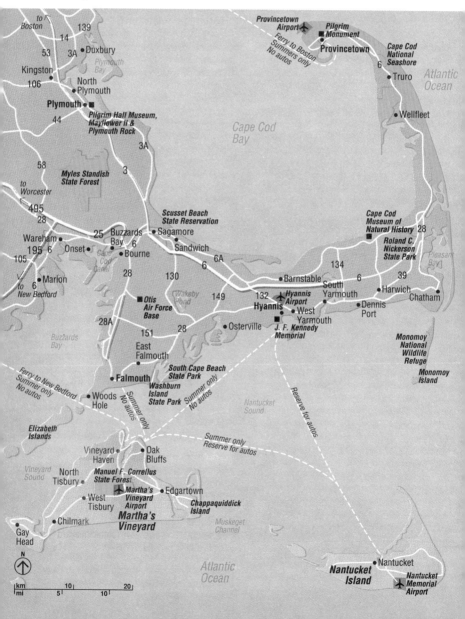

lead for gentle surf on the South Shore. Motor down -93 So to Rte 3A, the winding shore road to **Hingham** with its graceful town center, home of the **Old Ship Meetinghouse**, Main St, 749.1679. This is the oldest wooden church in continuous use in America, built in 1681, with pulpit, pews, and galleries dating from 1755. Visit a rare pastoral setting made by human design: **World's End Reservation**, a 250-acre part of a harborside estate designed by Frederick Law Olmsted, and one of the **Trustees of Reservations**' beautiful park holdings. It is located at the end of Martin's Lane, 749.8956. Forget about Boston's proximity until you reach the park's edge on the water, where you'll find unusual urban views. Then take a peek at **Boston Light**, the oldest operating lighthouse in America, easily viewed from **Nantasket Beach** on Rte 22 in **Hull**, a teeny town at the end of a peninsula stretching north of Hingham into **Boston Harbor**. Nantasket Beach is a 2-mile stretch of beach with bathhouse, playground, promenade, and some good body-surfing. The beach is also accessible by ferry from **Long Wharf** on Boston's waterfront, Bay State Cruises, 723.7800. Continue south on Rte 3A to **Duxbury** and **Duxbury Beach**, one of the finest barrier beaches on the Eastern shore and a paradise for birders and walkers year-round.

After Duxbury and on the way to Cape Cod, if you've plenty of time, visit **Plimouth Plantation** in Plymouth, Rte 3A, Exit 6 off 3 So, 508/746.6544, a living museum of 17th-century Plymouth, home of the famed **Plimouth Rock**. The costumed plantation residents and historic setting are the attractions. Also in Plymouth is **Cranberry World**, 225 Water St, 508/747.2350, with 3 outdoor working bogs—quite a sight, and you can buy the tart, delicious berry made into all sorts of treats.

Once a prosperous fishing and whaling center, **Cape Cod** is a large fishhook that curves 75 miles into the Atlantic and gleams with hundreds of freshwater ponds and lakes. Bordering **Cape Cod Bay** and the ocean are resort communities with beaches, clam shacks, summer theater, whale-watching, extending along the cape all the way to **Provincetown** at its tip where the **Pilgrims** first landed. Much of the cape has been intensely developed, causing erosion to whittle away some lovely land, but fortunately, residents are forcing the pace to slow. One of the state's great treasures is the **Cape Cod National Seashore**, a protected 30-mile-long system of pristine beaches, woodlands, marshes, culminating in the magnificent Provincetown sand dunes (headquarters: Marconi Station area, S. Wellfleet, info 508/349.3785). For information on Cape Cod, including campsites, call or write the **Cape Cod Chamber of Commerce**, Mid-Cape Highway, Hyannis 02601, 508/362.3225. By car take I-93 So to 3 So, and cross the **Sagamore Bridge** onto the Cape (Rte 6 E (and get a good look at the imposing **Cape Cod Canal**). Or ride the ferry from Commonwealth Pier on Boston's waterfront, Bay State Cruises, 723.7800. You can go round-trip in one day to Provincetown, although the best plan is to stay at least one night.

The first paper money in America was issued in 1690 by the Massachusetts Bay Colony, and was used to pay the soldiers who served on the ill-fated expedition attempting to capture Quebec from the French.

At **Falmouth** (So on Rte 28 from 3 So) visit the **Ashumet Holly Reservation and Wildlife Sanctuary**, open year-round, to see a small, unusual sanctuary with many holly varieties, 508/563.6390. Enjoy the Cape Cod natural environment at the **Mass. Audubon Society's Wellfleet Bay Wildlife Sanctuary** on the bay side of Rte 6, Wellfleet, 508/349.2615. Both **Wellfleet** and **Truro** are among Cape Cod's loveliest places. But the most special place to be—the timing depends on your tastes—is Provincetown with its stunning light. An artists' and Portuguese fishing community that welcomes everyone, Provincetown's population swells from 3800 to 25,000 people in summer. It's a gay haven that has a sensuous atmosphere and active tourist life from Memorial Day weekend until summer's end, but has a quiet side also. No matter what time of year, it feels comfortable and safe here; return in winter when *P-town* has shrunk and you'll feel as if you have the entire town and an entire ocean to yourself. Endowed with the loveliest National Seashore stretch, the town's outskirts are wonderful for bicycling and jogging. For a sweeping view of the tiny town and its ocean setting, climb the **Pilgrim Monument** (open year-round). The tallest granite structure in the United States, the tower always hovers high on the village skyline. Visit the funky, fascinating **Heritage Museum** near its base, open summer only. **Commercial St** is indeed the Main St of P-town, where the greatest concentration of restaurants, shops, and lodgings converge. The easiest way to find good accommodations and cuisine, including special off-season listings, is to call or write the very helpful **Provincetown Chamber of Commerce** office in advance, Box 1017, Provincetown 02657. The office is located at 307 Commercial St, MacMillan Wharf, 508/487.3424.

Martha's Vineyard, an island off Cape Cod, southeast of Boston, is a well-loved vacation spot; ferry reservations for cars are often sold out for summer weekends by Christmas. The Vineyard has wonderful beaches, sunsets, sailing, walking, picnicking, bicycling; bring the bug spray. Its population balloons from 12,000 to 100,000 in the summer. Down-island—the eastern side—are quiet **Vineyard Haven**, residential **Oak Bluffs**, and **Edgartown**. The latter is the most popular with tourists and has rich architectural styles from saltbox to Greek Revival. Up-island—the western side—are **Tisbury**, **Chilmark**, and **Gay Head**, known for its varicolored clay cliffs. The Vineyard, like Cape Cod and Nantucket, is as wonderful or more so out of season. To get there, ride the ferry from Woods Hole,

Day Trips

Steamship Authority, 508/540.2022; from New Bedford, Cape Island Express Lines, 508/540.2022, passengers only. (A historic and still-important seaport, **New Bedford** has an excellent whaling museum, 508/997.0046, and discount shopping too.) Seasonal, passengers-only ferries also leave for the Vineyard from Falmouth, 508/775.7185, and Hyannis, 508/548.4800. The island also has an airport in W. Tisbury, recorded information on all airlines 508/693.4776. For information on Vineyard events, places, accommodations, call or write the **Martha's Vineyard Chamber of Commerce**, P.O. Box 1698, Vineyard Haven 02568. The office is located on Beach Rd, 508/693.0085. **John** and **Mary Clarke** will take you sailing on their 54-foot *Alden* ketch out of Vineyard Haven for voyages of any length, call 508/693.1646. Eat fresh and delicious fish at the elegant, expensive **L'Etoile** in Edgartown, 508/627.5187; at the **Aquinnah** in Gay Head, 508/645.9654, for more basic and great seafood where you can also dine outdoors; or at **Feasts** in Chilmark at **Beetlebung Corner**, 508/645.3553, which is a little more hip and urban than you might anticipate, complete with picnic-packing service. A most curious site: wander among the **Carpenter Gothic Cottages** of Oak Bluffs, a Methodist revival campground of Victorian Gothic cottages from the late 1800s, oddly ornate with filigree trim.

Located 30 miles southeast off the mainland of Cape Cod, **Nantucket** is a pretty island known as the *Gray Lady of the Sea* for her gently weathering clapboards, possessing an adventurous history starring Indians, whaling, and ghosts. Nowadays, the island is referred to as a summer playground for the unflashy, monied crowd (keep an eye out for the famous Nantucket-red pants); it's considered expensive and a bit tricky to get to. For that very reason there are usually accommodations to be had, and by calling around you'll find reasonable rates. When it's hot-hot-hot in Boston, the sea breezes keep Nantucket cool and its serene weathered beauty is restorative, with gray-shingled houses and rose-covered cottages, moors of heather, cranberry bogs, scrub oak, gnarled pines. Absolutely no need for a car here because you can walk, bicycle, or moped from one end of the island to the other; magnificent sweeping views reward you. Arrive via ferry from Hyannis, Martha's Vineyard, Woods Hole (Steamship Authority, 508/540.2022). You can also fly to Nantucket Memorial Airport, 508/325.5300. For tourist information, call or write the **Nantucket Island Chamber of Commerce**, Main St, Nantucket 02554, 508/228.1700.

Little **Nantucket Town** is the exceedingly picturesque and quaint center of activity; pick up a street map at the **Nantucket Historical Society** at **Union** and **Main** streets. The town is crowded with expensive shops and restaurants, so you're as well off enjoying the natural attractions. However, reasonable eating places are scattered about, including many outside town offering portable fare, so keep an eye out and scan menus. Look for the giant donut and get a fresh hot one at the **Downey Flake**, S. Water St, 508/228.4533,

Day Trips

but beat the lines or they'll inevitably run out. For an all-out treat, enjoy splendid seafood with a view, reserve in advance at **Straight Wharf**, 508/228.4499. There are tranquil beaches and ones with dramatic surf; good fishing, especially for bluefish; golf and sailing. Try **Gail Johnson**'s tour of Nantucket Town and *Sconset* (**Siasconset**), 508/257.6557. The island has many charming inns and guest houses, one of the

best known being **The Jared Coffin House** in Nantucket Town, 508/228.2405; it is expensive.

Beyond the commonwealth's southern border, yet within a one- to 2-hour ride, are **Providence** and **Newport, Rhode Island**. Providence is the *Ocean State*'s capital and industrial and commercial center, as well as a major port. The city was founded by **Roger Williams**, who was banished from Boston by the single-minded and often intolerant Puritans. A city guide and map of landmarks is available at the **Greater Providence Convention and Visitors Bureau**, 30 Exchange Terrace 02903, 401/274.1636. It's worth a special trip to one of **George Germon** and **Johanne Killeen**'s renowned restaurants: **Al Forno** or **Lucky's**, both at 577 S. Main St, 401/273.9760. Al Forno offers rustic Italian-style decor and food, the latter mainly grilled over hardwood or roasted in a brick oven. Eat pizza. Lucky's tends toward French provincial in decor, but the cuisine is similar to Al Forno, with large portions at moderate prices. For an evening out, try going round trip by train from **South Station** in Boston.

South of Providence is Newport, which still echoes its origins as a colonial seaport. The town has always been associated with opulence and the sea: yachts, the Navy, competitive sailing, seaside palaces of the rich. Annual celebrations include the star-studded **Newport Jazz Festival**, the country's oldest. The **Cliff Walk** is Newport's other most popular attraction, a 3$\frac{1}{2}$-mile shoreline path and a **National Historic Walking Trail**, 800/458.4843, with the Atlantic Ocean on one side and the famous summer Newport mansions on the other.

Bests

Le Grand David
Cabot Street Cinema Theatre & Larcom Theatre, Beverly, Massachusetts

The **North Shore** has a week's worth of attractions all its own, and most are a short drive (or train ride along the old Boston & Maine railroad route) from the heart of the city. From **Beverly**, something of a crossroads for North Shore traffic, drive across the bridge to **Salem** (I do) and browse at the **Peabody Museum** (where America's 19th-century China trade seems still to bustle). Or take one of the **Essex Institute**'s guided tours of Salem's stately colonial houses. Lunch on the wharf at **Victoria Station** is always a favorite, though with children I might opt for a picnic at **Salem Willows**, where an antique carousel still spins you around for a quarter and you can rent a rowboat to explore the historic harbor.

You might enjoy equally a lunch at Beverly's **Union Grill** or at **Danvers' King's Grant Inn**, where your children will love chatting with the macaws in the tropical garden; and you'll appreciate the huge, varied menu at the **Lion's Head Tavern**. An afternoon drive up **Route 127** through **Beverly Farms**, Manchester, and **Magnolia** to **Cape Ann** will take you past some of the great estates built by turn-of-the-century Brahmins and, on a windy day, will provide some dramatic vistas of wave-swept coastline. In **Gloucester**, of a summer's day, take in a whale watch, or continue on to **Rockport**, the sometime art colony, and enjoy the scenery while looking over a painter's shoulder.

Justin Kaplan
Writer

Harvard Square—Variety, change.

Riding the **T**—Like a full-size model railroad.

Charles River—As close to flowing water as you can get without necessarily falling in.

Ice cream—Cambridge may be the world capital of ice cream consumption.

Getting out of town—You can be at **Walden Pond** in 1/2 hour; to the tip of **Cape Cod** in 2 1/2 hours.

Bookstores—They still exist here.

Museum of Science—Surprises—and giant toys.

Widener Library—One of the great intellectual resources of the world.

Harvard University—A giant outdoor architectural museum.

James Koch
Brewer, Samuel Adams Lager

Haymarket on Saturday morning—Boston's best social and ethnic melting pot —shopping for everything from live lobsters to potatoes by the 50-lb sack.

Harvard's Peabody Museum's miraculous glass flowers.

Cambridge's ridiculous **Lampoon Building** on Mt. Auburn Street, a building designed to show a 30-foot face.

Goodspeed's on Beacon Hill for old prints, maps, and signatures.

J.P. Lick's on Centre Street in Jamaica Plain for ice cream.

Le Jardin on Huron Ave in Cambridge for exotic flowers and vegetables; the **Bryn Mawr Bookstore** further down the street for used sets of classics.

The **Boathouse Bar** in Harvard Square for the most people under 25 drinking beer and having fun in a small bar.

Trio's pasta store on Hanover Street in the North End for the best homemade pasta.

The **Gardner Museum** on the Fenway, the best small and quiet museum.

The brewery tour of the **Samuel Adams Brewery** on Thursday and Saturday at 2PM for a taste of beer from a century ago.

David R. Godine
Publisher

Boston Museum of Fine Arts—One of the great collections in America, especially the Impressionists and Oriental Art.

Isabella Stewart Gardner Museum—Just as she left it, still the best place to spend a relaxed winter Sunday afternoon.

Jordan Hall—The best acoustics in Boston and invariably presenting a first-class roster of musicians and speakers. Many free concerts through the **New England Conservatory of Music**.

Arnold Arboretum—Well worth the trek to Jamaica Plain, but especially so in early to late spring to view their famous lilacs and flowering trees. One of the country's treasures for all forms of trees and shrubs from the northern temperate climates.

Locke-Ober—Boston dining at its most refined and for the money, most reasonable. The best Indian pudding in town.

Vose and **Child's Galleries**—These two are the old-line firms, both on Newbury Street, staffed by real experts with great taste. Excellent stock, much of it out of sight.

Ann Robert
Co-owner, Maison Robert

Arnold Arboretum—Beautiful, restful city space; lovely walk in every season.

Plum Island—a wildlife refuge site of great beauty; immense sky, green marsh, golden sandy beach and dunes, a refuge for kids, a place to share with children, visitors, and to enjoy alone.

Walk from **Beacon Hill** to **Back Bay** and over to the South End—lovely city spaces.

Boat ride in **Boston Harbor**—Makes clear to visitors the former history of Boston as a great port.

Hutchins Farm and **Concord**—History of New England becomes vivid as one walks the streets of this lovely New England city and Hutchins Farm, an organic farm, is a place of special interest with those who care about fresh produce.

Maison Robert—Unusually beautiful setting with an outdoor café terrace surveyed by the **statue of Benjamin Franklin**, historic rooms of the former city treasury, and the **Archives** of the **Old City Hall**. Even as its owner this unique and beautiful setting continues to please me.

V. Renato Burkhardt
General Manager, Locke-Ober Restaurant

Walking through the **Public Garden**, with its Swan Boats and beautifully kept gardens and historic statues.

An early Sunday morning stroll down **Charles Street** to **Rebecca**'s for breakfast.

Attending a competitive **Celtics** basketball game.

Attending a concert at the **Boston Symphony**.

A business lunch at **Locke-Ober**, one of the most prestigious *Power Lunch* spots in the country.

Strolling the **Charles River** watching the college crew boats.

Bests

Christmas shopping on **Newbury Street**.

Tea at the **Ritz**.

The view of Boston from the **Bay Tower Room**.

Spending a Saturday or Sunday afternoon at **Faneuil Hall Marketplace**.

C

The Standells, who came from **California**, recorded *Dirty Water—Aww Boston you're my home*—in 1966. The song reached No. 11 on *Billboard's* Top 100.

N

O

P

S

Boutiques, bars, bookstores, cafés, locksmiths, laundries, antiques galore, a great greasy-spoon, and the most understated convenience stores you'll ever see—all belong to the fascinating mishmash on Charles St. (Check the realtors' postings for the unbelievable rents a tiny 5th-floor walkup in an elevator-less building commands.) Charles St gets dull as it nears Cambridge St, so start at that end and head toward Beacon St, progressing from shade to sunlight, with the gracious Public Garden as your destination. Or try the opposite way and head toward the Esplanade along the Charles River. Come on a Saturday afternoon, when the whole world seems to be window-shopping here, then return Sunday morning to see how this hopping spot has been transformed into a quiet neighborhood byway.

Index

Boston Restaurant Index

Only restaurants with star ratings are listed below. All restaurants are listed alphabetically in the main index. Always telephone as far in advance as possible to confirm your table and ensure that a restaurant has not closed, changed its hours, or booked its tables for a private party.

Index

Boston Hotel Index

Boston Bests Index

Travel Notes

Credits

Since the publication of his first book in 1963, **Richard Saul Wurman** has distinguished his work with a singular passion: that for making information understandable. He has published over 50 books; **BOSTON** ACCESS® remains faithful to the motivating principles found in his previous works. Each project has been based on the premise that you understand something only in relation to what you already understand.

Receiving both bachelor's and master's degrees from the University of Pennsylvania, Wurman graduated in 1959 with highest honors. In the course of his studies, he established a close personal and professional relationship with architect Louis I. Kahn. A fellow of the American Institute of Architects, FAIA, Wurman is also a member of the Alliance Graphique Internationale and was Vice President of the American Institute of Graphic Arts. He has been the recipient of several grants from the National Endowment for the Arts, a Guggenheim fellowship, two Graham fellowships, and two Chandler fellowships.

Wurman has applied his design expertise to the field of cartography, creating several revolutionary works that have culminated in the **US**ATLAS project. CITIES: A Comparison of Form and Scale, published in 1963, focuses on the relative size and scale of 50 cities, allowing the reader to compare them accurately to one another. In 1967, Wurman developed city maps with standardized scale and legends, coauthoring them in a volume entitled *URBAN ATLAS: 20 American Cities*. One of his most notable mapmaking experiences was as a member of an archaeological expedition during the first year of exploration (1958) of the Mayan city of Tikal, in Guatemala, where he surveyed one-third of the city. In 1988 he wrote the paper *Mapping and Cartography in Metropolitan Areas* for the XVII Triennale in Milan.

Currently, Wurman is the co-owner of **ACCESS**®Press with HarperCollins and of The **Understanding** Business. **ACCESS**® travel guides to London, Paris, Rome, New York City, Los Angeles, San Francisco, Tokyo, and other major cities answer tourists' questions, from the most common to the most obscure; the latest in the non-travel series is *The Wall Street Journal Guide to Understanding Money & Markets*. Wurman restructured and redesigned the Pacific Bell Yellow Pages directories into the more coherently organized product, the *SMART Yellow Pages*®. *INFORMATION ANXIETY* (1989), his breakthrough guide to handling the information glut, has been published in six languages.

Wurman, his wife, novelist Gloria Nagy, and their four children live in Manhattan and in Bridgehampton, New York.

Project management: development, research, editing
Nancy Robins

Writing and research
Julia Collins

Editing
Melanie Falick

Restaurant consultant
Steven Raichlen

Urban history consultant
Arthur Krim

Reviewing
Margaret Reeve

Design
Tom Beatty
Joachim Müller-Lance

Maps
Julie Bilski
Michael Blum
Cheryl Fitzgerald
Kitti Homme
Patti Keelin
Michael Kohnke
Chris Middour
Laurie Miller

Text Styling
Jerry Stanton

Proofreading
Margie Lee
Karin Mullen
Caroline Scott

Cover Photograph
Reven T.C. Wurman

Printing and Otabind
Webcom Limited

Special Thanks
Mark Johnson
Ron Davis
Rajan Dev
Jean Linsteadt

ACCESS®PRESS

Creative Director
Richard Saul Wurman

Director
Jane Rosch

Editorial Director
Lise Friedman

Project Directors
Stuart L. Silberman
Mark Goldman

The following made significant contributions that are greatly appreciated:

Martin Bander, Massachusetts General Hospital
Philip Bergen, Bostonian Society
Susan Berk
John Codman, Jr.
Lorna Condon, Society for the Preservation of New England Antiquities
Sadie Brewer Faber
Firestone & Parson, Inc.
Alicia Gordon, Skinner, Inc.
Patricia Greeley
Christopher Hawes
Judith Hughes
George Joe, South Cove Neighborhood Council
Michele James
Harry Katz, Boston Athenaeum
John Krajovic
Alex Krieger
Claude Lee
Michael Malyszko
MBTA
Massport
Seth Minkoff
Thomas Palladino
Tom Pedulla
Dianne Pettipaw
Sally Pierce, Boston Athenaeum
Barbara Raymond
Ellie Reichlin, Society for the Preservation of New England Antiquities
Rick Shea, MASCO
Susan Turner
Ron Wallace
Michael Webb
Wendy Withington
Donald Woodward

Distinctive features of **ACCESS**® Travel Guides

- Organized by neighborhood, the way natives know a city and visitors experience it.
- Color-coded entries distinguish restaurants, hotels, shops, parks, architecture and places of interest.
- Generous use of maps with points of interest identified.

- Easy to use and a pleasure to read.
- Each city's flavor is conveyed by descriptions of its history, by lists of the personal favorites of people who know and love the city, by trivia and lavish illustrations of important buildings and places of interest.
- Perfect preparation for a visit, enjoyment of a city or recollection of a trip.

BARCELONAACCESS®
An up-to-the-minute guide to Spain's avant-garde city, home of the 1992 Summer Olympic Games.
144 pages, $16.95

BOSTONACCESS®
A guide to the many charms of America's Revolutionary capital, from historic landmarks to where to shop, stay and dine.
208 pages, $16.95

CHICAGOACCESS®
The key to inimitable Chicago style, from architecture to deep-dish pizza.
192 pages, $16.95

DCACCESS®
A comprehensive guide to the nation's capital with abundant descriptions of the beautiful and historic places that encircle it.
216 pages, $12.95

FLORENCE/VENICE/MILAN
ACCESS®
A grand tour through Northern Italy's three major cities, in one comprehensive guide.
240 pages, $16.95

HAWAIIACCESS®
Organized island by island...where to stay...what to see...what to do.
192 pages, $14.95

LAACCESS®
The city's characteristic urban sprawl and profusion of personalities rendered accessible.
224 pages, $16.95

LONDONACCESS®
The first winner from abroad of the London Tourist Board's Guidebook of the Year Award!
216 pages, $16.95

NYCACCESS®
For natives and visitors...the ultimate guide to the city famous for everything except subtlety and understatement.
312 pages, $16.95

PARISACCESS®
For the first-time and the veteran visitor, a guide that opens doors to the city's magic and nuances.
216 pages, $16.95

ROMEACCESS®
Award-winning guidebook, featuring favorite promenades of the Eternal City.
176 pages, $16.95

SAN FRANCISCOACCESS®
Our best-selling guide to the much-loved city...includes daytrips around the Bay Area.
208 pages, $16.95

To order these **ACCESS**®Guides, please see the other side of this page.

Praise for **ACCESS**® Guides

The **ACCESS**® Series offers literally thousands of bits of useful or surprising information, all color-coded and organized in odd but sensible ways that will satisfy both tourist and native.   **New York Magazine**

In a radical approach to the genre, **ACCESS**® Press has reinvented the wheel with a series of compact volumes that open up cities through striking graphics, terse copy and a tight format.   **Time Magazine**

For either the traveler or the armchair explorer who loves accurate detail and affectionate description, the **ACCESS**® Guides prove wonderful companions.
James A. Michener

About **NYC**ACCESS®
At last a guidebook to Manhattan that won't put you to sleep. **NYC**ACCESS® even has a section on teaching you how to talk like a *Noo Yawker*. But what's most remarkable about this lively little tome (and unusual for guidebooks) is that it not only tells you what to do, eat and see, but in no uncertain terms tells you what to avoid.
USA Today

ACCESS® GUIDES

Order by phone, toll-free: 1-800-**ACCESS**-4 or 1-800-345-8112

Name _____ Phone _____

Address _____

City _____ State _____ Zip _____

Please send me the following **ACCESS**®Guides:

☐ **BARCELONA**ACCESS®, $16.95
Available Fall 1991 BA92

☐ **BOSTON**ACCESS®, $16.95
BO91

☐ **CHICAGO**ACCESS®, $16.95
CH91

☐ **DC**ACCESS®, $12.95
DCØ288

☐ **FLORENCE/VENICE/
MILAN**ACCESS®, $16.95
FVM91

☐ **HAWAII**ACCESS®, $14.95
HIØ288

☐ **LA**ACCESS®, $16.95
LA91

☐ **LONDON**ACCESS®, $16.95
LN91

☐ **NYC**ACCESS®, $16.95
NY91

☐ **PARIS**ACCESS®, $16.95
PR91

☐ **ROME**ACCESS®, $16.95
RM91

☐ **SAN FRANCISCO**
ACCESS®, $16.95
SF91

Total for **ACCESS**®Guides:	$
For PA delivery please include sales tax:	
Add $4.00 for first book S&H, $1.00 per additional book:	
Total payment:	$

☐ Check or Money Order enclosed. Please make payable to **ACCESS**®PRESS

☐ Charge my credit card ☐ American Express ☐ Visa ☐ Mastercard

Card no. _____ Exp. date _____

Signature _____
WI91

☐ Please add my name to your mailing list for news of other **ACCESS**Guides.

Send orders to:
ACCESS®PRESS
P.O. Box 664
Holmes, PA 19043-9964

Send correspondence to:
ACCESS®PRESS
10 East 53rd. Street
New York, NY 10022

Praise for **ACCESS**® Guides

Finally, books that look at cities the way tourists do—block by block...**ACCESS**® may be the best series for the chronically lost.
USA Today

It combines the best of the practical directories with the superior artwork of the hardcover coffee-table books at an affordable price.
New York Times

Beautiful to behold, yet practical as a hammer and screwdriver.
Travel & Leisure Magazine

Each book is a piece of graphic ingenuity. Maps & diagrams lead its readers around the places where they go. The result for newcomer or native, is a pleasure to use and, for that matter, to peruse from the speculative comforts of home. The **ACCESS**® Guides are visual treats first and foremost.
Publisher's Weekly